学ぶ人は、
変えて
ゆく人だ。

目の前にある問題はもちろん、
人生の問いや、
社会の課題を自ら見つけ、
挑み続けるために、人は学ぶ。
「学び」で、
少しずつ世界は変えてゆける。
いつでも、どこでも、誰でも、
学ぶことができる世の中へ。

旺文社

JN172687

2023年度版

※ 本書に収録されている過去問は、公益財団法人 日本英語検定協会から提供を受けたもののみです。準会場・海外受験などの問題とは一致しない場合があります。また、二次試験のモデルスピーチはA日程のみ収録しています。

※このコンテンツは、公益財団法人 日本英語検定協会の承認や推奨、その他の検討を受けたものではありません。

英検®は、公益財団法人 日本英語検定協会の登録商標です。　旺文社

2022年度第2回　英検1級　解答用紙

【注意事項】

① 解答にはHBの黒鉛筆（シャープペンシルも可）を使用し、解答を訂正する場合には消しゴムで完全に消してください。

② 解答用紙は絶対に汚したり折り曲げたり、所定以外のところへの記入はしないでください。

③ マーク例

良い例	悪い例
●	◉ ✗ ◑

これ以下の濃さのマークは読めません。

解答欄 1

問題番号	1	2	3	4
(1)	①	②	③	④
(2)	①	②	③	④
(3)	①	②	③	④
(4)	①	②	③	④
(5)	①	②	③	④
(6)	①	②	③	④
(7)	①	②	③	④
(8)	①	②	③	④
(9)	①	②	③	④
(10)	①	②	③	④
(11)	①	②	③	④
(12)	①	②	③	④
(13)	①	②	③	④
(14)	①	②	③	④
(15)	①	②	③	④
(16)	①	②	③	④
(17)	①	②	③	④
(18)	①	②	③	④
(19)	①	②	③	④
(20)	①	②	③	④
(21)	①	②	③	④
(22)	①	②	③	④
(23)	①	②	③	④
(24)	①	②	③	④
(25)	①	②	③	④

解答欄 2

問題番号	1	2	3	4
(26)	①	②	③	④
(27)	①	②	③	④
(28)	①	②	③	④
(29)	①	②	③	④
(30)	①	②	③	④
(31)	①	②	③	④

解答欄 3

問題番号	1	2	3	4
(32)	①	②	③	④
(33)	①	②	③	④
(34)	①	②	③	④
(35)	①	②	③	④
(36)	①	②	③	④
(37)	①	②	③	④
(38)	①	②	③	④
(39)	①	②	③	④
(40)	①	②	③	④
(41)	①	②	③	④

※筆記4の解答欄はこの裏にあります。

リスニング解答欄

問題番号	1	2	3	4
Part 1 No.1	①	②	③	④
No.2	①	②	③	④
No.3	①	②	③	④
No.4	①	②	③	④
No.5	①	②	③	④
No.6	①	②	③	④
No.7	①	②	③	④
No.8	①	②	③	④
No.9	①	②	③	④
No.10	①	②	③	④
Part 2 A No.11	①	②	③	④
No.12	①	②	③	④
B No.13	①	②	③	④
No.14	①	②	③	④
C No.15	①	②	③	④
No.16	①	②	③	④
D No.17	①	②	③	④
No.18	①	②	③	④
E No.19	①	②	③	④
No.20	①	②	③	④
Part 3 F No.21	①	②	③	④
G No.22	①	②	③	④
H No.23	①	②	③	④
I No.24	①	②	③	④
J No.25	①	②	③	④
Part 4 No.26	①	②	③	④
No.27	①	②	③	④

2022年度第2回　Web特典「自動採点サービス」対応　オンラインマークシート

※検定の回によって2次元コードが違います。
※筆記1〜3, リスニングの採点ができます。
※PCからも利用できます（本書 p.8 参照）。

※実際の解答用紙に似せていますが、デザイン・サイズは異なります。

・指示事項を守り，文字は，はっきり分かりやすく書いてください。
・太枠に囲まれた部分のみが採点の対象です。

4 English Composition

Write your English Composition in the space below.

2022年度第1回 英検1級 解答用紙

【注意事項】
① 解答にはHBの黒鉛筆（シャープペンシルも可）を使用し、解答を訂正する場合には消しゴムで完全に消してください。
② 解答用紙は絶対に汚したり折り曲げたり、所定以外のところへの記入はしないでください。
③ マーク例

良い例	悪い例
●	◐ ✕ ◑

これ以下の濃さのマークは読めません。

解答欄 1

問題番号	1	2	3	4
(1)	①	②	③	④
(2)	①	②	③	④
(3)	①	②	③	④
(4)	①	②	③	④
(5)	①	②	③	④
(6)	①	②	③	④
(7)	①	②	③	④
(8)	①	②	③	④
(9)	①	②	③	④
(10)	①	②	③	④
(11)	①	②	③	④
(12)	①	②	③	④
(13)	①	②	③	④
(14)	①	②	③	④
(15)	①	②	③	④
(16)	①	②	③	④
(17)	①	②	③	④
(18)	①	②	③	④
(19)	①	②	③	④
(20)	①	②	③	④
(21)	①	②	③	④
(22)	①	②	③	④
(23)	①	②	③	④
(24)	①	②	③	④
(25)	①	②	③	④

解答欄 2

問題番号	1	2	3	4
(26)	①	②	③	④
(27)	①	②	③	④
(28)	①	②	③	④
(29)	①	②	③	④
(30)	①	②	③	④
(31)	①	②	③	④

解答欄 3

問題番号	1	2	3	4
(32)	①	②	③	④
(33)	①	②	③	④
(34)	①	②	③	④
(35)	①	②	③	④
(36)	①	②	③	④
(37)	①	②	③	④
(38)	①	②	③	④
(39)	①	②	③	④
(40)	①	②	③	④
(41)	①	②	③	④

※筆記4の解答欄はこの裏にあります。

リスニング解答欄

問題番号	1	2	3	4
Part 1 No.1	①	②	③	④
No.2	①	②	③	④
No.3	①	②	③	④
No.4	①	②	③	④
No.5	①	②	③	④
No.6	①	②	③	④
No.7	①	②	③	④
No.8	①	②	③	④
No.9	①	②	③	④
No.10	①	②	③	④
Part 2 A No.11	①	②	③	④
No.12	①	②	③	④
B No.13	①	②	③	④
No.14	①	②	③	④
C No.15	①	②	③	④
No.16	①	②	③	④
D No.17	①	②	③	④
No.18	①	②	③	④
E No.19	①	②	③	④
No.20	①	②	③	④
Part 3 F No.21	①	②	③	④
G No.22	①	②	③	④
H No.23	①	②	③	④
I No.24	①	②	③	④
J No.25	①	②	③	④
Part 4 No.26	①	②	③	④
No.27	①	②	③	④

2022年度第1回

Web特典「自動採点サービス」対応 オンラインマークシート

※検定の回によって2次元コードが違います。
※筆記1～3，リスニングの採点ができます。
※PCからも利用できます（本書 p.8 参照）。

※実際の解答用紙に似せていますが、デザイン・サイズは異なります。

切り取り線

・指示事項を守り，文字は，はっきり分かりやすく書いてください。
・太枠に囲まれた部分のみが採点の対象です。

4 English Composition

Write your English Composition in the space below.

2021年度第3回 英検1級 解答用紙

【注意事項】
① 解答にはHBの黒鉛筆（シャープペンシルも可）を使用し、解答を訂正する場合には消しゴムで完全に消してください。
② 解答用紙は絶対に汚したり折り曲げたり、所定以外のところへの記入はしないでください。

③ マーク例

良い例	悪い例
●	◔ ✖ ◕

これ以下の濃さのマークは読めません。

解答欄

問題番号	1	2	3	4
1	(1)	①	②	③	④
	(2)	①	②	③	④
	(3)	①	②	③	④
	(4)	①	②	③	④
	(5)	①	②	③	④
	(6)	①	②	③	④
	(7)	①	②	③	④
	(8)	①	②	③	④
	(9)	①	②	③	④
	(10)	①	②	③	④
	(11)	①	②	③	④
	(12)	①	②	③	④
	(13)	①	②	③	④
	(14)	①	②	③	④
	(15)	①	②	③	④
	(16)	①	②	③	④
	(17)	①	②	③	④
	(18)	①	②	③	④
	(19)	①	②	③	④
	(20)	①	②	③	④
	(21)	①	②	③	④
	(22)	①	②	③	④
	(23)	①	②	③	④
	(24)	①	②	③	④
	(25)	①	②	③	④

解答欄

問題番号	1	2	3	4
2	(26)	①	②	③	④
	(27)	①	②	③	④
	(28)	①	②	③	④
	(29)	①	②	③	④
	(30)	①	②	③	④
	(31)	①	②	③	④

解答欄

問題番号	1	2	3	4
3	(32)	①	②	③	④
	(33)	①	②	③	④
	(34)	①	②	③	④
	(35)	①	②	③	④
	(36)	①	②	③	④
	(37)	①	②	③	④
	(38)	①	②	③	④
	(39)	①	②	③	④
	(40)	①	②	③	④
	(41)	①	②	③	④

※筆記4の解答欄はこの裏にあります。

リスニング解答欄

問題番号	1	2	3	4
Part 1	No.1	①	②	③	④
	No.2	①	②	③	④
	No.3	①	②	③	④
	No.4	①	②	③	④
	No.5	①	②	③	④
	No.6	①	②	③	④
	No.7	①	②	③	④
	No.8	①	②	③	④
	No.9	①	②	③	④
	No.10	①	②	③	④
Part 2	A No.11	①	②	③	④
	A No.12	①	②	③	④
	B No.13	①	②	③	④
	B No.14	①	②	③	④
	C No.15	①	②	③	④
	C No.16	①	②	③	④
	D No.17	①	②	③	④
	D No.18	①	②	③	④
	E No.19	①	②	③	④
	E No.20	①	②	③	④
Part 3	F No.21	①	②	③	④
	G No.22	①	②	③	④
	H No.23	①	②	③	④
	I No.24	①	②	③	④
	J No.25	①	②	③	④
Part 4	No.26	①	②	③	④
	No.27	①	②	③	④

2021年度第3回 Web特典「自動採点サービス」対応 オンラインマークシート
※検定の回によって2次元コードが違います。
※筆記1〜3，リスニングの採点ができます。
※PCからも利用できます（本書 p.8 参照）。

※実際の解答用紙に似せていますが，デザイン・サイズは異なります。

切り取り線

・指示事項を守り，文字は，はっきり分かりやすく書いてください。
・太枠に囲まれた部分のみが採点の対象です。

4 English Composition

Write your English Composition in the space below.

2020年度第3回　英検1級　解答用紙

【注意事項】
① 解答にはHBの黒鉛筆（シャープペンシルも可）を使用し、解答を訂正する場合には消しゴムで完全に消してください。
② 解答用紙は絶対に汚したり折り曲げたり、所定以外のところへの記入はしないでください。

③ マーク例

良い例	悪い例
●	◐ ✗ ◕

 これ以下の濃さのマークは読めません。

解答欄

問題番号	1	2	3	4
(1)	①	②	③	④
(2)	①	②	③	④
(3)	①	②	③	④
(4)	①	②	③	④
(5)	①	②	③	④
(6)	①	②	③	④
(7)	①	②	③	④
(8)	①	②	③	④
(9)	①	②	③	④
(10)	①	②	③	④
(11)	①	②	③	④
(12)	①	②	③	④
1 (13)	①	②	③	④
(14)	①	②	③	④
(15)	①	②	③	④
(16)	①	②	③	④
(17)	①	②	③	④
(18)	①	②	③	④
(19)	①	②	③	④
(20)	①	②	③	④
(21)	①	②	③	④
(22)	①	②	③	④
(23)	①	②	③	④
(24)	①	②	③	④
(25)	①	②	③	④

解答欄

問題番号	1	2	3	4
(26)	①	②	③	④
(27)	①	②	③	④
2 (28)	①	②	③	④
(29)	①	②	③	④
(30)	①	②	③	④
(31)	①	②	③	④

解答欄

問題番号	1	2	3	4
(32)	①	②	③	④
(33)	①	②	③	④
(34)	①	②	③	④
(35)	①	②	③	④
3 (36)	①	②	③	④
(37)	①	②	③	④
(38)	①	②	③	④
(39)	①	②	③	④
(40)	①	②	③	④
(41)	①	②	③	④

※筆記4の解答欄はこの裏にあります。

リスニング解答欄

問題番号	1	2	3	4
No.1	①	②	③	④
No.2	①	②	③	④
No.3	①	②	③	④
No.4	①	②	③	④
Part 1 No.5	①	②	③	④
No.6	①	②	③	④
No.7	①	②	③	④
No.8	①	②	③	④
No.9	①	②	③	④
No.10	①	②	③	④
A No.11	①	②	③	④
No.12	①	②	③	④
B No.13	①	②	③	④
No.14	①	②	③	④
Part 2 C No.15	①	②	③	④
No.16	①	②	③	④
D No.17	①	②	③	④
No.18	①	②	③	④
E No.19	①	②	③	④
No.20	①	②	③	④
F No.21	①	②	③	④
G No.22	①	②	③	④
Part 3 H No.23	①	②	③	④
I No.24	①	②	③	④
J No.25	①	②	③	④
Part 4 No.26	①	②	③	④
No.27	①	②	③	④

2020年度第3回 **Web特典「自動採点サービス」対応オンラインマークシート**
※検定の回によって2次元コードが違います。
※筆記1～3，リスニングの採点ができます。
※PCからも利用できます（本書p.8参照）。

※実際の解答用紙に似せていますが、デザイン・サイズは異なります。

・指示事項を守り，文字は，はっきり分かりやすく書いてください。
・太枠に囲まれた部分のみが採点の対象です。

4 English Composition

Write your English Composition in the space below.

Introduction

はじめに

実用英語技能検定（英検®）は，年間受験者数410万人（英検IBA，英検Jr.との総数）の小学生から社会人まで，幅広い層が受験する国内最大級の資格試験で，1963年の第1回検定からの累計では1億人を超える人々が受験しています。英検®は，コミュニケーションに欠かすことのできない4技能をバランスよく測定することを目的としており，英検®の受験によってご自身の英語力を把握できるだけでなく，進学・就職・留学などの場面で多くのチャンスを手に入れることにつながります。

この『全問題集シリーズ』は，英語を学ぶ皆さまを応援する気持ちを込めて刊行しました。本書は，2022年度第2回検定を含む6回分の過去問を，皆さまの理解が深まるよう，日本語訳や詳しい解説を加えて収録しています。また正答率が高かった設問の解説には 正答率 ★75％以上 マーク（別冊p.3参照）がついているので，特におさえておきたい問題を簡単にチェックできます。

本書が皆さまの英検合格の足がかりとなり，さらには国際社会で活躍できるような生きた英語を身につけるきっかけとなることを願っています。

最後に，本書を刊行するにあたり多大なご尽力をいただきました松井こずえ先生，鴇﨑敏彦先生，浅場眞紀子先生，Ed Jacob先生に深く感謝の意を表します。

2023年　春

もくじ

Contents

本書の使い方 ……………………………………………… 3

音声について ……………………………………………… 4

Web特典について ………………………………………… 7

自動採点サービスの利用方法 …………………………… 8

英検インフォメーション ………………………………… 10

    試験内容／英検の種類／合否判定方法／英検（従来型）受験情報―2023年
度試験日程・申込方法

2022年度の傾向と攻略ポイント ……………………… 14

二次試験・面接の流れ …………………………………… 16

2022年度	第 2 回検定（筆記・リスニング・面接）……	17
	第 1 回検定（筆記・リスニング・面接）……	41
2021年度	第 3 回検定（筆記・リスニング・面接）……	65
	第 2 回検定（筆記・リスニング・面接）……	89
	第 1 回検定（筆記・リスニング・面接）……	113
2020年度	第 3 回検定（筆記・リスニング・面接）……	137

執　　筆：松井こずえ（アルカディア・コミュニケーションズ），鴇﨑敏彦（日本獣医生命科学大学），
　　　　　浅場眞紀子（Q-Leap），Ed Jacob
編集協力：斉藤 敦，鹿島由紀子，渡邉真理子，Jason A. Chau，株式会社鷗来堂
録　　音：ユニバ合同会社
デザイン：林 慎一郎（及川真咲デザイン事務所）
組版・データ作成協力：幸和印刷株式会社

本書の使い方

ここでは，本書の過去問および特典についての活用法の一例を紹介します。

本書の内容

| 過去問
6回分 | 英検
インフォ
メーション
(p.10-13) | 2022年度の
傾向と
攻略ポイント
(p.14-15) | 二次試験・
面接の流れ
(p.16) | Web特典
(p.7-9) |

本書の使い方

一次試験対策

情報収集・傾向把握
・英検インフォメーション
・2022年度の傾向と攻略ポイント

過去問にチャレンジ
・2022年度第2回一次試験
・2022年度第1回一次試験
・2021年度第3回一次試験
・2021年度第2回一次試験
・2021年度第1回一次試験
・2020年度第3回一次試験
　※【Web特典】自動採点サービスの活用

二次試験対策

情報収集・傾向把握
・二次試験・面接の流れ
・【Web特典】
　面接模範例

過去問にチャレンジ
・2022年度第2回二次試験
・2022年度第1回二次試験
・2021年度第3回二次試験
・2021年度第2回二次試験
・2021年度第1回二次試験
・2020年度第3回二次試験

過去問の取り組み方

1セット目 【本番モード】
本番の試験と同じように，制限時間を設けて取り組みましょう。どの問題形式に時間がかかりすぎているか，正答率が低いかなど，今のあなたの実力を把握しましょう。
「自動採点サービス」を活用して，答え合わせをスムーズに行いましょう。

2〜5セット目 【学習モード】
制限時間をなくし，解けるまで取り組みましょう。
リスニングは音声を繰り返し聞いて解答を導き出してもかまいません。すべての問題に正解できるまで見直します。

6セット目 【仕上げモード】
試験直前の仕上げに利用しましょう。時間を計って本番のつもりで取り組みます。
これまでに取り組んだ6セットの過去問で間違えた問題の解説を本番試験の前にもう一度見直しましょう。

3

音声について

一次試験・リスニングと二次試験・面接の音声を聞くことができます。本書とともに使い，効果的なリスニング・面接対策をしましょう。

収録内容と特長

 一次試験・リスニング

本番の試験の音声を収録	➡	スピードをつかめる！
解答時間は本番通り10秒間	➡	解答時間に慣れる！
収録されている英文は，別冊解答に掲載	➡	聞き取れない箇所を確認できる！

 二次試験・面接（スピーキング）

| 独自に制作したモデルスピーチを収録 | ➡ | 模範解答が確認できる！ |
| モデルスピーチは，別冊解答に掲載 | ➡ | 聞き取れない箇所を確認できる！ |

3つの方法で音声が聞けます！

音声再生サービスご利用可能期間
2023年2月24日～2024年8月31日
※ご利用期間内にアプリやPCにダウンロードしていただいた音声は，期間終了後も引き続きお聞きいただけます。
※これらのサービスは予告なく変更，終了することがあります。

① 公式アプリ「英語の友」(iOS/Android)でお手軽再生

リスニング力を強化する機能満載

- 再生速度変換（0.5～2.0倍速）
- お気に入り機能（絞込み学習）
- オフライン再生
- バックグラウンド再生
- 試験日カウントダウン

※画像はイメージです。

［ご利用方法］

1. 「英語の友」公式サイトより，アプリをインストール
   https://eigonotomo.com/ [英語の友 🔍]
   （右の2次元コードから読み込めます）

2. アプリ内のライブラリよりご購入いただいた書籍を選び，「追加」ボタンを押してください

3. パスワードを入力すると，音声がダウンロードできます
   ［パスワード：kjwysx］ ※すべて半角アルファベット小文字

※本アプリの機能の一部は有料ですが，本書の音声は無料でお聞きいただけます。
※詳しいご利用方法は「英語の友」公式サイト，あるいはアプリ内ヘルプをご参照ください。

② パソコンで音声データダウンロード（MP3）

［ご利用方法］

1 Web特典にアクセス　詳細は，p.7をご覧ください。

2 「一次試験［二次試験］音声データダウンロード」から
聞きたい検定の回を選択してダウンロード

※音声ファイルはzip形式にまとめられた形でダウンロードされます。
※音声の再生にはMP3を再生できる機器などが必要です。ご使用機器，音声再生ソフト等に関する技術的なご質問は，ハードメーカーもしくはソフトメーカーにお願いいたします。

③ スマートフォン・タブレットでストリーミング再生

［ご利用方法］

1 自動採点サービスにアクセス　詳細は，p.8をご覧ください。
　（右の2次元コードから読み込めます）

2 聞きたい検定の回を選び，
リスニングテストの音声再生ボタンを押す

※自動採点サービスは一次試験に対応していますので，一次試験・リスニングの音声のみお聞きいただけます。（二次試験・面接の音声をお聞きになりたい方は，①リスニングアプリ「英語の友」，②音声データダウンロードをご利用ください）
※音声再生中に音声を止めたい場合は，停止ボタンを押してください。
※個別に問題を再生したい場合は，問題番号を選んでから再生ボタンを押してください。
※音声の再生には多くの通信量が必要となりますので，Wi-Fi環境でのご利用をおすすめいたします。

CDをご希望の方は，別売『2023年度版 英検1級 過去6回全問題集 CD』
（本体価格3,300円+税）をご利用ください。

持ち運びに便利な小冊子とCD4枚付き。　※本書では，収録箇所を **CD 1** **1** ～ **11** のように表示。

Web特典について

購入者限定の「Web特典」を，みなさんの英検合格にお役立てください。

ご利用 可能期間	2023年2月24日〜2024年8月31日 ※本サービスは予告なく変更，終了することがあります。	
アクセス 方法	スマートフォン タブレット	右の2次元コードを読み込むと， パスワードなしでアクセスできます！
	PC スマートフォン タブレット 共通	1. Web特典（以下のURL）にアクセスします。 https://eiken.obunsha.co.jp/1q/ 2. 本書を選択し，以下のパスワードを入力します。 kjwysx ※すべて半角アルファベット小文字

〈特典内容〉

(1)自動採点サービス
リーディング（筆記1〜3），リスニング（Part1〜4）の自動採点ができます。詳細はp.8を参照してください。

(2)解答用紙
本番にそっくりの解答用紙が印刷できるので，何度でも過去問にチャレンジすることができます。

(3)音声データのダウンロード
一次試験リスニング・二次試験面接の音声データ（MP3）を無料でダウンロードできます。
※スマートフォン・タブレットの方は，アプリ「英語の友」(p.5)をご利用ください。

(4)1級面接対策
【面接模範例】入室から退室までの模範応答例を見ることができます。各チェックポイントで，受験上の注意点やアドバイスを確認しておきましょう。
【TOPIC CARD】面接模範例で使用しているトピックカードです。印刷して，実際の面接の練習に使ってください。

自動採点サービスの利用方法

正答率や合格ラインとの距離，間違えた問題などの確認ができるサービスです。

ご利用可能期間	2023年2月24日〜2024年8月31日 ※本サービスは予告なく変更，終了することがあります。	
アクセス方法	スマートフォン タブレット	右の2次元コードを読み込んでアクセスし，採点する検定の回を選択してください。
	PC スマートフォン タブレット 共通	p.7の手順で「Web特典」にアクセスし，「自動採点サービスを使う」を選択してご利用ください。

［ご利用方法］

1　オンラインマークシートにアクセスします

Web特典の「自動採点サービスを使う」から，採点したい検定回を選択するか，各回のマークシートおよび問題編の各回とびらの2次元コードからアクセスします。

2　「問題をはじめる」ボタンを押して筆記試験を始めます

ボタンを押すとタイマーが動き出します。制限時間内に解答できるよう，解答時間を意識して取り組みましょう。

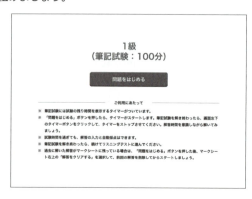

3 筆記試験を解答し終わったら，タイマーボタン  を押して
タイマーをストップさせます

4 リスニングテストは画面下にある音声再生ボタンを押して
音声を再生し，問題に取り組みましょう
一度再生ボタンを押したら，最後の問題まで自動的に
進んでいきます。

5 リスニングテストが終了したら，
「答え合わせ」ボタンを押して答え合わせをします

採点結果の見方

タブの選択で【あなたの成績】と【問題ごとの正誤】が切り替えられます。

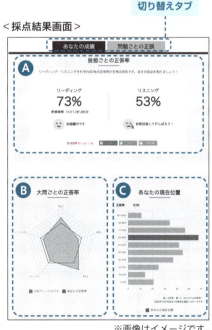

＜採点結果画面＞

【あなたの成績】
Ⓐ 技能ごとの正答率が表示されます。1級の合格の目安，正答率70％を目指しましょう。
Ⓑ 大問ごとの正答率が表示されます。合格ラインを下回る大問は，対策に力を入れましょう。
Ⓒ 採点サービス利用者の中でのあなたの現在位置が示されます。

【問題ごとの正誤】
各問題のあなたの解答と正解が表示されます。間違っている問題については色で示されますので，別冊解答の解説を見直しましょう。

※画像はイメージです。

9

英検®Information インフォメーション

出典：英検ウェブサイト

> **英検1級について**

1級では，「広く社会生活で求められる英語を十分理解し，また使用できる」ことが求められます。
転職や就職，単位認定，海外留学や入試など，多方面で幅広く活用される資格です。
目安としては「大学上級程度」です。

試験内容

一次試験 筆記・リスニング

主な場面・状況	家庭・学校・職場・地域（各種店舗・公共施設を含む）・電話・アナウンス・講義など
主な話題	社会生活一般・芸術・文化・歴史・教育・科学・自然・環境・医療・テクノロジー・ビジネス・政治など

筆記試験 ⏱100分

問題	形式・課題詳細	問題数	満点スコア
1	文脈に合う適切な語句を補う。	25問	
2	パッセージの空所に文脈に合う適切な語句を補う。	6問	850
3	パッセージの内容に関する質問に答える。	10問	
4	指定されたトピックについての英作文を書く。（200～240語）	1問	850

リスニング ⏱約35分 放送回数／1回

問題	形式・課題詳細	問題数	満点スコア
Part 1	会話の内容に関する質問に答える。	10問	
Part 2	パッセージの内容に関する質問に答える。	10問	850
Part 3	Real-Life形式の放送内容に関する質問に答える。	5問	
Part 4	インタビューの内容に関する質問に答える。	2問	

2022年12月現在の情報を掲載しています。試験に関する情報は変更になる可能性がありますので，受験の際は必ず英検ウェブサイトをご確認ください。

二次試験 　面接形式のスピーキングテスト

主な場面・題材	社会性の高い幅広い分野の話題
過去の出題例	科学の発展は常に有益か・芸術への財政的支援増加の是非・世界経済における日本の役割・選挙権の行使を義務化するべきか・遺伝子組み換え食品の安全性・公共の場における治安改善の必要性など

スピーキング　約10分

面接の構成	形式・課題詳細	満点スコア
自由会話	面接委員と簡単な日常会話を行う。	850
スピーチ	与えられた5つのトピックの中から1つ選び，スピーチを行う。（2分間）	
Q&A	スピーチの内容やトピックに関連した質問に答える。	

英検®の種類

英検には，実施方式が異なる複数の試験があります。実施時期や受験上の配慮など，自分に合った方式を選択しましょう。なお，従来型の英検とその他の英検の問題形式，難易度，級認定，合格証明書発行，英検CSEスコア取得等はすべて同じです。

▶英検®(従来型)
紙の問題冊子を見て解答用紙に解答。二次試験を受験するためには，一次試験に合格する必要があります。

▶英検S-CBT
コンピュータを使って受験。1日で4技能を受験することができ，申込時に会場・日程・ライティングの解答方式が選べます。原則，毎週土日に実施されています（級や地域により毎週実施でない場合があります）。ほかの実施方式で取得した一次試験免除の資格も申請可能です。

▶英検S-Interview
点字や吃音等，CBT方式では対応が難しい受験上の配慮が必要な方のみが受験可能。

受験する級によって選択できる方式が異なります。各方式の詳細および最新情報は英検ウェブサイト（https://www.eiken.or.jp/eiken/）をご確認ください。

11

合否判定方法

統計的に算出される英検CSEスコアに基づいて合否判定されます。Reading，Writing，Listening，Speakingの4技能が均等に評価され，合格基準スコアは固定されています。

▶▶ 技能別にスコアが算出される！

技能	試験形式	満点スコア	合格基準スコア
Reading（読む）	一次試験（筆記1〜3）	850	2028
Writing（書く）	一次試験（筆記4）	850	
Listening（聞く）	一次試験（リスニング）	850	
Speaking（話す）	二次試験（面接）	850	602

- 一次試験の合否は，Reading，Writing，Listeningの技能別にスコアが算出され，それを合算して判定されます。
- 二次試験の合否は，Speakingのみで判定されます。

▶▶ 合格するためには，技能のバランスが重要！

英検CSEスコアでは，技能ごとに問題数は異なりますが，スコアを均等に配分しているため，各技能のバランスが重要となります。なお，正答数の目安を提示することはできませんが，2016年度第1回一次試験では，1級，準1級は各技能での正答率が7割程度，2級以下は各技能6割程度の正答率の受験者の多くが合格されています。

▶▶ 英検CSEスコアは国際標準規格CEFRにも対応している！

CEFRとは，Common European Framework of Reference for Languages の略。語学のコミュニケーション能力別のレベルを示す国際標準規格。欧米で幅広く導入され，6つのレベルが設定されています。4技能の英検CSEスコアの合計「4技能総合スコア」と級ごとのCEFR算出範囲に基づいた「4技能総合CEFR」が成績表に表示されます。また，技能別の「CEFRレベル」も表示されます。

CEFR	英検CSEスコア	実用英語技能検定　各級の合格スコア				
C2	4000 〜 3300	■ CEFR算出範囲				1級 満点3400
C1	3299 〜 2600				準1級 満点3000	C1扱い 合格スコア 2630 3299
B2	2599 〜 2300		準2級 満点2400	2級 満点2600 B1扱い	合格スコア 2304 2599	2304
B1	2299 〜 1950	3級 満点2200	A2扱い	合格スコア 1980 2299	1980	
A2	1949 〜 1700	A1扱い 1949	合格スコア 1728	1728	CEFR 算出範囲外	CEFR 算出範囲外
A1	1699 〜 1400	合格スコア 1456 1699	1400 1400	CEFR 算出範囲外		
	1399 〜 0	CEFR 算出範囲外	CEFR 算出範囲外			

※ 4級・5級は4技能を測定していないため「4技能総合CEFR」の対象外。
※ 詳しくは英検ウェブサイトをご覧ください。

英検®（従来型）受験情報

※「従来型・本会場」以外の実施方式については，試験日程・申込方法が異なりますので，英検ウェブサイトをご覧ください。
※ 受験情報は変更になる場合があります。

◉ 2023年度 試験日程

	第 1 回	第 2 回	第 3 回
申込受付	3月31日 ▶ 5月2日	8月1日 ▶ 9月8日	11月1日 ▶ 12月14日
一次試験	6月 4日（日）	10月 8日（日）	1月 21日（日）2024年
二次試験	A 7月 2日（日） C 7月16日（日）	A 11月 5日（日） C 11月23日（木・祝）	A 2月18日（日）2024年 C 3月 3日（日）2024年

※ 一次試験は上記以外の日程でも準会場で受験できる可能性があります。
※ 二次試験にはA日程，B日程（2〜3級），C日程（1級，準1級）があり，受験級などの条件により指定されます。
※ 詳しくは英検ウェブサイトをご覧ください。

◉ 申込方法

団体受験	▶	学校や塾などで申し込みをする団体受験もあります。詳しくは先生にお尋ねください。
個人受験	▶	インターネット申込・コンビニ申込・英検特約書店申込のいずれかの方法で申し込みができます。詳しくは英検ウェブサイトをご覧ください。

お問い合わせ先

英検サービスセンター
TEL. 03-3266-8311
㊊〜㊎ 9：30 〜 17：00
（祝日・年末年始を除く）

英検ウェブサイト
www.eiken.or.jp/eiken/
試験についての詳しい情報を見たり，入試等で英検を活用している学校の検索をすることができます。

2022年度の傾向と攻略ポイント

2022年度第1回検定と第2回検定を分析し、出題傾向と攻略ポイントをまとめました。1級の合格に必要な正答率は7割程度と予測されます。正答率が7割を切った大問は苦手な分野だと考えましょう。

一次試験　筆記（100分）

1　短文の語句空所補充
問題数 **25**問　めやす **15**分

傾向　20～30語程度の短文中の空所に入るべき語句の4択問題が25問。(1)～(21)が単語、(22)～(25)が熟語の問題。単語は動詞、形容詞、名詞で、熟語は2語からなる句動詞。この2回では出題されなかったが、単語には副詞が1問含まれることが多い。また、句動詞は3語のこともある。

攻略ポイント　素早く状況を理解し、適切な語を選ぶ。高難度の語句が出題されるので、語彙力強化は必須。派生語や類語、語源の知識を利用した学習が効率的だろう。

2　長文の語句空所補充
問題数 **6**問　めやす **15**分

傾向　3段落からなる350語程度の長文2本で、文中の空所に入るべき語句を4つの選択肢から選ぶ問題が各3問（計6問）。

攻略ポイント　全体の構成を考えながら話の流れをしっかり追うことが最重要。特に接続表現が順接か逆接か、代名詞が何を指すか、に注意して読み進め、筋が通る選択肢を選ぼう。

3　長文の内容一致選択
問題数 **10**問　めやす **40**分

傾向　3段落からなる500語程度の長文2本と、7段落の800語程度の長文の計3本で、4つの選択肢から選ぶ内容一致問題が計10問。

攻略ポイント　先に設問を見てその答えを探しながら本文を読み進めたい。正解は本文とは違う表現を使って言い換えられているので、的確な読解力が必要となる。

4　英作文
問題数 **1**問　めやす **25**分

傾向　社会的問題に関する200～240語の英作文。3つの理由を提示し、「序論」「本論」「結論」で構成することが求められる。出題は、第1回が「賛成か反対か：遺伝子操作は将来の社会によい影響を与える」、第2回が「賛成か反対か：人間社会は常に環境に悪い影響を与えるだろう」。

攻略ポイント　明確な論理の展開ができるかを意識して、3つの理由とそれらの補足説明・例示を素早く決めてから、書き始めよう。時間を計って実際に書く練習が非常に有効。

一次試験　リスニング（約35分）

Part 1　Dialogues　問題数 10問

傾向　ダイアログに関する内容一致の4択問題が10問。家庭や職場など，日常のさまざまな場面における男女間の会話が扱われる（(10)のみ3人）。

攻略ポイント　日常会話で使われる句動詞や言い回しが出てくるので慣れておきたい。暗示的な発言の真意を問う設問が多く出題されるので，流れを正確に把握して聞く。

Part 2　Passages　問題数 10問

傾向　短い説明文が5本放送され，それぞれについて内容一致の4択問題が2問ずつ，計10問出題される。内容は学術的なものが多い。

攻略ポイント　最初に読まれるタイトルは内容を予測する上で重要な情報。専門用語や固有名詞が出てきても説明されるか文脈からわかる場合が多いので，慌てずに集中して聞く。

Part 3　Real-Life　問題数 5問

傾向　実生活におけるアナウンスや指示文などが放送され，問題用紙に印刷されている状況（Situation）に合致する内容を選ぶ問題が5問。

攻略ポイント　最初に設けられる10秒間で Situation と Question を素早く正確に把握することが最重要。音声が流れたら，状況に合った内容に的を絞って聞き取る。

Part 4　Interview　問題数 2問

傾向　3分〜3分半程度のインタビューが放送され，内容一致の4択問題2問に答える。質問は主にゲストの仕事に関するもの。

攻略ポイント　インタビューの直前にされるゲストの説明を聞き逃さないこと。聞き手からの質問は4つ程度。質問とその応答のポイントを整理して聞く。応答は長めなので適宜メモを取りたい。

二次試験　面接（約10分）

二次試験では5つのトピックが提示され，1分間で1つを選び準備をして，2分間のスピーチを行う。トピックは社会，政治経済，教育，科学など広い分野にわたる。本年度も，「文化遺産の保存」や「経済犯罪への処罰」など，さまざまな話題が取り上げられた。またどちらの回でも，「大企業は政策に影響を与え過ぎていないか」「非倫理的な活動にかかわっている企業を消費者は完全に避けることができるか」と企業活動に関するトピックが出題された。日ごろから問題意識を持ってニュースを読み，国内および国際問題に対して自分の意見をまとめてその根拠となる情報を集め，英語で伝える練習をしておこう。

二次試験・面接の流れ

(1) 入室
係員の指示に従い，面接室に入ります。面接カードを手渡し，指示に従って，着席しましょう。

(2) 氏名の確認と日常会話
面接委員があなたの氏名を確認します。その後，簡単な日常会話をしてから試験開始です。

(3) トピックカードの受け取りとスピーチの考慮
5つのトピックが書かれたトピックカードを受け取ります。1分間でトピックを1つ選び，スピーチの内容を考えます。メモを取ることはできません。

※トピックカードには複数の種類があり，面接委員によっていずれか1枚が手渡されます。本書では英検協会から提供を受けたもののみ掲載しています。

(4) スピーチ（2分間）
面接委員の指示に従い，スピーチをします。スピーチが終わる前に2分が経過してしまった場合は，言いかけていたセンテンスのみ，言い終えることが許可されます。

(5) Q&A（4分間）
2名の面接委員と，スピーチの内容やトピックに関する質疑応答が行われます。

(6) カード返却と退室
試験が終了したら，トピックカードを面接委員に返却し，あいさつをして退室しましょう。

2022-2

一次試験　2022.10.9 実施
二次試験　A日程　2022.11.6 実施
　　　　　C日程　2022.11.23 実施

Grade 1

試験時間

筆記：100分
リスニング：約35分

一次試験・筆記　　　　　p.18～32
一次試験・リスニング　　p.33～39
二次試験・面接　　　　　　　p.40

＊解答・解説は別冊p.5～56にあります。
＊面接の流れは本書p.16にあります。

2022年度第2回

Web特典「自動採点サービス」対応
オンラインマークシート

※検定の回によって2次元コードが違います。
※筆記1～3，リスニングの採点ができます。
※PCからも利用できます (本書 p.8 参照)。

一次試験
筆 記

---

1 To complete each item, choose the best word or phrase from among the four choices. Then, on your answer sheet, find the number of the question and mark your answer.

---

(1) *A:* Did the chairperson say why he was resigning?
B: No, he refused to (　　　) the reason. He said it was strictly a private matter.
1 divulge　　**2** condone　　**3** shun　　**4** elude

(2) The prime minister's position began to look increasingly (　　　) as more and more politicians left the party to join the new one.
1 propitious　**2** lustrous　　**3** precarious　**4** spasmodic

(3) Although the man did not tell the police any outright lies, he left out several (　　　) details that would have made it clear the accident had been his fault.
1 irate　　　**2** dilapidated　**3** ravenous　**4** salient

(4) While he was cleaning out his garage, Ken cut his hand on a sharp nail that was (　　　) from the wall.
1 fretting　　**2** mustering　**3** protruding　**4** replenishing

(5) Glen somehow (　　　) himself into thinking Heather was in love with him, even after she made it clear that she was not interested in him.
1 deluded　　**2** parried　　**3** quenched　**4** inundated

(6) Researchers have found that sharing a traumatic experience can create a feeling of (　　　) between people, often leading to lifelong friendships.
1 camaraderie **2** defamation　**3** calamity　**4** exuberance

(7) The police found no proof of the girl's (　　　) in the robbery committed by her boyfriend, so they let her go free.
1 mayhem　　**2** debacle　　**3** complicity　**4** gibberish

(8) The team's (　　　) performance this season has confused everyone. In one game, they might play very well, while in the next, they might make numerous mistakes.
1 scrupulous　**2** erratic　　**3** methodical　**4** gleaming

(9) The defendant's (   ) surprised everyone in the courtroom. They all thought the jury would return with a guilty verdict.
1 referral   **2** sojourn   **3** acquittal   **4** snare

(10) *A:* What's your new colleague like?
B: We don't get along very well. He's been (   ) toward me from day one. It's almost as though he's looking to fight with me.
1 eclectic   **2** intrinsic   **3** apathetic   **4** antagonistic

(11) The weather was warm and humid, so as soon as Percy left the hotel, he began to (   ) heavily. In no time at all, his shirt was stained with sweat.
1 patronize   **2** truncate   **3** perspire   **4** transcend

(12) After he was arrested for robbery, Brad called his sister and asked her to pay his (   ). However, she did not have the $10,000 needed for his release.
1 void   **2** effigy   **3** stint   **4** bail

(13) As a young boy, Evan was (   ) with a lung disease that made it impossible for him to participate in sports activities at school.
1 bolstered   **2** afflicted   **3** indulged   **4** confiscated

(14) *A:* Steve, can you explain this graph?
B: The blue lines (   ) our company's expenses, and the green lines represent the volume of sales we made last year.
1 denote   **2** smear   **3** decry   **4** squint

(15) The manager's assumption that his employee was stealing money proved to be (   ). An accounting mistake was the cause of the problem.
1 erroneous   **2** perpetual   **3** rigorous   **4** profuse

(16) The city council ordered the (   ) of the old building because it was too dangerous to leave it standing any longer.
1 intimation   **2** demolition   **3** allocation   **4** extortion

(17) Helen asked her neighbor to water her garden while she was away. Unfortunately, he forgot, and many of her flowers had (   ) by the time she returned.
1 tarnished   **2** polarized   **3** wilted   **4** slighted

(18) Although the film's subject matter is very serious, there are moments of (　　　) that prevent it from becoming too depressing.

1 levity **2** confluence **3** impetus **4** hegemony

(19) Yesterday, Andrew received a (　　　) e-mail from an unknown address. No matter how hard he tried, he could not understand what it was trying to say.

1 poignant **2** resilient **3** cryptic **4** delectable

(20) The handmade furniture brand is known for its (　　　) attention to detail. Each piece is crafted with great care.

1 relenting **2** tasteless **3** fastidious **4** insular

(21) When Roger tried to pick up his brother's baby for the first time, she (　　　) so much that Roger had trouble holding her properly.

1 squirmed **2** cleaved **3** scrounged **4** lampooned

(22) Peer pressure can have a powerful influence on teenagers. When (　　　) by friends, they can be persuaded to do some very foolish things.

1 bogged down **2** hitched up
3 goofed off **4** egged on

(23) When Michelle's neighbors have loud parties, she turns up her music to (　　　) the noise from next door.

1 fritter away **2** lap up **3** drown out **4** cave in

(24) The car company is working to (　　　) its old-fashioned image and appeal to young people by designing modern-looking cars with high-tech devices.

1 cast off **2** call out **3** dial up **4** box in

(25) The accusations of misconduct (　　　) the politician by former staff members have the potential to end his political career.

1 leveled at **2** drummed into
3 banked on **4** pitched for

---

2 *Read each passage and choose the best word or phrase from among the four choices for each blank. Then, on your answer sheet, find the number of the question and mark your answer.*

Spider Survival

A fascinating species of jumping spider found across the eastern United States called *Synemosyna formica* has been observed (**26**). Biologists theorize this behavior stems from the fact that the spiders, with their solitary lifestyles, tend to be attractive targets for many predators. Ants, on the other hand, are less appealing prey, owing to their powerful jaws and the fact that they are rarely unaccompanied; a predator attempting to feast on one ant, for instance, would likely have to fight off numerous other aggressive ones that come to its aid. Taking advantage of ants' fierce reputation, the spiders have developed certain behaviors to impersonate the insects, such as waving their front legs in a motion resembling that of ants' antennae. When successfully performed, this helps the spiders avert predatory attention.

S. formica has also come to bear a strong physical resemblance to ants. But while the adaptations are helpful for deceiving predators, they (**27**). The spiders' back legs appear to have evolved to be longer and thicker, and their bodies have become slender and segmented, accentuating their antlike appearance when viewed from above — a common vantage point for predators. Yet these changes appear to have rendered the spiders unable to perform the leaping action for which related species are known — a consequence, perhaps, of the constraints of an antlike structure and body weight, according to biologists. And since this ability, which is crucial for hunting prey, has diminished, the spiders' survival could be in jeopardy.

One mystery is how *S. formica* manages to (**28**). Most types of jumping spiders employ showy, elaborate rituals to entice prospective partners. Attracting partners is no less important for *S. formica*, but such acts of courtship in the open would likely draw unwanted attention from predators. To get around this, the spiders seemingly recognize each other from afar. Although they appear able to signal that they are not ants without sacrificing the guise of their antlike behavior, the exact mechanisms behind this discreet action remain unclear. Biologists hope that by expanding research into these peculiar creatures they can deepen their understanding of how survival instincts drive adaptations in animals.

(26) 1 trying to overpower larger species
2 significantly altering its diet
3 helping another species survive
4 mimicking another creature

(27) 1 also assist the spiders in other ways
2 have made some body parts useless
3 may have come at a cost
4 likely occurred for other reasons

(28) 1 locate new habitats
2 find potential mates
3 conceal its breeding locations
4 prevent predators from finding it

Valuing the Economy

The idea that war is beneficial for the economy is familiar to many people, and it is based on the assumption that major conflicts bring huge demand for production of supplies, stimulating job creation. Some experts, however, (**29**   ). Ultimately, most of what is created during massive arms-production efforts is used up or destroyed during battle, whereas the same funds and resources would provide significant long-term benefits if devoted to generating consumer goods and services. In fact, the experts note, this was observed after World War II, when the United States experienced a surprising period of prosperity following the government's dramatic reduction in military spending.

In recent years, economist Tyler Cowen has been an advocate for a revised theory of the economic merits associated with war. Accepting that military engagement itself cannot possibly be positive for economies, he argues that it is the (**30**   ) that is beneficial. Cowen contends that the recent stagnation of some economies around the world can be attributed to a pervading lack of urgency that slowly develops as a result of prolonged periods of peace. Citing examples such as the tremendous innovations that came out of the long period of hostility during the Cold War, when both the United States and the Soviet Union feared the other's tremendous military capabilities,

Cowen believes it is the potential for armed conflict that keeps governments on their toes, pressuring them to liberalize the economy and commit funds to science and technology, among other things.

Cowen is not proposing that nations should go around picking fights, however. In fact, he goes on to say that since weapons have become so much more destructive these days, the fallout that would occur if war actually broke out would be catastrophic, so economic stagnation might be a relatively good thing in today's world. He suggests, therefore, that it may be better (31   ). Just as there has been a recent realization that environmental devastation is not worth the benefits associated with the rampant use of fossil fuels, it is likely that the potential risks of constantly being on the verge of war cannot be justified by the rewards.

---

(29) **1** claim there is another reason for this
     2 point out that the idea is flawed
     3 underestimate the cost of war
     4 say the idea only applies to wars

(30) **1** spending on weapons
     2 threat of conflict
     3 gaining of territory
     4 aftermath of war

(31) **1** for nations to develop better technology
     2 to prevent short-term losses
     3 for people to use resources more efficiently
     4 to trade growth for peace

---

3 *Read each passage and choose the best answer from among the four choices for each question. Then, on your answer sheet, find the number of the question and mark your answer.*

Biopiracy

In their efforts to develop new medicines and foodstuffs,

multinational corporations frequently rely on indigenous peoples' knowledge of medicinal plants and other resources. This sometimes leads to accusations of biopiracy, a term referring to attempts to patent products found with the aid of indigenous peoples without providing them with fair compensation. It is generally agreed that when enlisting the aid of indigenous peoples in this way, it is essential to have informed consent regarding how the resources may be used, including the possibility that they will be turned into lucrative products. It is also important to draw up agreements detailing the rights and obligations of both parties before the start of any cooperation. However, such agreements often reflect fundamental differences between indigenous and other worldviews, which frequently lead to misunderstandings and exploitation. While Western societies, for instance, place emphasis on legal protections such as patents and trademarks, indigenous groups often find the concept of an individual or company possessing exclusive rights to natural resources and organisms to be incomprehensible. As a result, many indigenous groups have brought lawsuits against corporations that they say deceived them.

Furthermore, although legislation and international treaties have been enacted to combat biopiracy, creating unambiguous and comprehensive regulations has proved extremely challenging. In fact, the term biopiracy itself lacks a single unified definition, and regulations regarding it vary among nations, making it difficult to stamp out unethical practices. The Nagoya Protocol, for example, was designed to be a framework on which nations could build their own legislation to control access to genetic resources and ensure that benefits resulting from the use of such resources are shared. Yet the agreement has been interpreted and implemented in widely differing ways, and it has only been signed by a relatively small percentage of nations. These factors are a major reason why the practice of biopiracy has shown little sign of ending.

Legislation targeting biopiracy may also have unintended consequences. One group of scientists published an article arguing international agreements related to curbing biopiracy are already causing nations that are home to precious resources and organisms to throw up obstacles to urgently needed research. In particular, the science of taxonomy, which involves the discovery and classification of species for conservation purposes, has been significantly hampered by such international agreements. The scientists write that "biodiversity research has seemingly become suspect in the minds of many regulatory bodies, owing to fear that a taxonomic discovery today might conceivably translate into a commercial development tomorrow." Researchers in some countries have become reluctant to share specimens with scientists abroad, and others complain the regulatory hurdles they need to clear to obtain permits are hindering research, including conservation studies. On the other hand, the scientists who wrote the article note that, in the case of medical research, the development of advanced technologies such as genetic engineering means that obtaining access to organisms known to indigenous peoples could become less important. This would not only allow crucial scientific research to continue unimpeded but also cause current anti-biopiracy agreements to lose their relevance.

(32) When multinational corporations make agreements with indigenous peoples,

1 there has been a tendency for both parties to entrust the drawing up of legal rights such as patents and trademarks to an independent party.

2 there are often significant differences in the way that the parties involved understand fundamental concepts contained in the documents.

3 the parties involved generally disagree more about issues regarding medicines than they do about other types of products.

4 there is a need to explain not only the benefits indigenous peoples will receive but also the fact that their cooperation is vital to ongoing research.

(33) In the second paragraph, what does the author of the passage state about efforts to prevent biopiracy?

1 Legislation and treaties would be much more effective if both corporations and indigenous peoples were consulted during their creation.

2 There have been some signs that biopiracy is declining, but indigenous peoples say that the efforts have not gone far enough.

25

3 Local laws have generally been much more successful at decreasing biopiracy than international treaties have.

4 Their lack of success is largely the result of the difficulty of creating clear rules that every country will agree to follow.

(34) Which of the following statements would the scientists who wrote the article mentioned in the final paragraph most likely agree with?

1 Biopiracy is often disguised as conservation research, so this type of research should be more carefully regulated.

2 Although medical technologies like genetic engineering are advancing, they are creating greater risks of indigenous people being harmed by biopiracy.

3 Regulations designed to prevent biopiracy have the potential to interfere with essential research that could save endangered species.

4 Scientists' attempts to steal taxonomy research from one another present a far more serious problem than biopiracy does.

The Early Solar System

The origin of our solar system has long been the subject of speculation. The most widely accepted explanation is the nebular hypothesis, which argues that the solar system began as a massive cloud of interstellar gas and debris that collapsed under immense gravitational forces. The resulting mass of swirling matter eventually formed into pockets of material that then came together to become the sun and planets. While this accounts well for some aspects of the solar system's formation, other predictions derived from the hypothesis do not line up with the solar system's current state. For example, in computer simulations based on the hypothesis, the masses of certain planets and the regions in which those planets reside were inconsistent with current astronomical observations. The discrepancies, however, could be due to the fact that the nebular hypothesis was originally based on the assumption that planets in our solar system formed in their current locations and have mostly remained there.

Some of these mysteries may be close to being solved. The smaller planets of the inner solar system are believed to have formed from matter able to withstand the sun's tremendous heat, such as rock and metal. Conversely, the gas giants Jupiter and Saturn are thought to have formed in regions farther from the sun, beyond what is referred to as the frost line, as temperatures at this distance are low enough for the matter that makes up gas giants to solidify. Scientists, however, have observed Jupiter-like gas planets in distant solar systems — nicknamed "hot Jupiters" — orbiting their suns at surprisingly close distances. To explain this, scientists proposed the concept of planetary migration, and a scenario named the "grand tack" was modeled, using Jupiter's formation as a basis, to test the concept. In the scenario, Jupiter takes shape beyond the frost line, as is expected, but migrates toward the inner solar system, imitating hot Jupiters. However, as a result of gravitational forces from our solar system's other gas giant, Saturn, Jupiter is drawn back out to its current location farther from the sun. Despite sounding far-fetched, the scenario has been praised for plausibly explaining why hot Jupiters exist.

The grand tack scenario may also provide clarity for other apparent inconsistencies in our solar system. When the computer simulations based on the nebular hypothesis projected that Mars should be much larger than it currently is, the proposed grand tack migration of Jupiter suggested an explanation. By factoring in Jupiter's trajectory in the grand tack scenario, scientists realized the gas giant was likely scattering matter close to the sun that would otherwise have greatly increased Mars's mass. Furthermore, had Jupiter not made its migration, planets in the inner solar system, which includes the area where Earth is now, could very well have become larger, uninhabitable worlds shrouded by gas. The vast majority of the inner regions of other known solar systems are populated by such planets, so scientists believe our solar system may be extremely unique in this regard. If the grand tack scenario proves to be correct, humankind owes a great deal of gratitude to Jupiter for the planet's journey through the solar system.

(35) According to the author of the passage, what is one problem with the nebular hypothesis?

1 Although it accurately predicts that planets can change locations in the solar system, its predictions do not apply to other objects in space.

2 It does not sufficiently explain how gravitational forces affected the size and location of the sun during the early formation of our solar system.

3 Using it to model the history of our solar system has produced results that do not match what we currently know about certain planets.

4 It was based partly on inaccurate astronomical theories about the manner in which solar systems in distant areas of the universe formed.

(36) "Hot Jupiters" are significant because

1 they are evidence that the temperatures of frost lines detected in other solar systems have little connection to how planets are formed.

2 their size strongly implies that many of the other planets found in our solar system were once much smaller than they are now.

3 they support theories suggesting that the size of a star is directly related to the orbiting distance of its planets.

4 their existence appears to provide evidence to support the idea that planets do not always remain in the same orbits.

(37) What can be inferred about the "grand tack" scenario based on the third paragraph?

1 It could reasonably explain why Mars was not pulled into the sun and destroyed during the early days of the solar system.

2 The probability of life evolving on Earth would likely have been a great deal lower if it had never occurred.

3 There is a lower chance of life existing on large planets in solar systems where such events have taken place.

4 Solar systems where such events have never happened are likely to have planets that resemble Jupiter and Saturn.

The 1916 Irish Uprising

On the eve of World War I, Ireland, which had been absorbed into the United Kingdom around a century earlier, was on the verge of winning limited self-government, or Home Rule. Although Ireland had political representation in the British Parliament, it lacked its own government, which resulted in poverty, depopulation, and economic exploitation. As a result, nationalism had grown steadily throughout the 1800s, with the Home Rule movement becoming dominant within Irish politics. Since the 1870s, the Irish Parliamentary Party had pursued this agenda, which would allow Ireland a degree of independence in its domestic affairs while still keeping the country within the United Kingdom. The party, led by John Redmond, finally succeeded in getting a Home Rule Bill passed in the British Parliament in 1914.

There was to be no straightforward route to Home Rule, however. Ireland was divided along religious and political lines, with the South dominated by Catholics who tended to embrace nationalism to some degree, and the North by Protestants who felt more strongly tied to Britain politically and were resolved to remain under the jurisdiction of the British Parliament. In the South, a group known as the Irish Republican Brotherhood (IRB) found Home Rule to be insufficient because it did not offer true sovereignty. The IRB was so intent on achieving total independence for Ireland that it took up arms, yet it by no means represented mainstream views, even in the South. This became clear with Britain's involvement in World War I in August 1914: the IRB opposed Ireland's participation in the war, but the Irish Parliamentary Party supported it, accepting that the enactment of Home Rule would have to be postponed. The majority of the Irish public agreed, supporting the war in the same way as other UK nationals.

As Britain focused its military resources on fighting abroad, the IRB leadership believed that fewer soldiers would be available for security purposes in Ireland. So, on April 24, 1916, with Britain's attention diverted by its preparations for a large-scale military offensive near the Somme River in France, the IRB decided the time was ripe for action. Led by a military council that had been formed within the organization, it rose up in armed rebellion against British rule and proclaimed the formation of a republic.

Around 1,500 people — IRB members along with members of other nationalist groups — occupied various sites throughout Dublin, Ireland's capital. They had hoped their actions would inspire a wider uprising among the general population, but this did not occur. Moreover, lack of manpower meant they could not capture major railway stations and docks, or, most importantly, Dublin Castle, the British government's administrative headquarters. Consequently, Britain was able to move soldiers into the city unimpeded and retain control of its administrative center, which proved key. Thus, despite being initially caught off guard, the British quickly gained the upper hand through a swiftly organized counterattack. British troops flooded into the city, and heavy artillery was employed, leading to fire damage and civilian casualties.

Although they fought valiantly, the rebels were vastly outmanned and outgunned. They were forced back into a defensive position, and it was only a matter of time before they surrendered. The uprising ended on April 29, leaving approximately 450 dead and 2,000 injured, with much of the center of Dublin destroyed.

British retaliation was prompt and harsh: thousands of people suspected of involvement in the rebellion were rounded up and the leaders were tried and convicted by military courts. Fifteen of the rebels were executed by firing squad following trials that were conducted in secret and without defense attorneys, which British officials later ruled to have been in violation of established military judicial procedures. Given that the rebels had struck during wartime, a military response — including conducting the trials in military courts rather than civilian ones — was considered by some at the time to be justifiable. However, officials in the British government quickly became concerned about the manner in which the British commanding officer in Ireland was dealing with the rebels and the reaction this might provoke.

While further executions were halted, public opinion against British rule was galvanized as a result of the executions of men whom many Irish people regarded as patriots. The uprising had indirectly become a catalyst for a change in public sentiment. The Home Rule movement lost steam, and there emerged in its place widespread acceptance of the rhetoric of a political party called Sinn Féin, allowing the party to dominate the 1918 UK elections in Ireland. The party refused to take up its seats in the British Parliament and declared independence, which escalated into a guerrilla conflict that culminated in a large part of Ireland achieving the sovereignty the IRB had originally sought. Honored by statues and commemorated annually, the 1916 uprising is now regarded as a central event in Irish history.

(38) According to the passage, what is true regarding the political situation in Ireland in 1914?

  1 The outbreak of a major war had caused a conflict to arise between the Irish Parliamentary Party and various Protestant groups that had once supported it.

  2 Opposition to the Home Rule Bill had grown because support for the Irish Parliamentary Party had become much weaker.

  3 Although it lacked widespread public support, the Irish Republican Brotherhood (IRB) was determined that Ireland should become fully independent from Britain.

  4 The debate surrounding Home Rule helped to unite Protestants and Catholics in their opposition to fighting in World War I.

(39) What is one point the author of the passage makes about the uprising that occurred between April 24 and 29, 1916?

  1 If the IRB had waited until the start of the battle near the Somme River, the British may not have had sufficient troops to defeat the rebels.

  2 The rebels failed to secure important strategic sites that would have greatly weakened British troops' ability to defeat them.

  3 The British used a large amount of force to strike fear into civilians, thereby limiting the possibility that they might join the rebels.

  4 The rebels who took part included people who felt some loyalty to Britain, which made them less willing to harm British troops.

(40) The British reaction following the 1916 uprising was problematic on the grounds that

  1 thousands of rebels were found guilty in military courts,

despite the fact that few had played any significant role in the fighting.
2 it was later admitted by the government that its own troops had violated many of the same military laws it used to sentence the rebels.
3 the government made the situation worse by encouraging the commanding officer to conduct the rebels' trials in secret.
4 the way rebel leaders were tried and convicted did not adhere to the correct and proper procedures established by military law.

(41) Which of the following statements best describes the impact of the 1916 uprising?

1 The subsequent political success of Sinn Féin proved the electoral process should have been utilized from the beginning to facilitate change in Ireland.
2 Although the incident itself did not bring about immediate change, it eventually led to considerable progress being made toward the rebels' goal.
3 The uprising was significant because the military tactics employed during it would become invaluable in helping Ireland succeed in later conflicts.
4 Although the event resulted in destruction and loss of life, it was justified because it marked the end of Ireland's conflict with Britain.

4
- Write an essay on the given TOPIC.
- Give THREE reasons to support your answer.
- Structure: introduction, main body, and conclusion
- Suggested length: 200–240 words
- Write your essay in the space provided on Side B of your answer sheet. Any writing outside the space will not be graded.

TOPIC

Agree or disagree: Human societies will always have a negative effect on the environment

リスニング

―――――― Listening Test ――――――

There are four parts to this listening test.

Part 1	Dialogues: 1 question each	Multiple-choice
Part 2	Passages: 2 questions each	Multiple-choice
Part 3	Real-Life: 1 question each	Multiple-choice
Part 4	Interview: 2 questions	Multiple-choice

※**Listen carefully to the instructions.**

Part 1　　▶MP3　▶アプリ　▶CD 1　1～11

No. 1
1　Take a tour of the school.
2　Fill out an application form.
3　Speak with some of the students.
4　Go to the school's admissions office.

No. 2
1　He is having trouble understanding his work.
2　He needs help fixing some lights.
3　He may be too tired to do all his work.
4　He is moving to a new apartment.

No. 3
1　Reschedule the vacation for a later date.
2　Apply to become the jury coordinator.
3　Do her jury duty another time.
4　Come back from the vacation early.

No. 4
1　She does not know which products are safe.
2　The store will not give her a refund.
3　Her favorite product is only sold on the Internet.
4　The product's label is difficult to read.

No. 5　1 How much the bank will invest in the woman's company.
2 When the woman's loan will be approved.
3 Why the woman's business venture is risky.
4 What the woman needs to qualify for a loan.

No. 6　1 He will have to work longer hours in the future.
2 His boss does not recognize his achievements.
3 He could not choose which project to work on.
4 His boss has canceled his latest project.

No. 7　1 Fewer people will ride the bus downtown.
2 Businesses downtown need more support.
3 She will consider running for city council.
4 Repairing the sidewalks would be too costly.

No. 8　1 Inquire about a local baseball league.
2 Contact the karate school next month.
3 Sign Tyler up for a volunteer program.
4 Play softball as a family this weekend.

No. 9　1 Replace the filter more often.
2 Get rid of the shrimp in the tank.
3 Put less food in the tank.
4 Check the water quality every week.

No. 10　1 The discounts are not on all products.
2 The products they want are not available online.
3 They would not visit the store very often.
4 They think the membership fee is too high.

||||| Part 2 |||||||||||||||||||||||||||||||||||||||||||||||||||||||||| ◀)) ▶MP3 ▶アプリ ▶CD 1 **12**～**17**

(A)

No. 11
1 Evidence that shows people with dementia sleep more.
2 Various sleep disorders reported by young people.
3 Lifestyle changes as a treatment for dementia.
4 The sleep patterns of middle-aged people.

No. 12
1 Protein buildup is not always a sign of dementia.
2 Participants' sleep patterns were likely not caused by dementia.
3 Better treatments for dementia will soon be developed.
4 Middle-aged people generally have difficulty sleeping.

(B)

No. 13
1 Some kinds of meat were not readily available.
2 Studies showed they were healthier than meat.
3 They could be stored longer than other foods.
4 They were easier to process than other foods.

No. 14
1 The agriculture industry heavily promoted them in the 1960s.
2 Scientists learned how to make them taste like meat.
3 Their widespread use by parts of the food industry.
4 Cultural shifts in the second half of the twentieth century.

(C)

No. 15
1 It should target all available formats equally.
2 It is more likely to increase profits when done early.
3 It has been given less priority by studios recently.
4 It should not be handled by the studios alone.

No. 16
1 They often feature too many action scenes.
2 They have more impact after a movie's release.
3 They are more effective when seen repeatedly.
4 They are less interesting when seen in theaters.

(D)

No. 17
1 To supply goods to isolated regions.
2 To improve relationships with foreign countries.
3 To restore the ecology of desert areas.
4 To give them as gifts to senior military officers.

No. 18
1 They were captured to be sold to circuses.
2 They eventually spread across the desert.
3 Their population was too small to sustain itself.
4 They continued to be sighted for nearly 100 years.

(E)

No. 19
1 It is difficult to identify what kind of snake bit them.
2 Traditional medicines are generally unavailable.
3 They sometimes receive poor-quality antivenins.
4 Doctors often give them too much antivenin.

No. 20
1 It is more expensive than other antivenins.
2 Its production causes harm to animals.
3 It is only effective for mild snakebites.
4 It can be kept at room temperature.

|||||| Part 3 |||||||||||||||||||||||||||||||||||||||||||||||||||| ◀)) ▶MP3 ▶アプリ ▶CD 1 **18**～**23**

(F)

No. 21

Situation: You broke your ankle, but it does not hurt too badly. You have never used crutches before. At the hospital, a doctor tells you the following.

Question: What should you do next?

1 Ask for the tutorial.
2 Put on the special boot.
3 Get another x-ray.
4 Ask for a prescription.

(G)

No. 22

Situation: You are shopping for a vacuum cleaner. Your home has hardwood floors and several small rugs. You have a dog. A salesperson tells you the following.

Question: Which vacuum cleaner should you buy?

1 The ThunderClean 100.
2 The DeepVac.
3 The DustGuster.
4 The DustGuster Plus.

37

(H)

No. 23

Situation: You are on a business trip, and you just noticed that your suit jacket has a stain. It is 2 p.m., and you have a presentation tomorrow morning. The hotel receptionist tells you the following.

Question: What should you do with your jacket?

1 Send it to the Drop-and-Go service.
2 Bring it to the front desk.
3 Try to clean it yourself.
4 Take it to the nearby dry cleaner.

(I)

No. 24

Situation: You are driving from your home in Eastwick to your office downtown when you hear the following traffic report on the radio. You have not yet reached Battery Bridge.

Question: Which route should you take?

1 The Channel Freeway.
2 Battery Bridge.
3 The Martin Highway.
4 Sunset Road.

(J)

No. 25

Situation: It is your first day as an intern at an advertising company. You want to become a graphic designer but do not have any experience. Another intern is explaining your schedule.

Question: Who should you talk to this afternoon?

1 Martha.
2 Mark.
3 Hilda.
4 Carol.

|||| Part 4 |||||||||||||||||||||||||||||||||||||||||||||||||| ◀» ▶MP3 ▶アプリ ▶CD 1 **24**～**25**

No. 26

1 She noticed that people at fairs mostly bought records from the 1960s, '70s, and '80s.
2 She wanted to earn some pocket money by selling things she was not using.
3 She was inspired by her father making a lot of money selling records at markets.
4 She could not find a satisfactory teaching job and wanted to make money quickly.

No. 27

1 The shop was conveniently located near where the fairs were held.
2 The extra income from a second shop would allow her to quit teaching.
3 Customers wanted her to open a shop that specialized in signed records.
4 She wanted a larger shop but was hesitant to sell her original shop.

二次試験
面 接

A日程　◀))　▶MP3　▶アプリ　▶CD4 **1**～**5**

1. Do large corporations have too much influence on government policies?

2. Are growing populations an advantage or a disadvantage for developing countries?

3. Agree or disagree: The illegal trade in wild species is impossible to stop

4. Is Japan doing enough to protect its cultural heritage?

5. Do developed countries have a moral responsibility to lead the way in renewable energy research?

C日程

1. Is the global agriculture industry too dependent on the use of chemicals?

2. Should the gap between the rich and the poor in modern society be a bigger concern?

3. Are company hiring processes too focused on people's academic backgrounds?

4. Agree or disagree: The advantages of megacities outweigh the disadvantages

5. Is the problem of stress in modern workplaces being dealt with sufficiently?

（注）モデルスピーチと解説はA日程のみ収録しています。

2022-1

一次試験　2022.6.5実施
二次試験　A日程　2022.7.3実施
　　　　　C日程　2022.7.17実施

Grade 1

試験時間
筆記：100分
リスニング：約35分

一次試験・筆記　　　　　p.42〜56
一次試験・リスニング　　p.57〜63
二次試験・面接　　　　　　　p.64

＊解答・解説は別冊p.57〜108にあります。
＊面接の流れは本書p.16にあります。

2022年度第1回

Web特典「自動採点サービス」対応オンラインマークシート
※検定の回によって2次元コードが違います。
※筆記1〜3，リスニングの採点ができます。
※PCからも利用できます（本書 p.8 参照）。

一次試験
筆 記

1 To complete each item, choose the best word or phrase from among the four choices. Then, on your answer sheet, find the number of the question and mark your answer.

(1) The governor is often accused of (　　　) to the rich. He has repeatedly cut taxes for high-income earners during his time in office.
1 pandering　**2** pervading　**3** bemoaning　**4** sauntering

(2) Rather than (　　　) students in a narrow set of beliefs, a good teacher should encourage students to think critically by exposing them to a variety of perspectives.
1 emanating　　　　　　　**2** indoctrinating
3 usurping　　　　　　　　**4** forfeiting

(3) *A:* Why does Ben always wear dark glasses? Is there something wrong with his eyes?
　　B: No. He just wears them out of (　　　). He thinks they make him look cool.
1 rebuke　　**2** vanity　　**3** thrift　　　**4** piety

(4) At the (　　　) of her career, the novelist was writing two bestsellers a year. She never imagined she would have so much success.
1 dissent　　**2** payoff　　**3** zenith　　**4** proviso

(5) The CEO gave factory workers a raise after spending eight hours experiencing what it was like to do their job. He had never realized just how (　　　) it was.
1 grueling　**2** precocious　**3** concerted　**4** cursory

(6) Some critics are calling the book the greatest war novel ever written because it so perfectly (　　　) all the suffering, terror, and sadness of human conflict.
1 mollifies　　**2** ingratiates　　**3** encapsulates　**4** galvanizes

(7) *A:* There's no point in discussing politics if you're going to be so (　　　) about everything.
　　B: I'm sorry you feel that way. It's just that I have strong opinions about what's right and what's wrong.
1 dogmatic　　　　　　　**2** baffling
3 astronomical　　　　　　**4** hilarious

42

(8) *A:* How are you enjoying your new job, Harry?

B: It's great. It comes with a lot of (   ), too, including extra vacation days, free lunch at the cafeteria, and access to the company gym.

1 emblems   **2** statutes   **3** perks   **4** conceits

(9) Jenny was able to (   ) with Allen when he lost all the files on his computer, as the same thing had happened to her a few months earlier.

1 precipitate   **2** commiserate **3** abdicate   **4** explicate

(10) The judge reduced the criminal's sentence due to (   ) circumstances. His child needed an expensive operation, and this had led him to steal money from his employer.

1 phantom   **2** robust   **3** extenuating **4** aghast

(11) *A:* Honey, this is such a (   ) little village. Let's vacation here again soon.

B: Definitely! It feels like it's been frozen in time and hasn't changed for years.

1 terse   **2** grave   **3** quaint   **4** slanted

(12) Wasteful spending has led to the gradual (   ) of the company's financial resources, and now it is nearly bankrupt.

1 remuneration   **2** dissipation
3 conglomeration   **4** tribulation

(13) The prime minister never suspected her colleagues were secretly (   ) a plot to replace her with a new leader.

1 hatching   **2** bluffing   **3** venting   **4** chiding

(14) Some of the (   ) floating in the world's oceans is the result of spills from cargo ships and other boats, but most of it comes from sources on land, such as industrial waste.

1 debris   **2** dexterity   **3** remorse   **4** tedium

(15) When Susan's parents began to argue, she tried to (   ) the situation by suggesting they all go out to a restaurant together. Her plan worked, and her parents quickly calmed down.

1 bombard   **2** defuse   **3** torment   **4** mortify

(16) Despite being told that smartphones were forbidden in school, the boy continued to (   ) the rule openly. He sometimes even used his phone during class.

1 coax   **2** depict   **3** flout   **4** bind

(17) Before the trial, lawyers conducted a formal (　　) of the main witness in order to get a proper account of her story.
1 commendation　　　　　**2** tirade
3 schism　　　　　　　　**4** deposition

(18) The famous actor often stated in interviews that he came from a poor background. Journalists, however, could find no (　　) for his claim.
1 verification　**2** equilibrium　**3** consortium　**4** transgression

(19) The TV channel was criticized for showing a documentary that included (　　) details of murders that many viewers found disturbing.
1 supple　　　　**2** feudal　　　**3** lurid　　　　**4** dainty

(20) Police found two (　　) dogs in the abandoned building. The dogs were so thin they could barely move, so the officers rushed them to a veterinary clinic.
1 eponymous　**2** brusque　**3** fickle　　　　**4** emaciated

(21) The politician held a press conference in order to (　　) the myths about his proposed healthcare plan. He clearly outlined and explained every part of the plan.
1 jostle　　　**2** intersperse　**3** coddle　　　**4** debunk

(22) *A:* Heath, why are you (　　) in the desk drawers? Did you lose your keys again?
B: No, I have those. I can't find my wallet now.
1 shriveling up　　　　　**2** poking around
3 scooting over　　　　　**4** veering off

(23) The man was still in the airport restaurant when he heard the final announcement for his flight, so he quickly (　　) his meal and hurried to the boarding gate.
1 polished off　　　　　**2** softened up
3 tied back　　　　　　　**4** muddled through

(24) Last year, Peter struggled to pay his rent and buy groceries. He had to work two part-time jobs just to (　　) a living.
1 fuss over　**2** blurt out　**3** gloat over　**4** eke out

(25) Jacob wanted extra pocket money, so he tried to (　　) his mother by saying how nice she looked. However, she knew right away that he wanted something.
1 hem in　　　**2** dwell on　　**3** pine for　　**4** butter up

2

Read each passage and choose the best word or phrase from among the four choices for each blank. Then, on your answer sheet, find the number of the question and mark your answer.

The Science of Poison

During the Renaissance, the Swiss physician Paracelsus introduced a revolutionary medical concept. In those days, common wisdom held that toxic substances (**26**). However, Paracelsus, who was instrumental in establishing the role of chemistry in medicine, believed this to be nonsense. He argued instead that no substance was inherently lethal, and that when sufficiently diluted, any poison could be rendered harmless, or even prove beneficial. In fact, this principle has aided the development of various modern medicines, including digoxin, which is extracted from a potentially lethal plant called foxglove but is crucial in the treatment of certain heart conditions. Paracelsus also reasoned that an excessive quantity of usually healthful substances can prove fatal — there are even lethal dosages for substances such as water.

Paracelsus's principle has become standard in modern medicine and is often stated today as "the dose makes the poison." However, (**27**). Since Paracelsus's time, science has come to recognize cancer-causing substances, known as carcinogens. These are capable of mutating DNA, and even a single such alteration can cause cells to become malignant. This can result in uncontrolled cell growth, regardless of the fact that only a minuscule amount of the carcinogen served as a catalyst for the growth. Similarly, experiments have shown that low doses of some noroviruses cause infections in 50 percent of subjects, which would imply that there is no harmless dose for these organisms either.

The concept of dosage has been explored further in modern toxicology, particularly in the field of environmental science. "Sentinel species," for example, are organisms that can (**28**). Years ago, canaries were taken into mines because the birds are highly susceptible to harmful underground gases. The rapid rate at which toxins accumulate in canaries meant that miners knew it was urgent they evacuate the mine should the birds perish. In this way, such organisms essentially act as threshold dose indicators, facilitating the detection of environmental toxins and establishing the levels at which they become harmful. Dozens of sentinel species have since been identified, including crayfish for water contamination, suggesting that such organisms' vulnerability to poisons can be an invaluable predictor in the fight against ecological pollutants as well as help protect human safety.

---

(26) 1 actually had healing properties
     2 affected some people more than others
     3 could counteract other poisons
     4 were deadly in any amount

(27) 1 some chemicals have no fatal dose
     2 it has been criticized heavily
     3 there are exceptions to it
     4 the reasons remain a mystery

(28) 1 negatively affect other species
     2 signal potential danger
     3 survive exposure to toxins
     4 resist mutations to their DNA

Eyes in the Sky

While the use of artificial satellites in weather forecasting and broadcasting is widespread today, one rather surprising application has arisen in the financial world. Satellites are now being utilized to (**29**). Although there were once only a limited number of man-made satellites in orbit around Earth, they have recently become so ubiquitous that data on practically any area of the planet's surface can now be accessed in real time. Taking advantage of this capability, many leading financial firms now utilize such data to formulate projections of potential earnings on prospective investments. Estimating customer numbers by monitoring the number of vehicles in retailers' parking lots, for example, can be extremely valuable when determining whether to purchase shares in a business, as the value of a company's stock often rises dramatically when sales increase significantly.

While this strategy has generated tremendous wealth for some, critics argue that (**30**   ). Investors have always competed to acquire information of various types that would give them an edge when picking stocks. Satellite data, though, is generally only affordable to large investment firms with vast financial resources. According to economist Panos Patatoukas of the University of California, Berkeley, "Technology was supposed to level the playing field, but what I see is the fence separating sophisticated and unsophisticated investors growing higher." There have even been calls for laws that would ban the use of satellites in the investment world for precisely the same reasons that using inside information about a company to make stock purchases is prohibited.

However, allowing financial firms to utilize satellites (**31**   ). Stock purchases based on better-informed decisions, experts claim, will eventually culminate in stock prices that more accurately reflect the true value of companies. At any rate, the speed at which technology both matures and disseminates throughout society means that it is only a matter of time before individual investors gain access to satellite data. With a greater number of satellite imaging services springing up, advances in technology, coupled with increases in the number of users, will likely lead to cost reductions that make such services more widely affordable.

---

(29) **1** steal rivals' technologies
    2 determine new store locations
    3 control inventories in stores
    4 predict companies' revenues

(30) **1** such gambles are far too risky
    2 it creates an unfair advantage
    3 more-efficient methods exist
    4 retailers are being cheated

(31) **1** is not completely without merit
    2 should lead to fairer regulations
    3 has a number of hidden costs
    4 may already be an outdated concept

3 Read each passage and choose the best answer from among the four choices for each question. Then, on your answer sheet, find the number of the question and mark your answer.

Poinsettia and Poinsettismo

When the Mexican flower known as the *flor de Nochebuena* was first sent to the United States by the American botanist, diplomat, and politician Joel Poinsett in the 1820s, it was named the "poinsettia" in his honor. Mexicans in those days, however, created another word based on Poinsett's name: *poinsettismo*, to denote something entirely different. Poinsett, appointed as the first American ambassador to the nation of Mexico in 1825, soon became notorious in Mexico for both his meddling in state affairs and his arrogant, overbearing personality. Mexico had won its independence in a hard-fought war with Spain a few years earlier, and Poinsett's primary mission was to promote republicanism — a political system adopted by the United States in which people elect a president rather than having a hereditary monarch. To this end, Poinsett was constantly scheming to set up pro-American factions within Mexico and soon became known as a political puppeteer. It was such meddling that came to be described by the term *poinsettismo*.

At the time of Poinsett's appointment, the United States faced fierce competition from British trade interests in Mexico and the rest of Latin America, and it feared the influence that Spain still maintained even after Mexico had gained independence. Upon his arrival, Poinsett discovered that a pro-European faction known as the Escoceses, composed mainly of the country's politicians and generals, had an unrivaled and dominating influence in Mexico's government. Due to the animosity he encountered from this group, Poinsett worked to undermine its influence by assisting in the creation of a rival group known as the Yorkinos, which worked to promote republicanism. After the Yorkinos enjoyed an increasing number of political victories at the ballot box, an armed uprising by the Escoceses broke out in 1827, and one of their chief demands was Poinsett's expulsion. The uprising failed to gain widespread support and was quickly suppressed, eventually leading to one of Poinsett's allies, Vicente Guerrero — himself a member of the Yorkinos — assuming the country's leadership in 1829. By this time, though,

Poinsett's reputation as the instrument of a foreign power's attempt to pull strings had created so much hostility that he began receiving assassination threats, and Guerrero, realizing that Poinsett had become a liability, successfully petitioned the US government to recall him.

Poinsett was hailed as a hero upon his return to the United States, but he is not so fondly remembered in Mexico. Although he sought to uphold democratic ideals and saw himself as aiding Mexico's resistance to Europe's monarchies, in the eyes of the Mexican people, the fact that a foreigner had played such an extensive role in their region's political situation was intolerable. Poinsett's successor, Anthony Butler, followed in Poinsett's footsteps, and actually managed to further aggravate tensions between the United States and Mexico when he was caught resorting to bribery in his efforts to acquire what is now the state of Texas from the Mexican government. Together, the actions of Poinsett and Butler set the two nations on a course that would eventually result in armed conflict in 1846.

(32) In Mexico, Joel Poinsett's name

    1 came to signify the country's successful attempt to create a free society with no outside influence from European nations such as Spain.

    2 became associated with interference in government-related matters that was carried out with the purpose of promoting an American political agenda.

    3 was used for a type of flower that became widely adopted as a symbol of Mexico's attempt to gain freedom from Spanish rule.

    4 was used in reference to Americans who came to the country and were forced to choose between staying loyal to their homeland or supporting Mexico.

(33) According to the passage, which of the following statements about the Escoceses and Yorkinos is true?

    1 Their dislike of one another made Poinsett even more influential because he had given the Escoceses information that helped them to take power.

    2 Their internal disputes should be viewed more accurately as a

49

loss for European countries than a victory for Poinsett and his allies in Mexico.

3 Their struggle for power caused Poinsett so much stress that he had no choice but to give up his work in Mexico and return to the United States.

4 Their rivalry escalated into a conflict that not only led to a major victory for the Yorkinos but also forced Poinsett to leave Mexico.

(34) What conclusion does the author of the passage make about Poinsett's time in Mexico?

1 Although Poinsett had been a more successful ambassador than Anthony Butler, people at the time mistakenly believed the opposite to be true.

2 Although Poinsett likely felt he was acting with good intentions, he was partly responsible for a war that came to pass in later years.

3 Poinsett failed to fully understand the realities of Mexican politics, but he was able to improve the country's situation through some fortunate decisions.

4 If Poinsett had directed his diplomatic efforts toward the problem in Texas rather than issues in Mexico, tensions could have been reduced.

The Alvarez Hypothesis

While initially controversial, the theory that dinosaurs were wiped out by the impact of a giant asteroid is now taken for granted by the vast majority of the scientific community. The theory, known as the Alvarez hypothesis, originated when American geologist Walter Alvarez noticed that high levels of the element iridium were present worldwide in rock layers that corresponded with the geologic era in which dinosaurs became extinct. While extremely rare on Earth, iridium is common in asteroids, and Alvarez believed its presence was evidence of an asteroid collision that sent enormous dust clouds rising into the atmosphere, blocking out sunlight. This would have set off a chain reaction in which plant life died from a lack of sunlight, causing herbivores — and subsequently, their carnivore predators — to also perish. Later, the discovery of a gigantic crater in southeastern Mexico formed by the impact of a massive asteroid, which struck Earth near the present-day town of Chicxulub, made this hypothesis even more compelling.

A small minority of paleontologists, however, have resisted the Alvarez hypothesis for decades, and Gerta Keller of Princeton University is prominent among them. In her study of fossil records for the period in which the dinosaur extinction is thought to have occurred, she has gathered significant opposing evidence. Her research examined the fossils of marine organisms called foraminifers. Because these fossils are abundant and generally well-preserved, scientists can reliably assess foraminifer species' extinction patterns, so they are often used as an indicator of the well-being of the organisms that coexisted with them. Keller's examination of foraminifer fossils suggested foraminifer numbers had already been declining for hundreds of thousands of years before the Chicxulub impact. Furthermore, population numbers of foraminifers in proximity to the impact crater failed to experience the abrupt plunge that would have been expected based on the Alvarez hypothesis.

Keller presents an alternative explanation for the dinosaur extinction. Prior to the Chicxulub impact, temperatures had been rising globally, and the Deccan Traps — a vast area in India formed by solidified lava flows from eruptions of a network of prehistoric volcanoes — has long been viewed as a possible explanation for this phenomenon. Keller's evidence indicates that, although the eruptions occurred over hundreds of thousands of years, the most devastating eruptions occurred in the 60,000 years leading up to the extinction. These would have expelled so much poisonous gas and dust into the atmosphere that global warming and acid rain would have pushed ecosystems to what Keller calls a "point of no return." Keller's theory has been criticized, but additional evidence has emerged that suggests volcanism in the Deccan Traps region may have played at least a partial role in wiping out the dinosaurs. Researchers at the University of California, Berkeley, found that while the volcanic activity had been ongoing prior to the Chicxulub impact, there was an enormous surge in activity following it. Keller, however, sees such research merely as an attempt to modify a longstanding incorrect hypothesis, and remains adamant that volcanism was the sole main driver of the extinction. With evidence seemingly on both sides of the issue, consensus is likely still a way off.

(35) What first led to the development of the Alvarez hypothesis?

1 The discovery of an extremely large crater indicating that Earth was struck by an object from outer space in the distant past.

2 The widespread presence of a substance on Earth that appears to have arrived from outer space around the time the dinosaurs disappeared.

3 The identification of rare fossils of both plant- and meat-eating dinosaurs that lived just before dinosaurs became extinct.

4 The realization that the location of fossils in certain rock layers did not make sense based on the period that dinosaurs were thought to have become extinct.

(36) One reason Gerta Keller doubts the Alvarez hypothesis is that

1 fossils of foraminifers from just before the asteroid impact showed that some types had declined in number more quickly than others.

2 she discovered evidence of foraminifers' existence on Earth hundreds of thousands of years before the end of the dinosaur age.

3 foraminifers should have been affected over a large area rather than only near the area where the asteroid struck Earth.

4 she discovered evidence that there was a gradual decrease in the number of foraminifers rather than a sudden drop.

(37) Which of the following statements about the research from the University of California, Berkeley, would Keller most likely agree with?

1 The findings do not support her theory with regard to the dinosaur extinction but rather aim to sustain the Alvarez hypothesis by adjusting it.

2 The way in which the conclusions differed from her own indicates that the Alvarez hypothesis could be more accurate than she initially believed.

3 It should have been focused less on the Deccan Traps and more on the ways that the asteroid impact affected the atmosphere.

4 The fact that it failed to take climate change into account means the results should only be considered partially accurate.

The Wealth of Nations

Arguably the most famous economist of all time, Adam Smith may also be the most misunderstood. His highly influential work, *An Inquiry into the Nature and Causes of the Wealth of Nations*, was published in 1776 and is widely cited by advocates of free trade agreements and those who favor markets unrestricted by regulations. Yet a close reading of Smith's work reveals that many policies claiming to be based on it reflect misunderstandings or perversions of what he was actually trying to convey.

Much of what Smith laid out in *The Wealth of Nations* was in response to mercantilism, the dominant economic theory of his day. This doctrine was based on the assumption that there was only a finite amount of wealth in the world, and it claimed that the only way for a nation to prosper was by accumulating wealth in the form of gold and silver. This was to be achieved in a number of ways, from competing with rival nations to establish colonies whose resources could be exploited and exported to imposing tariffs on goods from other countries in order to maintain a favorable balance of trade.

Smith argued that this approach was misguided. Mercantilism viewed commerce as an activity that encouraged hostile competition among nations rather than unity and friendship. Smith felt that such an approach reflected a fundamental misconception about the nature of international trade. He held that nations should seek mutual prosperity through the exchange of goods, arguing that both free trade and the production of goods were key components that enabled a country to become truly wealthy.

The Wealth of Nations also proposed that allowing consumers, producers, and distributors a certain degree of free rein to do business as they saw fit was beneficial for society as a whole. Smith envisaged that individuals acting in their own self-interest would fulfill the needs and desires of others better than any planned economic system would. For example, consumers are more likely to purchase bread from a seller with lower prices, leading other sellers to adjust their prices to remain competitive without being forced to do so. The mechanism by which this principle operates was referred to by Smith in *The Wealth of Nations* as "the invisible hand."

Smith was not, however, making the simplistic argument that there should be no government intervention in markets whatsoever. The invisible hand was part of an appeal to governments to free individuals from constraints that benefited wealthy elites and were upheld by state power. In fact, the passage in *The Wealth of Nations* that explains the invisible hand is specifically condemning state interference that occurs at the insistence of powerful merchants. Ironically, though, Smith's ideas have become virtually synonymous with a political ideology known as neoliberalism, a system that favors policies such as deregulation, privatization, lower taxes, and reduced social services, and which continues to be highly influential in twenty-first-century politics. Many economists view these policies as the result of the influence of powerful corporations — the same influence that Smith believed was harmful to nations. Smith warned that business interests should not have too much influence on government policy decisions, as this would lead to situations where a lack of competitive pressure — due to special privileges or government-approved monopolies, for instance — could result in consumers being exploited by companies charging exorbitant prices for low-quality goods.

Smith was also aware that there were instances where the free market could not be relied upon to serve society's best interests. As the Nobel Prize-winning economist Joseph Stiglitz once wrote, the "reason that the invisible hand often seems invisible is that it is often not there." The invisible hand is incapable, for instance, of dealing with situations where market transactions among individuals have effects on society at large. Such effects, known as "externalities," include things such as the wider impact of natural resource depletion and water pollution resulting from manufacturing. This creates negative outcomes for society as a whole, despite the advantages gained by those involved in the transactions.

While Smith did not have faith in totally unregulated markets, he also believed politicians should not take over the roles traditionally carried out by merchants. Rather, it was his view that politicians needed to establish a regulatory environment in which legitimate business activities could be fruitfully pursued, while at the same time ensuring those same activities did not exploit any of the parties participating in the market. Unfortunately, however, he left no prescription for how this was to be accomplished. Furthermore, the phrase "invisible hand" appears only once in *The Wealth of Nations* and is never thoroughly explained. These facts, combined with the enormous changes in the world economy in the centuries since Smith's time, mean that Smith would almost certainly respond unfavorably to the way his work — and the concept of the invisible hand in particular — has been interpreted if he were alive today.

(38) What was Adam Smith's view on how countries should create wealth?

1 There needed to be a clear relationship between the amount of tariffs on goods and the amount of gold and silver a country possessed.

2 Since the total amount of wealth was limited, it was essential for nations to obtain as much as possible, even at the expense of other countries.

3 Mercantilism needed to be reformed so that colonies could provide more resources to the countries that established them.

4 Rather than attempting to build up stores of gold and silver, countries should attempt to develop mutually beneficial trading relationships.

(39) According to the author of the passage, neoliberalism is in opposition to Smith's ideas because

1 neoliberals have a very different idea about why the development of overly powerful corporations should be prevented.

2 it does not place as much emphasis as Smith did on the importance of wealthy corporations to the free market.

3 the policies that it promotes are created to benefit corporate interests rather than to encourage free and open trade.

4 it has a more negative view of what would happen if individuals were generally allowed to act in their own self-interest.

55

(40) What is one possible example of what Joseph Stiglitz meant when he said the invisible hand "is often not there"?

    1 Consumers having to pay high prices for a rare type of wood that must be imported at great expense to the merchant.

    2 Logging companies being permitted to cut down rain forests in response to increasing demand for wooden furniture.

    3 The profits of a manufacturer being reduced because of a new government regulation designed to protect natural habitats.

    4 A significant decrease in the demand for a product due to media claims about it being environmentally unfriendly.

(41) What is one problem with the way Smith presented his view of how markets should work?

    1 He did not explain how governments could create a balanced system that protected people yet allowed markets to operate efficiently.

    2 His distrust of governments caused him to overlook solutions that would allow the invisible hand to be used to properly control markets.

    3 He failed to acknowledge the importance of the role of government regulators because he had complete trust in the free market.

    4 His predictions regarding the many changes that would come about in the world economy turned out to be inaccurate.

4
- *Write an essay on the given TOPIC.*
- *Give THREE reasons to support your answer.*
- *Structure: introduction, main body, and conclusion*
- *Suggested length: 200–240 words*
- *Write your essay in the space provided on Side B of your answer sheet. Any writing outside the space will not be graded.*

TOPIC
Agree or disagree: Genetic engineering will have a positive influence on society in the future

一次試験
リスニング

────────── **Listening Test** ──────────

There are four parts to this listening test.

Part 1	Dialogues: 1 question each	Multiple-choice
Part 2	Passages: 2 questions each	Multiple-choice
Part 3	Real-Life: 1 question each	Multiple-choice
Part 4	Interview: 2 questions	Multiple-choice

※**Listen carefully to the instructions.**

Part 1   ▶MP3 ▶アプリ ▶CD 1 26〜36

No. 1
1　He will change the order of the paragraphs.
2　He will add some detailed information.
3　He will focus more on his communication skills.
4　He will describe his motivation more clearly.

No. 2
1　The company used poor materials to cut costs.
2　The company went out of business.
3　The company charged more than was initially agreed.
4　The company refused to redo the flooring.

No. 3
1　He was reluctant to accept the job.
2　His skill set may not be suitable for the position.
3　His technical knowledge is excellent.
4　He will be able to improve the department's finances.

No. 4
1　She should do more for the environment.
2　Her ideas will harm public transportation.
3　She will reduce government spending.
4　Her policies are not practical.

No. 5

1 The media has exaggerated the danger.
2 The police caught the convicts this morning.
3 Julian's friend is a bad influence on him.
4 It may not be safe to go out tonight.

No. 6

1 She stayed in the hospital longer than expected.
2 She has had to change to a stronger medication.
3 She will probably need to have another operation.
4 She may have to move to a retirement home.

No. 7

1 She is not earning enough money.
2 She meets clients more often than she expected.
3 She still has to deal with her old boss.
4 She has an unpredictable schedule.

No. 8

1 It is a worthwhile class to take.
2 It is only offered every few semesters.
3 There is not much lab work in it.
4 The professor is too demanding.

No. 9

1 Look for work off campus.
2 Concentrate on her studies.
3 Apply for financial aid.
4 Ask her parents for more money.

No. 10

1 Headquarters should focus more on airline services.
2 The women should explain their concerns to headquarters.
3 Some hotels will be sold despite the women's concerns.
4 The streamlining operation should have begun earlier.

||||| Part 2 |||||||||||||||||||||||||||||||||||||||||||||||| 🔊 ▸MP3 ▸アプリ ▸CD 1 37～42

(A)

No. 11
1 Nature behaves in predictable ways.
2 There are unique organisms in every ecosystem.
3 Everything in nature is connected.
4 Scientific discovery can happen anywhere.

No. 12
1 It led to the pollution of water sources.
2 It accelerated the disappearance of local animals.
3 It was partially responsible for serious landslides.
4 It forced indigenous people to leave the area.

(B)

No. 13
1 The use of real tanks and airplanes.
2 The presence of a famous military officer.
3 The movement of troops toward Normandy.
4 The fact that the army moved around frequently.

No. 14
1 It used too many resources.
2 Its sound effects were not realistic enough.
3 The German army gained knowledge of it.
4 It sometimes fooled Allied leaders.

(C)

No. 15
1 It reduces the health benefits of the nuts.
2 It requires the use of expensive machinery.
3 There is theft among workers.
4 Workers may face physical harm.

No. 16
1 It uses land needed for growing domestic food crops.
2 The nuts are being sold locally instead of being exported.
3 Farmers do not make enough money from the nuts.
4 Women are being forced to grow the nuts.

(D)

No. 17
1 It led to a decline in airline safety levels.
2 It is not the main reason for fares becoming cheaper.
3 It was followed by a temporary fare increase.
4 It resulted in air travel becoming less popular.

No. 18
1 Their economies have suffered.
2 Their airports have had to upgrade facilities.
3 Traffic at their airports has increased.
4 They have received bigger subsidies.

(E)

No. 19
1 Those that live in many different areas.
2 Those that eat the fewest types of foods.
3 Those that are over 5 million years old.
4 Those that are eaten by various animals.

No. 20
1 Their rate of evolution has slowed down.
2 Many species have gone extinct.
3 Their overall metabolic rate has not changed.
4 They have slower metabolisms than other animals.

60

||||| Part 3 |||||||||||||||||||||||||||||||||||||||||||||||||||| ◀») ▶MP3 ▶アプリ ▶CD 1 **43**〜**48**

(F)

No. 21

Situation: Your five-year-old son's birthday party is tomorrow, and you want to buy an educational gift for him. A toy-store salesperson tells you the following.

Question: Which item should you buy?

1 The volcano kit.
2 The electronics kit.
3 The dinosaur fossil dig set.
4 The action figure.

(G)

No. 22

Situation: You work in an office. You have received some strange e-mails recently but have not opened them. Your manager has called an emergency meeting and says the following.

Question: What should you do first?

1 Complete the online training.
2 Check your firewall settings.
3 Talk to your manager.
4 Fill out a security checklist.

(H)

No. 23

Situation: You need a sleeping bag for a summer backpacking trip next weekend. You will not take a tent, but rain has been forecast. A salesperson tells you the following.

Question: Which sleeping bag should you buy?

1 The Wilderness Dreamer.
2 The Trail Relax.
3 The Cozy Camper.
4 The Nature Cocoon.

(I)

No. 24

Situation: You have a stubborn weed that is growing very thickly throughout your whole yard. A neighbor gives you the following advice.

Question: What should you do to get rid of the weed?

1 Get a weed-killer containing dicamba.
2 Buy an organic weed-killer.
3 Put a plastic sheet over it.
4 Remove it by hand.

(J)

No. 25

Situation: You and your six-year-old son want to go on a guided hike in a nearby national park next week. You work weekday mornings. You call the park and are told the following.

Question: Which hike should you go on?

1 The Rainbow Hike.
2 The Bird-Watcher Hike.
3 The Sunset Hike.
4 The Lake Hike.

Part 4 ◆》 ▸MP3 ▸アプリ ▸CD 1 **49**〜**50**

No. 26
1 Find ways to stand out from other restaurants.
2 Use a variety of trusted suppliers.
3 Use only the highest-quality ingredients.
4 Add a wide range of dishes to their menus.

No. 27
1 Keeping prices low is usually the most important factor.
2 It is important to emphasize customer rewards programs.
3 Providing high-quality service should be a priority.
4 New dishes should be added to the menu frequently.

二次試験
面　接

[A日程]　◀》　▶MP3　▶アプリ　▶CD4 **6**～**10**

1. Are people today becoming less tolerant of different beliefs and cultures?

2. Agree or disagree: Some professional athletes' salaries have become too high to justify

3. Is it possible for consumers to completely avoid companies involved in unethical activities?

4. Should the government provide more funds to boost the economies of rural areas?

5. Should punishments for people who commit financial crimes be made stricter?

[C日程]

1. Has the global war on illegal drugs been lost?

2. Do young people today face more societal pressures than young people did in the past?

3. Is democracy facing more challenges today than it did in the 20th century?

4. Agree or disagree: Japan's low birthrate should be treated as a national crisis

5. Have industrialized nations made meaningful progress regarding climate change?

（注）　モデルスピーチと解説はA日程のみ収録しています。

2021-3

一次試験　2022.1.23実施
二次試験　A日程　2022.2.20実施
　　　　　C日程　2022.3.6実施

Grade 1

試験時間
筆記：100分
リスニング：約35分

一次試験・筆記　　　　　p.66〜80
一次試験・リスニング　　p.81〜87
二次試験・面接　　　　　　p.88

＊解答・解説は別冊p.109〜160にあります。
＊面接の流れは本書p.16にあります。

2021年度第3回　Web特典「自動採点サービス」対応
　　　　　　　オンラインマークシート
※検定の回によって2次元コードが違います。
※筆記1〜3，リスニングの採点ができます。
※PCからも利用できます（本書p.8参照）。

一次試験
筆 記

1 To complete each item, choose the best word or phrase from among the four choices. Then, on your answer sheet, find the number of the question and mark your answer.

(1) The door was so (   ) that when the boy kicked it, his foot went straight through the wooden panel.
1 musty   **2** fuzzy   **3** flimsy   **4** hazy

(2) Carl was threatened with (   ) from his apartment after not paying rent for several months. He was given one last chance to come up with the money.
1 altercation   **2** eviction
3 subordination   **4** nomination

(3) The conservative regime passed strict laws forbidding the (   ) of communist ideas. Anyone accused of spreading such ideas was severely punished.
1 propagation   **2** recuperation
3 injunction   **4** deregulation

(4) The children were so (   ) by the television show that none of them said a single word during the whole program.
1 undermined   **2** constricted   **3** dispelled   **4** mesmerized

(5) Paula tried to (   ) innocence when she was accused of stealing from the store. The unpaid-for clothes in her bag, however, proved that she was lying.
1 squash   **2** embark   **3** feign   **4** pamper

(6) In a recent speech, the mayor (   ) the city's educators for failing to properly prepare students for national achievement exams.
1 embossed   **2** berated   **3** mitigated   **4** squandered

(7) Toby fixed the hole in the fence between his yard and that of the (   ) house so that his neighbor's dog would not be able to get through.
1 adjacent   **2** errant   **3** flawless   **4** intrepid

(8) Elle is not (   ) by nature, so she always finds it hard to start up conversations with people and make new friends.
1 laconic   **2** pliable   **3** negligent   **4** amiable

66

(9) *A:* Bob, before you try to (   ) your opinion into a conversation, you might want to listen more carefully to what the other people are saying.

B: I know, I know. I just get so excited when it's a topic I really care about.

1 scorn　　　**2** neutralize　　**3** behold　　　**4** interject

(10) The motorist was given a ticket for a traffic (   ). She had been caught driving 25 kilometers per hour over the speed limit.

1 ensemble　**2** propensity　**3** nemesis　　**4** infraction

(11) The country's economy was so strong it remained (   ) from the financial crisis that affected the rest of the industrialized world.

1 ambivalent　**2** prescient　　**3** immune　　**4** lopsided

(12) *A:* Do you know anyone who would translate this document for me for $100?

B: Why don't you ask Joe? He knows French and is always looking for ways to (   ) his income.

1 nauseate　　**2** ostracize　　**3** alienate　　**4** augment

(13) The company president set a (   ) when he took all his employees on a trip to Hawaii. After that, they expected a trip every year, even when profits were down.

1 precedent　**2** malady　　**3** bounty　　**4** surcharge

(14) During the strike, the angry employees of the bus company stood outside the city hall, (   ), "Higher wages now!"

1 precluding　**2** dissuading　**3** chanting　　**4** enlisting

(15) Experts now believe the ancient tribe had been (   ), as new evidence suggests it did not live in any one region for any length of time.

1 innocuous　　　　　**2** nomadic

3 contemptuous　　　**4** erudite

(16) The escaped prisoner, who had been on the run for weeks, finally turned himself in to the police. He said he did not want to live the rest of his life as a (   ).

1 truant　　　**2** virtuoso　**3** socialite　**4** fugitive

(17) Passengers on the cruise ship were encouraged to (   ) themselves of the activities on offer. There were a variety of classes and shows for no extra charge.

67

    1 avail   **2** rehash   **3** nullify   **4** consign

(18) *A:* Tobias, have you had that (   ) on your neck looked at by a doctor yet? It could be something serious, you know.

     B: It doesn't hurt, but I'll make an appointment today. Thanks for reminding me.

     1 homage   **2** crevice   **3** lesion   **4** fiasco

(19) After the new employee made (   ) remarks about her boss in the coffee room, a coworker cautioned her to keep negative comments about others to herself.

     1 lethargic   **2** pensive   **3** derogatory **4** cerebral

(20) When the new worker was asked why he had not completed the task on time, he looked embarrassed and (   ) admitted that he had not understood the instructions.

     1 sheepishly **2** diabolically **3** gullibly   **4** fervently

(21) During the discussion on world history, the student eventually realized his own argument was (   ) and he knew he could not win.

     1 tenacious   **2** subliminal **3** untenable **4** nascent

(22) Jovanni needed a replacement part for his classic car, but the mechanic at the repair shop said that parts for it are hard to (   ) because the car is so old.

     1 come by   **2** tear into   **3** clam up   **4** filter out

(23) When the young zebra wandered away from its mother and the rest of the herd, it was (   ) by a lion waiting in the bushes nearby.

     1 picked off   **2** dumbed down

     3 spiced up   **4** eased back

(24) After receiving poor grades on her midterm progress report, Rosalind realized she needed to (   ) and study hard in the second half of the semester.

     1 hype up   **2** dash down **3** trip up   **4** buckle down

(25) *A:* What's taking so long with the sales project?

     B: Unfortunately, some unforeseen issues have (   ), and it'll take a while to solve them.

     1 dropped through   **2** cropped up

     3 floated around   **4** breezed in

2 Read each passage and choose the best word or phrase from among the four choices for each blank. Then, on your answer sheet, find the number of the question and mark your answer.

The Feminine Mystique

Betty Friedan's 1963 bestseller, *The Feminine Mystique*, addresses what the author called the "nameless aching dissatisfaction" experienced by women of her generation. Twentieth-century suburban life had brought an unparalleled degree of leisure and luxury to American women, and most seemed to embrace their roles as housewives. Beneath the placid surface, however, Friedan saw females struggling — but ultimately failing — to live up to what she dubbed "the feminine mystique," an indefinable feminine ideal regarding women's roles as mothers, housewives, and marriage partners. In Friedan's view, this ideal created in women a vague yet overwhelming sense that (**26**).

The feminine mystique, argued Friedan, (**27**). In previous generations, women had made clothes and household items and, in rural areas, tended crops and reared animals. Then, during World War II, they had filled the vacancies in traditionally male-oriented occupations as men went off to fight. In the postwar years, though, women contributed to the economy not by producing but by purchasing things, such as household appliances and frozen meals. Corporations and advertisers used the popular image of domestic bliss to sell these products, which were designed specifically to entice housewives aspiring to the feminine mystique. Friedan, however, saw this image as nothing more than an exploitative myth.

Although Friedan's book is provocative and passionate, it is not without flaws. First and foremost, it has been criticized for (**28**). Friedan was a White, highly educated graduate of an elite university, and *The Feminine Mystique* concentrates almost exclusively on housewives from the middle and upper classes. At the time of the book's publication, though, one-third of women were in the workforce, with many of them unable to stay at home due to economic necessity. Also disregarded are ethnic minorities, who receive only the briefest of mentions in the context of being hired as domestic help to relieve the pressures of taking care of children. Despite its shortcomings, the book touched a nerve with millions of

American women, serving as a catalyst for protests, media coverage of women's issues, and, most of all, a changed consciousness. Together, these contributed to the development of the feminist movement that remains active today.

---

(26) 1 their new roles could be beneficial
2 feminine stereotypes were empowering
3 validation from others was not important
4 they were not meeting society's expectations

(27) 1 reduced women to mere consumers
2 encouraged conflicts among women
3 preserved dangerous ideas from the past
4 affected men as much as it did women

(28) 1 unfairly blaming housewives
2 the change that it caused
3 presenting a narrow perspective
4 misrepresenting younger women

The Reid Technique

Developed in the 1950s, the Reid technique is employed by police agencies to extract confessions. The technique centers on obtaining admissions of guilt through verbal interrogations that are designed to reveal when suspects are lying. The Reid technique is reported to elicit confessions in almost 80 percent of interrogations, but critics claim that it is to blame for the incarceration of numerous innocent suspects. One major problem, they argue, is the technique's emphasis on (29   ). When the Reid technique was developed, psychology experts assumed that a suspect's constantly shifting gaze or verbal stumbles indicated a degree of outward nervousness, and that behind this appearance of unease was an attempt to deceive others. Research has since shown, however, that body language itself is not a reliable indicator of lying, as many people typically have difficulty remaining composed under intense questioning.

It has also been found that some suspects are likely to confess

70

to a crime when they (**30**   ). While the Reid technique was revolutionary for discouraging the once-common use of physical force to induce confessions, the use of stressors, such as isolation, verbal threats, and sleep deprivation, is still permissible. Under such pressure, admitting to a crime can seem like the easy way out, especially for those with positive perceptions of legal authorities, who believe they will eventually be exonerated. Unfortunately, though, a confession tends to trump all other forms of evidence. Once a person has admitted to a crime, even seemingly convincing contrary evidence tends to be ignored or viewed as irrelevant.

In recent years, various alternatives to the Reid technique have gained popularity. Rather than seeking confessions at any cost, these focus instead on the concept that (**31**   ). One such technique adopts a journalistic approach to interrogations. Investigators take detailed statements from a suspect and painstakingly compare them with available evidence and witness accounts. Then, the suspect is questioned further, and if inconsistencies appear, the suspect is asked to elaborate. When someone is being deceitful, the mental strain of recalling previous assertions and coming up with new falsehoods causes them to dig deeper holes for themselves, resulting in a cascade of erroneous testimony that eventually exposes their guilt.

---

(29) 1 frequently repeating accusations
　　2 looking for contradictions
　　3 detecting signs of anxiety
　　4 the suspect's background

(30) 1 are shown all the evidence
　　2 are able to speak to their victims
　　3 have a strong conscience
　　4 have faith in the justice system

(31) 1 people tend to trust reporters
　　2 lying requires great effort
　　3 most criminals lack willpower
　　4 many suspects are innocent

3 *Read each passage and choose the best answer from among the four choices for each question. Then, on your answer sheet, find the number of the question and mark your answer.*

Eisenhower vs. McCarthy

During the 1950s, the growing influence of Communism in Eastern Europe and heightened military tensions between the United States and the Soviet Union indirectly led to a major dilemma for then US President Dwight D. Eisenhower. A senator named Joseph McCarthy, who was a Republican like Eisenhower, had stoked the domestic fires of anti-Communist paranoia to the point of mass hysteria by making largely unfounded accusations that the US government had been infiltrated by Communist agents and sympathizers seeking to overturn America's democratic way of life. Eisenhower privately despised McCarthy for his part in stirring political unrest but vowed to aides that he would not "get into the gutter" with him. Refusing to publicly denounce McCarthy in order to maintain both party unity and presidential prestige, Eisenhower instead sought to weaken the senator's credibility.

At first, Eisenhower's tight-lipped responses whenever the senator's name was brought up were taken by many in the political sphere to indicate tacit consent to McCarthy's Communist witch hunts. Behind the scenes, however, Eisenhower commissioned a stealthy operation to subdue him. Evidence was unearthed that McCarthy and his right-hand man, Roy Cohn, had sought preferential treatment for one of their assistants who had been conscripted into military service. Eisenhower's aides discovered that McCarthy and Cohn had attempted to coerce military officials into awarding their assistant an undeserved officer's commission. The president bided his time until McCarthy took his anti-Communist crusade a step too far and accused the military of failing to take adequate precautions against Communist influence. Soon after, McCarthy was roundly denounced in the Senate, allegedly at the behest of Eisenhower, and several days later, a damning report that documented McCarthy and Cohn's shady activities was leaked to the media by the White House. Televised hearings documented McCarthy's tactics of intimidation and deceit, which, when combined with the leaked report, appalled the general public. Following this, Eisenhower again exerted his influence, and the Senate condemned McCarthy for conduct unbecoming of a senator, putting the final nail in his political coffin.

Many critics assert that Eisenhower's tactics, though ultimately successful, allowed McCarthy to rampage unchecked for years and ruin the careers and lives of various individuals accused of being Communist sympathizers or agents. Indeed, political expediencies caused Eisenhower to stand aside while McCarthy denounced General George Marshall, the president's mentor, causing Marshall to retire prematurely in disillusion. However, McCarthy thrived on confrontation and engaging in political mudslinging with him could easily have backfired, as seen when other politicians' antagonistic approaches to dealing with McCarthy only intensified his anti-Communist campaign. Although Eisenhower's subtle approach proved victorious against the senator in the long run, his subdued manner often caused him to appear to be an ineffectual leader. Yet the fact that he succeeded in both ending a war and lessening racial segregation during his presidency only proves the effectiveness of his method, of which there was no better example than his dealings with McCarthy. Had Eisenhower not taken the approach he did, McCarthy's anti-Communist purge may have had even more dire consequences.

(32) What do we learn about Dwight D. Eisenhower in the first paragraph?

    1 Although evidence of Communist influence within the US government was found to be accurate, his political enemies prevented him from taking action.

    2 To avoid causing widespread panic among the public, he decided not to expose Communist agents who had infiltrated the US government.

    3 The growing support for Communism within the US government caused him to doubt the trustworthiness of many of his closest political staff.

    4 He felt that speaking out against those who believed Communist sympathizers existed in the US government would harm his own party and reputation.

(33) How did Eisenhower deal with Joseph McCarthy?

    1 He released evidence of McCarthy's unethical use of power, which helped to discredit the senator in the eyes of ordinary Americans.

2 He was able to obtain sensitive information from a military official, which he used to threaten McCarthy with legal action.

3 He persuaded one of McCarthy's assistants to reveal secret information that could be politically harmful to the senator.

4 He convinced military officials to confront McCarthy about the senator's attempts to gain influence with Communist agents.

(34) What does the author of the passage suggest about Eisenhower's approach to dealing with McCarthy?

1 If Eisenhower had sought the help of General George Marshall, the president would have been able to build more political support against McCarthy.

2 Since other politicians' attempts to discredit McCarthy directly had failed, it seems that appearing to remain neutral was essential to Eisenhower's victory.

3 Although Eisenhower was responsible for many significant achievements, he lacked the political expertise to discredit someone like McCarthy.

4 Eisenhower was right to publicly debate with McCarthy, as this was the only way to force the senator into making a politically fatal mistake.

Darwin's Abominable Mystery

The flower may be one of nature's most exquisite creations, but it also proved problematic for Charles Darwin when he was promoting his theory of natural selection to a skeptical audience in the 1800s. Natural selection is based on the idea that evolution occurs through the gradual accumulation of slight alterations in the physical makeup of organisms, enabling them to adapt to and survive in their environment, and that this process can lead to the development of new species. When scientists at the time examined the fossil record for the two varieties of seed-bearing plants, gymnosperms and angiosperms, however, they found what appeared to be a major exception. The incremental evolution and expansion of gymnosperms, flowerless plants that produce cones, appeared to have occurred on the geologic timescale predicted by Darwin's theory, spanning the Paleozoic era about 390 million years ago and the Mesozoic era about 240 million years ago. Angiosperms, which reproduce through flowers, however, appeared to have emerged abruptly and with unexpected diversity about 100 million years ago during the Cretaceous period. Critics seized on this as a clear counterexample that greatly weakened the validity of Darwin's theory, leading Darwin to refer to it as "the abominable mystery."

Modern science, however, has gained a much clearer picture of prehistory thanks to more-detailed fossil records, knowledge of DNA, and advanced technology. Analysis of the oldest angiosperm fossils revealed a discrepancy between the fossils' estimated age and their molecular age — genetic testing indicates they are far more ancient. Attempting to explain this, researcher Daniele Silvestro of the University of Fribourg in Switzerland utilized a mathematical model that corrects for the scarcity of angiosperms when gymnosperms were ecologically dominant. Based on his results, Silvestro concluded that angiosperms likely date back to around 200 million years ago, earlier than was suggested by initial estimations of the age of angiosperm fossils. He also theorized that the lack of fossilized evidence from this period is possibly due to the fragility of flowers, which further reduced the odds of them becoming fossilized. Silvestro equates angiosperms to early mammals, which existed in the shadow of the dinosaurs for a time before going on to become dominant.

Another theory regarding the sudden increase of angiosperms in the past has gained momentum. Experts believe their ecological proliferation during the Cretaceous period in many regions of the earth was the result of angiosperms and pollinators, such as bees, influencing one another to evolve at an extremely rapid pace. For this to be true, however, there needs to be some factor that originally enabled angiosperms to obtain an advantage. Analysis of angiosperm DNA suggests that a process of "genome downsizing" occurred as angiosperms evolved, and the cellular transformations resulting from this process, experts say, allowed angiosperms to pack more cells into a smaller volume. This, in turn, made them far more efficient in terms of nutrient absorption and photosynthesis, the processes by which plants use sunlight to create sugars. While the abominable mystery may still be far from being completely solved, scientists are progressing ever closer to providing an explanation.

(35) Why did flowering plants present a problem for Charles Darwin's theory of natural selection?

1 The fossil record seemed to indicate that flowering plants had actually evolved before those that contained seeds.

2 The appearance of angiosperms occurred over a longer period of time than that which the theory of natural selection would predict.

3 It was impossible to find a common ancestor for the two major varieties of plants that produce seeds.

4 They seemed to contradict the idea that variation between species arose slowly due to a series of small changes.

(36) According to Daniele Silvestro,

1 gymnosperms were originally more ecologically successful than angiosperms due to significant molecular differences.

2 the dominance of gymnosperms during the age of the dinosaurs actually led to the rise of angiosperms in the Cretaceous period.

3 angiosperms appeared late in the fossil record, as they were unlikely to have been physically preserved when their numbers were low.

4 large numbers of angiosperms existed millions of years before early mammals lived, but other researchers failed to recognize them in the fossil record.

(37) What do some experts believe happened to angiosperms during the Cretaceous period?

1 The influence of pollinators led to an increase in their ability to identify and consume vital nutrients from the environment.

2 Genetic changes made their survival processes more effective and allowed them to thrive in many ecosystems.

3 Their ability to survive in a variety of regions was negatively affected as a result of severe changes in the levels of sunlight.

4 A mixing of gymnosperm and angiosperm DNA caused a change in the way angiosperms responded to pollinators.

Fernand Braudel and The Mediterranean

Fernand Braudel's *The Mediterranean* is perhaps the most significant piece of historical research written in the postwar era. Published in 1949, the conceptually challenging work takes as its subject not an individual, country, or event, but the Mediterranean region, and it examines how virtually every aspect of the land, people, and institutions shaped the region's history.

Braudel was prominent in the Annales school of history, which was founded earlier in the twentieth century, and *The Mediterranean* is often regarded as the pinnacle of Annales scholarship. The Annales school was established by Marc Bloch and Lucien Febvre, academic mavericks who rejected conventional approaches to history that focused on the study of influential individuals and their achievements. Instead of writing chronologically organized narratives describing notable political or military events, as was typical in history books of the day, Annales historians collaborated with academics from a wide variety of backgrounds to produce research with a greatly expanded scope.

Annales historians contended that disciplines such as geography, economics, psychology, and sociology could shed light on aspects of the past that would ordinarily be overlooked by conventional approaches to history. In fact, the Annales historians held that the activities of historical figures to whom so much attention was devoted in the books and articles of traditional historians were "surface disturbances, crests of foam that the tides of history carry on their strong backs." It was more illuminating, they argued, to study the day-to-day existence of peasants and merchants by analyzing anything from death certificates to business ledgers than it was to focus on prominent historical figures, such as Napoleon Bonaparte or Julius Caesar.

Nowhere is the Annales school's radical conception of history more evident than in *The Mediterranean*. The focus of conventional scholars on the lives of influential individuals and significant historical events meant that they rarely looked at periods longer than the life span of a single human being. Braudel, however, emphasized the concept of the "long duration," which he believed offered a more nuanced view of history. The first section of *The Mediterranean* begins with an examination of the geographical and climatic factors that have influenced the region. The text roams across the sea, over mountaintops, and through deserts, detailing the manner in which climate patterns and shifting topography have gradually and subtly shaped the Mediterranean region. Braudel emphasizes the constancy and continuity of geographical history, as change at this level is virtually imperceptible unless viewed on a geologic timescale.

The book's second section deals with periods measurable in centuries, moving away from a geologic timescale to examine the way that societal, economic, and political structures of Mediterranean civilizations have been defined by the natural forces described in the first section. Finally, Braudel moves on to the more conventional third section, where time is measured on the scale of human life spans. Here, he covers the reign of the Spanish king Philip II within the context of the previous two sections, demonstrating how the various civilizations of the Mediterranean have shaped historical events in the region that have often been the focus of conventional historical research.

In addition to its revolutionary conceptualization of historical timescales, *The Mediterranean* has been praised for Braudel's ability to avoid the pro-Western bias that many European and American historians of the time exhibited. Geography, climate, economies, and religions often transcend borders and races, so by the very nature of his approach to studying the region, Braudel dodges many of the traps that other historians of his generation fell into. By putting the deserts and plains of the Islamic world in the south of the region on an equal footing with the European areas to the north, and emphasizing the continuous exchange of technology, commodities, and even populations, Braudel reveals the complex and deeply rooted interconnectedness of groups and nations in the Mediterranean region that other historians had been blind to. Historian Richard Mowery Andrews cites Braudel's unconventional presentation of history as crucial to how *The Mediterranean* demonstrates that "no state or civilization enjoyed the luxury of self-determination; consciously or not, all were prisoners of interdependence."

Of course, *The Mediterranean* has not been entirely without critics. Braudel examines everything from the agricultural improvement in rural areas around the Mediterranean to peasants' wage patterns, and from demographic trends to the decline of Renaissance city-states. Overwhelmed by the mass of words and statistics, it is not uncommon for reviewers of Braudel's work to come away impressed but unable to comprehend what they have read. Historian Alan Macfarlane, for example, suggests that Braudel has "become lost in the woods of delightful data." In fact, Braudel's reluctance to make his thesis explicit has caused some to question whether he himself even had a firm grasp of it. Despite these criticisms, *The Mediterranean* is now considered a masterpiece of scholarship, and many of the approaches employed by Braudel have entered the mainstream of historical research.

(38) The Annales school of history believed that

1 many historians often went too far in making connections between the events of the past and various aspects of modern life.

2 accounts of the everyday lives of common people were unable to offer adequate insight into important historical events.

3 history should be examined from a variety of perspectives and not simply focus on well-known leaders and major events.

4 historical biographies should be expanded to show the effects that the actions of great people had on areas of life other than politics.

(39) In the first section of *The Mediterranean*, Fernand Braudel

1 argues that the impact of the Mediterranean Sea on the surrounding region was surpassed only by the influence of foreign economic powers.

2 describes environmental changes that are difficult to perceive but which he felt contributed to a more refined understanding of history.

3 demonstrates how a region's geographical features undergo so many transformations that it is impossible to definitively categorize them all.

4 shows how past historians had made serious mistakes in dating major events that had shaped the history of the Mediterranean region.

(40) Which of the following statements about *The Mediterranean* would Richard Mowery Andrews most likely agree with?

1 Its focus on nontraditional aspects of history allowed Braudel to reveal the importance of previously unnoticed connections between societies in the region.

2 Its lack of references to historical events in Western civilizations meant that Braudel's works were often not considered highly by foreign historians.

3 Braudel's emphasis on time allowed him to see how much faster countries in the north of the region developed in comparison with those in the south.

4 Braudel's view that a civilization's development depends on the determination of its people should have received more attention from other historians.

(41) What is one criticism of Braudel's approach to history?

1 Braudel's failure to understand the significance of various important events likely caused him to misinterpret some of the statistics he used.

2 His wandering focus on various periods in history meant that Braudel overlooked aspects of Mediterranean history that could have better supported his thesis.

3 Braudel was often less interested in the accuracy of his data than he was in trying to leave readers with a good impression of his work.

4 The detail and scope of Braudel's writing can make it difficult or impossible to understand the main point he was trying to convey.

4
- *Write an essay on the given TOPIC.*
- *Give THREE reasons to support your answer.*
- *Structure: introduction, main body, and conclusion*
- *Suggested length: 200–240 words*
- *Write your essay in the space provided on Side B of your answer sheet. Any writing outside the space will not be graded.*

TOPIC

Should investment in technology be a bigger priority for governments?

リスニング

─── **Listening Test** ───

There are four parts to this listening test.

Part 1	Dialogues: 1 question each	Multiple-choice
Part 2	Passages: 2 questions each	Multiple-choice
Part 3	Real-Life: 1 question each	Multiple-choice
Part 4	Interview: 2 questions	Multiple-choice

※**Listen carefully to the instructions.**

Part 1　　　　　▶MP3　▶アプリ　▶CD 2 **1**～**11**

No. 1
1　Make another appointment with the vet.
2　Choose a new brand of dog food.
3　See if her dog's food is on the list.
4　Leave her dog at the clinic for a few days.

No. 2
1　The woman should accept the new position.
2　The woman should request a higher salary.
3　The woman should spend more time at home.
4　The woman is better suited to marketing.

No. 3
1　He is being blamed for a project's delay.
2　Lisa is not satisfied with his work.
3　He discovered a problem with the intranet.
4　His manager wants him to lead a project.

No. 4
1　His choice of topic being too sensitive.
2　Not having done enough research.
3　Making too many controversial points.
4　Giving too much information.

No. 5	1 Having Jeffrey see a psychologist could be harmful.
	2 The teacher should have called about Jeffrey earlier.
	3 Jeffrey should stop playing soccer.
	4 Jeffrey was defending himself.

No. 6	1 He is having trouble finding a new job.
	2 His workload increased unexpectedly.
	3 He could not finish his project.
	4 He has little experience editing novels.

No. 7	1 Charlie should have attended.
	2 Noise levels should have been discussed further.
	3 There was too much focus on efficiency.
	4 Sharon was not to blame for the problem.

No. 8	1 The man's age will help him recover quickly.
	2 The man should change the way he exercises.
	3 The man does not need a scan.
	4 The man's pain was not caused by his training.

No. 9	1 She thinks her department may be eliminated.
	2 She thinks the new game will not be popular.
	3 The user tests will take longer than expected.
	4 The *Space Titans* game will not meet requirements.

No. 10	1 Bev's husband might change his mind.
	2 Bev's husband will probably never like children.
	3 Bev should give up on her dream.
	4 Bev should pressure her husband to have children.

‖‖‖ Part 2 ‖‖‖‖‖‖‖‖‖‖‖‖‖‖‖‖‖‖‖‖‖‖‖‖‖‖‖‖‖ ◀)) ▶MP3 ▶アプリ ▶CD 2 **12**〜**17**

(A)

No. 11
1 The workers involved were victims of violence.
2 It involved workers from many stations.
3 It was about more than money and living conditions.
4 Some White landowners actually supported it.

No. 12
1 The station owners agreed to a wage increase.
2 The government in Australia changed.
3 The Gurindji people ran out of money.
4 The government refused to support the workers.

(B)

No. 13
1 All of the claims made about the games are accurate.
2 It does not help users perform better at certain tasks.
3 It does not lessen the effects of Alzheimer's disease.
4 The memory problems it causes are temporary.

No. 14
1 The games become less challenging over time.
2 It could take time away from more-beneficial activities.
3 The content of the games is unrealistic.
4 It can be tiring on the brain.

(C)

No. 15
1 To propose a method for preventing counterfeit books.
2 To introduce an advantage of print on demand.
3 To show that small publishers dislike print on demand.
4 To illustrate a potential danger of counterfeit books.

No. 16
1 Ensure the prompt delivery of book orders.
2 Confirm the authenticity of the books they sell.
3 Charge lower prices for books.
4 Relax their policies toward authors.

(D)

No. 17
1 Some unqualified researchers received funding.
2 It often causes legal complications.
3 It rarely leads to useful products.
4 It contributes greatly to advances in technology.

No. 18
1 The government should get a share of any resulting profits.
2 The public should decide who receives the money.
3 Only nonprofit research organizations should be funded.
4 High-risk investments should be avoided.

(E)

No. 19
1 Fathers were not making enough use of it.
2 It did not treat fathers equally.
3 Mothers were unable to take time off.
4 It did not allow parents to receive pay.

No. 20
1 It led to increases in couples' medical bills.
2 It led to improvements in mothers' health.
3 It resulted in fathers working longer hours.
4 It caused psychological problems for fathers.

▮ Part 3 ▮▮▮▮▮▮▮▮▮▮▮▮▮▮▮▮▮▮▮▮▮▮▮▮▮▮▮ ◀» ▸MP3 ▸アプリ ▸CD 2 **18**〜**23**

(F)

No. 21

Situation: You are a third-year Japanese university student who has just transferred to a university abroad. You are attending an orientation for international students and first-year domestic students.

Question: What do you need to do first?

1 Create an account on the student portal website.
2 Meet with your academic adviser.
3 Register for required classes.
4 Attend your department orientation.

(G)

No. 22

Situation: You want to take weekly golf and tennis lessons for the lowest price. You are free after 6 p.m. on weekdays. A staff member at a sports club tells you the following.

Question: Which membership option should you choose?

1 Platinum Plus.
2 Gold Prime.
3 Flex Master.
4 Silver Saver.

(H)

No. 23

Situation: You are a department manager at a company. The company director has called an emergency staff meeting. You were given a blue nametag upon entering the conference room.

Question: What do you need to do first?

1 Contact former customers.
2 Research your company's competitors.
3 Investigate marketing strategies.
4 Evaluate the current product lineup.

(I)

No. 24

Situation: Your four-year-old son has a mild fever but no stomachache. He attends a day-care center near your home in Southport. You call a local hospital and are told the following.

Question: What should you do?

1 Take your son to the hospital for observation.
2 Call your son's day-care center in the morning.
3 Monitor your son's condition for the time being.
4 Try to reduce your son's fever.

(J)

No. 25

Situation: Due to a flight delay, you missed a connecting flight and had to buy another ticket. You speak to an airline representative at the airport.

Question: What should you do to get a full refund for the additional ticket?

1 Call the airline's customer service office.
2 Complete a form at the airport.
3 Apply through the airline's website.
4 Have the representative call you back later.

86

||||| Part 4 ||||||||||||||||||||||||||||||||||||||||||| ◀)) ▶MP3 ▶アプリ ▶CD 2 **24**〜**25**

No. 26
1 He was hired to perform magic for a major Japanese company.
2 He was asked to translate a magic book for Japanese customers.
3 He taught magic to successful businesspeople in his free time.
4 He made connections through people he studied Japanese history with.

No. 27
1 Despite his Japanese fluency, he struggled with cultural differences.
2 It was not possible to take vacations due to his irregular working hours.
3 The lack of a regular wage meant it was difficult to secure a visa.
4 He wanted to work in TV, but he could only find work at weddings.

87

二次試験
面　接

A日程　◀ッ　▶MP3　▶アプリ　▶CD 4 **11**～**15**

1. Does the economic future of Japan depend on labor from abroad?

2. Are international laws biased in favor of wealthy countries?

3. Agree or disagree: Promotion in the workplace should be based primarily on seniority

4. Should teachers be responsible for both the emotional development and academic development of students?

5. Is scientific research the key to improving human health in the future?

C日程

1. Should there be a mandatory retirement age for politicians?

2. Can the military invasion of other countries ever be justified?

3. Have internships become a way for companies to exploit young people?

4. Agree or disagree: Stem-cell research will revolutionize medical science

5. Should governments do more to promote free trade?

（注）モデルスピーチと解説はA日程のみ収録しています。

2021-2

一次試験　2021.10.10実施
二次試験　A日程　2021.11.7実施
　　　　　C日程　2021.11.23実施

Grade 1

試験時間

筆記：**100分**
リスニング：**約35分**

一次試験・筆記　　　　　p.90〜104
一次試験・リスニングp.105〜111
二次試験・面接　　　　　　p.112

＊解答・解説は別冊p.161〜212にあります。
＊面接の流れは本書p.16にあります。

2021年度第2回

**Web特典「自動採点サービス」対応
オンラインマークシート**

※検定の回によって2次元コードが違います。
※筆記1〜3，リスニングの採点ができます。
※PCからも利用できます（本書p.8参照）。

一次試験
筆 記

1 To complete each item, choose the best word or phrase from among the four choices. Then, on your answer sheet, find the number of the question and mark your answer.

(1) The ancient document was written in a script that for years no one could (   ). Then, finally, a brilliant young scholar worked out its meaning.
1 slander   **2** dawdle   **3** pledge   **4** decipher

(2) After the referee made several serious mistakes during the game, fans showed their (   ) by booing and shouting at him.
1 infamy   **2** clatter   **3** splendor   **4** disdain

(3) Gold is one of the most (   ) metals. This quality allows it to be shaped into many different forms and is one reason it is in such high demand.
1 bombastic   **2** malleable   **3** parched   **4** sordid

(4) The CEO said his company's success throughout the years was a clear (   ) to the wisdom of the policies of the company's past leaders.
1 prospectus   **2** abrasion   **3** testament   **4** reprisal

(5) During his first term, Governor Smith made many (   ). When he tried to get reelected, they supported his opponent, who easily won the election.
1 hermits   **2** prodigies   **3** adversaries   **4** protégés

(6) Aid agencies in the drought-affected region did their best to make sure emergency supplies were distributed (   ) to all citizens in need.
1 spuriously   **2** illicitly   **3** radiantly   **4** equitably

(7) As the coal strike spread and energy shortages became common, a number of industries found themselves in an increasingly (   ) condition.
1 crass   **2** acrid   **3** dire   **4** trite

(8) *A:* Your garden looks (   ). How do you keep it so neat and tidy?
B: To tell the truth, we hired a gardener to look after it.
1 immaculate   **2** warped   **3** intangible   **4** vulgar

(9) In 1993, the entire Internet was made up of just 130 websites. They have continued to (   ), however, and there are said to be over a billion today.

1 pulsate   **2** proliferate   **3** emancipate   **4** enumerate

(10) *A:* Those cakes look really good. Let's have one.
B: You go ahead. I'm on a diet, and I'm determined not to (   ) to temptation.

1 succumb   **2** perturb   **3** obliterate   **4** hassle

(11) In an effort to avoid an oncoming car, the driver (   ) off the side of the road.

1 swaggered   **2** cantered   **3** careened   **4** siphoned

(12) The patient suffers from a (   ) cough. He has been taking medicine for it, but it has continued for over six months.

1 chronic   **2** rustic   **3** tactful   **4** devious

(13) The army patrol encountered an (   ) on the way back to camp. A group of rebel fighters had been waiting for them as they entered a narrow valley.

1 ambush   **2** accolade   **3** epiphany   **4** inception

(14) The politician's popularity has (   ). Two years ago, his approval ratings were high. He then became the target of public criticism last year, but he has since regained support.

1 fluctuated   **2** concocted   **3** acceded   **4** tabulated

(15) Mary has long been a (   ) supporter of the city's plan to build a new highway. She believes it will have a hugely positive effect on the local economy.

1 residual   **2** staunch   **3** scandalous   **4** hereditary

(16) Kyle's back pain was so (   ) that he had a hard time even getting out of bed in the morning.

1 jocular   **2** derelict
3 excruciating   **4** endearing

(17) Trent caused a small fire in the kitchen when he forgot to turn the stove off. Luckily, he was able to (   ) the flames with a bucket of water before they spread.

1 recant   **2** disavow   **3** brandish   **4** douse

(18) Advancements in surgical techniques have allowed doctors to make smaller (   ) when they perform operations. This means that scars are much less noticeable.

1 conundrums 2 incisions

3 quagmires 4 caricatures

(19) The president was criticized for giving (   ) answers to questions at the press conference. The journalists who attended had hoped for more-straightforward replies.

1 oblique 2 lucrative 3 rotund 4 exquisite

(20) When Barbara was ill, someone from her family stayed at her side all day and all night. This (   ) continued until she was completely well again.

1 scourge 2 contour 3 cowardice 4 vigil

(21) Although Nina and Judy were twins, they behaved in very different ways at school. Nina was often rude and refused to obey her teachers, while Judy was always (   ).

1 omniscient 2 deferential 3 laborious 4 precipitous

(22) The ambassador decided to (   ) politeness and take a more aggressive stance on the issue after his initial approach failed to have any impact on the negotiations.

1 barge in 2 nibble at

3 pry out 4 dispense with

(23) The marathon runners were (   ) by the cheering crowds along the route. The support encouraged the runners to push hard until the end of the race.

1 spurred on 2 swept aside

3 put out 4 chipped in

(24) In an effort to reduce violent protests, the government has introduced laws to (   ) on large public gatherings.

1 churn out 2 crack down

3 grind up 4 swear in

(25) The soldiers received details of their new posting overseas soon after completing their training. They were ordered to (   ) to a base in West Africa.

1 ship out 2 chime in 3 ebb away 4 nod off

2

Read each passage and choose the best word or phrase from among the four choices for each blank. Then, on your answer sheet, find the number of the question and mark your answer.

Jewel Wasps and Cockroaches

The jewel wasp wields an ability that is vital to its reproduction, and the wasp's prey — the cockroach — plays an essential role. After grasping a cockroach in its jaws, the jewel wasp injects venom into its victim's body, instantly paralyzing the creature's front legs for a brief period. This immobility allows the wasp to deliver its second sting with the precise accuracy required to target specific areas of the cockroach's brain. There, the venom blocks the activity of certain neurons, interfering with the creature's ability to flee from the wasp. The fact that the wasp (**26**) in this way is considered one of the insect's most intriguing aspects.

After the venom takes effect, the cockroach is nearly ready to serve its role as nourishment for the wasp's larva. First, however, the cockroach engages in a prolonged self-grooming ritual while the wasp flies away and locates a hole in which to conceal its victim. Research suggests the cockroach's cleaning behavior is (**27**). It is unknown if the behavior benefits the wasp — for example, by ensuring a clean meal for the wasp's larva — but it was not exhibited when researchers subjected cockroaches to conditions similar to being pierced by a wasp's stinger. The behavior was also absent in cockroaches that simply experienced stress, including being grabbed, but not stung, by jewel wasps.

Upon the wasp's return, the cockroach is fully compliant to the will of its captor. After guiding the cockroach to the hole, the wasp lays an egg on its leg and departs. The wasp larva hatches and takes up residence inside the cockroach's body, using nutrients from the creature to cultivate its own development. But (**28**). Researchers have observed the larva producing a liquid substance that it deploys as a protective shield while in the cockroach's body cavity. The antibiotics within the substance inhibit the growth of bacteria that cockroaches harbor, which can be lethal to the jewel wasp's offspring during its incubation period. After surviving to maturation, the young wasp emerges from the shell of its host, ready to initiate its own search for an unfortunate victim.

(26) 1 risks its own safety   2 can attract prey to itself
     3 actually protects its victim   4 can manipulate its victim

(27) 1 essential to its survival
     2 a common response to stress
     3 a specific effect of the venom itself
     4 an attempt to confuse the wasp

(28) 1 the larva must make an important choice
     2 its environment is not without dangers
     3 predators can still locate the hole
     4 the larva's parent still has a role to play

Bertolt Brecht and Epic Theater

Widely considered one of the greatest directors and playwrights of the twentieth century, Bertolt Brecht was a pioneer of the innovative genre known as "epic theater." Though his work was consistently watchable and humorous, Brecht's plays evolved into acts of rebellion against theatrical conventions of the time. In particular, Brecht sought to overturn the common idea that art should (**29**   ). Productions of the time employed detailed props and scenery, utilized plots centered on contemporary subjects, and featured characters that audiences could easily relate to. Brecht's productions, however, turned traditional scriptwriting and staging on their head, purposely reminding audiences at every turn that they were viewing a heavily dramatized, theatrical interpretation of everyday life rather than a real event occurring before their eyes.

Brecht particularly despised the principle of catharsis — the release of emotions created when audience members sympathize with characters in ordinary plays. This most harmful of theatrical traditions, he argued, (**30**   ). Brecht therefore employed minimalist scenery and sets, and had his characters address the audience directly or hold up signs expressing their character's traits. By doing so, Brecht intentionally caused his audience to maintain an emotional distance from the characters and events on stage, creating a highly intellectual theater experience. His dramatic devices, Brecht hoped, would provoke the general public into reflecting thoughtfully on the play's themes.

Brecht's plays were almost invariably an expression of his political and philosophical principles, foremost among these being the concept that (31   ). One way that he conveyed this was through the use of historical material. Brecht felt such subject matter served to make audiences aware that seemingly momentous and universal events, such as wars, come to an end, and that the way those events were interpreted was often very different after the events themselves had ended. Brecht held the view that human civilization was progressing toward a utopian society and believed that theater could act both as a reminder that life is not static and as a motivator to help people work toward such a goal. While his utopian political views are today sometimes regarded as a weakness, he is revered for his groundbreaking and influential contribution to theater.

---

(29) **1** be a mirror of reality   **2** unite rather than divide
     3 challenge our assumptions   **4** always use original ideas

(30) **1** inevitably led to disappointment
     2 appealed mainly to playwrights
     3 often served to ridicule audiences
     4 kept audiences from thinking logically

(31) **1** all individuals are equal
     2 nothing is permanent
     3 even small acts have consequences
     4 history always repeats itself

---

3 *Read each passage and choose the best answer from among the four choices for each question. Then, on your answer sheet, find the number of the question and mark your answer.*

Usury and Sin

Though widely accepted today, charging interest on loaned money, also known as usury, was once considered a major sin. Usury laws were common in the past, and the Roman Catholic Church in particular was known for harshly resisting the practice during the medieval period, expelling those who were guilty of it from the church.

Prohibitions against usury originally arose due to the way that debt and credit were viewed as a system of benevolent aid and trust. People in the poor, rural populations of medieval times formed strong communal ties due to the way that families and friends relied on sharing and lending goods to help one another. Expecting compensation, therefore, for an act that was considered one's social duty was regarded as morally wrong, and this belief persisted following the shift from goods to money as a medium of exchange. Individuals who were destitute or had suffered financial misfortune, however, were forced to turn to the church or the nobility due to their large reserves of capital. And in keeping with the belief at the time regarding the moral nature of debt and credit, lenders who profited from something that was part of one's social and religious responsibility were viewed as sinful.

Some, however, attempted to circumvent church and legal bans on usury in order to profit from moneylending. Various methods emerged to do so, such as complex schemes that involved repaying loans in foreign currencies to use shifting exchange rates as a way to camouflage earned interest. Another method routinely employed by financiers was the "triple contract." This was a combination of contracts that, while separately permissible under laws at the time, together allowed moneylenders to gain interest by becoming business partners with the recipients of their loans. After moneylenders became part of the businesses they had authorized loans to, they were technically earning a profit from their capital rather than illegally gaining interest.

As trade expanded and developed, problems created by usury laws became obvious. Medieval opposition to generating money from money was due to the commonly held view of money as a means of exchange lacking inherent value. Shortages of gold and silver coins and the difficulty of making payments to clients in distant lands, however, led to the development of banks with branches in multiple cities and the emergence of moneychangers who could convert foreign currencies. As wealth spread throughout society, it became clear that moneylenders were not, in fact, receiving "money for nothing." Just as a farmer who lends someone a cow is deprived of the chance to obtain milk and calves from it, the lender of money is deprived of the opportunity to invest in other means of obtaining profits. Along with the changing nature of lending, a greater appreciation arose for the risk that moneylenders were burdened with upon parting with their capital. Over time, the acknowledgment of these factors by the church and scholars helped reframe the debate around usury, prompting the evolution from an outright ban on the charging of interest to the modern usury laws that protect ordinary consumers from excessive charges by loan sharks and credit card companies.

(32) In medieval society, prohibitions surrounding usury

    1 were a manifestation of the belief that it was a sin to request aid from anyone except relatives when one had financial problems.

    2 reflected the idea that people with money should not take unfair advantage of something that was considered a charitable act.

    3 were a demonstration of how the church and the nobility abused their access to large sums of money to exploit the poor.

    4 suggested that people did not have a sufficient understanding of debt and credit to make a lending system work effectively.

(33) According to the passage, what is true about the methods used to profit from moneylending?

    1 They were an example of how views about moneylending were not always the same in different countries and various industries.

    2 They illustrated that the way interest payments were made in medieval times could cause legal disputes between business partners.

    3 They were an indication of how people in medieval times believed that profit and interest were two entirely unconnected concepts.

    4 They showed how some people used indirect ways of earning interest on loans while appearing to obey the law.

(34) Which of the following statements would the author of the passage most likely agree with?

1 Abolishing usury laws in medieval times was only considered after the agricultural industry outgrew the limitations of the financial system.
2 A change in leadership within the church led to a reevaluation of the laws surrounding the borrowing and lending of money.
3 New attitudes toward moneylending were partly a result of increased understanding of the potential losses that could occur from giving out loans.
4 Banks and moneychangers pressured the church to relax its policy on usury as a way to boost profits from international trade.

The Classification Debate

Three varieties of the striolated puffbird in the Brazilian Amazon are virtually identical in appearance, but their songs differ subtly in rhythm and tone. When one scientist approached a committee in charge of bird species classification to advocate for reclassifying the three types into separate species, the committee members faced a dilemma. Were the distinctions sufficient to warrant the creation of two additional species? They eventually added just one. Their decision, however, sparked yet another controversy in the world of taxonomy, the branch of science that deals with identifying and defining the multitude of organisms found in nature.

The number of new species identified worldwide has been increasing as technological advances allow for closer examination of Earth's organisms. The number of bird species in South America alone has grown by over 150 since the year 2000. The vast majority of these, however, were not discovered based on expeditions into the deepest corners of the rain forest. Rather, they were created by reclassifying variants of existing species as a result of breakthroughs in recording technology or genetic classification. And while some argue the nuances detectable in recent years justify such reclassifications, others find the distinctions arbitrary. Bird expert James Remsen sees the current state of bird taxonomy as "trying to make the best of a bad situation," explaining that "we're trying to apply artificial barriers on a continuum."

These disputes have renewed debate over the "species problem," a fundamental issue in taxonomy regarding how to distinguish between species. The problems inherent in the attempts to answer this question underscore Remsen's view. The Biological Species Concept (BSC), for example, has long been a prominent guideline for biologists, defining a species as organisms that can only successfully reproduce with each other and produce healthy, fertile offspring. Using reproduction in this way to draw distinct lines between species causes complications, though. In cases where species have been split into two or more groups for geographical reasons, proponents of the BSC believe that this isolation justifies distinct species classification. It is impossible, they say, to know if these groups would naturally reproduce with each other because they do not meet.

Today, in addition to the BSC, biologists are guided by analysis of both DNA and the evolutionary history of groups of organisms. An example is the taxonomic debate over dingoes in Australia. For centuries, dingoes have been subject to eradication in rural areas due to the threat they pose to livestock. One reason they have not been granted protection is because they are classified as wild dogs, belonging to the same species as domestic dogs. Researchers examined factors including dingoes' bone structure, genetics, and historical lack of domestication, and in 2019, it was determined that a distinct species designation is warranted. This contradicted previous findings that were based on the BSC and which argued that dingoes' interbreeding naturally with domestic dogs shows they are not a distinct species. Considering dingoes' important role in controlling populations of pests such as foxes, the issue shows how taxonomic classification can have major implications both for the management of species and for entire ecosystems.

(35) Why does the author of the passage mention the controversy that arose over the classification of striolated puffbirds?

    1 It is an example of the issues related to classifying birds solely based on less-remarkable things like their appearance instead of more-important factors.

    2 It shows that the minor distinctions between varieties of animals can make it difficult to be certain if new species classifications are appropriate.

    3 It is an example of the problems that occur when scientists reject existing information about birds in favor of new data gained through fieldwork.

4 It shows that many of the small differences once thought to be significant in classifying species are not actually important at all.

(36) The Biological Species Concept can be problematic because

1 the opportunities that would normally exist for members of the same species to reproduce are sometimes affected by external factors.

2 it was established based on observations of interbreeding between animals kept in captivity rather than observations of animals in their natural habitats.

3 classification factors designed to apply to a specific species are often mistakenly applied to many different organisms.

4 the guidelines it is based on do not attempt to address the basic question of how to assess whether a group of organisms is a distinct species.

(37) What is evident from the situation concerning dingoes?

1 Close analysis of an animal's breeding habits over a long period of time can reveal the importance of that animal to the ecosystems it inhabits.

2 The 2019 research findings will likely result in Australian farmers being given more rights to exterminate dingoes that attack their livestock.

3 Judgments related to the classification of species are likely to be ignored if it is clear that maintaining animal populations leads to economic gain.

4 The decision regarding whether an animal should be considered a distinct species can significantly impact the way it is treated by humans.

The Trail of Tears

Known today as the Trail of Tears, the forcible removal and

migration of approximately 100,000 Native Americans from their ancestral homelands in the southeastern United States during the 1830s marks a dark moment in US history. The route to the new territories extended thousands of kilometers across nine states, and approximately 15,000 men, women, and children are believed to have perished during the removals and subsequent journey.

Prior to the Trail of Tears, a policy of cultural assimilation had been in place. Though Native Americans faced tremendous pressure to embrace Christianity and Western education, their right to retain their ancestral territories was generally acknowledged. In 1830, however, the US Congress passed President Andrew Jackson's Indian Removal Act, a piece of legislation that allowed the government to move tribes from their homelands to new homes in "Indian Territory," located in present-day Oklahoma. The policy faced difficulties, though, when an attempt in 1832 to seize Cherokee-owned land in Georgia was ruled unconstitutional by Chief Justice John Marshall of the Supreme Court. Recognizing the Cherokee tribe as a sovereign nation, the ruling set what appeared to be an important legal precedent. Jackson, though, undeterred and defiant, reportedly reacted to the ruling with the words, "John Marshall has made his decision; now let him enforce it."

Jackson's justifications for Native American removals were almost entirely unfounded. Despite the tribes' efforts to "civilize" themselves, they were criticized for their overreliance on hunting and failure to adopt modern agricultural practices. At the time, James Fenimore Cooper's novel *The Last of the Mohicans* was contributing to the romanticized American myth that Native Americans and their cultures were in the process of vanishing, and Jackson took advantage of this notion, arguing that without relocation, Native Americans and their cultures were doomed. In reality, however, Native American populations were stable and possibly even growing at the time.

According to historian Claudio Saunt, the Native American deportations should be seen in the context of capitalist expansion at the time. White slave owners and investors knew Native American holdings represented some of the most fertile land in the nation, ready to be exploited for farming and construction. Saunt chronicles how banks on the East Coast collaborated with Southern speculators to finance the dispossession of Native American lands, which White men, especially slave owners, saw as a golden opportunity to expand their business enterprises. While the removals were supposedly benign measures carried out to avert Native Americans' extinction, those behind the planning and execution of the removals saw Native American territory in the same way that they viewed slaves — a God-given resource to be exploited economically.

Saunt also documents how Southern politicians and Northern allies created a network of offices, soldiers, and administrators to manage the removals. These efforts were incredibly expensive, but the land, when cultivated with the free labor of Black slaves, was seen as worth the costs. East Coast bankers were quickly growing wealthier by financing the dual enterprises of slavery and expulsion, and this, in turn, provided capital for railroads and other large-scale development projects. As horrific as the Trail of Tears was, some argue that it brought technological advancement and infrastructure that were essential for America's emergence as a nation stretching from coast to coast.

The expulsions resulting from the Indian Removal Act provoked different reactions depending on the tribe. Some went voluntarily, while others resisted fiercely. One of the most tragic cases was that of the Cherokees. Faced with enormous pressure, a tiny minority of the tribe's members took it upon themselves to enter into negotiations with the government about moving west, resulting in the Treaty of New Echota. The document was considered invalid by the vast majority of the Cherokees, who argued that the so-called representatives responsible for brokering the terms were not their recognized leaders, and a petition requesting that the treaty be nullified received over 15,000 signatures. Congress, however, passed the treaty legislation, sealing the Cherokees' fate.

Despite a two-year deadline to leave, only about 2,000 Cherokees had set out for Indian Territory by 1838. In an effort to expedite the process, some 7,000 soldiers were ordered into Cherokee territory, where they dragged the Cherokees from their homes at gunpoint and locked them up while looting their homes and belongings. Unsheltered and lacking even basic supplies, the Cherokees were forced to endure long marches in extreme heat and cold. Water scarcity and meager food rations caused them to become malnourished, with many surrendering to deadly diseases. By the time the Cherokees had reached Indian Territory, approximately one-fourth had perished.

By about 1840, most of the tribes had settled on land that the government promised would remain theirs forever. However, they found themselves in a harsh, unfamiliar environment, and suffered appallingly in the coming years. Furthermore, as railroads opened up the American West, large numbers of White settlers flooded Indian Territory, gradually reducing its size until it had completely disappeared by the early twentieth century.

(38) During the 1830s, President Andrew Jackson

1 began attempting to use the courts to remove Native Americans from their lands after realizing that his assimilation policies were not effective.

2 was forced to negotiate and alter the way the Indian Removal Act worked after it was rejected by the nation's highest court.

3 ignored a legal decision which stated that the government did not have the authority to remove Native Americans from their lands without their consent.

4 was left with no choice but to extend special treatment to the Cherokees that had been denied to people of other tribes.

(39) Which of the following statements would Claudio Saunt most likely agree with?

1 Though many Native American tribes struggled with poor harvests and decreasing food sources, books often portrayed their lives in a glamorous way.

2 Though presented as an attempt to aid Native Americans, plans for their removal were actually motivated by the potential for economic gain.

3 Though many policies were introduced to restrict the influence of Native American cultures, some innovative business ideas helped popularize them.

4 Though the government was mainly to blame for the removals, Native Americans' cooperation with business leaders created many of their problems.

(40) The Trail of Tears is said to have fueled American expansion

1 because the rivalry between wealthy businessmen from the

North and the South helped lower the costs of expansion projects and speed up their construction time.

2 because many of the resettled Native Americans were offered jobs in the railroad and construction industries, which proved vital in opening up the country.

3 due to many Native Americans using the money they received from the expulsions and their knowledge of farming to relocate to and cultivate other lands.

4 due to a profitable industry being created around the expulsions, generating wealth that was then used for infrastructure development across the country.

(41) Which of the following statements regarding the Treaty of New Echota is true?

1 The deadline that the Cherokees had been given to sign the treaty did not allow them enough time to make a decision on such an important matter.

2 The petition to have the treaty passed as law was dismissed by officials who felt that there was not enough support from the Cherokees to justify such an action.

3 Many of the Cherokees were upset as they believed that the group responsible for the treaty did not have the authority to enter into negotiations on their behalf.

4 A group of Cherokee leaders felt that the treaty was far less favorable than similar kinds of treaties other tribes had been offered in the past.

4
- *Write an essay on the given TOPIC.*
- *Give THREE reasons to support your answer.*
- *Structure: introduction, main body, and conclusion*
- *Suggested length: 200–240 words*
- *Write your essay in the space provided on Side B of your answer sheet. Any writing outside the space will not be graded.*

TOPIC

Can individual privacy be protected in the modern world?

104

リスニング

—————— **Listening Test** ——————

There are four parts to this listening test.

Part 1	Dialogues: 1 question each	Multiple-choice
Part 2	Passages: 2 questions each	Multiple-choice
Part 3	Real-Life: 1 question each	Multiple-choice
Part 4	Interview: 2 questions	Multiple-choice

※**Listen carefully to the instructions.**

Part 1   ▶MP3 ▶アプリ ▶CD 2 26〜36

No. 1
1 They are made from low-quality materials.
2 They are difficult to adapt for use in Africa.
3 Throwing them away can be dangerous.
4 Donating them is not always a good thing.

No. 2
1 He will succeed in saving the wetlands.
2 He uses his position to do favors for certain people.
3 He works hard to protect the environment.
4 He is popular with his ordinary constituents.

No. 3
1 He worked late the night before.
2 He had an early morning meeting.
3 He has been working alone too often.
4 He did not finish the advertising contract.

No. 4
1 He is not a threat to her.
2 He should be hired as a manager.
3 He seems too confident.
4 He has poor communication skills.

No. 5
1 She has more chores than before.
2 Her exhibition has been successful.
3 She has more time for herself now.
4 Her gallery has closed down.

No. 6
1 He will be angry.
2 He will not notice.
3 He will overreact.
4 He will be understanding.

No. 7
1 The man does not need to repay anything.
2 She will not lend the man money.
3 She is also short of money now.
4 The man misled her on purpose.

No. 8
1 The man is too generous with his time.
2 The vice president does too much overtime.
3 The vice president owes her a favor.
4 The man is not qualified for his position.

No. 9
1 It will affect his work more than it will the woman's.
2 It might help staff expand their professional knowledge.
3 It means he will have to drive more than he currently does.
4 It may help staff strengthen existing client relationships.

No. 10
1 The women's input will be ignored.
2 It will probably be the last one they have to complete.
3 His boss wants to see it before human resources does.
4 It could lead to changes in the workplace.

Part 2 ◀» ▶MP3 ▶アプリ ▶CD 2 37～42

(A)

No. 11
1 It focused only on Internet-based relationships.
2 It was funded by an Internet company.
3 The researchers used outdated technology.
4 The length of the study was inadequate.

No. 12
1 They tend to misuse data from people's profiles.
2 They often ignore factors related to compatibility.
3 They may contribute to creating strong marriages.
4 They have simplified their algorithms recently.

(B)

No. 13
1 They can match the quality of the best natural diamonds.
2 They are unsuitable for use in high-tech tools.
3 They have a different chemical makeup from natural diamonds.
4 They can be more expensive than natural diamonds.

No. 14
1 By operating fewer mines in developing countries.
2 By reducing the size of their workforce.
3 By utilizing environmentally friendly methods.
4 By increasing their production capacity.

(C)

No. 15
1 Improve worker performance through competition.
2 Encourage workers to cooperate with other workers.
3 Teach workers how to cope better with stress.
4 Make it easier to recruit highly skilled workers.

No. 16
1 The true sources of employee motivation.
2 The importance of focusing on success.
3 The skills needed for interacting with customers.
4 The need for companies to minimize costs.

21年度第2回 リスニング

107

(D)

No. 17
1 The emergence of new marine predators.
2 The development of much stronger fins.
3 The absence of food sources in the ocean.
4 The ability to better detect food sources there.

No. 18
1 The location of their eyes remained unchanged.
2 They likely became able to hunt in a different way.
3 It caused some of them to react faster.
4 It led to harmful effects in the long term.

(E)

No. 19
1 Soldiers had better body armor.
2 More soldiers survived serious wounds.
3 Certain types of weapons were banned.
4 Injuries to soldiers were greatly reduced.

No. 20
1 She made masks using newly discovered materials.
2 She was a plastic surgeon before becoming an artist.
3 She was known for the accuracy of her masks.
4 She was a mental health professional.

Part 3 ◀)) ▶MP3 ▶アプリ ▶CD 2 **43**~**48**

(F)

No. 21

Situation: You are a Japanese executive arriving at a conference in Australia. You have business cards and an international driver's license, but your passport is at your hotel. You hear the following announcement.

Question: What should you do first?

1 Show your international driver's license at reception.
2 Hand a business card to security as you enter the building.
3 Collect your conference pass at reception.
4 Obtain some forms at the security desk.

(G)

No. 22

Situation: You have brought your car to an automobile repair shop for maintenance before a road trip. Safety is important, but you want to avoid unnecessary repairs. The mechanic tells you the following.

Question: What work should you ask the mechanic to do now?

1 Replace the engine coils.
2 Change the oxygen sensor.
3 Adjust the wheel alignment.
4 Replace the brake pads.

(H)

No. 23

Situation: It is April. You need to take beginner-level German classes before June. You work weekdays until 8 p.m. You call a language school and are told the following.

Question: Which course should you choose?

1 Introduction to German.
2 Basic German for Travel.
3 Intensive German.
4 Private German Online.

(I)

No. 24

Situation: You work at a graphic-design firm and hope to be promoted. Your assistant has not been working on the museum project. Your manager left you the following voice mail.

Question: What should you do?

1 Continue with the museum project as planned.
2 Meet with your assistant to explain his new role.
3 Prepare materials for your performance review.
4 Contact the president with your plan for the client.

(J)

No. 25

Situation: You recently bought a racing bicycle. You want assistance on how to position your feet on the pedals. Your budget is $400. You call the bicycle store and are told the following.

Question: Which option should you choose?

1 The Standard Fit Program.
2 The Dynamic Fit Program.
3 The Biomechanical Tuning Service.
4 The Perfect Fit Tutor.

110

| Part 4 | ◀)) ▶MP3 ▶アプリ ▶CD 2 **49**〜**50**

No. 26

1 She is often impressed by the strength of her students' arguments.
2 It can be hard to apply the grading criteria objectively.
3 She sometimes disagrees with the professors' grades.
4 It is the most interesting aspect of being a teaching assistant.

No. 27

1 Make sure that they can explain the material clearly.
2 Try not to be too intimidating toward students.
3 Accept the fact that they will occasionally make mistakes.
4 Allow the students to express themselves during seminars.

二次試験
面 接

A日程　◀》　▶MP3 ▶アプリ ▶CD 4 **16**〜**20**

1. Agree or disagree: Urbanization inevitably leads to a lower quality of life

2. Has online media destroyed traditional print journalism?

3. Is a society free of crime an unattainable goal?

4. Has the traditional five-day workweek become outdated in the modern world?

5. Can the technology gap between developed and developing nations ever be eliminated?

C日程

1. Are modern methods of food production sustainable in the long term?

2. Should governments prioritize domestic issues over international issues?

3. Are airline companies doing enough to become more environmentally friendly?

4. Should athletes who take performance-enhancing drugs be banned for life?

5. Agree or disagree: Public surveillance is justified if it helps prevent crimes

（注）モデルスピーチと解説はA日程のみ収録しています。

2021-1

一次試験　2021.5.30実施
二次試験　A日程　2021.6.27実施
　　　　　C日程　2021.7.11実施

Grade 1

試験時間

筆記：**100分**
リスニング：約35分

一次試験・筆記　　　　p.114～128
一次試験・リスニングp.129～135
二次試験・面接　　　　　　p.136

＊解答・解説は別冊p.213～264にあります。
＊面接の流れは本書p.16にあります。

2021年度第1回　Web特典「自動採点サービス」対応
オンラインマークシート
※検定の回によって2次元コードが違います。
※筆記1～3，リスニングの採点ができます。
※PCからも利用できます（本書p.8参照）。

一次試験

筆 記

1 To complete each item, choose the best word or phrase from among the four choices. Then, on your answer sheet, find the number of the question and mark your answer.

(1) Cell phones have become a permanent (　　) in modern society. Most people could not imagine living without one.
1 clasp　　　**2** stint　　　**3** fixture　　　**4** rupture

(2) Colin did not have enough money to pay for the car all at once, so he paid it off in (　　) of $800 a month for two years.
1 dispositions　　　　　　**2** installments
3 enactments　　　　　　**4** speculations

(3) When she asked her boss for a raise, Melanie's (　　) tone of voice made it obvious how nervous she was.
1 garish　　　**2** jovial　　　**3** pompous　　　**4** diffident

(4) The religious sect established a (　　) in a rural area where its followers could live together and share everything. No private property was allowed.
1 dirge　　　**2** prelude　　　**3** repository　　　**4** commune

(5) The famous reporter was fired for (　　) another journalist's work. His article was almost exactly the same as that of the other journalist.
1 alleviating　　**2** plagiarizing　**3** inoculating　　**4** beleaguering

(6) Now that the local steel factory has closed down, the streets of the once-busy town are lined with (　　) businesses. Most owners have abandoned their stores.
1 rhetorical　　**2** volatile　　**3** defunct　　　**4** aspiring

(7) The ambassador's failure to attend the ceremony held in honor of the king was considered an (　　) by his host nation and made already bad relations worse.
1 elucidation　　**2** affront　　**3** impasse　　　**4** ultimatum

(8) US border guards managed to (　　) the escaped prisoner as he tried to cross into Canada. He was returned to jail immediately.
1 apprehend　　**2** pillage　　**3** exalt　　　　**4** acclimate

(9) Anthony enjoyed his first day at his new job. The atmosphere

114

was (   ), and his colleagues did their best to make him feel welcome.

1 congenial   **2** delirious   **3** measly   **4** implausible

(10) **A:** I just learned I've been (   ) to second violin in the school orchestra. I knew I should've practiced more.

B: Well, if you work hard, I'm sure you can get your previous position back.

1 relegated   **2** jeopardized   **3** reiterated   **4** stowed

(11) After the politician received death threats on social media, many news outlets said that such behavior was (   ) and should be punished.

1 incalculable   **2** reprehensible
3 bumbling   **4** virtuous

(12) As an increasing number of vehicles are being designed to operate (   ), drivers will be free to relax or get some work done while their cars drive themselves.

1 listlessly   **2** forlornly
3 autonomously   **4** semantically

(13) The opera singer (   ) in the audience's applause on the final night of the show. She knew she had given the best performance of her life.

1 clamored   **2** basked   **3** floundered   **4** trampled

(14) It is important to check the expiration date of seeds before planting them. If they are too old, there is a strong chance that many of them will not (   ).

1 sprout   **2** forestall   **3** lunge   **4** rescind

(15) **A:** It's such a beautiful night! What's the name of that (   ) over there?

B: That's Orion. You can tell by the row of three stars in the middle.

1 constellation   **2** exodus
3 tenet   **4** redemption

(16) The official report said that foreign governments were using the Internet to (   ) democracy. It pointed to fake news stories published on various popular websites to influence voters.

1 salivate   **2** hoist   **3** placate   **4** subvert

21年度第1回　筆記

115

(17) Roderick was in a car accident last year, but luckily he was not ( ) for any of the damage as it was the other driver's fault.
1 impervious **2** redolent **3** impalpable **4** liable

(18) Guests at the opening of the new national museum had to dress in formal ( ). A few people who wore jeans and T-shirts were turned away at the door.
1 pageant **2** attire **3** parlance **4** attrition

(19) From an early age, the child had an ( ) ability to guess what other people were thinking. His schoolteachers said they had never seen anything like it before.
1 impetuous **2** idyllic **3** uncanny **4** odious

(20) The actor is now at the ( ) of his career, having recently received universal praise and numerous awards for his latest film role.
1 pinnacle **2** figment **3** relapse **4** vortex

(21) Reza thinks his boss is too ( ). He finds it frustrating because she always wants to discuss small, unimportant details.
1 unseemly **2** indignant **3** apolitical **4** pedantic

(22) The meeting was supposed to ( ) by noon, but it was still going at 1:30 p.m. By then, most of the people were very hungry.
1 wind up **2** shell out **3** wear in **4** spill over

(23) The new prime minister's economic policy focuses on ( ) inflation. He has promised to get prices under control as quickly as possible.
1 sounding out **2** stitching up
3 reining in **4** locking away

(24) The detective spent several months ( ) the circumstances surrounding the murder before he was able to discover who had done it.
1 tilting at **2** swinging around
3 digging into **4** bracing for

(25) *A:* Carlos, did you ( ) the dates for your time off this summer? I was hoping we could make our vacation plans soon.
B: Not yet, honey. I'll talk to the boss about it tomorrow and then make a decision.
1 shy away **2** settle on **3** strip out **4** hang back

116

2

Read each passage and choose the best word or phrase from among the four choices for each blank. Then, on your answer sheet, find the number of the question and mark your answer.

Jediism

Based on the *Star Wars* science fiction movies, Jediism is a pop-culture philosophy with a substantial worldwide following. Its practitioners seek to emulate a group of spiritual warriors from the movies who are masters of a phenomenon called "the Force," an energy that underlies all creation and gives the warriors supernatural abilities. Followers see Jediism as a legitimate religion, but as a spiritual practice anchored in fiction it is the focus of frequent ridicule. In response, however, believers point out that many members of other religions (**26**). Major religions commonly use stories to communicate moral or spiritual lessons, and these often contain fantastical elements — talking animals, for example — which strongly suggest that they do not describe actual historical events. Yet just as this does not necessarily discredit such faiths, so practitioners of Jediism feel its origin in fiction should not affect its validity.

Following a movie-based philosophy can, however, (**27**). In the case of Jediism, followers are well known for enthusiastically investing substantial amounts of money in costumes, imitation weapons, and other paraphernalia. While it can be argued that many elements in the movies are purposely designed to facilitate the purchase of related merchandise, such behavior appears contrary to the prohibition against excessive ownership of material goods expounded in the movies. Most followers simply ignore the inconsistency, though some do attempt to recycle or take other measures to reduce their possessions.

Gaining official recognition has presented difficulties for Jediism. In the United Kingdom, an application for tax-exempt status was rejected on the basis of Jediism's lack of both structure and a unifying system of belief. Yet despite its failure to attain official designation, Jediism is evidence of (**28**) in the West. As Western culture has been influenced by Eastern religions such as Buddhism, which may not have concepts of God that are recognizable to many Westerners or which lack the type of worship found in Christianity, clear lines that could be used to characterize and legitimize religious practices have become difficult to draw. Commentators frequently depict Jediism as exemplifying both the decline in authoritarian, highly structured organizations and the rise of groups focused on their members' personal fulfillment.

---

(26) 1 often claim religious ignorance
 2 are not supportive of wild beliefs
 3 have been persecuted in the past
 4 do not take all their sources literally

(27) 1 cause many to reject the movies
 2 give rise to ironic situations
 3 place excessive hardship on followers
 4 lead to antisocial attitudes

(28) 1 new governmental approaches toward religion
 2 a surge in general religious sentiment
 3 a shift in the way religion itself is perceived
 4 society's influence on older religions

Webster's Third

When the most prominent dictionary maker in the United States, Merriam-Webster, published its *Webster's Third New International Dictionary* in 1961, it expected the dictionary to be received as a groundbreaking reference tool for the modern era. Influenced by recent trends in linguistics, *Webster's Third* took an innovative "descriptivist" approach, focusing on how English is actually written and spoken by ordinary people in everyday life. Critics, however, charged that the dictionary's authors had (**29**). They argued that dictionaries are meant to be "prescriptive"; that is, their role is to make authoritative pronouncements on correct usage and pronunciation. Some even complained that the abandonment of prescriptivism was sending the English language down a slippery slope into linguistic chaos. They were particularly irate about the alleged endorsement of slang terms like "ain't," which *Webster's Third* asserted was "used orally . . . by many cultivated speakers."

It can be said, however, that *Webster's Third* was rooted in (**30**). From the late 1700s, dictionaries had been embraced just as fully by the lower classes as by the highly educated elite. Marginalized and oppressed minorities used them as a path to attain the literacy forbidden to them, and immigrants to the country viewed dictionaries as indispensable learning tools to aid linguistic and cultural assimilation. *Webster's Third* epitomized this egalitarian mentality, utilizing, for example, sentences not just from Shakespeare and the Bible but from Hollywood actors and other nontraditional sources as well, further reinforcing its accessibility and inclusivity.

Superficially, the uproar *Webster's Third* created among the elite and academics was a conflict about whether words like "ain't" should be labeled with disparaging terms such as "incorrect" and "illiterate," or with more diplomatic ones such as "nonstandard." On a deeper level, though, it reflected a radical cultural shift in which absolute ideas about right and wrong were fading and pressures to conform were declining, as exemplified by the growing feminist movement and the rejection of authority by young people that occurred in the 1960s. Therefore, when considered in the context of such movements, *Webster's Third* is a pioneering work in the field of linguistics as well as (**31**).

---

(29) **1** acted in an irresponsible way
      2 misunderstood descriptivism
      3 made things needlessly complicated
      4 fallen behind the times

(30) **1** a disturbing American tendency
      2 incorrect assumptions about American society
      3 the influence of the American upper class
      4 the American attitude toward dictionaries

(31) **1** a result of extreme compromise
      2 a reflection of social change
      3 an attempt to profit from a trend
      4 an extension of academic biases

3 Read each passage and choose the best answer from among the four choices for each question. Then, on your answer sheet, find the number of the question and mark your answer.

Conspicuous Consumption

According to the economic law of demand, there is a negative correlation between the price of an item and the demand for it. Significant price increases of a product by a company, therefore, should motivate consumers to switch to a competitor that provides an equivalent product at a more reasonable price. In 1899, however, economist Thorstein Veblen coined the term "conspicuous consumption," arguing that specific segments of society were unconcerned with the market value of certain products and would spend lavishly on anything that provided opportunities to display their wealth and prominence. These goods — items such as rare and fine wines and handcrafted watches — have subsequently become known as "Veblen goods." Unlike ordinary consumer goods, the price increase — even a substantial one — of Veblen goods will not have an adverse effect on the volume of their sales to wealthy consumers and may even add to their appeal. Veblen based his theory on observations of American millionaires, such as William Randolph Hearst and Andrew Carnegie, whose opulent concert halls, mansions, and museums appeared to have been built as much to reflect the owners' affluence as for any practical purpose. Veblen saw such displays as the manifestation of an innate desire that "prompts us to outdo those with whom we are in the habit of classing ourselves."

Conspicuous consumption, however, has also been observed in other segments of society where visible displays of opulence imply wealth beyond that of the purchaser's actual status. For such individuals, purchasing luxury goods is seen more as a tool by which they might appear to be a member of a higher social class. Economists point out that to avoid the stigma associated with poverty, people tend to splurge on visible indicators of affluence, regardless of price changes. A case in point is the role emerging economies play in driving the luxury goods market. Consumers in growing markets such as Russia, China, and Saudi Arabia, economists note, have become essential drivers of growth in luxury goods sales in recent decades, despite the fact that average incomes are significantly lower than they are in developed nations, such as the United States or Japan. In fact, it

120

is common, economists say, for less-affluent consumers to spend beyond their means and purchase status symbols in order to emulate wealthy individuals.

Veblen's theory paints an incomplete picture, however. Recent research shows that wealthy people flaunting their money signifies a phase of economic maturity, and that this visibly extravagant spending tends to fade as the wealth gap narrows. As individuals, classes, or countries begin to enjoy higher levels of affluence, patterns of "inconspicuous consumption" begin to emerge, and access to exclusive services becomes increasingly sought-after and valuable. Luxury goods still retain some semblance of importance as status symbols, but these services begin to account for an increasing proportion of expenditure and prioritize self-improvement and exclusivity. As such, experiences such as having a life coach, joining a boutique health clinic, or attending an invitation-only event become better demonstrators of the economic class to which an individual belongs than simply owning a designer watch.

(32) What is one thing that we learn about "Veblen goods"?

1 Their popularity among some consumers is defined more by the degree of wealth they signify than by the price of the goods themselves.

2 Because they are subject to frequent shifts in demand, manufacturers that produce them often do so at a considerable risk.

3 Consumers looking for bargains are often drawn to them as the goods frequently experience periods where they are lower in price.

4 They are more likely to follow the law of demand than ordinary consumer goods due to their superior quality.

(33) According to the passage, which of the following statements would economists most likely agree with?

1 The trend of purchasing luxury goods is strongest among those who have just recently advanced to a higher social class.

2 Luxury goods are more accessible to wealthy people in developing nations than they are to people with similar levels of wealth in developed ones.

3 Despite being unable to afford luxury goods, some people buy them to avoid appearing as though they are from a low-income background.

4 While luxury goods are highly popular among the wealthy at first, they lose their luxury status as they begin to be purchased by poor people.

(34) The author of the passage suggests that Thorstein Veblen's theory does not account for

1 recent cycles of economic downturn, which prohibit people from all segments of society from accumulating greater levels of wealth.

2 the increase of financial prosperity as a result of economic growth, which leads to a decline in the use of luxury goods to represent status.

3 a proportion of people across all wealth groups who are rejecting luxury goods as a means of displaying their wealth and status in society.

4 the promotion of inconspicuous luxury goods affordable to members of lower economic classes becoming a more common occurrence.

Fossil-Fuel Subsidies

A report by the International Monetary Fund (IMF) revealed that governments provided $5.2 trillion in subsidies to fossil-fuel companies in 2017. In light of evidence that fossil-fuel-related pollution causes millions of deaths each year, supporting the use of fossil fuels appears both morally questionable and in direct opposition to government pledges to reduce carbon emissions. However, the subsidy total is misleading in that it includes both pretax and posttax subsidies. The former are what most people associate with the word "subsidy" — things like cash handouts and tax breaks for oil companies that are designed to lower the cost of production, resulting in lower prices for consumers. The vast majority of the subsidies in the report, however, are of the posttax variety. These represent the additional burden on taxpayers that is the consequence of our dependence on fossil fuels — everything from oil-spill cleanup bills to increased traffic congestion and road accidents. Numerous critics contest the IMF's definition of subsidies, pointing out that there is obviously a high degree of subjectivity with regard to whether such costs should be included in these calculations. When posttax subsidies are excluded, the amount decreases to $424 billion, a fraction of the original sum.

While the inclusion of posttax subsidies may have been deceptive, a closer look at their societal costs is troubling. Many in society indeed gain an advantage from the economic and lifestyle benefits afforded from consumption of fossil-fuel-based energy, but the approximately 200,000 air-pollution-related deaths recorded annually in the United States reflect the unfortunate price that some are forced to pay. Furthermore, research indicates that there are racial and socioeconomic disparities in the extent to which the consequences of fossil-fuel use have a positive or negative impact on individuals' lives. Studies show, for example, that White Americans are responsible for 17 percent more air pollution than they are subjected to, while Black and Hispanic Americans are exposed to well over 50 percent more than they cause.

The indirect nature of posttax subsidies, however, makes them much harder to deal with than pretax subsidies. And while pretax subsidies are declining worldwide, their removal could be a double-edged sword. Since they do decrease the direct financial burden on consumers, removing them would add stress to low-income households, and in some cases drive very poor individuals to use cheaper fuels that release even greater amounts of pollutants than fossil fuels do. At the same time, these very households experience a disproportionate amount of suffering and hardship as a result of the activity the subsidies encourage. Experts say a more effective strategy for governments is to focus on the broader societal costs. There can be initiatives, for example, to tax companies that extract and produce fossil fuels on the emissions they release and redistribute the money to those their activities affect the most. This would impose a degree of accountability on the fossil-fuel industry while easing the impacts on low-income households. It would also, and perhaps more importantly, result in higher prices for fossil fuels, mitigating the degree of damage they cause by incentivizing the research and development of energy from cleaner sources.

(35) According to the author of the passage, the subsidy total reported by the International Monetary Fund is misleading because

1 the organization calculates the amounts of pretax subsidies directly based on an estimation of what it believes posttax subsidies should be.

2 the subsidy total does not take into account the future costs of commitments by governments to reduce emissions of harmful greenhouse gases.

3 the organization ignores the fact that pretax subsidies often do not help lower production costs or pass on cheaper fuel costs to the general public.

4 the subsidy total includes a large portion of various costs paid by taxpayers that do not fit the conventional idea of what makes up a subsidy.

(36) In the second paragraph, what does the author of the passage reveal about fossil fuels?

1 If current trends in fossil-fuel use continue, the people who consume more of them will suffer the most severe health consequences.

2 The worst of the negative effects on the public that result from the burning of fossil fuels have been discovered to be unrelated to air pollution.

3 There is an imbalance between the benefits minorities receive from fossil-fuel subsidies and the negative effects they suffer from fossil-fuel use.

4 The specific ways in which fossil fuels are consumed by some minorities have little effect on the amount of pollution fossil fuels ultimately cause.

(37) Which of the following would likely be part of the strategy that experts recommend?

1 Removing posttax subsidies paid to fossil-fuel companies and redirecting the money to industries that work to improve air quality.

2 Introducing policies that hold fossil-fuel companies directly responsible for the pollution they cause while ensuring low-income households benefit financially.

3 Providing pretax subsidies to companies in clean-energy industries and rewarding them for making clean energy more accessible to low-income households.

4 Ensuring that any cuts to pretax subsidies are carried out at the same rate as reductions in posttax subsidies are.

Plant Intelligence

Taking it for granted that a central nervous system — and a brain in particular — is a prerequisite for intelligence, scientists have long asserted that only humans and animals are capable of thinking. Based on this view, research into intelligence has been defined by IQ tests and other objective measurements of the ability to do things like answering written questions, solving physical puzzles, and demonstrating memory skills through actions.

Proponents of an emerging field known as plant neurobiology, however, have disputed the scientific consensus, arguing that the lack of a central nervous system does not necessarily preclude plants from possessing some form of intelligence. They contend that ordinary biological, chemical, and genetic mechanisms in plants do not adequately explain the wide array of highly sophisticated behaviors that they exhibit. Advocates claim, therefore, that plants are not simply passive elements in their environment, but are, in fact, capable of sensing and assessing stimuli from multiple environmental factors in order to coordinate appropriate responses. Such assertions, however, have been met with skepticism and even outright hostility in the scientific community.

Research by Monica Gagliano of the University of Western Australia attempted to validate some of plant neurobiology's controversial claims using the mimosa plant, which is known for defensively curling its leaves in reaction to being touched or disturbed. Gagliano's experiment involved exposing over 50 mimosa plants to weekly sessions of controlled, harmless dropping motions. She observed that, over time, some of the plants stopped reacting defensively, indicating they had learned that danger was not imminent. To discount the possibility that the plants' lack of reaction to being dropped could be attributed to fatigue or something similar, Gagliano exposed some of the plants to a sudden shaking motion.

Though the process of adapting to being dropped had been gradual, the shaking motion instantly returned the plants to their normal defensive behavior. When she exposed them to the dropping motions again, the plants "remembered" what they had previously learned, suggesting that they were purposely altering their response to being dropped based on experience.

Research like this supports the growing argument that while plants may not have brains, their behavior in reaction to environmental stimuli is evidence of a brainlike information-processing system. Scientists who support this theory have also noted that, on a biological level, the chemical signaling systems found in the nervous systems of animals have been identified in plants, too.

Despite the mounting research lending support to the concept of plant intelligence, Gagliano and others who advocate for further studies into this field have come under fire from those who doubt the validity of such research. In direct response to Gagliano's experiment, some argue that dropping a plant is not a common occurrence in nature, and thus cannot be considered a reliable trigger for the type of learning Gagliano ascribes to her plants. Instead, they describe the behavior of Gagliano's plants as the result of evolutionary adaptation, an automatic reaction programmed by nature over many generations. In response, Gagliano points out that the stimulus in her experiment was artificial, so it does not make sense that plants could have undergone an evolutionary adaptation to something that does not occur in their natural environment. Her argument that the plants' response could not be innate is further supported by the fact that some of her plants learned faster than others.

Stefano Mancuso, the director of the International Laboratory of Plant Neurobiology in Florence, Italy, approaches the controversy in a different way. His research has revealed unusual levels of electrical activity and oxygen consumption in the roots of plants, possibly hinting at a "root brain." A firm advocate of plant neurobiology, Mancuso believes that plant intelligence is analogous to the distributed intelligence observed in swarm behavior. In bird flocks, for example, birds follow rules for the collective good of the group, such as maintaining appropriate distances between each other when flying. This type of collective behavior, he suggests, is not unlike the manner in which individual roots of a plant act in a coordinated manner to benefit the entire organism.

The contention surrounding plant neurobiology has reignited a broader debate about intelligence. According to Mancuso, our reluctance to apply intelligence to other organisms may be due to psychologically based biases. In his opinion, we are able to accept the concept of artificial intelligence in the machines we build, for example, because they serve us and are our own creations. On the other hand, our hostility to plant intelligence, he believes, could be a manifestation of the somber realization that while a world without plants would be disastrous for humans, the opposite would likely not be an issue for plants. Considering Mancuso's perspective, perhaps the simplification of plant intelligence as just a consequence of electrical signals exchanged between cells could be deemed unfairly dismissive.

(38) Why is plant neurobiology controversial in the scientific community?

1 It argues that the very same methods used by scientists to determine a human subject's level of intelligence should also be applied to other organisms.

2 It proposes that the biological, chemical, and genetic processes observed in plant behavior operate differently from those in humans and animals.

3 It implies that mechanisms previously thought to underlie the human central nervous system do not function as scientists have always believed.

4 It makes claims regarding the fundamental mechanisms behind intelligence that are in opposition to the ideas held by a majority of scientists.

(39) Monica Gagliano's experiment on the mimosa plant suggests that

1 since the plant displayed delayed defensive behavior when presented with threats, it is unable to react quickly to danger.

2 the plant's ability to act upon what it has remembered is greatly affected by the degree of fatigue that it is experiencing at any one time.

3 the plant demonstrates the capacity to distinguish between various types of sensory input as well as exhibit different reactions to them.

4 since there were inconsistencies in the ways the plant reacted to being shaken, learning speed is not the same between species.

(40) According to the passage, which of the following statements would Gagliano most likely agree with?

1. Testing plants with a stimulus they do not experience in nature helps to show that their response is actually based on learning.
2. The way plants adapt over generations is actually more similar to the way humans learn than most researchers believe.
3. The consensus among scientists that plants are in possession of a nervous system provides enough justification to compare plant behavior with that of animals.
4. Though plants' information-processing systems work much more slowly than those of humans, it does not mean they are necessarily inferior.

(41) What does Stefano Mancuso imply regarding plant intelligence?

1. If researchers chose to compare plants to animals other than humans, the field of plant neurobiology would advance far more quickly.
2. Despite some similarity between how humans and plants formulate various behaviors, it is irresponsible to assume that this relates to intelligence in the same way.
3. Human attitudes toward the concept of intelligence in plants may be related to how we understand and rationalize our relationship with them.
4. The fact that electrical-activity levels are similar in plant roots and the brains of birds suggests that they may operate similarly.

4
- *Write an essay on the given TOPIC.*
- *Give THREE reasons to support your answer.*
- *Structure: introduction, main body, and conclusion*
- *Suggested length: 200–240 words*
- *Write your essay in the space provided on Side B of your answer sheet. <u>Any writing outside the space will not be graded.</u>*

TOPIC
Are economic sanctions a useful foreign-policy tool?

リスニング

―― Listening Test ――

There are four parts to this listening test.

Part 1	Dialogues: 1 question each	Multiple-choice
Part 2	Passages: 2 questions each	Multiple-choice
Part 3	Real-Life: 1 question each	Multiple-choice
Part 4	Interview: 2 questions	Multiple-choice

※**Listen carefully to the instructions.**

Part 1 ▶MP3 ▶アプリ ▶CD 3 **1**〜**11**

No. 1
1 Her back pain became less severe.
2 She was worried about side effects.
3 Her doctor suggested it might not be safe.
4 She heard it was ineffective against back pain.

No. 2
1 He did not get along with the staff.
2 Employee turnover was high.
3 He had to deal with many complaints.
4 Product quality was better.

No. 3
1 The declining quality of school meals.
2 The proposal to open a snack shop.
3 The lack of convenient restaurants in the area.
4 The increasing cost of school meals.

No. 4
1 He is planning to leave the company.
2 He is away on business for much of the year.
3 His current project has become complicated.
4 His boss will not extend the deadline.

No. 5

1 It is not being advertised well.
2 The location of the house might put buyers off.
3 There are better houses available in the area.
4 The asking price for the house may be too high.

No. 6

1 She may stop buying organic food.
2 She has reduced her shopping budget.
3 She is committed to helping the environment.
4 She has found a cheaper organic-food store.

No. 7

1 Contact the insurance company.
2 Renegotiate the payments on the car.
3 Purchase a more fuel-efficient vehicle.
4 Spend less money on other things.

No. 8

1 The job's salary is not as high as he expected.
2 His wife places too much emphasis on money.
3 The job would force him to change his lifestyle.
4 His family may go further into debt.

No. 9

1 Replace her car's brake drums.
2 Go to a cheaper garage.
3 Get her car repaired as soon as possible.
4 Pay for the repairs in advance.

No. 10

1 The agencies have found some ideal candidates.
2 Dan should lower his expectations.
3 Philip Johnson's sales record is not outstanding.
4 Dan should make the final hiring decision.

|||||| Part 2 |||||||||||||||||||||||||||||||||||||||||||||||||||||||||||||||| ◀)) ▶MP3 ▶アプリ ▶CD3 **12**〜**17**

(A)

No. 11
1 Our brains do not age in the same way as our bodies do.
2 Electrical stimulation may cause serious mental issues.
3 Learning is not connected to other brain functions.
4 Synchronizing brain waves improves memory function.

No. 12
1 It has potential uses beyond improving memory and learning.
2 It has helped to identify previously unknown conditions.
3 It has demonstrated long-term effectiveness.
4 It has proved unsuitable for treating brain disorders.

(B)

No. 13
1 It was once covered in dense rain forest.
2 It has several distinct ecological environments.
3 It attracted many species from other landmasses.
4 It remains isolated from modern civilization.

No. 14
1 By comparing it to wildlife on other islands.
2 By recruiting local people as guides.
3 By examining past changes in the climate.
4 By copying methods used in other countries.

21年度第1回 リスニング

131

(C)

No. 15
1 Germany's nuclear program depended on it.
2 It prevents atoms from splitting.
3 German scientists thought it was unsafe.
4 No neutrons can pass through it.

No. 16
1 Germany had stolen nuclear technology from the US.
2 Britain had not developed a nuclear program.
3 An air attack on Vemork would not have succeeded.
4 The US needed Vemork to produce heavy water.

(D)

No. 17
1 They would have been more conclusive using x-rays.
2 The imaging technology he used limited their accuracy.
3 They revealed it was made of wood rather than bronze.
4 His analysis differed from that of Roman scientists.

No. 18
1 It is older than similar ancient devices that have been found.
2 Some of the information it revealed was incorrect.
3 It may not have been the first of its kind.
4 The way it was originally used was not efficient.

(E)

No. 19
1 It was started by homeless people living in the city.
2 Environmental conditions helped it to spread quickly.
3 It did not affect buildings in the business district.
4 Firefighters thought they had brought it under control.

No. 20
1 The height of new buildings was restricted.
2 Reconstruction resulted in population growth.
3 Famous architects overcharged for their services.
4 Officials ignored fire codes to speed up reconstruction.

|||||| Part 3 |||||||||||||||||||||||||||||||||||||||||||||||||| ◀)) ▶MP3 ▶アプリ ▶CD3 **18**~**23**

(F)

No. 21

Situation: You have recently started an entry-level job at an automobile parts manufacturer. You work in the legal department. At a staff meeting, the company president says the following.

Question: What do you need to do first?

1 Review the standards for manufacturing goods.
2 Create a summary of legal requirements for recalls.
3 Check the procedures for amending existing contracts.
4 Investigate lawsuits the company might face.

(G)

No. 22

Situation: You live in the US and need to fly to Canada in one week due to a family emergency. Your Japanese passport expires in two months. A travel agent tells you the following.

Question: What should you do?

1 Consult with officials at the airport in Canada.
2 Apply for a temporary passport online.
3 Go downtown to get a new passport.
4 Visit a Japanese consulate after arriving in Canada.

21年度第1回 リスニング

133

(H)

No. 23

Situation: You and your family recently moved abroad. You are enrolling your daughter in a primary school. She completed her vaccinations in Japan. A school administrator tells you the following.

Question: What should you do before the first day of school?

1 Submit the signed permission forms.
2 Have a doctor give your daughter a checkup.
3 Submit proof of immunization.
4 Get a letter from your employer.

(I)

No. 24

Situation: Your Gold membership with E-Zonia Travel will expire soon, and you would like to renew it. Your total budget for the year is $3,000. An agency representative gives you the following advice.

Question: What should you do?

1 Raise your spending to the E-Zonia minimum.
2 Apply for an E-Zonia credit card.
3 Book a flight through E-Zonia before the year's end.
4 Reserve four nights at an E-Zonia partner hotel.

(J)

No. 25

Situation: You are an American citizen living overseas. You want to transfer money from your US bank account to your daughter's account. You call your bank, and a representative tells you the following.

Question: What should you do first to obtain an access code?

1 Change your account password.
2 Reconfirm your e-mail address.
3 Visit a bank branch in person.
4 Answer two security questions.

|||| Part 4 |||||||||||||||||||||||||||||||||||| ◀)) ▶MP3 ▶アプリ ▶CD 3 **24**〜**25**

No. 26

1 They do not fully understand the value of their jewelry.
2 They are overly attached to worthless sentimental pieces.
3 They rely too much on market prices for gold and silver.
4 They often neglect to check the reputation of the jeweler.

No. 27

1 It has led to some jewelry makers leaving the profession.
2 It has reduced his profits, despite the high price of gold.
3 It is similar to destroying a valuable work of art.
4 It is occurring less frequently than it did in the past.

21
年度第**1**回

リスニング

二次試験
面 接

A日程　◀)) ▶MP3 ▶アプリ ▶CD 4 **21**〜**25**

1. Should democratic nations try to force democracy on other nations?

2. Information in the Internet age — too much or not enough?

3. Could genetic engineering be the solution to human health problems?

4. Is there too much emphasis on technology in professional sports today?

5. Agree or disagree: A single world government would benefit the planet

C日程

1. Agree or disagree: Business monopolies can be beneficial to society

2. Should the decentralization of power be a key goal of the government?

3. Is more regulation the answer to cybercrime?

4. Has news objectivity become impossible in the age of social media?

5. Should more be done to promote awareness of mental health issues?

（注）モデルスピーチと解説はA日程のみ収録しています。

2020-3

一次試験　2021.1.24実施
二次試験　A日程　2021.2.21実施
　　　　　B日程　2021.2.28実施

Grade 1

試験時間

筆記：**100分**
リスニング：**約35分**

一次試験・筆記　　　　　p.138〜152
一次試験・リスニングp.153〜159
二次試験・面接　　　　　　p.160

＊解答・解説は別冊p.265〜316にあります。
＊面接の流れは本書p.16にあります。

2020年度第3回

Web特典「自動採点サービス」対応
オンラインマークシート

※検定の回によって2次元コードが違います。
※筆記1〜3，リスニングの採点ができます。
※PCからも利用できます（本書 p.8 参照）。

一次試験
筆　記

1 To complete each item, choose the best word or phrase from among the four choices. Then, on your answer sheet, find the number of the question and mark your answer.

(1) The new president of RC Computers (　　　) several decisions made by the previous president. He believed that they had been mistakes and were hurting the company's sales.
1 perpetuated　**2** prefaced　　**3** overrode　　**4** satiated

(2) Brendan has been an (　　　) supporter of the Greenville Wolves basketball team since he was a child. Every season, he goes to as many of their games as he can.
1 elusive　　　**2** ardent　　　**3** ornate　　　**4** apathetic

(3) After the church began offering weekend religious education programs for children, its (　　　) grew steadily, with new families joining every month.
1 partition　　**2** compilation　**3** inhibition　　**4** congregation

(4) Owing to the sudden (　　　) in the value of the currency this year, the prices of imported goods have risen sharply.
1 depreciation　　　　　　　**2** rendition
3 demarcation　　　　　　　**4** extraction

(5) The new tax was highly unpopular, so the finance minister decided to wait until public criticism had (　　　) before introducing any further taxes.
1 abated　　　　**2** permeated　**3** corroded　　　**4** instigated

(6) *A:* Honey, I want this new house, but what if we can't sell the one we live in now?
B: We'll make the purchase agreement (　　　) on the sale of our current house. So if we can't sell it, we won't have to buy the new one.
1 plenary　　　**2** appalling　**3** filial　　　　**4** contingent

(7) Lucy sustained a mild (　　　) in the car accident and was treated at a local hospital. The doctor said her head would hurt for the next couple of weeks.
1 conciliation　**2** conurbation　**3** contraption　**4** concussion

(8) The climb to the top of the tower turned out to be more

138

(   ) than the tourists had expected. By the time they reached the top, most of them felt exhausted.

1 arduous   **2** shattered   **3** barbarous   **4** decrepit

(9) When Tim moved to the city, he could only afford to rent an old, run-down apartment. When his mother visited, she was shocked at the (   ) conditions he lived in.

1 colossal   **2** auxiliary   **3** squalid   **4** inadvertent

(10) Many people were shocked by the new biography of the wartime leader. They accused the author of (   ) a great man by reporting unproven rumors.

1 deviating   **2** soliciting   **3** denigrating   **4** incubating

(11) The president was concerned about the sudden increase of enemy troops on the border. He feared his country could be invaded and (   ) by its powerful neighbor.

1 annexed   **2** yielded   **3** vacillated   **4** proffered

(12) People tend to judge an academic institution by the success of its graduates, but that is not the only (   ) for determining how good a school is.

1 allegory   **2** yardstick   **3** exponent   **4** blurb

(13) As a young politician, Ramesh had been widely (   ) as a future leader. After falling seriously ill, however, he was forced to give up his political career.

1 touted   **2** pulverized   **3** fermented   **4** pared

(14) Many cheeses from Europe are well known for having (   ) aromas, but those who love eating them do not mind their smell at all.

1 pungent   **2** truculent   **3** dreary   **4** murky

(15) *A:* Gina, you look (   ). What's wrong?
B: I spent the whole day taking care of my sister's three kids. I was totally exhausted after just a couple of hours.

1 frazzled   **2** awry   **3** insufferable   **4** overt

(16) The criminal's detailed knowledge of the bank's security led the police to believe that he must have had an (   ) inside the organization.

1 electorate   **2** autocrat   **3** extrovert   **4** accomplice

(17) *A:* Have you seen the latest opinion polls on the prime minister?

B: Yes, he's doing terribly. After that last public debate, his approval ratings have dropped to a (   ) 10 percent.

1 candid   2 virulent   3 petulant   4 paltry

(18) When Roland learned his business partner had been overcharging clients, he quit and (   ) all ties with the company. He did not want to be associated with such activity.

1 presaged   2 instilled   3 repatriated   4 severed

(19) The police concluded that the murder was (   ). It was clear from the evidence that the killer had planned every last detail of the crime.

1 premeditated   2 embittered
3 threaded   4 gleaned

(20) Mr. Garcia was shocked when one of his staff members had the (   ) to ask for a pay raise on the same day that she overslept and arrived late for work.

1 sham   2 wrath   3 gall   4 piety

(21) Initial attempts to market the new product in creative ways were only (   ) successful, so the company decided to rethink its sales strategy.

1 heartily   2 marginally   3 vehemently   4 intently

(22) When the school administrators found out that some students had cheated on their final exams, they were quick to (   ) punishments to everyone involved.

1 dish out   2 tear off   3 wire up   4 dive into

(23) Franklin was (   ) by the news that his sister had won $50 million in the lottery. He never thought that anyone he knew would become so rich overnight.

1 blasted off   2 blown away   3 bashed in   4 boiled over

(24) Although young tigers can (   ) themselves by the age of 18 months, they usually stay with their mother until they are around two-and-a-half years old.

1 skirt around   2 lag behind   3 fend for   4 tangle with

(25) The news photographer was (   ) by a hotel worker that a film star was vacationing there, so he rushed to the hotel to try to get a picture.

1 tipped off   2 scrimped on
3 worked over   4 clogged up

140

2

Read each passage and choose the best word or phrase from among the four choices for each blank. Then, on your answer sheet, find the number of the question and mark your answer.

The Mitchell Map

In 1750, John Mitchell, an American doctor living in England, was tasked with creating a map of North America by the Earl of Halifax, a high-ranking British official. Britain's relations with France were tense at the time, with ongoing disputes over control of North American colonial territories, where France was constructing military fortifications. Halifax, in charge of managing these colonies, was determined to rally government support for a campaign to resist the intrusions. The map he commissioned Mitchell to make (26   ). Mitchell was a supporter of Britain's claims over North America, and this bias was noticeable in the borders he drew and the numerous annotations regarding British territorial claims in early versions of his map. That sentiment was further apparent in subsequent publications of the map, with even less land being recognized as belonging to France. This helped sway public and political opinion, hastening a series of events that led to the two nations competing fiercely over colonial interests.

While France's defeat in the ensuing conflict resulted in a massive territorial acquisition for Britain, the vast amounts of money it had poured into the war caused British national debt to soar. In an attempt to offset this loss, Britain passed the Stamp Act in 1765, which exacted the first direct tax on the American colonies. Protests erupted throughout the colonies in retaliation, culminating in the American Revolution. With another military conflict so soon after its previous one, Britain's victory against France had clearly (27   ).

The Revolutionary War, fought between Britain and its American colonies over eight years, concluded in 1783. It was an auspicious ending for the Americans, who not only broke free from Britain's grasp but also gained possession of a generous amount of land, thanks to the British and American negotiators using Mitchell's map to draw up the new territorial boundaries. Given the contrast between the original intention behind the map's creation and its eventual role in the aftermath of the war, there is little doubt that Mitchell himself — had he been alive to witness the signing — would have disapproved of (**28**). Mitchell's map, by playing a key role in helping encourage conflict with the French, ultimately paved the way for American independence from the British.

---

(26) 1 led him to change his mind
     2 had been created far too late
     3 succeeded in this objective
     4 helped the opposite to occur

(27) 1 reduced its appetite for war
     2 threatened other nations
     3 come at a high price
     4 helped it gain new allies

(28) 1 the benefits afforded to Britain
     2 how American requests were denied
     3 the simplifications made to his map
     4 how his map had been put to use

Acting and the Brain

An actor's role is to inhabit a variety of different characters with mind-sets that can differ substantially from their own. It has been suggested, however, that (**29**). Crucial to the success of an actor's performance is a phenomenon known as "suspension of disbelief," which involves convincing audiences to cast aside critical thinking and disregard the knowledge that the actor is not, in reality, the character being portrayed. Yet it is the ability of actors to lose themselves in the characters they play that makes suspension of disbelief possible, and many actors claim that the lengths they go to in their attempts to immerse themselves in characters' emotions take a psychological toll. This is said to be particularly true when actors portray individuals in stories dealing with domestic violence or sexual assault.

It now appears that (**30**). A research team at a Canadian university monitored actors as they responded to a series of questions under different conditions, including responding as themselves and also "in character" after preparing for a role in a Shakespeare play. The researchers found that when subjects had "become" the character in the play, they experienced a large decrease in activity in areas of the brain associated with the processing of self-related information. This suggests actors do, in fact, run the risk of compromising their own identity when they transform into a character.

The Canadian researchers tested their ideas about self even further by instructing the actors to respond to questions using a foreign accent but without "becoming" someone who would naturally speak in that accent. The brain activity monitored during this experiment suggested that simply talking in an uncommon way could facilitate the weakening of the self. This is supported by another study involving ordinary people, in which subjects were asked questions about their own personality and that of a friend. Later, when asked about their own personality again, the subjects responded in a manner that suggested they had subconsciously shifted perception of their own personality closer to that of their friend's, highlighting how even ordinary people's brains experience a degree of instability when processing identity. The findings, it seems, underline a fragility to people's sense of self that (**31**   ).

---

(29) **1** only certain types of actors can do this
      2 this can sometimes be harmful to actors
      3 an actor's true purpose is different
      4 this is actually impossible for an actor

(30) **1** this applies more to the least-skilled actors
      2 the mind is not that easily influenced
      3 this concern should be taken seriously
      4 performing strengthens relationships among actors

(31) **1** can only be understood by some
      2 is not simply limited to actors
      3 may damage relationships
      4 many actors refuse to accept

143

3 *Read each passage and choose the best answer from among the four choices for each question. Then, on your answer sheet, find the number of the question and mark your answer.*

Business and Sustainability

In 2015, the United Nations unanimously adopted the Sustainable Development Goals (SDGs)—an initiative calling on governments, businesses, and ordinary citizens alike to help realize a more prosperous and sustainable global future by tackling poverty and protecting the environment. While many businesses have seemed to enthusiastically embrace the SDGs, there appears to be a worrying disconnect between what these companies say and what they actually do. According to one study conducted by the global investment management firm PIMCO, the fact that a large number of firms reference the SDGs in corporate reporting indicates a widespread awareness regarding their existence and importance. Fewer than one in ten firms, however, provided figures indicating quantifiable progress toward targets, and the report's authors concluded that "most companies still lack the expertise to identify activity and targets that can add business value."

While it is true that the disparity could be the result of the relative newness and unfamiliarity of the SDGs, others have taken a more cynical view. Numerous corporations have been accused of "greenwashing," a term referring to attempts to deceive the general public into thinking that firms care more about the environment than they really do. A significant number of the 17 SDGs directly address issues like clean energy and the protection and restoration of ecosystems, and critics point out that it is all too easy to take existing practices, as well as projects already in the pipeline, and manipulate them into a form resembling an SDG target, with the ambiguous wording of the SDGs making them highly susceptible to this practice. In addition, some firms have also been accused of double-dealing in the name of SDG compliance by, for example, attempting to beef up their public image with substantial contributions to environmental groups but failing to pay living wages to their employees. Since the SDGs were intended to be catalysts for innovation and transformation that are universally beneficial, these practices are clearly missing the mark.

Accusations against companies suspected of greenwashing often portray SDG reporting in an unflattering light, but there may be a silver lining to the controversy surrounding the practice. Any degree of SDG reporting opens a company up to increased scrutiny of its sustainability practices. In recent years, it has become extremely common for public opinion to spur even the most uncompromising corporation to expand sustainability efforts, yet this inevitably leads to an avalanche of greenwashing accusations. Erica Charles, lecturer at Glasgow Caledonian University London, however, suggests that just a miniscule, public-relations-inspired shift in practices at a multinational corporation can have a significant "impact and ripple effect on the rest of the industry to review their approach to business." Some would argue that for this reason it is essential that critics exercise a degree of restraint in their accusations against what they perceive as insufficient reporting, since an excessively harsh media backlash could deter corporations from doing anything at all. Even a failed or insincere corporate effort made under the guise of environmental sustainability, it appears, may not be an entirely wasted endeavor after all.

(32) According to the study conducted by PIMCO,

    1 the slowdown in progress toward SDG targets set by companies since 2015 indicates that firms fear the targets will negatively affect profits.

    2 distrust of the United Nations' motives is the main reason that many companies have been slow to acknowledge the importance of the SDGs.

    3 companies appear to be attempting to hide their violations of the SDGs by falsifying the numbers in the reports that they provide.

    4 many corporations approve of the SDGs but have been unable to determine how to implement them in a way that is beneficial to their business.

(33) What is one reason that firms get accused of "greenwashing"?

    1 The unclear wording of some of the SDGs has caused so much confusion that misunderstandings about their policies are almost certain to arise.

    2 Some have been attempting to make it appear that things they were already doing are part of their efforts to comply with the SDGs.

3 The unrealistic targets set in many of the SDGs have forced some companies to pretend that they are meeting every single one of the goals.

4 Companies know that since many of the SDGs are unrelated to the environment, it is easier to focus on those and neglect the environment-related ones.

(34) How can Erica Charles's comment best be interpreted in the context of the passage?

1 Large companies are trying to undermine SDG reporting by influencing other firms in their industry to resist environmental regulation.

2 Rather than focusing on the largest corporations in an industry, it is important for critics to look at all businesses responsible for greenwashing.

3 When large companies implement minor changes that do not appear significant, it may be unwise to be overly critical of them.

4 The majority of SDG reporting at large companies is so poorly conducted that an entirely new system needs to be developed.

Rent Control

In the face of skyrocketing housing costs in major metropolises throughout the United States, numerous municipalities have imposed rent-control legislation designed to ensure stable access to housing for low-income residents. These laws are generally set by a city-run committee and ensure that housing costs will not rise by more than a very small percentage annually. While on the surface rent control can be seen as shielding vulnerable citizens from economic hardship, these restrictions are almost universally condemned by economists. They argue that since rent control has the effect of limiting landlord income, the laws reduce incentives to construct new properties. Available rental units inevitably become scarcer, and in accordance with the principles of supply and demand, rents for the housing that is exempt from rent control are driven up. In addition, tenants fortunate enough to occupy rent-controlled units tend to stay in them even when their economic circumstances improve, greatly amplifying the negative effect on the housing supply available to people with lower incomes. It is apparent then, economists argue, that rent-control laws aggravate the very issue they are intended to remedy.

On the other hand, rent-control advocates point out that recently constructed housing is generally exempt from rent-control legislation. Studies have, in fact, indicated that most rent-control regulation does not adversely affect new housing construction in cities where it is imposed on preexisting properties in the market. Economists argue, though, that rent control instead pushes landlords to take steps such as converting rental properties into for-sale units, or even selling them to their longtime occupants, further contributing to shortfalls in the rental-housing supply.

Both economists and proponents of rent-control measures agree on one thing: limiting rents lowers the risk of financially disadvantaged people being displaced from their homes. What is more, researchers who examined the addresses and migration histories of residents in San Francisco found that low-income people, and especially minorities, who had lived in a rent-controlled unit were more likely to continue residing in the city even after vacating the rent-controlled unit. While this is a positive finding for a subset of low-income people, economists say the measures do not address the problem of others unable to find housing because of the lack of affordable options resulting from the short supply of rental units.

Often overlooked by economists, however, is the issue of housing stability. US tax laws grant homeowners significant benefits in the form of tax breaks; people lacking sufficient funds to purchase a home are unable to take advantage of these. Without rent controls, low-income renters are therefore at especially high risk of being evicted because of financial hardship. The damaging effect of forced moves on mental and physical health is well documented, and it has been shown to impact women more severely than men. This is particularly concerning given that children of women who experience stress during pregnancy suffer long-term psychological consequences, and children with little residential stability are also less likely to graduate from high school. While the quantitative arguments economists make when decrying rent control do have some validity, city officials must not overlook its broader, more positive implications.

(35) One common criticism made by economists about rent control is that

1 it has been unable to compensate for the sharp rise in rents resulting from building booms in recent years.

2 the city committees that regulate rental apartments can be easily influenced by landlords to force people to leave rent-controlled units.

3 it actually limits the living choices that are available to residents who may not be as economically advantaged as others.

4 although it helps increase the supply of available apartments in a city, it also contributes to reduced demand for them.

(36) Which of the following statements would supporters of rent control most likely agree with?

1 While rent control may be a result of temporary housing shortages, these are balanced out in the long run by an increase in construction.

2 Since many older buildings are not subject to rent control, rental-housing shortages are actually the result of a lack of new construction projects.

3 The measures taken by landlords in response to rent-control laws actually tend to lead to an increase in the availability of housing.

4 Rent control affects the housing market less than economists claim because the laws usually only affect rental properties already available.

(37) What does the author of the passage imply about rent control in the last paragraph?

1 While economists' warnings about rent-control laws make little sense at present, the issue will need to be reconsidered by future generations.

2 Despite any drawbacks of rent-control laws, they play an important role in society that cannot be measured by economic analysis alone.

3 The negative consequences that rent-control laws have on the housing market outweigh the social benefits they can lead to.

4 The benefits that rent-control laws provide for wealthier

populations eventually end up being available to society as a whole.

Nasser and Pan-Arabism

In 1952, a group of army officers seized power from the British-backed monarchy in Egypt, forcing the nation's king, Farouk I, into exile. The rebels were part of a nationalist movement within the military forces of Egypt, known as the Free Officers, which had formed around the anticolonialist ideology of its leader, a young Egyptian officer named Gamal Abdel Nasser. Its official head at the time of the coup was Mohammed Naguib, a senior army officer and war hero, whom Nasser installed as a figurehead. Nasser was taking advantage of Naguib's tremendous renown among the general public to legitimize the new regime since he himself lacked the prestige necessary for the role at the time. When Naguib overstepped his bounds by attempting to defy Nasser, however, he was removed from power and Nasser emerged from the shadows, assuming the country's leadership in 1954.

During his long years in power, Nasser remade Egypt. He instituted a far-reaching modernization program that included free education and medical care, improved housing, and labor reforms. A feudal system of land ownership during the monarchy had created an unequal distribution of wealth, which Nasser addressed with reforms that improved conditions for farmers and limited the amount of land individuals could own. Nasser came from humble beginnings and presented himself as a man of the people. "Nasserism," as his ideology became known, was rooted in socialism and wealth redistribution, and unlike previous rulers, Nasser remained free of corruption.

This is not to say, however, that his rule was benign. Dissent was mercilessly crushed, and Nasser expressed open contempt for democracy. He saw both his egalitarian social programs and harsh enforcement tactics as essential for attaining his vision of Arab unity, or pan-Arabism, across the Middle East. If Egypt were to take the dominant role in a unified Arab world, it would first have to bolster its economy and improve social welfare domestically while ensuring that any opponents who might undermine Nasser's policies were kept off the political stage.

Anticolonialism was the foundation of Nasser's foreign policy, and he supported liberation movements throughout Africa. Aided by his charisma and public-speaking talents, Nasser not only transformed Egyptian society but also provided a model to which other Arab nations could aspire. Nasser stepped into the international spotlight in 1956, when he nationalized the strategically and economically important Suez Canal. Despite its location within Egyptian territory, it had been jointly owned and operated by Britain and France, but Egyptian soldiers seized control of the canal. Israeli, French, and British forces invaded the country, quickly defeating Egyptian forces in the Suez region and precipitating what became known as the "Suez Crisis." Egypt enjoyed greater success on the diplomatic front, however. The Soviet Union was courting Egyptian favor at the time with a view to greater influence in the region in the future, and condemned what it saw as an example of Western imperialism. The Soviets even went so far as to threaten a nuclear strike against Western Europe if the invaders failed to withdraw. A horrified United States intervened behind the scenes to avert a confrontation with the Soviets, resulting in a humiliating withdrawal by the European and Israeli invaders. Nasser emerged from the Suez Crisis having not only defied the West but triumphed against long odds, albeit due in part to the fortuitous intercession of the Americans and Soviets. Nasser's actions nonetheless resulted in mass displays of public adulation throughout the Middle East and the consolidation of his leadership role within it.

At the height of Nasser's power, Arab unity seemed a genuine possibility. Having shaken off colonial rule, nations in the Middle East stood together in solidarity and identified as an independent geopolitical bloc. Yet the 1958 formation of the United Arab Republic, a union between Egypt and Syria, was short-lived owing to Syrian dissatisfaction with Nasser-imposed centralization policies. The notion that Arab nations could unify was smashed in 1967, when Egypt led surrounding Arab countries into a disastrous war with Israel, the result of which was not only a significant loss of territory but also a deep, abiding wound inflicted upon the Arab psyche.

Nasser's popularity waned in the years before his death in 1970, but he remains an icon to many throughout the Middle East, even though disunity and conflict today have lessened the prospect of pan-Arabism. In post-Nasser Egypt, the gulf between rich and poor continues to fluctuate, and Nasser's goal of social equality appears unlikely to come to fruition. Despite the nostalgia for Nasser's rule, however, some commentators insist his charisma made Egyptians blind to his failings, such as the fact that his wealth-redistribution policies encouraged an economic overreliance on the state by the work force which continues to this day. While there is truth in such accusations, in the end, since Nasser's popularity has always been primarily a product of his ideology rather than his accomplishments, the nostalgia will likely endure for years to come.

(38) What can be inferred about the Free Officers?

1 Gamal Abdel Nasser believed it would be necessary to break up the group after Mohammed Naguib attempted to alter its leadership structure.

2 Though the group's actions received widespread support due to Naguib's reputation, the loss of his position showed he was not an essential figure.

3 There was conflict between Nasser and Naguib over the degree of democracy the group would allow after it took power.

4 While its principles were based on Naguib's ideas, Nasser felt he himself had to be in control to ensure the coup was peaceful rather than violent.

(39) According to the author of the passage, what was the primary reason for Nasser's harsh political policies?

1 His ultimate objective of uniting the Arab world under Egyptian leadership required that domestic policies be introduced without obstacles.

2 He feared the increased wealth and education of ordinary people could lead to the rise of political opponents who favored socialism.

3 He feared his humble origins and lack of wealth would lead both the Egyptian public and other politicians to view him as a weak leader.

4 His opposition to the monarchy was not shared by most people, who believed their quality of life had been better under the previous government.

(40) Which of the following statements best describes the outcome of the "Suez Crisis"?

1 What at first appeared as a victory turned out to have done irreparable damage to Egypt's relationship with crucial Western allies.

2 Although Nasser gained a slight advantage near the end of the crisis, Egypt's military losses demonstrated that long-term success was impossible.

3 While Nasser initially appeared to side with the Soviets, his policy change at the end of the crisis demonstrated he was actually allied with the United States.

4 Nasser was able to win a significant political victory against Western powers, although it was partly due to factors beyond his control.

(41) What explanation does the author of the passage give for the way that many modern Egyptians feel about Nasser and his rule?

1 The working class in Egypt has not forgiven Nasser for damage resulting from the war with Israel despite its admiration for him as a person.

2 It is influenced more by the philosophy and vision that Nasser represented for Egypt than by the changes that arose from his policies.

3 The changes in social welfare and education for all Egyptians that Nasser introduced have had long-term benefits despite subsequent leaders' failings.

4 It has been shaped by people who fail to understand how much Nasser's personality and charisma inspired Egyptians during his rule.

4
- *Write an essay on the given TOPIC.*
- *Give THREE reasons to support your answer.*
- *Structure: introduction, main body, and conclusion*
- *Suggested length: 200–240 words*
- *Write your essay in the space provided on Side B of your answer sheet. Any writing outside the space will not be graded.*

TOPIC

Agree or disagree: Globalization is a positive force in today's world

リスニング

―――― Listening Test ――――

There are four parts to this listening test.

Part 1	Dialogues: 1 question each	Multiple-choice
Part 2	Passages: 2 questions each	Multiple-choice
Part 3	Real-Life: 1 question each	Multiple-choice
Part 4	Interview: 2 questions	Multiple-choice

※**Listen carefully to the instructions.**

Part 1 ▶MP3 ▶アプリ ▶CD 3 26～36

No. 1
1 The woman should consider improving her skill set.
2 The woman has set her standards too high.
3 He deserves to be considered for the position.
4 He can cover until they find the right person.

No. 2
1 Consult with his sales staff.
2 Reschedule the feedback meeting.
3 Cut the salaries of his staff.
4 Request additional staff.

No. 3
1 She plays for the New York symphony orchestra.
2 She just started teaching the violin.
3 She demands a lot from her students.
4 She prefers to work with beginners.

No. 4
1 He missed an appointment with his boss.
2 He forgot to make copies for his boss.
3 He broke the copier by accident.
4 He failed to get the copier fixed.

No. 5	1 Change their advertising strategy.
	2 Wait for the results of the TV ads.
	3 Carry out more marketing polls.
	4 Cancel the direct-mail campaign.

No. 6
1 He does not feel competent yet.
2 His clients at RCB are dissatisfied.
3 He is not used to having tight deadlines.
4 He does not think RCB's products will sell.

No. 7
1 The man should keep calling the number.
2 The man should use this experience to become a salesman.
3 The man should make use of the filing system.
4 The man should give up hope of getting his money back.

No. 8
1 Search for a more convenient location.
2 Decide to rent the office space.
3 Look for something smaller elsewhere.
4 Move again within a few years.

No. 9
1 It is not close enough to public transportation.
2 It would cost them too much to repair themselves.
3 It could be dangerous for elderly visitors.
4 It does not have space outside to build a ramp.

No. 10
1 The curriculum is the wrong level for students.
2 Helen is not fulfilling her responsibilities.
3 Margaret is too strong and overly bossy.
4 The teachers are creating too many materials.

|||||| Part 2 |||||||||||||||||||||||||||||||||||||||||||||||||||||||||| ◀⑴ ▶MP3 ▶アプリ ▶CD 3 **37**～**42**

(A)

No. 11
1 Children of strict parents are more likely to rebel.
2 Family values have little to do with political beliefs.
3 The way people are raised affects their political views.
4 People try to take different viewpoints from their parents.

No. 12
1 It seems to be caused by biological factors.
2 It makes people ignore negative stimuli.
3 It only develops in the brain during adulthood.
4 It affects liberals more than conservatives.

(B)

No. 13
1 The decreasing proportion of young adults.
2 Senior citizens living alone after a spouse dies.
3 Fewer divorced people remarrying.
4 Greater wealth leading to a higher divorce rate.

No. 14
1 They struggle to provide for their families.
2 They tend to seek educated spouses.
3 They often have children immediately after marriage.
4 They now get married later in life.

(C)

No. 15
1 Mental illness must be treated immediately.
2 External factors are not what make people happy.
3 People should be less individualistic.
4 Mental illness is more common than people think.

No. 16
1 It is more expensive than traditional therapies.
2 It takes a long time to be effective.
3 It could affect treatment for mentally ill patients.
4 It has no effect in preventing mental illness.

(D)

No. 17　1 They were given health tonics that contained it.
　　　　2 They were required to apply it to their fingers.
　　　　3 They put radium-covered brushes into their mouths.
　　　　4 They used it to clean their brushes.

No. 18　1 It proved that radium in paint was not dangerous.
　　　　2 It showed the women's exposure levels were low.
　　　　3 It successfully avoided lawsuits.
　　　　4 It used biased research results.

(E)

No. 19　1 They will improve the utilization of robots.
　　　　2 They greatly improve security in companies.
　　　　3 They are essential for human survival.
　　　　4 They are unavoidable in future workplaces.

No. 20　1 The technology could easily be stolen.
　　　　2 The safety of such devices is still uncertain.
　　　　3 The microchips may produce inaccurate data.
　　　　4 The implants are known to cause health issues.

||||| Part 3 |||||||||||||||||||||||||||||||||||||||||||||||||||||||||| ◀» ▸MP3 ▸アプリ ▸CD 3 **43**～**48**

(F)

No. 21

Situation: You are purchasing a diving watch, and the store clerk is telling you about maintenance. You usually go scuba diving five times a year.

Question: What should you do?

1 Have the watch serviced every three years.
2 Purchase the recommended cleaner and brush.
3 Keep some replacement parts handy.
4 Replace the battery every five years.

(G)

No. 22

Situation: An airline lost your baggage several weeks ago, and you want to be compensated in some way. You fly on a regular basis. A lawyer gives you the following advice.

Question: What should you do?

1 Call the airline for a cash settlement.
2 Have a lawyer represent you in court.
3 Submit a claim form with receipts.
4 Wait for an offer of travel vouchers.

20
年度第**3**回

リスニング

(H)

No. 23

Situation: You are on a business trip. You listen to a voice mail that a coworker left you over three hours ago. You will be in a conference meeting tomorrow morning until noon.

Question: What should you do?

1 Send the client a revised contract.
2 Answer the client's questions by e-mail.
3 Wait for the client to call.
4 Contact the client after he returns from Brazil.

(I)

No. 24

Situation: You are discussing your investments with your financial adviser. You want to earn at least 3 percent interest on your holdings, but you also want to minimize your risk.

Question: What should you do with your money?

1 Keep it in the American money-market account.
2 Invest it in the American real-estate investment trust.
3 Shift it to the Australian money-market account.
4 Move it to a Japanese bond-investment fund.

(J)

No. 25

Situation: You are buying lottery tickets for the first time. You want to increase your chances of winning. The clerk gives you the following advice.

Question: What should you do if you do not win on the first drawing?

1 Open an online account and submit your ticket numbers.
2 Download a claim form from the lottery's website.
3 Send your tickets to the state lottery office.
4 Take losing tickets to any lottery retailer.

| | **Part 4** | ◀)) ▶MP3 ▶アプリ ▶CD 3 **49**～**50** |

No. 26
1 People have free time in summer because the financial year ends in March.
2 Excellent teamwork means people change jobs less often than in other industries.
3 Those who can handle the pressures of the job usually become reliable coworkers.
4 New recruits need three years of experience before they work with clients.

No. 27
1 The United Nations must do more to help companies protect the environment.
2 The majority of companies now feel that it is important to their business.
3 Investors should fund efforts by companies to do work in the community.
4 Many companies ignore it to focus on charity events and art projects.

二次試験
面　接

A日程　◀))　▶MP3　▶アプリ　▶CD 4 **26**〜**30**

1. Would the global economy benefit from a single world currency?
2. Can labor unions effectively support workers in the modern business world?
3. Agree or disagree: The traditional family unit has lost its central role in modern society
4. Do the advantages of jury trials outweigh the disadvantages?
5. Will the human race one day be the cause of its own downfall?

B日程

1. Can Japan ever repeat the successful economic performance it enjoyed in the past?
2. Should essential workers such as doctors and firefighters be allowed to strike?
3. Can political violence ever be justified?
4. Agree or disagree: Interpersonal communication skills are becoming less important in the digital age
5. Should companies abandon the concept of lifetime employment for their employees?

（注）　モデルスピーチと解説はA日程のみ収録しています。

2023年度版

文部科学省後援

英検®1級
過去6回全問題集

別冊解答

2023年度版

英検®は、公益財団法人 日本英語検定協会の登録商標です。

旺文社

2023年度版

文部科学省後援

英検®1級
過去6回全問題集

別冊解答

英検®は、公益財団法人 日本英語検定協会の登録商標です。　旺文社

2022-2

一次試験
筆記解答・解説　　　p.6〜24

一次試験
リスニング解答・解説　p.25〜52

二次試験
面接解答・解説　　　p.53〜56

解 答 一 覧

一次試験・筆記

1

(1)	1	(10)	4	(19)	3
(2)	3	(11)	3	(20)	3
(3)	4	(12)	4	(21)	1
(4)	3	(13)	2	(22)	4
(5)	1	(14)	1	(23)	3
(6)	1	(15)	1	(24)	1
(7)	3	(16)	2	(25)	1
(8)	2	(17)	3		
(9)	3	(18)	1		

2

(26)	4	(29)	2
(27)	3	(30)	2
(28)	2	(31)	4

3

(32)	2	(35)	3	(38)	3
(33)	4	(36)	4	(39)	2
(34)	3	(37)	2	(40)	4
				(41)	2

4　解答例は本文参照

一次試験・リスニング

Part 1

No. 1	1	No. 5	4	No. 9	4
No. 2	3	No. 6	2	No.10	3
No. 3	3	No. 7	2		
No. 4	1	No. 8	1		

Part 2

No.11	4	No.15	2	No.19	3
No.12	2	No.16	3	No.20	4
No.13	1	No.17	1		
No.14	4	No.18	3		

Part 3

No.21	1	No.23	4	No.25	3
No.22	2	No.24	4		

Part 4

No.26	2	No.27	4

一次試験・筆記 1 | 問題編 p.18～20

(1) ― 解答 1

訳 A：会長はなぜ辞職するのか言ってた？

B：いや，彼は理由を明かすのを拒んだんだ。それは完全に私的なことだと言っていたよ。

語句 1「(秘密など) を漏らす」　　2「～を許す」

3「～を避ける」　　4「～を逃れる」

解説 辞職理由 (it) はまったくの私事だと会長は言ったのだから，彼は理由を divulge「(秘密など) を打ち明ける，漏らす」のを拒んだのだ。

(2) ― 解答 3

訳 新党に参加するために党を離れる政治家が次第に増えるにつれて，首相の立場はますます危ういように見え始めた。

語句 1「幸先のよい」　　2「光沢のある」

3「不安定な，危険な」　　4「発作的な，断続的な」

解説 党を去る政治家が増えているのだから，首相の立場を述べる空所には悪い意味合いの語が入る。precarious は「(状況などが) 不安定な，危険な」。

(3) ― 解答 4

訳 その男は警察にあからさまなうそは一つもつかなかったが，事故が彼の過失だったことを明らかにしたであろういくつかの重要な詳細を言わなかった。

語句 1「ひどく怒った」　　2「(建物などが) 荒廃した」

3「非常に飢えている」　　4「目立った，重要な」

解説 男が警察に言わなかった (left out) 詳細は，彼の過失を明らかにするものなので，salient「目立った，(問題点・特色などが) 重要な」な詳細だ。

(4) ― 解答 3

訳 車庫を片付けていて，ケンは壁から突き出ているとがったくぎで手を切った。

語句 1「やきもきしている」　　2「～を集めている」

3「突き出ている」　　4「～を補充している」

解説 くぎで手を切ったのだから，くぎは壁から protruding「突き出ている」状態だったのだ。動詞 protrude「突き出る」= pro (前へ) + trude < thrust(突き出す)。

(5) ― 解答 1

訳 グレンは，ヘザーが彼に興味がないと明らかにした後でも，どういうわ

けかヘザーは彼に恋していると思い込んだ。

語句 1「(心・判断) を惑わせた」　　2「～をかわした」
3「～を抑えた」　　　　　　　　4「～を水浸しにした」

解説 ヘザーがグレンに興味がないと明白にした後なので，彼女が彼に恋して
いるというのはグレンの思い込み。delude *oneself* into thinking
(that) ...「…だと思い込む」。

(6) ― 解答 **1**

訳 研究者たちは，トラウマになるような経験を共有することは人々の間に
仲間意識を生み出すことがあり，しばしば生涯続く友情をもたらすこと
を発見した。

語句 1「仲間意識」　　　　　　　　2「名誉毀損，誹謗中傷」
3「災難，惨事」　　　　　　　　4「あふれるばかりの活気」

解説 つらい経験の共有が作り出す感情で生涯の友情になり得るのだから，そ
の感情は camaraderie「(仲間であることの) 友情，仲間意識」だ。

(7) ― 解答 **3**

訳 警察は，ボーイフレンドが犯した強盗で少女が共謀した証拠が見つから
なかったので，彼女を自由にした。

語句 1「(収拾のつかない) 大混乱」　2「総崩れ，失敗」
3「共謀，共犯」　　　　　　　　4「わけのわからない話」

解説 ボーイフレンドが犯した強盗なのだから，警察は少女の complicity「共
謀，共犯」を疑ったのだ。類義語は collusion，「共犯者」は
accomplice。

(8) ― 解答 **2**

訳 今シーズンのそのチームのむらがあるプレーは皆を困惑させている。あ
る試合で彼らはとても上手にプレーするかもしれないが，次の試合では
数多くのミスをするかもしれない。

語句 1「良心的な，きちょうめんな」　2「一定しない，とっぴな」
3「順序[秩序]立った」　　　　　4「キラリと光る」

解説 ある試合でうまくても次の試合ではミス連発かもしれないのだから，チ
ームのプレーは erratic「一定しない，(人・行動が) とっぴな」だ。

(9) ― 解答 **3**

訳 被告の無罪判決は法廷にいる皆を驚かせた。彼ら全員が，陪審員団は有
罪評決を持って戻ると思った。

語句 1「参照，紹介」　　　　　　　2「滞在」
3「無罪判決」　　　　　　　　　4「(輪なわの) わな」

解説 有罪評決 (guilty verdict) が出ると全員が思ったのだから，法廷の皆
を驚かせたのは予想とは逆の acquittal「無罪判決」だ。動詞は acquit
「～に無罪を宣告する」。陪審は別室で評議するので，return with a ...

7

verdict という言い方をしている。

(10) －解答 **4** ●●●●●●●●●●●●●●●●●●●●●●●●●●●●●●●●●●

[訳] A：新しい同僚はどんな感じだい？
B：あまりうまくいってないわ。彼は初日からずっと私に けんか腰 なの。何だか，どうにかして私とけんかしたいかのようよ。

[語句] 1「取捨選択による」　　　　　2「本来備わっている」
3「無感動な，無関心な」　　　4「敵対する」

[解説] 自分とけんかしたいようだと B が言っているのだから，新しい同僚は B に対して antagonistic「敵対する，敵意を持つ」だ。

(11) －解答 **3** ●●●●●●●●●●●●●●●●●●●●●●●●●●●●●●●●●●

[訳] 天候は暖かく湿度が高かったので，パーシーはホテルを出るとすぐにひどく 汗をかき 始めた。あっという間に彼のシャツに汗染みができた。

[語句] 1「～をひいきにする」　　　2「～の先端を切る」
3「汗をかく」　　　　　　　　4「～を越える」

[解説] 暖かく湿度が高い中での外出でシャツに汗染みができたのだから，彼は perspire「汗をかく」だったのだ。名詞は perspiration「汗」。

(12) －解答 **4** ●●●●●●●●●●●●●●●●●●●●●●●●●●●●●●●●●●

[訳] 強盗で逮捕された後，ブラッドは姉に電話して 保釈金 を払ってくれるように頼んだ。しかし，彼女は彼の釈放に必要な 10,000 ドルを持っていなかった。

[語句] 1「虚空」　　　　　　　　　2「（人の）像，肖像」
3「割り当てられた仕事［任期］」　4「保釈（金）」

[解説] ブラッドは逮捕されたのだから，彼の釈放（his release）に必要な 10,000 ドルとは bail「保釈金」だ。句動詞 bail out は「～の保釈金を払う」。

(13) －解答 **2** ●●●●●●●●●●●●●●●●●●●●●●●●●●●●●●●●●●

[訳] 少年のころ，エバンは学校のスポーツ活動に参加するのを不可能にした肺病で 苦しんだ。

[語句] 1「支えられた」　　　　　　2「苦しめられた」
3「甘やかされた」　　　　　　4「没収された」

[解説] 学校でスポーツ活動ができなかったのだから，エバンは肺病で was afflicted「苦しめられた」のだ。be afflicted with a disease「病気で苦しむ」。

(14) －解答 **1** ●●●●●●●●●●●●●●●●●●●●●●●●●● 正答率 ★**75%以上**

[訳] A：スティーブ，このグラフを説明してくれる？
B：青い線は当社の経費を 示し，そして緑の線は去年当社が販売した売上高を表します。

[語句] 1「～を示す」　　　　　　　2「～を塗って汚す」

3「～を（公然と）非難する」　　4「目を細める」

解説 グラフを説明するのだから，青線は経費を…とくれば denote「～を示す」だ。続いて緑線が表すものを述べていることが裏付けとなる。

(15) – 解答 **1**

訳 従業員がお金を盗んでいたという部長の憶測は間違いだとわかった。会計処理のミスが問題の原因だった。

語句 1「誤った」　　2「永久の」　　3「厳しい」　　4「豊富な」

解説 会計ミスが原因だったのだから，従業員が盗んだという憶測は erroneous「誤った」ものだったのだ。名詞は error「誤り」，動詞は err「誤る」。

(16) – 解答 **2**

訳 危険過ぎてこれ以上立ったままにしておけないので，市議会はその古い建物の取り壊しを命じた。

語句 1「ほのめかし」　　　　　　　　2「（建物などの）取り壊し」
3「割り当て（額［量］）」　　　　　4「（金銭などの）強要，強奪」

解説 立ったままでは危険過ぎる建物なのだから，市が命じたのは建物の demolition「破壊，取り壊し」だ。動詞は demolish「～を取り壊す」。

(17) – 解答 **3**

訳 ヘレンは留守の間に庭に水をやってくれるように隣人に頼んだ。残念ながら彼は忘れて，彼女が戻るまでに花の多くはしおれてしまった。

語句 1「（金属などが）光沢を失った」　2「二極化した」
3「（草花などが）しおれた」　　　　4「～を軽視した」

解説 隣人は庭の水やりを忘れたのだから，花は wilted「しおれた」のだ。wilt の類義語は wither, shrivel, droop など。

(18) – 解答 **1**

訳 その映画の主題は非常に深刻だけれども，重苦しくなり過ぎるのを防ぐお気楽な瞬間がある。

語句 1「軽薄」　　　　　　　　　　2「（川などの）合流」
3「起動力，勢い」　　　　　　　　4「覇権」

解説 深刻な映画が重苦しくなり過ぎないためのものなので，「深刻，重苦しさ」の反意語が入りそうだ。levity「軽薄，不まじめ，（口調などの）軽さ」。

(19) – 解答 **3**

訳 昨日アンドリューは知らないアドレスから謎めいたメールを受信した。どんなに懸命に努力しても，それが言おうとしていることが理解できなかった。

語句 1「痛切な」　　　　　　　　　　2「立ち直りの早い」
3「謎の，不可解な」　　　　　　　4「（飲食物が）おいしい」

9

解説 どんなにがんばっても内容が理解できなかったのだから，受信したメールは cryptic「謎の，（暗号のように）不可解な」であったのだ。

(20) – 解答 ③

訳 その手作り家具のブランドは細部にまで細心の注意を払うことで知られている。一つ一つが非常に注意深く作られている。

語句 1「態度が和らいでいる」　　　2「味のない」
3「細心の，気難しい」　　　　4「島の，狭量な」

解説 Each piece (of furniture) がとても注意深く作られているのだから，細部に払われる注意は fastidious「細心の（注意を要する）」だ。

(21) – 解答 ①

訳 ロジャーが初めて兄の赤ちゃんを抱き上げようとしたとき，赤ちゃんがすごく身をくねらせたので，ロジャーは彼女をきちんと抱っこするのに苦労した。

語句 1「身をくねらせた［よじった］」　2「くっ付いた」
3「せびった」　　　　　　　　　4「〜を風刺した」

解説 きちんと抱っこするのが困難だったのだから，赤ん坊（she）は squirmed「身をくねらせた［よじった］」のだ。squirm の類義語は twist，wriggle。

(22) – 解答 ④

訳 仲間からの圧力は 10 代の若者に強い影響を与え得る。友達にけしかけられると，彼らは非常に愚かなことをするように説得されることがある。

語句 1「泥沼にはまり込んで」　　　2「ぐいと引き上げられて」
3「怠けた」　　　　　　　　　4「けしかけられて」

解説 仲間の圧力は強い影響力があるのだから，友人に be egged on「けしかけられる」と愚行をするのだ。egg on「〜にけしかける，〜をそそのかす」。

(23) – 解答 ③

訳 ミシェルの隣人たちが騒がしいパーティーを開くと，彼女は隣からの騒音をかき消すために音楽の音量を上げる。

語句 1「（金・時間など）を浪費する」　2「〜を楽しむ」
3「（音）をかき消す」　　　　　4「〜を陥没させる」

解説 隣人のパーティーは騒がしいのだから，ミシェルが音量を上げるのは，隣からの騒音を drown out「（大きな音が小さな音）をかき消す」ためだ。

(24) – 解答 ①

訳 その自動車会社は時代遅れのイメージを捨て去り，ハイテク装備でモダンな感じの車を設計することで若者を引き付けるように努力している。

語句 1「〜を投げ捨てる」　　　　　2「〜を大声で言う」

3「〜に電話をする」　　　4「〜を閉じ込める」

解説 ハイテクでモダンな車で若者にアピールしたいのだから，時代遅れという自社イメージを cast off「投げ捨てる」のだ。cast「投げる」，off「離れて」おのおのから意味を推測できそうだ。

(25)―解答

訳 元のスタッフたちによるその政治家に向けられた不正行為の告発は，彼の政治的キャリアを終わらせる可能性がある。

語句 1「〜に向けられた」　　　2「〜にたたき込まれた」
3「当てにされた」　　　　4「〜に合うように調節された」

解説 彼の政治生命を絶つかもしれないのだから，告発は政治家に leveled at「向けられた」ものだ。level *A* at *B*「*A*（銃・非難など）を *B* に向ける」。

一次試験・筆記 2　問題編 p.20〜23

全文訳　**クモの生存**

　米国東部の各地で見つかる Synemosyna formica というハエトリグモの非常に興味深い種は，ほかの生き物に擬態することが観察されている。生物学者たちは，この行動は孤立性の生活様式を持つこのクモが多くの捕食者にとって格好の標的になりがちだという事実から生じている，という説を立てた。一方でアリは，その強力な顎とめったに単独ではいないという事実のためあまり好ましくない獲物であり，例えば，1匹のアリをおいしくいただこうとする捕食者は，助けに来る数多くのほかの攻撃的なアリたちをおそらく撃退せざるを得なくなるだろう。アリの凶暴な評判をうまく利用して，クモはこの昆虫のふりをするために，アリの触角の動きに似た動きで前脚を揺り動かすなど特定の行動をするようになった。うまく行くと，これはクモが捕食者の注意をそらすのに役立つ。

　S. formica はまた，身体的にアリによく似るようにもなった。しかし，その適応は捕食動物を欺くのに役立つ一方で，かなりの犠牲を伴ったのかもしれない。そのクモの後脚はより長く太く進化したように見え，そして胴体は細く体節のあるものになり，一般に捕食者が見渡すのに有利な地点である上方から見ると，アリのような外見を際立たせる。だが，これらの変化はこのクモに，近縁種がすることで知られている跳ぶ動作をできなくさせたようであり，これはおそらくアリのような形態と体重による制約の結果であると生物学者たちは言う。そして，獲物を捕らえるのに極めて重要なこの能力が衰えたので，このクモの生存は危ういかもしれない。

　1つの謎は，いかにして S. formica はつがう可能性のある相手をなんとか見つけるのか，である。ほとんどの種類のハエトリグモは，パートナーになる見込みのある相手を誘うために，派手で入念な儀式を行う。パートナーの気を引くことは S. formica に

とっても同様に重要だが，戸外におけるそのような求愛行動は，おそらく捕食者からの不要な注意を引くだろう。これを回避するために，このクモはどうやら遠くから互いを認識しているようだ。アリのような行動の偽装を損なわずに自分たちはアリではないと合図で知らせることができるようだが，この目立たない行動の正確な仕組みはわからないままだ。生物学者たちは，これらの一風変わった生き物へと研究を拡大することによって，どのように生存本能が動物の適応を推し進めるのかについての理解を深められることを望んでいる。

> 語句　jumping spider「ハエトリグモ」，theorize「～という理論を立てる」，solitary「孤立性の，群居しない」，unaccompanied「同伴者のない」，feast on ～「～をごちそうになる」，impersonate「～になりすます，～のふりをする」，antennae「触角」(antenna の複数形)，avert「～をそむける，そらす」，segmented「体節のある」，accentuate「～を目立たせる」，vantage point「見通しの利く地点」，in jeopardy「危うくなって」，showy「派手な，目立つ」，entice「～を誘惑する」，courtship「求愛行動」，from afar「遠くから」，guise「見せかけ，ふり」，discreet「慎重な，控えめな」

(26) ― 解答 ④

> 解説　このクモは何をするのが観察されているか，が空所に入る。空所文以降で，このクモは単独で生活するため捕食者の格好の標的になるが，アリは凶暴で標的になりにくいので，impersonate the insects「この昆虫（アリ）のふりをする」ようになったことが述べられている。これを mimicking another creature「ほかの生き物に擬態する」と言い換えた **4** が正解。

(27) ― 解答 ③

> 解説　アリに身体的に似るという適応は，役立つ一方でどうなのか，が空白に入る。第2段落後半で述べているのは，この変化はクモに leaping action「跳ぶ動作」をできなくさせたが，跳ぶ能力は獲物を狩るのに極めて重要なので「このクモの生存は危ういかもしれない」こと。このことを「かなりの犠牲（cost）を伴ったかもしれない」と言い換えた **3** が正解。come at a cost「（かなりの）犠牲・代償を伴う」。

(28) ― 解答 ②

> 解説　クモが何をする方法が謎なのか，が空白に入る。第3段落によると，S. formica の acts of courtship「求愛行動」では遠くから互いを認識しており，アリに偽装したまま自分はアリでないと合図しているようだが，その行動の exact mechanisms ... remain unclear「正確な仕組みはわからないままだ」という。よって，謎なのは求愛行動の仕組みであり，これを find potential mates「つがう可能性のある相手を見つける」と言い換えた **2** が正解。

全文訳 経済を評価する

　戦争は経済に有益であるという考えは多くの人々によく知られており，大きな紛争は物資の製造に膨大な需要をもたらし雇用創出を促す，という前提に基づいている。しかし，その考えには欠陥があると指摘する専門家もいる。結局，大量の武器製造に取り組む間に作られるものの大部分は，戦闘中に使い尽くされるか破壊されるかだが，一方でその同じ資金と資源がもし消費者向けの物品やサービスを生み出すのにつぎ込まれたら，大きな長期的利益をもたらすだろう。実際，これは第2次世界大戦後に見られたことで，その時期に，政府が軍事支出の大幅削減を行った後に米国は驚くべき繁栄の時代を経験した，と専門家は言う。

　近年，経済学者タイラー・コーエンは戦争関連の経済的利点に関して修正した学説を提唱してきた。軍事衝突そのものは経済に対して有益ではとうていあり得ないと認め，有益なのは戦争の脅威であると彼は主張する。コーエンは，世界各地のいくつかの国における近年の不況は，長引く平和な時代の結果としてゆっくり展開する，緊迫感の欠如のまん延のせいと考え得ると強く主張する。米国とソビエト連邦の双方が相手国のとてつもない軍事力を恐れた冷戦中，長期にわたる敵対心の結果ものすごいイノベーションが出てきたことなどの例を挙げて，コーエンは，政府を油断させずにおくのは武力衝突の可能性であり，それが経済を自由化し科学技術などに資金を投入する圧力を政府にかけるのだと考える。

　だがコーエンは，国はけんかを売って回るべきだと提案しているのではない。事実，彼は続けて，今日では武器はずっと破壊的になってきたため，もし実際に戦争が勃発したら生じる結果は壊滅的だろうから，景気低迷は今日の世界では比較的よいことなのかもしれない，と言う。それ故，成長と引き換えに平和を手に入れる方がよいのかもしれない，と彼は提言する。環境破壊は化石燃料の野放図な使用に関連する利益に見合わないことが最近認識されてきたのと同様に，常に戦争の瀬戸際にいることの潜在的リスクはその報酬によって正当化できなさそうだ。

> **語句** stagnation「停滞，不況」，pervade「〜に広がる，まん延する」，prolong「〜を長引かせる」，on *one's* toes「気を張りつめて，油断のない」，liberalize「〜を自由化する」，go around *doing*「いつも〜して回る」，pick a fight「けんかを売る」，fallout「付随的な結果」，catastrophic「壊滅的な」，devastation「破壊，破滅」，rampant「はびこる」

(29) – 解答 ②

> **解説** 冒頭の「戦争は経済に有益だ」という考えに逆接 however で続く空所文は，この考えに否定的な内容だろう。実際，空所文以降では，同じ資源を戦争で失うものにではなく消費者物品などに費やせば大きな長期的利益をもたらすことが述べられている。つまり，冒頭の考えは flawed「欠陥・間違いがある」ものなのだ。よって **2** が正解。

13

(30) ─解答 **2** ・・

解説 第2段落で示されているコーエンの考えでは，近年の不況は平和による緊迫感欠如のせいであり，緊迫していた米ソ冷戦時代にものすごい革新が出たように，政府に緊迫感を持たせ利益（経済自由化や科学技術などへの資金投入）を導くのは，戦争そのものではなく potential for armed conflict「武力衝突の可能性」だ。これを threat of conflict「戦争の脅威」と言い換えた**2**が正解。

(31) ─解答 **4** ・・

解説 第2段落で，平和は経済不況を招くが（平和→不況），戦争の脅威は経済に有益（戦争脅威→経済成長）だと示された。第3段落第2文「戦争が起これば壊滅的な結果になるだろうから，不況は比較的よいことだ」というのはつまり「（壊滅を起こしかねない戦争脅威が招く）経済成長よりも（平和が招く）不況の方がよい」ということ。このことを trade growth for peace「成長と引き換えに平和を手に入れる」と言い換えた**4**が正解。

一次試験・筆記 **3** | 問題編 p.23 ～ 32

全文訳 *バイオパイラシー*

　新しい薬や食料品を開発しようとして，多国籍企業はしばしば薬草やほかの資源についての先住民族の知識を頼る。このことは時に，バイオパイラシーだという非難を引き起こす。バイオパイラシーは，先住民族に公正な報酬を払わずに，彼らの協力を得て見つけた産物の特許を取ろうとすることを指す用語である。このように先住民族に協力を頼むときは，その資源がもうかる製品に変えられる可能性を含め，どのように使われることがあるかについて十分説明をして相手の同意を得ることが不可欠だ，というのが一般的な合意である。また，何らかの協力を始める前に，双方の権利と責務を詳しく述べた協定を作成することも重要だ。しかし，そのような協定はしばしば先住民族とほかの人々の世界観の根本的な違いを反映しており，たびたび誤解と搾取につながる。例えば，西洋社会は特許権や商標権のような法的保護に重きを置くが，先住民族はしばしば，個人や企業が天然資源や生物に対して独占権を持つという概念は理解し難いと感じる。その結果，多くの先住民族が，彼らが自分たちをだましたと言う企業に対して訴訟を起こしてきた。

　その上，バイオパイラシーと闘うために法律や国際条約が制定されてきたが，曖昧でなく包括的な規則を作るのは極めて困難だとわかった。実際，バイオパイラシーという用語それ自体に統一された単一の定義がなく，バイオパイラシーに関する規則が国によってさまざまであることが，倫理に反する行いを撲滅するのを困難にしている。例えば，名古屋議定書は，遺伝資源の入手を管理してそのような資源の利用がもたらす利益が共

有されるのを確実にするため，各国が独自の法律を策定する上での枠組みとなるように作られた。けれども，この協定は非常に異なって解釈され施行されており，また比較的低い割合の国が署名しただけだ。これらの要因が，バイオパイラシーの行いが終わる兆しがほとんど見られない主な理由だ。

また，バイオパイラシーに的を絞った法律は意図せぬ結果をもたらすかもしれない。ある科学者たちのグループは，バイオパイラシーの抑制に関連する国際協定は既に，貴重な資源や生物を持つ国々に，急務となる研究を妨げる障壁を設けさせている，と主張する論文を発表した。特に，保全を目的とする種の発見と分類を伴う分類学は，そのような国際協定により著しく阻まれてきた。その科学者たちは，「今日の分類上の発見がことによると明日の商業的開発に変わるかもしれないことを恐れるせいで，多くの規制機関が生物多様性の研究を疑わしく思うようになっているようだ」と書いている。研究者たちが海外の科学者に標本を分けるのを嫌がるようになった国もあれば，許可を得るために乗り越えねばならない規制上の障害が，保全研究などの研究を妨げていると不満を言う国もある。一方で，その論文を書いた科学者たちは，医学研究の場合に遺伝子工学のような先進技術の発展が意味するのは，先住民族に知られている生物を入手することがさほど重要でなくなるかもしれないことだ，と述べている。このことは，極めて重要な科学研究を妨げられずに継続できるようにするばかりでなく，現在の反バイオパイラシー協定の意義を失わせもするであろう。

語句 enlist「（協力など）を得る」，informed consent「十分な説明に基づく同意，インフォームドコンセント」，lucrative「もうかる」，incomprehensible「理解できない」，enact「（法律など）を制定する」，unambiguous「曖昧でない」，stamp out「～を撲滅する，根絶する」，unethical「非倫理的な」，taxonomy「分類学」，hamper「～を妨げる」，biodiversity「生物多様性」，taxonomic「分類学の」，conceivably「考えられる限りでは」，translate into ～「～に変わる」，hinder「～を妨げる」，unimpeded「妨げられていない」

(32) – 解答 ②

問題文の訳 多国籍企業が先住民族と協定を結ぶとき，

選択肢の訳
1 特許や商標のような法律的権利事項の作成を第三者に任せる傾向が両者にある。
2 当事者たちが文書に含まれる基本概念を理解する方法に，しばしば大きな相違がある。
3 当事者たちは一般に，ほかの種類の製品についてよりも医薬品に関する問題についての方が意見が合わない。
4 先住民族が受ける利益ばかりでなく，彼らの協力が進行中の研究に不可欠だという事実もまた説明する必要がある。

解説 協定を結ぶときのことについては第1段落後半にある。西洋では特許権など法的保護を重視するが，先住民族は個人や企業が天然物の独占権を

持つという概念が理解し難いことを例に，「協定はしばしば先住民族とほかの人々の世界観の根本的な違い（fundamental differences）を反映」する（第5文）と述べている。このことを言い換えた **2** が正解。

(33) − 解答 ④

問題文の訳 第2段落で，この文章の筆者はバイオパイラシーを防ぐ取り組みについて何と述べているか。

選択肢の訳 1 法や条約は，もし策定中に企業と先住民族の両方が意見を求められたら，はるかに効果的になるだろう。
2 バイオパイラシーが減っている兆候はいくつかあるが，その取り組みは十分ではないと先住民族たちは言う。
3 現地の法律は一般的に，バイオパイラシーを減らす上で国際条約よりもずっと成功してきた。
4 その取り組みが成功しないのは，主として，各国が従うことに同意する明確な規則を作ることが難しいことの結果だ。

解説 第2段落前半で，バイオパイラシーと闘う取り組みで「曖昧でなく包括的な規則を作るのは極めて困難」だとわかったが，この用語に単一の定義はなく「規則が国によってさまざま」なので撲滅し難い（成功しない），後半では名古屋議定書を例に「この協定は非常に異なって解釈され施行されて」いるのでバイオパイラシーが終わる兆しがない（成功しない）と述べている。明確な規則があればこのような違いは起こらないので，取り組みが成功しないのは，**4** のように「明確な規則を作ることが難しいことの結果」だと言える。

(34) − 解答 ③

問題文の訳 最終段落で言及されている論文を書いた科学者たちは，次の記述のどれに同意する可能性が最も高いだろうか。

選択肢の訳 1 バイオパイラシーはしばしば環境保全研究を装うので，この種の研究はより注意深く規制されるべきだ。
2 遺伝子工学のような医療技術が進歩しているが，それらは先住民がバイオパイラシーによって被害に遭う，より大きなリスクを作り出している。
3 バイオパイラシーを防ぐために策定された規則は，絶滅危惧種を救うかもしれない極めて重要な研究を妨げる可能性がある。
4 科学者たちがお互いに分類学研究を盗もうとする試みは，バイオパイラシーよりもはるかに深刻な問題を呈する。

解説 第3段落第2，3文で述べられている論文の主張は，バイオパイラシー抑制のための協定により資源のある国が障壁を設け，急務の（→極めて重要な）研究，特に保全目的（→絶滅危惧種を救うなど）で種の発見や分類をする分類学が妨げられていること。これを言い換えた **3** が正解。

16

全文訳 初期の太陽系

　私たちの太陽系の起源は長いこと考察の対象となってきた。最も広く受け入れられている説明は星雲説で，太陽系は非常に大きな重力を受けて崩壊した星間ガスとちりの巨大な雲として始まった，と主張する。結果として生じた渦巻く物質の集まりが最終的にいくつものまとまった物質となり，次にそれらが集まって太陽や惑星になった。これは太陽系形成のいくつかの側面をうまく説明する一方で，この仮説から導かれるほかの予測は太陽系の現在の状況と一致しない。例えば，この仮説に基づいたコンピューター・シミュレーションでは，特定の惑星の質量とそれらの惑星が存在する領域は現在の天体観測とは矛盾していた。しかしその矛盾は，星雲説は元々，私たちの太陽系にある惑星が現在の場所で形成されほぼそこにとどまっているという前提に基づいていた，という事実のせいかもしれない。

　これらの謎のいくつかは，もう少しで解明されるかもしれない。内太陽系の比較的小さな惑星は，岩石や金属など，太陽の途方もない熱に耐え得る物質からできたと考えられている。逆に，巨大ガス惑星である木星と土星は，凍結線と呼ばれるものを越えた，太陽からもっと遠い領域で形成されたと考えられている。この距離での温度は，巨大ガス惑星を構成する物質が固体化するほど十分低いからである。しかし，科学者たちは，「ホット・ジュピター」というニックネームが付けられた，遠い太陽系外惑星系の木星に似た巨大ガス惑星が，驚くほど近い距離でその太陽（中心にある恒星）を周回するのを観測している。このことを説明するために，科学者たちは惑星移動という概念を提案し，そしてこの概念を検証するために，木星の形成を土台として使って「グランド・タック」と名付けられたシナリオがモデル化された。シナリオでは，木星は予想どおりに凍結線の外側で形成されるが，ホット・ジュピターに倣って内太陽系に移動する。しかし，私たちの太陽系のもう1つの巨大ガス惑星である土星から重力を受ける結果，木星は太陽からもっと遠い現在の位置へと外側に引き戻される。信じ難い話に聞こえるにもかかわらず，このシナリオは，ホット・ジュピターが存在する理由をもっともらしく説明していると称賛されている。

　また，グランド・タックのシナリオは，私たちの太陽系において矛盾と思えるほかのことをはっきりさせるかもしれない。星雲説に基づいたコンピューター・シミュレーションが，火星は今の大きさよりもずっと大きいはずだと予想したとき，提案された木星のグランド・タックの移動が1つの説明を示唆した。グランド・タックのシナリオにおける木星の軌道を計算に入れることによって，この巨大ガス惑星は太陽の近くの物質をたぶん追い散らしていた，そうでなければ火星の質量を著しく増やしていたであろう，と科学者たちは気付いた。その上，木星が移動していなかったら，地球が今ある場所を含む内太陽系の惑星は，ガスで包まれたもっと大きくて人の住めない世界になっていた可能性が十分にある。ほかの既知の太陽系外惑星系の中心に近い領域の大部分がそのような惑星で占められているので，科学者たちは，私たちの太陽系はこの点において極めて独特なのかもしれないと考えている。もし，グランド・タックのシナリオが正しいと判明すれば，人類は，木星が太陽系を通って旅をしたことに対して木星に大いに感謝し

なければならない。

語句 solar system「太陽系，太陽系外惑星系」，nebular「星雲の」，interstellar「星間の」，gravitational「重力の，引力の」，mass「集団，質量」，swirl「渦巻く」，pocket「小集団」，line up with ～「～と一致する」，inconsistent「一貫性のない，矛盾する」，astronomical「天文学の」，discrepancy「不一致，矛盾」，conversely「逆に」，gas giant「巨大ガス惑星」，solidify「～を凝固させる」，planetary「惑星の」，far-fetched「信じ難い」，plausibly「もっともらしく」，inconsistency「矛盾」，factor in ～「～を要素として含める，計算に入れる」，trajectory「軌道」，uninhabitable「住めない」，shroud「～を覆う，包む」，populate「～に住みつく」

(35) − 解答 ③

問題文の訳 この文章の筆者によれば，星雲説に関して何が１つの問題か。

選択肢の訳
1 それは，惑星が太陽系で位置を変えられることを正確に予測するけれども，その予測は宇宙のほかの物体には当てはまらない。
2 それは，私たちの太陽系の形成初期に，重力が太陽の大きさと位置にどのように影響を与えたかを十分に説明していない。
3 私たちの太陽系の来歴をモデル化するのにそれを使うと，特定の惑星について私たちが現在知っていることと合致しない結果が出た。
4 それは，宇宙の遠い領域にある太陽系外惑星系が形成された方法について，不正確な天文学的理論に部分的に基づいていた。

解説 第１段落第４，５文で，星雲説に基づく予測には太陽系の現状と合わないものがあり，その例として「シミュレーションでは，特定の惑星の質量とそれらの惑星が存在する領域は現在の天体観測とは矛盾していた」と述べており，この不一致が星雲説の１つの問題だ。このことを言い換えた **3** が正解。本文の do not line up with, were inconsistent with, 第６文の discrepancies, **3** の do not match はどれも「不一致（である），矛盾（する）」ことを示す。

(36) − 解答 ④

問題文の訳 「ホット・ジュピター」が重要なのは，

選択肢の訳
1 それらは，ほかの太陽系外惑星系で見つかる凍結線の温度が，惑星が形成された方法とほとんど関係がないことの証拠だからである。
2 それらの大きさは，私たちの太陽系に存在するほかの惑星の多くはかつて，現在よりもずっと小さかったことを強く暗示するからである。
3 それらは，星の大きさはその惑星の軌道距離と直接関係していることを示唆する理論を裏付けるからである。
4 それらの存在が，惑星は必ずしも同じ軌道にとどまるわけではないという考えを裏付ける証拠となるようだからである。

18

解説 第2段落に注目。木星などの巨大ガス惑星は中心である太陽から遠く離れた低温域で形成されたと考えられるが，ほかの惑星系には，中心近くを周回する巨大ガス惑星であるホット・ジュピターがある。この存在は，凍結線の外側から内側へと惑星が移動するというシナリオで説明できる。つまり，惑星が移動したことの証拠がその存在であるため，ホット・ジュピターは重要なのだ。惑星が移動することを「必ずしも同じ軌道にとどまるわけではない」と言い換えた**4**が正解。

(37) − 解答 **2**

問題文の訳 第3段落に基づくと，「グランド・タック」のシナリオについて何が推論され得るか。

選択肢の訳
1 それは，火星が太陽系の初期に太陽に引き込まれて破壊されなかった理由を合理的に説明できるかもしれない。
2 それが一度も起こらなかったとしたら，地球上で進化する生命の見込みはおそらくずっと低かっただろう。
3 そのような出来事が起こった太陽系外惑星系にある大きな惑星では，生命が存在する可能性はより低い。
4 そのような出来事が一度も起こらなかった太陽系外惑星系には，木星や土星に似た惑星がありそうだ。

解説 第3段落第4文にグランド・タック，すなわち木星の移動が起こらなければ，地球は「人の住めない（→人類がいない）世界になっていた可能性が十分にある」とある。このことを「地球上で進化する生命の見込みはおそらくずっと低かっただろう」と言い換えた**2**が正解。最終文の，シナリオが正しければ（→木星が移動したなら）人類は木星に感謝すべきだ，という記述が裏付けになっている。**3**はlowerでなくhigherなら正解となり得る。

全文訳 1916年のアイルランド蜂起

第1次世界大戦の前夜，その100年ほど前にイギリスに吸収されていたアイルランドは，ホームルールという限定された自治を勝ち取る寸前だった。アイルランドはイギリス議会に議席を持っていたけれども，自らの政府はなく，そのことが貧困，人口減少，経済的搾取をもたらした。結果として，1800年代を通してナショナリズムが着実に高まっており，ホームルール運動はアイルランドの政界で優勢になった。1870年代以来アイルランド議会党は，国をイギリス内にとどめながらも国内問題においてはある程度の独立をアイルランドに認めることになる，この議題を推し進めていた。ジョン・レドモンドに率いられたその党は，1914年にイギリス議会でホームルール法案を通過させることついに成功した。

しかし，ホームルールへと真っすぐ進める道があるはずはなかった。アイルランドは宗教的路線と政治的路線の違いによって分断されており，南部はナショナリズムをある

程度受け入れる傾向のあったカトリック教徒が多数派を占め，北部は政治的にイギリスにより強いつながりを感じイギリス議会の管轄下にとどまることを決心していたプロテスタントが多数派を占めていた。南部では，アイルランド共和主義同盟（IRB）として知られるグループが，ホームルールは真の主権を与えないので十分ではないと考えていた。IRBはアイルランドの完全独立の達成を強く決意していたので武器を取ったが，南部においてさえ，それは決して主流派の意見を代表するものではなかった。このことは，1914年8月のイギリスの第1次世界大戦への参戦とともに明らかになった。すなわち，IRBはアイルランドが戦争に参加することに反対したが，アイルランド議会党はそれを支持し，ホームルールの立法化が延期されねばならないことを受け入れたのである。アイルランドの人々の大半は同意し，ほかのイギリス国民と同じように戦争を支持した。

イギリスが軍事資源を海外での戦いに集中して投じたので，IRBの指導者たちは，アイルランドにおける治安目的で使える兵士が減るだろうと考えた。そのため，1916年4月24日に，フランスのソンム川近くでの大規模軍事攻撃の準備によってイギリスの注意がそれたことで，IRBは行動を起こす機が熟したと判断した。組織内で結成されていた軍事評議会に率いられ，IRBはイギリス支配に反対する武装蜂起を起こして共和国の設立を宣言した。

約1,500人が——IRBのメンバーがほかのナショナリストグループのメンバーとともに——アイルランドの首都ダブリン中のさまざまな場所を占拠した。彼らは自分たちの行動がより広範な一般民衆の蜂起を引き起こすことを望んでいたが，そうはならなかった。その上，人員不足のせいで，彼らは主要な鉄道駅や波止場，そしてこれが最も重要なのだが，イギリス政府の行政本部であるダブリン城を占領することができなかった。それ故，イギリスは妨げられずに兵士を市内に移動させ行政の中心地の支配を維持できたが，これが結局決め手となった。このようにして，初めは不意を突かれたにもかかわらず，イギリス側は迅速に編成された反撃を通してすぐさま優位に立った。イギリス軍が市内になだれ込み，重砲が使われ，火災による被害や民間人の死傷者が出た。

反乱者たちは果敢に戦ったけれども，人員と武器の数で大幅に負けていた。彼らは守勢に回らざるを得ず，降伏するのは時間の問題でしかなかった。蜂起は4月29日に終わり，およそ450人が死んで2,000人が負傷し，ダブリンの中心の大部分が破壊された。

イギリスの報復は素早く厳しかった。反乱への関与を疑われた数千の人々が検挙され，指導者たちは軍事法廷で裁かれ有罪判決を受けたのである。反乱者のうち15人は，秘密裏に被告側弁護士なしで行われた裁判に続いて銃殺隊によって処刑されたが，その裁判は，定められた軍事司法手続きに違反していたとイギリスの当局者たちが後に裁定を下した。反乱者たちが戦時中に攻撃を加えたことを考えると，民事法廷でなく軍事法廷で裁判を行ったことを含む軍部の対応は正当化できると当時は考える者もいた。しかし，イギリス政府の当局者たちは，アイルランドでイギリスの指揮官が反乱者たちを扱っていたやり方と，これが招くかもしれない反発をすぐに懸念したのである。

それ以上の死刑執行は停止されたが，多くのアイルランド人が愛国者だと見なした男

性たちが処刑された結果，イギリス支配に反対する世論は活気づいた。蜂起は間接的に，大衆の感情に変化を起こすきっかけとなっていたのだ。ホームルール運動は勢いを失い，その代わりにシン・フェインと呼ばれる政党の弁論が広く受け入れられるようになり，その政党はアイルランドにおいて 1918 年のイギリス選挙で多数を占めることができた。その政党はイギリス議会で議席を取ることを拒否して独立を宣言したが，それがゲリラ戦に発展して，IRB が元々求めていた主権をアイルランドの大部分がついに獲得するに至った。1916 年の蜂起は，彫像でたたえられ毎年祝われて，今日ではアイルランドの歴史で重要な出来事と見なされている。

語句 uprising「反乱，蜂起」，self-government「自治」，depopulation「人口減少」，line「路線，方針」，resolved to *do*「〜することを決心して」，enactment「（法律の）制定，立法」，ripe「熟した」，unimpeded「妨げられていない」，be caught off guard「不意を突かれる」，gain the upper hand「優位に立つ」，counterattack「反撃」，valiantly「果敢に」，outman「〜より人数が多い」，outgun「〜より軍事力で勝る，多くの武器を持っている」，retaliation「仕返し，報復」，round up「〜を検挙する，逮捕する」，firing squad「銃殺隊」，justifiable「正当化できる」，galvanize「〜を活気づかせる」，patriot「愛国者」，catalyst「触媒，（変化などの）きっかけ」，lose steam「勢いが衰える」，rhetoric「美辞麗句，大げさな言葉」，commemorate「〜を（記念式や行事などで）祝う」

(38) – 解答 3

問題文の訳 この文章によると，1914 年のアイルランドの政治情勢に関してどれが正しいか。

選択肢の訳
1 大戦争の勃発が，アイルランド議会党とかつてその党を支持していたさまざまなプロテスタント系グループとの間に争いを引き起こしていた。
2 アイルランド議会党への支持が非常に低下していたので，ホームルール法案への反対が大きくなっていた。
3 一般市民からの幅広い支持はなかったが，アイルランドはイギリスから完全に独立すべきだとアイルランド共和主義同盟（IRB）は決意していた。
4 ホームルールを取り巻く議論は，第 1 次世界大戦で戦うことに反対の立場であるプロテスタントとカトリック教徒が団結するのに役立った。

解説 ホームルール法案の議会通過や第 1 次世界大戦へのイギリスの参戦があった 1914 年のアイルランドの政情は，第 2 段落で述べられている。第 2 段落第 4 文に①「IRB はアイルランドの完全独立の達成を強く決意していた」，②「それ（完全独立）は決して主流派の意見を代表するもの

ではなかった」とあり，②を「一般市民からの幅広い支持はなかった」と言い換えた**3**が正解。本文の was ... intent on は**3**では was determined で言い換えられている。

(39) – 解答 ②

問題文の訳 1916年4月24日から29日に起こった蜂起について，この文章の筆者が述べている1つの論点はどれか。

選択肢の訳
1 もし IRB がソンム川近くでの戦いの開始まで待っていたら，イギリスは反乱者たちを打ち負かすのに十分な部隊を持たなかったかもしれない。
2 反乱者たちは，自分たちを倒すイギリス軍の能力を大いに弱めていたであろう戦略的に重要な場所を確保できなかった。
3 イギリスは民間人に恐怖心を吹き込むために膨大な軍事力を使い，それによって彼らが反乱者たちに加わるかもしれない可能性を制限した。
4 関与した反乱者たちには，イギリスに対していくばくかの忠義を感じていた人々が含まれており，そのことで彼らはイギリス軍に危害を加えるのをためらうようになった。

解説 1916年4月24〜29日の状況は第3〜5段落にある。第4段落第3，4文に，反乱者たちが（戦略的に重要な場所である）主要な駅や港，ダブリン城を占拠できなかった結果，イギリスはスムーズに兵士を市内に移動させ中心地の支配を維持できたことが決め手（key）だったとある。つまり，もし反乱者たちが重要な場所を占拠できていれば，イギリスは兵士を市内に送り込めず，軍力は弱まっていたはずだ。このことを言い換えた**2**が正解。

(40) – 解答 ④

問題文の訳 1916年の蜂起に続くイギリスの反応には問題があったが，その根拠は，

選択肢の訳
1 戦いで何かしらの重要な役割を果たした者はほとんどいなかったにもかかわらず，数千の反乱者たちが軍事法廷で有罪となったことである。
2 政府自身の軍隊が，反逆者たちを刑に処するのに使ったのと同じ軍法の多くに違反していたことを，政府が後に認めたことである。
3 政府が指揮官に秘密裏に反乱者たちの裁判を行うよう促したことで，状況をさらに悪化させたことである。
4 反乱の指導者たちが裁判にかけられて有罪判決を受けたやり方は，軍法で定められた正しく適切な手続きを守っていなかったことである。

解説 蜂起後のことは第6段落以降にある。第6段落第1，2文で，反乱の指導者15名が秘密裏に弁護士なしで行われた裁判で有罪判決を受けて処刑されたが，この裁判は定められた軍事裁判の手続きに違反していたと

後にイギリス当局者たちが裁定したことが述べられている。この違反を述べた **4** が正解。

(41) - 解答

問題文の訳 次の記述のどれが，1916年の蜂起の影響を最もよく述べているか。

選択肢の訳
1 それに続くシン・フェインの政治的成功は，アイルランドの変化を促すためには最初から選挙のプロセスが使われるべきであったことを証明した。
2 事件そのものはすぐに変化を引き起こさなかったが，最終的には反乱者たちの目的へとかなり前進することにつながった。
3 その間に用いられた軍事戦術が後の争いでアイルランドが勝利するのを助けるのに極めて有益になるので，蜂起は重要だった。
4 その出来事は破壊と人命の損失に終わったけれども，アイルランドのイギリスとの争いに終わりを告げたので，正当化された。

解説 蜂起した IRB の目的は「アイルランドの完全独立（すなわち主権）」（第2段落）だったが，鎮圧された（→すぐの変化はない）。しかし後に世論が活気づき，1918年の選挙で多数を占めたシン・フェインによる独立宣言がゲリラ戦に発展して結果的に「IRB が元々求めていた主権をアイルランドの（目的だった全部でなくとも）大部分がついに獲得するに至った」（第7段落）。このことを「目的へとかなり前進」したと言い換えた **2** が正解。

一次試験・筆記 4 問題編 p.32

解答例　Although it is undeniable that human societies currently inflict damage upon the environment worldwide, I disagree that this will be the case indefinitely. I believe green technologies, government policies, and societal attitudes will evolve to better accommodate environmental conservation.

　Green technology has blossomed into a vibrant global industry, and revolutionary developments are being made on a regular basis. Over the coming decades, the negative effects resulting from drilling for oil or mining for coal can be negated as the fossil fuel industry is increasingly displaced by maturing green technology.

　Additionally, more governments are codifying policies vital to the environment. Such efforts safeguard the habitats of wild species, particularly endangered ones, and highlight a growing trend toward conservation. This will help liberate these species from potential dangers posed by the expansion of urbanization.

Furthermore, societal attitudes toward nature are constantly changing for the better as humans are becoming ever more aware of their environmental footprints. Over the last century, consumerism has become a defining element of people's lives. However, this is gradually being supplanted by an increasingly popular lifestyle that champions minimalism and sustainability over excess and wastefulness. As this lifestyle spreads, the holistic effect of human activities on the environment will become more positive.

In summary, due to the collective efforts of those working to develop new technologies, government policymakers, and the global populace as a whole, human societies will not always have a negative effect on the environment.

トピックの訳 「賛成か反対か：人間社会は常に環境に悪い影響を与えるだろう」

解説 解答例はトピックに対して否定の立場から「人間社会は必ずしも環境に悪影響を及ぼすわけではない」と述べている。

3つの理由と根拠は，①環境に優しい技術：グリーンテクノロジーの発展により化石燃料が置き換えられて悪影響をなくす，②政府の政策：多くの政府が環境にとって重要な政策を成文化し絶滅危惧種の生息地を都市化から守る，③社会の姿勢：環境を意識した生活をする人の増加により人間活動はもっと環境によくなる，である。それぞれ順に具体例の中に，化石燃料，絶滅危惧種，大量消費主義を挙げているが，どれも現代社会の長年にわたる問題なので理解しやすく説得力のある主張となっている。

また，このトピックは always が使われた肯定文だが，このような場合，1つでも not である例を示せば always が崩れることになるので，一般的には not の側に立つ方が論理的に強い主張が展開できる。この解答例から受ける説得力の強さには，この点も寄与していそうだ。

さらに，解答例には高度な単語や表現が全体的にちりばめられており，格調高い文章となっている。例えば，「損害を与える」は cause [do] damage を使ってもまったく問題ないのだが，解答例のように inflict damage とすると格が一段上がる。ほかにも動詞 protect, support ではなく safeguard, champion を使っているところに注目したい。なお，解答例の語数は 239 語で絶妙だ。

一次試験・リスニング Part 1

問題編 p.33〜34

No.1 —解答 ① 正答率 ★75%以上

スクリプト
★: Welcome to St. Alphonsus College, Ms. West. I'm Jonathan MacDonald, admissions director.
☆: Nice to meet you. St. Alphonsus is at the top of my list of prospective schools.
★: Wonderful. This morning, I'll show you around the school, and we can sit in on some classes in session so you can witness our rigorous academic program.
☆: Will I get to speak with any current students? I'd like to hear about their experiences as well.
★: Absolutely. I've put aside some time for that in the afternoon. And at around two o'clock, we'll return to the admissions office to discuss the application process.
☆: That sounds great.

Question: What will the woman probably do next?

全文訳
★: セント・アルフォンサス・カレッジへようこそ, ウェストさん。入学事務局主事のジョナサン・マクドナルドです。
☆: 初めまして。セント・アルフォンサスは私の志望校リストの中でトップに位置しています。
★: よかったです。本日の午前中は, 校内をご案内して, 授業中のクラスをいくつか参観できますので, 本校の厳格な学問的プログラムをご覧いただけます。
☆: 在学生と話をする機会はありますか？ 彼らの体験談も聞きたいのですが。
★: もちろんです。午後にそのための時間を少し取ってあります。そして2時ごろに, 入学事務局に戻って申請手続きについて話し合いましょう。
☆: それはどうもありがとうございます。

質問: 女性はおそらく次に何をするか。

選択肢の訳
1 学校見学に参加する。
2 申請書に必要事項を記入する。
3 学生数名と話をする。
4 学校の入学事務局に行く。

解説 男性の2つ目の発言の This morning, I'll show you around the school, and we can sit in on some classes in session から, まずは校内を案内してもらい, 授業をいくつか参観するはずなので, 正解は **1**。3は午後に予定されており, 4も3の後に予定されていることなので誤

25

り。rigorous「厳格な」。

No.2 −解答 ③

スクリプト ☆ : You look kind of bleary-eyed, Martin. Are you doing a lot of overtime these days?

★ : I'm a little sleep-deprived. They installed new lighting around the grounds of my apartment complex, and it's a bit too well-lit. The LEDs are bright, and the light shines right through my curtains.

☆ : I've heard that LED light can disrupt sleep.

★ : It's definitely true in my case. I'm going shopping for new curtains this weekend.

☆ : Hopefully, you'll be able to sleep better once you get them put up. Till then, let me know if you need help with any of your work.

★ : Thanks, Claire.

Question: Why does the woman offer to assist the man?

全文訳 ☆ : ちょっと目が充血しているようね，マーティン。最近は残業が多いのかしら？

★ : 少し睡眠不足なんだ。共同住宅の敷地の周りに新しい照明が設置されて，それがちょっと明る過ぎるんだよ。LED が輝いていて，光がカーテンを突き抜けてまぶしいんだ。

☆ : LED ライトは睡眠を妨げることがあるって聞いたことがあるわ。

★ : 僕の場合が間違いなくそうだよ。今週末に新しいカーテンを買いに行く予定なんだ。

☆ : それを取り付けたら，もっとよく眠れるようになるといいわね。それまでの間，もし何か仕事で手助けが必要だったら知らせてね。

★ : ありがとう，クレア。

質問：女性はなぜ男性を援助すると申し出ているのか。

選択肢の訳 **1** 彼は仕事を理解するのに苦労している。

2 彼は照明を修理するのを手伝ってもらう必要がある。

3 彼はあまりに疲れていて仕事をすべてこなせないかもしれない。

4 彼は新しいアパートへの引っ越しを予定している。

解説 カーテン越しに差し込んでくる外灯の光が原因で sleep-deprived「睡眠不足の」状態に陥っている男性に対して，女性は最後の発言で let me know if you need help with any of your work と申し出ている。つまり，女性は男性の仕事に支障が生じる可能性があると考えていることになる。bleary-eyed「目のかすんだ，充血した」。

No.3 −解答 ③

スクリプト ☆ : Honey, I just received a notification to report for jury duty next month.

★： That's a good thing, right? You'll be doing your part as a member of society.

☆： Yeah, but it's during the week we've booked for our vacation.

★： Oh no! Can you request a deferral?

☆： I'm not sure. I heard the jury coordinator can excuse people if they apply with a valid reason.

★： I doubt you can get out of it altogether, but you may be able to postpone it.

☆： That's probably true. I'll look into it.

Question: What will the woman try to do?

全文訳 ☆： あなた，来月陪審義務のために出頭するようにとの通知を今しがた受け取ったの。

★： それはいいことだよね？ 社会の一員としての役割を果たすことになるよ。

☆： そうね，でも私たちが休暇を予定していた週の間なのよ。

★： そんな，まさか！ 延期を要請できるかな？

☆： わからないわ。正当な理由を添えて申請すれば，陪審員団のコーディネーターが免除してくれることもあるとは聞いたけど。

★： 君が完全にその役から逃れられるとは思わないけど，延期はできるかもしれないよ。

☆： おそらくそのとおりね。調べてみるわ。

質問：女性は何をしようとするか。

選択肢の訳 1　休暇の予定をもっと遅い日程に変更する。

2　陪審員団のコーディネーターになることを志願する。

3　別の時に陪審義務を果たす。

4　休暇から早く戻ってくる。

解説 女性が陪審員として出頭する日程と，男性と過ごす休暇の予定が重なってしまった男女の会話。陪審義務の免除は無理でも，延期なら可能かもしれないという男性の発言に対して，女性は最後の発言で同意し，I'll look into it. と述べている。したがって，正解は **3**。deferral「延期」。

No.**4** −解答 **1**

スクリプト ☆： Excuse me, I'd like to return this laundry detergent.

★： Is there a problem with it?

☆： Actually, yes. The label says it's safe for sensitive skin, but it caused my son to break out in hives. It's not safe for my family.

★： I'm so sorry. Of course, we'll provide you with a full refund.

☆： Thank you. I'm reluctant to trust the claims on any of these products now, and there are so many conflicting reviews on the

27

Internet.

★： I recommend you speak with our pharmacist. She might be able to suggest an appropriate detergent.

Question: What is one problem the woman has?

全文訳 ☆： すみません，この洗濯用洗剤を返品したいのですが。

★： 何か問題がございますか？

☆： 実は，そうなんです。ラベルには敏感肌にも安全だと書いてありますが，洗剤が原因で息子にじんましんが出てしまいました。私の家族には安全ではありません。

★： 誠に申し訳ありません。もちろん，全額を返金いたします。

☆： ありがとう。今こういった製品のどんなものにも書かれているうたい文句は信用する気になれませんし，インターネット上には相反するレビューが本当にたくさんありますよね。

★： 当店の薬剤師に相談なさることをお勧めします。適切な洗剤をご提案できるかもしれません。

質問：女性が抱える問題の１つは何か。

選択肢の訳 **1** 彼女はどの製品が安全なのかがわからない。
2 店は彼女に返金しないだろう。
3 彼女のお気に入りの製品はインターネット上でしか売られていない。
4 製品のラベルが読みにくい。

解説 敏感肌にも安全と書かれた洗剤を使用したが，息子に hives「じんましん」が出たと店員に話す女性は，最後の発言で the claims on any of these products は信用したくないし，ネット上には相反するレビューがあふれていると述べている。つまり，どの製品が安全かを判断できなくなっているので，正解は **1**。

No.5 − 解答 ④

スクリプト ★： Welcome to Steele International Bank. How can I help you today?

☆： I'm a small-business owner, and I'm interested in financing for entrepreneurial start-ups. I know this type of loan is harder to acquire than some other types, and I'd just like some more information.

★： You're right. With entrepreneurial ventures, there is more risk involved for the lender, so that complicates things. If you have assets to serve as collateral, however, there are some options we can talk about.

☆： OK. But first I think you'd better tell me what kinds of assets would be acceptable.

Question: What will the man probably explain next?

28

全文訳 ★： スティール国際銀行へようこそお越しくださいました。本日はどのような ご用件でしょうか？

☆： 私は小規模企業の経営者なのですが，起業家のスタートアップへの融資 に興味があるんです。この種のローンを獲得するのは他種のローンより も難しいことはわかっていまして，とにかくもう少し情報が欲しいんで す。

★： おっしゃるとおりです。ベンチャー企業に関しましては，貸し手により 大きなリスクが伴いますので，事態は複雑化します。ですが，担保にな る資産をお持ちでしたら，相談できる選択肢がいくつかございます。

☆： わかりました。でもその前に，どんな種類の資産が認められるのかを教 えていただければと思います。

質問：男性はおそらく次に何を説明するか。

選択肢の訳 1 銀行が女性の会社に投資する額。

2 女性のローンが承認される時期。

3 女性の投機的事業にリスクが伴う理由。

4 女性がローンの審査に通るために必要なもの。

解説 スタートアップへの融資に興味がある女性と銀行員の男性の会話。男性 は2つ目の発言で，女性に collateral「担保」になる資産があれば選択 肢をいくつか相談できると述べている。そして，女性は続く最後の発言 で，まずは担保として認められる資産の種類の説明を求めている。それ を違う表現で言い換えた **4** が正解。

No.6 – 解答 ②

スクリプト ☆： Hi, Lars. How was your performance review?

★： It left a bad taste in my mouth.

☆： Oh, really? Was your boss hard on you?

★： I'd say so. Her criticisms were so petty. She focused on little things that didn't go right with the projects I've been working on and gave me no credit for all my successes.

☆： At least she lets you manage your own projects.

★： For now, but she said she wants to be more involved in my next project. I'm worried that I'll have less control in the future.

Question: What is one reason the man is annoyed?

全文訳 ☆： こんにちは，ラース。勤務評価はどうだった？

★： 後味の悪さが残ったよ。

☆： あら，本当に？ 上司はあなたに厳しかったの？

★： そう言えるだろうね。彼女の批判はごくささいなことだったよ。僕が取 り組んできたプロジェクトでうまくいかなかった細かなことばかりに目 を向けて，うまくいったことはどれもまったく評価してくれなかったん

だ。

☆： 少なくとも担当プロジェクトの管理は任されているわよね。

★： 今のところはそうだけど，僕の次のプロジェクトにはもっとかかわりたいと言っていたな。今後はあまり思うようにできなくなるのではないかと心配だよ。

質問：男性が悩んでいる理由の1つは何か。

選択肢の訳
1 今後はもっと長い時間働かなければならないだろう。
2 上司が彼の業績を認めていない。
3 どのプロジェクトに取り組むかを決められなかった。
4 上司が彼の最新のプロジェクトを中止した。

解説 勤務評価に納得のいかない様子の男性は，2つ目の発言で，上司の批判は非常に petty「ささいな」ことで，プロジェクトでの little things that didn't go right ばかりに注目し，all my successes を評価しなかったと説明している。この上司の姿勢を「業績を認めていない」とまとめた **2** が正解。

No.7 - 解答 ②

スクリプト ☆： Hey, Tom. Did you hear the city council is raising parking fees downtown?

★： Yes, it's ridiculous.

☆： I guess they're concerned about traffic congestion. Maybe they're hoping more people will ride the bus.

★： But I heard some council members are pushing to raise the bus fares, too.

☆： Really? Well, repairing the sidewalks downtown should be a priority. They're in terrible condition. Fixing them would encourage more people to walk around downtown, which would provide a real boost to local businesses. You know how they've been struggling recently.

★： That's a good idea. Maybe you should run for city council!

Question: What does the woman imply?

全文訳 ☆： ねえ，トム。市議会が中心街の駐車料金を値上げする予定だって聞いた？

★： ああ，ばかげているよね。

☆： 交通渋滞のことを心配しているんでしょうね。たぶんもっと多くの人にバスに乗ってほしいと思っているのよ。

★： だけど一部の議員はバス料金の値上げも推し進めているって聞いたよ。

☆： 本当に？ でもね，中心街の歩道の補修が優先されるべきだわ。ひどい状態だもの。歩道を補修すれば，もっと多くの人たちが中心街を歩き回るようになって，そのことが地元企業を大きく後押しするはずよ。このと

30

ころずっと業績不振なのは知っているでしょう。
- ★：それはいい考えだね。市議会に立候補した方がいいかもしれないよ！

質問：女性は暗に何と言っているか。

選択肢の訳
1 中心街でバスに乗る人が減るだろう。
2 中心街の企業はより多くの支援を必要としている。
3 市議会への立候補を検討するだろう。
4 歩道の補修には費用がかかり過ぎるだろう。

解説 女性は3つ目の発言で，ひどい状態の歩道を補修すれば中心街を歩く人が増え，そのことが業績不振にあえぐ地元企業にとってa real boost「大きな後押し」になると予測している。つまり，中心街の企業にはもっと支援が必要だと暗に言っていることになる。

No.8 －解答

スクリプト
- ★：Brenda, the karate school said that they currently don't have space for new students, so we should check back in a month.
- ☆：I wasn't thrilled about signing Tyler up for karate, anyway. I still feel he's too young.
- ★：How about baseball? He said he wanted to play, and there's that local kids' league.
- ☆：Sure. I heard they're looking for a volunteer coach, too, and you love watching baseball.
- ★：Yes, but you actually played softball in college. You'd be more competent than I would.
- ☆：I do have free time on the weekends. Let's contact them and see what they say.

Question: What will the couple likely do?

全文訳
- ★：ブレンダ，空手教室の話では，今のところ新規生を受け入れる余裕はないから，1カ月後にもう一度問い合わせてほしいということだよ。
- ☆：いずれにしても，私はタイラーを空手教室に入れることにあまり乗り気ではなかったわ。幼過ぎると今でも思っているの。
- ★：野球はどうだい？ 本人もやってみたいと言っていたし，例の地元の子供リーグがあるじゃないか。
- ☆：そうよね。ボランティアのコーチを探しているとも聞いたし，あなたは野球を見るのが大好きよね。
- ★：ああ，でも君は実際に大学でソフトボールをしていたよね。君の方が僕より適任じゃないかな。
- ☆：確かに週末には自由な時間があるわ。連絡を取って意見を聞いてみましょう。

質問：夫婦はおそらく何をするか。

選択肢の訳　**1**　地元の野球リーグについて問い合わせる。
2　来月空手教室に連絡を取る。
3　タイラーをボランティアプログラムに参加させる。
4　今週末に家族でソフトボールをする。

解説　息子を空手教室に入れることに乗り気ではなかった妻に対して，夫は地元に子供リーグがある野球を提案し，妻も賛成している。そして，ソフトボール経験者でコーチも務められそうな妻が，最後の発言で Let's contact them and see what they say. と述べているので，正解は **1**。夫婦の考えは空手から野球へと移っているので，**2** は誤り。

No.**9** – 解答 ④

スクリプト　★： Excuse me. I'm having some problems with my new aquarium. Can you help me?

☆： I'll do my best. What's your problem?

★： Well, for whatever reason, I can't seem to keep my fish alive.

☆： Oh dear, that *is* a problem. Have you checked the water's pH and ammonia levels?

★： I didn't know I was supposed to.

☆： You need to test the water regularly — at least once a week. This kit has everything you need to test and adjust the pH balance.

★： OK, I'll try it. My next problem is that the water keeps getting cloudy and green.

☆： That's easy to solve. We sell filters that will purify the water. Also, do you have any bottom feeders in your tank?

★： I have a couple of shrimp in there at the moment.

☆： Well, I recommend that you buy a few catfish, too. They will go a long way to keeping your tank clean by eating the extra food and waste that settles on the bottom.

Question: What is one thing the man is advised to do?

全文訳　★： すみません。新しい水槽のことで困っているんですが。助けてもらえますか？

☆： できるだけのことはいたします。どんなことでお困りですか？

★： えー，どんな理由かはわからないんですが，どうも魚を生かしておくことができないんです。

☆： おやまあ，それは本当に問題じゃないですか。水の pH 値とアンモニア値は調べましたか？

★： そんなことをしなくてはならないとは知りませんでした。

☆： 水は定期的に検査する必要があります。最低週 1 回ですね。このキットに，pH バランスを検査して調節するのに必要な物が全部入っています。

32

★：わかりました，やってみます。次の問題は，水がだんだん濁って緑色になってくることです。
☆：それは簡単に解決できます。当店では水を浄化するフィルターを販売しています。それと，タンクには何か底魚を入れていますか？
★：今のところ小エビを数匹入れています。
☆：そうですね，ナマズも2，3匹ご購入されることをお勧めします。ナマズは，余分な食べ物や底にたまるごみを食べてくれるので，タンクをきれいに保つのにとても役に立ちます。

質問：男性がするように勧められていることの1つは何か。

選択肢の訳
1 もっと頻繁にフィルターを交換する。
2 タンク内の小エビを取り除く。
3 タンクに入れる食べ物を少なくする。
4 毎週水質を調べる。

解説 ペットを扱う店での店員（女）と客（男）の会話。アドバイスをしているのは女性なので，彼女の発言に注目する。彼女のアドバイスは「定期的に水質を検査する」「浄化フィルターを設置する」「底魚を入れる」の3つ。このうち1つ目のアドバイスが **4** と合致する。「底魚」とは海底や川底に住む魚のこと。go a long way to *do*「～するのに大いに役立つ」。

No.10 解答 正答率 ★75%以上

スクリプト
☆：Thank you for shopping at Riverside Organic Foods. Would you be interested in joining our frequent buyer program?
○：I don't know. How would we benefit?
☆：You'd receive a 10% discount on all products in our store and 5% off at our restaurant. Up to four family members could take advantage of the discounts.
★：That sounds good. How much does membership cost?
☆：It's free as long as you purchase $300 of our products a year. You'd receive the 10% discount on those products, so it's a great deal.
○：What happens if we don't spend the $300?
☆：In that case, we would charge you a membership fee of $30 for the year.
★：It's worth considering. I like the fact that everything you sell is organic, and your restaurant is great.
○：True, honey, but we don't get out this way very often. Once or twice a year at most.
☆：It's easy to order online. We can ship to anywhere in the country. You'd have to pay a shipping fee, of course.

★： Hmm . . . The shipping fee makes the deal less attractive.

○： And we can already get a fair selection of organic products at our local supermarket. I think we'll pass for now.

☆： That's fine. Here's our brochure with details of the program in case you change your mind.

Question: What is one reason the couple rejects the frequent buyer program?

全文訳 ☆： リバーサイド・オーガニック食品でお買い物いただきありがとうございます。当店のお得意さまプログラムへの加入に関心はございませんか？

○： わからないわ。どんなメリットがあるの？

☆： 店内の全商品が10%引きに，当店のレストランが5%引きになります。ご家族4名さままでが割引をご利用になれます。

★： それはよさそうだ。会費はいくらかな？

☆： 当店の商品を年間300ドルご購入さえしていただければ無料です。その商品も10%引きになりますから，とてもお得です。

○： その300ドルを使わなかったらどうなるの？

☆： その場合，その年は会費30ドル請求させていただきます。

★： 検討する価値はあるね。こちらで売っている物が全部オーガニックというところが気に入っているし，レストランはとてもおいしいしね。

○： そうだけど，あなた，こっち方面にはそうしょっちゅうは出かけないわよ。せいぜい年に1度か2度だわ。

☆： インターネットで注文していただくのが簡単です。全国どこでも配送いたします。もちろん送料はお支払いいただかなければなりませんが。

★： ふむ……送料がかかるとなるとお得感が薄れるな。

○： それに，今では地元のスーパーマーケットでかなりの品ぞろえのオーガニック商品が買えるわよ。今のところは見送ろうと思うわ。

☆： 結構ですよ。お気が変わったときのために，プログラムの詳細が載ったパンフレットをどうぞ。

質問： 夫婦がお得意さまプログラムを断る理由の1つは何か。

選択肢の訳 **1** 全商品が割引になるわけではない。

2 彼らの欲しい商品がインターネットでは手に入らない。

3 彼らはあまり頻繁にはその店に行かないだろう。

4 彼らは会費が高過ぎると思っている。

解説 当初，夫は前向きだが，慎重な妻は後半で we don't get out this way very often と冷静にコメントしている。そして，夫もオンラインショッピングに送料がかかると知ると，考えを変えて less attractive と言っている。妻が言うように来店の機会が少ないことが，断っている理由である。したがって **3** が正解。

A

スクリプト **Sleep and Dementia**

Researchers in France have been studying possible causes of dementia, a condition in which a person experiences a severe loss of cognitive function. They investigated whether the amount of sleep a person gets in middle age plays a role in the development of the condition. Using self-reported sleep data from a large-scale lifestyle survey, the researchers looked at 8,000 participants who had been research subjects since 1985. The team found that, compared to participants who reported sleeping seven hours per night in their 50s and 60s, those who regularly got six hours of sleep or less per night were 30% more likely to develop dementia in later decades.

While this finding suggests that insufficient sleep could be a contributing factor in the development of dementia, it is not conclusive. It could be that lack of sleep in middle age is actually an early symptom of dementia, rather than a cause. However, a neurologist who commented on the study thinks this is probably not the case, as the poor sleeping habits arose such a long time before any of the subjects were diagnosed with dementia. Additionally, she points out that the first biological change that leads to dementia — the buildup of certain proteins in the brain — typically does not begin that early on.

Questions

No.11 What is one thing the researchers in France examined?
No.12 What does the neurologist believe?

全文訳 **睡眠と認知症**

フランスの研究者たちは，人が認知機能の深刻な喪失を経験する病気である認知症の考えられる原因について研究し続けてきた。彼らは中高年期の人が取る睡眠時間がこの病気の発症に役割を果たしているかどうかを調査した。大規模な生活様式調査から得た自己申告の睡眠データを使って，研究者たちは1985年から研究対象者となっていた8千人の参加者を調べた。研究チームは，50代と60代で一晩当たり7時間の睡眠を申告した参加者と比べると，一晩当たり6時間以下の睡眠時間を規則的に取っていた参加者の方が，その後数十年で認知症を発症する可能性が30%高くなることを発見した。

この調査結果は睡眠不足が認知症の発症の一因になっている可能性を示唆しているが，決定的なものではない。中高年期における睡眠不足は，実際は認知症の初期症状であって，原因ではないかもしれないのだ。しかしながら，その研究についてコメントした神経学者は，これはおそらく事実ではないと考えている。どの被験者も認知症と診断されるずっと以前に，不適切な睡眠習慣が発生していたからだ。さらに彼女は，認知症

へとつながる最初の生物学的変化，つまり脳内でのある種のタンパク質の蓄積は，通常，そこまで早い時期に始まることはないと指摘している。

語句　dementia「認知症」，conclusive「決定的な」，neurologist「神経学者」，buildup「蓄積」

No.11解答 ④ ....

質問の訳　フランスの研究者たちが調査したことの1つは何か。

選択肢の訳　**1**　認知症を患った人たちは睡眠時間が長くなることを示す証拠。
2　若者たちによって報告されたさまざまな睡眠障害。
3　認知症の治療としての生活様式の変化。
4　中高年の人たちの睡眠パターン。

解説　第1段落前半に，the amount of sleep a person gets in middle age が認知症の発症に果たす役割を調査したとあり，段落の最後で，50代と60代で一晩の睡眠時間が異なる参加者を比較したところ，後の認知症の発症率に差異があることがわかった，と述べられている。よって，正解は **4**。

No.12解答 ② ....

質問の訳　その神経学者はどう考えているか。

選択肢の訳　**1**　タンパク質の蓄積は必ずしも認知症の兆候ではない。
2　参加者の睡眠パターンはおそらく認知症が原因ではなかった。
3　認知症のよりよい治療法が間もなく開発されるだろう。
4　中高年の人たちは一般に眠るのに苦労している。

解説　第2段落中ほどの，神経学者がおそらく事実ではないと考えている this とは，中高年期の睡眠不足が認知症の初期症状の可能性があること。その理由として，認知症の診断よりもずっと以前に睡眠不足の習慣があったことが挙げられ，最後に，認知症につながる the first biological change がそれほど早く表れることは通常はないと指摘している，とあるので，正解は **2**。

B

スクリプト　**Soybeans in the United States**

Vegetarian products made with soybeans are commonplace on American supermarket shelves today, but, surprisingly, efforts to introduce such products started over a century ago. In 1917, the US government commissioned Yamei Kin, a Chinese-born American scientist, to go to China. Her mission was to research soybeans as a substitute for meat products to address wartime food shortages. Kin had been promoting soy products because their production was far less resource-intensive than that of meat. Upon her return, she experimented with processing methods, knowing that to be successful in the US, not only

36

did soy products need to taste good but they also had to look appealing.

Other scientists were impressed with the range of foods that Kin produced from soybeans. In some instances, they could not distinguish soy products from meat. However, when wartime scarcities ended, so did interest in soybeans, meaning that Kin would not live to see soy products take hold among the US public. Nevertheless, the agriculture industry adopted soybeans for use as food for livestock and as a source of oil. Later, in the 1960s and '70s, American fascination with Eastern spiritual practices and increasing interest in healthy eating finally led to soy products becoming available in American supermarkets.

Questions

No.13 Why was the US government interested in soybeans in 1917?

No.14 What helped soy products to become popular with the American public?

全文訳 **米国の大豆**

大豆を使って作られたベジタリアン製品は，今日では米国のスーパーマーケットの棚に当たり前に置かれているが，驚いたことに，そういった製品の導入への努力は百年以上前に始まっていた。1917 年に，米国政府は中国生まれの米国の科学者であるヤメイ・キンに中国に行くよう依頼した。彼女の任務は，戦時中の食糧不足に対処するために，大豆を肉製品の代用品として使う研究をすることだった。大豆製品の生産は肉製品の生産と比べるとはるかに消費する資源が少なかったので，キンは大豆製品をずっと推奨していたのだ。帰国後すぐに，彼女は複数の加工方法を試してみた。米国で成功するためには，大豆製品に味のよさが必要なのはもちろんのこと，見た目も魅力的でなければならないことがわかっていたからだ。

ほかの科学者たちは，キンが大豆から作った食品の幅に感銘を受けた。場合によっては，彼らは大豆製品と肉とを区別することができなかった。しかしながら，戦時中の食糧不足が終わると，大豆への関心も終わりを告げ，キンは大豆製品が米国国民の間に定着するのを見ることなく亡くなることになった。それでも，農産業界は家畜の餌や油の原料として使用するために大豆を導入した。その後，1960 年代と 70 年代に，米国人が東洋の精神修行に魅力を感じ，健康的な食事への関心が高まったことで，最終的に米国のスーパーマーケットで大豆製品が入手できるようになったのだ。

語句 resource-intensive「資源消費型の」，take hold「根づく」

No.**13** 解答 **1**

質問の訳 なぜ米国政府は 1917 年に大豆に興味を持ったのか。

選択肢の訳 **1** 一部の種類の肉が簡単には手に入らなかった。
2 研究により肉よりも健康的であることが示された。
3 ほかの食品よりも長く保存することができた。
4 ほかの食品よりも加工するのが簡単だった。

解説 第1段落前半で、米国政府は1917年にキンを中国に派遣し、その任務は wartime food shortages に対処するために大豆を a substitute for meat products として使う研究をすることだった、とある。つまり、肉が不足していたことが理由なので、正解は **1**。

No.14 解答 ④

質問の訳 大豆製品が米国国民の間で人気を得るのに役立ったことは何か。

選択肢の訳
1 農産業界が1960年代に盛んに推奨した。
2 科学者たちが肉のような味にする方法を学んだ。
3 一部の食品業界による広範な使用。
4 20世紀後半における文化的変化。

解説 第2段落最後に、1960年代・70年代に米国人が Eastern spiritual practices に魅了され、healthy eating への関心が高まったことが、最終的に大豆製品の普及へとつながった、と述べられている。この時期に起きた米国人の変化を cultural shifts「文化的変化」と簡潔にまとめた **4** が正解。

スクリプト **Marketing Movies**

When movie studios market films, they face tough decisions about promotional advertising. Movies usually open in theaters first and are later released in various formats, such as DVDs and digital streaming. One option is for studios to put all their resources into promoting the initial theater release in the hope of maximizing box-office profits. Alternatively, studios can divide their budget so that advertising funds are available when the film is released in other formats. A group of marketing researchers investigated which approach offers the most earning potential. They found that, generally, advertising becomes less effective at influencing people's purchasing decisions over time, which indicates that a massive push during the initial theater release is the ideal strategy.

Additionally, it seems the genre of the movie may be a factor in how much should be spent on advertising. Science fiction movies, for example, appear to make the largest profits when large prerelease campaigns with lots of ads are used. This is because advertising for these movies has what the researchers call "wear-in appeal": the more the ads are viewed, the greater their impact. Action movies, on the other hand, tend to make bigger profits with less prerelease advertising because viewers appear to quickly tire of such ads.

Questions
No.15 What did the researchers find about movie advertising in general?
No.16 What do we learn about ads for science fiction movies?

全文訳 映画をマーケティングする

映画をマーケティングするとき，映画製作会社は販売促進広告に関して厳しい決断を迫られる。映画は通常，最初に劇場で公開され，後に DVD やデジタルストリーミングといった，さまざまなフォーマットで発売される。選択肢の 1 つは，興行収入の最大化を期待して，映画製作会社が最初の劇場公開の宣伝にすべての資金を投入することだ。あるいは，映画製作会社は予算を分割して，映画がほかのフォーマットで発売されたときに広告資金を使えるようにしておくこともできる。マーケティング研究者のグループが，どちらの手法が最も多くの収益をもたらす可能性があるのかを調査した。彼らがわかったのは，一般に，広告は時間がたつにつれて人々の購買決定への影響という点で効果が低下するということで，これは，最初の劇場公開中の大規模な売り込みが理想的な方策であることを示している。

それに加えて，映画のジャンルが，広告に費やすべき金額を決める要因である可能性があるようだ。例えば，SF 映画は，多くの広告を用いた大々的な公開前のキャンペーンが活用されたときに，最も大きな利益が得られるようだ。これは，こういった映画の広告には，広告を目にする回数が増えれば増えるほどその影響が大きくなるという，研究者たちが「ウェア・イン・アピール」と呼ぶものがあるからだ。一方，アクション映画は，視聴者が公開前の広告にすぐに飽きてしまうようなので，そういった広告が少ない方がより大きな利益を上げる傾向がある。

語句 box-office profit「興行収入」，prerelease「一般公開前の」

No.15 解答 ②

質問の訳 一般的な映画広告について研究者たちは何がわかったか。

選択肢の訳 1 利用可能なすべてのフォーマットを平等に対象にすべきだ。
2 早く実施されると利益が増える可能性が高くなる。
3 最近は映画製作会社による優先度が低くなっている。
4 映画製作会社だけで担当するべきではない。

解説 研究者たちが発見した一般論は，第 1 段落最後で語られている。そこには，概して広告は時間の経過とともに less effective になり，このことは最初の劇場公開中の a massive push「大規模な売り込み」が the ideal strategy だと示している，とある。よって，正解は **2**。フォーマットの違いによって生じる利益の差については触れられていないので，**1** は誤り。

No.16 解答 ③

質問の訳 SF 映画の広告について何がわかるか。

選択肢の訳 1 あまりに多くのアクションシーンを頻繁に売りにしている。
2 映画の公開後の方が影響が大きくなる。
3 繰り返し目にすると効果が高まる。
4 劇場で見た方が面白くない。

解説 第2段落中ほどで，SF映画の広告には研究者たちがwear-in appealと呼ぶものがあって，目にする回数が多ければ多いほど，その影響が大きくなる，と述べられている。このことを，繰り返し目にするとmore effectiveであると言い換えた **3** が正解。

#

スクリプト American Camels

  Today, camels are an iconic symbol of the Middle East and North Africa. Surprisingly, however, evidence indicates that they originated in North America. Fossils suggest that the last indigenous camels in North America died out many thousands of years ago. Then, in the mid-1800s, the US government imported several dozen camels to deliver military supplies to remote areas. It was thought that the animals would be well-suited to the harsh desert climate of the southwestern United States. Indeed, initial field exercises were so successful that a high-ranking official suggested acquiring an additional thousand camels. When the American Civil War broke out shortly after the camels had been put to work, however, the plan was abandoned.

  Some of the camels that had been brought over were sold to private businesses such as circuses and mining operations for their value as entertainment and labor, but a few were released and continued living in the desert. Although there were several wild-camel sightings over the following decades, their numbers were too few to create a stable population, and it is thought they disappeared completely. Now, over 100 years later, some scientists are considering reintroducing camels a second time.

Questions
No.17 Why did the US government import camels in the mid-1800s?
No.18 What do we learn about the camels that were released into the wild?

全文訳 米国のラクダ

  今日では，ラクダは中東や北アフリカを象徴する存在になっている。ところが，驚いたことに，北米が原産だったことが証拠により示されている。化石から，最後の北米原産のラクダが何千年も前に絶滅したことが示唆されているのだ。その後，1800年代半ばに，米国政府は遠隔地域に軍事物資を輸送するために数十頭のラクダを輸入した。その動物は米国南西部の厳しい砂漠気候に適していると考えられていた。実際に，最初の野外演習は大成功を収めたので，ある高級官僚は追加で千頭のラクダを入手することを提案した。しかしながら，ラクダが働き始めた直後に米国南北戦争が勃発し，その計画は中止になった。

  持ち込まれたラクダのうちの何頭かは，娯楽や労働力としての価値があるので，サーカスや採鉱会社といった民間企業に売り渡されたが，数頭は解放され，砂漠で生き続けた。その後数十年の間に，野生のラクダが数回目撃されたが，その数は安定した個体群

を形成するにはあまりに少なく，完全に絶滅したと考えられている。百年以上が経過した今，一部の科学者はもう一度ラクダを再導入することを検討している。

> 語句　iconic「象徴的な」，sighting「目撃」，reintroduce「（動植物）を再導入する」

No.17 解答 ①

質問の訳　なぜ米国政府は 1800 年代半ばにラクダを輸入したのか。

選択肢の訳
1　隔絶した地域に物資を供給するため。
2　外国との関係を改善するため。
3　砂漠地帯の生態系を回復させるため。
4　高級将校に贈り物として渡すため。

解説　第 1 段落中ほどの to deliver military supplies to remote areas から，米国政府がラクダを輸入したのは，軍事物資を遠隔地域に輸送するためだったことがわかる。1 では，この目的の deliver military supplies を supply goods と簡潔に表現し，remote areas を isolated regions と言い換えている。

No.18 解答 ③

質問の訳　野生に放されたラクダについて何がわかるか。

選択肢の訳
1　サーカスに売り渡すために捕獲された。
2　最終的に砂漠の至る所に分布した。
3　個体数が少な過ぎて存続できなかった。
4　百年近くの間，目撃され続けた。

解説　第 2 段落中ほどに，野生のラクダは数が少な過ぎたために create a stable population できなかった，とある。この状況を sustain itself「存続する」ことができなかったと言い換えた 3 が正解。サーカスに売り渡されたのは野生に放されなかったラクダなので，1 は誤り。野性のラクダの目撃情報は数件しかなく，目撃され続けたのは数十年の間のことなので，2 と 4 も誤り。

E

スクリプト　**Antivenins**

Every year, millions of people are bitten by venomous snakes. Although treatments known as antivenins exist, lives that could be saved are being lost due to supply problems and substandard products. In developing countries, snakebite victims who cannot afford proper treatments often receive partial doses or cheap antivenins that are ineffective for the snakes that bit them. To make matters worse, when these low-grade antivenin treatments are unsuccessful, victims turn instead to traditional healers. As a result, antivenin sales fall, causing some manufacturers to stop producing them altogether.

Currently, antivenins are made by injecting snake venom into animals so that the animals produce proteins called antibodies, which are then extracted. These negate the effects of the venom. However, such products often have serious side effects. Furthermore, they have to be stored at low temperatures, meaning that victims must often travel for hours to hospitals, during which time their symptoms worsen. However, a new antivenin is being developed that may solve these problems. It is an artificial substance that does not need to be refrigerated. As a result, it could be kept on hand and administered immediately after a snakebite, greatly improving victims' chances of survival.

Questions

No.19 What is one problem for snakebite victims in developing countries?

No.20 What is one thing we learn about the new antivenin?

全文訳 **蛇毒血清**

　毎年，何百万という人たちが毒蛇にかまれている。蛇毒血清として知られる治療薬は存在するが，供給の問題や規格外製品が原因で，救われるはずの命が失われている。発展途上国では，蛇にかまれても適切な治療を受ける余裕のない被害者が，服用量の一部だけを投与されたり，かんできた蛇には効果がない安価な蛇毒血清を投与されることが多い。さらに悪いことに，これらの低品質な蛇毒血清による治療が失敗に終わると，被害者はその代わりに伝統治療者を頼りにする。その結果，蛇毒血清の売り上げは落ち込み，完全に生産を中止してしまう製造業者も出てくるのだ。

　現在，蛇毒血清は，動物が抗体と呼ばれるタンパク質を作り出せるよう，蛇の毒液を動物に注入することによって作られており，抗体は後に採取される。この抗体が毒液の効果を打ち消すのだ。ところが，そういった製品は深刻な副作用を伴うことが多い。さらに，低温で保管する必要があることから，被害者は何時間もかけて病院まで移動しなければならないことが多くなり，その間に症状が悪化する。しかしながら，これらの問題を解決するかもしれない新たな蛇毒血清が目下開発中である。それは冷蔵しておく必要のない人工物質である。結果として，それを手元に置いておき，蛇にかまれた直後に投与できれば，被害者の生存の可能性が大幅に向上するかもしれないのだ。

語句 antivenin「蛇毒血清」，venomous「毒のある」，substandard「標準以下の」，healer「信仰療法家」，venom「毒液」，negate「～を打ち消す」

No.**19** 解答 **3**

質問の訳 発展途上国における蛇にかまれた被害者にとっての問題の１つは何か。

選択肢の訳
1 　かんできた蛇の種類を特定するのが難しい。
2 　伝統的な薬は通例手に入らない。
3 　時々低品質の蛇毒血清を投与される。
4 　医者が頻繁に過度な量の蛇毒血清を投与する。

42

解説 第1段落中ほどで，発展途上国では，proper treatments を受ける余裕のない被害者は，partial doses であったり，かんできた蛇には効かない cheap antivenins を投与されることが多いと述べられている。**3** では，この問題点を時々poor-quality antivenins を投与されると言い換えている。

No.20 解答

質問の訳 新たな蛇毒血清についてわかることの1つは何か。
選択肢の訳
1 ほかの蛇毒血清よりも高価である。
2 生産することで動物に害が及ぶ。
3 蛇に軽くかまれた場合にしか効果がない。
4 室温で保管することができる。

解説 新たな蛇毒血清に関する情報は第2段落後半で語られている。そこには，冷蔵しておく必要のない an artificial substance なので，手元に置いておいて，かまれた後すぐに投与できるようになる，とある。この冷蔵の必要がないという利点を room temperature で保管できると言い換えた **4** が正解。

F

You have 10 seconds to read the situation and Question No. 21.

Well, the good news is your x-ray showed you've got a clean break. Over-the-counter painkillers will probably be sufficient to manage the pain. But, if it becomes unbearable, I can write a prescription for you. Now, you'll be in this cast for a few weeks. The cast immobilizes your ankle so that you won't interfere with the healing process by moving it around. Once the cast is off, we'll check your progress and see if you'll need to wear a special boot for a few more weeks. While you're in the cast, be sure to keep your ankle elevated higher than your knee whenever you can. This helps reduce any swelling. Now, let's get you some crutches to help you get around. We can adjust them for your height, and if it's your first time using them, you can ask a nurse to give you a quick tutorial.

Now mark your answer on your answer sheet.

全文訳
さて，よい知らせですが，レントゲン写真から，きれいに折れていることがわかりました。市販の鎮痛剤でおそらく十分に痛みに対処できるでしょう。ですが，我慢できな

くなるようでしたら，処方箋を書くこともできます。今後，数週間はこのギプスをはめていただきます。ギプスは，足首を動かしても治癒過程の妨げにならないように，足首を固定します。ギプスが外れたら，経過を確認して，さらに数週間特別なブーツを履いていただく必要があるかどうかを調べます。ギプスをはめている間は，できる限り足首を膝よりも高く上げておくように心がけてください。これはむくみの軽減に役立ちます。それでは，歩行補助用の松葉づえをお持ちしましょう。身長に合わせて調節できますし，使うのが初めてでしたら，看護師に頼んで簡単な個人指導も受けられます。

No.21 解答 ①

状況の訳 あなたは足首を骨折したが，痛みはそれほどひどくはない。あなたはこれまで一度も松葉づえを使ったことがない。病院で，医者があなたに次のことを告げる。

質問の訳 あなたは次に何をすべきか。

選択肢の訳
1 個人指導を依頼する。
2 特別なブーツを履く。
3 もう一度レントゲン検査を受ける。
4 処方箋を依頼する。

語句 over-the-counter「（薬が）店頭で買える，市販の」，cast「ギプス」，immobilize「～を固定する」，tutorial「個人指導」

解説 今後の治療方針を一通り説明した後，医者はあなたに松葉づえを渡すと告げ，使うのが初めてなら看護師に頼んで a quick tutorial を受けるようにと指示している。したがって，次にすべきことは **1**。**2** は数週間後の診断の結果次第であり，**4** は痛みに耐えられなくなったときのことなので誤り。

G

スクリプト

You have 10 seconds to read the situation and Question No. 22.

This vacuum cleaner, the ThunderClean 100, is hands down our most powerful model. It has no trouble sucking up large volumes of debris, including pet hair. But be aware it's so powerful that when it's used on a rug, it may actually start sucking up the rug itself and get stuck, so it's recommended only for hard floors or fixed wall-to-wall carpeting. Next up is the DeepVac. It's got enough power to suck up everything from pet hair to sand, and it has six power settings to accommodate all surfaces, including rugs and tiles. And then there's the DustGuster. Its unique shape makes it the best for cleaning hard-to-reach corners of the house. The same goes for its sister model, the DustGuster Plus, which is lighter and has longer battery life. Neither of these is quite as effective as the other models when it comes to removing pet hair, though.

Now mark your answer on your answer sheet.

全文訳

　こちらの掃除機は，サンダークリーン100と言いまして，間違いなく当店で最も強力な機種です。ペットの毛を含め，大量のごみを何の問題もなく吸い取ります。ですが，大変強力なため，ラグの上で使うと実際にラグ自体を吸い上げ始めて詰まってしまう可能性があるので，堅木の床か敷き詰めて固定されたカーペットにのみ推奨されていることをご承知おきください。次にご紹介するのはディープヴァックです。ペットの毛から砂まで何でも吸い取る十分なパワーがありますし，6段階のパワー設定が備わっていて，ラグやタイルを含め，どんな表面にも対応できます。そして次はダストガスターです。独自の形状により，家の届きにくい角を掃除するのに最適です。姉妹機種のダストガスター・プラスにも同じことが言えますが，そちらの方が軽量で，バッテリーの寿命が長いです。ですが，ペットの毛の除去という点では，これら2機種はどちらもほかの機種ほどは効果を発揮しません。

No.22 解答 ②

状況の訳　あなたは掃除機を買いに来ている。あなたの家には堅木の床と数枚の小さなラグがある。あなたは犬を飼っている。販売員があなたに次のことを告げる。

質問の訳　あなたはどの掃除機を買うべきか。

選択肢の訳　**1**　サンダークリーン100。
　2　ディープヴァック。
　3　ダストガスター。
　4　ダストガスター・プラス。

語句　hands down「間違いなく」，wall-to-wall「床一面を覆う」

解説　状況で述べられている条件から，あなたが買うべきなのは，ペットの毛から砂まで何でも吸い取るパワーがあり，6段階のパワー設定によりラグにも対応可能だと紹介された**2**のディープヴァックである。**1**はパワーがあり過ぎてラグには推奨されておらず，**3**と**4**はペットの毛の掃除には不向きなので誤り。

H

スクリプト

You have 10 seconds to read the situation and Question No. 23.

We offer a range of different laundry services for hotel guests. If you need several items cleaned, I recommend our Drop-and-Go service. I can provide you with a laundry bag. Just put the items you want to be washed inside the bag and leave it outside your door. We send all our laundry to an off-premises service, so turnaround is generally about 24 hours. If you have items that need

45

to be dry-cleaned, like a suit jacket or slacks, we can take those here at the front desk. Those are also sent out to a service and are usually returned within 24 hours. Of course, we know that not all guests have time to wait, so we can also recommend an express dry cleaner a few blocks from here. They normally only take a few hours to clean a garment, and we've never had a guest complain about their services.

Now mark your answer on your answer sheet.

全文訳

　私どもはホテルのお客さまにさまざまな種類のランドリーサービスを提供しています。何点かクリーニングが必要でしたら，当ホテルのドロップ・アンド・ゴー・サービスをお勧めします。お客さまにランドリーバッグをお渡しします。そのバッグの中に洗濯をご希望される物を入れて，ドアの外に置いていただくだけです。お預かりした洗濯物はすべて外部のサービスに送りますので，所要時間は通常約 24 時間です。スーツのジャケットやスラックスなど，ドライクリーニングが必要な物をお持ちでしたら，こちらのフロントでお預かりすることができます。そちらもサービスに出して，通常 24 時間以内に戻ります。もちろん，待つ時間があるお客さまばかりではないことは承知していますので，ここから数ブロック先のスピード仕上げのドライクリーニング店もお薦めできます。通常は衣類 1 点のクリーニングに数時間しかかかりませんし，その店のサービスに関してお客さまから苦情をいただいたことは一度もありません。

No.23 解答 ④

状況の訳　あなたは出張中で，スーツのジャケットに染みが付いていることに今気が付いた。時刻は午後 2 時で，あなたは明日の午前中にプレゼンテーションがある。ホテルの受付係があなたに次のことを告げる。

質問の訳　あなたはジャケットをどうすべきか。

選択肢の訳　1　ドロップ・アンド・ゴー・サービスに送る。
　2　フロントに持って行く。
　3　自分できれいにしてみる。
　4　近くのドライクリーニング店に持って行く。

語句　off-premises「敷地外の」，turnaround「（受注から引き渡しまでの）所要時間」

解説　現在の時刻は午後 2 時で，明日午前中のプレゼンテーションまでにクリーニング済みのジャケットの受け取りが可能という条件を満たすのは，衣類 1 点を数時間でクリーニングしてくれて，サービスも安心だと紹介された近くの an express dry cleaner のみである。1 は引き渡しまでに通常約 24 時間かかり，2 も 24 時間かかる可能性があるので誤り。3 に関しては触れられていない。

(スクリプト)

You have 10 seconds to read the situation and Question No. 24.

Here's your 8 a.m. commuter traffic update. A major five-car accident near Exit 4 on the Channel Freeway, heading into downtown, has resulted in the closure of four lanes there. Traffic is at a standstill from the start of the Channel Freeway, at Battery Bridge, all the way to the downtown area. Road crews are busy clearing the lanes, but this could take all morning. Commuters currently stuck on Battery Bridge are being advised to access downtown via the Martin Highway, which is accessible from Exit 5, which is one kilometer past the bridge. Commuters coming from the Randall Heights or Eastwick areas should use the exit just before the approach to the bridge to get on Sunset Road toward the Ocean Tunnel. It's your best bet as far as alternate routes downtown go. We'll be back in 15 minutes with another update.

Now mark your answer on your answer sheet.

(全文訳)

　午前8時の通勤交通の最新情報をお届けします。チャンネル高速道路の上り方面，4番出口付近にて車5台が絡む大事故が発生したため，現場では4車線が通行止めになっています。チャンネル高速道路の起点であるバッテリー橋から，街の中心部までの全区間で車の流れは止まっています。路上作業員が急いで車線の開通作業をしていますが，これには午前中いっぱいかかるかもしれません。現在バッテリー橋で動けなくなっている通勤者の方々には，マーティン街道経由で中心街に入ることをお勧めしています。マーティン街道には，橋の1キロ先にある5番出口から入ることができます。ランドールハイツあるいはイーストウィック地区からの通勤者の方々は，橋への進入路直前の出口を利用して，サンセット通りに降り，オーシャントンネルに向かってください。中心街への別ルートという点では，それが最善の選択です。15分後に次の最新情報をお届けします。

No.24 解答

(状況の訳) あなたはイーストウィックにある自宅から中心街の勤務先に車で向かっている最中に，ラジオで次の交通情報を聞く。あなたはまだバッテリー橋に到着していない。

(質問の訳) あなたはどのルートを通るべきか。

(選択肢の訳)
1　チャンネル高速道路。
2　バッテリー橋。
3　マーティン街道。
4　サンセット通り。

(語句) standstill「停止」，best bet「最善の策」

> **解説** イーストウィック地区からの通勤者に対しては，バッテリー橋への進入路直前の出口からサンセット通りに降り，オーシャントンネルに向かうのが，中心街への別ルートとして最善だと案内されている。あなたはまだ橋の手前にいるので，正解は **4**。**1** は中心街まで交通が止まっており，**3** はバッテリー橋で渋滞につかまっている通勤者に対して推奨されているルートなので誤り。

J

スクリプト

You have 10 seconds to read the situation and Question No. 25.

In the afternoon, we're supposed to check in with the full-time staff to see how we can help them. I usually check in with Martha first, but it really depends on what sort of work you're interested in. If writing is your thing, Martha writes copy for the ads. If you don't have experience, she'll probably ask you to begin with some basic spell-checking. Mark is in charge of everything related to graphic design. If you're confident in your skills, he will probably have some work for you. Otherwise, you can talk to his teammate, Hilda. She does the same kind of work, but her project has some easier tasks that she might want help with. Finally, if you want to work on fundamental business skills, you can assist the boss, Carol. She's always looking for help responding to clients' inquiries.

Now mark your answer on your answer sheet.

全文訳

午後には，私たちは社員に連絡を入れて，どんな手伝いができるか確認することになっています。普段，私はまずマーサに連絡を入れますが，とにかくあなたが興味を持っている職種次第ですね。書くことに関心があるなら，マーサは広告用のコピーを書いています。経験がない場合，たぶん基本的なスペルチェックから始めるよう頼まれるでしょう。マークはグラフィックデザインに関するあらゆることの責任者です。スキルに自信があるなら，たぶん彼はあなたに任せる仕事を持っているでしょう。自信がないなら，彼のチームメイトのヒルダと話してもいいでしょう。彼女は同種の仕事をしていますが，彼女のプロジェクトには，手伝いが欲しいかもしれない比較的簡単な作業がいくつかあります。最後に，基本的なビジネススキルを身に付けたいなら，上司のキャロルを手伝ってもいいでしょう。いつも彼女はクライアントからの問い合わせに対応するのに助けを求めています。

No.25 解答

状況の訳 あなたは広告会社のインターンとしての初日を迎えている。あなたはグラフィックデザイナーになりたいと思っているが，経験はまったくない。別のインターンがあなたのスケジュールを説明している。

質問の訳 あなたは今日の午後に誰と話をすべきか。
選択肢の訳
1 マーサ。
2 マーク。
3 ヒルダ。
4 キャロル。

語句 check in with ～「～に連絡を入れる」, *one's* thing「～の関心事」

解説 グラフィックデザイン関係の仕事をしているのは **2** のマークと **3** のヒルダの 2 人だが，**2** のマークは，あなたがスキルに自信がある場合に話をすべき人なので誤り。経験のないあなたは，手助けができそうな some easier tasks を含むプロジェクトを担当している **3** のヒルダと話をすべきである。**1** のマーサについては，If you don't have experience, she'll probably ask you to ... という表現に惑わされないように。

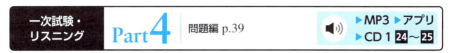

スクリプト

This is an interview with Aisha Chopra, who runs two vintage record shops.

Interviewer (I): Thanks for tuning in. Today, we're talking to Aisha Chopra. Welcome, Aisha.

Aisha Chopra (A): Thanks for having me.

I: Could you tell us a little about what you do?

A: Sure. I own and manage two shops that deal in vintage vinyl records and music merchandise, mainly from the 1960s, '70s, and '80s. I opened my first shop just over 15 years ago and my second one 5 years ago.

I: Interesting. How did you get into this kind of work?

A: My parents would always play music in the house, so I kind of grew up listening to old bands and musicians like Janis Joplin, the Doors, the Beatles, stuff like that. Plus, my dad loved to collect old stuff, which he kept all over the house — T-shirts from famous concerts, posters of rock stars, books, magazines, and, of course, thousands of old records. Then, when I was around eight or nine years old, he would take me to shows and fairs where all of this stuff was on sale. I started using my pocket money to buy things, and before I knew it, my collection had grown substantially; so much so, I was running out of space to keep it all.

I: What made you decide that you should start selling things yourself?

A: It just kind of happened. Actually, I wanted to teach, and that's what I started to do. Then, one of my friends took me to the flea market, where people were selling all kinds of used goods. Surprisingly, though, there weren't many people selling music. My collection of records was mainly in storage at the time, so I thought I'd get some of it sent to me and make a little money on the side. I was selling everything I put on sale, and before I knew it, I was making hundreds of dollars just from a few markets every month. From there, I started getting a bit more serious about it as a source of income.

I: And that led to opening your shops?

A: Yeah, kind of. One of my regular customers from the markets became my husband, and to cut a long story short, his parents used to run a small furniture store, but they closed it because they wanted to retire. My husband didn't want to take over the furniture store, so he suggested I use it to sell records and other things. His parents agreed, so I was very lucky to get that opportunity.

I: It sounds like it was a big success.

A: Not at first. Business was slow, and I was still working as a teacher for about a year so that we could afford to pay our rent. I'd teach during the week, then run to the shop on weekends. I was still going to fairs and spending countless hours combing the Internet for things to resell. I focus on rare goods, so, slowly but surely, word got out that my shop was the only place in town to get some very hard-to-find items. For example, I had records signed by people like David Bowie, Bob Dylan, and John Lennon. When business really picked up, I thought about moving to a bigger space, but the shop had a lot of sentimental value because my husband's parents had owned it. Instead, I decided to open a second shop, which is also doing great.

I: Well, Aisha, that's all the time we have today. Thanks so much for coming in, and I wish you continued success.

A: Thank you. I had a great time.

Questions

No.26 How did Aisha first become interested in selling vintage records and merchandise?

No.27 What is one reason Aisha decided to open a second shop?

全文訳

これは2軒のビンテージレコード店を経営しているアイシャ・チョプラとのインタビューです。

聞き手 (以下「聞」): チャンネルを合わせてくれてありがとう。今日は,アイシャ・チョプラとお話しします。ようこそ,アイシャ。

アイシャ・チョプラ (以下「ア」): お招きいただきありがとうございます。

聞: あなたのお仕事について少し教えていただけますか。

ア：わかりました。私は2軒の店を所有，経営していまして，主に1960年代，70年代，そして80年代のビンテージのアナログレコードと音楽関連商品を扱っています。15年と少し前に最初の店をオープンして，2軒目は5年前でした。

聞：興味深いですね。どういった経緯でこの種の仕事を始めたのですか。

ア：両親がいつも家で音楽をかけていたので，ジャニス・ジョプリンやドアーズ，ビートルズといったような，昔のバンドやミュージシャンを聴きながら育ったようなものです。それに加えて，父は古いものを集めるのが大好きで，家の至る所に保管していました。有名なコンサートのTシャツやロックスターのポスター，本，雑誌，そして，もちろん，何千枚という古いレコードもです。その後，私が8歳か9歳くらいだったころに，父は私をこういったものすべてが販売されているショーやフェアによく連れて行ってくれました。私は自分のお小遣いを使って買い物をし始め，いつの間にか，私のコレクションは膨大な数になっていて，あまりに増えたために，そのすべてを保管しておくにはスペースが足りなくなりました。

聞：ご自身で販売を始めることに決めたのはなぜですか。

ア：本当に偶然そうなったようなものです。実は，なりたかったのは教師で，それが私が最初にした仕事です。そして，友人の1人が私をフリーマーケットに連れて行ってくれて，そこでは人々があらゆる種類の中古品を販売していました。ですが，驚いたことに，音楽を販売している人はあまりいませんでした。私が収集したレコードは，その当時，ほとんどが倉庫に入っていたので，その一部を送ってもらって，少し副収入を得ようと思ったのです。売りに出した物は全部売れて，いつの間にか，毎月数回マーケットに参加するだけで数百ドルも稼いでいました。そこから，それが収入源になるのではないかと少し真剣に考えるようになりました。

聞：そして，そのことがお店のオープンにつながったのですね？

ア：ええ，そんなところです。マーケットでの常連客の1人が私の夫になって，手短に話しますと，彼の両親は以前に小さな家具店を経営していたのですが，引退したいという理由で閉店しました。夫は家具店を継ぎたくなかったので，私にそこを使ってレコードやその他の物を売ったらどうかと提案しました。彼の両親も賛成したので，私は非常に幸運なことにその機会に恵まれました。

聞：大成功だったようですね。

ア：最初は違いました。売り上げは振るわなかったですし，家賃を支払う余裕を得るために，およそ1年間はまだ教師として働いていました。平日は教師をして，週末は店に駆け付けていました。フェアにもまだ行っていましたし，転売する物を求めてインターネットをくまなく検索するのに膨大な時間を費やしていました。レアものに重点を置いていますので，ゆっくりですが着実に，私の店は入手が非常に難しい商品を買うことができる町で唯一の場所だといううわさが広まりました。例えば，デビッド・ボウイやボブ・ディラン，そしてジョン・レノンといった人たちのサイン入りレコードを持っていました。売り上げが本当に好転したときに，もっと広い場所に移転しようかと考えましたが，夫の両親が所有していた店でしたので，そこには大きな思い入

れがありました。その代わりに，2号店をオープンすることに決めたのですが，そこもとても順調です。

聞：それでは，アイシャ，今日はここで時間となりました。来ていただいたことに感謝するとともに，今後ますますのご活躍をお祈りします。

ア：ありがとう。とても楽しかったです。

> 語句 vinyl record「アナログレコード」，merchandise「商品」，comb *A* for *B*「Bを求めてAをくまなく捜す」，resell「～を転売する」，word gets out that ...「…ということがうわさになる」，sentimental value「（思い出をそそるなどの）心情的な価値」

No.26 解答 ②

質問の訳 アイシャはどのような経緯でビンテージのレコードや商品を売ることに興味を持ち始めたのか。

選択肢の訳
1 フェアに来る人たちは主に1960年代，70年代，そして80年代のレコードを買うことに気が付いた。
2 使っていなかった物を売ることで小遣いを稼ぎたいと思った。
3 父親がマーケットでレコードを売って大金を得ていることに刺激を受けた。
4 満足のいく教師の仕事を見つけることができず，手っ取り早く金を得たいと思った。

解説 アイシャは4つ目の発言で，友人と行ったフリーマーケットでは音楽を販売している人が少なく，My collection of records はほとんどが倉庫に眠っていたので，その一部を売って副収入を得ようと考えたと述べている。この経緯を，使用していない物を売って earn some pocket money「小遣い稼ぎをする」ことを望んだと言い換えた**2**が正解。

No.27 解答 ④

質問の訳 アイシャが2号店をオープンすることに決めた理由の1つは何か。

選択肢の訳
1 その店はフェアの開催地の近くという便利な場所にあった。
2 2号店から追加の収入があれば教師を辞めることができるだろう。
3 顧客たちは彼女がサイン入りのレコードに特化した店をオープンすることを望んでいた。
4 もっと広い店を求めていたが，最初の店を売るのをためらっていた。

解説 アイシャの6つ目の発言から，最初は振るわなかった売り上げが好転したときに，moving to a bigger space を検討したが，元は夫の両親が所有していた店舗には a lot of sentimental value があったので，移転はせずに2号店をオープンすることに決めたことがわかる。この理由を was hesitant to sell her original shop という表現を使って言い換えた**4**が正解。

52

二次試験・面接 | **トピックカード** **A** **日程** | 問題編 p.40 | ▶MP3 ▶アプリ ▶CD 4 **1**～**5**

22年度第2回 面接

ここでは，A日程の5つのトピックをモデルスピーチとしました。

A日程

1. Do large corporations have too much influence on government policies?

  From my point of view, large corporations have a lot of influence over government policies. I'll focus on corporate lobbyists, tariffs and duties, and corruption. The most harmful way that corporations influence government is through lobbying. Lobbyists hired by various industries donate millions of dollars to political campaigns, and politicians become so dependent on their funding that policy decisions can be affected. For example, people often say that America's lack of environmental protection laws is the result of lobbying by the energy and automotive industries. Many government tariffs and duties are also the result of corporate pressure on politicians. Governments often impose taxes on foreign imports on the pretext of protecting domestic companies. However, these are extremely harmful to consumers as they raise prices, and they can result in trade wars. Corruption is another huge problem. When businesspeople are elected to public office, there is often a huge temptation for them to use their influence to enrich the companies they control. Furthermore, many politicians have friends or relatives who control large corporations, and there have been many cases in which they passed laws that favored or were influenced by such companies. To sum up, I think it's clear that large corporations are having a terrible effect on governments, so it's time that something was done to reduce their influence.

解説 「大企業は政府の方針に影響力を持ち過ぎているか」

①企業のロビー活動，②関税及び諸税，③政治腐敗の3つを論点に選び，大企業は政府の方針に対して悪い影響を与えていると主張している。また，それぞれの理由について The most harmful way，extremely harmful，another huge problem などの表現でいかに悪影響が大きいかを強調し，その後で具体的にわかりやすい例を加えている。lobby，impose taxes，corruption など政治に関する単語も発話でしっかり使えるようになりたい。

2. Are growing populations an advantage or a disadvantage for developing countries?

53

In my opinion, the advantages of growing populations in developing countries outweigh the disadvantages. Some of the main reasons are that they provide larger workforces, they allow for larger domestic markets, and they can better support senior citizens. First, for developing countries to achieve prosperity, large workforces are a must. Large populations provide huge numbers of workers, who, in turn, can produce huge numbers of goods. This has been a major factor in China's rise to become one of the world's economic superpowers. Large populations also mean that there are larger domestic markets. China has also benefited from its huge population because there are over a billion consumers to support internal trade. It also allows China to be largely self-reliant if there are slowdowns in global markets. Finally, when populations are growing, the young people are able to support the elderly financially. When developing countries have huge numbers of young workers, they don't face problems like Japan does with our graying population. This allows citizens to enjoy comfortable retirements. In conclusion, I think it's clear that developing nations are best off when their populations are increasing because of the benefits from larger workforces and markets, and due to the ability to provide financial support for seniors.

解説 「増え続ける人口は発展途上国にとって有利か不利か」

冒頭で，人口増加のメリットはデメリットを outweigh する「上回る」，という表現で人口増加は途上国にとって利点が多いという結論を述べている。outweigh は使えると便利な語なので覚えておこう。3つの理由として①労働人口の増加，②国内市場の拡大，③高齢者への支援，を挙げている。これは国の自然な成長過程を示しているので，時系列もきちんと考えられたスピーチと言える。このように，3つの理由をどの順番で話せば自然な展開ができるかを準備時間内に検討できると理想的だ。

3. Agree or disagree: The illegal trade in wild species is impossible to stop

Although the poaching of wild animals has been a serious problem for many years, I'm optimistic that it can be stopped. I believe we can put an end to it because of technology, education, and international cooperation. Technology will be the biggest factor. These days, devices such as drones, tracking chips, and security cameras are making it much harder for poachers to catch wild animals. As technology continues to advance, even more can be done to protect them. I also think education will be important. Today, more and more people in developing countries are being educated. Education offers many opportunities to teach people about the importance of preserving threatened species and it will encourage people to find more practical ways to co-exist

54

with these species. Finally, international cooperation is going to reduce poaching as well. In the past, one country might have made efforts to crack down on it, but in other countries, laws were not enforced well. However, as globalization continues, there will be more international aid and cooperation that will make it easier for all countries to prevent poaching. Although poaching is a difficult problem to solve, I feel that there has been so much progress in technology, education, and international cooperation that the world will someday be free of this serious problem.

解説 「賛成か反対か：野生動物の不法取引を止めることは不可能である」

トピックに反対の立場からのスピーチ。可能か不可能かと聞かれた場合，「可能である」と答える方が理由や具体例をとっさに見つけやすいかもしれない。ここでは①テクノロジー，②教育，③国際協力，の 3 つの分野の進展により不法取引を止められると主張している。具体的で直接的な効果のある対策から国際協力というやや大局的な解決法まで，幅広く具体例を出している。poaching「密猟」，poacher「密猟者」，crack down on ～「～を取り締まる」などの専門的な用語が使えると，時間的に効率よく話せるだろう。

4. Is Japan doing enough to protect its cultural heritage?

While Japan has made efforts to preserve our cultural heritage, much more needs to be done. In particular, we need to do more to preserve our traditional architecture, performing arts, and crafts. Unfortunately, when Japan was rebuilding its economy after World War II, we lost a lot of old buildings. Although the government preserved some historic structures, much of our unique architecture was torn down as a result of efforts to modernize and enrich the economy. To preserve what is left, the government should pass preservation laws and subsidize preservation efforts. Traditional performing arts are also in danger. Although the government has built some wonderful venues and subsidizes arts like bunraku, the audiences have been shrinking. Such performing arts are attractive to tourists and are an important part of Japan's international image, so more needs to be done to support them. Similarly, many traditional crafts are in danger of dying out. Recently, young people have not been attracted to jobs that take a long time to become skilled at such as making kimonos, and the pay is often below average. The government should offer young people more incentives to train in these crafts. This will revitalize the traditional crafts industry. Japan has a unique and valuable culture, so I believe we must do more to preserve it, especially in the vulnerable areas I just mentioned.

55

解説 「日本は文化遺産を守るために十分な対策をしているか」

Is 〜 doing enough to ...? という頻出の設問タイプ。トピックに反対の立場から，①伝統的建築物，②伝統芸能，③伝統工芸の3つを特に差し迫った分野として挙げ，今残されたものをどうやって守っていくかに焦点を当てた意見となっている。First, Second, ... という一般的なつなぎ方をせず，自然な文脈の流れに沿って Unfortunately, Traditional performing arts are ...., Similarly でそれぞれの理由の説明を始めているが，これも冒頭で3つの論点を明示しているからこそ可能な，効果的なスタイルである。

5. Do developed countries have a moral responsibility to lead the way in renewable energy research?

I believe developed countries are morally responsible for leading the way in renewable energy research. This responsibility has arisen because of developed countries' past actions, the costs involved, and the urgency of the problem. Firstly, it's clear developed countries caused the climate crisis. Because we continued burning fossil fuels even when we were warned that it was warming the planet, we have to take responsibility now. Renewable energies are the best way to slow global warming, so we're morally obligated to develop them. Another reason is the tremendous cost. Developing technologies like fusion energy requires massive investments, and poorer countries cannot afford the huge research budgets. Therefore, developed countries have to step up and help those that cannot afford to develop alternative energies on their own. Finally, we must take into account the urgency of the climate crisis. Global warming is quickly worsening and is bringing floods, droughts, and other disasters that could kill millions. Developed countries have a moral duty to save lives worldwide by developing alternative energies. In conclusion, due to our past actions, the costs involved, and the urgent need to stop global warming, countries like Japan and America have an ethical obligation to develop renewable energies.

解説 「先進国には再生可能エネルギーの研究を率先するべき道徳的責任があるか」

トピックに賛成の立場からのスピーチで，その根拠を①先進国の過去の行動，②開発コスト，③問題の緊急性，の3つに置いている。it's clear, we have to, we must などを使って，先進国の気候変動に対する責任を厳しく追及するトーンとなっている。このようにスピーチ全体のトーンを統一することで，自分の考えをより正確に聞き手に届けることができる。

2022-1

一次試験
筆記解答・解説　　　　p.58〜76

一次試験
リスニング解答・解説　p.77〜104

二次試験
面接解答・解説　　　　p.105〜108

解 答 一 覧

一次試験・筆記

1

(1)	1	(10)	3	(19)	3
(2)	2	(11)	3	(20)	4
(3)	2	(12)	2	(21)	4
(4)	3	(13)	1	(22)	2
(5)	1	(14)	1	(23)	1
(6)	3	(15)	2	(24)	4
(7)	1	(16)	3	(25)	4
(8)	3	(17)	4		
(9)	2	(18)	1		

2

(26)	4	(29)	4
(27)	3	(30)	2
(28)	2	(31)	1

3

(32)	2	(35)	2	(38)	4
(33)	4	(36)	4	(39)	3
(34)	2	(37)	1	(40)	2
				(41)	1

4　　解答例は本文参照

一次試験・リスニング

Part 1	No. 1	2	No. 5	4	No. 9	2
	No. 2	1	No. 6	3	No.10	3
	No. 3	2	No. 7	4		
	No. 4	4	No. 8	1		

Part 2	No.11	3	No.15	4	No.19	1
	No.12	3	No.16	1	No.20	3
	No.13	2	No.17	2		
	No.14	4	No.18	1		

Part 3	No.21	4	No.23	3	No.25	3
	No.22	2	No.24	4		

Part 4	No.26	1	No.27	3

| 一次試験・筆記 | **1** | 問題編 p.42〜44 |

(1) ─解答 **1**

訳 知事は金持ちにおもねっているとしばしば非難されている。彼は在任中,何度も高所得者に減税をしている。

語句 1「おもねる」　　　　　　　　　2「〜の隅々に広がる」
3「〜を嘆く」　　　　　　　　　4「ぶらぶら歩く」

解説 第2文の high-income earners は第1文の the rich の言い換え。たびたび金持ちに減税をしているということは,知事は金持ちを優遇する政治をしていることになる。pander to 〜 は「〜におもねる,〜の歓心を買おうとする」という意味。

(2) ─解答 **2** ★75%以上

訳 狭いひとまとまりの信条を生徒に教え込むのではなく,よい教師は,多様な視点に生徒の目を向けさせることによって,批判的に考えるよう生徒を促すべきだ。

語句 1「発する」　　　　　　　　　　2「〜に教え込む」
3「〜を不正に奪う」　　　　　　4「〜を没収される」

解説 indoctrinate は,特定の考え・教義などを「〜に教え込む,たたき込む」という意味。indoctrinate *A* with [in] *B*「A に B を教え込む」の形でよく用いられる。

(3) ─解答 **2**

訳 A：どうしてベンはいつも黒いサングラスをかけているの? 目の具合が悪いの?
B：いや,見えでかけているだけだよ。ああすればクールに見えると思っているんだ。

語句 1「叱責」　　2「見え」　　3「倹約」　　4「敬虔」

解説 B の第2文から,ベンは単に格好をつけるためにサングラスをかけているのだとわかる。vanity は「見え,虚栄心」という意味で,形容詞は vain。

(4) ─解答 **3**

訳 キャリアの頂点にいるとき,その小説家はベストセラーを年に2作書いていた。自分がそれほど成功するとは思ってもいなかった。

語句 1「異議」　　2「賄賂」　　3「頂点」　　4「ただし書き」

解説 ベストセラーを年に2作送り出すという状況は,小説家キャリアのzenith「頂点,絶頂」だと考えられる。zenith の類義語は height, peak, pinnacle など。

58

(5) — 解答 **1** ․․

訳 CEO は工場労働者の仕事をするのがどんなものかを 8 時間費やして経
験した後，工場労働者の給料を上げた。その仕事がどれだけ過酷なもの
か，彼はまったく認識していなかった。

語句 **1**「過酷な」　　**2**「早熟な」　　**3**「協調した」　　**4**「急いだ」

解説 工場労働者の仕事を自ら経験した後で賃上げしたのだから，CEO はそ
の仕事がいかに grueling「過酷な，極度にきつい」ものかを知り，そ
れに見合う給与レベルにしたのだと考えられる。

(6) — 解答 **3** ․․

訳 その戦争小説は人間の争いの苦悩と恐怖と悲しみをとても完璧に要約し
ているので，これまで書かれた最高の戦争小説と呼んでいる批評家もい
る。

語句 **1**「～をなだめる」　　　　　　　　**2**「～を気に入られるようにする」
3「～を要約する」　　　　　　　　**4**「～を刺激する」

解説 encapsulate は，en-（中に）＋ capsule（カプセル）＋ -ate（動詞語尾）
からイメージできるように，カプセルの中に押し込むようにぎゅっと
「要約する」こと。

(7) — 解答 **1** ․․

訳 A：君が何にでもそんなに独善的になるつもりなら，政治について議論
しても意味がないよ。
B：あなたがそんなふうに感じるのは残念だわ。物事の善悪について強
い意見を持っているだけのことよ。

語句 **1**「独善的な」　　**2**「当惑させる」　　**3**「天文学的な」　　**4**「陽気な」

解説 「物事の善悪について強い意見を持って」いて他人の考えに耳を貸さな
いことを dogmatic「独善的な，独断的な」と言う。そういう人とは議
論にならない。

(8) — 解答 **3** ․․

訳 A：新しい仕事は楽しめている，ハリー？
B：素晴らしいよ。福利厚生もたくさん付いていて，特別休暇，社員食
堂の無料ランチ，会社のジムの利用などがあるね。

語句 **1**「記章」　　　　**2**「法令」　　　　**3**「福利厚生」　　**4**「うぬぼれ」

解説 B が including 以下で挙げているのは，給料以外に与えられる perk
「福利厚生，特典」の例である。perk は perquisite の略語だが，perk
を用いるのが一般的で，通例 perks と複数形で使う。

(9) — 解答 **2** ․․

訳 アレンがコンピューターのファイルを全部なくしたとき，ジェニーは彼
に同情することができた。数カ月前に自分にも同じことが起きたからだ。

語句 **1**「～を突然引き起こす」　　　　　　**2**「同情する」

22
年
度
第
1
回
　
筆
記

59

3「退位する」　　　　　　　　**4**「〜を詳細に説明する」

解説　自分にも同じトラブルが起きたのだから，ジェニーはアレンの気持ちを理解できるはず。commiserate は sympathize とほぼ同義だが，同情を感じるだけでなく，「慰めの言葉をかける」というニュアンスもある。

(10) – 解答　**3**

訳　裁判官は，情状酌量の余地があるとして犯人の刑を減刑した。彼の子供は高額の手術が必要で，そのため彼は雇い主からお金を盗んだのだった。

語句　**1**「幻影の」　　**2**「強健な」　　**3**「酌量できる」　**4**「ぎょっとして」

解説　extenuating circumstances「酌量すべき情状，軽減事由」は，このフレーズで覚えておきたい。問題文では，子供の手術費用を得るためだったことが酌量すべき情状ということになる。mitigating circumstances [factors] という言い方もある。

(11) – 解答　**3**

訳　A：あなた，ここはとても古風で趣のある小さな村だわ。またすぐにここで休暇を過ごしましょう。

　　　B：絶対そうしよう！ ここは時が完全に止まって，長年変わっていないような感じがする。

語句　**1**「簡潔な」　　　　　　　　　　**2**「重大な」
　　　　3「古風で趣のある」　　　　　　**4**「斜めの」

解説　また来ようというA の提案にB が全面的に同意していることから，2人とも村が気に入ったとわかる。quaint は，古風さが魅力になっていることを表す形容詞。

(12) – 解答　**2**

訳　無駄の多い支出のせいでその会社の財源は徐々に浪費され，今や会社は倒産寸前である。

語句　**1**「報酬」　　　　**2**「浪費」　　　**3**「集合（体）」　**4**「苦難」

解説　動詞 dissipate には「（霧など）を散らす，（心配など）を消す」に加え，「（金・時間など）を浪費する」という意味もある。dissipation はその名詞。

(13) – 解答　**1**

訳　首相は，自分を新しい指導者とすげ替える陰謀を同僚たちがひそかにたくらんでいるとは疑ってもいなかった。

語句　**1**「〜をたくらむ」　　　　　　　**2**「〜にはったりをかける」
　　　　3「（感情など）を爆発させる」　**4**「〜を叱る」

解説　hatch には「（卵が）かえる，（卵）をかえす」に加え，「（陰謀など）を企てる，たくらむ」という意味がある。hatch a plot は典型的な用法。

(14) – 解答　**1**　　　　　　　　　　　　　　　　　　正答率　★75%以上

訳　世界の海に浮かぶごみの一部は貨物船をはじめとする船からの流出物に

60

よるものだが，大半は産業廃棄物など陸地の発生源に由来する。

語句 **1**「ごみ」　　**2**「器用さ」　　**3**「深い後悔」　　**4**「退屈」

解説 船からの流出物や産業廃棄物に由来するのだから，空所には「ごみ」を意味する語が入ると考えられる。debris には「残骸，がれき」のほかに，marine debris「海洋ごみ」，space debris「宇宙ごみ」といった用法がある。

(15) – 解答 ②

訳 両親が言い争いを始めると，スーザンは，みんな一緒にレストランに出かけようと提案することでその場を和らげようとした。彼女の作戦は功を奏し，両親はすぐに落ち着いた。

語句 **1**「～を爆撃する」　　　　　　　**2**「～の危険性を弱める」
3「～を苦しめる」　　　　　　　**4**「～に屈辱を与える」

解説 defuse は defuse a bomb「爆弾の信管（fuse）を除去する（de-)」といった使い方が本義だが，比喩的に「(危険な状況など）を和らげる，落ち着かせる」という意味で用いられる。

(16) – 解答 ③

訳 学校ではスマートフォン禁止だと言われていたのに，少年はその規則を公然と無視し続けた。時には授業中に電話を使うことさえあった。

語句 **1**「～をおだてて…させる」　　**2**「～を描く」
3「～をばかにして無視する」　　**4**「～を縛る」

解説 授業中にスマートフォンを使うこともあったとあるので，空所には規則を「無視する」に類する語が入る。flout は，法や規則などをあからさまに無視すること。

(17) – 解答 ④

訳 裁判を前に弁護士たちは，主要な証人の説明の正規の供述を得るため，彼女に正式な証言録取を行った。

語句 **1**「称賛」　　　　　　　　　　　**2**「長い非難演説」
3「分裂」　　　　　　　　　　　**4**「証言録取」

解説 deposition「証言録取，デポジション」は法律用語。証人が真実を述べると宣誓した上で，裁判の前に行う証言のこと。記録され法廷に提出される。

(18) – 解答 ① 正答率 ★75%以上

訳 その有名俳優は，自分は貧しい出自だとインタビューでしばしば語った。しかし，彼の主張が真実だという証拠を記者たちは見つけられなかった。

語句 **1**「立証，証明」　**2**「平衡」　　　**3**「共同事業体」　**4**「逸脱」

解説 動詞 verify は「～の正しさを確認する［立証する］」という意味で，verification はその名詞。類義語は confirmation。

(19) – 解答 **3** ･･････････････････････････････････････

訳 そのテレビチャンネルは，多くの視聴者が不快だと感じた殺人事件の<u>ぞっとするような</u>細部を含むドキュメンタリーを放送して批判された。

語句 **1**「しなやかな」 **2**「封建制度の」 **3**「恐ろしい」 **4**「きゃしゃな」

解説 lurid は「恐ろしい，ぞっとするような」という意味で，暴力的な要素を含む記述や映像について用いるのが普通。「(色が) けばけばしい」という意味もある。

(20) – 解答 **4**

訳 警察はその打ち捨てられた建物の中で2匹の<u>やせ衰えた</u>犬を見つけた。犬たちはあまりにやせていてほとんど身動きできなかったので，警官たちは急いで動物病院に連れて行った。

語句 **1**「題名と同じ名の」 **2**「ぶっきらぼうな」
3「移り気な」 **4**「やつれた」

解説 第2文から，犬たちはかなり衰弱していたと考えられる。emaciated は病気や飢えで「やつれた，やせ衰えた」という意味。

(21) – 解答 **4** ･･････････････････････････････････････

訳 その政治家は，自身が提案した医療プランに関する流説は<u>誤りだと証明する</u>ために記者会見を開いた。彼はそのプランのあらゆる部分の要点を明快に述べ説明した。

語句 **1**「～を (乱暴に) 突く」 **2**「～を点在させる」
3「～を甘やかす」 **4**「～の誤りを暴く」

解説 空所の後の myths は「広く流通する誤った考え」つまり「流説，流言」の意味なので，記者会見を開いた目的は，自分のプランを正しく知ってもらい流説が「誤りだと証明する」ことだと考えられる。

(22) – 解答 **2**

訳 A : ヒース，どうして机の引き出しを<u>捜し回っている</u>の？ また鍵をなくしたの？
B : いや，鍵は持っている。今度は財布が見つからないんだよ。

語句 **1**「しわが寄る」 **2**「捜し回る」
3「席を詰める」 **4**「(進路など) を外れる」

解説 文脈から，空所には「捜す」という意味の語句が入るとわかる。poke around は，物を動かしたりかき分けたりしながら「捜し回る」というニュアンス。

(23) – 解答 **1** ･･････････････････････････････････････

訳 その男性は搭乗便の最終アナウンスが聞こえたとき，まだ空港のレストランにいたので，さっさと食事を<u>食べ終えて</u>搭乗ゲートへと急いだ。

語句 **1**「(食事) をさっと平らげた」 **2**「～の気持ちを和らげた」
3「(髪) を後ろで結んだ」 **4**「～を何とか切り抜けた」

解説 polish off は問題文のように食べ物に使うことが多いが,「(仕事)を手早く片付ける,(本)をさっさと読み終える」といった意味もある。

(24) – 解答 ④

訳 去年ピーターは,家賃を払い食料や雑貨を買うのに苦労した。生計を何とか立てるためだけに,アルバイトを2つ掛け持ちしなければならなかった。

語句 1「～で騒ぎ立てる」　　　　2「～を出し抜けに言い出す」
3「～にほくそ笑む」　　　　4「(生計)を辛うじて立てる」

解説 eke out にはいくつか意味があるが,eke out a living「辛うじて生計を立てる,細々と生活する」は決まり文句なので,このまま覚えておきたい。

(25) – 解答 ④

訳 ジェイコブは小遣いを多めに欲しかったので,すごくきれいだよと言って母親にごまをすろうとした。しかし,彼には欲しいものがあるのだと彼女はすぐにわかった。

語句 1「～を取り囲む」　　　　　2「～をくよくよ考える」
3「～を思い焦がれる」　　　　4「～におべっかを使う」

解説 butter up は,こちらの利益になるように「～におべっかを使う,ごまをする」こと。同じ意味の句動詞に suck up to ～ がある。

一次試験・筆記 **2** 問題編 p.45 ～ 47

全文訳 **毒の科学**

ルネサンス期に,スイスの医師パラケルススは革命的な医学概念を導入した。当時の一般常識では,毒物はどんな量でも死をもたらすと考えられていた。しかし,医学における化学の役割を確立する上で大きな力となったパラケルススは,これはばかげていると考えていた。彼が代わりに主張したのは,いかなる物質も本来的に致死性を持つわけではなく,十分に薄めればどんな毒も無害にすることができ,有益だとわかることすらある,ということだった。事実,この原則はさまざまな現代の医薬品の開発に役立ってきており,その中には,ジギタリスという潜在的に致死性を持つ植物から抽出されるが,ある種の心臓病の治療に極めて重要なジゴキシンも含まれている。パラケルススはまた,通常は健康によい物質でも過剰な量だと命取りになることがあると推論した——水のような物質にすら致死的な用量が存在するのである。

パラケルススの原則は現代医学において標準になっており,今日ではしばしば「服用量が毒を作る」と表される。しかし,それには例外がある。パラケルススの時代以来,科学は,発がん性物質として知られるがんの原因となる物質の存在を認めるようになっている。これらは DNA を突然変異させることができ,たった1つのそうした変化です

63

ら，細胞が悪性化する原因になり得る。ごく微量の発がん性物質しか細胞増殖の触媒として働いていなかったとしても，これが統制のない増殖を招くことがある。同様に，一部のノロウイルスを低量服用すると被験者の50％に感染を引き起こすことが実験で明らかになっているが，これは，これらの有機体にも無害な服用量などないことを暗に示すだろう。

　服用量という概念は，現代の毒物学，特に環境科学の分野において，さらに探求されてきた。例えば「指標種」は，潜在的危険の合図をすることができる生物である。昔は，有害な地下ガスの影響を非常に受けやすいという理由で，カナリアは鉱山の中に連れて行かれた。毒素が速い速度でカナリアの体内に蓄積することから，万一この鳥が死ねば緊急に鉱山から退避する必要があると鉱山労働者たちは知ったのである。このように，こうした生物は本質的に閾値量の指標として働き，環境毒素の検知を容易にしてその毒素が有害になるレベルを確定する。その後，数十の指標種が特定されているが，その中には水の汚染を示すザリガニもおり，そうした生物が毒に侵されやすいことは，生態系の汚染物質との闘いにおける貴重な予測因子になり得ると同時に，人間の安全を守る上で有用であることを示唆している。

> 語句　inherently「本質的に，固有に」，lethal「致死（性）の」，dilute「～を薄める」，foxglove「ジギタリス」，dosage「（1回分の）服用量」，carcinogen「発がん性物質」，mutate「～を突然変異させる」，malignant「悪性の」，minuscule「微小の」，catalyst「触媒」，norovirus「ノロウイルス」，toxicology「毒物学」，toxin「毒素」，threshold「閾値（ある反応を起こすのに必要な最小量）」，vulnerability「弱さ，（病気などの）かかりやすさ」，predictor「予測するもの」，pollutant「汚染物質」

(26) – 解答 ④　　　　　　　　　　　　　　　　　正答率 ★75％以上

解説　空所後のHoweverの文のthisは，toxic substances（　）を指す。これがばかげていると考えたパラケルススが主張したのは，どんな毒も薄めれば無害にでき，有益なものすらある，ということ。つまり，「毒物はどんな量でも死をもたらす」という当時の常識をパラケルススは否定した，と考えると文脈に合う。

(27) – 解答 ③

解説　空所前のthe dose makes the poisonというパラケルススの原則は，第1段落に書かれているように，毒になるか薬になるかは服用量次第という考え方。一方，空所後では，ごく微量の発がん性物質がんの原因になるといった例が紹介されている。つまり，微量なら毒は無害だというパラケルススの考え方に当てはまらない例外も存在することになる。

(28) – 解答 ②

解説　sentinel speciesは何をすることができるか。空所後のカナリアの例によると，カナリアは有毒ガスに敏感なので，鉱山の中でカナリアが死ね

ば，人は危険が差し迫っていることを知り鉱山から退避した。これを「潜在的危険の合図をする」と表した**2**が正解。

全文訳 空の目

　人工衛星は天気予報と放送で今日広く用いられているが，いささか驚くべき1つの応用法が金融界で出現している。人工衛星は今では，企業の収益を予測するために利用されているのである。地球を周回する軌道にはかつては限られた数の人工衛星しかなかったが，最近は至る所に存在するようになったので，地球の表面のほとんどの地域のデータにも，今ではリアルタイムでアクセスすることができる。この能力を活用し，今では多くの主要金融企業が，今後の投資から見込める収益の予測を立てるためにそうしたデータを利用している。例えば，小売店の駐車場の車両数を継続的に観察して顧客数を推定することは，店の株を購入するかどうかを決断する際に極めて有益なことがある。売り上げが大幅に伸びれば，企業の株価はしばしば急騰するからである。

　この戦略は一部に巨大な富を生んだ一方で，不公平な優位性をつくり出すと批判者たちは論じる。投資家は株を選ぶ際に，自分に有利になるようなさまざまな種類の情報を獲得しようと常に競ってきた。だが衛星データを買う金銭的余裕があるのは，一般に，豊かな資金を持つ大手投資会社だけである。カリフォルニア大学バークレー校の経済学者パノス・パタトウカスによると，「テクノロジーによって誰もが同じ条件で競争できるようになるはずだったのに，私が目にしているのは，洗練された投資家と洗練されていない投資家を隔てる塀が次第に高くなっている状況だ」。企業に関する内部情報を用いて株を購入することは禁止されているが，それとまったく同じ理由で投資業界における衛星の利用を禁じるような法律を求める声すら上がっている。

　しかし，衛星の利用を金融企業に認めることにまったく価値がないわけではない。より詳しい情報を得た上での決定に基づく株の購入は，最終的には，企業の真の価値をより正確に反映した株価に行き着く，と専門家は主張する。いずれにせよ，テクノロジーが成熟しかつ社会に行き渡る速度を考えれば，個人投資家が衛星データを利用できるようになるのは時間の問題にすぎない。より多くの衛星画像サービスが次々と現れれば，テクノロジーの進歩に利用者の増加が加わることでおそらくコスト削減につながり，それによりそうしたサービスはより多くの人の手の届く価格になるだろう。

（語句）ubiquitous「至る所に存在する」，affordable「安価な，手頃な」，culminate in ～「（最終的に）～となる」，disseminate「普及する」

(29) – 解答 **4** ・・

解説 人工衛星は金融界でどのように利用されているか。空所後の記述によると，金融企業は衛星からリアルタイムで得られるデータを formulate projections of potential earnings on prospective investments のために役立てている。これを短く言い換えた**4**が正解。なお，タイトルに使われている eye in the sky という表現は「上空の監視装置」といった意味合い。

(30) – 解答 **2** ••••••••••••••••••••••••••••••••••••• 正答率 ★**75%以上**

解説 空所後に書かれているのは，衛星データを利用できるのは豊富な資金力を持つ投資会社だけだということ。つまり，空所前の some「一部」だけが有利な立場に立つ不公平な状況が生じていることになる。sophisticated investor は十分な資金・実績・経験・知識を持つ投資家を指す業界用語だが，そうした投資家とそうでない投資家との格差が拡大する一方だとパタトゥカスは指摘していることになる。

(31) – 解答 **1** •••

解説 空所文が However で始まっていることから，衛星利用のネガティブな面を記述している前段落とは違う内容が空所に入ると考えられる。より詳しい情報に基づいて株を購入すれば株価は企業の真の価値を反映したものになる，という次の文の内容は衛星利用を肯定的に捉えたものなので，それを merit「価値」と表した **1** が正解となる。

一次試験・筆記 3 問題編 p.48～56

全文訳 **ポインセチアとポインセチスモ**

　flor de Nochebuena（スペイン語で「聖夜の花」）として知られるメキシコの花が米国の植物学者・外交官・政治家ジョエル・ポインセットによって1820年代に初めて米国に送られたとき，その花は彼に敬意を表して「ポインセチア」と名付けられた。しかし当時のメキシコ人は，ポインセットの名前を基に，まったく違うことを意味する「ポインセチスモ」という別の語を作った。1825年に初代駐メキシコ米国大使に任命されたポインセットは，内政に干渉することと尊大で高圧的な性格の両方ですぐにメキシコで悪名をはせた。メキシコは数年前にスペインとの激烈な戦争で独立を勝ち取っており，ポインセットの第一の使命は，米国が採用している，世襲君主を置くのではなく人々が大統領を選挙で選ぶ政治システムである共和制を促進することだった。この目的を果たすため，ポインセットは，メキシコ内部に親米派を作ろうと絶えずたくらみ，すぐに政界の黒幕として知られるようになった。「ポインセチスモ」という語で表されるようになったのは，そうした干渉だった。

　ポインセットが任命された当時，米国は，メキシコとその他のラテンアメリカにおける英国の貿易利権との激しい競争にさらされており，メキシコが独立を獲得した後でもスペインがなお保持している影響力を恐れていた。着任したポインセットは，スコットランド派として知られる，主に国の政治家と将軍で構成される親ヨーロッパ派が，メキシコ政府に対して他を圧する支配的な影響力を持つことを知った。このグループから敵意で迎えられたため，ポインセットは，ヨーク派として知られる対抗グループの創設を援助することでスコットランド派の影響力をそごうと努め，ヨーク派は共和制を促進しようと努めた。ヨーク派が投票で政治的勝利を収めることが増えてから，1827年にス

コットランド派による武装蜂起が起き，彼らの主な要求の１つはポインセットの追放だった。蜂起は幅広い支持を得られず直ちに鎮圧され，最終的に，ポインセットの同盟者の１人であり，自身もヨーク派のメンバーだったビンセンテ・ゲレロが 1829 年に国のリーダーシップを握る結果となった。だがこのころには，ポインセットは強大な外国が影響力を行使しようとする試みの道具だという世評が非常に強い反感を生んでいたため，彼は暗殺の脅迫を受けるようになり，ポインセットが厄介者になったと気付いたゲレロは，彼を呼び戻すよう米国政府に要請して成功した。

　米国に戻ったポインセットは英雄として歓迎されたが，メキシコではそれほど好意的に記憶されているわけではない。彼は民主主義の理念を擁護しようと努め，自分はヨーロッパ君主国へのメキシコの抵抗を援助していると考えていたが，メキシコの民衆の目からすれば，自分たちの領域の政治状況において外国人がそれほど広範な役割を演じたことは耐え難かった。ポインセットの後継者アンソニー・バトラーはポインセットと同じ道を歩み，現在のテキサス州をメキシコ政府から手に入れようと賄賂に訴えて捕まったとき，ものの見事に米国とメキシコの緊張をさらに悪化させてしまった。ポインセットとバトラーの行動が合わさって，この２国は，最終的に 1846 年の武力衝突へと至る成り行きをたどることとなった。

(語句) botanist「植物学者」，meddling「干渉」，overbearing「高圧的な」，hard-fought「激戦の」，republicanism「共和制」，hereditary「世襲の」，puppeteer「人形遣い，黒幕」，unrivaled「競争相手のない」，animosity「憎悪，敵意」，ballot box「投票」，expulsion「追放」，pull strings「影響力を行使する」，liability「不利になるもの，お荷物」，fondly「優しく」，aggravate「〜を悪化させる」，bribery「贈収賄」

(32) – 解答 **2**

問題文の訳　メキシコでジョエル・ポインセットの名前は，

選択肢の訳　**1**　スペインなどのヨーロッパ諸国からの外部の影響がない自由な社会を作る国の試みが成功したことを意味するようになった。

2　米国の政治的課題を促進する目的で行われた，政府に関連する事柄への干渉と結び付けて考えられるようになった。

3　スペインの支配から自由を獲得しようとするメキシコの試みの象徴として広く採用されるようになった種類の花に用いられた。

4　国にやって来て祖国への忠誠を維持するかメキシコを支援するかを選ぶよう強いられた米国人に関して用いられた。

解説　ポインセットの名前に由来する poinsettismo という造語が何を意味したかを読み解く。メキシコに米国と同じ共和制を採用させることがポインセットの使命で，そのために彼は内政干渉すら行った。第１段落最終文にあるように，そうした干渉が poinsettismo と呼ばれるようになった。**2** が 本 文 の meddling in state affairs を interference in government-related matters と，republicanism を an American

67

political agenda と言い換えている。

(33) – 解答 ④

問題文の訳 この文章によると，スコットランド派とヨーク派に関する以下の記述のどれが正しいか。

選択肢の訳
1　ポインセットはスコットランド派が権力を握るのに役立つ情報を彼らに与えていたので，両派が互いを嫌っていたことによってポインセットの影響力はさらに増した。
2　両派の内紛は，より正確には，ポインセットと彼のメキシコにおける同盟者の勝利というより，ヨーロッパ諸国の敗北と見なされるべきだ。
3　両派の権力闘争はポインセットに大きなストレスをもたらしたので，彼はメキシコでの仕事を放棄して米国に戻らざるを得なかった。
4　両派の対立関係は，ヨーク派の大勝利につながっただけでなくポインセットにメキシコを去ることをも余儀なくさせた争いにエスカレートした。

解説 第2段落に書かれているのは，the Escoceses に嫌われたポインセットが対抗勢力として the Yorkinos を支援し，the Escoceses の蜂起が失敗して the Yorkinos が権力を握ったものの，ポインセットは the Yorkinos にとって厄介者となり米国に戻された，という流れ。それを**4**が短くまとめている。

(34) – 解答 ②

問題文の訳 この文章の筆者は，ポインセットがメキシコにいた期間についてどのような結論を下しているか。

選択肢の訳
1　ポインセットはアンソニー・バトラーよりも大使として成功したのに，当時の人々はその反対が本当だと誤って考えていた。
2　ポインセットは善意で行動していると感じていたのだろうが，彼には後年に起きた戦争の部分的責任があった。
3　ポインセットはメキシコ政治の現実を十分には理解できなかったが，いくつかの幸運な決定によってその国の状況を改善することができた。
4　もしポインセットが外交的努力をメキシコの諸問題ではなくテキサスの問題に向けていたら，緊張は緩和されたかもしれない。

解説 筆者は最終段落で，ポインセットは民主主義の理念に従いメキシコを支援しているつもりだったと書いている。これが**2**の「善意で行動していると感じていた」に対応する。また，彼の行動と後任のバトラーの行動が合わさって，後の米国とメキシコとの武力衝突を招くことになったとも書いている。これが**2**の「後年に起きた戦争の部分的責任があった」と合致する。

68

全文訳 **アルバレス仮説**

　恐竜は巨大小惑星の衝突により滅亡したという説は，当初は賛否両論あったものの，今では科学界の圧倒的多数によって当然視されている。アルバレス仮説として知られるこの説は，米国の地質学者ウォルター・アルバレスが，恐竜が絶滅した地質時代と一致する世界中の岩石層にイリジウムという元素が高濃度で存在することに気付いたときに始まった。イリジウムは地球では極めてまれだが小惑星では普通に見られ，それが存在することは，特大のちりの雲を大気に噴き上げて日光を遮断した小惑星衝突の証拠だとアルバレスは考えた。これが，日光の欠乏で植物が死に絶え，それが原因で草食動物──そして引き続きそれらを捕食する肉食動物──も滅亡した連鎖反応を引き起こしたのだろう。後年，メキシコ南東部で，現在のチクチュルーブという町の付近で地球にぶつかった巨大小惑星の衝突によって形成された巨大クレーターが発見されたことで，この仮説は一層説得力を増した。

　しかし，ごく少数の古生物学者は数十年来アルバレス仮説に抵抗しており，プリンストン大学のゲルタ・ケラーはその筆頭である。彼女は恐竜の絶滅が起きたと考えられている時代の化石記録を調査し，重要な反証を集めた。彼女の研究は，有孔虫という海洋生物の化石を調べることだった。これらの化石は豊富に存在し一般に保存状態が良好なので，科学者は有孔虫種の絶滅パターンを確実に評価でき，そのためそれらの化石は，共存していた生物の健康状態の指標としてしばしば用いられる。ケラーによる有孔虫の化石の調査は，チクチュルーブの衝突の数十万年前から有孔虫の数が既に減少しつつあったことを示唆していた。さらに，衝突でできたクレーター近辺の有孔虫の生息数は，アルバレス仮説に基づけば想定されるような突然の急落を経験していなかった。

　ケラーは恐竜の絶滅について，別の説明を提案している。チクチュルーブの衝突の前は全世界的に気温が上昇し続けており，デカン・トラップ──有史以前，網状に存在した火山の噴火による溶岩流が固まって形成されたインドの広大な地域──がこの現象の説明として考え得ると長年見なされてきた。これらの噴火は数十万年にわたって起きたのだが，最も壊滅的な噴火は絶滅に至る6万年の間に起きたことをケラーの証拠は示している。これらは非常に多くの有毒ガスとちりを大気中に放出しただろうし，そのため地球温暖化と酸性雨が，ケラーが「回帰不能点」と呼ぶものへと生態系を追い込んだのだろう。ケラーの説は批判されているが，恐竜を滅亡させる上でデカン・トラップ地域の火山活動が少なくとも部分的役割を果たしたかもしれないことを示唆するさらなる証拠が出現している。チクチュルーブの衝突前に火山活動は継続していたものの，衝突後は活動がすさまじく上昇したことをカリフォルニア大学バークレー校の研究者たちが発見したのである。しかしケラーは，そうした研究は長年の誤った仮説を手直ししようとする試みにすぎないと見なし，火山活動が絶滅の唯一の主原動力だったと頑強に主張し続けている。見たところ問題のどちら側にも証拠があるようなので，合意はたぶんまだ先のことになるだろう。

　語句 asteroid「アステロイド，小惑星」，geologist「地質学者」，iridium「イリジウム」，geologic「地質の」，herbivore「草食動物」，carnivore「肉

食動物」，gigantic「巨大な」，paleontologist「古生物学者」，reliably「信頼して，確実に」，coexist「共存する」，proximity「近接」，plunge「急落」，solidify「固まる」，lava「溶岩」，prehistoric「有史以前の」，expel「～を放出する」，volcanism「火山活動」，adamant「断固主張して」

(35) − 解答 ②

問題文の訳 最初に何がアルバレス仮説の発展につながったか。

選択肢の訳
1 遠い昔に宇宙からの物体が地球にぶつかったことを示す極めて大きなクレーターの発見。
2 恐竜が姿を消したのと同じころに宇宙からやって来たと思われる物質の，地球の広範囲にわたる存在。
3 恐竜が絶滅する直前に生きていた，植物を食べる恐竜と肉を食べる恐竜双方の珍しい化石の特定。
4 恐竜が絶滅したと考えられた時代に基づくと，ある岩石層の化石の位置が理屈に合わないという認識。

解説 第1段落第2文の originated が設問の first に対応している。その文以降の記述によると，恐竜が絶滅した時代の世界中の岩石層に地球ではまれなイリジウムという物質が高濃度で存在することの発見が，小惑星の衝突で恐竜が絶滅したとするアルバレス仮説の始まりだった。それを，本文の worldwide を widespread と，iridium を substance と言い換えてまとめた 2 が正解。1 は段落最終文と合致するが，仮説を補強する証拠であり，仮説の始まりではない。

(36) − 解答 ④

問題文の訳 ゲルタ・ケラーがアルバレス仮説を疑う1つの理由は，

選択肢の訳
1 小惑星の衝突直前のころの有孔虫の化石が，一部の種類がほかの種類よりも速く数が減少したと示していたことである。
2 恐竜時代の終わりの数十万年前に地球上に有孔虫が存在していた証拠を発見したことである。
3 小惑星が地球にぶつかった地域の近くだけでなく，広い地域にわたって有孔虫が影響を被っていたはずだということである。
4 有孔虫の数は突然減少したのではなく徐々に減ったという証拠を発見したことである。

解説 第2段落によると，ケラーは有孔虫の化石という信頼できる指標を用いて調査を行った。アルバレス仮説のとおりなら，小惑星が衝突したときに有孔虫は激減したはずだが，そうではなく，有孔虫はその数十万年前から減りつつあった。これが，ケラーがアルバレス仮説を疑う理由である。4 が，数十万年前から減っていたことを gradual decrease とまとめ，本文の abrupt plunge を sudden drop と言い換えている。

(37) – 解答 ①

問題文の訳 カリフォルニア大学バークレー校の研究に関する以下の記述のうち，ケラーはどれと意見が一致する可能性が最も高いだろうか。

選択肢の訳 1 研究結果は恐竜の絶滅に関する彼女の説を裏付けるものではなく，むしろアルバレス仮説を微調整して支持することが目的である。

2 研究の結論が彼女自身の結論とどのように異なっていたかは，アルバレス仮説が彼女が当初考えていたより正確かもしれないことを示している。

3 研究はデカン・トラップより，小惑星の衝突がどのように大気に影響したかの方にもっと焦点を当てるべきだった。

4 研究が気候変動を考慮に入れなかったことは，結果は部分的にしか正確ではないと考えられるべきだということを意味する。

解説 ケラーはアルバレス仮説を否定し，火山活動が恐竜絶滅の唯一の原因だったとする。一方，第3段落後半に書かれているカリフォルニア大学バークレー校の研究は衝突と火山活動を関連させるもので，ケラーにとってそれは「長年の誤った仮説を手直ししようとする試みにすぎない」。つまり，**1** のように，その研究は結局ケラーの説ではなくアルバレス仮説を支持するものだというのがケラーの意見ということになる。選択肢の adjusting は本文の modify の言い換え。

全文訳 **国富論**

　おそらく史上最も有名な経済学者であるアダム・スミスは，最も誤解されている経済学者でもあるかもしれない。非常に大きな影響力を持つ彼の著作『諸国民の富の本質と原因の研究』（『国富論』）は1776年に出版され，自由貿易協定の主張者と，規制に制限されない市場を支持する人たちによって広く引き合いに出されている。だがスミスの著作を精読すれば，それに基づくと主張する多くの政策が，彼が実際に伝えようとしていたことの誤解と曲解を反映していることが明らかになる。

　スミスが『国富論』で詳述したことの多くは，彼の時代の支配的な経済理論だった重商主義への返答として書かれたものだった。この学説は，世界には限られた量の富しかないという想定に基づくもので，国家が繁栄する唯一の方法は金と銀の形態で富を蓄積することだと主張した。これは，資源を開発し輸出できる植民地を建設するためにライバル国と競い合うことから，有利な貿易収支を維持するために他国からの商品に関税を課すことまで，いくつかの方法で達成されるとされた。

　このアプローチは見当違いだとスミスは論じた。重商主義は，商業とは団結と友愛ではなく敵対的競争を諸国間に促す活動だと考えた。そうしたアプローチは国際貿易の本質に関する根本的誤認を反映しているとスミスは感じた。諸国家は商品の交換を通して相互の繁栄を追求すべきだと彼は考え，自由貿易と商品生産の両方が，国が真に豊かになることを可能にする重要な構成要素だと論じた。

また『国富論』は，消費者と生産者と流通業者に自分たちが適切と思うように商売をする裁量をある程度与えることは，社会全体にとって有益だと提案した。利己心で行動する個人は，いかなる計画的経済制度よりもうまく他者の必要と欲望を満たすだろうとスミスは予想した。例えば，消費者は価格がより低い売り手からパンを購入する可能性の方が高く，そうするとほかの売り手は，強制されなくても，競争力を保つために自分の価格を調整することになる。この原理が働く仕組みを，スミスは『国富論』の中で「見えざる手」と呼んだ。

　しかしスミスは，市場への政府の介入は決してあってはならない，という単純過ぎる主張をしていたわけではない。見えざる手は，富裕なエリートを利し国家権力に擁護されていた制約から個人を解放するように，という諸政府への訴えの一部だった。事実，見えざる手を説明する『国富論』の一節は，有力な商人の強い求めで行われる国家の干渉をとりわけ糾弾している。だが皮肉なことに，スミスの理念は，新自由主義として知られる政治イデオロギーと実質的に同義になってしまった。新自由主義は，規制緩和，民営化，減税，社会サービス削減といった政策を支持し，21世紀の政治において非常に強い影響力を持ち続けているシステムである。多くの経済学者は，これらの政策は有力企業の影響力がもたらしたものだと見なしている——スミスが諸国家にとって有害だと考えたのと同じ影響力である。スミスは，財界は政府の意思決定に影響力を持ち過ぎるべきではないと警告した。なぜなら，そうなれば，例えば特別な特権や政府に認可された独占権による競争圧力の欠如の結果，低品質の商品に対して法外な価格を請求する企業によって消費者が搾取されかねないからである。

　スミスは，自由市場が最も社会のためになると当てにできない事例があることも認識していた。ノーベル賞を受賞した経済学者ジョセフ・スティグリッツはかつて，「見えざる手がしばしば見えないように思える理由は，しばしばそこに存在しないからだ」と書いた。見えざる手は，例えば，個人間の市場取引が社会全体に影響を与える状況に対処することはできない。「外部性」として知られるそうした影響には，天然資源の枯渇によるより広い影響や，製造業に起因する水質汚染といった事柄が含まれる。これは，取引に関与する人たちが得るメリットにもかかわらず，社会全体にとってはマイナスの結果を生むのである。

　スミスは規制がまったくない市場を信頼していなかったが，政治家は伝統的に商人が担ってきた役割を引き継ぐべきではないとも考えていた。むしろ彼の考え方は，正当な事業活動を実り多い形で追求できる一方で，同時にその同じ活動が市場に参加する当事者を誰一人搾取することのない規制された環境を，政治家は築き上げる必要がある，というものだった。しかし残念なことに，彼はどうすればこれが達成されることになるかの処方箋を残さなかった。さらに，「見えざる手」という文言が『国富論』に登場するのは一度きりで，徹底した説明はまったくされていない。これらの事実に，スミスの時代以来の数世紀で世界経済に起きた途方もない変化を加味して考えれば，スミスがもし今日生きていたとしたら，自分の著作——そして特に見えざる手という概念——がどのように解釈されてきたかに対し，ほぼ間違いなく拒否的な反応をするだろう。

語句 arguably「おそらく」，perversion「曲解」，mercantilism「重商主義」，finite「限られた」，prosper「繁栄する」，balance of trade「貿易収支」，misguided「誤った考えに導かれた」，misconception「誤解，誤認」，self-interest「利己心」，simplistic「過度に単純化した」，synonymous with ～「～と同義の」，neoliberalism「新自由主義，ネオリベラリズム」，deregulation「規制緩和」，privatization「民営化」，exorbitant「法外な」，externality「外部性」，depletion「枯渇」，fruitfully「実り多く」，unfavorably「好意的でなく」

(38) – 解答 ④

問題文の訳 諸国が富を築くべきやり方に関するアダム・スミスの考えはどのようなものだったか。

選択肢の訳
1 商品に課す関税の額と国が所有する金と銀の量には明確な関係がある必要がある。
2 富の総量は限られているのだから，諸国家は他国を犠牲にしてでもできるだけ多くを手に入れることが必須だ。
3 植民地を建設した国により多くの資源が植民地から供給できるよう，重商主義は改善される必要がある。
4 金と銀の蓄えを増強しようと試みるのではなく，諸国は相互に有益な貿易関係を発展させようと試みるべきだ。

解説 第2段落に重商主義の説明，第3段落にそれを批判するスミスの基本的な考え方が書かれている。敵対的競争を排し，自由貿易による商品の交換によって諸国は豊かになるべきだというのがスミスの理念。**4**がそれを mutually beneficial「相互に有益な」という表現を用いてまとめている。**2**は重商主義の考え。

(39) – 解答 ③

問題文の訳 この文章の筆者によると，新自由主義はスミスの理念と対立する。なぜなら，

選択肢の訳
1 過度に強力な企業の発展がなぜ妨げられるべきなのかについて，新自由主義者は大きく違う考え方を持っているからである。
2 自由市場にとっての富裕な企業の重要性を，新自由主義はスミスほど重視しないからである。
3 新自由主義が推進する政策が，自由で開かれた貿易を促すためではなく，企業の利益を有利にするために作られているからである。
4 個人が利己心で行動することが広く許されればどうなるかについて，新自由主義の方が否定的な見解を持っているからである。

解説 第5段落の記述によると，スミスの理念は，経済活動への政府の干渉を排する点では新自由主義とほぼ同じだが，政府の意思決定に対する企業からの影響力を否定する点で新自由主義とは異なる。自由競争が段落最

終文にある competitive pressure「競争圧力」を生み出し（第4段落のパンの例），それが社会全体の利益につながるというのがスミスの基本理念だから，**3** のように，自由競争を阻害し企業の利益だけを追求する新自由主義とは相いれないことになる。

(40) – 解答 **2**

問題文の訳 見えざる手が「しばしばそこに存在しない」とジョセフ・スティグリッツが述べた際に言いたかったことの考え得る1つの例は何か。

選択肢の訳
1 商人に多大な費用を負わせて輸入されなければならない珍しい種類の木材に消費者が大金を払わなければならないこと。
2 木製家具の需要増加に対応して伐採企業が熱帯雨林を切り倒すのを許可されること。
3 自然生息地保護を目的とする新しい政府規制のために製造業者の利益が減らされること。
4 ある製品が環境に害を与えるというメディアの主張によってその製品の需要がかなり減少すること。

解説 「そこに存在しない」とは，見えざる手がそもそも働き得ない状況を言う。本文では2つの例を挙げ，externalities「外部性」という用語でそれを説明している。「取引に関与する人たちが得るメリットにもかかわらず，社会全体にとってはマイナスの結果を生む」ことが外部性なのだから，それに合致するのは **2** である。熱帯雨林を伐採して家具を作れば企業はもうかるが，地球温暖化を促して社会全体にはマイナスの影響を与えると考えられる。

(41) – 解答 **1**

問題文の訳 市場はどう作用すべきかに関する考え方をスミスが提示したやり方の1つの問題は何か。

選択肢の訳
1 人々を保護しながらも市場が効率的に機能することを可能にするバランスの取れたシステムを諸政府はどうすれば作ることができるのかを，彼は説明しなかった。
2 諸政府に対する不信が原因で，市場を適切に規制するために見えざる手を利用することを可能にするだろう解決策を彼は見逃した。
3 彼は自由市場に全面的信頼を置いていたので，政府の規制当局の役割の重要性を認めなかった。
4 世界経済に起きるだろう多くの変化に関する彼の予言は，結果的に不正確だった。

解説 最終段落前半に，市場と規制に関するスミスの考えが書かれている。簡単にまとめると，誰もが自由に利益を追求でき，しかも誰もが互いに搾取することのないようにする規制のある市場が彼の理想だった。そしてそれを達成するための「処方箋（＝説明，提言）」を書き残さなかった

ことが，問題文の one problem に対応する。理想的な市場を a balanced system という表現を用いてまとめた **1** が正解である。

一次試験・筆記 **4** 問題編 p.56

解答例 Although still in its infancy, genetic engineering will be a tremendous boon to future societies. Specifically, the technology will eliminate genetic diseases, help protect wildlife, and stabilize the global food supply.

Genetic engineering has potentially life-changing health applications. For example, the technology has opened the door to the possibility of identifying fatal diseases early or neutralizing genetic defects before birth. In addition to the improvement in individual quality of life, the long-term significance of healthier populations only reinforces the importance of this technology.

The environmental implications of genetic engineering are also pertinent. Accelerated by unprecedented industrialization, global warming has become one of many factors behind the dwindling number of wildlife species. Genetic engineering, however, could help bring back extinct species and strengthen the genes of endangered ones, which would benefit society greatly as healthy ecosystems are a key source of many resources indispensable for modern needs.

Finally, genetic engineering offers modern-day solutions that promise lasting impacts on future generations. Growing populations are putting greater strain on the global food supply, which is already at the mercy of worsening climate change. Genetic modification, however, could boost yields and create more-resilient crops, both of which would prove vital in famine-stricken areas and regions with poor climates.

Therefore, tackling human health issues, the issue of endangered species, and the escalating food crisis via genetic engineering underscores just how invaluable a tool such technology will be for effecting positive societal change in the future.

トピックの訳 「賛成か反対か：遺伝子操作は将来の社会によい影響を与える」

解説 解答例はトピックに agree の立場から，遺伝性疾患の根絶，野生動物

の保護，世界の食糧供給の安定という３つの理由を挙げて，遺伝子操作は将来の社会に途方もない恩恵をもたらすとしている。冒頭の「まだ初期段階にあるものの」のように多少の条件を付け，手放しで賛成しているだけではないことを示すテクニックは参考になる。あるいはもう一歩進んで，食品の安全性や医療の倫理性の問題，生態系に与え得る悪影響などの具体例を挙げ，「懸念を持つ人もいるが」のように始めて，視野の広さをアピールするのも有効である。

解答例は５段落で，トピックへの立場を表明し３つの理由を示す導入の段落，理由について述べる本論の段落が３つ，最後にまとめの段落という基本に則った構成。第３段落の also，そして Finally，Therefore といった語を用いてスムーズにつなげている。耳から情報が入る面接のスピーチでは，Firstly, Secondly, ... のように区切りを明確にする必要があるが，作文では段落が改まったことが視覚的にわかるので，スピーチほどの厳格さは必要はない。それでも，副詞（句）や接続詞を適度に交えてめりはりをつけ，平板な印象を与えないようにする工夫は作文でも必須である。

本論は，それぞれ，第１文で遺伝子操作がいかに期待できるかを述べ，遺伝子操作をどのように活用できるかという具体例を挙げ，その結果社会にどのようなよい影響を与えるか，という流れでまとめられている。具体例としては，遺伝性疾患については致死的疾患を早期に特定することと出生前に遺伝的欠陥を無効化すること，野生動物保護については絶滅種の復活と絶滅危惧種の遺伝子の強化，世界の食糧供給については収穫量の増加とより回復力のある作物の開発と，ある程度現実味のある活用例が取り上げられているので，説得力がある。

最後のまとめの段落では，３つの理由を別の言葉で言い換えた上で，トピックに賛成する立場を再確認している。理由については，genetic diseases → human health（一般的な概念への言い換え），wildlife → endangered species（本論で用いた語句を再利用した言い換え），global food supply → escalating food crisis（本論を踏まえた新しい語句での言い換え）と，それぞれ異なるパターンが用いられていることに注目したい。もちろん，最初に挙げた際の表現をそのまま使っても構わないのだが，表現力や語彙の豊富さをアピールするにはこうした言い換えは非常に有効なので，ぜひ参考にしたい。

一次試験・リスニング Part 1

問題編 p.57〜58

No.1 – 解答 ②　　　　　　　　　　　　　　　　　　　　　正答率 ★75%以上

スクリプト
☆: I've finished looking over your cover letter for your job application, Ramone.
★: Thanks. Do you think I highlighted my communication skills sufficiently?
☆: I do. And I think the first paragraph, where you talk about your motivation for applying, will really appeal to the company.
★: Great. I'm a bit concerned about the second paragraph, though. Any thoughts on that?
☆: It was somewhat vague. For instance, instead of just saying you're good at cost-cutting and time management, perhaps you could add some concrete figures to indicate how you exceeded your targets at your previous job.
★: Thanks. That's a good idea.

Question: How will the man probably change his cover letter?

全文訳
☆: 求職用のカバーレターに目を通し終わったわよ,ラモーン。
★: ありがとう。コミュニケーションスキルを十分強調できていると思う？
☆: ええ。あと,最初のパラグラフ,応募の動機を述べているところね,ここは会社にすごくアピールすると思う。
★: バッチリだね。だけど,2つ目のパラグラフがちょっと気になっているんだ。それに関して何か考えはある？
☆: 多少漠然としていたわね。例えば,コスト削減と時間管理が得意だと言うだけじゃなくて,前職でどうやって目標を超えたかを示すために,具体的な数字を少し加えてみたらどうかしら。
★: ありがとう。いい考えだ。

質問: 男性はカバーレターをおそらくどのように変更するか。

選択肢の訳
1　パラグラフの順序を変更する。
2　詳しい情報を少し加える。
3　もっとコミュニケーションスキルに的を絞る。
4　動機をもっと明確に説明する。

解説 男性のカバーレターについてアドバイスをする女性は,最後の発言で,具体的な数字を加えるよう提案し,男性も同意している。concrete figures を detailed information と言い換えた **2** が正解。コミュニケーションスキルと動機はよく書けているというのが女性の評価なので,**3** と **4** は不適。

No.2 − 解答 ① ･･･････････････････････････

(スクリプト) ☆： Hey, Jack. Did you say you got your kitchen renovated last year?

★： Actually, it was two years ago, but yes.

☆： We're thinking of getting ours done, and we were wondering if you'd recommend the renovation company you hired.

★： Well, they charged us a fortune and justified it by saying their work would last for years, but it's now clear they cut corners to save a few bucks. They obviously selected inferior materials for the flooring, as it already needs redoing.

☆： Ouch. I'm beginning to wish I hadn't asked.

★： Sorry, it's a sore subject. I'd steer well clear of them if I were you.

Question: What does the man say about the renovation company?

(全文訳) ☆： こんにちは，ジャック。去年台所をリフォームしてもらったって言ってた？

★： 実際は2年前だけど，そうだね。

☆： うちでもやってもらおうと考えていて，あなたが雇ったリフォーム会社はお薦めかどうかと思っていたんだけど。

★： うーん，大金を請求して，自分たちの仕事なら何年ももつと言って正当化したのに，わずかな金を節約するために手抜き工事をしたのは今では明らかだよ。質の悪い材料を選んでフローリングに使ったのは明白だね，もうやり直しが必要なんだから。

☆： あらまあ。質問しなきゃよかったと思い始めたわ。

★： 悪いね，触れたくない話題なんだ。僕が君なら，あの会社には決して近づかないだろう。

質問：そのリフォーム会社について男性は何と言っているか。

(選択肢の訳) **1** その会社は費用削減のため質の悪い材料を使った。

2 その会社は倒産した。

3 その会社は最初の取り決めよりも高額を請求した。

4 その会社はフローリングをやり直すことを拒否した。

(解説) 台所をリフォームしてもらった会社がお薦めかどうか聞かれた男性は，2つ目の発言で，高額を請求したのに手抜き工事をし，もうやり直しが必要だと言っている。会話の save a few bucks を cut costs と，inferior materials を poor materials と言い換えた **1** が正解。cut corners「手抜きをする」，steer clear of ～「～を避ける」。

No.3 − 解答 ② ･･･････････････････････････

(スクリプト) ★： Have you met the new manager yet?

☆： Yeah. He seems like a pleasant guy. He said that his entire career has been in finance, though.

78

★ : This is the first time we've had someone in charge who wasn't promoted from within, isn't it? I guess the company wants a fresh perspective.

☆ : I'm worried it'll be a little too fresh. We're a software development company, and managing this department requires a strong technical background.

★ : I'm sure the company wouldn't have hired him if they didn't think he was up to the job.

☆ : I hope you're right.

Question: What does the woman suggest about the new manager?

全文訳
★ : 新しい部長にはもう会った？

☆ : うん。感じのいい人みたいね。ずっと財務畑一筋だって言ってたけど。

★ : 内部で昇進したのではない責任者が来たのは初めてじゃない？ 会社は新鮮な視点を欲しがっているんだろうな。

☆ : ちょっと新鮮過ぎることにならないか心配だわ。うちはソフト開発会社だし，この部を管理するには技術分野でのしっかりした経歴が必要だもの。

★ : 彼にその仕事をするだけの力がないと会社が思ったら，きっと雇っていないよ。

☆ : そうだといいんだけど。

質問：新しい部長について女性は何を示唆しているか。

選択肢の訳
1　彼はしぶしぶその仕事を引き受けた。
2　彼のスキルセットは役職に適していないかもしれない。
3　彼の技術的知識は卓越している。
4　彼は部の財務状況を改善することができる。

解説 女性の最初の発言の though から，前キャリアが財務という新部長の経歴に疑問を感じていることがわかる。そのキャリアを新鮮な視点と捉える男性に対し，女性は，ソフト開発会社の部長に必要な技術的経歴がないことに不安を感じるといったことを言っている。つまり，**2**のように，財務だけの skill set は役職に適さないと感じていることになる。

No.**4** – 解答 **4** .... 正答率 ★75%以上

スクリプト
★ : Did you catch the election debate last night?

☆ : Yes. I have to say, I was quite impressed with Janet Goldstein's ideas about expanding public transportation and providing more funding for recycling.

★ : I wonder how feasible those goals are, though. She also says she'll reduce taxes for the middle class, but how can she do that if she's going to shell out huge amounts of money for her other promises?

☆： Well, there's a budget surplus at the moment.

★： But that won't last long. If she has her way, the country will be running a deficit before you know it.

Question: What does the man imply about Janet Goldstein?

全文訳 ★： 昨日の夜の選挙討論会は見た？

☆： うん。確かに，公共交通機関を拡大してリサイクルにもっとお金を投入するというジャネット・ゴールドスタインの考えにはとても感心したわ。

★： それらの目標がどれだけ実行可能なのかと思うけどね。中産階級に減税するとも彼女は言うけど，ほかの公約に大金を出すつもりなら，どうすればそんなことができるんだろう。

☆： うーん，今のところ予算が黒字だし。

★： だけどそれも長くは続かない。彼女が好きなようにやれば，いつの間にか国は赤字を出していることになるよ。

質問：男性はジャネット・ゴールドスタインについて暗に何と言っているか。

選択肢の訳 **1** 彼女はもっと環境のためになることをすべきだ。

2 彼女の考えは公共交通機関を害する。

3 彼女は政府支出を減らす。

4 彼女の政策は実際的でない。

解説 女性は候補者の公約を高く評価している。一方男性は，それらの公約に加え減税まですれば国は赤字になる，と財源について疑問視している。男性の2つ目の発言の I wonder how feasible those goals are が男性の考えを端的に表しており，**4** が feasible を practical と言い換えている。

No.5 －解答 **4** 　　　　　　　　　　　　　　　正答率 ★75%以上

スクリプト ☆： Honey, did you hear there are two convicts on the loose in town? It's all over the news.

★： Yes, I heard about it late last night. Have there been any sightings?

☆： The news said they may have been involved in a burglary at a liquor store this morning.

★： Wow, that's really frightening. Are they armed?

☆： I think so. Listen, Julian said he wanted to bike to his friend's house tonight, but I think we have to tell him to stay home, even though there are extra police patrols now.

★： Yes, absolutely. I don't want him out on the streets tonight.

Question: What is one thing we learn from this conversation?

全文訳 ☆： あなた，囚人が2人，町を逃走中だって聞いた？　そのニュースで持ち

80

切りよ。

★： うん，昨日の夜遅くに聞いたよ。目撃情報はあったの？

☆： 今朝酒屋に強盗が入って，それに関与しているかもしれないってニュースで言っていた。

★： うわー，それはすごく恐ろしいな。武器は持っているの？

☆： 持っていると思う。あのね，ジュリアンが今夜自転車で友達の家に行きたいって言っていたんだけど，家にいるよう言わなきゃならないと思うの。今は警察がパトロールを増やしているにしてもよ。

★： それはもちろんそうだ。今夜は街に出てほしくないね。

質問：この会話からわかる１つのことは何か。

選択肢の訳　**1**　メディアが危険を誇張した。
2　今朝警察が囚人を捕まえた。
3　ジュリアンの友人は彼に悪影響を与えている。
4　今夜外出するのは安全でないかもしれない。

解説　逃走中の２人の囚人を巡る会話。今朝の強盗事件に関与した可能性がある，警察がパトロールを増やしている，などの情報から，２人はまだ捕まっていないことがわかる。また，たぶん息子であるジュリアンに今夜の外出をやめさせようというやり取りからも，**4**のように，夜間に街に出るのは依然として危険だと判断できる。

No.6 – 解答 ③　　正答率 ★75%以上

スクリプト　☆： I heard your mother was discharged from the hospital yesterday. That must be a big relief after such a serious operation.

★： Yes, it's good to have her back home with us. It's not all good news, though. The physician said follow-up surgery will likely be required in the months to come.

☆： That'll be hard on her. She's in her 70s, right?

★： Yeah. The medication the doctors are giving her seems to be effective at controlling the symptoms for now, but unfortunately that won't be enough in the long term.

Question: What is one thing the man says about his mother?

全文訳　☆： 昨日お母さんが退院されたそうね。あんな大手術の後だから，さぞほっとしたことでしょう。

★： うん，家に帰って来てくれてうれしいよ。いい知らせばかりではないんだけどね。医者が言うには，今後何カ月かの間に再度の手術が必要になりそうなんだ。

☆： それはお母さんには厳しいわね。お母さんは70代だったわよね？

★： ああ。医者が出している薬は今のところ症状を抑えるのに効果的なようなんだけど，残念ながら長期的にはそれじゃ十分ではないんだ。

81

質問：男性が母親について言っている 1 つのことは何か。

選択肢の訳　**1**　思ったより長く入院していた。
　2　より強い薬に変えなければならなかった。
　3　おそらくまた手術を受ける必要がある。
　4　老人ホームに移らなければならないかもしれない。

解説　男性が母親について言っているのは，数カ月後に follow-up surgery
「再度の手術」が必要になりそうなこと，そして，今は症状を抑えてい
る薬もいずれ効かなくなること。**3** が follow-up surgery を another
operation と言い換えている。

No.7 – 解答 ④ ····················· 正答率 ★75%以上

スクリプト　★：How's your new freelancing career going, Annika?

☆：It's great! My overall earnings have exceeded what I was making
before, and I'm certainly enjoying the independence.

★：It must be nice not having a boss looking over your shoulder all
the time. Are there any downsides?

☆：Well, some weeks, I'm expecting things will be quiet, and then I
suddenly get swamped with a huge project out of the blue. And
then the following week, I'm sitting on my hands because a
client has postponed something.

★：I can imagine that might be stressful.

Question: What does the woman say about her work?

全文訳　★：フリーランスの仕事を始めて調子はどう，アニカ？

☆：すごくいいの！ 全体的な収入は以前の稼ぎを超えたし，独立して間違い
なく楽しいわ。

★：何か起きやしないかと始終監視している上司がいないのはいいだろう
な。何かマイナス面はある？

☆：そうね，週によっては，落ち着いた状況になるだろうと思っていたら，
突然，出し抜けに大規模プロジェクトに忙殺されたりするの。そしてま
た次の週は，クライアントが何かを延期したので手をこまねいていたり
するのよね。

★：それはストレスがたまるかもしれない，想像できるよ。

質問：女性は自分の仕事について何と言っているか。

選択肢の訳　**1**　彼女は十分なお金を稼いでいない。
　2　彼女は予想していたより頻繁にクライアントと会っている。
　3　彼女はまだ以前の上司と取引をしなければならない。
　4　彼女のスケジュールは予測できない。

解説　フリーランスのマイナス面を聞かれた女性は，2 つ目の発言で，落ち着
いていると思っていたら突然忙しくなったり，クライアントの都合でま

82

た暇になったり，といったことを話している。それを unpredictable schedule と表した **4** が正解。be looking over *a person's* shoulder 「(人) がしていることを監視している」，get swamped with ～「～に忙殺される」，sit on *one's* hands「手をこまねいている」。

No.**8** – 解答 ①　　　　　　　　　　　　　　　　正答率 ★75%以上

スクリプト ☆： Did you say that you'd taken Chemistry 203 already, Charles?

★： Yes, I took it a couple of semesters ago. It was tough, but the things I learned from Professor Bedi have been invaluable in my other courses.

☆： I was wondering if I should take it. It's not mandatory, right?

★： Right, it's not, but a couple of my professors said the lab skills you acquire in it are extremely useful to have if you're majoring in chemistry.

☆： In that case, I'll definitely be signing up for it.

Question: What does the man say about Chemistry 203?

全文訳 ☆： 化学 203 はもう取ったって言ってた，チャールズ？

★： うん，2 学期前に取った。難しかったけど，ベディ教授から学んだことはほかの授業でもとても貴重なものになっているよ。

☆： 私も取った方がいいのかなと思っていて。必修ではないんだよね？

★： そうだね，必修ではないけど，化学を専攻するのなら，その授業で得られる実験スキルは持っていればものすごく役に立つって僕の担当教授が 2 人，言っていたよ。

☆： それなら，絶対受講届を出すわ。

質問：男性は化学 203 について何と言っているか。

選択肢の訳 **1** 取る価値のある授業だ。

2 数学期に 1 回しか開講されない。

3 実験室での作業があまりない。

4 教授の要求が多過ぎる。

解説 Chemistry 203 について聞かれた男性は，最初の発言で It was tough と言っているが，続く invaluable と 2 つ目の発言の extremely useful から，難しくてもとても役に立つ授業だと思っていることがわかる。それを worthwhile とまとめた **1** が正解。

No.**9** – 解答 ②　　　　　　　　　　　　　　　　正答率 ★75%以上

スクリプト ★： I understand that you need to find a part-time job to help cover your expenses at university. Is that correct, Kirsten?

☆： Yes, my parents gave me what they thought was enough to cover my first year, but I'm going through my money a lot faster than I expected. That's why I came here to the Student Services Office

83

for help.

★ : Well, there are many part-time jobs on campus. There are openings for office assistants, if you're interested.

☆ : Sounds perfect. When can I apply?

★ : Before we get to that, I just realized this is your first semester. How are your studies coming along?

☆ : Classes are quite challenging, but I'm getting by.

★ : As part of university regulations, students must refrain from working during their first semester. Then, if their grades are fine, they can apply for work at the beginning of the second semester. Does that sound OK to you?

☆ : Can't you make an exception? I could really use the money.

★ : I'm afraid we can't help you.

Question: What does the man suggest the student do?

全文訳 ★ : 大学の費用を賄う助けになるようアルバイトを見つける必要がある，ということだね。それで合っているかな，カーステン？

☆ : はい，両親は1年目を賄うのに足りると思ったお金をくれたんですが，思ったよりずっと速くお金を使い果たしつつあって。なので，助けてもらえないかと学生支援課に来たというわけです。

★ : さて，学内にはアルバイトがたくさんある。興味があるなら，事務補助員に空きがあるよ。

☆ : 願ってもないです。いつ応募できますか？

★ : その話をする前に，今気が付いたけど，これが最初の学期だよね。勉強の進み具合はどうなの？

☆ : 授業は結構大変ですが，何とかやっています。

★ : 大学の規則にあるんだけど，学生は最初の学期の間はアルバイトを自粛しなければならないんだ。その後，成績に問題がなければ，第2学期の初めにアルバイトを申し込むことができる。それで大丈夫そうかな？

☆ : 例外は作れないんですか？ 本当にお金が必要なんです。

★ : 悪いけど力になれないね。

質問：男性は学生が何をすることを提案しているか。

選択肢の訳 **1** 学外で仕事を探す。
2 勉強に集中する。
3 金銭的支援を申し込む。
4 もっとお金が欲しいと両親に言う。

解説 お金に困っている学生の話を最初は親身に聞く男性だが，学生がまだ最初の学期だと知ると，最初の学期はアルバイト禁止という規則を持ち出して態度を一変させている。その規則によると，their grades are fine

84

なら第2学期からはアルバイトをしていいのだから，**2**のように，最初の学期の間は勉強に集中すべきだと言っていることになる。

No.**10** 解答 ③

スクリプト
○： Dave, in the next long-range planning meeting, I'd like to recommend expanding the hotel division.

★： I'm afraid it's not in the cards.

○： Why not? I think we'll see a steady increase in guest numbers over the next few years.

★： My sources say headquarters wants to downsize our holdings in that division by selling a few hotels, and then focus on the airline business.

☆： That'd be a mistake. The hospitality industry was struggling during the economic slump, but since then our hotel business has been looking up.

○： If the company really wants to sell, we'd be better off waiting until we can show several years of consistent profit.

☆： We're already in the black for the year, and things will only improve as the weather warms up.

★： I agree, but headquarters wants to streamline operations. They're looking to offload any ventures that aren't directly related to the airline business.

○： But I think a case for the connection between the airline business and the hotel industry could certainly be made.

★： Well, I don't think they're interested, and rumor has it a few companies have already expressed interest in a couple of our hotels. I wouldn't be surprised if headquarters accepts an offer sooner rather than later.

Question: What does the man believe?

全文訳
○： デイブ，次回の長期計画会議ではホテル部門の拡大を勧めたいの。

★： それは見込みがないんじゃないかな。

○： どうして？ 向こう数年間，客数は着実に伸びることになると思う。

★： 情報筋の話では，本部はホテルを何軒か売ってその部門のうちの持ち株を縮小して，それから航空事業に注力したいようだよ。

☆： それは間違いでしょうね。ホスピタリティ産業は不況の間苦労していたけど，それ以来うちのホテル事業は上向いてきているもの。

○： 会社が本当に売りたいのなら，数年は安定した利益を出せるようになるまで待った方がいいわ。

☆： 今年は既に黒字だし，暖かい気候になるにつれてよくなる一方よ。

85

★：同感だけど，本部は事業活動を合理化したいんだ。航空事業に直接関係しないベンチャー事業は処分しようとしているんだよ。
○：だけど，航空事業とホテル産業の間には関連があると主張することもきっとできるんじゃないかと思う。
★：うーん，会社は興味がないと思うし，うわさでは数社が既にうちのホテル2軒に関心を示しているらしい。本部が早々にオファーに応じても驚かないね。

質問：男性はどう考えているか。

選択肢の訳
1　本部は航空事業にもっと注力すべきだ。
2　女性たちは懸念を本部に説明すべきだ。
3　女性たちの懸念にもかかわらずいくつかのホテルは売られる。
4　合理化作業はもっと早く始まるべきだった。

解説　ホテル事業拡大に楽観的な見通しを持つ女性2人に対し，会社の内部事情に詳しい男性は，ホテル事業を縮小する本部の考えが覆ることはないと思っている。つまり，**3**のように，女性たちが何を言おうとホテルは売却される，というのが男性の考えということになる。in the cards「ありそうな」，offload「〜を処分する」。

一次試験・リスニング　Part 2　問題編 p.59〜60　

A

 Alexander von Humboldt

Alexander von Humboldt made many contributions to science during the nineteenth century, but perhaps the most significant was the way he explained nature as an intricate web in which no single element could exist independently. This was in sharp contrast to the dominant view of his day, which focused on individual organisms and considered them in isolation. Humboldt's idea began to take shape when he embarked on a voyage that would last five years.

Humboldt traveled extensively throughout the Americas, observing indigenous peoples, plants, and animals. It was during his travels that he began to realize that nature is best understood as the balance of countless living and nonliving elements, and that human interference can disrupt this delicate balance. For instance, Humboldt noticed that logging in what is now Venezuela had an unforeseen impact on the local environment: a lack of trees caused water sources to disappear and the soil to become loose. When heavy rains fell, this soil was the source of devastating landslides. Because of his work, Humboldt is credited with being one of the first scientists to describe

the concept that human influence can impact nature on a wider scale.
Questions
No.11 What is one idea that Alexander von Humboldt introduced?
No.12 What did Humboldt observe about logging in Venezuela?

全文訳　アレクサンダー・フォン・フンボルト

　アレクサンダー・フォン・フンボルトは19世紀の間科学に多くの貢献をしたが，もしかすると最も重要なのは，自然とはただ1つの要素も独立して存在することのできない複雑な網の目だ，と説明したやり方だったかもしれない。これは，個々の生物に焦点を当てそれらを切り離して考察した当時の支配的な考え方とは明確な対照を成していた。5年続くことになる長旅に乗り出したとき，フンボルトの考えが具体化し始めた。

　フンボルトは両アメリカ大陸をくまなく広範囲に旅し，土着の民族と動植物を観察した。自然とは無数の生命のある要素と生命のない要素の均衡だと理解するのが最適なこと，そして，人間の干渉はこの微妙な均衡を乱しかねないことに彼が気付き始めたのは，この旅の間のことだった。例えば，現在のベネズエラでの伐採が現地の環境に予期しない影響を与えたことをフンボルトは見て取った。樹木がなくなったことが原因で水源が消失し，土壌が緩くなったのである。大雨が降ると，この土壌は壊滅的な土砂崩れのもとになった。フンボルトはその仕事により，人間の影響はより広い規模で自然に影響を与え得るという考え方を述べた最初の科学者の1人であるという功績を認められている。

語句　intricate「複雑な」，unforeseen「予期しない」

No.11 解答 　　　　　　　　　正答率 ★75%以上

質問の訳　アレクサンダー・フォン・フンボルトが導入した1つの考えは何か。
選択肢の訳　1　自然は予測可能な形で振る舞う。
　　　　　　2　あらゆる生態系に独特な生物がいる。
　　　　　　3　自然のすべては関連している。
　　　　　　4　科学的発見はどこででも起こり得る。
解説　フンボルトの最も重要な貢献は，自然を an intricate web in which no single element could exist independently と説明したことだと前半で述べられている。それを短くまとめた**3**が正解。

No.12 解答

質問の訳　フンボルトはベネズエラでの伐採について何に気付いたか。
選択肢の訳　1　水源の汚染につながった。
　　　　　　2　現地の動物の消失を加速させた。
　　　　　　3　ひどい土砂崩れの部分的原因になった。
　　　　　　4　現地の人々にその地域を去ることを強いた。
解説　フンボルトがベネズエラで気付いたのは，伐採により水源が消失して土壌が緩くなり，土砂崩れの原因になること。したがって**3**が正解。**3**の

partially は，大雨という別の要因が関与することを指す。森林では土壌に染み込んだ雨水が地下水として水源となるが，伐採はその森林の機能を失わせ，土壌が水を含んだままになり災害を招くという構造をフンボルトは見抜いたことになる。

B

スクリプト **The Ghost Army**

On June 6, 1944, the Allies launched the D-Day invasion of World War II to free Europe from Nazi Germany. The attack occurred in the French region of Normandy. However, prior to the invasion, the Allied forces used a military unit known as the Ghost Army to deceive the German forces into focusing on defending another possible target about 150 miles from Normandy. The Ghost Army employed fake vehicles and used sound recordings to mimic invading forces. Crucial to the success of the trick was the role of the famed general George Patton as the unit's commanding officer. Patton was considered unfit for a real command because of a recent scandal, so he was assigned as leader of the pretend army to make the threat more believable.

The D-Day deception was highly successful, as the Nazis moved many troops away from the Allies' intended target of Normandy. After the invasion, the Ghost Army continued its operations. These were so successful that they occasionally caused a problem: Allied commanders themselves were tricked into believing, for example, that the unit's sound effects were actual Allied tanks moving out of position. On the whole, though, the Ghost Army is believed to have greatly reduced Allied casualties by weakening Nazi resistance in battles across Europe.

Questions

No.13 What was one thing that made the Ghost Army's D-Day operation seem realistic?

No.14 What was one problem associated with the Ghost Army?

全文訳 **ゴーストアーミー**

1944年6月6日，ナチスドイツからヨーロッパを解放するため，連合軍は第2次世界大戦のDデー侵攻を開始した。攻撃はフランスのノルマンディー地域で行われた。しかし，連合軍は侵攻に先立ち，ノルマンディーからおよそ150マイル離れた別の考え得る目標地点を防御するようドイツ軍を欺くため，ゴーストアーミーとして知られる部隊を用いた。ゴーストアーミーは偽の車両を用い，侵攻軍に成り済ますため録音した音声を使った。この策略の成功に必須だったのは，高名な将軍ジョージ・パットンの部隊司令官としての役割だった。パットンは直前に起こしたスキャンダルのため実際に軍の指揮を執るには適さないと考えられたので，脅威の信ぴょう性を高めるために偽の軍隊の指導者の役を振られたのである。

連合軍が予定していたノルマンディーの目標地点からナチスが多くの部隊を移動したことで，Dデーの偽装はまんまと成功した。侵攻後，ゴーストアーミーは軍事行動を継続した。これらはうまくいき過ぎて時々問題を引き起こした。連合軍の司令官たち自身がだまされて，例えば，部隊の音響効果が持ち場を離れる実際の連合軍の戦車だと信じてしまったのである。だが全体的には，ゴーストアーミーはヨーロッパ全域での戦闘でナチスの抵抗を弱めることによって，連合軍の死傷者を大きく減らしたと考えられている。

　　　語句　mimic「～をまねる」

No.13 解答　②

質問の訳　ゴーストアーミーのDデー作戦を本物らしく見せた1つのことは何だったか。

選択肢の訳　1　本物の戦車と飛行機の使用。
　　　　　　2　有名な将校の存在。
　　　　　　3　部隊のノルマンディー方面への移動。
　　　　　　4　軍が頻繁に動き回ったこと。

解説　ゴーストアーミーが用いたのは，偽の車両と録音した音声という物理的作戦と，実際の指揮を外されていたパットン将軍を司令官に据えて信ぴょう性を高めるという心理的作戦。将軍について，famed general を famous military officer と言い換えた **2** が正解。

No.14 解答　④

質問の訳　ゴーストアーミーに関係する1つの問題は何だったか。

選択肢の訳　1　あまりに多くの資源を用いた。
　　　　　　2　音響効果が十分に本物らしくなかった。
　　　　　　3　ドイツ軍がそれについて知った。
　　　　　　4　連合軍の指導者たちをだますこともあった。

解説　ゴーストアーミーの問題については，Allied commanders themselves were tricked into believing ... 以下で，音響効果を本物の戦車の音と勘違いしたという具体例が挙げられている。commanders を leaders と，tricked を fooled と言い換えた **4** が正解。**2** はまったく逆である。

スクリプト　**Cashew Nuts**

As more people adopt vegetarian diets, cashew nuts are becoming an increasingly popular source of healthy fats and protein. However, like many export crops grown in developing countries, their production is problematic. Cashew nuts must be removed from their shells by hand. However, the shells contain a toxic oil, and some workers who handle them suffer from blisters and skin rashes because they are not given gloves for protection. One international human rights organization has even reported cases of patients at drug rehabilitation centers being forced to process the nuts and experiencing abuse if they refuse to comply.

As demand for cashew nuts grows, the government in Ghana, already a major producing country of the nuts, is encouraging even more farmers to use their land to grow cashew nuts for export. While many farmers benefit from the increased income generated by cashew-nut production, some agencies warn that the decrease in land available for domestic food-crop production may threaten the country's food security. Moreover, unlike domestic food-crop farming, which Ghanaian women are heavily involved in, the cultivation of cash crops, such as cashew nuts, for export is generally controlled by men. This means that Ghana's goals for gender equality could become harder to realize.

Questions

No.15 What does the speaker say about cashew-nut processing?

No.16 What is one concern agencies have about cashew-nut farming in Ghana?

全文訳 **カシューナッツ**

　ベジタリアン食を取り入れる人が増えるにしたがい，健康によい脂肪とタンパク質の摂取源としてカシューナッツの人気が次第に高まっている。しかし，発展途上国で栽培される多くの輸出用作物同様，その生産は問題含みである。カシューナッツは手で殻から取り出さなければならない。しかし，殻には有毒な油が含まれ，殻を扱う労働者の中には，保護用の手袋をもらえないため水膨れと皮膚の発疹を患う者がいる。ある国際人権組織は，薬物リハビリセンターの患者が服従を拒むと，ナッツの加工処理を強制され虐待を経験する事例すら報告している。

　カシューナッツの需要が増えるにしたがい，既にこのナッツの主要生産国であるガーナの政府は，さらに多くの農家に，自分の土地を利用して輸出向けカシューナッツを栽培することを奨励している。多くの農家がカシューナッツ生産で生み出された所得増加で利益を得る一方，国内用の食糧作物生産に利用できる土地の減少は国の食糧安全保障を脅かすかもしれない，と警告する政府機関もある。さらに，ガーナ人女性が多く関与している国内用の食糧作物農業と異なり，カシューナッツなどの輸出向け換金作物の耕作は一般的に男性が掌握している。これは，ジェンダー平等に向けたガーナの目標の実現がより困難になるかもしれないことを意味している。

語句 problematic「問題のある」，blister「水膨れ」，rash「発疹」

No.15 解答 ④　　　　　　　　　　　　　　正答率 ★75%以上

質問の訳 カシューナッツの加工処理について話者は何と言っているか。

選択肢の訳 **1** このナッツが健康にもたらす利点を減らす。

90

2 高価な機械類の使用を必要とする。
3 労働者の間に盗難がある。
4 労働者が身体的危害に直面するかもしれない。

解説 前半で，カシューナッツの生産は problematic だとして，素手で殻からナッツを取り出すと殻に含まれる有毒成分により blisters and skin rashes「水膨れと皮膚の発疹」を患う労働者がいたり，加工処理を強制される人たちがいたりする，と指摘されている。**4** が，それを physical harm という一般的な表現で言い換えている。

No.16 解答

質問の訳 ガーナのカシューナッツ農業について政府機関が持っている1つの懸念は何か。

選択肢の訳
1 国内用の食糧作物の栽培に必要な土地を利用する。
2 このナッツは輸出される代わりに現地で販売されている。
3 農家はこのナッツから十分なお金を稼いでいない。
4 女性がこのナッツを栽培するよう強制されている。

解説 後半の some agencies warn ... 以下で，2つの懸念が挙げられている。1つは，カシューナッツの栽培が国内用作物の耕作地を奪い，国の食糧安全保障を脅かしかねないこと。もう1つは，多くの女性がかかわる国内用作物農業と違いカシューナッツなどの耕作は男性が支配しているので，ジェンダー平等に逆行するかもしれないこと。**1** が前者と一致する。

##

スクリプト **Airline Deregulation**

Until 1978, when the United States deregulated its airline industry, the government controlled everything from airfares to the routes that airlines could fly. Today, however, only airline safety remains under government control. Many people have hailed deregulation as a success, citing the fact that fares have declined by around 50 percent since the 1970s. Research, however, has shown that fares actually declined faster in the years leading up to deregulation than in the years after it, and that such declines have had more to do with the development of fuel-efficient planes than with freer competition.

Furthermore, as a result of deregulation, airlines are no longer required to schedule flights to smaller cities. Since it is harder to fill seats on planes to less-popular destinations, many airlines quickly eliminated these routes. Because airports and frequent air service are key to regional development, this has had an adverse effect on smaller, less populous cities, causing them to miss out on the economic benefits that come with heavier air traffic. In fact, since deregulation, many smaller cities have been compelled to provide economic incentives such as subsidies to encourage airlines to fly to their

airports.
Questions
No.17 What has research shown about airline-industry deregulation?
No.18 What has been one effect of airline deregulation on smaller cities?

　全文訳　航空規制緩和

　米国が国の航空産業の規制を緩和した1978年まで，政府は，航空運賃をはじめ航空会社が飛行できる路線に至るまであらゆることを管理していた。しかし今日では，いまだに政府の管理下にあるのは航空の安全だけである。多くの人が，1970年代以来運賃が5割前後下がったことを挙げて，規制緩和は成功だとたたえている。しかし，運賃の値下げは規制緩和後の年月より規制緩和に至る年月の方が実際は速かったこと，そして，そうした値下げはより自由な競争よりも燃料効率の高い飛行機の開発と大きく関係していたことが，研究で明らかになっている。

　さらに，規制緩和の結果，航空会社は中小都市への便を時刻表に入れることをもはや求められていない。人気の低い目的地に向かう飛行機の座席を埋める方が難しいのだから，多くの航空会社はそうした路線をすぐさま廃止した。空港と頻繁な航空便は地域の発展の鍵なので，これは人口の少ない中小都市に悪影響を与えており，そのためそれらの都市は，飛行機の往来が多くなれば付いてくる経済的メリットを逃している。事実，規制緩和以来，多くの中小都市は，自分たちの空港に乗り入れるよう航空会社を促すため，補助金などの経済的インセンティブを出すことを余儀なくされている。

　語句　deregulation「規制緩和」，deregulate「～の規制を緩和する」，airfare「航空運賃」

No.17 解答　②

質問の訳　航空産業の規制緩和について研究は何を明らかにしたか。
選択肢の訳　1　航空の安全レベルの低下につながった。
2　運賃が安くなったことの主な理由ではない。
3　続いて一時的に運賃が上昇した。
4　結果的に空の旅の人気が下がった。
解説　規制緩和で航空運賃が安くなったという話に続き，Research, however, has shown ... 以下で，運賃が急速に下がったのは規制緩和の後ではなく前であることと，価格競争より燃料効率の向上の方が大きくかかわっていたことが説明されている。つまり，**2**のように，規制緩和は運賃値下げの主な理由ではないことになる。

No.18 解答　

質問の訳　航空規制緩和が中小都市に与えている1つの影響は何か。
選択肢の訳　1　中小都市の経済が被害を被った。
2　中小都市の空港が設備を更新しなければならなくなった。
3　中小都市の空港での飛行機の往来が増えた。

4 中小都市はより多い補助金を受け取った。

解説 規制緩和が中小都市に与えた影響として挙げられているのは，路線が減ったことと，それにより経済的メリットを逃していること。**1** が後者を「経済が被害を被った」と表している。

E

スクリプト **Metabolism and Extinction**

The metabolic rate is the rate at which an organism uses energy to perform essential functions. Researchers have discovered a possible link between an organism's metabolic rate and the probability it will go extinct. The study, which examined a period of around 5 million years, looked at fossils and living species of mollusks, such as snails and clams. The researchers found that, overall, mollusks with faster metabolisms were more likely to go extinct.

Organisms with faster metabolisms require more energy, so when environmental changes decrease the amount of available nutrition, these organisms are at greater risk of starvation. However, the researchers also found that this risk is lower for species that are more widespread. Widespread species are usually better equipped to survive in diverse conditions and consume a greater variety of foods, so they are more able to adapt to environmental changes.

One finding the researchers did not expect was that the average metabolic rate of all mollusks remained consistent throughout the period studied. If mollusks with low metabolisms are better able to avoid extinction, it seems logical to expect that the average metabolic rate would drop over time. However, the research findings suggest that when species with fast metabolisms go extinct, other species with fast metabolisms fill the gap they leave.

Questions

No.19 Which organisms with fast metabolisms are least likely to go extinct?

No.20 What finding about mollusks surprised the researchers?

全文訳 **代謝と絶滅**

代謝率とは，生物が必要不可欠な機能を実行するためにエネルギーを使う割合のことである。研究者たちは，生物の代謝率とその生物が絶滅する見込みの間には関連があるかもしれないことを発見した。その研究は 500 万年前後の期間を調査したもので，カタツムリや二枚貝など軟体動物の化石と現存種を調べた。研究者たちは，全体的に，代謝の高い軟体動物の方が絶滅する可能性が高いことを突き止めた。

代謝の高い生物の方が多くのエネルギーを必要とするので，環境の変化によって手に入る栄養の量が減ると，これらの生物の方が飢えるリスクが大きくなる。しかし研究者たちは，このリスクは分布域が広い種の方が低いことも突き止めた。分布域が広い種の方が，通例，多様な条件で生き延びる力をより多く備えており，摂取する食物がずっと

93

多種多様なので，環境の変化に適応する能力がより高いのである。

　研究者たちが予期しなかった1つの発見は，調査した期間全体にわたり，すべての軟体動物の平均代謝率が常に一貫していたことだった。代謝の低い軟体動物の方が絶滅を免れる能力に優れているなら，平均代謝率は時とともに低下すると予想するのが論理的に思える。しかし，代謝の高い種が絶滅すると，それらが残した空白を代謝の高いほかの種が埋めることを研究結果は示唆している。

　語句　metabolism「代謝」，metabolic rate「代謝率」，mollusk「軟体動物」，clam「二枚貝」

No.19 解答 ①

質問の訳　代謝の高いどんな生物が最も絶滅する可能性が低いか。

選択肢の訳　**1**　多くの異なる地域にすむ生物。
　　　　　　2　最も少ない種類の食物を食べる生物。
　　　　　　3　500万年以上前からいる生物。
　　　　　　4　さまざまな動物に食べられる生物。

解説　第1段落最後の mollusks with faster metabolisms were more likely to go extinct から，代謝の高い方が絶滅しやすいことがわかる。質問は，その中でも絶滅の可能性が低いものは何かを問うている。それに該当する説明は第2段落の this risk is lower for species that are more widespread なので，widespread を live in many different areas と表した **1** が正解となる。

No.20 解答 ③

質問の訳　軟体動物に関するどんな発見が研究者を驚かせたか。

選択肢の訳　**1**　進化の速度が緩やかになった。
　　　　　　2　多くの種が絶滅した。
　　　　　　3　全体的な代謝率が変化していない。
　　　　　　4　ほかの動物より代謝が低い。

解説　質問の surprised に対応するのは第3段落の did not expect。研究者たちが予期しなかったのは the average metabolic rate of all mollusks remained consistent だったこと。remained consistent を has not changed と言い換えた **3** が正解。

F

スクリプト

You have 10 seconds to read the situation and Question No. 21.

We've got a range of items that make great gifts. This big display is for the volcano kit. It's fun to build and includes instructions for making fake lava, which appeals to kids who like science. It's out of stock, unfortunately, but we should receive more in about a week. We also have an electronics kit. There's one over here for customers to try out. It's very entertaining, but, to be honest, it doesn't really live up to its promise to teach kids about circuitry. Over here is our dinosaur fossil dig set, which my seven-year-old daughter loves. However, the box can be misleading. It says, "Ages four and up," but in my experience, kids under seven aren't likely to have the patience for it. Finally, we have this superhero action figure. Don't be fooled. It actually teaches about anatomy. If you push these buttons, the various body parts light up, and a voice recording explains what they are.

Now mark your answer on your answer sheet.

全文訳

当店は素晴らしい贈り物になる商品を幅広く置いています。この大きな展示は火山キットのものです。楽しく組み立てられて，模造溶岩を作る説明書も入っています。模造溶岩は，科学好きの子供に人気があります。あいにく在庫を切らしていますが，1週間後くらいにもっと入るはずです。電子回路キットもございます。こちらにお客さまのお試し用のものが1つあります。とても面白いですが，正直申しますと，子供に回路のことを教えるといううたい文句にはあまり沿いません。こちらが当店の恐竜化石発掘セットで，うちの7歳の娘のお気に入りです。ですが，箱が誤解を招きかねません。「4歳以上」と書かれていますが，私の経験では，7歳未満の子供はたぶん根気が続きません。最後に，このスーパーヒーローのアクションフィギュアがございます。だまされないでください。これは実は体の構造について教えてくれます。これらのボタンを押すとさまざまな体の部位が明るくなり，録音された声が，それらが何なのかを説明します。

No.21 解答 ④

状況の訳　5歳の息子の誕生日パーティーが明日あり，あなたは知育関係の贈り物を息子にあげたいと思っている。玩具店の店員があなたに次のように言う。

質問の訳　あなたはどの商品を買うべきか。

選択肢の訳　**1**　火山キット。

95

2　電子回路キット。
　　3　恐竜化石発掘セット。
　　4　アクションフィギュア。
語句　lava「溶岩」，circuitry「回路」，anatomy「解剖，（解剖学的）構造」
解説　火山キットは条件に合うように思えるが，在庫がなく入荷は約1週間後なので，明日のパーティーには間に合わない。電子回路キットは，店員が薦めていない。恐竜化石発掘セットは，店員によると7歳未満の子供には向かない。スーパーヒーローのアクションフィギュアはeducationalという条件に合わないように思えるが，体の構造を教える仕組みになっているので，これを買うのが無難ということになる。

スクリプト

You have 10 seconds to read the situation and Question No. 22.

Recently, there have been reports of spam getting through our e-mail filter. Our IT department is working on improving the filter, but going forward we must be more vigilant about our Internet security. Firstly, and I know you've been told this before, be cautious with e-mails from unknown addresses, and do not open any unsolicited attachments, as they could contain viruses. If you have opened any recently, let me know immediately. As a basic precaution, please also confirm that your firewall is on as soon as you have returned to your computers. In addition, I'll be asking you all to take a mandatory online training program. I'll send the link in an e-mail after this meeting. I apologize for the short notice, but please complete the training by the end of the week, as we would like to introduce a daily security checklist as soon as possible.

Now mark your answer on your answer sheet.

全文訳

最近，スパムがわが社のメールフィルターをすり抜けているという報告があります。IT部がフィルターの改善に取り組んでいますが，今後はインターネットのセキュリティーにもっと注意しなければなりません。まず，この話は前にもしましたが，知らないアドレスからのメールに用心し，こちらから頼んだものではない添付ファイルは一切開かないでください。ウイルスが含まれているかもしれませんから。最近1通でも開いた人は，直ちに私に知らせてください。基本的な予防策として，自分のコンピューターに戻り次第，ファイアウォールがオンになっていることも確認してください。加えて，全員にお願いしますが，義務付けられたオンライントレーニングプログラムを受けてください。この会議後にメールでリンクを送ります。急な通知で申し訳ありませんが，今週中にはトレーニングを完了してください。できるだけ早く毎日のセキュリティーチェックリストを導入したいので。

No.22 解答 ②

状況の訳 あなたはオフィス勤務である。最近妙なメールが数件届いたが，開いていない。部長が緊急会議を招集し，次の話をする。

質問の訳 あなたはまず何をすべきか。

選択肢の訳
1 オンライントレーニングを完了する。
2 ファイアウォールの設定を確認する。
3 部長と話す。
4 セキュリティーチェックリストに記入する。

語句 going forward「今後は」，vigilant「用心深い」，unsolicited「求めたものではない」

解説 選択肢の事項について，まず部長は，怪しい添付ファイルを開いた人は直ちに知らせるように言っているが，あなたはメールを開いていないので3は外れる。続いて，自分のコンピューターに戻ったら2のファイアウォールの設定を確認するように言っている。1のオンライントレーニングは今週末までに終えればよい。4のセキュリティーチェックリストは1の後になる。したがって，まずすべきなのは2ということになる。

H

スクリプト

You have 10 seconds to read the situation and Question No. 23.

We have sleeping bags to fit all camping styles and conditions. This one's my personal favorite, the Wilderness Dreamer. It's filled with high-quality goose down, and it's waterproof, too, so you'll be warm even on winter nights. I wouldn't use it during summer or when warm weather is expected, though, as you'd be uncomfortably hot. Over here, we have the Trail Relax and the slightly more expensive Cozy Camper. They're both three-season bags, which means they'll keep you comfortable in every season except winter. Both models are filled with synthetic material, so they're light and easy to wash, but the Cozy Camper has the extra protection of a waterproof outer shell. This means you can camp without a tent or any other shelter. Finally, there's the Nature Cocoon. This one's so popular it's out of stock for the next month. It's filled with down and has a waterproof shell.

Now mark your answer on your answer sheet.

全文訳

　当店はあらゆるキャンプスタイルと条件に合う寝袋をそろえています。これは私の個人的なお気に入り，ウィルダネスドリーマーです。フィリングは高品質のグースダウンで，防水性もありますから，冬の夜でも暖かいです。夏の間や暖かい天気が予想されるときは，不快なくらい暑くなるので，私なら使いませんけれど。こちらにあるのが，トレイルリラックスと，もう少し値の張るコージーキャンパーです。両方ともスリーシー

ズン用の寝袋で、つまり、冬を除く季節はいつでも快適さを保ちます。どちらのモデルもフィリングは合成素材なので軽くて洗いやすいですが、コージーキャンパーは防水のアウターシェルで余分に保護されています。つまり、テントやほかの雨よけは一切なくてもキャンプできるということです。最後にネイチャーコクーンがあります。こちらはとても人気があるので、向こう1カ月は在庫がありません。フィリングはダウンで、シェルは防水です。

No.23 解答 ③

状況の訳 あなたは来週末の夏のバックパック旅行用に寝袋が必要である。テントは持って行かないが、雨が予報されている。店員があなたに次のように言う。

質問の訳 あなたはどの寝袋を買うべきか。

選択肢の訳
1 ウィルダネスドリーマー。
2 トレイルリラックス。
3 コージーキャンパー。
4 ネイチャーコクーン。

語句 shell「シェル、表地」

解説 ウィルダネスドリーマーは防水性があるが夏は不快なくらい暑くなるので自分なら使わないと店員は言っている。トレイルリラックスとコージーキャンパーはどちらも夏でも快適だが、コージーキャンパーは防水性がある。防水性のあるネイチャーコクーンが夏向きかどうかはわからないが、1カ月は在庫がないのでいずれにせよ来週には間に合わない。そうすると、コージーキャンパーが最も適していることになる。

スクリプト

You have 10 seconds to read the situation and Question No. 24.

Well, any weed-killer with dicamba in it would be highly effective, and it wouldn't harm your grass at all. The thing is, though, that chemical has been included in the recent herbicide ban in our state. However, you can get organic products like Broadleaf Natural at most garden stores. They might work if the weed is not well-established yet. One easy solution if the weed is in an isolated patch is just to put a plastic sheet over it to shut out the sun for a couple of weeks. Otherwise, you'll need to first rake any areas containing the weed. That helps to loosen it and makes it easier to pull out by hand. Be sure to wear gloves when you do it to prevent blisters. And whatever you do, you'll have to buy some grass seed and fertilizer to fix the areas the weed has been removed from.

Now mark your answer on your answer sheet.

> 全文訳

えー，ジカンバの入った除草剤なら何でもとても効果的で，芝を傷つけることはまったくないでしょう。ただ問題は，うちの州で最近できた除草剤禁止令にその化学薬品が含まれていることですね。ですが，ブロードリーフナチュラルのような有機製品はほとんどの園芸店で手に入りますよ。雑草がまだ定着していなければ効くかもしれません。雑草がほかから離れた区画にある場合の1つ簡単な解決策は，ただビニールシートをかぶせて2，3週間日光を遮ることです。そうでなければ，雑草を含んだ場所があったらまずは全部レーキでかく必要があります。そうすることで雑草を緩める助けになるし，手で抜くのがより簡単になります。まめができないよう，そうするときは必ず手袋をはめてください。それから，どうするにせよ，雑草を取り除いた場所を修復するために，芝の種と肥料を買わなくちゃなりませんね。

No.24 解答 ④

> 状況の訳

あなたの庭全体の至る所にしつこい雑草がびっしり生えている。近所の人があなたに次のアドバイスをする。

> 質問の訳

雑草を除去するためにあなたは何をすべきか。

> 選択肢の訳

1 ジカンバを含む除草剤を手に入れる。
2 有機除草剤を買う。
3 雑草にビニールシートをかぶせる。
4 雑草を手で取り除く。

> 語句

herbicide「除草剤」，well-established「定着した」

> 解説

ジカンバ入りの除草剤はよく効くが，that chemical（＝ジカンバ）は最近州で禁止されたので手に入らない。有機製品が効くのは雑草が定着していない場合なので，しつこい雑草には効果がない。ビニールシートは雑草が一部分にしかない場合の対策なので，庭全体の至る所に生えていては意味がない。そうすると，最後に説明されているように，レーキでかいて雑草を緩めてから**4**のように手で取り除くしかない。

> スクリプト

You have 10 seconds to read the situation and Question No. 25.

This is a great time of year to hit the trails. There are four guided hikes offered this season. The three-hour Rainbow Hike begins every day at 1 p.m. and goes through an area where the fall colors are currently at their peak. There are steep climbs, though, so it's not recommended for kids under 12. Then, there's the all-day Bird-Watcher Hike, which takes you near the habitats of the park's most beautiful birds. That hike begins every weekday morning at nine. The Sunset Hike will take you to a meadow where, on a clear evening, you can get a breathtaking view of the sun setting behind the mountains. This easy hike begins every Saturday at 4 p.m. Finally, the Lake Hike, which is another evening hike, is popular with kids because of all the fireflies along the trail, but current repair work means the trail won't be open until next month.

Now mark your answer on your answer sheet.

全文訳

今はトレイルに行くには絶好の時期です。今シーズンは，4つのガイド付きハイキングをご用意しています。3時間のレインボーハイキングは毎日午後1時出発で，紅葉が現在真っ盛りの地域を通ります。ですが，急な登りがありますから，12歳未満のお子さんにはお薦めしません。それから，終日のバードウォッチャーハイキングがございまして，公園で最も美しい鳥の生息場所の近くにお連れします。そのハイキングは，平日の毎日午前9時出発です。サンセットハイキングは，晴れた夕方には太陽が山々の後ろに沈む素晴らしい眺めを見ることのできる草原にお連れします。このお手軽なハイキングは，毎週土曜日の午後4時出発です。最後にレイクハイキングですが，これも夕方のハイキングで，トレイル沿いの実にたくさんの蛍のおかげでお子さんに人気がありますが，現在補修工事中のため，トレイルは来月までオープンしません。

No.25 解答 ③

状況の訳 あなたと6歳の息子は，来週近くの国立公園でガイド付きハイキングに行きたいと思っている。あなたは平日の午前中は仕事がある。公園に電話し，次のように言われる。

質問の訳 あなたはどのハイキングに行くべきか。

選択肢の訳 1 レインボーハイキング。
2 バードウォッチャーハイキング。
3 サンセットハイキング。
4 レイクハイキング。

語句 hit「～に出かける」

解説 まずレインボーハイキングは12歳未満の子供には向かないので外れる。バードウォッチャーハイキングは平日の午前中なので，仕事があって行けない。サンセットハイキングは毎週土曜日の午後4時からで，年齢については何も言っていないので条件に合う。レイクハイキングも夕方からなので条件に合いそうだが，トレイルが工事中で来月まで使えないと最後に言っているので，来週行けるのはサンセットハイキングということになる。

スクリプト

This is an interview with Jason Windham, who runs a restaurant consulting company.

Interviewer (I): Jason, thanks for being on our program today.

Jason Windham (J): Thank you for having me.

I: So, to begin with, could you tell us a bit about exactly what a restaurant consultant does?

J: Sure. Basically, my job is to fill in the gaps in a restaurant owner's knowledge. Many restaurateurs are experts when it comes to the food preparation side of the business, but they may not be as adept at advertising, managing staff, or maximizing profits. Approximately one-third of restaurants fail in their first year of operation, and another third just barely scrape by. I try to provide advice that will move restaurants into the final one-third that thrive. I come in and observe their operations, carry out customer surveys, and provide recommendations on things they can improve.

I: Why do so many restaurants fail?

J: Well, one of the main reasons is the cutthroat competition. In today's economy, finding a way to differentiate yourself is essential. We work closely with our clients to research what customers in their area want and then find ways to provide it. It could be anything from an innovative menu to a more-welcoming décor. One of our clients, for example, was on the verge of bankruptcy even though her dishes were some of the tastiest in the city. We helped her to innovate by taking traditional foods and serving them in a unique way, which helped her get back into the black within just a few months.

I: Many people may have the impression that consultants are just for big restaurant chains. Do you do any work for smaller, independent restaurants?

J: Yes, in fact, that's the largest segment of our business. Of course, some businesses have initial concerns about whether or not they can afford our fees, but in the long term, they almost always end up with more money in their pockets as a result of our recommendations.

I: Can you elaborate on how you help your clients?

J: Well, one of the things we do is collect a great deal of data. For example, we're able to give restaurant owners a new perspective on their menu by analyzing each dish based on factors including popularity, price, and cost of ingredients. We then often suggest that the owner either remove or rework items that are eating into their profits. For instance, we may help them find a new supplier that will save them money without sacrificing quality. We also offer menu redesigns that can increase sales by up to 30 percent. By emphasizing the dishes with high profit margins, you can increase orders of those foods that will improve your earnings the most.

I: Does your firm have a specialty?

J: Well, one thing we always focus on is improving customer loyalty. A lot of businesses just give out cards that offer rewards to repeat customers, but we go far beyond that. We've found that while people will put up with an occasional slip-up in the kitchen that leads to an overcooked dish, they won't tolerate servers who are rude or inattentive. Therefore, we stress thorough training programs that produce knowledgeable, courteous servers. That can have a huge impact on a customer's impression of their dining experience and makes them much more likely to come back. We've also found that engaging with customers using social media is highly effective. Responding to customers who leave online reviews, even negative ones, can do wonders for a business. Not only does it provide excellent feedback, but it helps greatly with word-of-mouth advertising.

I: Well, it sounds like a fascinating line of work. Thanks so much for telling us about it today.

J: It was my pleasure.

Questions

No.26 According to Jason, what must restaurants do to survive?

No.27 What does Jason say about getting customers to return?

全文訳

これは飲食店コンサルティング会社を経営しているジェイソン・ウィンダムとのインタビューです。

聞き手（以下「聞」）： ジェイソン，今日は当番組にご出演いただきありがとうございます。

ジェイソン・ウィンダム（以下「ジ」）： お招きいただきありがとうございます。

聞： では，まず初めに，飲食店コンサルタントとは一体どんな仕事なのか，少しお話しいただけますか。

ジ： わかりました。基本的に，私の仕事は，飲食店オーナーの知識の欠けている部分を埋めることです。多くの飲食店経営者は，商売の調理の面では専門家ですが，広告やスタッフ管理や利益の最大化にはそれほど熟達していないこともあります。飲食店のおよそ3分の1は営業1年目でつぶれ，もう3分の1はぎりぎりで持ちこたえています。私は，繁盛している最後の3分の1に飲食店を入れるようなアドバイスを提供

するよう努めています。店内に入って業務を観察し，顧客アンケートを実施し，飲食店が改善できることに関する助言を行います。

聞：どうしてそんなに多くの飲食店がつぶれるのでしょうか。

ジ：そうですね，主な理由の１つは激しい競争です。今日の経済では，差別化する方法を見つけることが必須です。私たちはクライアントと緊密に協力して，クライアントの地域の顧客が何を欲しているかを調査し，そしてそれを提供する方法を見つけようとします。革新的なメニューでも，もっと温かい雰囲気の装飾でも，どんなものでも可能性があるでしょう。例えばクライアントの１人は，作る料理は市内で一番おいしい部類に入るのに，倒産寸前でした。私たちは，伝統的な料理を取り入れてそれを独自のやり方でお客さまに出すことで，新しいことに挑戦するよう彼女を手助けし，そのおかげで彼女はほんの数カ月以内にまた黒字に戻ることができました。

聞：多くの人は，コンサルタントは大手飲食店チェーンのためだけのものだというイメージを持っているかもしれません。もっと小さな独立系の飲食店の仕事をされることもありますか。

ジ：はい，実はそれが私たちの会社の最も大きな部分です。もちろん，私たちの料金を払う金銭的余裕があるかどうか，最初は心配する店もありますが，長い目で見れば，私たちの助言の結果，ほとんどいつも最終的には懐に入るお金が増えることになります。

聞：どうやってクライアントの手助けをするのか，もっと詳しく教えてもらえますか。

ジ：えー，私たちがすることの１つは，大量のデータを集めることです。例えば，人気と価格と材料コストを含む要素に基づいてそれぞれの料理を分析することで，飲食店オーナーにメニューに関する新しい視点を与えることができます。そして，利益を圧迫している品目をオーナーが外すか手直しすることをしばしば提案します。例えば，質を犠牲にせずともお金の節約になる新しい仕入れ業者をオーナーが見つけるお手伝いをできるかもしれません。また，売り上げを最大３割伸ばすことのできるメニューの再構築を提案しています。利益率の高い料理を目立たせることで，収益を最も改善するそうした料理の注文を増やすことができるんです。

聞：御社に得意分野はありますか。

ジ：えー，私たちがいつも重点を置いている１つのことは，顧客の忠誠心を高めることです。多くの店は常連客に特典を提供するカードを配るだけですが，私たちはそのはるか上を行きます。人々は厨房で時々ちょっとしたミスがあって，火を通し過ぎた料理が出てきても我慢する一方で，無礼だったり不注意だったりする給仕は許容しないことに，私たちは気付きました。ですから私たちは，知識を持っていて礼儀正しい給仕を育てる徹底したトレーニングプログラムを重視しています。これは，顧客が食事の経験に持つ印象にとても大きな影響を与えることがありますし，顧客が戻ってくる可能性をはるかに高くします。また，ソーシャルメディアを利用して顧客に積極的にかかわることも非常に効果的だとも気付きました。ネットにレビューを残す顧客に返答することは，たとえそのレビューが否定的なものだったとしても，店にとってもの

すごく大きなメリットになり得ます。これは素晴らしいフィードバックとなるだけでなく，口コミの宣伝にもとても役立ちます。

聞：えー，とても魅力的なお仕事のようですね。今日はそのお話をしていただきどうもありがとうございました。

ジ：こちらこそありがとうございました。

語句 restaurateur「飲食店経営者」, adept at ～「～に熟練した」, scrape by「何とかやっていく」, cutthroat「激烈な」, décor「装飾」, elaborate on ～「～についてさらに詳しく述べる」, rework「～を手直しする」, redesign「再設計」, slip-up「ちょっとした誤り」, inattentive「不注意な」, knowledgeable「物知りの」, word-of-mouth「口伝えの」

No.26 解答

質問の訳 ジェイソンによると，飲食店は生き残るために何をしなければならないか。

選択肢の訳
1 ほかの飲食店より目立つ方法を見つける。
2 信頼を置いているさまざまな仕入れ業者を使う。
3 最高級の材料のみを使う。
4 メニューに幅広い料理を加える。

解説 多くの飲食店がつぶれる理由を尋ねられたジェイソンは，3つ目の発言で，finding a way to differentiate yourself is essential と言い，メニューを刷新して成功した例について述べている。differentiate yourself を stand out from other restaurants と言い換えた **1** が正解。ジェイソンが言っているのはメニューを innovative にすることで，**4** のように品数を増やすことではない。

No.27 解答

質問の訳 顧客に戻って来てもらうことについてジェイソンは何と言っているか。

選択肢の訳
1 価格を低く抑えることがたいてい最も重要な要素だ。
2 顧客特典プログラムに力を入れることが重要だ。
3 質の高いサービスを提供することが優先事項であるべきだ。
4 メニューに頻繁に新しい料理を加えるべきだ。

解説 ジェイソンの6つ目の発言の customer loyalty は，顧客が特定の店やブランドに信頼や愛着を持ち繰り返し利用することで，質問の getting customers to return はそれに対応している。ジェイソンは，**2** の顧客報奨プログラムより重要なのは knowledgeable, courteous servers を育てることで，それにより顧客が戻ってくる可能性が高くなると言っている。つまり，**3** のように，質の高いサービスの提供を最優先させるべきだというのがジェイソンの考えということになる。

104

二次試験・面接 トピックカード A 日程 問題編 p.64

ここでは，A日程の5つのトピックをモデルスピーチとしました。

A日程

1. Are people today becoming less tolerant of different beliefs and cultures?

Although there is still a lot of conflict between people of different beliefs and cultures today, I think that intolerance is actually decreasing overall due to government policies, increased knowledge of other cultures, and mass media. First of all, many modern constitutions and government laws make discrimination of things like religion illegal. The fact that these types of laws had enough public support to be passed is evidence that more people understand the importance of accepting other beliefs and cultures. Secondly, people are becoming more aware of the positive aspects of other cultures. For example, in the past, many Westerners thought their cultures were superior to indigenous cultures. However, indigenous knowledge about things like ecology and herbal medicines has made more people realize that indigenous cultures deserve more respect. Finally, I think that books and movies are making people more tolerant. Many countries that previously had poor relations have been brought closer together by the popularity of music, movies, or TV programs. These have brought increased understanding and tolerance, especially among younger generations. In conclusion, I'm very optimistic that the trends of legal changes, increased respect for foreign cultures, and shared entertainment will continue to make people more tolerant in the future.

解説 「最近の人々は異なる信条や文化に対して許容力が低下しているか」

トピックに反対の立場からのスピーチ。「現代では正しい情報に基づいて人々の異文化への意識が高まっている」という大きな観点をベースに，具体的な理由を①多くの憲法や法律が差別を違法なものと見なしている，②人々は異文化のよい点に気付き始めている，③本，音楽，映画といったものを通して異文化理解が進んでいる，の3つとしている。「正しい情報」の共有，という抽象的な理由をかなり具体的なものに落とし込むことで3つの理由が重複しないように工夫している。

2. Agree or disagree: Some professional athletes' salaries have become too high to justify

It is not unusual for professional athletes these days to receive millions of dollars in salary. Although some people say these amounts are unjustifiable, I think that athletes deserve them. First, professional athletes provide an amazing service to society. They entertain millions of people, increase cities' and countries' pride, and inspire young people to work harder and try to achieve their dreams. Since they provide such an important service, it is natural that they receive a huge salary. Secondly, athletes' salaries reflect the free market. Since there is a huge demand for tickets to sporting events, it makes sense that ticket prices would be expensive and that the athletes would be highly paid. It would be wrong for the government or some other organization to try to prevent athletes from being compensated based on the huge demand for their services. Finally, due to the competitive environment in sports, most athletes can only be active while they are young and physically fit. There will always be even younger athletes who are ready to take over the roles of those who are older. Therefore, it is reasonable for athletes to be paid high salaries to support their lives after their short careers. For these reasons, I think elite athletes deserve every penny that they are paid.

> **解説** 「賛成か反対か：一部のプロスポーツ選手の報酬は正当化できないほど高額になった」
>
> Although some people say ～ と賛成の立場の人への理解を示しながらも，反対の立場から具体的な理由を3つ挙げている。①人，社会，国に与えるポジティブな影響の大きさ，②公平な市場価値の反映，③競争の激しさと選手生命の短さ，といった説得力のある理由をきちんと展開している。それぞれの理由のすべてに「～という理由から選手は十分な報酬を受けるべきである」という結論が繰り返されているところも，このスピーチをとても印象深く，強いものにしている。

3. Is it possible for consumers to completely avoid companies involved in unethical activities?

Nowadays, some consumers try to completely avoid supporting companies that have unethical business practices. However, I would like to tell you why I don't think this is really possible. First, how can a consumer accurately judge whether a company is an ethical one? These days, supply chains are so complicated that even companies themselves may not know where all their products and raw materials come from. Therefore, consumers cannot be expected to research every product that they buy to make sure the company is operating ethically. In addition, consumers may sometimes have limited choices over the businesses they use. For example, significant services in the

Internet industry are driven by a few big companies. Many people cannot easily find similar services or move their data to other websites simply because they heard about the companies' unethical practices. Finally, unless a consumer is rich, it is not realistic to expect someone to buy only products produced by ethical companies. Things like organic products and electric cars are so expensive that many people cannot afford them. While most people would like to buy ethically produced products, it is just not practical for everyone. Consumers should try to make ethical choices when using money, but I think it would be going too far to say everyone needs to completely avoid companies involved in unethical activities.

解説 「消費者は非倫理的な活動にかかわっている企業を完全に避けることができるか」

トピックに対して「現実的ではない」という否定の立場から，①流通が複雑な今日では，消費者がすべての商品情報を知るのは難しい，②利用できる企業の選択肢が少ないこともある，③価格を考えると誰にとっても現実的というわけではない，の3点を論拠に反論している。First で始まる文のように，効果的に疑問文を使うテクニックはぜひマスターしたい。実際には自分で問いを出し，自分で答えるのだが，それでも聞き手に対してインタラクティブに働きかけている印象を残すだろう。

4. Should the government provide more funds to boost the economies of rural areas?

These days, many rural areas are facing a crisis due to depopulation. Therefore, I think the government should provide more funds to boost their economies. As Japanese cities have expanded, more and more young people have been moving to urban areas. Unfortunately, this has created serious problems for the people who remain in the countryside. Local economies are suffering from labor shortages and lack of consumers, so they require stimulation. Another reason for increasing funding to rural areas is to enable local governments to protect the environment. If the number of taxpayers declines, so will tax revenue, and there will be less money available for environmental protection. Economic stimulation would increase funds for environmental protection, so it is extremely important. My final reason is agriculture. Many farmers are struggling financially, and it would be terrible if their problems worsened or they went bankrupt. Not only would there be terrible suffering among farming families, but it would create problems in the food supply. In conclusion, I think the government should do more to stimulate rural economies. Due to depopulation, the need for environmental protection, and the importance of the agricultural industry, it is urgent that the government take action before it is too late.

解説「地方経済を成長させるために政府はより多くの資金を投入すべきか」

冒頭で地方の根本的な問題である過疎化に触れた後，トピックに賛成の立場を明確にしている。資金投入をすべきだという根拠は，①若者が都市部に流れ空洞化した地方経済には景気刺激が必要，②環境保全の予算を確保するため，③地方の農業をサポートするため，の3つ。どれも地方の急激な人口減少が引き起こしている問題なので，冒頭でこれに言及しておいたのは効果的だ。このスピーチでは，最後に it is urgent that ～「～は喫緊の課題である」とさらに積極的な態度で意見を述べている。

5. Should punishments for people who commit financial crimes be made stricter?

I strongly believe in stricter penalties for people who commit financial crimes. Many people are more worried about violent crimes, but financial crimes often have more-serious consequences. Although no one is directly harmed physically, financial crimes often have far-reaching and long-lasting consequences. For example, if a financial adviser steals money from clients, it could cause the clients to become homeless, have trouble paying medical bills, or lose their retirement savings. Secondly, stricter punishments would help to deter crimes. There are many financial crimes in the news these days, so they seem to be becoming extremely common. If people were more afraid of the penalties, it might help to prevent them from breaking the law. Finally, it is unfair that people who commit financial crimes tend to be punished less harshly. Actually, many financial criminals who receive prison sentences only receive fairly short ones. If the point of prison is either to reform criminals to become productive citizens or to prevent them from committing crimes again, longer sentences are necessary for achieving either of these aims. In conclusion, due to financial crimes' seriousness, the need to prevent them, and the purpose of prison sentences, I believe that the law should be amended so that people who commit such crimes would receive harsher punishments.

解説「経済犯罪を犯した人たちへの刑罰をより厳しくすべきか」

トピックに賛成であることを述べてから，経済犯罪の影響力の大きさ，深刻さについて丁寧に具体例を交えて説明している。3つの理由は，①経済犯罪は人々が思うより深刻な被害を与える，②経済犯罪を未然に防ぐため，③刑罰の重さの公平性の観点から。①が十分に展開されていることで②③の理由の重要さが聞き手により正確に伝わる。commit a crime や receive prison sentences，amend the law など基本の法律用語は1級受験者にはマストなので，ぜひ使えるようにしておこう。

108

2021-3

一次試験
筆記解答・解説　　p.110〜128

一次試験
リスニング解答・解説　p.129〜156

二次試験
面接解答・解説　　p.157〜160

解 答 一 覧

一次試験・筆記

1

(1)	3	(10)	4	(19)	3
(2)	2	(11)	3	(20)	1
(3)	1	(12)	4	(21)	3
(4)	4	(13)	1	(22)	1
(5)	3	(14)	3	(23)	1
(6)	2	(15)	2	(24)	4
(7)	1	(16)	4	(25)	2
(8)	4	(17)	1		
(9)	4	(18)	3		

2

(26)	4	(29)	3
(27)	1	(30)	4
(28)	3	(31)	2

3

(32)	4	(35)	4	(38)	3
(33)	1	(36)	3	(39)	2
(34)	2	(37)	2	(40)	1
				(41)	4

4　解答例は本文参照

一次試験・リスニング

Part 1

No. 1	3	No. 5	1	No. 9	1
No. 2	1	No. 6	2	No.10	1
No. 3	1	No. 7	4		
No. 4	4	No. 8	2		

Part 2

No.11	3	No.15	4	No.19	1
No.12	2	No.16	2	No.20	2
No.13	3	No.17	4		
No.14	2	No.18	1		

Part 3

No.21	4	No.23	4	No.25	1
No.22	2	No.24	3		

Part 4

No.26	1	No.27	3

一次試験・筆記 **1** 問題編 p.66 ～ 68

(1) ―解答 3 ....
訳 ドアはとても薄っぺらだったので，少年が蹴ると足が木製のパネルを突き破った。
語句 1「かび臭い」　2「けば立った」　3「薄っぺらな」　4「かすんだ」
解説 足がパネルを突き破ったのだから，flimsy「薄っぺらな，もろい」ドアだったことになる。flimsy には「（証拠などが）説得力のない」という意味もある。

(2) ―解答 2 ....
訳 カールは家賃を数カ月払わなかった後，アパートからの立ち退きを迫られていた。彼は家賃のお金を工面する最後のチャンスを与えられた。
語句 1「口論」　　2「立ち退き」　　3「従属」　　4「指名」
解説 滞納している家賃を払う最後のチャンスを与えられたという第2文から，お金を工面できなければカールはアパートから出ていかざるを得ないと考えられる。eviction は動詞 evict「～を立ち退かせる」の名詞。

(3) ―解答 1 ....
訳 保守政権は，共産主義思想の拡散を禁じる厳格な法律を成立させた。そうした思想を広めた罪に問われた者は，誰でも厳罰に処せられた。
語句 1「普及，拡散」　　　　　2「回復」
3「（裁判所が出す）命令」　　4「規制撤廃」
解説 動詞 propagate は第2文の spread と同義だが，特に「（思想・情報など）を広める，拡散させる」という意味で用いられる。propagation はその名詞。

(4) ―解答 4 ....
訳 子供たちはそのテレビ番組にすっかり魅了されていたので，番組の最初から最後まで誰も一言も発しなかった。
語句 1「徐々にむしばまれた」　　2「締め付けられた」
3「一掃された」　　　　　　　4「魅了された」
解説 ずっと無言だったのだから，子供たちは番組に釘付けだったと推測される。mesmerize「～を魅了する」は通例受け身で用いられる。類義語は fascinate。

(5) ―解答 3 ....
訳 その店で盗みを働いたととがめられたとき，ポーラは無実を装おうとした。しかし，彼女のバッグの中の未払いの服が，彼女がうそをついていることを証明した。
語句 1「～を押しつぶす」　　　　　2「～を乗船させる」

110

3「〜を装う」　　　　　　　　　4「〜を甘やかす」

解説 feign は feign illness [surprise]「病気を装う［驚いたふりをする］」のように，状態や感情を表す名詞を直接目的語に取ることが多い。類義語 pretend にも同じ用法はあるが，pretend to be ill [surprised] と to *do* を用いる方が一般的。

(6) ―解答 **2**

訳 市長は最近行った演説で，生徒たちに全国学力試験の適切な準備をさせなかったことで市の教育者たちを叱責（しっせき）した。

語句 1「〜に浮き彫りを施した」　　　2「〜を叱責した」
　　　　3「〜を和らげた」　　　　　　　4「〜を浪費した」

解説 試験の準備が不十分だったのなら，結果はよくなかったはず。それに対して市長が「怒った」と考えるのが妥当である。berate は scold の堅い語。

(7) ―解答 **1**

訳 トビーは自宅の庭と隣家の庭の間にある柵の穴を修理し，隣の犬が通り抜けられないようにした。

語句 1「隣接した」　　　　　　　　　2「正道から外れた」
　　　　3「欠点のない」　　　　　　　　4「恐れを知らない」

解説 文脈から，「隣の」という意味の語が入ると考えられる。adjacent の類義語に adjoining があるが，*A* adjacent to *B*「B に隣接する A」のような叙述用法は adjacent にしかない。問題文のような限定用法ではどちらも用いられる。

(8) ―解答 **4**

訳 エルは生来愛想がよくないので，人と会話を始めて新しい友達を作るのはいつも難しく感じる。

語句 1「簡潔な」　　2「曲げやすい」　3「不注意な」　　4「愛想のよい」

解説 amiable は「(人・振る舞いが) 愛想のよい，感じのよい」という意味。似た形容詞 amicable は「(事柄が) 友好的な，協調的な」という意味なので，区別して覚えておこう。語頭の a の発音が異なることにも注意。

(9) ―解答 **4**

訳 A：ボブ，会話に自分の意見を不意に差し挟もうとする前に，ほかの人たちが言っていることをもっと注意して聞いた方がいいよ。

　　B：はいはい，わかってるよ。とても気になる話題だと，つい熱くなるんだ。

語句 1「〜を軽蔑する」　　　　　　　2「〜の効果をなくす」
　　　　3「〜を見る」　　　　　　　　　4「(言葉) を不意に差し挟む」

解説 話の流れから，A は人の会話に割り込むボブの癖について注意しているのだと考えられる。interject は，人の話を遮って言葉を発すること。

(10) – 解答 **4** ･･･

訳 その自動車運転者は交通違反で切符を切られた。彼女は制限速度の時速
25 キロオーバーで運転して捕まった。

語句 1「アンサンブル」　　　　　　　2「性向，性癖」
3「（勝ち目がない）強敵」　　　4「違反」

解説 制限速度をオーバーして捕まったのだから，交通「違反」をしたことに
なる。infraction は violation と同義で，「（規則・法律などの）違反」
という意味。

(11) – 解答 **3** ･･･

訳 その国の経済はとても強力だったので，世界のほかの工業国を襲った金
融危機から免れたままだった。

語句 1「相反する感情を抱く」　　　2「予知する」
3「免れた，影響されない」　　4「不均衡な」

解説 immune は「（病気に）免疫のある」が本義だが，問題文のように，ネ
ガティブな事柄の影響から免れることに広く用いられる。

(12) – 解答 **4** ･･･

訳 A：この文書を 100 ドルで翻訳してくれる人を誰か知らない？
B：ジョーに頼んでみたら？ フランス語がわかるし，収入を増やす方法
をいつも探しているよ。

語句 1「～に吐き気を催させる」　　2「～を排斥する」
3「（人）を遠ざける」　　　　　4「～を増加させる」

解説 augment「～を増やす，増加させる」は increase の堅い語。デジタル
情報を現実に付加する技術「拡張現実」の略語 AR は augmented
reality から来ている。

(13) – 解答 **1** ･･･

訳 その社長は，全社員をハワイ旅行に連れて行った際に先例を作った。そ
れ以後，利益が下がったときでも，社員は毎年旅行があるものと思った。

語句 1「先例，前例」　　　　　　　2「深刻な問題」
3「（自然などの）豊かな恵み」　4「追加料金」

解説 ハワイ旅行の後は毎年の旅行が当たり前になったのだから，ハワイ旅行
は社員旅行の precedent「先例」になったことになる。動詞 precede
「～に先立つ」，名詞 precedence「先行」もまとめて覚えよう。

(14) – 解答 **3** ･･･

訳 ストライキ中，バス会社の怒った従業員たちは市役所の外に立って「今
こそ賃上げを！」とシュプレヒコールを上げた。

語句 1「～を妨げている」　　　　　2「～に思いとどまらせている」
3「～と連呼している」　　　　　4「（協力など）を得ている」

解説 chant は大勢の人が声をそろえて同じ言葉を叫ぶこと。ストライキやデ

112

モでは「～とシュプレヒコールを上げる」という意味になる。

(15) – 解答 **2** ・・・

訳 その古代部族がわずかな時間でも1つの地域には決して住まなかったと新しい証拠が示唆していることから，専門家は，その部族は遊牧民だったと今では考えている。

語句 **1**「悪意のない」 **2**「遊牧の」 **3**「軽蔑を示す」 **4**「博識な」

解説 文の後半から，その部族は1つの土地に定住せず移動し続けていたことがわかる。そのような人を nomad「遊牧民」と言い，nomadic はその形容詞。

(16) – 解答 **4** ・・・

訳 何週間も逃走していた脱獄囚は，ついに警察に出頭した。人生の残りを逃亡者として生きたくはない，と彼は言った。

語句 **1**「ずる休みする生徒」 **2**「巨匠，名手」
3「(社交界の) 名士」 **4**「逃亡者」

解説 on the run「逃走中で」の状態を続けている人を fugitive「逃亡者，逃走犯」と言う。turn *oneself* in は「自首する，出頭する」の意味。

(17) – 解答 **1** ・・・

訳 そのクルーズ船の乗客は，提供されているアクティビティーを利用するよう促された。追加料金なしで，さまざまな講座とショーがあった。

語句 **1**「(avail *oneself* of で) ～を利用する」
2「(古い考えなど) を焼き直す」
3「～を無効にする」
4「～を厄介払いする」

解説 動詞 avail は「(～の) 役に立つ」が本義だが，avail *oneself* of ～ で「(提供されたもの・機会など) を利用する」という意味になる。問題文では，さまざまなアクティビティーが on offer「利用できて，提供されて」いる状況である。

(18) – 解答 **3** ・・・

訳 A：トバイアス，首のその病変はもう医者に診てもらった？ 重いものかもしれないじゃない。
B：痛みはないんだけど，今日予約を入れるよ。注意してくれてありがとう。

語句 **1**「敬意」 **2**「(岩・壁の) 裂け目」
3「病変」 **4**「大失敗」

解説 病院に行くのだから，首にあるのは lesion「病変」。lesion はけがや病気が原因で皮膚・脳・内臓などにできる異変のこと。

(19) – 解答 **3** ・・・

訳 その新入社員が休憩室で上司について軽蔑的な発言をした後，ほかの人

への否定的な意見は胸にしまっておくよう同僚が警告した。

- 語句 1「無気力な」 2「物思いに沈んだ」
- 3「軽蔑的な」 4「脳の」
- 解説 後半の negative から，新入社員は上司を悪く言ったのだと考えられる。動詞 derogate「〜をけなす」も覚えておきたい。

(20) − 解答 **1**

- 訳 なぜ仕事を時間どおりに終わらせなかったのかと尋ねられた新入社員は，ばつの悪そうな顔をし，指示を理解していなかったとおずおずと認めた。
- 語句 1「おずおずと」 2「悪魔のように，ひどく」
- 3「だまされやすく」 4「熱心に」
- 解説 形容詞 sheepish は，特に自分のしたことへの罪悪感から「おどおどした，きまりの悪い」という意味で，sheepishly はその副詞。この文では，指示を理解しないまま時間を無駄にしたことを恥じているという意味合いである。

(21) − 解答 **3**

- 訳 世界史に関する議論中，その学生は，自身の立論が批判に耐えられないものだとようやく気付き，自分は勝てないと悟った。
- 語句 1「粘り強い」 2「潜在意識の」
- 3「批判に耐えられない」 4「発生期の」
- 解説 議論で勝てないのだから，空所には「弱い」に類する語が入ると考えられる。untenable は「（立場・意見などが）批判［攻撃］に耐えられない」という意味。

(22) − 解答 **1**

- 訳 ジョバンニは所有するクラシックカーの交換部品が必要だったが，修理工場の整備士は，車がとても古いのでそれ用の部品は手に入れるのが難しいと言った。
- 語句 1「〜を手に入れる」 2「〜を激しく攻撃する」
- 3「口を閉ざす」 4「ろ過して〜を除去する」
- 解説 come by 〜 は be hard [easy] to come by「手に入れるのが難しい［容易だ］」というフレーズで用いられることが多い。

(23) − 解答 **1**

- 訳 その若いシマウマが母親や群れのほかのシマウマからはぐれると，近くの茂みで待っていたライオンに狙いを定めて仕留められた。
- 語句 1「狙いを定めて仕留められた」 2「易しくされた」
- 3「興趣を添えられた」 4「ゆっくり元に戻された」
- 解説 pick off は「〜に狙いを定めて（銃で）撃つ」が基本の意味だが，ライオンなので，「撃つ」ではなく「仕留める」という意味で用いられている。

(24) – 解答 **4** ••

訳 中間成績表で悪い点を取った後，ロザリンドは，学期の後半は**身を入れ**て一生懸命勉強する必要があると気付いた。

語句 **1**「～を誇大に宣伝する」 **2**「～を一気に書く」
3「失敗する」 **4**「本気で取りかかる」

解説 buckle down and work [study] hard は決まり文句。同じ意味の句動詞に knuckle down がある。progress report は，学習の進度状況を評価した報告書。

(25) – 解答 **2** ••

訳 Ａ：販売プロジェクトはどうしてこんなに時間がかかっているの？
Ｂ：あいにく想定外の問題がいくつか**持ち上がり**まして，解決にはしばらくかかります。

語句 **1**「～を通って落ちた」 **2**「(不意に) 持ち上がった」
3「(うわさなどが) 流れた」 **4**「すっと入ってきた」

解説 crop up は「(予想外の事柄が) 持ち上がる，生じる，現れる」という意味。同じ意味の句動詞に come up がある。

一次試験・筆記 **2** | 問題編 p.69～71

全文訳 **女性らしさの神秘**

　ベティ・フリーダンの 1963 年のベストセラー『女性らしさの神秘』は，著者の世代の女性が経験する，「何とも言いようのないうずくような不満」と著者が呼んだものを取り上げている。20 世紀の郊外の暮らしは類を見ない度合いの余暇とぜいたくをアメリカの女性にもたらしており，ほとんどのアメリカの女性は主婦としての役割を喜んで受け入れているように思えた。しかし，その穏やかな表面の下にフリーダンが見たのは，彼女が「女性らしさの神秘」と名付けた，母親と主婦と結婚のパートナーとしての女性の役割に関する説明し難い理想の女性像にかなうために悪戦苦闘する——だが最終的に失敗する——女性たちだった。フリーダンの考えでは，この理想が，自分たちは社会の期待に応えていないという漠然としてはいるが圧倒的な感覚を女性にもたらしたのである。

　女性らしさの神秘は女性をただの消費者に変えた，とフリーダンは論じる。それ以前の世代では，女性は衣服と家庭用品を作っていたし，農村地域では作物を世話し動物を育てていた。さらに第 2 次世界大戦中には，男性が戦いに出向いたので，女性は伝統的に男性向けだった職業の空白を埋めていた。だが戦後の年月には，女性は生産することによってではなく，家電製品や冷凍食品といった物を購入することによって経済に貢献した。企業と広告主は，家庭の幸せという通俗的なイメージを用いてこれらの製品を売ったが，それらの製品は，女性らしさの神秘を熱望する主婦を誘い込むことを特に意図したものだった。しかしフリーダンは，このイメージは (女性を) 搾取する神話にすぎ

115

ないと見なした。

　フリーダンの本は挑発的で情熱的だが，欠点がないわけではない。まず何よりも，この本は狭い視野を示していると批判されている。フリーダンはエリート大学で高等教育を受けた白人卒業生であり，『女性らしさの神秘』はほぼ中流階級と上流階級出身の主婦だけを集中的に扱っている。だが，この本が出版された当時，女性の3分の1は労働者であり，その多くは経済的必要から家庭にとどまることができない人たちだった。同じく軽視されているのは人種的マイノリティーで，子供の世話をする重圧を軽減するため家事手伝いとして雇われるという文脈でごく短く言及されているにすぎない。確かに欠点はあるものの，この本は数百万人のアメリカの女性の痛いところを突き，抗議活動，女性問題のメディア報道，そしてとりわけ，変化した意識の触媒としての役を担った。これらがまとまって，今日なお活発なフェミニズム運動の発展に寄与したのである。

> 語句　mystique「神秘的雰囲気」，nameless「名状し難い」，unparalleled「並ぶもののない」，placid「穏やかな」，dub *A B*「A を B と呼ぶ，名付ける」，indefinable「説明できない」，bliss「至福」，entice「～を誘う」，exploitative「搾取した」，provocative「挑発的な」，disregard「～を軽視する」，touch a nerve「痛いところを突く」，catalyst「触発するもの」

(26) —解答　④

> 解説　フリーダンの著作のテーマが見かけの豊かさの裏に潜む女性の dissatisfaction であり，空所文の this ideal（＝理想の母親と主婦と結婚のパートナー）にかなうことは結局できない，という前文の内容を考えると，空所にはネガティブな内容が入る。理想の女性像を society's expectations と言い換えている **4** が正解。

(27) —解答　①

> 解説　空所後では，昔の女性と第2次世界大戦後の女性が対比されている。昔の女性は，物を作ったり男性の代わりをしたりと，by producing で経済に貢献した。しかし戦後の女性は by purchasing でしか経済に貢献しなかった。つまり，女性は「ただの消費者」になったことになる。

(28) —解答　③

> 解説　空所後のフリーダンに対する批判は，エリートであるフリーダンは中流と上流階級の主婦を対象とし，多くの働く女性や人種的マイノリティーを軽視したというもの。**3** の「狭い視野」がこれを的確に表している。

全文訳　リード・テクニック

　1950年代に開発されたリード・テクニックは，自白を引き出すため警察機関によって用いられている。このテクニックの核となるのは，容疑者がいつうそをついているのかを明らかにするよう設計された口頭尋問によって，罪を認めさせることである。リード・テクニックは尋問の8割近くで自白を引き出すと報告されているが，批判的な人た

116

ちは，無実の容疑者を多数投獄している責任があると主張する。1つ大きな問題は，このテクニックが不安の兆候の検知を重視することだと彼らは論じる。リード・テクニックが開発されたときに心理学の専門家が仮定したのは，容疑者の絶えず移動する視線や言い間違いは外に現れた緊張の度合いを示すものであり，この不安の様子には人をだまそうという企てが潜んでいるということだった。しかし，以後の研究で，厳しい取り調べを受けている状況下で平静を保つのは多くの人にとって概して困難なので，ボディーランゲージそれ自体はうそをついていることの信頼に足る指標ではないことが明らかになっている。

　司法制度を信頼する一部の容疑者は罪を自白する可能性が高いこともわかっている。自白を誘い出すためにかつては当たり前だった身体的暴力の使用をやめさせる上でリード・テクニックは革命的だったが，隔離，言葉での威嚇，睡眠を奪うといったストレス要因の使用は今でも許容されている。そうした重圧の下では，罪を認めることが楽な解決策のように思えることもあり得る。特に，司法当局を肯定的に認識し，最終的に自分の嫌疑は晴れると考える人はそうである。だが残念なことに，自白はほかのあらゆる形態の証拠に勝る傾向がある。ひとたび人が罪を認めてしまうと，説得力があると思える反対の証拠ですら，無視されたり関連がないと見なされたりする。

　近年では，リード・テクニックに代わるさまざまな選択肢が人気を得ている。何が何でも自白を得ようとするのではなく，代わりにこれらが重視するのは，うそをつくことは多大な努力を要するという考え方である。そうした1つのテクニックは，尋問に対するジャーナリズム的なアプローチを採用している。捜査員は容疑者から詳細な供述を取り，それを，手に入る証拠ならびに目撃者の話と丹念に比較する。それから容疑者はさらに取り調べを受け，矛盾が浮かび上がれば，容疑者は詳しく説明するよう求められる。人を欺こうとしている人は，以前の主張を思い起こすことと新しいうそを考え出すことの精神的緊張が原因で，自らをさらに窮地に追い込むことになり，その結果次々に誤った証言をして，それがついには罪を暴くのである。

（語句）extract「（情報など）を無理に引き出す」，interrogation「尋問」，elicit「（真相など）を引き出す」，incarceration「投獄」，stumble「間違い」，unease「不安」，composed「落ち着いた」，stressor「ストレス要因」，deprivation「剥奪」，permissible「許される」，way out「解決法」，exonerate「～の嫌疑を晴らす」，trump「～をしのぐ」，painstakingly「労を惜しまず」，inconsistency「矛盾したこと」，deceitful「人を欺く」，falsehood「うそ」，a cascade of ～「大量の～」，erroneous「誤った」

(29) –解答 **3** ‥‥‥‥‥‥‥‥‥‥‥‥‥‥‥‥‥‥‥ 正答率 ★75%以上

解説　空所後の記述によると，リード・テクニックには，定まらない視線や言い間違いといった outward nervousness「外に現れた緊張」や appearance of unease「不安の様子」を示す容疑者は怪しいという前提があったが，必ずしもそうではないことが研究で明らかになっている。これらを signs of anxiety「不安の兆候」と言い換えた **3** が正解。

117

(30) — 解答 4

解説 罪を自白する可能性が高いのはどんな容疑者なのかを考えながら読み進めると，ストレスを受けると罪を認めるのが楽だと思う人もいる，特に司法当局を肯定的に認識する人はそうだという内容が書かれている。本文の with positive perceptions of legal authorities を **4** が全体的に言い換えている。

(31) — 解答 2

解説 空所後では，容疑者の供述と証拠の矛盾点をあぶり出して容疑者を追い詰める手法が取り上げられている。うそを重ねてつじつまを合わせようとすると mental strain「精神的緊張」を強いられるので，結局最後はぼろを出す，という考え方である。つまり，**2** のように，「うそをつくことは多大な努力を要する」という考えということになる。

一次試験・筆記 3 問題編 p.72 ～ 80

全文訳 **アイゼンハワー対マッカーシー**

　1950 年代の間，東欧における共産主義の影響力拡大と，米国とソ連との軍事的緊張の高まりによって，当時の米国大統領ドワイト・D・アイゼンハワーは大きなジレンマを間接的に抱えることとなった。アイゼンハワーと同じく共和党員だったジョセフ・マッカーシーという名の上院議員が，米国の民主的な生き方を転覆させようとする共産主義のスパイとシンパが米国政府に潜入しているというおおむね根拠のない非難を行って，国内で燃え盛っていた反共産主義パラノイアをかき立てて集団ヒステリーにまで至らせたのである。アイゼンハワーは，政治不安を引き起こすことに関与したとして内心マッカーシーを忌み嫌っていたが，彼とともに「どぶにはまる」つもりはないと側近たちに誓った。党の結束と大統領の威信の両方を保つため，マッカーシーを公の場で非難することを拒んだアイゼンハワーは，その代わり，この上院議員の信用を弱めようと努めた。

　最初，この上院議員の名前が話題に出たときのアイゼンハワーの反応がいつもだんまりだったことを，政界の多くの人は，マッカーシーによる共産主義者の魔女狩りに暗黙の同意を示すものと受け取った。しかし舞台裏で，アイゼンハワーは彼を制圧するひそかな作戦を委嘱した。マッカーシーとその右腕ロイ・コーンが，兵役に取られた助手の 1 人のために特別待遇を得ようとした証拠が明るみに出た。マッカーシーとコーンが軍の高官に，自分たちの助手に不相応な将校の任務を授けるよう強要しようとしたことを，アイゼンハワーの側近たちは突き止めたのである。大統領は，マッカーシーが反共産主義運動の限度を一歩踏み越えて，共産主義の影響に対し十分な予防措置を取らなかったと軍を非難するまで，時機をうかがった。その後間もなく，伝えられるところではアイゼンハワーの指令により，マッカーシーは上院で徹底的に非難され，数日後，マッカーシーとコーンのいかがわしい活動を記録した，罪を立証する報告書がホワイトハウスに

118

よってメディアにリークされた。テレビで放送された公聴会はマッカーシーが用いた脅しと欺きの策略を記録し，リークされた報告書とそれが合わさって，一般大衆の背筋を凍らせた。これに続きアイゼンハワーは再度影響力を行使し，上院はマッカーシーの上院議員にあるまじき振る舞いを糾弾して彼の政治生命にとどめを刺した。

　多くの批判者たちは，アイゼンハワーの策略は最終的には成功したとはいえ，マッカーシーが何年も野放しで荒れ狂い，共産主義のシンパやスパイだと非難されたさまざまな人たちのキャリアと人生を破滅させるのを許したと主張する。確かに，大統領のよき助言者だったジョージ・マーシャル大将をマッカーシーが公然と非難している間，アイゼンハワーは政治的方便のため傍観しており，幻滅したマーシャルに早過ぎる引退をさせた。しかし，マッカーシーは対決の場面で力を発揮し，ほかの政治家のマッカーシーへの敵対的対処法が彼の反共産主義運動を強化したにすぎなかった際に見られたように，彼との政治的泥仕合にかかわれば裏目に出る可能性が十分あった。アイゼンハワーの遠回しの手法は長期的には上院議員に対し勝利を収めたものの，生ぬるいやり方が原因で，彼はしばしば指導力を欠く指導者に見られた。だが，大統領在任中に戦争の終結と人種隔離の軽減の両方に成功したことは彼の方法の有効性の証明にほかならず，その例として，マッカーシーへの対処ほどの好例はなかった。アイゼンハワーが実際に取った手法を取らなかったとしたら，マッカーシーによる反共産主義の粛清はいっそう悲惨な結果を招いたかもしれない。

（語句）stoke「(感情など) をかき立てる」，paranoia「被害妄想，パラノイア」，hysteria「ヒステリー」，unfounded「根拠のない」，infiltrate「(スパイなどが)〜に潜入する」，aide「側近」，gutter「どぶ」，tight-lipped「口をつぐんだ」，tacit「暗黙の」，stealthy「ひそかな」，subdue「〜を制圧する」，unearth「(新事実など) を明るみに出す」，preferential「優先的な」，conscript「〜を徴兵する」，coerce *A* into *B*「A に B を強要する」，undeserved「(賞などが) 受けるに値しない」，bide *one's* time「時機を待つ」，roundly「完全に，徹底的に」，at the behest of 〜「〜の命令［要請］で」，damning「有罪を証明する」，shady「いかがわしい」，intimidation「脅し」，deceit「だますこと」，appall「〜をぞっとさせる」，unbecoming「ふさわしくない」，a nail in *A's* coffin「A の命取りになるもの」，rampage「たけり狂う」，expediency「方便」，disillusion「幻滅」，thrive on 〜「〜にうまく対処できる」，mudslinging「泥仕合」，backfire「裏目に出る」，antagonistic「敵対的な」，ineffectual「無力な」，segregation「(人種などによる) 隔離」，purge「粛清」，dire「悲惨な」

(32) – 解答　4

（問題文の訳）第 1 段落からドワイト・D・アイゼンハワーについて何がわかるか。

（選択肢の訳）**1** 米国政府内における共産主義の影響の証拠が正確だとわかったのに，彼の政敵が，彼が行動を起こすことを阻んだ。

2 大衆の間に広範囲のパニックを引き起こすことを避けるため，彼は米国政府に潜入していた共産主義のスパイを暴露しないことにした。

3 米国政府内における共産主義の支持の拡大が原因で，彼は自分に最も近い政治スタッフの信頼性を疑った。

4 米国政府に共産主義シンパが存在すると信じる者に公然と反対意見を述べることは，自身の党と名声に害を及ぼすと感じた。

解説 1950年代は東西冷戦真っただ中の時代だったという基礎的知識は持っておきたい。本文冒頭の文の indirectly は，冷戦という国際問題がマッカーシーによって国内問題化されたという構図を指して使われている。第1段落最終文の publicly denounce を speak out against と言い換え，party unity and presidential prestige を party and reputation と短くまとめた **4** が正解。

(33) −解答 ①

問題文の訳 アイゼンハワーはどのようにジョセフ・マッカーシーに対処したか。

選択肢の訳 **1** マッカーシーの非倫理的な権力利用の証拠を公表し，それが，普通の米国人の目から見れば上院議員の信用を失わせることに役立った。

2 軍の高官から機密情報を入手することができ，それを用いて，法的措置を取るとマッカーシーを脅した。

3 マッカーシーの助手の1人を説得し，上院議員を政治的に傷つけ得る秘密情報を暴露させた。

4 軍の高官を説き伏せ，共産主義のスパイに影響力を得ようとする上院議員の企てについてマッカーシーと対決させた。

解説 第2段落によると，アイゼンハワーは舞台裏で策を講じた。マッカーシーが軍に圧力をかけて不当に便宜を図らせた証拠をつかみ，それをメディアに流し，さらにテレビ放送された公聴会で暴露した。これに合致するのは **1** である。マッカーシーの不正を unethical という語でまとめている。

(34) −解答 ②

問題文の訳 この文章の筆者は，アイゼンハワーのマッカーシーへの対処法について暗に何と言っているか。

選択肢の訳 **1** もしアイゼンハワーがジョージ・マーシャル大将の助力を求めていたら，大統領はマッカーシーに反対する政治的支援をもっと築くことができただろう。

2 直接マッカーシーの信用を失わせようというほかの政治家の企ては失敗していたのだから，中立を保つように見えることがアイゼンハワーの勝利に不可欠だったと思える。

3 アイゼンハワーは多くの重要な成果を上げた功績があるものの，マッカーシーのような人の信用を失わせるための政治的専門知識を欠いて

いた。

4 マッカーシーと公の場で討論することが，政治上致命的な誤りを犯すよう上院議員に強いる唯一の方法だったので，アイゼンハワーがそうしたのは正しかった。

> **解説** 最後の段落は，アイゼンハワーの策略への批判で始まる。しかし，However 以降で，直接対決はマッカーシーの思うつぼであり，対決を選んだほかの政治家は失敗したのだから，アイゼンハワーのやり方が結果的に正解だった，という筆者の肯定的評価が述べられている。自分は表に出ず傍観するアイゼンハワーの策略を appearing to remain neutral と表した **2** が正解。

全文訳　ダーウィンの忌まわしい謎

　花は自然が創造した最も精緻なものの１つかもしれないが，1800 年代，自らの自然選択説を懐疑的な受け手たちに売り込もうとしていたチャールズ・ダーウィンにとっては，難儀な問題ともなった。自然選択の基礎となる考えは，生物の身体的構成のわずかな変化が徐々に積み重なることによって進化が生じ，それにより生物は置かれた環境に適応し生存し続けられるようになり，そして，このプロセスは新しい生物種の発展につながり得る，というものである。しかし，裸子植物と被子植物という，種をつける２種類の植物の化石記録を調査した当時の科学者は，大きな例外と思えるものを発見した。花をつけずに球果をつくる植物である裸子植物の漸進的進化と拡大は，３億９千万年前の古生代と２億４千万年前の中生代にわたる，ダーウィンの説が予測する地質学的な時間的尺度で生じたらしかった。しかし，花によって生殖する被子植物は，白亜紀の間，約１億年前に突如として思いもよらない多様性を持って出現したようだった。批判者たちは，ダーウィンの説の妥当性を大いに弱める明らかな反証だとしてこれに飛び付き，そのためダーウィンはこれを「忌まわしい謎」と呼ぶことになった。

　しかし現代科学は，より詳細な化石記録，DNA に関する知識，そして先進技術のおかげで，より鮮明な先史時代のイメージを手にしている。最も古い被子植物の化石を分析すると，化石の推定される年代と分子的な年代の間に不一致があることが明らかになった——遺伝子検査は，化石がはるかに古代のものだと示している。これを説明しようと，スイスのフリブール大学の研究者ダニエル・シルベストロは，裸子植物が生態学的に優位だったときの被子植物の希少性を加味して補正する数学モデルを用いた。シルベストロは自らの結果に基づき，被子植物はたぶんおよそ２億年前，つまり被子植物の化石の年代の当初の推定が示唆するよりも前にさかのぼると結論付けた。また彼は，この時代の化石化した証拠の欠如は，もしかすると花がひ弱だったせいであり，それによって花が化石化する見込みが一層減ったのだ，という説を打ち出した。シルベストロは被子植物を，しばらくの間恐竜の陰に隠れて存在し，続いて優位を占めるようになった初期哺乳類と同等と見なす。

　被子植物の過去の急増に関する別の説が勢いを得ている。地球の多くの地域で白亜紀

の間に被子植物が生態学的に急増したことは，被子植物とミツバチなどの送粉者が影響し合って非常に速いペースで進化したことの結果だと専門家は考えている。しかしこれが本当であるためには，そもそも被子植物が優位性を得ることを可能にした何らかの要因がなければならない。被子植物 DNA の分析は，被子植物が進化するにつれ「ゲノムの小型化」というプロセスが起きたことを示唆しており，このプロセスの結果生じた細胞の変化によって，被子植物はより多くの細胞をより小さな体積に詰め込むことができたのだと専門家は言う。その結果，被子植物は栄養の吸収の点で，そして植物が日光を用いて糖を作るプロセスである光合成の点で，はるかに効率がよくなった。忌まわしい謎はまだ完全解決には程遠いかもしれないが，科学者はあとわずかで説明できるところまで迫りつつある。

語句 abominable「忌まわしい」，makeup「構成」，gymnosperm「裸子植物」，angiosperm「被子植物」，incremental「漸進的な」，cone「球果」，geologic「地質学の」，timescale「時間的尺度」，Paleozoic era「古生代」，Mesozoic era「中生代」，Cretaceous period「白亜紀」，counterexample「反証」，prehistory「先史時代」，discrepancy「不一致」，fossilize「〜を化石化する」，fragility「虚弱」，equate *A* to *B*「A を B と同等と見なす」，pollinator「送粉者」，downsizing「小型化」，cellular「細胞の」，photosynthesis「光合成」

(35) – 解答 ④

問題文の訳 なぜ花をつける植物がチャールズ・ダーウィンの自然選択説にとって問題となったのか。

選択肢の訳
1 化石記録は，花をつける植物が実際には種を含む植物の前に進化していたことを示すように思えた。
2 被子植物の出現は，自然選択説が予測しただろうよりも長い期間をかけて生じた。
3 種をつくる 2 つの主要な種類の植物の共通の祖先を見つけるのは不可能だった。
4 花をつける植物は，生物種の間の相違は一連の小さな変化によりゆっくり生じるという考えに矛盾するように思えた。

解説 第 1 段落によると，花をつけない裸子植物は 1 億年以上の長い時間をかけて進化し拡大したので自然選択説に合うが，花をつける被子植物は多様性を持って突然現れたので，自然選択説では説明できない。これに合致するのは 4 で，本文の through the gradual accumulation of slight alterations を slowly due to a series of small changes と言い換えている。

(36) – 解答 ③

問題文の訳 ダニエル・シルベストロによると，

選択肢の訳 1 重大な分子の違いのため，裸子植物の方が当初は被子植物より生態学

122

的に成功した。

2 恐竜時代の間に裸子植物が優勢だったことが実は白亜紀における被子植物の台頭につながった。

3 被子植物は数が少なかったときに物理的に保存された可能性が低かったので，化石記録に現れるのが遅かった。

4 初期哺乳類が生きていたころより数百万年も前に大量の被子植物が存在していたが，ほかの研究者たちは化石記録にそれらがあることに気付かなかった。

解説 第2段落冒頭によると，被子植物の化石はそれまでの推定よりはるかに古いとわかっている。シルベストロは，被子植物の出現は当初の推定の1億年前ではなく2億年前だと示し，被子植物の花がひ弱だったせいで化石化する見込みが低かったという説を立てた。化石化することをphysically preserved と表し，本文の reduced the odds を unlikely を使って言い換えた **3** が正解。

(37) – 解答 **2**

問題文の訳 白亜紀の間に被子植物に何が起きたと一部の専門家は考えているか。

選択肢の訳 **1** 送粉者に影響され，必須栄養素を環境から特定し摂取する能力が増大することとなった。

2 遺伝子の変化により生存プロセスがより効率的になり，多くの生態系で繁栄することが可能になった。

3 日光の量がひどく変化した結果，多様な地域で生存できる能力が悪影響を受けた。

4 裸子植物と被子植物の DNA が混ざり合ったことが原因で，被子植物が送粉者に反応する方法が変化した。

解説 最後の段落によると，被子植物の急速な進化は「ゲノムの小型化」のおかげで，細胞の数が増えて栄養吸収と光合成がより効率的になった。genome downsizing を genetic changes という一般的な表現で言い換え，栄養吸収と光合成を survival processes とまとめた **2** が正解。選択肢の thrive in many ecosystems は，段落前半の ecological proliferation に対応している。

全文訳 **フェルナン・ブローデルと『地中海』**

フェルナン・ブローデルの『地中海』は，もしかすると戦後期に書かれた最も重要な歴史研究書かもしれない。1949 年に刊行された難解なコンセプトを持つこの作品は，個人や国，出来事ではなく地中海地方を主題としており，土地と人々と制度のほとんどすべての側面がこの地域の歴史をどのように形成したかを考察している。

ブローデルは 20 世紀初期に創始されたアナール歴史学派の中でも傑出した存在で，『地中海』はしばしばアナール派の学問の頂点と見なされる。アナール学派を創設した

のはマルク・ブロックとリュシアン・フェーヴルで，彼らは，影響力のある個人とその業績に焦点を当てる旧来的な歴史へのアプローチを退けた学界の異端児だった。当時の歴史書に典型的だったように，年代順に整理された物語を書いて注目すべき政治的出来事や軍事的出来事を描写するのではなく，アナール派の歴史家は，幅広いさまざまな経歴を持つ学者と共同作業を行って，大きく範囲を拡大させた研究を生み出した。

アナール派の歴史家は，地理学，経済学，心理学，社会学といった学問分野は旧来的な歴史へのアプローチが普通見逃してしまうような過去の諸側面の解明に役立ち得ると主張した。実際，アナール派の歴史家は，伝統的な歴史家の著作と論文において非常に多くの注目が向けられていた歴史上の人物の活動は「表面の乱れであり，歴史の潮がその力強い背に乗せて運ぶ泡の頂」だと考えていた。ナポレオン・ボナパルトやユリウス・カエサルのような傑出した歴史上の人物に焦点を当てるより，死亡証明書から商売台帳までどんなことでも分析して，農民と商人の日々の暮らしを研究する方が啓発的だと彼らは主張した。

歴史に対するアナール学派の急進的な考え方が最もはっきり表れているのは『地中海』である。旧来の学者が影響力のある個人の生涯と重要な歴史的出来事に焦点を当てたことは，つまり，彼らが一個人の寿命より長い時代についてめったに検討しなかったことを意味した。しかし，ブローデルは「長期持続」という概念を強調し，それがより陰影に富む歴史観を提示すると考えていた。『地中海』の第1部は，この地域に影響を与えてきた地理的要素と気候的要素の考察から始まる。テキストは海を渡り，山々の頂を越え，砂漠を通り抜けて転々とし，気候パターンと移り変わる地形が，次第に，ほんの少しずつ，どのようにして地中海地方を形成してきたかを詳述する。ブローデルは地理的歴史の恒久性と連続性を強調するが，それは，地質学的な時間の尺度で見ない限り，このレベルでの変化はほぼ知覚し得ないからである。

この本の第2部は世紀単位で測定できる時代を扱い，地質学的な時間の尺度を離れて，地中海諸文明の社会的・経済的・政治的構造が第1部で記述された自然の諸力によってどのように定められてきたかを考察している。最後にブローデルはより旧来的な第3部へと移り，そこでは，時間は人間の寿命の尺度で測られる。ここで彼は，先行する2部の文脈の範囲内でスペイン王フェリペ2世の治世を扱い，地中海のさまざまな文明が，しばしば旧来の歴史研究の焦点となってきた地域における歴史的出来事をどのように形作ってきたかを証明している。

歴史的な時間の尺度の画期的な概念化に加え，『地中海』は，当時の多くのヨーロッパとアメリカの歴史家が示した西洋寄りのバイアスをブローデルが免れ得たことで称賛されてきた。地理と気候と経済と宗教はしばしば国境と人種を超越するので，この地域についての彼の研究法の本質それ自体によって，ブローデルは，同世代のほかの歴史家が陥ったわなの多くを巧みに回避している。この地域南部のイスラム世界の砂漠と平原を北方のヨーロッパ地域と対等な立場に置くことによって，そして科学技術，商品，人々ですら連綿と交換されていたことを強調することによって，ほかの歴史家には見えなかった地中海地方の諸集団と諸国家の複雑で深く根付いた相互の結び付きを，ブロー

デルは明らかにしている。歴史家リチャード・マワリー・アンドリューズは，ブローデルの型にはまらない歴史の提示方法を挙げ，「いかなる国家や文明も自決主義というぜいたくを味わうことはなく，意識していたにせよそうでないにせよ，すべては相互依存の捕らわれの身だった」ことを『地中海』がどう証明するかに，それが決定的に重要だったと言っている。

　もちろん，『地中海』を批判する人がこれまで皆無だったわけではない。ブローデルは，地中海周囲の農村地域の農業改良から小作農の賃金パターンまで，また人口統計学的動向からルネサンス期の都市国家の衰退まで，あらゆるものを考察している。大量の文字と統計に圧倒されたブローデルの作品のレビュアーが，感銘は受けたが自分の読んだものを理解できずに読了するのも珍しいことではない。例えば歴史家アラン・マクファーレンは，ブローデルは「楽しいデータの森で迷子になった」のではないかと言っている。実際，ブローデルが主張を明確にしたがらないため，彼自身がそもそも自らの主張をしっかり理解していたのかを疑う者も出ている。これらの批判にもかかわらず，今では『地中海』は学術研究の傑作と見なされており，ブローデルが用いたアプローチの多くは歴史研究の主流になっている。

21年度第3回　筆記

(語句) conceptually「概念的に」，pinnacle「頂点」，scholarship「学問」，maverick「異端者」，chronologically「年代順に」，crest「頂上」，illuminating「啓発的な」，ledger「元帳，台帳」，nuanced「微妙な違いのある」，climatic「気候の」，topography「地形」，constancy「不変性」，imperceptible「感知できない」，geologic「地質学の」，timescale「時間的尺度」，conceptualization「概念化」，transcend「～を越える」，dodge「～を巧みにかわす」，footing「関係，立場」，interconnectedness「相互に連結していること」，unconventional「因習にとらわれない」，interdependence「相互依存」，demographic「人口統計学の」，city-state「都市国家」，come away「（ある印象を抱いて）去る」，thesis「主張」

(38) –解答 ③ ....

問題文の訳　アナール歴史学派は，

選択肢の訳
1　過去の出来事と現代生活のさまざまな側面を結び付けることにおいて，多くの歴史家はしばしば度が過ぎていると考えていた。
2　庶民の日々の生活の説明は重要な歴史的出来事を十分に解き明かすことができないと考えていた。
3　歴史は多様な観点から考察されるべきで，有名な指導者と重大な出来事ばかりに焦点を当てるべきではないと考えていた。
4　歴史上の人物の伝記を膨らませて，偉人の行いが政治以外の生活分野に与えた影響を示すべきだと考えていた。

解説　第2段落によると，アナール派は influential individuals や notable political or military events を基調とする歴史記述を否定し，a wide

125

variety of backgrounds を持つ学者と共同研究を行った。**3** がそれと一致する。

(39) – 解答 **2**

問題文の訳 『地中海』の第 1 部でフェルナン・ブローデルは,

選択肢の訳 1 地中海が周囲の地域に与えた影響をしのぐのは外国の経済大国の影響力だけだったと論じている。

2 知覚するのが難しいが,より洗練された歴史理解に貢献すると彼が感じた環境の変化を記述している。

3 ある地域の地理的特徴は非常に多くの変化を遂げるので,そうした変化のすべてを明確に分類するのは不可能だと証明している。

4 地中海地方の歴史を形成してきた主要な出来事の時代を特定する際に,過去の歴史家が重大な誤りを犯していたことを示している。

解説 第 4 段落によると,「長期持続」が陰影に富む歴史観を提示すると考えるブローデルは,気候的要素と長期的にしか知覚し得ない地理的要素の変化に着目して地中海地方の形成を論じた。本文の imperceptible を difficult to perceive と,nuanced を refined と言い換え,気候と地理を environmental とまとめた **2** が正解である。

(40) – 解答 **1**

問題文の訳 リチャード・マワリー・アンドリューズは『地中海』に関する以下の記述のどれに同意する可能性が最も高いか。

選択肢の訳 1 歴史の非伝統的な側面に焦点を当てることによって,ブローデルは,この地域の諸社会のそれまで気付かれていなかった結び付きの重要性を明らかにすることができた。

2 西洋文明の歴史的出来事への言及がないことは,ブローデルの作品が外国の歴史家からしばしば高く評価されなかったことを意味した。

3 時間を強調することによって,ブローデルは,この地域の北部諸国が南部諸国と比べてどの程度速く発達したかを理解することができた。

4 文明の発達は人々の決断力にかかっているというブローデルの見解は,ほかの歴史家からもっと注目されてしかるべきだった。

解説 第 6 段落に出てくるアンドリューズの言う prisoners of interdependence は 本文 の the complex and deeply rooted interconnectedness に対応し,さまざまなものの交換による地中海各地域の結び付きを言う。それに合致するのは **1** で,本文の unconventional を nontraditional と言い換え,ほかの歴史家がそうした結び付きに blind to だったことを unnoticed という語で表している。

(41) – 解答 **4**

問題文の訳 ブローデルの歴史へのアプローチに対する 1 つの批判は何か。

選択肢の訳 1 おそらくさまざまな重要な出来事の重要性を理解しなかったことが原

因で，ブローデルは自分が用いた統計の一部を誤って解釈した。

2 歴史のさまざまな時代にとりとめなく焦点を当てたことは，自らの主張をもっとよく裏付けることができただろう地中海の歴史の側面をブローデルが見逃したことを意味した。

3 しばしばブローデルは，自分の作品へのいい印象を読者に残そうとすることより，用いたデータの正確さへの関心の方が低かった。

4 ブローデルが書いたものの詳細さと範囲のせいで，彼が伝えようとした主眼点を理解するのが難しかったり不可能だったりすることがある。

解説 ブローデルへの批判は最終段落に書かれている。あらゆるものを考察しようとするブローデルの作品は大量の文字と統計から成るので，読み手は内容を理解できないことも多い。**4** がそれを全体的に言い換えている。もう 1 つの批判は，ブローデル本人が何を主張したいのかよくわかっていなかったのではないかというもので，アラン・マクファーレンはそれを「データの森で迷子になった」と表している。

一次試験・筆記 **4** 問題編 p.80

解答例 Governments should prioritize investment in technology, as the benefits of doing so can curb the emerging problems associated with climate change, the worsening health epidemic, and global labor shortages.

As the fallout from global warming continues to threaten the survival of humankind, technology is proving to be an invaluable tool. The encouraging progress being made in areas such as alternative energy exemplifies the role that technology can play in combating this problem. While such technologies offer undeniable benefits, their development requires steady financial backing, which governments have a moral responsibility to provide.

The rise of modern health issues is another problem that can benefit from government-level investment. Although rates of obesity and coronary diseases continue to escalate, breakthroughs in surgical procedures and innovations in preventative medicine provide hope. Yet without monetary support from governments, securing budgets for the rigorous research and testing required for mass production and adoption of these technologies will be a

21年度第3回　筆記

127

struggle.

Additionally, labor shortages are necessitating research into technologies such as artificial intelligence and automation. Rising labor demands in the construction industry, for example, can be answered with on-site robots that not only automate menial tasks but also improve workflow efficiency. The broad implementation of such technologies, however, requires state-level subsidies and grants to offset high up-front costs.

Considering the potential of technology to mitigate the effects of modern-day environmental, medical, and labor problems, boosting investment in technologies related to such issues is imperative for governments.

トピックの訳「科学技術への投資は諸政府にとってより優先される事項であるべきか」

解説 トピックでは bigger という比較級が用いられているが，比較の対象は明示されていない。科学技術の発展のためには政府の投資が欠かせないとする解答例では，現在の状況と今後の展望を比較しながら論を進めている。一方，トピックに対して No の立場を取るなら，例えば貧困問題の解決，教育格差の解消，世界平和の実現などへの投資の方がより優先されるべきだ，と具体的に比較することもできるだろう。もう1つトピックで注意したいのは，governments と無冠詞の複数形が用いられていること。求められているのはグローバルな視点で論じることなので，記述が日本の事情だけに偏ることがないようにしたい。

解答例の構成は，トピックへの立場を表明し3つの理由を挙げる導入の段落，それぞれの理由について個別に論じる3つの段落，理由をまとめて立場を再確認する結論の段落，という基本的な形を踏襲している。理由を3つ挙げるよう指定されている限り，この構成を変える必要はない。

3つの理由は，気候変動，悪化する健康問題のまん延，全世界的な労働力不足。3つとも「現在こういう問題がある」→「その解決のためには科学技術の発展が必要だ」→「それにはお金がかかるので政府の投資が欠かせない」という同じパターンで書かれており，論旨が明快にまとまっている。それぞれについて，代替エネルギー，外科手術と予防医学，建設現場のロボットと具体例を示していることも説得力を増している。

表現面で注目したいのは，段落の最後で政府の投資の必要性を述べる3つの文が，言いたいことは同じでも，まったく異なる書き方をされていること。似たような文を繰り返すのではなく，このように表現に幅を持たせることが重要である。また，最後の段落で3つの理由を environmental, medical, and labor problems と短くまとめている手際のよさは，ぜひとも参考にしたい。

一次試験・リスニング Part 1 　問題編 p.81～82

No.1 - 解答 ③

[スクリプト] ☆: So, do you know what's wrong with my dog?
★: Well, he clearly has stomach issues, and they're causing him considerable discomfort. Has he swallowed any plastic or other objects?
☆: I haven't witnessed him eating anything like that.
★: And what about alterations to his diet?
☆: He's started eating a new type of dog food that's supposed to be specially formulated for older dogs.
★: Do you recall the brand?
☆: Not off the top of my head. Sorry.
★: Well, here's a list of reputable brands. If the one you use isn't on there, try one that is. Come back in a few days if the problem persists.

Question: What should the woman do first?

[全文訳] ☆: それで，うちの犬がどうしたのかわかりますか？
★: えー，明らかに胃に問題があって，それがかなりの不快感を引き起こしています。プラスチックとかそういう物を飲み込みませんでしたか？
☆: そういった物を食べるのを見かけたことはありません。
★: それから，食事の変更はどうですか？
☆: 高齢犬用に特別に調合されたことになっている新しいタイプのドッグフードを食べ始めました。
★: ブランドを思い出せますか？
☆: すぐには出てきません。すみません。
★: えー，こちらが評判のいいブランドのリストです。お使いのブランドが載っていなければ，載っているのを試してください。問題がずっと続くようなら，2，3日後にまた来てください。

質問： 女性はまず何をすべきか。

[選択肢の訳] 1　別の日に獣医の予約を取る。
2　新しいドッグフードのブランドを選ぶ。
3　飼い犬のフードがリストにあるか見てみる。
4　飼い犬を2，3日クリニックに預ける。

[解説] 犬を連れて来た女性と獣医の会話は途中からフードの話題になり，最近与え始めた新しいブランドを思い出せるかと問われた女性は，Not off the top of my head. と答えている。このフレーズが「すぐには思い付

かない」という意味だとわかるかどうかがポイント。帰宅したら，その
フードが獣医に渡されたリストにあるかを確認するのが最初にすべきこ
と。

No.**2** – 解答 **1** .... 正答率 ★**75%以上**

スクリプト ☆： I have some news, honey. The company asked if I'd be willing to
take a position in human resources.

★： Well, you've always spoken highly of that department. And you
said marketing has changed for the worse, right?

☆： Yeah, but the post would involve assisting overseas branches with
hiring and salary negotiations. I'd be away for weeks at a time.

★： Well, that's not ideal, but I think you should focus on your career
at this point. I'd miss you, of course, but making some sacrifices
now will pay off in the long run.

Question: What does the man imply?

全文訳 ☆： 知らせたいことがあるんだけど，あなた。人事部の役職に就く気はある
かと会社に聞かれたの。

★： うーん，君はいつもその部のことは高く評価していたよ。それに，マー
ケティングは悪い方に変わったって確か言っていたよね？

☆： うん，だけどこのポストに就くと，採用と給与の交渉で海外支社の補助
をすることになる。一度に何週間も家を空けることになるわ。

★： うーん，理想的じゃないけど，今の時点ではキャリアに集中するのがい
いと思う。もちろん君がいないと寂しいけど，今少し犠牲を払っても，
長い目で見れば報われるよ。

質問： 男性は暗に何と言っているか。

選択肢の訳 **1** 女性は新しい役職に就くべきだ。
2 女性は昇給を希望すべきだ。
3 女性は家庭で過ごす時間を増やすべきだ。
4 女性はマーケティングの方が適している。

解説 会社から提示された役職は長期の海外出張を伴うので，女性は男性の反
応をうかがおうとしている。男性の最後の発言の you should focus on
your career や making some sacrifices now will pay off in the
long run から，女性が新しい役職に就くことを積極的に後押ししてい
ることがわかる。

No.**3** – 解答 **1** ....

スクリプト ★： Lisa, do you ever think about quitting?

☆： Why do you ask? Did you get passed over for promotion again,
Gerry?

★： No. Even worse. The upgrade of the company's intranet has been a disaster. The project's weeks behind schedule. I don't think it'll be ready in time for the new fiscal year.

☆： How does that relate to you?

★： Well, I helped them with some data analysis early on, which was all double-checked, but now the manager's holding me responsible for the problems. It's unbelievable!

☆： Maybe it's time for you to polish up your résumé.

Question: What do we learn about Gerry?

全文訳 ★： リサ，会社を辞めようと思うことはある？

☆： どうしてそんなことを聞くの？ また昇進を見送られたの，ジェリー？

★： いや。もっと悪い。会社のイントラネットのアップグレードが悲惨なことになっているんだ。プロジェクトは予定から何週間も遅れている。新会計年度に間に合うように準備できないと思う。

☆： それがあなたとどんな関係があるの？

★： えー，最初のころ僕もデータ分析を少し手伝って，それは全部ダブルチェックしたんだけれど，今になって部長が，問題の責任は僕にあると言っているんだ。あり得ないよ！

☆： 履歴書に磨きをかける頃合いなのかもね。

質問：ジェリーについて何がわかるか。

選択肢の訳 1 プロジェクトの遅延が彼のせいにされている。

2 リサが彼の仕事に満足していない。

3 イントラネットに問題を見つけた。

4 部長は彼がプロジェクトを率いることを望んでいる。

解説 ジェリーの2つ目の発言から会社で問題が起きていること，3つ目の発言からその責任を負わされていることがわかる。responsible を blame を用いて言い換えた 1 が正解。polish (up) *one's* résumé は「アピール度の高い履歴書を書く」という意味の決まり文句なので，リサも転職を勧めていることになる。

No.4 – 解答 ④

スクリプト ☆： Imran, do you have a minute?

★： Sure, Professor Holmes. Is there a problem?

☆： Far from it. I just wanted to congratulate you on your presentation. The way you laid out the time line of Buddhism's spread from India was easy for everyone to follow.

★： Thanks.

☆： Also, I was impressed with the quality of your research. The biographical details you provided on the key historical figures added depth to the entire presentation.

★： That's a relief. I was worried I'd gone overboard there. In fact, I was on the verge of cutting those details.

☆： It's a good thing you didn't.

Question: What was the man worried about?

全文訳 ☆： イムラン，ちょっと時間ある？

★： いいですよ，ホームズ教授。何か問題でも？

☆： 全然，そんなのじゃないの。あなたの発表のことでおめでとうと言いたくて。仏教のインドからの広まりを年代を追って詳しく説明したやり方は，誰もが簡単に理解できたわ。

★： ありがとうございます。

☆： それに，あなたの調査の質の高さにも感心した。重要な歴史的人物についてあなたが述べた伝記的詳細は，発表全体に深みを加えていたわ。

★： そう言っていただけるとほっとします。その点についてはやり過ぎたんじゃないかと心配だったんです。本当は，あの詳細はカットするところだったんです。

☆： そうしなくてよかったわね。

質問：男性は何を心配していたか。

選択肢の訳 **1** 選んだ論題が微妙過ぎること。

2 十分な調査をしなかったこと。

3 議論を呼ぶ主張を多くし過ぎたこと。

4 情報を多く与え過ぎたこと。

解説 学生の発表を褒める教授が 3 つ目の発言で言及した The biographical details について，学生は I'd gone overboard there が心配だったのでカットするところだったと言っている。go overboard は「度を超す，やり過ぎる」という意味なので，その details が詳し過ぎるのではないかと心配していたことになる。details を information で言い換えた **4** が正解。

No.5 – 解答 ①

スクリプト ☆： Jeffrey's teacher contacted me today. She said he punched a child during recess again.

★： Really?

☆： We need to do something about his temper.

★： OK. Let's speak to him, but it's not as if he's aggressive all the time.

☆： Maybe not at home, but he also pushed a kid at soccer practice last week. We should probably consult a child psychologist.

★： That might make him think something's wrong with him, which could make him feel insecure.

132

☆： Well, assuming he'll just grow out of this seems unwise to me.

Question: What does the man imply?

全文訳 ☆： 今日ジェフリーの先生から連絡があったの。先生の話では，また休み時間に子供を殴ったんだって。

★： そうなの？

☆： すぐにかっとなるのは何とかしなくちゃね。

★： よし。言って聞かせることにしよう，だけどいつも攻撃的というわけじゃないんだから。

☆： 家ではそうじゃないかもしれないけど，先週もサッカーの練習で子供を押したのよ。たぶん児童心理学者に相談した方がいいわ。

★： そうすると自分はどこかおかしいと思ってしまうかもしれないし，そうなれば不安な気持ちになるかもしれない。

☆： うーん，成長すればこういうことがなくなると仮定するのは賢明じゃないと私には思えるけど。

質問：男性は暗に何と言っているか。

選択肢の訳 **1** ジェフリーを心理学者に診てもらうのは有害かもしれない。
2 先生はもっと前にジェフリーのことで電話をくれればよかった。
3 ジェフリーはサッカーをするのをやめるべきだ。
4 ジェフリーは自分の身を守っていた。

解説 ほかの子供に暴力を振るうジェフリーについて，母親は児童心理学者に相談するという積極的な治療策を提案している。一方父親は，母親が最後に assuming he'll just grow out of this とまとめているように，様子見の立場を取っており，児童心理学者に相談することについても，息子を不安にさせるかもしれないと反対している。その反対理由を **1** が harmful とまとめている。

No.6–解答 ② ··· 正答率 ★75%以上

スクリプト ☆： Hi, Miguel. How's things at the publishing company?

★： Busier than ever. Two of our editors took leave this month. Each of them was in the middle of editing a novel, and I had to take over their unfinished projects.

☆： Sounds like you have a lot on your plate.

★： It wouldn't be so bad if my boss had given advance notice that everything would fall on my shoulders. If I'd known, I would've left some space in my schedule.

☆： That sort of thing is typical at my company, too.

Question: What is the man's problem?

全文訳 ☆： こんにちは，ミゲル。出版社はどんな調子なの？

★： これまでになく忙しいよ。編集者のうち2人が今月休暇を取ったんだ。

それぞれ小説の編集の真っ最中で，僕が2人の未完成のプロジェクトを引き継がなければならなかったんだよ。

☆：仕事がてんこ盛りって感じね。

★：全部僕の肩にかかってくると上司が事前に通告してくれていれば，こんなにひどくはなかったんだけど。知っていれば，スケジュールに空きを残しておいたのに。

☆：そういった類いのことはうちの会社でもありがちね。

質問：男性の問題は何か。

選択肢の訳　**1**　新しい仕事を見つけるのに苦労している。
　　　　　　2　仕事量が不意に増えた。
　　　　　　3　自分のプロジェクトを終わらせられなかった。
　　　　　　4　小説を編集した経験がほとんどなかった。

解説　男性は1つ目の発言で，休暇を取った2人の仕事が回ってきたこと，2つ目の発言で，それに関する事前通告がなかったことを話している。前者を His workload increased，後者を unexpectedly とまとめた **2** が正解。

No.7 – 解答 ④

スクリプト　★：Well, that was a waste of time.

☆：Yeah. The agenda Sharon sent out said we'd be brainstorming ways to increase efficiency so we can reduce overtime.

★：Right. But in the hour we were in that room, I think no more than five minutes were spent even touching on the subject of efficiency. Ironic, isn't it?

☆：To be fair, Sharon kept trying to bring us back to the topic. But Charlie wouldn't stop rambling on about the noise levels in the shared workspaces.

★：Yeah. He's really starting to annoy me.

Question: What does the woman imply about the meeting?

全文訳　★：いやー，時間の無駄だった。

☆：うん。シャロンが送ってきた議題には，残業を減らせるよう効率をアップする方法のブレーンストーミングをすると書いてあったのに。

★：そうだね。だけど僕たちがあの部屋にいた1時間で，効率というテーマに触れたのはせいぜい5分あったかどうかだと思う。皮肉じゃないか？

☆：公平に言うと，シャロンはずっとその話題に戻そうとしていた。だけどチャーリーが，共有ワークスペースの雑音レベルのことをぐだぐだ話してやめようとしなかったのよね。

★：うん。あいつにはすごく腹が立ってきた。

質問：女性は会議について暗に何と言っているか。

選択肢の訳 1 チャーリーは出席すべきだった。
2 雑音レベルについてもっと議論すべきだった。
3 効率が話の中心になり過ぎていた。
4 シャロンに問題の責任はなかった。

解説 本来議題となるはずだった効率アップが会議でほとんど取り上げられなかったことが，会話の前半からわかる。その理由について女性は，シャロンが話をその話題に戻そうとしてもチャーリーが違う話をやめようとしなかったからだと言っている。したがって **4** が正解。選択肢の the problem は，会議で効率アップの話をほとんどできなかったこと。

No.**8**-解答 **2** ·························· 正答率 ★**75**%以上

スクリプト ☆： What seems to be the problem, Mr. Sunak?
★： Well, Doctor, I was lifting weights and felt a popping sensation in my lower back, followed by intense pain.
☆： It's likely a herniated disk, but we'll do a scan to confirm it.
★： When can I get back to the gym?
☆： You'll need at least two weeks of physical therapy.
★： That long?
☆： At least. You know, it's unrealistic to think you can train the same way as you did when you were in your 20s. The spine becomes more prone to injury as you age.

Question: What does the doctor imply?

全文訳 ☆： どうされましたか，スナクさん？
★： えー，先生，バーベルを上げていたら腰にずきんとする感覚があって，その後激痛が来たんです。
☆： おそらく椎間板ヘルニアでしょうが，確認のためスキャンを撮ります。
★： いつごろジムに戻れますか？
☆： 最低2週間の理学療法が必要になりますね。
★： そんなに長く？
☆： 最低でも，ですよ。いいですか，20代のころにしていたのと同じようにトレーニングできると思ったら大間違いです。背骨は加齢とともにけがをしやすくなりますから。

質問：医師は暗に何と言っているか。

選択肢の訳 1 男性の年齢が，急速に回復する助けになる。
2 男性は運動するやり方を変えるべきだ。
3 男性はスキャンの必要がない。
4 男性の痛みの原因はトレーニングではなかった。

解説 腰を痛めた男性と医師の会話。早くトレーニングを再開したい男性に対して，医師は，背骨は加齢とともに弱くなるので若いころと同じやり方

135

では駄目だとくぎを刺している。つまり，**2**のように，年齢相応のトレーニング法に変えた方がいいと忠告していることになる。herniated disk「椎間板ヘルニア」，physical therapy「理学療法」。

No.9 – 解答 ①

スクリプト

★： Neela, did you see the e-mail from management?

☆： Yeah, I can't believe the domestic development department is taking over our new game prototype.

★： Especially since the game is supposed to be sold exclusively overseas.

☆： I know the international development department is small, but why even have us if they're not going to let us do the work?

★： Exactly. Well, domestic development will have their work cut out dealing with international specifications and requirements.

☆： I agree. But what do you think is behind this move? I hope it's not a sign we're being phased out.

★： I doubt it. It's probably because we're still working on the update of the *Space Titans* game.

☆： But that's only because we've been waiting to get the results of the user tests. They knew up front it would take at least 90 days.

★： I think you're worrying too much. Maybe they're trying to do us a favor by taking the pressure off a bit.

☆： I hope you're right, but I think we should arrange a meeting and let them know we can handle the work.

Question: Why is the woman concerned?

全文訳

★： ニーラ，経営陣からのメールを見た？

☆： ええ，国内開発部が私たちの新しいゲームの試作品を引き継ぐなんて信じられない。

★： 特に，このゲームは海外のみで販売されることになっているからね。

☆： 国際開発部は確かに小さいけど，私たちにその仕事をさせるつもりがないのなら，なぜわざわざ私たちを置いているのかしら。

★： そのとおり。まあ，国内開発は国際規格と要件の対応にかなり苦労するだろう。

☆： 同感。だけど，この動きの裏にあるのは何だと思う？ 私たちの部が徐々に廃止されている兆しじゃないといいけど。

★： それは違うと思う。おそらく，僕たちがまだ『スペース・タイタンズ』ゲームのアップデートに取り組んでいるからだよ。

☆： だけど，それは単に，ユーザーテストの結果が出るのをずっと待っているからよ。少なくとも90日はかかるって経営陣は前もって知っていた

136

わ。
★：心配し過ぎだと思う。もしかすると、僕たちのためを思って、プレッシャーを少し取り除こうとしてくれているのかもしれない。
☆：そうならいいけど、会議を設定して、私たちがその仕事を処理できると経営陣に知らせるべきだと思う。

質問：なぜ女性は心配しているのか。

選択肢の訳
1 自分の部が廃止されるかもしれないと思っている。
2 新しいゲームは人気が出ないと思っている。
3 ユーザーテストが予想より時間がかかる。
4 『スペース・タイタンズ』ゲームが要件を満たさない。

解説 新しいゲームの開発を別の部に奪われたことに関して、女性は2つ目の発言で why even have us という疑問、3つ目の発言で we're being phased out という懸念を述べている。つまり、女性は自分の部が不要になり廃止されようとしているのではないかと心配していることになる。phased out を eliminated と言い換えた **1** が正解。have *one's* work cut out「難しい仕事を抱えている、相当苦労する」。

No.10 解答 正答率 ★75%以上

スクリプト
○：What's up, Bev? You don't look happy.
☆：I'm not sure what to do, Lucy. I suggested having kids to Tom the other day, and he didn't seem very interested.
○：What was his reason?
☆：He thinks kids will restrict our freedom. He wants to be able to drop everything and take a trip whenever he feels like it.
★：How about you?
☆：I like freedom, but I've always wanted a family. Tom seemed OK with that before we got married.
○：He probably just doesn't have much experience with kids.
★：Yeah, raising kids is a huge responsibility that can scare anyone off.
☆：He's great with his niece, but he says the difference is that he can go back home to a quiet house after spending time with her.
○：I'm sure he'd feel differently if you actually had kids. Give him some more time to get comfortable with the idea.
☆：I don't know. Maybe I should give up my dream of being a mother.
★：It's not over yet, Bev. To tell you the truth, I didn't want kids, either. But after I realized how much it meant to my wife, we decided to have a baby. Once my son was born, my view

137

changed completely.

☆： Thanks, George. I'll give him some time to think it over.

Question: What do the man and woman think about Bev's situation?

全文訳 ○： どうしたの，ベブ？ 浮かない顔ね。

☆： どうすればいいかわからなくて，ルーシー。この間トムに子供をつくらないかと言ってみたら，彼はあまり関心がないようだったの。

○： 理由は何だって？

☆： 子供は私たちの自由を束縛すると彼は思っているの。気が向いたらいつでも全部なげうって旅行に行きたいのよ。

★： 君はどうなの？

☆： 自由は好きだけど，子供が欲しいとずっと思っていた。結婚する前は，トムはそれで構わないようだったんだけど。

○： 彼はたぶん子供を扱った経験があまりないだけよ。

★： うん，子供を育てるのは，誰もが尻込みしかねないものすごく大きな責任だからね。

☆： 彼は自分のめいにはとても優しいんだけど，何が違うかというと，めいと時間を過ごした後で静かな家に戻って来られることだと言うの。

○： 実際に子供を持てば，きっと彼の気持ちも変わるわ。子供を持つという考えを素直に受け入れられるよう，もう少し時間をあげなさいよ。

☆： どうかしら。母親になる夢は諦めた方がいいのかもしれない。

★： まだ終わりじゃないよ，ベブ。本当のことを言うと，僕も子供は欲しくなかったんだ。だけど，それが妻にどれほど大きな意味を持つかに気付いてから，僕たちは赤ん坊を持とうと決めたんだ。息子が生まれたとたんに僕の考え方は完全に変わったよ。

☆： ありがとう，ジョージ。じっくり考える時間を少しあげることにするわ。

質問：男性と女性はベブが置かれている状況についてどう思っているか。

選択肢の訳 1 ベブの夫は考えを変えるかもしれない。

2 ベブの夫が子供好きになることはたぶん決してない。

3 ベブは夢を諦めるべきだ。

4 ベブは子供を持つよう夫にプレッシャーをかけるべきだ。

解説 自分は子供が欲しいのに，自由と静かな生活を手放したくない夫が子供を欲しがらないのがベブの悩み。相談に乗る2人のうち女性は he'd feel differently if you actually had kids と，子供ができれば気持ちが変わると言い，自分も子供は欲しくなかったと話す男性も Once my son was born, my view changed completely. と女性の考えに同調している。これらを change his mind と表した **1** が正解。

138

一次試験・リスニング Part2　問題編 p.83～84

A

スクリプト **The Wave Hill Station Strike**

Until the late 1960s, many Australian Aboriginal people whose land had been forcibly taken from them by White landowners were employed on cattle-grazing lands called stations. Wave Hill Station was one of many stations that exploited these Aboriginal workers. Wages were extremely low, water and sanitation were lacking, and local Aboriginal people were the victims of routine violence at the hands of White landowners. In 1966, an elder of the Gurindji people, whose traditional land included Wave Hill Station, led the workers on a strike. About 200 Aboriginal employees and their families walked off the station. Though the strike was seen by many people as being about workers' pay and living conditions, for the Gurindji people, the primary focus was reclaiming their land.

The strike went on for a number of years until the Australian political situation changed with the election of the Labor Party. One of its policies was resolving the issue of Aboriginal land rights. In the mid-1970s, the Gurindji people had a portion of their traditional land returned, marking a turning point in their long struggle. The strike is recognized as one of the factors behind the Aboriginal Land Rights Act of 1976, which gave legal recognition to Aboriginal land claims.

Questions
No.11 What did many people fail to understand about the strike?
No.12 What was one important factor that led to the end of the strike?

全文訳　**ウエーブヒル・ステーションのストライキ**

　白人土地所有者に力ずくで土地を取り上げられた多くのオーストラリア先住民の人々は，1960年代後期まで，ステーションと呼ばれる牛の放牧地で雇われていた。ウエーブヒル・ステーションは，こうした先住民の労働者を搾取していた多数のステーションの1つだった。賃金は極めて低く，水と衛生設備は不足し，その地の先住民の人々は白人土地所有者による日常的な暴力の被害を受けていた。1966年に，先祖代々の土地がウエーブヒル・ステーションを含んでいたグリンジの人々の長老が，労働者を率いてストライキを起こした。200人ほどの先住民の従業員とその家族が，ステーションでの仕事を放棄した。ストライキは労働者の給与と生活状態に関するものだと多くの人は考えたが，グリンジの人々にとり，最も重要な焦点は自分たちの土地を取り戻すことだった。

　労働党が選出されてオーストラリアの政治状況が変わるまで，ストライキは数年続いた。労働党の政策の1つは，先住民の土地権問題を解決することだった。1970年代半

ばに，グリンジの人々は先祖代々の土地の一部を返還してもらい，彼らの長い闘いのターニングポイントとなった。このストライキは，先住民の土地所有の権利を法的に認めた 1976 年の先住民土地権法の背景にあった要因の 1 つだと認められている。

語句 walk off ～「（職務など）を放棄する」，reclaim「～を取り戻す」

No.11 解答 ③

質問の訳 多くの人がこのストライキについて理解できなかったことは何か。

選択肢の訳 1　関与した労働者は暴力の被害を受けていた。
2　多数のステーションの労働者が関与していた。
3　お金と生活状態以上のことに関するものだった。
4　実際に支援した白人土地所有者もいた。

解説 前半の最後で，the strike was seen by many people as being about workers' pay and living conditions だったが，実際は土地を取り戻すことが焦点だったと言っている。土地を取り戻すことを more than money and living conditions と表した 3 が正解。

No.12 解答 ②

質問の訳 ストライキが終結するに至った 1 つの重要な要因は何だったか。

選択肢の訳 1　ステーションの所有者たちが昇給に同意した。
2　オーストラリアの政府が変わった。
3　グリンジの人々のお金が尽きた。
4　政府が労働者を支援することを拒否した。

解説 ストライキは the Australian political situation changed with the election of the Labor Party まで続いたと言っている。つまり，政権交代が起きたことがストライキ終結の契機になったことがわかる。したがって 2 が正解。

B

スクリプト **Mind Games**

　As the US population ages, many seniors have turned to so-called brain-training computer games in an attempt to preserve their mental abilities. Some makers of such games claim that playing them benefits users in many ways, from improving memory to preventing conditions that cause cognitive decline, such as Alzheimer's disease. A group of scientists has examined these claims. The scientists did find indications that such brain training helped users to perform better at certain specialized tasks. However, there was little evidence that this had resulted from overall improvements in brain function. Furthermore, the scientists could find no compelling evidence for the claim that playing brain-training games can prevent Alzheimer's disease or lessen its effects.

　A further issue with brain-training games is related to the concept of opportunity cost. This is the idea that when people choose to do something, they miss the chance to gain the benefits that would have come from making a different choice. Users who become glued to their smartphones or computers for hours each day playing brain-training games may neglect to spend time reading or exercising, activities for which there is clear evidence of benefits for the aging brain and body.

Questions

No.13 What is one thing the scientists' research suggested about playing brain-training games?

No.14 What is one possible problem with playing brain-training games?

全文訳 頭のゲーム

　米国の人口が高齢化するにつれ，多くの高齢者が知力を維持しようと，いわゆる脳トレコンピューターゲームをするようになっている。そうしたゲームのメーカーの中には，それらをすることは記憶力の改善から認知機能低下の原因となるアルツハイマー病などの疾患の予防まで，多くの点でユーザーのメリットになると主張するところもある。科学者のグループが，こうした主張について検討した。そうした脳のトレーニングが，ある特定の専門化したタスクをユーザーがよりよくこなす上で役立つというしるしを，科学者たちは確かに見つけた。しかし，これが脳の機能の全体的な向上に起因したという証拠はほとんどなかった。さらに，脳トレゲームをすることがアルツハイマー病を予防したりその影響を減らしたりできるという主張の説得力のある証拠を，科学者たちは見つけられなかった。

　脳トレゲームのさらなる問題は，機会費用という概念に関連している。これは，何かをする選択をすると，別の選択をすることで生じるだろうメリットを得る機会を失う，という考えである。脳トレゲームをして毎日何時間もスマートフォンやパソコンにかじり付きになっているユーザーは，読書や運動をして時間を費やすことを怠っているかもしれないが，こうした活動には，老化する脳と体に対するメリットの明らかな証拠が存在するのである。

　　　　語句 glued to ～「～にくぎ付けになって」

No.**13** 解答 **3**

質問の訳 科学者たちの研究が脳トレゲームをすることについて示唆していた1つのことは何か。

選択肢の訳 **1** ゲームについてなされた主張はすべて正確だ。

　　　　　　2 ある特定のタスクをユーザーがよりよくこなす上で役に立たない。

　　　　　　3 アルツハイマー病の影響を減らさない。

　　　　　　4 ゲームをすることが原因の記憶障害は一時的なものだ。

解説 前半の A group of scientists ... 以降によると，脳トレゲームについて科学者が発見したのは，①特定の専門化したタスクをうまくこなせるよ

うになる，②それが脳の機能の向上によるものだという証拠はほとんどない，③アルツハイマー病の予防や影響を減らすのに役立つという証拠はない，の3つ。**3**が③と合致する。

No.14 解答 ②　　　　　　　　　　　　　正答率 ★75%以上

質問の訳　脳トレゲームをすることで起こり得る1つの問題は何か。

選択肢の訳
1　時間がたつとゲームが難しくなくなる。
2　よりメリットのある活動の時間を奪うかもしれない。
3　ゲームの内容が非現実的だ。
4　脳を疲れさせることがある。

解説　後半では，脳トレゲームの別の問題を opportunity cost「機会費用」という概念を用いて説明している。脳の老化を防ぐ効果が証明されていない脳トレゲームに熱中することによって，脳と体の老化を防ぐメリットが実際に証明されている読書や運動に費やす時間が犠牲になる，というのがその構図。読書や運動を more-beneficial activities と表した **2** が正解である。

スクリプト **Online Books**

　Print on demand, or POD, is a publishing method in which books are printed only after customers order them. POD has helped more authors get their books out into the world, as it allows small numbers of books to be printed quickly and cheaply. However, some people say it has also made it easier to produce counterfeit books. They say that works by popular authors are sometimes copied word for word and printed, or texts are altered slightly and released under new titles. The consequences of this illegal activity could potentially be more serious than just lost revenue for the true author. For example, if medical professionals unknowingly purchased counterfeit copies of manuals that contain incorrect information, it could lead to errors in the treatment of patients.

　Critics believe some online booksellers are not doing enough to police their stores for counterfeit books. They say the policy of the booksellers is to assume that the books supplied to them have been sent in good faith. The critics believe this is problematic and recommend that online booksellers become more proactive in eliminating counterfeit books. In response, some online booksellers have said they take a zero tolerance approach to counterfeiting and have programs in place to prevent it.

Questions
No.15 Why does the speaker mention medical professionals?
No.16 What do some critics want online booksellers to do?

全文訳　**オンライン書籍**

　オンデマンド印刷，すなわち POD は，客が注文して初めて書籍が印刷される出版方法である。POD は少ない部数の書籍を迅速かつ安価に印刷することを可能にするので，より多くの著者が自著を世に出すのに役立ってきた。しかし，POD によって，偽造書籍を作ることもより簡単になったと言う人もいる。人気のある著者の作品が一言一句たがわずコピーされて印刷されることがあったり，本文が少し改変されて新たなタイトルで発売されたりする，と彼らは言う。この違法活動がもたらすものは，本当の著者が単に収益を失うことより，もしかすると深刻かもしれない。例えば，誤った情報を含むマニュアルの偽造コピーを医療専門家がそうと知らずに購入すれば，患者の治療の過誤につながるかもしれない。

　偽造書籍がないか店を監視する取り組みを十分にしていないオンライン書店もある，と批判的な人たちは考えている。それらの書店のポリシーは，自分たちに供給される書籍は当然善意で送られたものだと考えることだ，と彼らは言う。これは問題があると批判的な人たちは考え，オンライン書店が偽造書籍の排除により能動的に取り組むことを提案している。それに応え，一部のオンライン書店は，偽造を一切許容しない姿勢で臨み，偽造を防止するプログラムを整えていると言っている。

　語句　counterfeit「偽の」，unknowingly「知らずに」，police「～を監視する」，problematic「問題のある」，proactive「能動的な」

No.15 解答 ④

　質問の訳　話者はなぜ医療専門家に言及しているのか。

　選択肢の訳　1　偽造書籍を防止する方法を提案するため。
　　2　オンデマンド印刷の利点を紹介するため。
　　3　小規模出版社がオンデマンド印刷を嫌っていることを示すため。
　　4　偽造書籍の潜在的危険を例証するため。

　解説　前半ではオンデマンド印刷のメリットとデメリットを述べている。デメリットは偽造書籍が簡単に作られることで，その結果，著者が収益を失うこと以上に深刻な問題が生じるかもしれないと言っている。その例として For example 以下で medical professionals を取り上げているこ とから，4 が正解。

No.16 解答 ②　　　　　　　　　　　　　正答率 ★75%以上

　質問の訳　一部の批判的な人たちはオンライン書店にどうしてほしいと思っているか。

　選択肢の訳　1　書籍の注文の迅速な配送を確実にすること。
　　2　販売する書籍が本物だと確認すること。
　　3　書籍の請求価格を下げること。
　　4　著者に対するポリシーを緩めること。

　解説　偽造書籍をチェックしていないオンライン書店があるというのが批判者

の 主 張 で, The critics ... recommend that online booksellers become more proactive in eliminating counterfeit books. から, 彼らの望みはオンライン書店から偽造書籍を排除すること, つまり **2** のように本物の書籍のみを販売することだとわかる。

D

スクリプト **Government Funding of Research**

Government funding of research in the US has been cut in recent years, but a new study has shown that this may be a mistake. The study's researchers examined patents, the licenses giving inventors exclusive rights to their inventions. They found that government funding facilitated the creation of a significant percentage of patents issued. Additionally, their analysis indicated that the patents created as a result of government funding contributed the most to the development of other inventions and were therefore more influential in the creation of future technologies.

According to one economist, one problem with the funding system is that the government frequently shares the risks but rarely gets any of the rewards. If it pumps a massive amount of money into research that comes to nothing, it will be severely criticized, but it is usually not rewarded when the research pays off. The economist believes that the government should continue funding research but, like any investor, should insist on financial returns when a project leads to a successful product. The economist says this would make voters aware of the importance of government funding, and it would also make them more accepting when failures occur.

Questions

No.17 What did the study reveal about government-funded research?

No.18 What is one thing the economist says about government funding of research?

全文訳 **研究への政府出資**

米国では研究への政府出資が近年削減されているが, これは間違いかもしれないことが新たな調査でわかっている。この調査の研究者たちは, 自らの発明に対する独占権を発明者に与える免状である特許について検討した。政府出資が, 交付された特許のかなりの割合の創出を促進したことを彼らは発見した。加えて, 政府出資の結果として創出された特許は, ほかの発明の開発に最も貢献し, したがって将来の科学技術の創出により大きな影響を及ぼすことを, 彼らの分析は示した。

ある経済学者によると, 出資制度の 1 つの問題は, 政府はしばしばリスクを共有するが, ほとんどの場合報酬は一切受け取らないことである。何の成果も生まない研究に巨額のお金を注ぎ込めば政府は厳しく批判されることになるが, 研究がうまくいっても通例報酬は与えられない。政府は研究への出資を続けるべきだが, どの投資者もそうであ

るように，プロジェクトが成功した産物を生んだなら金銭的見返りを強く求めるべきだ，とその経済学者は考えている。そうすれば，有権者は政府出資の重要性を意識するようになり，また，失敗が生じたときでも有権者がより受け入れやすくなるだろう，とその経済学者は言う。

　　　語句　facilitate「～を容易にする，促進する」

No.17 解答　④

質問の訳　その調査は政府に出資された研究の何を明らかにしたか。
選択肢の訳　1　一部の資格のない研究者が資金を受け取った。
　　　　　2　しばしば法的に厄介な問題を引き起こす。
　　　　　3　役に立つ産物を生むことがめったにない。
　　　　　4　科学技術の発展に多大な貢献をする。
解説　冒頭の a new study が明らかにしたのは，政府出資によって多くの特許が創出されたこと，そして，そうした特許がさらなる発明に寄与し，新たな科学技術を創出していること。放送文の more influential in the creation of future technologies を全体的に言い換えた **4** が正解。

No.18 解答　①

質問の訳　その経済学者が研究への政府出資について言っている1つのことは何か。
選択肢の訳　1　結果的に何か利益が出たら，政府は分け前をもらうべきだ。
　　　　　2　誰がそのお金を受け取るかを大衆が決めるべきだ。
　　　　　3　非営利研究組織だけに出資すべきだ。
　　　　　4　高リスクの投資は避けるべきだ。
解説　出資する政府はリスクを共有するのに報酬を受け取らないことが問題だと指摘する経済学者は，プロジェクトが成功したなら政府は金銭的見返りを求めるべきだと言う。**1** が，放送文の financial returns を share と，successful product を resulting profits と言い換えている。

E

スクリプト　**Parental Leave in Sweden**

　Today, many countries around the world offer maternity leave to women who give birth. Sweden, however, has offered both parents paid time off since the mid-1970s. Under this parental-leave program, each couple originally received six months of leave, which could be divided between the parents as they saw fit. But while both parents were entitled to use the leave, in the majority of cases, fathers signed their leave over to mothers. To discourage this, the Swedish government has gradually added restrictions. Now, couples get more leave that they can share between them, but each parent has a minimum of 90 days that they cannot transfer to the other parent. The revised system has been successful, and the percentage of the total leave used by fathers has risen significantly.

According to a study by university researchers, the flexibility to take time off that this revised system has afforded Swedish men has also benefited mothers. When fathers took advantage of the system in the period immediately after the birth of a child, it significantly reduced the chances of mothers needing medical care for childbirth-related physical complications. It also decreased the odds that they would need medications to treat anxiety.

Questions
No.19 What was one problem with Sweden's parental-leave system at first?
No.20 What did the study find about the revised system?

全文訳　スウェーデンの育児休暇

今日では世界中の多くの国が，出産する女性に産休を与えている。しかし，スウェーデンは1970年代半ばから両親に有給休暇を与えてきた。この育児休暇制度では，当初，それぞれの夫婦が半年の休暇をもらい，それを両親は自分たちが都合のいいと思うように分けることができた。だが，両親双方が休暇を利用できる権利を持っていたのに，大多数の場合，父親は書類にサインして自分の休暇を母親に譲っていた。これをやめさせるため，スウェーデン政府は徐々に制限を加えてきた。今では，夫婦間で分け合うことのできる休暇は増えたが，それぞれの親は，最低90日はもう一方の親に譲渡できない。この改正された制度は成功しており，父親が利用する全休暇の割合は大きく上昇している。

大学の研究者の調査によると，この改正された制度がスウェーデンの男性にもたらした休みを取る柔軟性は，母親の利益にもなっている。子供が生まれた直後の時期に父親がこの制度を活用すると，出産関連の身体的合併症で母親が医療的ケアを必要とする可能性は大きく減った。また，不安を治療する薬を母親が必要とするだろう見込みも減少した。

語句　sign A over to B 「A（権利など）を書類に署名してBに譲渡する」

No.19 解答　

質問の訳　最初，スウェーデンの育児休暇制度の1つの問題は何だったか。
選択肢の訳
1　父親が制度を十分に利用していなかった。
2　制度は父親を公平に扱っていなかった。
3　母親は休みを取ることができなかった。
4　親が給料をもらうことを認めていなかった。

解説　前半の To discourage this「これをやめさせるため」がポイント。そのためにスウェーデン政府は制度を改正したのだから，this が問題だったと考えられる。this が指すのは直前の fathers signed their leave over to mothers で，**1** がその内容と合致する。

No.20 解答 ②　　正答率 ★75%以上

質問の訳 その調査から，改正された制度について何がわかったか。

選択肢の訳
1 夫婦の医療費の増加につながった。
2 母親の健康の改善につながった。
3 父親の労働時間が増える結果になった。
4 父親に心理的問題を引き起こした。

解説 後半の According to a study … 以下によると，改正された制度は benefited mothers であり，その具体例として，出産による合併症の治療と，不安を治療する薬が必要になる可能性の減少が挙げられている。これらを improvements in mothers' health とまとめた **2** が正解。

スクリプト

You have 10 seconds to read the situation and Question No. 21.

These next two weeks before classes begin can be hectic, so we'll lay out what you need to do. It'll be important to familiarize yourself with our new student portal, which is your online hub for making appointments to see your academic adviser, registering for classes, paying tuition, registering for accommodation, and so on. You will all have your department orientation the day after tomorrow, where you'll be given a personal code to set up your new student portal account. Domestic students should already have registered for classes on the old portal, but you'll need a new personal code to use the new portal. International students, after setting up your account, you must make an appointment to meet with your academic adviser before registering for classes. Your adviser will explain which classes are required and answer any questions you may have. Registration will open three days from now.

Now mark your answer on your answer sheet.

全文訳

授業が始まるまでのこれからの2週間はばたばたすることもありますから，何をする必要があるか，詳しく説明します。本学の新しい学生用ポータルサイトに慣れ親しむことが重要になります。ポータルサイトは，アカデミックアドバイザーに面会する予約を取ったり，授業の登録をしたり，授業料を払ったり，宿泊施設の登録をしたりといったもろもろのことをオンラインでするハブです。皆さんの学部のオリエンテーションはあさってで，そこで学生用ポータルサイトに新しいアカウントを作成するための個人コードをもらえます。国内の学生は以前のポータルサイトで既に授業の登録を済ませている

はずですが，新しいポータルサイトを使うには新しい個人コードが必要になります。留学生はアカウントを作成後，授業の登録をする前にアカデミックアドバイザーと面談する予約を取らなければなりません。アドバイザーはどの授業が必修かを説明し，質問があれば何でも答えてくれます。登録は今から3日後に始まります。

No.21 解答 ④

状況の訳 あなたは外国の大学に転学したばかりの日本人の大学3年生である。留学生と国内の1年生向けのオリエンテーションに参加している。

質問の訳 あなたはまず何をする必要があるか。

選択肢の訳 1 学生用ポータルサイトでアカウントを作る。
2 アカデミックアドバイザーと面談する。
3 必修授業の登録をする。
4 学部のオリエンテーションに参加する。

語句 hectic「やたらに忙しい」，portal「ポータルサイト」

解説 新しい学生用ポータルサイトの重要性を力説する話者は，あさって行われる学部のオリエンテーションでポータルサイトにアカウントを作成するための個人コードをもらえると言っているので，**4 → 1**の順になる。続いて留学生への指示によると，**1**のアカウント作成後に**2**，そして**3**という流れになるので，まずは**4**をすることになる。

G

スクリプト

You have 10 seconds to read the situation and Question No. 22.

We offer a variety of monthly membership plans. Platinum Plus provides unlimited access to all facilities 24 hours a day and includes lessons for up to five activities. It's just $160 a month. Gold Prime offers access to all facilities from 9 a.m. to 9 p.m. on weekdays and until 11 p.m. on weekends. It includes two free lessons a week for any activities of your choice, and it's a great deal at $110. Our most popular plan is Flex Master, which costs $90. It includes access to all facilities, with the exception of golf-related facilities. It's valid on weekdays until 9 p.m. and on weekends between 1 p.m. and 9 p.m. Finally, we offer the Silver Saver plan, which is just $60. You get access to our main facilities, which are the gym, the tennis courts, and the pool, but it's limited to weekdays from 9 a.m. to 9 p.m. and does not include lessons.

Now mark your answer on your answer sheet.

全文訳

当クラブはバラエティーに富んだ月々の会員プランをご用意しています。プラチナムプラスでは1日24時間，すべての設備を無制限に利用でき，最大5つのアクティビティーのレッスンが含まれます。月々わずか160ドルです。ゴールドプライムでは，平

日午前 9 時から午後 9 時と週末の午後 11 時まで，すべての設備をご利用いただけます。お好みのどんなアクティビティーでも週に 2 回の無料レッスンが含まれ，110 ドルと大変お値打ちです。一番人気のプランはフレックスマスターで，料金は 90 ドルです。ゴルフ関連の設備を除き，すべての設備のご利用が含まれます。平日は午後 9 時まで，週末は午後 1 時から午後 9 時まで有効です。最後にご用意しているのはシルバーセイバープランで，わずか 60 ドルです。ご利用できるのは当クラブの主要な設備であるジムとテニスコートとプールですが，平日の午前 9 時から午後 9 時限定で，レッスンは含まれません。

No.22 解答 ②

状況の訳 あなたは最も安い料金で毎週ゴルフとテニスのレッスンを受けたい。平日午後 6 時以降は暇である。スポーツクラブのスタッフが以下の話をする。

質問の訳 あなたはどの会員の選択肢を選ぶべきか。

選択肢の訳
1 プラチナムプラス。
2 ゴールドプライム。
3 フレックスマスター。
4 シルバーセイバー。

語句 of *one's* choice「好みの」

解説 状況の the lowest price と after 6 p.m. から，金額と時間に関する数字が多く出てくると予測できる。丁寧にメモを取ることが重要である。プラチナムプラスは「毎週ゴルフとテニスのレッスン」と「平日午後 6 時以降」という 2 つの条件を満たして 160 ドル。ゴールドプライムも 2 つの条件を満たして 110 ドル。フレックスマスターはゴルフが除外され，レッスンについては何も言っていない。シルバーセイバーはゴルフの設備が使えず，レッスンもない。そうすると **2** が条件に合って最も安い。

H

スクリプト

You have 10 seconds to read the situation and Question No. 23.

As you all know, sales have fallen sharply over the last six months. We need to explore the causes and respond quickly. We all have some ideas about why this has happened and what to do about it, but we need a thorough analysis. You've been given a color-coded nametag that assigns you to a working group. Those with a red tag will research our competitors' customer services to see how they compare to ours. Blue tags will investigate the reasons for the increase in customer contract cancellations by performing surveys of customers who've canceled and then make recommendations based on the results. Yellows will examine our current marketing strategies and suggest new promotion ideas. Oh, and department managers will also need to reexamine our current product offerings to see if they're up-to-date and cost competitive. Please do this prior to taking on other tasks. All right. That's it. Thanks, everyone.

Now mark your answer on your answer sheet.

全文訳

　皆さん知ってのとおり，この半年で売り上げが激減しました。原因を調査し，速やかに対応する必要があります。なぜこうなったのか，どうすればいいのか，全員が何らかの考えを持っているわけですが，徹底的な分析が必要です。皆さんを作業グループに割り当てる，色分けされた名札を渡してあります。赤い名札の人たちは競合他社の顧客サービスを調査し，わが社の顧客サービスと比較してどうなのかを調べます。青い名札は，契約を取り消した顧客に調査を行って顧客の契約取り消し増加の理由を探り，そしてその結果に基づいて提案をします。黄色はわが社の現在のマーケティング戦略について検討し，販売促進の新しいアイデアを提案します。ああ，それから各部長は，わが社が現在提供している製品が時代に乗り遅れていないか，コスト競争力があるかどうかを調べるため，製品について再検討する必要もあります。これは，ほかの任務に取りかかる前に行ってください。それでは，以上です。皆さんありがとう。

No.23 解答 ④

状況の訳 あなたは会社の部長である。取締役が緊急スタッフ会議を招集した。あなたは会議室に入ると青の名札を渡された。

質問の訳 あなたはまず何をする必要があるか。

選択肢の訳
1　以前の顧客に連絡する。
2　競合他社を調査する。
3　マーケティング戦略を研究する。
4　現在の製品ラインアップを評価する。

語句 color-coded「色分けされた」，nametag「名札」

解説 質問に first「まず」があるということは，することが複数あり，その順序を問われていることになる。青の名札の任務には契約を取り消した顧客への調査が含まれるので 1 が該当するが，最後に，department managers はその前に reexamine our current product offerings をするよう指示されている。したがって，まずすべきなのは 4 である。慌てて 1 を選ばないように注意。

I

スクリプト

You have 10 seconds to read the situation and Question No. 24.

Parents often think a child with a fever needs to see a doctor, or the fever

150

needs to be reduced immediately, but that's usually not the case. A fever is the body's way of fighting infection, so lowering it too soon could actually delay your son's recovery. Children often develop high temperatures with common colds, so just keep an eye on him. If his condition worsens or the fever rises sharply over the next few hours, call us again. Actually, having said all that, there's been an outbreak of food poisoning at the elementary school in Southport. If your son is a student there, I'd suggest bringing him in for observation, but only if he has a stomachache in addition to the fever. Otherwise, plenty of water and a good night's sleep is probably all he needs for now.

Now mark your answer on your answer sheet.

全文訳

　熱のある子供は医者に診てもらう必要があるとか，熱は直ちに下げる必要があるとか親は思いがちですが，たいていそんなことはありません。熱は体が感染と闘う方法ですから，あまりに早く下げると，実際は息子さんの回復を遅らせるかもしれません。子供はただの風邪でしばしば高熱を出しますから，とにかく目を離さないようにしてください。今から数時間の間に状態が悪化したり熱が急激に上がったりしたら，また電話してください。実は，そうは言うものの，サウスポートの小学校で食中毒が発生しています。息子さんがそこの生徒なら，連れて来てもらって容態を見るのがいいでしょうが，熱に加えて腹痛がある場合に限ります。そうでないのなら，水をたっぷり飲んで一晩ぐっすり眠れば，今のところほかに必要なことはたぶんありません。

No.24 解答 ③　　　正答率 ★75%以上

状況の訳　あなたの4歳の息子が微熱を出しているが，腹痛はない。息子は自宅に近いサウスポートの保育園に通っている。あなたは地元の病院に電話し，以下のことを言われる。

質問の訳　あなたは何をすべきか。

選択肢の訳　1　その病院に連れて行って容態を見てもらう。
　　　　　　　2　午前中に息子の保育園に電話する。
　　　　　　　3　差し当たり息子の状態を注視する。
　　　　　　　4　息子の熱を下げるよう努める。

語句　food poisoning「食中毒」

解説　前半で，子供の発熱はよくあることだから keep an eye on him でよいと言っているので，動詞 monitor を使って言い換えた **3** が該当する。後半では小学校で発生した食中毒の話になるが，息子が通っているのは保育園であること，また，熱に加え腹痛があったら病院に連れて来るのがよいという内容から，前半の指示のように，取りあえずは様子見でいいことになる。

151

(スクリプト)

You have 10 seconds to read the situation and Question No. 25.

We deeply apologize for the inconvenience caused. You have a few options. As a special courtesy, we can provide 10,000 bonus miles. This is enough for two free round-trip domestic flights, so I highly recommend this option. You'd just need to complete this form here. Alternatively, we can offer cash and miles. This would be 5,000 miles together with an amount equal to half the purchase price of your additional ticket. If you often travel alone, this is a great choice, since 5,000 miles would earn you a free domestic flight. You can apply for this option through our website. Finally, if you simply want your money back, our customer service office can help you arrange it. It's closed today because it's a Sunday, but you can reach the office tomorrow. The phone lines are often busy, so please be patient. Use the number here on this card.

Now mark your answer on your answer sheet.

(全文訳)

ご迷惑をおかけし大変申し訳ございません。お客さまにはいくつか選択肢があります。特別ご優待として，1万マイルのボーナスマイルを差し上げることができます。これですと無料の国内往復便を2回余裕で使えますから，この選択肢は非常にお勧めです。こちらの書式に記入していただくだけです。あるいは，現金とマイルを差し上げることもできます。こちらは，別の航空券の購入代金の半額相当の金額に加えて5千マイルになります。お一人で移動されることが多いのなら，5千マイルあれば無料の国内便が手に入りますから，これはとてもお得な選択肢です。この選択肢は，当社のウェブサイト経由でお申し込みいただけます。最後に，単にお金を返してほしいということでしたら，当社のお客さま相談室がその手配のお手伝いをできます。今日は日曜日なので閉まっていますが，明日は相談室に連絡できます。電話が込み合っていることが多いので，ご辛抱ください。このカードのこちらの番号におかけください。

No.25 解答

(状況の訳) 搭乗便の遅延のため，あなたは乗り継ぎ便に間に合わず，別の航空券を買わなければならなかった。あなたは空港で航空会社の係員と話す。

(質問の訳) 別の航空券の全額払い戻しを受けるには，あなたはどうすべきか。

(選択肢の訳)
1 航空会社のお客さま相談室に電話する。
2 空港で書式に記入する。
3 航空会社のウェブサイト経由で申請する。
4 係員に後で電話をかけ直してもらう。

(語句) round-trip「往復の」

(解説) 質問の get a full refund が条件になると予測して聞く。係員は選択肢

を3つ提示しているが，最初の選択肢はマイルのみ，2つ目は現金とマイルの組み合わせなので条件に合わない。Finally 以下の最後の選択肢の simply want your money back が get a full refund に相当するので，指示どおり customer service office に電話すればよい。したがって **1** が正解。

(スクリプト)
This is an interview with Shaun Parker, who works as a magician.
Interviewer (I): Thanks for tuning in. Today, we're talking to Shaun Parker. Welcome, Shaun.
Shaun Parker (S): Thank you for inviting me.
I: So, how did you first become interested in magic?
S: When I was just a young boy, I used to watch a famous comedian who got many of his laughs by deliberately making his magic tricks fail. I loved him, but I decided that I wanted to do magic properly. After that, it became a bit of an addiction.
I: How did that then become a job?
S: Well, it's a bit of a long story, but I used to enter talent competitions in my hometown when I was in high school. At first, I didn't really get very far because I was copying other people rather than trying to develop my own style. But I started showing more of my personality and making more jokes, and I won a national talent competition a year later. From there, I started to do paid shows on weekends. However, I also wanted to get a good education so that if the magic didn't work out full time, I could pursue a different career. My other passion aside from magic is Japanese history, so I went on to study it at university. I came to Japan straight after I graduated and landed a job as a translator. Although that job wasn't great, to be honest, I got to meet a lot of successful businesspeople through work. At a party one time, I did some tricks, and I was then invited to do an official show for one of the biggest companies in Japan. That changed everything for me. It led to similar offers, and within a year, I was making enough just from magic to do it full time. That was over 20 years ago, and I've been working as a professional magician ever since.
I: Are there any challenges to working in Japan?
S: Well, I now read and speak Japanese fluently, so though the language used

to be a problem, it isn't now. The main issue I had when I first started was with visas. Not having a regular income or employer meant that it wasn't always easy to convince the government to give me a visa. I had to jump through a lot of bureaucratic hoops most years. Eventually, I realized that the only way I was going to be able to settle was to start my own entertainment company, which solved the problem. Also, this type of work means that I mainly work evenings and weekends, which is sometimes tough these days because I have a family. That's not unique to Japan, but the late nights tend to be a little later here, so that means a lot of my shows are crammed into a short space of time quite late at night.

I: Sounds tough! Who are your main clients now?

S: Nowadays, I mainly perform for corporate clients and occasionally do TV commercials. Until about five years ago, though, I mostly performed at weddings. I used to do up to four weddings every weekend, up and down the country, which was exhausting. As I said, I have a family now, so I have reduced the amount of evening and weekend work I do. Otherwise, I'd never see my wife and kids.

I: Well, Shaun, thanks for coming in today. That was great.

S: My pleasure.

Questions

No.26 What event led to Shaun becoming a professional magician in Japan?

No.27 What is one challenge Shaun faced early on in his career as a magician?

全文訳

これはマジシャンの仕事をしているショーン・パーカーとのインタビューです。

聞き手（以下「聞」）：チャンネルを合わせていただきありがとうございます。今日はショーン・パーカーとトークをします。ようこそ，ショーン。

ショーン・パーカー(以下「シ」)：お招きいただきありがとうございます。

聞：さて，最初はどうしてマジックに興味を持ったのですか。

シ：まだ子供だったころ，手品をわざと失敗して多くの笑いを取る有名なコメディアンをよく見ていました。彼が大好きだったのですが，自分はきちんとマジックをやりたいと心に決めました。それ以降，マジックがちょっと病みつきになりました。

聞：それがそれからどうやって仕事になったのですか。

シ：えー，ちょっと長い話なのですが，高校生のころ，地元のタレントコンテストによく出場していました。最初は，自分だけのスタイルを開拓しようとするより，ほかの人たちのまねをしていたので，大して上位には入れませんでした。ですが個性をもっと発揮して，ジョークを増やし始めると，1年後に全国タレントコンテストで優勝しました。そのときから，週末はお金をもらってショーをするようになりました。しか

154

し，マジックがフルタイムの仕事としてうまくいかなければ違うキャリアを積めるよう，いい教育も受けたいと思いました。マジック以外にもう1つ熱烈に好きなのが日本の歴史なので，大学でその勉強を続けました。卒業後すぐに日本に来て，翻訳者の仕事を得ました。正直なところあまりいい仕事ではありませんでしたが，仕事を通じて，成功した実業家にたくさん会う機会を得ました。あるときパーティーで少し手品をしたら，日本の最大手企業の1つで正式のショーをするよう招かれました。それで何もかも変わりました。同様のオファーが来るようになり，1年もたたないうちに，フルタイムでマジックをするのに十分な稼ぎをマジックだけで得ていました。それが20年以上前のことで，それ以来ずっとプロのマジシャンの仕事をしています。

聞：日本で働くことに何か困難な点はありますか。

シ：えー，今では日本語をすらすら読んで話すので，以前は言葉が問題でしたが，今はそうではありません。最初に始めたころの主な問題は，ビザに関するものでした。定期的な収入もなく雇用者もいませんでしたから，ビザを出してくれるよう政府を納得させるのは必ずしも簡単ではありませんでした。ほとんどの年月は，官僚主義的な困難をたくさん切り抜けなければなりませんでした。結局，定住できるようになる唯一の方法は自分のエンターテインメント会社を立ち上げることだと気付き，それで問題が解決しました。また，この種の仕事だと，主に夜と週末に働くことになり，家族がいますから，近ごろはつらいこともあります。それは日本特有のことではありませんが，夜遅い時間はこちらの方が少し遅い傾向がありますから，ということは，私のショーの多くはかなり夜遅く，短い時間にぎゅっと詰め込んだものだということです。

聞：大変そうですね！ 今の主な顧客はどんな人たちですか。

シ：最近は主に企業の顧客向けにショーをしていて，時々テレビコマーシャルをやっています。ですが，5年くらい前まではほとんど結婚式でショーをしていました。以前は毎週末，国中を行ったり来たりして最大4つの結婚式をこなして，疲れ果てていました。さっき言ったように今では家族がいますから，夜と週末にする仕事の量は減らしました。そうしなければ，妻と子供たちの顔を決して見られないでしょう。

聞：さて，ショーン，今日はご出演いただきありがとうございました。とてもいいお話でした。

シ：どういたしまして。

語句　jump through hoops「多くの試練を受ける」，cram「～を詰め込む」

No.26 解答

質問の訳　どんな出来事がきっかけでショーンは日本でプロのマジシャンになったのか。

選択肢の訳　1　日本の大企業でマジックをするよう雇われた。
2　マジックの本を日本の顧客向けに翻訳するよう依頼された。
3　暇な時間に，成功した実業家にマジックを教えた。
4　共に日本の歴史を学んだ人たちを通じて人脈を作った。

解説 ショーンは3つ目の発言で，マジックが仕事になった経緯を説明している。その後半で，日本では翻訳の仕事をしていたが，パーティーで手品を披露したら大企業でショーをするよう招かれ，それが契機となってプロのマジシャンに専念できるようになったと述べている。was ... invited to do an official show for one of the biggest companies in Japan を言い換えた **1** が正解。

No.27 解答 ③

質問の訳 ショーンがマジシャン人生の初期に直面した1つの困難は何か。

選択肢の訳
1 日本語は流ちょうだったが，文化の違いに苦労した。
2 不規則な労働時間のため，休暇を取ることが不可能だった。
3 定期的な賃金がなかったので，ビザを手に入れるのが困難だった。
4 テレビの仕事が欲しかったが，結婚式の仕事しか見つからなかった。

解説 続けて，日本で働くことの困難について問われたショーンは，The main issue I had when I first started was with visas. と言っている。started は「（マジシャンの仕事を）始めた」ということ。ビザについては，Not having a regular income or employer が理由で政府がなかなかビザを発行してくれなかった，といったことを述べている。**3** がそれを The lack of a regular wage という表現を使ってまとめている。

156

二次試験・面接　トピックカード　A 日程　問題編 p.88

ここでは，A日程の5つのトピックをモデルスピーチとしました。

A日程

1. Does the economic future of Japan depend on labor from abroad?

I believe that foreign labor will be necessary for Japan's economic survival. This is due to Japan's aging society, globalization, and the need for more diversity. Firstly, Japan is famous for its low birthrate and high number of elderly citizens. If Japan fails to attract immigrants, there will be serious worker shortages. Without enough workers, how can Japan compete against countries with huge populations like India and China? Secondly, as companies become globalized, it will be important to have foreign workers. Many Japanese firms currently lack staff who speak foreign languages and are familiar with other cultures. Without such employees, it will be difficult for them to sell their products and services abroad. Finally, Japanese companies need more diversity. One of the best ways to increase diversity is by having more foreign workers, because they have a lot of different experiences and ideas to share with their companies. In this way, Japanese companies will be able to compete globally in terms of innovation. Although Japan has been very successful economically up until now, I think that if we don't meet the challenges of our aging population, globalization, and the need for greater diversity, we could be left behind in the future.

> **解説**「日本の経済的未来は外国人労働者に依存するか」
> トピックに対して肯定の立場からのスピーチ。最初に自分の意見とその理由をまとめてリストして，①高齢化社会に伴う労働力の不足，②企業のグローバル化の促進，③多様性の強化によるイノベーション競争力の向上，の3つを具体的に展開している。日本の現状を「労働者が足りない」→「外国語を話せる社員も足りない」→「多様性が足りない」とロジカルにつなげることで自然な流れが生まれ，聞き手にとってわかりやすいスピーチとなっている。未来への懸念を強調した結論も伝わりやすい。

2. Are international laws biased in favor of wealthy countries?

I disagree with the idea that international laws are biased in favor of wealthy nations. I'll discuss human rights, environmental treaties, and arms control agreements. To me, the most important international laws are those dealing with human rights. These laws offer essential protections to everyone equally, regardless of how much money they have or where they live. Without them, it would be much easier for rich countries to exploit people in less wealthy ones. Similarly, environmental treaties are a form of international law that protects all nations, not just rich, powerful ones. These agreements are usually signed by the vast majority of the world's countries, and all countries have rights and responsibilities under them. Furthermore, they have been used to prevent companies in highly developed countries from doing environmental damage in developing nations. Finally, I think that arms control agreements are important for protecting people in less wealthy countries. Today, one of the biggest threats to humanity is the danger of weapons of mass destruction. Like human rights laws, these treaties keep everyone safe from nuclear, biological, and chemical weapons, no matter where they live. In conclusion, I feel that international laws, such as human rights laws, environmental agreements, and arms control treaties have a strong benefit for any country, developed or developing.

解説 「国際法は経済力のある国に有利な内容に偏っているか」

トピックに反対の立場からの意見。I'll discuss ～ とこれから議論される観点を冒頭で紹介し、①人権法、②環境条約、③軍縮協定の3つの国際法において経済力のない国々も十分に守られているという主張をそれぞれ丁寧に展開している。①の To me, the most important ～, ②の Similarly, ③の Finally, I think ～ と自分にとって重要度の高いものから話しているところはスピーチのストラテジーとしてぜひ参考にしたい。自分に引き寄せて話すことで、難しめのトピックでも発話のボリュームが担保されやすくなるだろう。

3. Agree or disagree: Promotion in the workplace should be based primarily on seniority

In the past, many companies used to promote workers based on seniority, but I think it is better to promote staff based on merit. The most important reason is the success of the company. In order to be more competitive than their rivals, firms need to have the best workers in leadership positions, regardless of age. There are many cases where younger workers have more ability than older employees, so they should be in charge if they have better skills. Secondly, promotion based on merit is fairer. If one employee has more ability and is more efficient than his or her coworkers, then he or she should get a more responsible position and more money. Workers these days

158

understand that people should be rewarded based on their performance. Thirdly, companies that adopt a meritocracy will be able to allocate costs well and reward employees who truly deserve it. As long as companies introduce a fair evaluation system, workers will feel motivated to exceed their expectations. Therefore, companies can more easily maintain the cost of human resources while their employees will have an increase in morale. Society has changed greatly in recent decades, and companies have to change with it, so I feel strongly that a merit-based promotion system is better.

解説 「賛成か反対か：職場での昇進は主に年功によって決められるべきだ」

トピックに対して反対の立場からの意見を，「実力主義」の利点を中心に展開している。①会社の成功のため，②公平性のため，③コスト効率のため，の3つを挙げているが，このままではやや抽象的な理由なので，それぞれについて具体例を掘り下げ，「理由の理由」または「その効果」をしっかりと説明したことでとても説得力のあるスピーチとなっている。日本人スピーカーの発話は具体的な理由に乏しく，抽象的な理由を繰り返す傾向が往々にして見られるので，ぜひ参考にするとよいだろう。

4. Should teachers be responsible for both the emotional development and academic development of students?

In my opinion, teachers should not only be responsible for students' academic development but for their emotional development as well. The most obvious reason is that parents are getting much busier these days. More women are remaining in the workforce after they give birth, so they have less time to spend with their children. In the past, parents were able to provide more emotional support to children, but they now tend to have less time for this role, so they need help from teachers. Secondly, emotional development is strongly connected with academic development. If students have teachers who inspire them to love learning and show them how to control their emotions, they will have better motivation and self-discipline. Without these things, students cannot reach their academic potential. Finally, teachers should remember that education is about much more than learning from books. Students need social skills to succeed in their future lives. To provide these skills and nurture well-rounded human beings, schools need to emphasize emotional development as well as academics. Based on the reasons I've given, I think it is essential that teachers make sure to help their students develop emotionally as well as academically.

解説 「教師は生徒の精神面と学業面，双方の成長に対して責任を負うべきか」

トピックに対して肯定の立場からのスピーチ。①両親が仕事で忙しい，

②精神面の成長と学業面の成長は分けては考えられない，③教育とは学業だけでなく社会的スキルを教え全人格的に人を育てるもの，の3つを理由に挙げて意見を展開している。ここでは最も具体的でわかりやすい理由①から②，③へと抽象度が上がる解答になっているが，抽象度が上がっても聞き手が具体的なイメージを持てるように丁寧に説明を加えている。このように抽象度の高いものを異なる表現で言い換える力を1級受験者は磨くとよいだろう。

5. Is scientific research the key to improving human health in the future?

If humans want to live longer, healthier lives in the future, it is essential that we continue to make progress in scientific research. First, just think about all the treatments for diseases that science has brought us. Many illnesses that used to kill millions of people can now be cured, and treatments for many others have improved greatly. There is also promising research for curing diseases like diabetes and HIV, so it is important that scientists continue this important work. Another promising area is in treating injuries and birth defects. Many problems that once caused people to live their whole lives in wheelchairs can now be treated or cured. Furthermore, there is the potential that scientific research will give humans the ability to grow organs or other body parts in order to undo the effects of injuries or aging. Finally, there have been many advancements in preventive medicine, in which major diseases can be identified and treated at an early phase. Nowadays, doctors can look at genetics or environmental factors to predict the risks that patients have for developing a disease. They can use screening technology to detect, for example, signs of cancer cells. Preventive medicine will likely have an increasingly larger role in healthcare. For these reasons, I believe scientific research is the key to improving human health in the future.

解説　「科学的研究は今後人間の健康を向上させるための鍵なのか」

トピックに賛成の立場から，人間の健康にとって科学の発展が重要かつ不可欠であることを主張している。その理由として，科学的研究のおかげで①病気の治癒，②けがや生まれつきの障害からの回復，③予防医学の発達，の3つが大幅に改善されてきたことを説明している。①〜③の具体例が重複せず，多面的に話し手の主張を裏付けているところが素晴らしい。医療系のトピックは birth defects や preventive medicine など，簡単な言い換え表現が見つからないものも多いので，日ごろからニュースなどに触れて語彙を養っておきたい。

160

2021-2

一次試験
筆記解答・解説　　p.162〜180

一次試験
リスニング解答・解説　p.181〜208

二次試験
面接解答・解説　　p.209〜212

解 答 一 覧

一次試験・筆記

1

(1)	4	(10)	1	(19)	1
(2)	4	(11)	3	(20)	4
(3)	2	(12)	1	(21)	2
(4)	3	(13)	1	(22)	4
(5)	3	(14)	1	(23)	1
(6)	4	(15)	2	(24)	2
(7)	3	(16)	3	(25)	1
(8)	1	(17)	4		
(9)	2	(18)	2		

2

(26)	4	(29)	1
(27)	3	(30)	4
(28)	2	(31)	2

3

(32)	2	(35)	2	(38)	3
(33)	4	(36)	1	(39)	2
(34)	3	(37)	4	(40)	4
				(41)	3

4　解答例は本文参照

一次試験・リスニング

Part 1

No. 1	3	No. 5	3	No. 9	2
No. 2	2	No. 6	4	No.10	4
No. 3	1	No. 7	3		
No. 4	1	No. 8	1		

Part 2

No.11	4	No.15	1	No.19	2
No.12	3	No.16	1	No.20	3
No.13	1	No.17	4		
No.14	3	No.18	2		

Part 3

No.21	4	No.23	4	No.25	3
No.22	1	No.24	1		

Part 4

No.26	2	No.27	1

一次試験・筆記 **1** | 問題編 p.90～92

(1) ―解答 4 ·· 正答率 ★75%以上

訳 その古文書は，長年にわたって誰も解読できない手書き文字で書かれていた。その後，ついに優秀な若い学者がその意味を解明した。

語句 **1**「～を中傷する」 **2**「（時）をぶらぶらして過ごす」
3「～を固く約束する」 **4**「～を解読する」

解説 ついに意味を解明したのだから，それまでは誰も decipher「解読する」ことができなかったのだ。work out「（問題など）を苦労して解く」。

(2) ―解答 4 ···

訳 審判員が試合中にいくつか大きなミスをした後，ファンたちはブーイングや彼に向かって怒鳴ることで侮蔑の態度を示した。

語句 **1**「悪名，不名誉」 **2**「カタカタいう音」
3「豪華さ，輝き」 **4**「軽蔑」

解説 何度も重大ミスをした審判。ファンがブーイングと怒鳴ることで何を表すのか，を考えると disdain「軽蔑」だ。類義語は scorn, contempt。

(3) ―解答 2 ···

訳 金は最も可鍛性のある金属の1つだ。この性質が金をさまざまな形に成形することができるようにし，金がとても需要の高い1つの理由だ。

語句 **1**「大言壮語の」 **2**「可鍛性の」
3「干上がった」 **4**「汚い」

解説 さまざまな形にすることができる性質を持つのだから，金は malleable（= easy to press into different shapes）「可鍛性の」金属だ。

(4) ―解答 3 ···

訳 CEO は，ここ何年にもわたる会社の成功は，会社の過去のリーダーたちが取った方針の知恵の明白な証しだと言った。

語句 **1**「（事業などの）説明書」 **2**「摩滅，皮膚のすりむけ」
3「証明するもの」 **4**「報復」

解説 長年の会社の成功は先人たちの知恵の何か，を考えて選択肢を見ると testament「証明するもの」が適切。a testament to ～「～の証し」。

(5) ―解答 3 ···

訳 最初の任期中にスミス知事は多くの敵を作った。彼が再選を目指したとき，彼らは対立候補を支持し，対立候補はやすやすと選挙に勝った。

語句 **1**「隠遁者」 **2**「神童」 **3**「敵」 **4**「被保護者」

解説 2文目の they が指す対象が文中にないので，they に当たる語が空所に入る。they は対立候補を支持したのだから，知事が作ったのは adversaries「敵」だ。

162

(6) ― 解答 4 ・・・・・・・・・・・・・・・・・・・・・・・・・・・・・ 正答率 ★75%以上

訳 干ばつに襲われた地域の援助機関は，緊急救援物資が援助を必要としているすべての市民に公平に分配されることを確実にするため，ベストを尽くした。

語句 **1**「偽って」 **2**「不法に」 **3**「光り輝いて」 **4**「公平に」

解説 救援物資は困っている全市民にどのように分配されるべきか，を考えると副詞 equitably「公平に」が適切。名詞形は equity「公平」。

(7) ― 解答 3 ・・・

訳 炭鉱でのストライキが広がりエネルギー不足がよく起こるにつれ，いくつかの業界は自分たちがますます悲惨な状況に陥っているのに気付いた。

語句 **1**「愚かな，粗野な」 **2**「(味などが) ぴりっとする」
3「悲惨な，ひどい」 **4**「使い古された，陳腐な」

解説 エネルギー不足がよくあるのだから，いくつかの産業界の状態は dire「悲惨な」のだ。類義語は terrible, dreadful。

(8) ― 解答 1 ・・・

訳 A：あなたの庭は非の打ち所がないようね。どうやって，きちんと整えておくの？
B：実を言うと，手入れをしてくれる庭師を雇ったんだ。

語句 **1**「汚れ [欠点] のない」 **2**「ゆがんだ」
3「触れることができない」 **4**「下品な，低俗な」

解説 庭師が手入れをした，とても neat and tidy「きちんと整って」いる庭なのだから，immaculate「欠点のない」庭なのだ。

(9) ― 解答 2 ・・・

訳 1993 年にインターネット全体はたった 130 のウェブサイトでできていた。しかし，それらは急増し続け，今日では 10 億を超えると言われている。

語句 **1**「脈打つ」
2「急増する」
3「～を (束縛などから) 解放する」
4「～を列挙する」

解説 たった 130 だったのが今では 10 億を超えているのだから，ウェブサイトは proliferate「急増する」ことを続けているのだ。類義語は multiply。

(10) – 解答 1 ・・

訳 A：あれらのケーキ，本当においしそうだ。1 つ食べようよ。
B：どうぞ。私はダイエット中で，誘惑に負けないと決心しているの。

語句 **1**「負ける，屈する」 **2**「～の心をかき乱す」
3「～を (完全に) 消す」 **4**「口論する」

解説 ダイエット中なのだから，B がしないと決めているのは succumb to

163

temptation「誘惑に負ける」だ。succumb to ～「～に負ける，屈する」。

(11) －解答 **3** ･･

(訳) 対向車を避けようとして，運転手は路肩を外れて揺れながら突っ走った。

(語句) **1**「いばって歩いた」

2「(馬が) 緩い駆け足で行った」

3「(車などが) 揺れながら疾走した」

4「(液体が) サイフォンを通った」

(解説) 対向車を避けるためなのだから，車は路肩を離れて careened「(制御が困難で左右に) 揺れながら疾走した」のだ。

(12) －解答 **1** ･･････････････････････････････ 正答率 ★75%以上

(訳) その患者は慢性のせきで苦しんでいる。彼はそのための薬を服用してきたが，せきは 6 カ月以上も続いている。

(語句) **1**「慢性の」 **2**「田舎の」 **3**「如才ない」 **4**「狡猾な」

(解説) 患者のせきは薬を服用しながらも半年以上続いているのだから，chronic「慢性の」なのだ。反意語は acute「(病気が) 急性の」。

(13) －解答 **1** ･･

(訳) 陸軍巡察隊は駐屯地に戻る途中で待ち伏せ攻撃に遭った。彼らが狭い谷間に入ると，反乱兵のグループが彼らを待っていた。

(語句) **1**「待ち伏せ (攻撃)」   **2**「称賛」

3「直観的把握」   **4**「初め，始まり」

(解説) 反乱兵たちは巡察隊が来るのを狭い谷間で待ち構えていたのだから，巡察隊が出くわしたのは ambush「待ち伏せ攻撃」だ。

(14) －解答 **1** ･･

(訳) その政治家の人気は変動した。2 年前は彼の支持率は高かった。その後，彼は昨年国民の批判の標的となったが，それ以来支持を取り戻してきた。

(語句) **1**「変動した」   **2**「混ぜ合わせて作った」

3「同意した，継承した」   **4**「表にまとめた」

(解説) 時系列では「高い支持率→国民の批判の的→支持を取り戻す」となっているのだから，政治家の人気は fluctuated「変動した」のだ。

(15) －解答 **2** ･･

(訳) メアリーは長いこと新しい幹線道路を建設する市の計画の忠実な支持者だ。それは地元の経済に大きなプラスの影響を与えると，彼女は信じている。

(語句) **1**「残りの」 **2**「忠実な」 **3**「恥ずべき」 **4**「遺伝 (性) の」

(解説) 新しい幹線道路は地元経済に大きなプラス効果があると信じているメアリーは，計画の staunch「忠実な，断固たる」支持者だ。

(16) －解答 **3** ･･

(訳) カイルの背中の痛みはとてもひどかったので，朝ベッドから出るのさえ

164

大変だった。

（語句）　**1**「おどけた」　　　　　　　　**2**「（家屋などが）見捨てられた」
　　　　3「ひどく痛い，苦しめる」　　**4**「人に好かれる」

（解説）　ベッドから出るのにさえ苦労するのだから，背中の痛みは excruciating
「ひどく痛い」のだ。excruciating pain「耐え難いほどの痛み，激痛」。

(17) – 解答　❹

（訳）　トレントはこんろを止めるのを忘れて台所で小さな火事を起こした。幸
いにも，彼は炎が広がる前にバケツ1杯の水をぶっかけて炎を消すこと
ができた。

（語句）　**1**「～を取り消す」　　　　　　**2**「～を否認する」
　　　　3「（武器など）を振り回す」　　**4**「～に（水などを）ぶっかける」

（解説）　Luckily があるので，消火できたのだ。バケツの水を炎に…とくれば
douse「～に（水などを）ぶっかける，（火など）を（水をかけて）消
す」だ。

(18) – 解答　❷

（訳）　外科技術の進歩で，手術を行うときに医者はより小さな切開ができるよ
うになった。これは傷がずっと目立たなくなることを意味する。

（語句）　**1**「なぞなぞ，難問」　　　　　**2**「切開，切り込み」
　　　　3「沼地」　　　　　　　　　　**4**「風刺画」

（解説）　傷が目立たなくなるのだから，医者は手術時にもっと小さな incision
「切開」をすることができるようになったのだ。

(19) – 解答　❶

（訳）　社長は記者会見で質問に対して遠回しの回答をしたことを批判された。
参加したジャーナリストたちはもっと明快な返答を望んでいた。

（語句）　**1**「遠回しの」　　　　　　　　**2**「もうかる」
　　　　3「丸い」　　　　　　　　　　**4**「この上なく優れた」

（解説）　もっと明快な返答が望まれていたのだから，批判された社長がしたのは
oblique「遠回しの」回答だ。

(20) – 解答　❹

（訳）　バーバラが病気だったとき，家族の誰かが昼も夜もずっと彼女のそばに
いた。この寝ずの番は，彼女が全快するまで続いた。

（語句）　**1**「難儀，厄難」　　　　　　　**2**「輪郭（線）」
　　　　3「臆病」　　　　　　　　　　**4**「寝ずの番」

（解説）　昼夜を問わず誰かが病気のバーバラのそばにいたのだから，彼女が全快
するまで続いたのは vigil「寝ずの番」だ。

(21) – 解答　❷

（訳）　ニーナとジュディーは双子だったが，学校ではまったく違った態度を取
った。ニーナはしばしば失礼で教師の指示に従うのを拒み，一方ジュデ

21
年度第2回　筆記

165

ィーはいつも敬意を表した。

（語句） **1**「全知の」 **2**「敬意を表する」
3「（仕事などが）骨の折れる」 **4**「絶壁の（ような）」

（解説） 態度がまったく違う 2 人なのだから，失礼で教師に従わないニーナと違って，ジュディーの態度は deferential「敬意を表する」だったのだ。

(22) －解答 **4**

（訳） 大使は最初の取り組み方が何ら交渉に影響を与えられなかった後，礼儀正しさをなしにしてその問題についてもっと積極的な態度を取ることを決めた。

（語句） **1**「（部屋などに）どかどか入り込む」
2「〜を少しずつかじる」
3「（情報など）を探り出す」
4「〜なしで済ます」

（解説） 最初のやり方が失敗した後なので，最初のやり方が空所直後の politeness で，これをやめて aggressive にすると決めたと考えると理にかなう。

(23) －解答 **1**

（訳） マラソン走者たちは，沿道で声援を送る観衆によって鼓舞された。そのサポートが走者たちをレースの最後までがんばるように励ました。

（語句） **1**「鼓舞された」 **2**「掃いて脇へどけられた」
3「外に出された」 **4**「（金銭が）出し合われた」

（解説） 観衆の声援で走者は spurred on「鼓舞された」と考えられる。2 文目「そのサポート（声援）が走者のがんばりを促した」が裏付けとなる。

(24) －解答 **2**

（訳） 暴力的な抗議行動を減らそうとして，政府は街頭での大人数の集会を厳しく取り締まる法律を制定した。

（語句） **1**「〜を大量生産する」 **2**「厳しく取り締まる」
3「ひいて粉にする」 **4**「〜を宣誓就任させる」

（解説） 暴力的抗議行動を減らすために導入した法律なのだから，大人数の集会について crack down「断固たる処置を取る，厳しく取り締まる」ものだ。

(25) －解答 **1**

（訳） 兵士たちは訓練の完了後すぐに，海外の新しい配属の詳細を受け取った。彼らは西アフリカの基地へ出発するように命じられた。

（語句） **1**「（別の任地へ）出発する」 **2**「（話に）加わる」
3「衰える，弱る」 **4**「居眠りをする」

（解説） 兵士は新しい配属の詳細を受け取ったのだから，命じられたのは西アフリカの基地へ ship out「出発する」ことだ。ship out は軍務で別の場所に出発するときに使われることが多い。

| 一次試験・筆記 | **2** | 問題編 p.93 〜 95 |

全文訳 宝石バチとゴキブリ

宝石バチは生殖に欠かせないある能力を使う。そして，このハチの獲物であるゴキブリが極めて重要な役割を果たす。宝石バチは，顎でゴキブリをつかんだ後，獲物の体内に毒を注入し，瞬時にその生き物の前脚を短時間まひさせる。こうして動かなくなることで，ハチは，ゴキブリの脳の特定部位を狙うために必要となる確かな精度で2回目の針を刺すことができる。そこで毒液が特定の神経細胞の活動を遮断し，その生き物がハチから逃げる能力を妨げる。このハチがこのように獲物を操ることができるという事実は，この昆虫の最も興味深い特徴の1つだと考えられている。

毒が効くと，ゴキブリがハチの幼虫の栄養物としての役割を果たす準備がほとんど整う。しかしまず，ハチが飛び去って獲物を隠す穴を決めている間に，ゴキブリは長い身づくろいの儀式を行う。研究によると，ゴキブリの清浄行動は毒自体の特定の効果である。この行動が，例えばハチの幼虫にきれいな食事を確保することでハチに利益をもたらしているかどうかはわかっていないが，研究者たちがゴキブリをハチの針で刺されたのと同じような状態にしたときには，この行動は見られなかった。この行動はまた，宝石バチに捕まえられても刺されていない状態など，単にストレスを経験しただけのゴキブリにもなかった。

ハチが戻ると，ゴキブリは完全に捕獲者の意のままだ。ハチは，ゴキブリを穴に誘導すると，その脚に卵を1つ産んで去る。ハチの幼虫がふ化し，ゴキブリの体内に居を定め，自分自身の成長を養うために，その生き物からの栄養を利用する。しかし，その環境に危険がないわけではない。研究者たちは，ゴキブリの体腔内にいる間に防御用の盾として配備する液状物を，幼虫が出すのを観察している。この液状物に含まれる抗生物質は，（ゴキブリの体内での）潜伏期に宝石バチの子孫を死に至らせる可能性がある，ゴキブリが体内に持つ細菌の増殖を抑える。成熟するまで生き延びると，若いハチは宿主の外皮から出てきて，不運な獲物を自ら探し始める準備が整う。

語句 venom「（蛇・クモ・ハチなどの）毒液，毒」，paralyze「〜をまひさせる」，neuron「ニューロン，神経単位」，flee「逃げる」，intriguing「興味をそそる」，larva「幼虫」，prolonged「長引く」，self-grooming「独り身づくろい」，subject *A* to *B*「AにBを受けさせる」，pierce「〜を刺す」，compliant「従順な」，captor「捕獲者」，cavity「空洞，穴」，inhibit「〜を抑制する」，harbor「〜を住まわせる」，incubation「潜伏」，maturation「成熟」

(26) – 解答 ❹ ·· 正答率 ★75%以上

解説 ハチはこの方法で何をするのか，が空所に入る。この段落の説明によると，宝石バチは捕まえたゴキブリに毒を注入して前脚が動かない状態にした上で，再度脳の特定部位に毒を注入して逃げる能力を奪う。これが

167

in this way に相当するので，ハチはゴキブリを「操ることができる」と考えるのが自然。また，ゴキブリが行う清浄行動（第2段落）やハチの意のままになること（第3段落冒頭）が補強となっている。

(27) – 解答 3 ·····

解説 ゴキブリの清浄行動は何であるか，が空所に入る。第2段落後半で「ハチに刺されたのと同様の状態にしても，捕まえられても刺されないなどストレスを経験させても清浄行動は見られなかった」と述べられているので，この行動は **3**「毒自体の特定の効果」だと考えられる。空所文の直後で「この行動が……ハチに利益を与えているかどうかはわかっていない」と述べられているので **1** は誤りである。

(28) – 解答 2 ·····

解説 第3段落後半で，幼虫は（ゴキブリの体内での）潜伏期に，ゴキブリが体内に持つ細菌の増殖によって死ぬ可能性があるという危険が述べられている。このことを「環境に危険がないわけではない」と言い換えた **2** が正解。

全文訳 **ベルトルト・ブレヒトと叙事演劇**

　20世紀の偉大な演出家・劇作家の1人と広く認められているベルトルト・ブレヒトは，「叙事演劇」として知られる革新的なジャンルの先駆者であった。彼の作品は常に見て楽しくユーモアがあったが，ブレヒトの演劇は，当時の演劇の慣習に反抗する行為へと発展した。特に，ブレヒトは，芸術は現実を映し出す鏡であるべきという一般的な考えを覆そうとした。当時の作品は細かく作り込んだ小道具と舞台装置を使い，今日的な問題を中心とする筋書きを利用し，観客が簡単に共感できる登場人物を主役にしていた。しかし，ブレヒトの作品は従来の脚本術と演出法を覆し，観客に，自分たちが見ているのは目の前で起こっている実際の出来事ではなく，大幅に脚色され芝居じみた日常生活の解釈であることを，至る所で意図的に思い出させた。

　ブレヒトは特に，普通の演劇において観客が登場人物に共感するときに生み出される感情の放出である，カタルシスの原理をひどく嫌った。これは演劇の伝統の中で最も有害で，観客を論理的に考えないようにさせる，と彼は主張した。それ故にブレヒトは必要最低限の舞台装置とセットを使って，登場人物に直接観客に話しかけさせたり，自分の特徴を表すプラカードを掲げさせたりした。そうすることで，ブレヒトは意図的に，観客に舞台の登場人物と出来事から心理的距離を保たせ，非常に知的な劇場体験を作り出したのだ。ブレヒトは，自分の劇の工夫が一般大衆を刺激してその戯曲の主題をじっくりと考えさせることを願った。

　ブレヒトの戯曲は，ほとんど常に彼の政治的・哲学的な信念の表現で，その中で真っ先に挙げられるのは，永遠のものはない，という観念だった。彼がこれを伝えた1つの方法は，歴史的題材の使用を通してだ。戦争のように見たところ重大で普遍的な出来事には終わりが来ること，そして，そうした出来事がどのように解釈されるかは出来事そ

のものが終わった後ではたいてい非常に異なることを，観客に気付かせるのに，そのような題材は役立つとブレヒトは感じていた。ブレヒトは，人類の文明はユートピア的社会に向かって進んでいるという考えを抱いており，演劇は，人生は静的ではないことを思い出させるものとして，また，人々がそのような目標を目指して励むのを助けるための意欲を与えるものとしての両方の役割を果たし得ると信じていた。彼のユートピア的な政治観は，今日では弱さと見なされることもあるが，演劇に与えた革新的で多大な貢献のために，彼はあがめられている。

語句 watchable「見て楽しい」，rebellion「反乱，反逆」，theatrical「劇の，芝居じみた」，prop「小道具」，scenery「（背景を含む）舞台装置」，turn ~ on its head「~をひっくり返す」，at every turn「至る所で」，dramatize「~を脚色する」，despise「~を軽蔑する，嫌悪する」，employ「~を使用する」，trait「特徴」，device「工夫，方策」，reflect on ~「~を熟考する」，invariably「常に，いつも」，convey「~を伝える」，momentous「重大な」，universal「全世界の，普遍的な」，static「静的な，固定的な」，revere「~をあがめる，崇敬する」

(29) – 解答 **1**

解説 ブレヒトが覆そうとした一般的な考えとは何かを，空所以降の記述から読み取る。ブレヒト以前の演劇が重視したのは，作り込んだ小道具と舞台装置，今日的な筋書き，観客が共感できる登場人物，つまり実際の出来事（a real event）が舞台で起きているかのように見せることだった。それに合うのは，**1**「現実を映し出す鏡」である。

(30) – 解答 **4**

解説 ブレヒトが最も有害な伝統だと嫌悪するカタルシスは何をするのか，が空所に入る。ブレヒトは，観客に登場人物などから心理的距離を取らせて知的な劇場体験を作り出し，観客が演劇の主題をじっくり考える（reflecting thoughtfully on the play's themes）ことを望んだ（第2段落後半）のだから，彼が嫌うのはそれとは逆のことなので，**4**「観客を論理的に考えないようにさせる」が適切。

(31) – 解答 **2**

解説 空所に入るのは，ブレヒトの信念の中で先頭に来る観念（concept）の内容。彼はこの観念を伝えるのに歴史的題材を使ったが，それは「見たところ重大で普遍的な出来事には終わりが来る」こと，また，同じ出来事の解釈が出来事の後では大きく変わることを観客に気付かせるのに役立つから（第3段落第3文）。これらのことで伝えられるのは**2**「永遠のものはない」という観念だ。

21年度第2回　筆記

一次試験・筆記 **3** 問題編 p.95 〜 104

全文訳 **高利貸しと罪**

　貸した金に対して利息を請求することは高利貸しとしても知られ，今日では広く受け入れられているが，かつては大きな罪と見なされていた。昔は，高利貸し規制法は普通のことで，特にローマカトリック教会は，中世の時代にこの行いに厳しく反対することで知られており，その罪を犯した者を教会から追放した。

　元々高利貸しが禁止されるようになったのは，借金と信用貸しが，善意による援助と信頼のシステムと考えられていたことによる。中世の貧しい農村部の人々は，家族と友人が助け合うために物を共有し貸すことに頼ることによって，強い共同社会のつながりを形成した。それ故，人の社会的義務と考えられている行為に対して報酬を期待するのは，道徳的に間違っていると見なされ，そしてこの考えは，交換の媒体が物からお金へと変化した後もずっと続いた。しかし，貧窮していたり金銭上の不運に苦しんでいたりした人たちは，教会や貴族が資本を多量に蓄えていたので，彼らに頼らざるを得なかった。そして，借金と信用貸しの道徳的な本質に関する当時の考えに沿って，人の社会的・宗教的責任の一部であるものから利益を得る金貸しは，罪深いと見なされた。

　しかし，貸金業から利益を得るために，教会と高利貸しの法的禁止の抜け道を見つけようとする者もいた。そうするために多様な方法が出現した。例えば，稼いだ利息を隠す方法として変動する為替レートを利用しようと，外貨で借金を返済することを伴う複雑な策略などである。ほかの方法で貸金業者が日常的に用いたのは「3つ組み契約」だ。これは複数の契約を組み合わせたもので，契約は個別なら当時の法律で許可されていたが，合わせると，貸金業者は貸し付ける金の受取人の共同経営者となることで利息を得ることができた。貸金業者は自分が貸し付けを認めた先である企業の一部となった後，違法に利益を得るのではなく，厳密に言えば自分の資本から利益を得ていたのだ。

　取引が拡大し成長するにつれ，高利貸し規制法によって引き起こされる問題が明らかになった。お金からお金を生み出すことに対する中世の反発は，交換手段としてのお金には内在的価値が欠けているという一般的な考え方のせいだった。しかし，金貨と銀貨の不足と遠方にいる顧客への支払いの困難さが，多数の都市に支店を持つ銀行の発展と，外貨を両替できる両替商の出現につながった。富が社会の隅々にまで行き渡ると，実のところ貸金業者は「何もしないでお金」を受け取っているわけではないことが明らかになった。誰かに雌牛を貸す農夫がその牛から乳と子牛を得る機会を奪われているのとまったく同じように，貸金業者は利益を得るほかの方法に投資する機会を奪われている。貸し付けの性質が変化するとともに，貸金業者が資金を手放すときに負うリスクがより深く理解されるようになった。時がたつにつれ，これらの要因は教会や学者によって認められて高利貸しに関する議論を組み立て直すのに役立ち，利息請求の全面的禁止から，一般消費者を高利貸し業者とクレジットカード会社が課す法外な料金から守る現代的な高利貸し規制法への進化を促した。

170

語句 usury「高利貸し」，benevolent「善意の，優しい」，communal「共同社会の」，destitute「極貧の」，misfortune「不運」，nobility「貴族（階級）」，sinful「罪深い」，circumvent「（法律など）の抜け道を見つける」，camouflage「〜を偽装する，隠す」，financier「金融業者，貸金業者」，permissible「許される」，technically「正式には，厳密には」，moneychanger「両替商」，be deprived of 〜「〜を奪われている」，reframe「〜を作り直す，再構成する」，loan shark「高利貸し（業者）」

(32) – 解答 ②

問題文の訳 中世の社会で，高利貸しを取り巻く禁止事項は，

選択肢の訳
1 人が金銭的問題を抱えたときに親族以外の誰かに援助を求めるのは罪である，という信念の現れだった。
2 お金がある人々は慈善行為と見なされることを不当に利用するべきではない，という考えを反映していた。
3 教会と貴族が，貧民を搾取するために，大金を使える機会をどのように悪用したか，の実証であった。
4 人々が，貸付制度を効果的に機能させるのに十分な借金と信用貸しの理解を持っていなかったことを示唆した。

解説 第2段落に高利貸し禁止の経緯がある。中世の貧しい相互扶助社会で，物の貸し借りは「善意による援助と信頼のシステム」であり「人の社会的義務」と見なされ「故に報酬を得るのは道徳的に間違っている」という考えが発生し，これに沿って「義務である行為で利益を得る貸金は罪」となった。このことをまとめた **2** が正解。**2** の charitable act は本文の benevolent aid の言い換え。

(33) – 解答 ④

問題文の訳 この文章によると，貸金業から利益を得るために使われた方法についてどれが正しいか。

選択肢の訳
1 それらは，貸金業についての考えが，さまざまな国といろいろな産業によって必ずしも同じとは限らないことの例だった。
2 それらは，中世で利息が支払われた方法が，共同経営者たちの間に法的な争いを起こし得ることの例証だった。
3 それらは，中世の人々が利益と利息は2つのまったく無関係な概念だと信じていたことを示すものだった。
4 それらは，一部の人々が法に従うように見えながらも，貸付で利息を稼ぐ間接的な方法を使ったことを示した。

解説 第3段落冒頭に，貸金業から利益を得るために法的禁止を回避しようとした者もいたとあり，以下でその方法が説明されている。変動する為替レートを利用して利息を隠す，法的に許される別々の契約を組み合わせ

21年度第2回　筆記

て「違法に利息を得る（illegally gaining interest）のではなく」資本から利益を得る方法など。これらを「法に従う（obey the law）ように見える間接的な（indirect）方法」と述べた **4** が正解。

(34) – 解答 ③

問題文の訳 この文章の筆者は，以下の記述のどれと意見が一致する可能性が最も高いだろうか。

選択肢の訳
1 中世に高利貸し規制法を廃止することは，農業が金融システムの限界より大きくなった後にやっと検討された。
2 教会内部での指導者層の交代が，お金の貸し借りを取り巻く法律の見直しにつながった。
3 貸金業に対する新たな姿勢は，部分的には，貸付金を与えることによって起こり得る潜在的損失に対する理解が深まったことの結果だった。
4 銀行と両替商が，国際貿易からの利益を押し上げる方法として，高利貸しに関する方針を緩和するよう教会に圧力をかけた。

解説 第4段落で，貸金業者が負う①利益を得るほかの方法に投資する機会を奪われるリスクが「より深く理解されて（a greater appreciation arose）」，②高利貸しの議論の見直しに役立ったことが述べられている。このことをまとめた **3** が正解。**3** では，①は potential losses，②は New attitudes toward moneylending に言い換えられている。

全文訳 **分類論争**

　ブラジルのアマゾンに生息する3つの変種のタテフオオガシラは，見た目はほぼ同一だが，鳴き声はリズムと音色が微妙に違う。1人の科学者が，この3つの変種を別々の種に分類し直すことを提唱するために，鳥の種の分類を担当する委員会に話を持ちかけたとき，委員たちはジレンマに陥った。その違いは，追加で2つの種を作る正当な理由となるのに十分だったのか？結局，彼らは1つだけ追加した。しかし彼らの決定は，自然界に見られる多くの生物の特定と定義を扱う科学分野である分類学の世界で，さらにもう1つの論争を巻き起こした。

　技術の進歩によって地球の生物をより詳しく調べることが可能となるにつれて，世界中で特定される新種の数は増えてきている。南米だけで，鳥の種の数は2000年以来150以上増えた。しかし，これらの大部分は，熱帯雨林の奥深い隅々に遠征して発見されたのではなかった。むしろ，記録技術や遺伝的分類における飛躍的進歩の結果として，既存の種の変種を分類し直すことで作り出されたのだった。そして，近年検知可能となった微妙な差異はそのような再分類を正当化すると主張する者がいる一方で，その区別を恣意的だと考える者もいる。鳥類専門家のジェイムズ・レムセンは，鳥の分類学の現状を「悪い状況で最善を尽くそうとしている」と見ており，「私たちは1つの連続するものに人為的な境界をつけようとしているのです」と説明する。

172

これらの議論により，種の区別方法に関する分類学における根本的な問題である「種の問題」を巡る論争が再び始まった。この問いに答えようとする試みに固有の問題は，レムセンの見解を際立たせる。例えば，生物学的種の概念（BSC）は生物学者にとって長い間有名な指針で，相互間でのみうまく生殖できて健康で繁殖力のある子孫を産むことができる生物，として種を定義する。しかし，種の間に明確な線引きをするためにこのように生殖を使うとややこしい問題が起こる。地理的な理由で種が2つ以上のグループに分かれた場合，BSCの支持者は，この分離が別個の種の分類を正当化すると考える。これらのグループは出会わないのだから，相互間で自然生殖するであろうかどうかを知るのは不可能だ，と彼らは言う。

今日では，BSCに加えて，生物学者は，生物のグループのDNAと進化の歴史の両方の分析によって手引きされる。1つの例は，オーストラリアに生息するディンゴを巡る分類上の論争だ。ディンゴは家畜に及ぼす脅威のため，何世紀にもわたって農村部で駆除の対象になってきた。それらが保護されてこなかった1つの理由は，野生の犬で，家畜犬と同じ種に属すると分類されているからである。研究者たちがディンゴの骨格，遺伝的特徴および歴史的に家畜化されていないことなどの要因を調べ，2019年に，別個の種の指定が正当だと決定された。これは，BSCに基づいて，ディンゴが自然に家畜犬と行う交配は彼らが別個の種ではないことを表す，と主張する以前の結論を否定した。キツネなど有害生物の個体数を抑制するのにディンゴが果たす重要な役割を考えると，この問題は，分類学的な分類が種の管理にも生態系全体にも重大な影響を及ぼし得ることを表している。

> 語句　subtly「微妙に」，reclassify「～を再分類する」，taxonomy「分類学」，multitude「大勢，多数」，nuance「微妙な差異」，detectable「探知できる」，continuum「連続（体）」，underscore「～を強調する」，fertile「繁殖力のある」，proponent「支持者」，eradication「根絶，撲滅」，genetics「遺伝的特徴［構成］」，domestication「家畜化」，interbreeding「交配」

(35) – 解答　②

> 問題文の訳　なぜこの文章の筆者はタテフオオガシラの分類に関して起こった論争に言及しているのか。

> 選択肢の訳
> 1　もっと重要な要因ではなく，見た目のようなあまり注目に値しないことだけに基づく鳥の分類に関連する問題の例である。
> 2　動物の変種間のささいな違いが，新しい種の分類が適切かどうかを確かにするのを困難にし得ることを示している。
> 3　科学者たちが，実地調査を通して得られた新しいデータを支持し，鳥についての既存の情報を退けるときに起こる問題の例である。
> 4　種の分類でかつては重要だと考えられたわずかな違いの多くは，実はまったく重要ではないことを示している。

> 解説　第1段落に，外見は同じだが鳴き声が微妙に違うタテフオオガシラの3

つの変種を別々の種に分類することを提案されたとき，鳴き声の微妙な違いは2つの新種を作るほどのものか，というジレンマに委員会が陥ったことが述べられており，**2**の内容の具体的な例示となっている。

(36) – 解答 ①

問題文の訳 生物学的種の概念に問題があり得る理由は，

選択肢の訳
1 同じ種のメンバーが生殖するために通常あるであろう機会は，時に外的要因に影響されることだ。
2 それが，自然生息地での動物の観察ではなく，飼育された動物間の交配の観察に基づいて制定されたことだ。
3 特定の種に適用するように作られた分類の要因が，しばしば誤って多くの異なる生物に適用されることだ。
4 基にしている指針が，ある生物のグループが別の種であるかどうかを評価する方法という根本的な問題に対処しようとしていないことだ。

解説 生物学的種の概念（BSC）の問題は第3段落後半にある。同じ種が地理的な理由で複数のグループに分かれた場合にほかのグループと出会わないために，相互間で自然生殖するかがわからず，BSCの考えでは別個の種になること。ほかのグループとの出会いを「生殖のために通常ある機会」，地理的な理由を「外的要因」と言い換えた**1**が正解。

(37) – 解答 ④

問題文の訳 ディンゴに関する状況から明らかなのはどれか。

選択肢の訳
1 長期にわたる動物の繁殖習性の綿密な分析が，それが生息する生態系に対するその動物の重要性を明らかにし得る。
2 2019年の調査結果により，家畜を襲うディンゴを駆除するより多くの権利がオーストラリアの農民に与えられることになりそうだ。
3 動物の個体数を維持することが経済的利益につながることが明確なら，種の分類に関連する判断はおそらく無視される。
4 ある動物が別個の種と見なされるべきかどうかについての決定は，人間によるその動物の扱われ方に大きな影響を及ぼし得る。

解説 第4段落に，「有害生物の抑制で重要な役割を果たすにもかかわらず，野生の犬と分類されていたので長年駆除の対象であり保護されなかった」というディンゴの状況が，「分類が種の管理に重大な影響を及ぼし得ることを表す（最終文）」と述べられている。この最終文の部分を言い換えた**4**が正解。本文のmajor implicationsは**4**ではsignificantly impactに，management of speciesはway it is treated by humansに言い換えられている。

全文訳 **涙の道**

今日では涙の道として知られているが，約10万人のアメリカ先住民が，1830年代

の間に米国南東部にある先祖代々の居住地から強制的にさせられた移動および移住は，アメリカ史における暗い時期を表す。新たな土地へ行くルートは9つの州を横断して数千キロメートルにわたり，およそ1万5千人の男性，女性，子供が立退きとそれに続く旅の間に亡くなったと考えられている。

　涙の道に先立って，文化的な同化政策が実施されていた。アメリカ先住民はキリスト教と西洋教育を受け入れるように求める非常に大きな圧力に直面したが，彼らが先祖代々の土地を保有する権利は，たいてい認められた。しかし，1830年にアメリカ議会はアンドリュー・ジャクソン大統領の政権下でインディアン移住法を可決したが，これは部族を彼らの居住地から現在のオクラホマ州に位置する「インディアン居留地」にある新たな生活の地へと移動させることを，政府ができるようにする法律だった。しかし，1832年にチェロキー族が所有するジョージア州の土地を没収しようとしたことについて，最高裁判所のジョン・マーシャル長官が違憲判決を下したとき，この政策は困難に直面した。この判決は，チェロキー族を主権国家として認め，重要な判例のようなものを作った。しかし，ジャクソンはくじけることなく反抗的で，伝えられるところによれば，「ジョン・マーシャルが判決を下したのだ。さあ，彼にそれを実行させろ」という言葉で判決に応じた。

　ジャクソンがアメリカ先住民の強制移住を正当化した理由は，ほぼ全面的に事実無根だった。部族は自らを「文明化」しようと努力したにもかかわらず，狩猟への過度の依存と近代的な農業方式を導入しないことで非難された。当時ジェイムズ・フェニモア・クーパーの小説『モヒカン族の最後』が一因で，アメリカ先住民と彼らの文化は消滅しつつある，というロマンチックに描かれたアメリカの神話があり，ジャクソンはこの考えをうまく利用して，移住しないとアメリカ先住民と彼らの文化は滅びる運命にあると主張した。しかし実際には，当時アメリカ先住民の人口は安定しており，おそらく増えてさえいた。

　歴史学者のクローディオ・ソーントは，アメリカ先住民の強制移住は当時の資本主義の拡大という文脈で捉えるべきだ，と言う。白人の奴隷所有者と投資家は，アメリカ先住民の保有地が全国で最も肥沃な土地のいくつかであり，農業経営と建設のためにすぐに利用できることを知っていた。アメリカ先住民の土地の所有権奪取を白人，特に奴隷所有者が事業を拡大する絶好の機会と見て，これに出資するためにどのように東海岸の銀行が南部の投機家と協力したのかを，ソーントは年代記として描いている。強制移住は，アメリカ先住民の絶滅を防ぐために行われる親切な対策だとされていたが，強制移住の立案と実行の背後にいた人々は，奴隷を経済的に利用されるために神から与えられた資源だと考えていたのと同じように，アメリカ先住民の土地を見ていた。

　ソーントはまた，南部の政治家たちと北部の協力者たちが強制移住を何とかやり遂げるために，どのように役所・軍人・行政官のネットワークを作り上げたのかも記録している。これらの取り組みには信じられないほど費用がかかったが，その土地は，黒人奴隷の無料の労働者を使って耕せばコストに見合うと見なされた。東海岸の銀行家たちは，奴隷所有と強制移住の二重の事業に出資することで急速に裕福になっており，そしてこ

175

のことが次に，鉄道やほかの大規模開発事業の資金を提供した。涙の道は恐ろしかったけれども，太平洋岸から大西洋岸まで広がる国としてのアメリカの出現に不可欠であった技術的進歩とインフラをもたらした，と主張する者もいる。

インディアン移住法から生じた強制移住は，部族によって異なる反応を引き起こした。自発的に行く者がいる一方で，激しく抵抗する者もいた。最も悲劇的な事例の1つは，チェロキー族であった。非常に大きな圧力にさらされて，部族のごく少数の人々が西への移動について政府と交渉を始めることを独断で決め，ニューエコタ条約を結んだ。チェロキー族の大多数がその文書を無効と見なし，条件の仲介に関与した代表者とやらは自分たちが認めたリーダーではないと主張し，この条約を無効にするよう求める請願書には1万5千を超える署名が集まった。しかし，議会はその条約を可決して法律と認め，チェロキー族の運命は決まった。

退去の期限は2年であったが，1838年までにインディアン居留地に向かったチェロキー族は約2千人だけであった。その進行をはかどらせるため，約7千人の兵士がチェロキー族の土地へ行くように命じられ，そこで銃を突き付けてチェロキー族を家から引きずり出して閉じ込め，その間に彼らの家と持ち物を略奪した。保護施設をあてがわれず基本的な物資さえもなかったので，チェロキー族は極度の暑さと寒さの中で長距離の行進に耐えなければならなかった。水不足とわずかな食料の配給のせいで彼らは栄養失調になり，多くの者が死に至る病に屈した。チェロキー族がインディアン居留地に到着するころには，およそ4分の1が亡くなっていた。

1840年ごろまでに，ほとんどの部族は，永久に彼らのものであり続けると政府が約束した土地に定住していた。しかし，彼らは自分たちが厳しく不慣れな環境にいることがわかり，それから何年間もひどく苦しんだ。さらに，鉄道がアメリカ西部を開くにつれて多くの白人移住者がインディアン居留地に押し寄せたので，その規模は徐々に縮小し，20世紀初頭には完全に消滅していた。

(語句) forcible「強制的な」，ancestral「祖先の」，perish「死ぬ」，assimilation「同化」，unconstitutional「違憲の」，sovereign nation「主権国家」，undeterred「くじけない」，defiant「反抗的な」，unfounded「根拠のない」，civilize「～を文明化する」，overreliance「過度の依存」，romanticize「～をロマンチックに描く」，doomed「破滅する運命にある」，deportation「強制退去」，holdings「保有財産」，fertile「（土地が）肥えた」，chronicle「～を年代記に載せる」，speculator「投機家」，dispossession「（不動産の）所有権奪取」，golden opportunity「絶好の機会」，benign「優しい，慈悲深い」，avert「～を避ける，防ぐ」，slavery「奴隷所有」，expulsion「排除すること，追放」，horrific「恐ろしい」，take it upon *oneself* to *do*「～することを独断で決める」，invalid「無効の」，broker「～の仲介をする」，nullify「～を無効にする」，seal「（運命・死など）を決める」，expedite「～を促進する」，loot「～を略奪する」，unsheltered「保護

されていない」, scarcity「欠乏，不足」, meager「わずかな」, malnourished「栄養失調の」, appallingly「ぞっとするほど」

(38) – 解答 ③

問題文の訳 1830 年代の間，アンドリュー・ジャクソン大統領は，

選択肢の訳
1 彼の同化政策は効果がないとわかった後，アメリカ先住民を彼らの土地から追い出すために，裁判所を利用しようとし始めた。
2 インディアン移住法が国の最高裁で却下された後，その法律が機能する方法を協議して変えるよう強いられた。
3 政府はアメリカ先住民を彼らの土地から本人の同意なしに追い出す権力を持たない，と述べる法的判断を無視した。
4 ほかの部族の人々には与えなかった特別待遇をチェロキー族に与える以外選択肢がなかった。

解説 チェロキー族所有のジョージア州の土地を政府が没収することは違憲だと最高裁で判決が下されたが，ジャクソンはくじけず反抗的だった（第2段落後半）のだから，彼はこの法的判断を無視したのだ。3で述べている法的判断（legal decision）の内容はこの言い換え。彼は裁判所を利用しようとしておらず，移住法は最高裁で却下されていないので 1，2 は誤りである。

(39) – 解答 ②

問題文の訳 クローディオ・ソーントは以下の記述のどれと意見が一致する可能性が最も高いだろうか。

選択肢の訳
1 多くのアメリカ先住民の部族が不作と食料源の減少に苦労したが，書物はたいてい彼らの生活を華やかに描いた。
2 アメリカ先住民を支援するための試みとして提示されたが，彼らの強制移住は実は経済的利益の可能性によって動機付けられていた。
3 アメリカ先住民の文化の影響を規制するために多くの政策が導入されたが，いくつかの革新的なビジネスアイデアがそれらを世に広める助けとなった。
4 政府が強制移住の主な責めを負うべきだが，アメリカ先住民が実業界のリーダーたちと協力したことが先住民の多くの問題を引き起こした。

解説 第4段落の冒頭で，強制移住は資本主義の拡大の一環だというソーントの立場が明示されている。具体的な記述が続いた後，最終文に「強制移住の建前はアメリカ先住民の絶滅防止のためだが，その立案・実行をした人々は先住民の土地を経済的に利用できる資源と見ていた」ことが示されている。このことを言い換えた 2 が正解。

(40) – 解答 ④

問題文の訳 涙の道がアメリカの拡大に勢いをつけたと言われているのは，

21年度第2回　筆記

177

選択肢の訳　1　北部と南部の裕福な実業家たちの間の競争が，拡大事業のコストを減らし建設のピッチを上げる助けになったからだ。
2　別の場所に定住させられた多くのアメリカ先住民には鉄道業と建設業の仕事が与えられたが，そのことが国を開拓するのに不可欠だったと判明したからだ。
3　多くのアメリカ先住民が強制移住で受け取ったお金と農業の知識を，ほかの土地に引っ越して耕作するために使ったからだ。
4　強制移住を巡ってもうかる産業が作り出され，その後全国でインフラ開発に使われた富を生んだからだ。

解説　涙の道とはアメリカ先住民の強制移住のこと（第1段落冒頭）。第5段落で，先住民の土地を耕作させるための奴隷所有と強制移住への事業出資で裕福になった銀行家が，次に鉄道など大規模開発事業に資金提供したので，広いアメリカに必要なインフラができたことが述べられている。このことを「強制移住を巡って産業が作られ」と言い換えた**4**が正解。

(41) – 解答

問題文の訳　ニューエコタ条約に関する以下の記述のどれが正しいか。
選択肢の訳　1　チェロキー族が条約に署名するために与えられた期限は，そのような重要な事柄について決定を下す余裕を彼らに与えなかった。
2　条約を法律として通過させてほしいという請願書は，そのような活動を正当化するのに十分な支持がチェロキー族からはない，と感じた役人たちによって退けられた。
3　その条約に関与したグループには自分たちを代表して交渉を始める権限がないと信じていたので，チェロキー族の多くが動揺した。
4　チェロキー族のリーダーたちのグループが，その条約は過去にほかの部族が提示された同じような種類の条約よりもずっと好ましくないと感じた。

解説　ニューエコタ条約については第6段落にある。この条約は部族のごく少数が独断で政府と交渉してまとめたが，彼らは自分たちが認めたリーダーではないと大多数のチェロキーが主張してこの条約を無効と見なし，条約破棄を求めたことが述べられている。このことを言い換えた**3**が正解。**3**では自分たちが認めたリーダーではないことを「自分たちを代表して交渉する権限がない」と言い換えている。

一次試験・筆記 **4** 問題編 p.104

解答例　Technological advancements have undoubtedly brought convenience to our lives. However, the commodification of personal data, digitization of society, and scarcity of laws have eroded our ability to protect individual privacy in the modern world.

The Internet has paved the way for the accumulation and trading of data regarding users' online habits. Scandals involving the sale of users' social media data, for example, are proof that our digital footprints are now lucrative commodities. Moreover, penalties for selling this data are a fraction of the revenues gained from the activity, which may incentivize corporations to continue violating people's privacy.

Additionally, as society becomes ever more digitized, individuals are being compelled to disclose more personal data. Registering private information on governmental sites, for example, may afford citizens access to vital public services such as healthcare. Once registered, however, it may not be possible for citizens to control how their data is used, thereby making the safeguarding of their personal details unfeasible.

The struggle to maintain individual privacy is further exemplified by a conspicuous lack of legislation. Devising and authorizing laws is a protracted process, requiring meticulous consideration. The massive effort required to safeguard the huge amounts of data generated by our daily activities has left lawmakers struggling to keep up.

Thus, in the face of capitalist greed and intrusive governance, both of which are escaping the reach of overwhelmed judicial systems, protecting individual privacy has become an impossible task.

トピックの訳　「個人のプライバシーは現代世界において守ることができるか」

解説　解答例はトピックに対して No で「個人のプライバシーは守れない」との立場。導入部で述べる 3 つの理由とその根拠は，①個人データの商品化 (commodification of personal data)：データの売買がもうかるので，罰金を払っても売買を続ける企業がある，②社会のデジタル化 (digitization of society)：ネットのサービス利用時に登録が必要とな

る個人データが，どう使われるかわからない，③法律の不足 (scarcity of laws)：法不足のため個人情報保持に苦労しているが，法制定にかかる作業は長く膨大で追い付かない，である。

3つの理由はどれも技術的進歩に関連するもの。導入部でこれらの理由を列挙することによって予想される内容の範囲を冒頭で絞り込むため，読み手が理解しやすいエッセーとなっている。

難しい単語を多く使っているので，全体が引き締まっている。日ごろからエッセーに使えそうな単語，この例では commodification「商品化」，digitization「デジタル化」，scarcity「不足，欠乏」，feasible「実行可能な」などは，スペルを間違えずに書けて使えるようにしておきたい。

また，導入部分（第1段落）で示した理由①②③を，結論部分（第5段落）で，①を資本家の欲 (capitalist greed)，②を押し付けがましい管理 (intrusive governance)，③を司法制度の力の及ぶ範囲から逃れる (escaping the reach of ... judicial systems)，と言い換えているのは見事だ。なお，解答例は236語で理想的な長さだ。

| 一次試験・リスニング | **Part 1** | 問題編 p.105 ~ 106 | ▶MP3 ▶アプリ ▶CD 2 26~36 |

No.1 – 解答 ③

スクリプト
☆: Is that a new cell phone, Martin?

★: Yeah, I got it yesterday.

☆: What about your old one?

★: Donated it. A friend works for an organization that sends used phones to people in Africa who can't afford new ones.

☆: That's great.

★: Yeah, and it reduces the garbage created by discarded cell phones. Did you know they contain hazardous chemicals?

☆: No, I didn't. Actually, I've been thinking about getting a new phone. Can I pass on my old one when I do?

★: Sure.

Question: What does the man imply about cell phones?

全文訳
☆: それって新しい携帯電話かしら，マーティン？

★: そうだよ，昨日買ったんだ。

☆: 古いのはどうしたの？

★: 寄付したよ。新しい携帯電話を買う余裕がないアフリカの人たちに中古のものを送っている団体で，友達が働いているんだ。

☆: それは素晴らしいわね。

★: そうだね，それにそうすることで，携帯電話を捨てることによって生じるごみが減少するんだ。携帯電話には危険な化学物質が含まれているって知っていたかい？

☆: いいえ，知らなかったわ。実は，ずっと新しい携帯電話を買おうと思っていたの。買ったら古いのを預けてもいいかしら？

★: もちろん。

質問： 携帯電話について男性は暗に何と言っているか。

選択肢の訳
1 低品質の素材で作られている。
2 アフリカで使えるように改造するのは難しい。
3 捨てると危険な場合がある。
4 寄付することは必ずしもよいことではない。

解説 男性は3つ目の発言で，携帯電話を寄付すればごみになる携帯電話が減ることと，携帯電話には hazardous chemicals が含まれていることを指摘している。つまり，携帯電話を throw away「捨てる」ことは危険を伴う場合があると暗に言っていることになる。

21年度第2回 リスニング

No.2 −解答 ②

スクリプト ★： Patricia, I heard you sent a letter to Congressman Taylor. What's he up to this time?

☆： He's pushing this stupid industrial development near the Fairfield Wetlands.

★： Unbelievable!

☆： Some friends and I are campaigning to get protected status for the wetlands. It's just like when he tried to turn the old Weller Farmstead into a golf course.

★： I'm sure you'll get a lot of support. It's about time Taylor started helping his ordinary constituents, not just his rich friends in business.

Question: What does the man imply about Congressman Taylor?

全文訳 ★： パトリシア，テイラー議員に手紙を送ったって聞いたけど。彼は今度は何をしようとしているんだい？

☆： フェアフィールド湿地帯の近くで工業開発なんていうばかげたことを推し進めているのよ。

★： 信じられない！

☆： 友人数人と私で湿地の保護指定を獲得するために運動しているの。テイラー議員が昔のウェラー農園をゴルフ場にしようとしたときとまったく同じよ。

★： きっと支持をたくさん得られるよ。もういいかげん，テイラーは仕事上の金持ちの友達だけじゃなくて，普通の有権者を助け始めるべきだよ。

質問：テイラー議員について男性は暗に何と言っているか。

選択肢の訳 **1** 湿地を救うのに成功するだろう。

2 ある特定の人たちに特別な計らいをするために地位を利用している。

3 環境を保護するために尽力している。

4 普通の有権者に人気がある。

解説 開発推進派のテイラー議員に対して女性は環境保護派で，男性は女性に全面的に賛同しているという構図は明快である。正解 **2** の certain people は，最後の男性の発言の his rich friends in business を指している。

No.3 −解答 ①　　　　　　　　　　　　　　正答率 ★**75%以上**

スクリプト ☆： Richard, you look really beat. What's going on?

★： I was here most of the night finishing that new advertising contract. The sales department said that they need it by nine this morning.

☆： You finished it by yourself?

★： Yes, unfortunately.

☆： That's rough. Can I get you a cup of coffee or something?

182

★： That sounds like just what the doctor ordered.

Question: What's the matter with Richard?

全文訳 ☆： リチャード，疲れ切っているわね。どうしたっていうの？

★： ほとんど一晩中ここにいて，例の新しい広告契約書を仕上げていたんだ。今朝9時までに必要だと営業部に言われてさ。

☆： 1人で仕上げたの？

★： ああ，残念ながら。

☆： ひどい話ね。コーヒーか何か持って来てあげようか。

★： それは願ったりかなったりだ。

質問：リチャードはどうしたのか。

選択肢の訳 **1** 昨夜遅くまで働いた。

2 早朝会議があった。

3 1人で働くことが多過ぎる。

4 広告契約書を仕上げられなかった。

解説 男性の最初の発言の I was here most of the night finishing that new advertising contract. から，ほぼ徹夜で仕事をしていたことがわかるので正解は **1**。昨夜は1人で働いたが，**3** のように too often という内容は会話にない。just what the doctor ordered「まさに必要なもの」。

No.4 – 解答 ①

スクリプト ★： Well, we've interviewed all the candidates, and now it's decision time.

☆： Hmm . . . I was impressed with the last applicant. He was well qualified and very articulate. And he has copywriting experience.

★： That's true. He also seemed ambitious. Are you sure you can stand the competition, Ruth?

☆： Come off it. He wasn't that good.

★： Actually, I think he could be future management material.

☆： In that case, maybe you should watch your own back, Bob!

Question: What does the woman imply about the applicant?

全文訳 ★： さて，候補者全員の面接が終わりましたから，結論を出す時間です。

☆： うーん……私は最後の志願者が印象に残りました。資格も十分にあり，発言もとてもはっきりしていました。それに，コピーライターの経験もあります。

★： そうですね。それに意欲的にも見えました。彼との競争に耐えられると思いますか，ルース。

☆： ばかなことを言わないでくださいよ。彼はそんな大したことなかったです。

★： いや，彼は将来の管理職になるだけの人材じゃないかと思いますよ。

☆：もしそうなら，追い上げられないように注意した方がいいかもしれませんね，ボブ！

質問：この志願者について女性は暗に何と言っているか。

選択肢の訳
1. 彼女にとっての脅威ではない。
2. 管理職として採用されるべきだ。
3. 自信があり過ぎるように見える。
4. コミュニケーション能力が弱い。

解説 Are you sure you can stand the competition, Ruth?「彼との競争に耐えられると思いますか，ルース」と聞かれた女性は，2つ目の発言で Come off it.「ばかなことを言わないで」（= Stop joking!）と答えているので，1 が正解。

No.5 －解答

スクリプト
★：Judy, I guess you have a lot of free time now that both your kids have gone away to college.

☆：Well, definitely more. But I still manage to fill the time doing things around the house.

★：Don't you ever find yourself getting bored?

☆：Not at all! There are so many things I want to do. I haven't mentioned this before, but . . . I'm going to exhibit some of my paintings at a small gallery downtown.

★：That's great! Congratulations. You know, I always thought you had some hidden talent. I guess it was just a matter of getting your foot in the door.

☆：Having my own exhibition's been something I've always dreamed about, but I never imagined it would actually happen.

★：Good for you. Definitely send me an invitation.

Question: What do we learn about the woman?

全文訳
★：ジュディー，子供が2人とも大学に入って家を出たんだから，今は自由な時間がたくさんあるんじゃないのかい。

☆：そうね，確かに増えたわ。でも家のことをやっていればまだ何とか時間をつぶせるわね。

★：飽きてくることはないの？

☆：全然！ やりたいことが山ほどあるのよ。このことは今まで言っていなかったけど……街中の小さなギャラリーで私の描いた絵をいくつか展示してくれることになったの。

★：すごいね！ おめでとう。まあ，君には隠れた才能があると常々思っていたよ。あとは始めの一歩を踏み出すかどうかだけだったと思うよ。

☆：自分の展覧会を開くのは昔からの夢だったんだけど，それが実現するな

んて想像もしなかったわ。

★： よかったね。必ず招待状を送ってよ。

質問：女性についてわかることは何か。

選択肢の訳　**1**　彼女は前よりも家事が増えた。

2　彼女の展覧会は成功だった。

3　彼女は今の方が自分のための時間が増えた。

4　彼女のギャラリーは閉鎖された。

解説　1つずつ確認しよう。「増えた」のは家事ではなく自由時間なので**1**は誤り。展覧会はまだ開かれていないので**2**も誤り。自分のギャラリーを持っているわけではないので**4**も誤り。女性は最初の発言で「（自由な時間が）増えた」と述べているので，**3**が正解。絵画や展覧会の話もこれにまつわることである。

No.**6** – 解答　④

スクリプト　★： Mr. Lang isn't going to be happy when he finds this mistake in our data.

☆： Yeah, but I don't think he'll overreact. He's usually pretty considerate.

★： Sure, but remember the last time we messed things up?

☆： Yeah, but this time it's nothing major. I'm sure he'll cut us some slack.

★： I sure hope so. We were up all night on this.

Question: How does the woman predict the boss will react?

全文訳　★： 僕たちのデータのこの間違いを見つけたら，ラングさんは不満に思うだろうね。

☆： ええ，だけど過剰に反応することはないと思うわ。普段はかなり思いやりがある人だもの。

★： 確かにそうだけど，前回僕たちが大失敗したときのことを覚えている？

☆： ええ，だけど今回のは大したことないわ。きっと大目に見てくれるわよ。

★： 本当にそうだといいんだけど。僕たちは徹夜でこれに取り組んだんだから。

質問：上司がどう反応すると女性は予測しているか。

選択肢の訳　**1**　怒る。

2　気付かない。

3　過剰に反応する。

4　理解を示す。

解説　会話中で Mr. Lang や he と呼ばれているのが2人の上司。仕事でミスをした2人だが，女性の方は一貫して楽観的で，上司は considerate だし今回のミスは nothing major だから，大事にはならないと考えてい

185

る。したがって **4** が正解。cut ～ some slack「～を大目に見る」。

No.7 – 解答 ③ ··

スクリプト ☆： Hey, Francis. I'm glad I caught you. Do you happen to have that money I lent you?

★： Sorry. I've been meaning to talk to you about that. Is it OK if I give you half now and the rest after my next payday?

☆： Seriously? You promised it wouldn't be a problem to repay me this month.

★： I know, but I've had a couple of unexpected expenses.

☆： It'll put me in a bit of a bind. We all have bills to pay, you know. Still, I guess half is better than nothing.

★： Thanks. I really appreciate it.

Question: What does the woman imply?

全文訳 ☆： こんにちは，フランシス。捕まってよかったわ。私が貸したあのお金だけど，持ち合わせているかしら。

★： ごめんよ。そのことについてずっと君と話すつもりでいたんだ。今半分を返して，残りは次の給料日の後でも構わないかな？

☆： 本気なの？ 今月に返済するということで問題ないって約束したわよね。

★： わかっているけど，予定外の出費がいくつかあったんだ。

☆： それはちょっと困るわ。私たちの誰もが，支払わなければならない請求書を抱えているんだから。それでも，ゼロよりは半分の方がましかもしれないわね。

★： ありがとう。本当に感謝するよ。

質問：女性は暗に何と言っているか。

選択肢の訳 **1** 男性は何も返済する必要はない。
2 彼女は男性に金を貸さないだろう。
3 彼女も今，金が不足している。
4 男性は故意に女性を欺いた。

解説 金を貸した男性から，約束の全額ではなく，取りあえず半額の返済を提案された女性は，3つ目の発言で，It'll put me in a bit of a bind. We all have bills to pay と言っている。つまり，女性も支払いを抱えて金が不足していることがわかる。put ～ in a bind「～を困らせる」。

No.8 – 解答 ① ··

スクリプト ☆： Steve, were you making photocopies for the board meeting again this morning?

★： Yeah, the vice president asked me to lend him a hand because his assistant's off sick.

☆： Maybe it's none of my business, but aren't you too busy for that

186

sort of thing? You're a section manager, not an assistant.

★： Maybe, but you never know when the shoe will be on the other foot.

☆： I doubt the vice president would return the favor.

★： Not him necessarily, but we're all in this together, right? And taking an extra 15 minutes to make copies isn't the end of the world.

☆： Suit yourself.

Question: What does the woman imply?

全文訳 ☆： スティーブ，今朝また取締役会用にコピーを取っていたわよね。

★： ああ，アシスタントが病気で休みだから手を貸してくれないかと副社長が頼んできたんだ。

☆： 私には関係ないことかもしれないけど，そんなことをしている暇はないんじゃない？ あなたは課長であって，アシスタントではないのよ。

★： そうかもしれないけど，いつ逆の立場になるかわからないからね。

☆： 副社長が恩返しをするとは思えないけど。

★： 彼がそうするとは限らないけど，僕たちは一心同体だよね？ それに，コピーを取るのに 15 分余分な時間がかかっても大したことじゃないよ。

☆： 好きにすればいいわ。

質問：女性は暗に何と言っているか。

選択肢の訳 1　男性はあまりに惜しげもなく自分の時間を割く。

2　副社長はあまりにも残業が多い。

3　副社長は彼女に借りがある。

4　男性は現在の地位にふさわしくない。

解説 本来の仕事ではないことまで引き受けてしまう男性を女性は心配しているが，男性はいつ the shoe will be on the other foot「立場が逆転する」かわからないし，自分たちは一心同体であり，コピーを取ることくらい the end of the world「大変なこと」ではない，と答えている。そして，女性は最後の発言で Suit yourself.「お好きなように」と述べているので，正解は **1**。

No.9 −解答 ②

スクリプト ★： Man, I'm glad that meeting is over. What do you think of the proposed change for the sales department, Bev?

☆： Honestly, I'm in shock. Each of us has spent all this time developing proficiency in a specific field to better serve clients, and now they want to assign us to customers simply based on location!

★： I mean, I know we sometimes have to travel a long way to get to a client, but I thought giving them the expertise they needed and building up a relationship was worth the time and mileage.

☆： Right. Being restricted to a certain geographic area could cost us dozens of our existing client relationships. And building new ones will take time, too.

★： Well, it's done now. I guess we'll just have to share as much information about existing customers as we can with the guys in the other regions. I see one upside, though: instead of just working in one specialist area, we'll get a chance to learn new things.

☆： I suppose. But I still think we risk losing some of our big accounts if we make this switch.

★： Seems like management thinks the long-term savings in time and money will be worthwhile.

☆： Well, we'll just have to wait and see, but I won't be holding my breath.

Question: What is one thing the man says about the proposed change?

全文訳 ★： やれやれ，あの会議が終わってうれしいよ。営業部の改革案をどう思う，ベブ？

☆： 正直言って，ショックを受けているわ。顧客によりよいサービスを提供しようと，私たち一人一人が特定の分野での熟練度を高めることにずっと時間を費やしてきたのに，今度は，場所だけを基に私たちを顧客に割り当てたいと言うんだもの！

★： つまりさ，確かに顧客のところに行くのに長い距離を移動しなければならないことも時にはあるけど，顧客が必要とする専門知識を提供して関係を構築することには，その時間と移動距離をかける価値があると僕は思っていたよ。

☆： そうよね。特定の地理的エリアに限定されれば，私たちが今持っている顧客との関係を何十も失うかもしれないわ。それに，新しい関係を築くのに時間もかかるだろうし。

★： まあ，もう決まったことだ。現在の顧客情報をできるだけ多く，ほかの地域の連中と共有しなければならないだろうね。だけど，1ついい点があることも認めるよ。1つの専門的分野だけで働く代わりに，新しいことを学ぶ機会を得ることになるね。

☆： そうでしょうね。だけど，やっぱり，この変更をすると大きな得意先をいくつか失う危険があると思うわ。

★： 時間とお金の長期的節約はやってみる価値がある，と経営陣は思ってい

るようだね。
☆：まあ，成り行きを見守るしかないでしょうけど，期待はしないわね。
質問：改革案について男性が言っていることの1つは何か。
選択肢の訳　1　女性の仕事よりも男性の仕事の方に大きな影響を与える。
　　　　　　2　スタッフが専門的知識を広げるのに役立つかもしれない。
　　　　　　3　今よりも長距離を運転しなければならなくなることを意味する。
　　　　　　4　スタッフが現在の顧客との関係を強化するのに役立つかもしれない。
解説　質問の the proposed change とは，営業部員がエリアに関係なく得意分野に応じて顧客を担当していたこれまでのやり方を変えて，エリアごとに営業部員を配置すること。一貫して懐疑的な女性に男性はおおむね同調しているが，3つ目の発言の後半で I see one upside と言って，we'll get a chance to learn new things という利点を挙げている。**2** がこの利点を言い換えている。account「得意先」, not hold *one's* breath「期待を持たない」。

No.10 解答

スクリプト　★：Hey, did you guys fill out the year-end review yet?
☆：The one we use to evaluate last year's projects?
★：Yeah. We're supposed to turn it in by the end of this week.
○：I hate doing that. It's always about 10 pages long.
☆：Me, too. The instructions are so complicated.
★：I've already spent two hours on it, and I'm not even halfway through.
☆：Well, I'm not going to spend so much time on it. It's just going to end up in a pile on our boss's desk like it always does.
○：I agree. I've never gotten any feedback regarding anything I've submitted.
★：Actually, our boss is not going to see it. It's going straight to human resources. New policy.
○：You mean there's a chance our suggestions about how to improve some processes might actually get heard?
★：Could be. They're specifically asking for feedback about project management.
☆：In that case, it might be worth taking seriously. There's no way I'll get to it today, though.
★：Let's go through some of the key points over lunch tomorrow. If we present a united front, they might actually listen.
☆：OK.
○：I guess it couldn't hurt.

Question: What does the man imply about this year's review?

全文訳
★： ねえ，君たちは年末評価書にもう記入した？

☆： 去年の企画を評価するために使うやつ？

★： うん。今週末までに提出することになっているよ。

○： 私，あれをするのは嫌い。いつも 10 ページくらいあるんだもの。

☆： 私も。指示がすごく複雑なのよね。

★： 僕はもう 2 時間かけてやっているけど，半分も終わっていないよ。

☆： うーん，私はあれにそんなに時間はかけないわ。毎度そうだけど，結局上司の机に山積みになるだけじゃない。

○： 本当よね。提出したものに関して何ひとつ反応が返ってきたためしがないんだもの。

★： 実はね，上司が見ることはないんだ。人事部へ直行するんだよ。新しい方針なんだ。

○： いくつかの工程をどう改善するかについての私たちの提案が，実際に聞いてもらえるかもしれないチャンスがあるっていうこと？

★： かもね。特に企画管理についての意見を求めているよ。

☆： そういうことなら，真剣に取り組む価値があるかもしれないわね。今日取りかかるのは絶対無理だけど。

★： 明日ランチを食べながら，大事なポイントをいくつか検討しようよ。共同戦線を張れば，実際に耳を傾けてくれるかもしれないよ。

☆： わかったわ。

○： やって損になることはないわね。

質問：今年の評価書について男性は暗に何と言っているか。

選択肢の訳　**1**　女性たちの意見は無視される。

2　おそらく彼らが記入しなければならない最後の評価書になる。

3　人事部が見る前に上司が見たがっている。

4　職場の変化につながるかもしれない。

解説　同僚 3 人の会話。これまで評価書は放置されていたが，男性は 4 つ目の発言で，評価書は人事部に直行すると言っている。新しい方針なので，今年からそうなることを意味する。そして，それを知った女性の 1 人が，our suggestions about how to improve some processes を聞いてもらえるかもしれないと言い，男性も肯定している。つまり，今年の評価書は，社員の声が職場に反映される可能性を与えるものということになる。present a united front「共同戦線を張る」。

A

(スクリプト) **Digital Relationships**

There has been considerable concern about the effects of the Internet on people's social well-being. An influential study at one university found that subjects felt increasingly socially isolated the more time they spent online. This confirmed a common belief that the Internet weakens personal bonds by emphasizing the quantity of one's so-called friends over the quality of relationships. Superficial interactions are encouraged, leaving people feeling lonelier and less connected to one another. However, the university study has been the subject of some criticism. Among other problems, it focused on novice Internet users over a short duration. Many of the same subjects, when contacted years after the study ended, stated that continued Internet use had actually had a positive effect on their social well-being.

More-recent research suggests that Internet use may have other benefits. For example, searching for romantic partners online can lead to successful relationships. Some dating sites utilize complicated algorithms to match people with each other. This may help people find their ideal partner and form long-term romantic partnerships. Moreover, in some studies, spouses who had met online reported increased marital satisfaction and may therefore face a lower risk of divorce than those who met offline.

Questions

No.11 What is one criticism that has been raised about the university study?
No.12 What is one thing the speaker suggests about dating sites?

(全文訳) **デジタルな人間関係**

インターネットが人々の社会生活の充足感に与える影響に関しては相当な懸念が持たれてきた。ある大学の有力な研究で，被験者がオンラインで費やす時間が長いほど，彼らはますます社会的な孤立感を深めるようになることがわかった。このことにより，インターネットは人間関係の質よりもいわゆる友達の数の多さを重要視することで個人的な結び付きを弱める，という通説が正しいと確認された。表面的な交流が促されて，人々はより孤独感を深め，お互いのつながりが薄くなっていると感じてしまうのだ。しかしながら，その大学の研究は一部で批判の対象となっている。ほかにも問題はあるが，その研究は短期間の間に初心者のインターネットユーザーに焦点を当てた。研究が終了した数年後に連絡を取ってみたところ，同じ被験者の多くは，継続してインターネットを利用したことが実際に自身の社会生活の充足感にプラスの影響を与えたと明言した。

さらに最近の調査では，インターネットの利用にはほかにも利点があるかもしれない

ことが示唆されている。例えば，オンラインで恋人を探すと良好な関係につながる可能性があるのだ。一部の出会い系サイトは，人同士を引き合わせるために複雑なアルゴリズムを活用している。このことが人々にとって理想の相手を見つけ，長期的な恋愛関係を形成するための手助けとなるかもしれない。さらに，一部の研究では，オンラインで出会った配偶者たちは結婚満足度が高まったと報告しており，それ故，オフラインで出会った人たちよりも離婚のリスクが低くなるかもしれない。

語句 subject「被験者，対象」，spouse「配偶者」

No.11 解答 ④

質問の訳 その大学の研究について唱えられている批判の1つは何か。

選択肢の訳
1 インターネットに基づいた人間関係にのみ焦点を当てた。
2 インターネット会社から資金提供を受けた。
3 研究員たちが時代遅れの技術を利用した。
4 研究の期間が不十分であった。

解説 第1段落後半に，novice Internet users を対象とした短期間の研究であることが問題点の1つだとあり，続く最終文で，数年後には同じ被験者の多くが continued Internet use にプラスの側面があったと明言したと述べられている。このことを研究期間が inadequate「不十分だ」と表現した 4 が正解。

No.12 解答 ③ 　　　　　　　　　　　　　　　　　正答率 ★75%以上

質問の訳 話者が出会い系サイトについて示唆していることの1つは何か。

選択肢の訳
1 人々のプロフィールから得たデータを悪用する傾向がある。
2 相性に関連する要因をしばしば無視する。
3 強い夫婦関係を築くのに貢献するかもしれない。
4 最近になってアルゴリズムを単純化した。

解説 第2段落最終文で，オンラインで出会った配偶者たちが increased marital satisfaction を報告している研究があり，オフラインで出会った人たちよりも離婚のリスクが低下する可能性があると述べられている。このことを creating strong marriages に貢献する可能性があると言い換えた 3 が正解。

B

スクリプト **Synthetic Diamonds**

Although laboratory-made diamonds have been used in machinery and cutting tools for decades, they have rarely been used for jewelry. That may be changing, however. Some laboratories have even succeeded in producing Type IIa diamonds, the purest category. This is significant, as only a very small percentage of all naturally mined diamonds are Type IIa. The new, high-quality synthetic diamonds are chemically identical to their natural counterparts, and they are now challenging natural diamonds for a share of the consumer jewelry market.

Quality, though, is not the only factor attracting consumers to synthetic diamonds. Mining for natural diamonds has a reputation for oppressive working conditions and environmental unsustainability. Synthetic-diamond manufacturers claim their production methods avoid labor concerns and result in fewer carbon dioxide emissions than mining. However, closing diamond mines could have detrimental effects on local communities. In some developing nations, diamond mines are one of the few means of employment. Therefore, some people argue that it is better to improve pay and conditions for miners than to take away their jobs. Efforts have been made by diamond-mining companies to address environmental concerns. In response to pressure from environmental groups, some diamond-mining companies have adopted carbon-capture technology, with the aim of becoming carbon neutral.

Questions

No.13 What do we learn about synthetic diamonds?

No.14 What is one way some diamond-mining companies are trying to improve their practices?

[全文訳] **合成ダイヤモンド**

　実験室で作られたダイヤモンドは，何十年もの間機械や切削工具に使用されてきたが，宝飾品のために使用されることはめったになかった。ところが，このことが変わりつつあるようだ。最高純度に分類されるタイプⅡaダイヤモンドの製造に成功した実験室すらある。これは大きな意義のあることだ。というのも，すべての天然採掘のダイヤモンドの中でタイプⅡaダイヤモンドはほんのわずかな割合しかないからだ。その新しい高品質の合成ダイヤモンドは，天然のものと化学的に同一で，現在，宝飾品の消費者市場のシェアをかけて天然ダイヤモンドに挑んでいるところである。

　だが，品質が消費者を合成ダイヤモンドに引き付けている唯一の要因ではない。天然ダイヤモンドの採掘には，過酷な労働条件と環境の非持続可能性という評判があるのだ。合成ダイヤモンドの製造業者は，自分たちの製造方法は労働問題を回避しており，結果的に二酸化炭素の排出量が採掘よりも少なくなると主張している。しかしながら，ダイヤモンド鉱山を閉鎖することは地元の地域社会に悪影響を及ぼす可能性がある。一部の発展途上国では，ダイヤモンド鉱山が数少ない雇用手段の1つになっている。それ故，鉱山労働者の給料と条件を改善する方が，彼らの職を奪うよりも望ましいと主張する人もいる。環境問題に対処するために，ダイヤモンド採掘企業によって努力がなされてきた。環境保護団体からの圧力に応え，一部のダイヤモンド採掘企業は，カーボンニュートラルになることを目指して，炭素回収技術を採用している。

(語句) synthetic「合成の」，unsustainability「非持続可能性」，detrimental「有害な」

No.13 解答 ①

質問の訳 合成ダイヤモンドについて何がわかるか。

選択肢の訳
1 最高の天然ダイヤモンドの品質に匹敵する。
2 ハイテク機器への使用には適さない。
3 天然ダイヤモンドとは化学組成が異なっている。
4 天然ダイヤモンドよりも高額な場合がある。

解説 第1段落前半で，天然でもごくわずかしかない最高純度の合成ダイヤモンドの製造に成功したこと，また，後半で，新たな高品質の合成ダイヤモンドは their natural counterparts，つまり天然ダイヤモンドと化学的に同一であることが述べられている。これらを品質の点で can match「匹敵する」と言い換えた **1** が正解。

No.14 解答 ③

質問の訳 一部のダイヤモンド採掘企業が慣行の改善を試みている方法の1つは何か。

選択肢の訳
1 発展途上国で運営する鉱山の数を減らすことによって。
2 従業員の規模を縮小することによって。
3 環境に優しい方法を利用することによって。
4 生産能力を高めることによって。

解説 第2段落後半で，ダイヤモンド採掘業者は environmental concerns に対処するために努力を続けていると述べられた後，続く最終文に，一部の業者は carbon neutral になることを目指して carbon-capture technology「炭素回収技術」を採用している，とある。よって，正解は **3**。

スクリプト **Gamification**

These days, many businesses are incorporating features common to games through a practice known as gamification. Customer-support centers, for instance, may allow customers to award points to customer-service agents based on the quality of the service they provide. The agents get rewards, such as additional pay, based on the number of points they receive. Their scores are also displayed to other agents, and some managers believe this can create an atmosphere where employees try to compete with one another to satisfy customers. Some managers also believe this element of competition can make the work more enjoyable, which could prove especially useful in jobs where wages are low and employee turnover is high.

Critics of gamification argue that it reduces employee morale in the long term. Research has demonstrated that the most powerful motivators for employees are independence, skill development, and the satisfaction that comes from being engaged in meaningful work. External rewards may fail to satisfy these needs. Furthermore, it could be argued that such reward systems focus too much on success. According to one expert on game design, including more possibilities for failure would encourage workers to stay more committed to their work.

Questions
No.15 What do some managers believe gamification can do?
No.16 According to critics, what does gamification fail to address?

全文訳　ゲーミフィケーション

　最近では，多くの企業がゲーミフィケーションとして知られる手法を通じて，ゲームと共通の特徴を取り入れている。例えば，顧客サポートセンターが顧客に対して，顧客サービス担当者が提供するサービスの質に基づいてその担当者にポイントを付与することを認めることもある。受け取ったポイント数に基づいて，担当者は割増賃金などの報酬を手にする。彼らの得点はほかの担当者にも開示されており，このことにより従業員たちがお互いに競い合って顧客を満足させようとする雰囲気を作り出すことができると考えている経営者もいる。また，一部の経営者は，この競争の要素によって仕事がより楽しめるものとなり，そのことが，賃金が低く従業員の離職率が高い仕事では，結果的に特に役に立つかもしれないと考えている。

　ゲーミフィケーションに批判的な人たちは，長期的に見るとそれが従業員の士気を低下させると主張している。調査によって，従業員にとっての最強の動機付け要因は，自立，能力開発，そして，有意義な仕事に従事することから得られる満足感であることが証明されている。外的報酬ではこれらの要求を満たすことができないかもしれない。さらに，そういった報酬制度は成功に重点を置き過ぎていると論じることもできる。あるゲーム設計の専門家によると，失敗の可能性をより多く含めておくことで，労働者はより熱心に仕事に取り組み続ける気になるようだ。

語句　gamification「ゲーミフィケーション（ゲームの要素をゲーム以外の活動に応用すること）」，turnover「離職率」

No.15 解答 　　　　　　　　　　　　　　　　　　　正答率 ★75%以上

質問の訳　一部の経営者はゲーミフィケーションに何ができると考えているか。
選択肢の訳　**1** 競争を通じて労働者の業績を向上させる。
　　　　　　2 労働者にほかの労働者と協力するよう促す。
　　　　　　3 労働者により優れたストレスの対処法を教える。
　　　　　　4 高度な技術を持った労働者を採用しやすくする。
解説　一部の経営者の考えは第1段落後半で語られている。そこには，ポイント制の導入で従業員が顧客の満足を得るために競い合うようになり，その競争の要素によって仕事がmore enjoyableになる，とある。つまり，競争によって従業員のperformanceが向上すると考えていることにな

るので，**1** が正解。

No.16 解答

質問の訳 批判的な人たちによると，ゲーミフィケーションは何に対処できないか。

選択肢の訳
1 従業員の動機付けの真の源。
2 成功に重点を置くことの重要性。
3 顧客との交流に必要とされる技能。
4 企業がコストを最小限に抑える必要性。

解説 第2段落で批判的な人たちの主張が述べられており，中ほどに External rewards may fail to satisfy these needs. とある。この these needs はその前の文で挙げられた3つの the most powerful motivators for employees のことを指しているので，正解は **1**。external rewards は成功に対して与えられる昇進や昇給のことだが，そのための競争をあおるより，失敗を許容するなどして従業員のやる気や満足感を引き出す方が結果的に有益だというのが批判派の考えということになる。

D

スクリプト **Land-Based Vertebrates**

All land-based vertebrates — animals with a spine — are believed to have evolved from sea creatures. Scientists had long speculated that the move onto land occurred when some sea creatures' fins became stronger. Having stronger fins would have allowed creatures to move onto land to escape predators that could only swim. Recent research, however, indicates that sea creatures began to leave the ocean because they experienced a dramatic increase in eye size. This development meant that they were better equipped to spot potential food sources, like insects, on land, and it triggered a transition to searching out such prey.

Another evolutionary adaptation involving vision coincided with the move to land. The eyes of some creatures began moving toward the tops of their heads. This would not have benefited creatures when looking through water, as water restricts visual range, but the change would have allowed them to see more clearly when above the surface. These developments in visual ability may also have contributed to a change in neural circuitry. Such a change may have helped land-based vertebrates to develop skills such as planning when they hunted, rather than relying solely on quick reaction times.

Questions

No.17 According to recent research, what caused sea creatures to move onto land?

No.18 What does the speaker say about the development of land-based vertebrates?

全文訳 陸生の脊椎動物

　すべての陸生の脊椎動物，つまり背骨を持つ動物は，海洋生物から進化したと考えられている。科学者たちは長らく，陸上への移動が起こったのは一部の海洋生物のひれがより強くなったときだと推測してきた。より強いひれを持つことで，生物は陸上に移動し，泳ぐことしかできない捕食者から逃れることが可能になったのであろう。ところが，最近の研究では，海洋生物が海を離れ始めたのは，目の大きさの劇的な拡大を経験したためであることが示されている。この発達が意味したのは，これらの海洋生物に備わる，陸上にいる昆虫のような潜在的な食糧源を見つける能力が以前よりも高まったということであり，そのことが，そういった獲物の探索への移行を引き起こした。

　視覚に関連したもう１つの進化的適応が，陸への移動と同時に発生した。一部の生物の目が頭頂部に向かって移動し始めたのだ。水は視界を制限するので，このことは水中で見る際には生物に恩恵をもたらさなかったであろうが，その変化によって，水面から出たときによりはっきりと見ることができるようになったであろう。また，これらの視覚能力の発達は，神経回路に変化をもたらす一因になったかもしれない。そういった変化のおかげで，陸生の脊椎動物は，狩りをする際に，単に素早い反応時間に頼るのではなく，計画を立てるといった能力を伸ばすことができたかもしれないのだ。

　　語句 land-based「陸生の」，vertebrate「脊椎動物」，neural circuitry「神経回路」

No.**17** 解答 **4**

　質問の訳 最近の研究によると，何が原因で海洋生物は陸上に移動したのか。

　選択肢の訳 1　新たな海洋捕食者の出現。
　　　　　　　2　はるかに強いひれの発達。
　　　　　　　3　海中における食糧源の欠乏。
　　　　　　　4　そこで食糧源を発見する能力の向上。

　解説 最近の研究成果は第１段落後半で語られている。そこには，海洋生物が陸上に移動したのは a dramatic increase in eye size を経験したからで，この発達は to spot potential food sources, like insects, on land の能力が向上したことを意味した，とある。よって，正解は **4**。強いひれの発達が原因というのは従来の考え方なので，**2** は不適。

No.**18** 解答 **2**

　質問の訳 陸生の脊椎動物の発達について話者は何と言っているか。

　選択肢の訳 1　目の位置は変化しないままだった。
　　　　　　　2　異なる方法で狩りをすることができるようになったようだ。
　　　　　　　3　一部の脊椎動物の反応がより速くなる原因となった。
　　　　　　　4　長期的に見ると悪影響をもたらした。

　解説 第２段落後半で，視覚能力の発達は neural circuitry「神経回路」の変化をもたらし，そういった変化が，狩りをする際に計画を立てるといっ

197

た能力の発達に役立った可能性があると述べられている。つまり，狩り
の方法に変化が生じた可能性があると指摘しているので，正解は **2**。

E

（スクリプト） **Masking War Injuries**

World War I was brutal in many ways. The use of machine guns and other
powerful weapons caused terrible destruction. In addition, much of the fighting
took place in long, deep ditches known as trenches. Although trenches
protected soldiers' bodies, their heads were often exposed, leaving them
vulnerable to machine gun and sniper fire. As a result, many soldiers suffered
injuries to their faces. In contrast to previous wars, however, advancements in
surgical techniques allowed increased survival rates for those with serious
wounds. Still, many soldiers were left with facial injuries for life, and some
felt ashamed of their injuries.

Around the same time, the field of cosmetic surgery was emerging. Artists
began helping injured soldiers by creating facial parts made from metal,
including complete masks made from thin sheets of copper. Sculptor Anna
Coleman Ladd became famous for her mask-making skills. She took great
care to ensure that the features on her masks were accurate and that the color
matched the patient's skin color exactly. She was able to create a new face that
was amazingly similar to the original by using photos of the victims before
they were injured. These developments gave many soldiers the confidence to
resume productive lives.

Questions

No.19 What is one way that World War I was different from previous conflicts?

No.20 What is true of Anna Coleman Ladd?

（全文訳） **戦傷を仮面で隠す**

　第1次世界大戦は多くの点で残酷だった。機関銃をはじめとする強力な武器を使用し
たことでひどい破壊が引き起こされた。さらに，戦闘の多くは，塹壕として知られる長
く深い溝の中で行われた。塹壕は兵士たちの体を守ったが，彼らの頭部は露出している
ことが多く，機関銃や狙撃手の射撃を受けやすい状態にあった。その結果，多くの兵士
が顔に傷を負った。しかしながら，それまでの戦争と比べて，外科技術の進歩によって，
重傷を負った人たちの生存率を上げることができた。それでも，多くの兵士は生涯顔に
傷を負ったままであり，その傷を恥ずかしく思う者もいた。

　同じ時期に，美容整形という分野が生まれつつあった。芸術家たちが，薄い銅板でで
きた完全な仮面を含め，金属でできた顔のパーツを作り出すことによって，負傷した兵
士たちを助け始めた。彫刻家のアンナ・コールマン・ラッドは仮面制作の技術で有名に
なった。彼女は細心の注意を払って，仮面の顔立ちが正確であるように，そして，色が
患者の皮膚の色と正確に一致するように努めた。負傷する前の被害者の写真を使うこと

で，彼女は元の顔に驚くほど似た新たな顔を作り出すことができた。これらの進歩が多くの兵士に，有意義な人生を取り戻す自信を与えたのだ。

語句 trench「塹壕」，vulnerable「攻撃されやすい」

No.19 解答 ②

質問の訳 第1次世界大戦がそれまでの紛争と異なっていた点の1つは何か。
選択肢の訳
1 兵士たちがより優れた防弾服を持っていた。
2 より多くの兵士が重傷を乗り切った。
3 特定の種類の武器が禁止された。
4 兵士たちの負傷が大幅に減少した。

解説 第1段落後半で，これまでの戦争と比べて，外科技術の進歩によって those with serious wounds の生存率の上昇が可能になったと述べられている。この点を survived serious wounds という表現を使って言い換えた **2** が正解。防弾服と武器の禁止に関しては触れられていないので，**1** と **3** は不適。多くの兵士が顔を負傷したので，**4** も不適。

No.20 解答 ③

質問の訳 アンナ・コールマン・ラッドについて当てはまることは何か。
選択肢の訳
1 新たに発見された素材を用いて仮面を作った。
2 芸術家になる前は形成外科医だった。
3 仮面の正確さで知られていた。
4 精神衛生の専門家だった。

解説 第2段落中ほどで her mask-making skills で有名になったと述べられた後，続く文に，細心の注意で仮面の顔立ちの正確さと皮膚の色の正確な一致を目指した，とある。**3** がこの彼女の技術の特徴を，accuracy という語を使って「仮面の正確さ」と簡潔にまとめている。

F

スクリプト

You have 10 seconds to read the situation and Question No. 21.

Welcome to the conference. Due to increased security, we ask that you keep your conference pass with you at all times. If you are just arriving, please proceed directly to reception to check in and receive your pass. Valid ID will be required. Australian nationals may present any government-issued ID, such as a driver's license. For international attendees, a valid passport will be required. If you do not have your passport with you, an international driver's license is acceptable, but you will first need to fill in some additional forms to confirm your personal details. These are available at the security desk. Please note that a company business card will not be accepted as a valid ID. We ask for your patience while these security checks are being completed. Thank you for your cooperation and understanding.

Now mark your answer on your answer sheet.

全文訳

　会議にようこそいらっしゃいました。セキュリティー強化のため，会議の入場許可証を常に携帯いただきますようお願い申し上げます。到着されたばかりの方は，そのまま受付にお進みいただき，お手続きをして入場許可証をお受け取りください。有効な身分証明書が必要になります。オーストラリア国籍の方は，例えば運転免許証など，政府発行の身分証明書でしたら，どれをご提示いただいても構いません。外国人の出席者の方は，有効なパスポートが必要になります。パスポートがお手元にない場合は，国際運転免許証でも受け付けておりますが，まず追加の用紙数枚に必要事項を記入していただいて，詳細な個人情報を確認させていただかなければなりません。この用紙は警備デスクにてご用意しております。会社の名刺は有効な身分証明書として受け付けておりませんのでご注意ください。これらのセキュリティーチェックが完了するまでの間，しばらくお待ちいただきますようお願い申し上げます。ご協力とご理解に感謝し上げます。

No.21 解答 ④ ....

状況の訳　あなたは日本人の重役で，オーストラリアで開かれる会議に到着したところである。あなたは名刺と国際運転免許証を持っているが，パスポートはホテルにある。あなたは次のアナウンスを聞く。

質問の訳　あなたはまず何をすべきか。

選択肢の訳　1　受付で国際運転免許証を提示する。
2　建物に入る際に警備員に名刺を渡す。
3　受付で会議の入場許可証を受け取る。
4　警備デスクで数枚の用紙を入手する。

語句　attendee「出席者」

解説　名刺と国際運転免許証は所持しているが，パスポートはホテルに置いてきたあなたは，国際運転免許証で受け付けてもらうことになる。その場合は，まず some additional forms を完成させる必要があると告げられた後，その用紙は警備デスクで入手可能との説明を受ける。よって，正解は **4**。**1** と **3** は追加の用紙を完成させた後ですべきことなので不適。

G

スクリプト

You have 10 seconds to read the situation and Question No. 22.

We've checked your vehicle. You said a warning light sometimes tells you to check the engine. The problem seems to be aging engine coils. If they're faulty, the engine will sometimes misfire or stall. I'd recommend getting those changed now. They could be a safety hazard, especially if you'll be on the road for long periods. We also checked your oxygen sensor, which could fail to detect toxic emissions if it's worn out, but it's working. We also noticed that your wheel alignment was off. This could have been very dangerous, so we went ahead and adjusted that for you. Your brake cables are in good shape and shouldn't need any repairs for the time being. It's been a while since you replaced the brake pads, though, so next time you bring the car in, you might want to consider getting that done.

Now mark your answer on your answer sheet.

全文訳

お客さまのお車を点検しました。時々警告灯がついて，エンジンを点検するようにとの指示が出るとおっしゃっていましたね。問題はエンジンの点火コイルが古くなっていることのようです。点火コイルに不具合がありますと，エンジンが点火しなかったり，止まったりすることが時々あります。今交換されることをお勧めします。特に長期間車でお出かけになる場合は，安全上問題となるかもしれません。酸素センサーも点検しまして，劣化すると有害排出物を検知できなくなることもあるのですが，作動しています。ホイールアライメントが狂っていることもわかりました。このままではとても危険だったかもしれないので，お客さまのために先に調整しておきました。ブレーキケーブルはよい状態ですので，当分の間何も修理する必要はないでしょう。ですが，ブレーキパッドは取り換えてからしばらくたっていますので，次にお車を持ち込まれたときに，お取り換えをご検討なさるとよろしいかもしれません。

No.22 解答 ①

状況の訳　あなたは車で旅行する前に整備をしてもらうため，自動車修理工場に車を持ち込んだ。安全は重要だが，必要のない修理は避けたいと思っている。整備士はあなたに次のことを告げる。

質問の訳　あなたは今整備士にどの作業をするように頼むべきか。

選択肢の訳　1　エンジンの点火コイルを取り換える。
2　酸素センサーを交換する。
3　ホイールアライメントを調整する。
4　ブレーキパッドを取り換える。

語句　coil「（エンジンの）点火コイル」，misfire「点火しない」，wheel alignment「ホイールアライメント（自動車の車輪の整列具合）」

解説　整備士は問題となっている aging engine coils の交換を勧めており，特に長期間の旅行では a safety hazard になる可能性があると告げている。よって，現時点で頼むべき作業は 1。2 の the oxygen sensor は作

21年度第2回　リスニング

201

動していて，**3** の the wheel alignment は調整済みであり，**4** の the brake pads の交換は次回の点検時に検討すればよいことなので不適。

H

(スクリプト)

You have 10 seconds to read the situation and Question No. 23.

We offer several options. Introduction to German is held on Mondays from 8 p.m. to 9 p.m. and runs from June 1st to July 15th. We also offer Basic German for Travel on Wednesdays and Saturdays from 5 p.m. to 7 p.m. This is a one-month course and begins from the first of each month. You'd need to attend both sessions each week. Of course, the fastest way to learn a language is through immersion, and our three-week Intensive German course beginning this month will get you speaking the language in no time, with a class every weekday from 7 p.m. to 9 p.m. Finally, there's our Private German Online course. This beginners' course costs more than group classes, but lessons can be arranged to fit your schedule. And no matter which course you choose, you are welcome to attend our open conversation sessions on Saturday afternoons from noon to 4 p.m.

Now mark your answer on your answer sheet.

(全文訳)

当校では複数の選択肢を提供しております。「ドイツ語入門」は毎週月曜日午後8時から午後9時の間に開講され，6月1日から7月15日まで続きます。毎週水曜日と土曜日の午後5時から午後7時の間に「旅行のための基礎ドイツ語」も提供しております。こちらは1カ月間の講座で，毎月初めから始まります。毎週両方の授業に出席していただくことになります。もちろん，言語を学ぶ一番の近道は没入法でして，今月始まる3週間の「集中ドイツ語」講座ですと，平日毎日午後7時から午後9時までの授業を受ければ，あっという間にドイツ語を話し始めているでしょう。最後に，「オンライン個別ドイツ語」講座がございます。この初級者向けの講座は集団の授業よりも費用はかかりますが，個人の予定に合うようにレッスンを調整することができます。そして，どの講座をお選びになったとしても，毎週土曜日の午後，正午から午後4時まで行われている参加自由の会話セッションにいつでもご参加いただけます。

No.23 解答

(状況の訳) 今は4月である。あなたは6月になる前に初級者レベルのドイツ語の授業を受ける必要がある。あなたは平日午後8時まで働いている。あなたは語学学校に電話をして，次のことを告げられる。

(質問の訳) あなたはどの講座を選ぶべきか。

(選択肢の訳)
1 ドイツ語入門。
2 旅行のための基礎ドイツ語。
3 集中ドイツ語。
4 オンライン個別ドイツ語。

語句 immersion「没入法，イマージョン（外国語だけで授業を行う教育法）」
解説 状況で述べられている条件から，あなたが選ぶことができるのは，初級者向けの講座であり，自身の予定に合わせてレッスンの調整が可能と紹介された **4** の「オンライン個別ドイツ語」のみである。**1** は 6 月 1 日から始まり，**2** は水曜午後 5 時開始の授業に参加できず，**3** は平日午後 7 時開始なので不適。

スクリプト

You have 10 seconds to read the situation and Question No. 24.

Hi. Great news. G-P Industries wants us to come up with a whole new image for them, and you're my first choice to head the project. I know you're currently committed to the museum project, so it's up to you whether to stay on that or take this on. The president will keep a close eye on this new project, so it would be a good opportunity to get her attention, especially with performance reviews coming up in a couple of months. Maybe your assistant could step up and replace you on the museum project if he's already involved? If not, the museum director wouldn't be happy about any staff changes this late in the game, so I'd recommend playing it safe. We don't want to jeopardize the chances of future work with the museum, and I'm sure you'll have other opportunities to impress the president.

Now mark your answer on your answer sheet.

全文訳

もしもし。とてもいい知らせです。G-P インダストリーズが私たちに自社のまったく新しいイメージを考案してほしいとのことで，あなたがそのプロジェクトを指揮してほしいと私が最初に選んだ人です。あなたが現在，博物館のプロジェクトに全力を注いでいることはわかっていますので，それをそのまま続けるか，これを引き受けるかどうかはあなた次第です。社長はこの新たなプロジェクトを注視するでしょうから，特に業績評価が数カ月後に迫っているので，彼女に注目されるいい機会になるでしょう。あなたのアシスタントが博物館のプロジェクトに既に携わっていたら，おそらく昇進してあなたの後任になることができるのではないでしょうか？ もし携わっていなかったら，博物館の館長はこんな遅過ぎるタイミングではいかなるスタッフの変更も不満に思うでしょうから，安全策を取ることをお勧めします。博物館との今後の仕事の機会を危うくすることを私たちは望んでいないし，あなたが社長に好印象を与える機会はきっとまたあると思います。

No.24 解答

状況の訳 あなたはグラフィックデザイン会社に勤務しており，昇進を望んでいる。あなたのアシスタントは博物館のプロジェクトに取り組んできていな

203

い。あなたの部の部長はあなたに次のボイスメールを残した。

質問の訳 あなたは何をすべきか。

選択肢の訳 1 予定どおり博物館のプロジェクトを続ける。
2 新たな役割を説明するためにアシスタントと打ち合わせをする。
3 自身の業績評価のための資料を準備する。
4 クライアント向けのプランを携えて社長と連絡を取る。

語句 step up「昇進する」, late in the game「タイミングが遅過ぎて」, jeopardize「～を危うくする」

解説 新たなプロジェクトを引き受けるかどうかはあなた次第。社長も注視するはずなので, 昇進を望むあなたには絶好の機会だが, 現在注力している博物館のプロジェクトにアシスタントが携わっておらず, 後任の適任者が不在なので, 部長の忠告どおり play it safe「安全策を取る」, つまり今回の昇進は諦めて博物館のプロジェクトを続ける方が無難である。

J

スクリプト

You have 10 seconds to read the situation and Question No. 25.

OK, our Standard Fit Program, priced at $200, uses precise measurements to make sure your bike's geometry and setup are appropriate for standard use. The Dynamic Fit Program, which is $250, measures your power output on a test bike with high precision. We work from those results to make adjustments that will give you maximum power. The Biomechanical Tuning Service, for $350, includes the key features of those two programs and adds data capture and video analysis to fine-tune your ride. This really helps with the positioning of the seat and your shoes, so your feet lock into your pedals at the optimal angle. Finally, the Perfect Fit Tutor also offers a premium tuning service performed by our trained physiotherapist. She'll analyze your movements to spot physical problems affecting your riding technique and give you exercises to address them. That option's normally $550 but is discounted by $50 right now.

Now mark your answer on your answer sheet.

全文訳

わかりました, 当店のスタンダード・フィット・プログラムは, 料金は200ドルとなっていまして, 正確な測定法を用いて, お客さまの自転車のジオメトリーとセッティングが標準的な使用に適しているかどうかを確認します。ダイナミック・フィット・プログラムですが, 250ドルでして, 試乗自転車を使ってお客さまの出力を高い精度で測定します。その結果を基に作業して, お客さまが最大限の力を発揮できるように調整します。バイオメカニカル・チューニング・サービスは, 350ドルとなっていますが, それら2つのプログラムの主要な特徴が含まれていまして, 乗り心地を微調整するためにデータ収集とビデオ分析が加わります。これはサドルと靴の位置を調整するのに本当に

役に立つので，お客さまの足は最適な角度でペダルに固定されます。最後に，パーフェクト・フィット・チューターも，当店の熟練した理学療法士が実施する質の高い調整サービスを提供します。彼女がお客さまの動きを分析して，乗車技術に影響を与えている身体的な諸問題を発見し，それらに対処するための運動をお伝えします。そちらをお選びになると，通常は550ドルですが，今ですと50ドル割引いたします。

No.25 解答 　　　　　　　　　　　　　　　　正答率 ★75%以上

状況の訳 あなたは最近，レース用自転車を購入した。あなたは足をペダルのどの位置に乗せるかについて助力がほしいと思っている。あなたの予算は400ドルである。あなたは自転車店に電話をして，次のことを告げられる。

質問の訳 あなたはどの選択肢を選ぶべきか。

選択肢の訳
1 スタンダード・フィット・プログラム。
2 ダイナミック・フィット・プログラム。
3 バイオメカニカル・チューニング・サービス。
4 パーフェクト・フィット・チューター。

語句 geometry「ジオメトリー，幾何学的配置」，setup「セッティング（サドルの高さやハンドルまでの距離などの調整）」，fine-tune「～を微調整する」，optimal「最適な」，physiotherapist「理学療法士」

解説 ペダルに置く足の位置を決める方法を教えてもらえて，予算は400ドルまでという条件を満たすのは，the positioning of the seat and your shoes に本当に役立つものであり，価格は350ドルだと紹介された **3** のバイオメカニカル・チューニング・サービスのみである。**4** も a premium tuning service を提供するが，割引後の価格でも500ドルと予算オーバーなので不適。

  問題編 p.111

スクリプト

This is an interview with Christine Baker, a graduate student and teaching assistant at a university.

Interviewer (I): Welcome to *Voices on Campus*. Christine, thanks for joining us today.

Christine Baker (C): Thanks for having me.

I: So, could you tell us a little about what you do as a teaching assistant?

C: Well, I help teach small seminar classes focusing on specific areas the students are working on.

I: What do you enjoy most about it?

C: Well, the students come from diverse ethnic, cultural, and religious backgrounds, so there are a lot of interesting and sometimes heated debates in the seminars. Plus, I feel like a sort of minor celebrity. I teach about 80 students over the course of each semester, and now everywhere I go on campus somebody recognizes me. I've met all kinds of people I wouldn't have gotten to know otherwise.

I: That's great. And what would you say are the biggest challenges you face in your job?

C: Well, to be honest, it's taken a while to get used to evaluating the students' writing assignments. Fortunately, the professors have helped me get a good handle on grading procedures. Sometimes, though, students question their grades. Usually, I can defend the scores I give, but at first, I found myself changing grades more often than I would've liked. So, a skill I had to work on was applying each professor's grading criteria consistently and not being influenced by other factors. Things like whether I agreed with the argument the student was making in the paper. I have to put my feelings about the content aside and focus on whether the paper meets the criteria for the assignment. That's made things a lot easier.

I: Interesting. So, what advice would you give to new teaching assistants?

C: Well, when I started teaching, I was intimidated by the things people told me. Stuff like, "Never let the students know you're nervous," and "Never apologize." I second-guessed myself sometimes because I really wanted to measure up to what I imagined their standards for a teacher were. But, quite often, the students would say they were really getting a lot out of my seminars. So, I gradually learned that for the students, the seminars are more about the material they're there to learn and less about the person that's helping them to learn it. I would say that the key is to be thoroughly familiar with the material beforehand. Not just having a firm grasp on it yourself but making sure you can convey what's in your head to a group of students, some of whom will be very quick on the uptake. Anyway, when I began focusing on the students' needs rather than my own worries, things started going a lot better.

I: That sounds like good advice. Thanks for sharing your experiences with us today, Christine.

C: It was my pleasure.

Questions

No.26 What does Christine say about grading students' writing assignments?

No.27 What does Christine say is one important thing for teaching assistants to do?

全文訳

これは大学院生で，大学で教育助手をしているクリスティーン・ベーカーとのインタビューです。

聞き手（以下「聞」）：「キャンパスの声」にようこそ。クリスティーン，今日はご参加いただきありがとうございます。

クリスティーン・ベーカー（以下「ク」）：お招きいただきありがとうございます。

聞：では，教育助手としてどんなことをされているのか，少しお話しいただけますか。

ク：えー，学生たちが取り組んでいる特定の分野に焦点を合わせた少人数のゼミクラスを教えるのを手助けしています。

聞：それをしていて一番楽しいと感じることは何ですか。

ク：そうですね，学生たちはさまざまな民族的，文化的，そして宗教的背景を持っていますので，ゼミでは多くの興味深い，そして時には白熱した議論が行われます。それに，私はまるでちょっとした有名人のような感じがしています。私は各学期を通じて約80人の学生を教えていて，今ではキャンパスのどこへ行っても，誰かが私に気が付きます。教育助手をしていなかったらおそらく知り合いになることはなかったさまざまな人たちと私は出会いました。

聞：それは素晴らしいですね。では，仕事をする上で直面する最大の課題は何だとお考えですか。

ク：うーん，正直に言いますと，学生たちのレポート課題の評価に慣れるのに少し時間がかかりました。ありがたいことに，教授たちが手助けをしてくれて，採点の手順をしっかりと理解することができました。ですが，学生たちが自身の評点に疑問を抱くことが時々あります。たいていは，自分がつける点数の正当性を主張することができるのですが，最初のうちは，気が付くと，思っていた以上に頻繁に評点を変えていました。ですから，私が磨かなければならなかった技能は，各教授の採点基準を一貫して適用して，その他の要因には影響を受けないことでした。学生がレポートで論じている主張に私が賛同したかどうか，といったようなことです。内容についての私の感想は脇に置いておいて，レポートがその課題の基準を満たしているかどうかに重点を置かなければなりません。そうすることで物事がずっと進めやすくなりました。

聞：興味深いですね。それでは，新人の教育助手に向けてどのようなアドバイスを送りますか。

ク：そうですね，私が教え始めたときは，人から言われたことで臆病になっていました。「絶対に学生たちに緊張していることを知られてはいけない」とか「絶対に謝ってはいけない」といったようなことです。私はあれでよかったのだろうかと後で思うことが時々あったのですが，それは，そういう人たちが教師に求める基準だと私が想像したものに本当に到達したいと思っていたからなのです。ですが，学生たちは，かなりの頻度で，私のゼミから本当に多くのことを学んでいると言ってくれました。それで，徐々にわかってきたのが，学生たちにとってゼミは，そこで学ぶ題材の方がより重要

21年度第2回 リスニング

207

であって，それを学ぶ手助けをする人はそれほど重要ではないということです。鍵となるのは，前もって題材に完全に精通しておくことだと言えるでしょう。自分自身がしっかりと題材を理解するだけではなく，自分が考えていることを学生グループに確実に伝えることができるようにしておくと，理解がとても早くなる学生が出てくるでしょう。とにかく，私自身の心配よりも学生たちのニーズの方に重点を置き始めてから，はるかに順調に物事が進み始めました。

聞：よいアドバイスになりそうですね。今日はご自身の経験を私たちにお話しいただきありがとうございました，クリスティーン。

ク：どういたしまして。

> 語句 get a handle on ～「～を理解する」，defend「～の正当性を主張する」，intimidate「～を臆病にする」，second-guess「～に後でとやかく言う」，measure up to ～「～に達する」，be quick on the uptake「理解が早い」

No.26 解答 ②

質問の訳 学生たちのレポート課題を採点することについてクリスティーンは何と言っているか。

選択肢の訳
1 学生たちの主張の力強さにたびたび感銘を受けている。
2 客観的に採点基準を適用することが難しい場合がある。
3 教授たちの評点に賛同できないときがある。
4 教育助手としての最も興味深い側面である。

解説 クリスティーンは4つ目の発言で，evaluating the students' writing assignments に慣れるのに少し時間がかかり，各教授の採点基準の一貫した適用と，自分の意見など，その他の要因の影響の除外に取り組む必要があったと述べている。このことを objectively「客観的に」採点基準を適用するのが難しい場合があると言い換えた **2** が正解。

No.27 解答 ①

質問の訳 教育助手がするべき重要なことの1つは何であるとクリスティーンは言っているか。

選択肢の訳
1 確実に題材の明快な説明ができるようにしておく。
2 学生たちに対して威圧的になり過ぎないように心がける。
3 時には間違えることがあるという事実を受け入れる。
4 学生たちがゼミの最中に自分の考えを述べるのを許可する。

解説 新人の教育助手へのアドバイスを求められたクリスティーンは，5つ目の発言で，前もって the material に精通しておくことが鍵であり，自分自身がしっかり理解するだけではなく，what's in your head を確実に伝えられるようにしておくことで，学生の早い理解に結び付くと述べている。このアドバイスを explain the material clearly という表現を使って言い換えた **1** が正解。

208

二次試験・面接　トピックカード　A　日程　問題編 p.112

ここでは，A日程の5つのトピックをモデルスピーチとしました。

A日程

1. Agree or disagree: Urbanization inevitably leads to a lower quality of life

I disagree with the idea that urbanization has led to a lower quality of life. Not only has the spread of cities helped make people better off economically, but it has also provided better access to various services and benefited the environment. Firstly, cities are the backbone of economic growth. With large populations living in dense areas, they provide large workforces for factories and corporations. As companies grow, they pay workers' salaries and give out benefits, leading to a higher standard of living. Another advantage is the ease of access to a multitude of services that improve our daily lives. Everything from medical care to education to food shopping is much more widely available in urban areas. This improved access to so many different kinds of services has led to better health, increased literacy, and improved nutrition. Finally, by concentrating populations, cities greatly reduce people's environmental impact. They allow for efficient public transportation, and apartment living greatly reduces the amount of building materials and energy needed for housing. This means cities produce far less carbon per person than rural areas do. Without urbanization, I think it's clear that society would not be nearly as advanced, and billions of people would not enjoy the quality of life that they have today.

解説　「賛成か反対か：都市化による生活の質の低下は避けられない」

トピックに対して反対の立場から，その理由として①労働力が集中することで企業が発展する，②医療から教育まであらゆるサービスが提供されている，③資源の効率化により1人当たりの二酸化炭素の排出量が減る，という3点を挙げ，都市化により逆に生活の質は上がると主張している。賛成意見を述べたい場合は，人口が集中することによる競争の激化，生活費の高騰，精神的ストレス，などを理由にできるだろう。重複しない理由を3つ言えればベストだが，2つしか思い付かない場合は丁寧に具体例を入れよう。

2. Has online media destroyed traditional print journalism?

I think it would be an exaggeration to say that online media has destroyed print journalism. I'd like to discuss magazines' and newspapers' circulation, prestige, and quality to explain why. Firstly, while magazine and newspaper circulations have definitely declined, they are still read by hundreds of millions of people every single day. Reading on paper is easier on your eyes and makes it easier to concentrate, so there are still a huge number of people who prefer reading news and articles in this way. Furthermore, print publications still have a huge amount of prestige. Names like the New York Times and Time are far more trusted and respected than most online news sources. In fact, much of the news that you read online is actually based on reporting by journalists working for print publications. Perhaps the biggest reason is that the quality of most print publications still surpasses that of online sources. Readers of print publications tend to be more demanding of careful fact-checking and high-quality reporting. There will always be readers who are willing to pay for quality print journalism. As a result of its still-substantial circulation, prestige and quality, I think that traditional print journalism will be around for a long time.

> **解説** 「インターネットメディアは伝統的な紙媒体のジャーナリズムを破壊したか」
>
> 冒頭の10秒ほどで自分の意見とその理由を含むスピーチ構成を無駄なく伝え，聞き手の気をそらさない工夫がある。トピックに対して反対の立場から，紙媒体のメディアについて①必要とする人は多く発行部数もまだ多い，②知名度も高くネットを含む多くのニュースの発信源である，③信頼度と質で他に勝っている，という3点からその優位性を主張している。冒頭で I think it would be an exaggeration ... としているように，新しいメディアによる影響は認めつつも「破壊」は言い過ぎではないか，という一貫した立場を取っている。

3. Is a society free of crime an unattainable goal?

Crime has been around as long as human civilization, and I think that, unfortunately, while it can be reduced and controlled, it can never be eliminated. The most important reason is that science has shown that criminal behavior is built into some people's brains. Many people may hope, for example, that social programs can reform criminals. However, due to people having a fixed nature, it is actually impossible to manipulate people into acting in ways that coincide with society's idealized behavior. Secondly, there is a huge amount of conflict between people with different politics, religions, and cultures these days. Because of this, there will always be some people who feel the only solution to their problems is violence, and that explains the constant threat of terrorism. Since ideological and cultural conflict has existed throughout all of human history, the crimes that stem from this will never disappear. Lastly, I'd like to discuss inequality in modern society. Poverty has always been a major cause of crime. As the gap between rich and poor increases, it seems certain that not having enough income will cause people to commit more crimes. When you look at all of these factors together, eliminating crime completely cannot ever be achieved.

解説　「無犯罪社会は達成不可能な目標か」

　　　　自分の意見を表明する前に人類史における犯罪について言及したことで視野の広さを感じさせる。このようにスピーチの最初で聞き手の心をぐっとつかめると効果的だ。トピックを肯定する立場から「犯罪は減らせても完璧になくすことは不可能」を前提に，以下の3点を理由としている：①科学的見地から犯罪性は一部の人間の本質である，②複雑化する社会の中で思想や文化の衝突は避けられず暴力が解決策となってしまう場合も多い，③貧富の差が広がる中で貧困層による犯罪は避けられない。客観的で論理性の高い優れたスピーチなのでお手本にしたい。

4. Has the traditional five-day workweek become outdated in the modern world?

　These days, there are a lot of reports in the media about four-day workweeks, and I think they're very likely to become a reality in the near future. In this speech, I'd like to share my thoughts about why five-day workweeks are outdated. One very important reason is technology. Thanks to AI and robots, many things that once had to be done by humans can now be done by technology. This means that workers can maintain their productivity without working as many hours. Next, reducing energy consumption is imperative in modern society, and four-day workweeks can contribute to this. When workers don't have to commute as often, fossil fuel use is reduced. Additionally, if companies can close down one extra day per week, it reduces electricity use as well. Finally, society is placing much more importance on work-life balance these days. Five-day workweeks make it harder for people to spend time with their friends or family, so more workers are demanding an increase in their leisure time. Furthermore, many studies have shown that work-life balance is important for workers' physical and mental health. Based on technological advances, the environmental benefits, and the advantages in terms of work-life balance, I feel that four-day workweeks are definitely going to replace five-day ones.

　　解説　「伝統的な週5日勤務は現代社会では時代遅れか」

トピックに対して賛成の立場から挙げている３つの理由は，①テクノロジーによる効率性の向上，②通勤を減らすことによる省エネへの貢献，そして③ワークライフバランスの重要性，である。このスピーチの冒頭部分で使っている I'd like to share my thoughts about why ～「自分がなぜ～と思うのかをお伝えしたい」という表現は，押し付けがましくなく洗練された言い回しなので覚えておくことをお勧めする。また，最後の結論部分で簡潔に３つの理由をまとめているところも，基本のテクニックとはいえ忘れがちなことなのでぜひ参考にしたい。

5. Can the technology gap between developed and developing nations ever be eliminated?

The technology gap between developed and developing nations is a serious problem, but, fortunately, I think it is solvable due to globalization, climate change awareness, and the portability of technology. The main reason is globalization. In the past, when nations created new technologies, governments and businesses were able to control their spread. Now, however, science and the economy have become globally connected, so there is much more transfer of technologies internationally. Second, increased awareness of the climate change crisis has made technology-sharing a top priority for many developed countries. It has been recognized that all nations require advanced technologies to work together in keeping global warming under control. To this end, many governmental, technological and non-profit organizations are working hard to ensure that technologies are spread where they are needed the most. A third reason is that technology itself is becoming much more portable. Devices like smartphones and laptop computers can easily be carried anywhere in the world, no matter how isolated an area is. This miniaturization has helped billions of people get their hands on various technologies, and they will be able to use them to develop new technologies of their own. As you can see, I'm very optimistic about closing the technology gap due to globalization, climate change awareness, and the portability of technology.

解説 「先進国と発展途上国の間のテクノロジー格差は埋められるか」

トピックに対し，①グローバリゼーションによる技術移転，②地球温暖化に対応するための地球規模の技術共有の必要性，③デバイスの携帯化による技術の拡散，の３点から，格差解消は可能であるとしている。３つに共通するのは「グローバル化による技術の透明化と普遍化」だが，それをさらに具体的に落とし込むことで独立した理由にして発話を充実させている。選んだトピックに対し，１つの大きな理由しか思い付かない場合，できるだけ具体的なものに分けてみるとこのスピーチのように発話量をぐっと伸ばせるので試してみよう。

212

2021-1

一次試験
筆記解答・解説　　p.214〜232

一次試験
リスニング解答・解説　p.233〜260

二次試験
面接解答・解説　　p.261〜264

解 答 一 覧

一次試験・筆記

1

(1)	3	(10)	1	(19)	3
(2)	2	(11)	2	(20)	1
(3)	4	(12)	3	(21)	4
(4)	4	(13)	2	(22)	1
(5)	2	(14)	1	(23)	3
(6)	3	(15)	1	(24)	3
(7)	2	(16)	4	(25)	2
(8)	1	(17)	4		
(9)	1	(18)	2		

2

(26)	4	(29)	1
(27)	2	(30)	4
(28)	3	(31)	2

3

(32)	1	(35)	4	(38)	4
(33)	3	(36)	3	(39)	3
(34)	2	(37)	2	(40)	1
				(41)	3

4　解答例は本文参照

一次試験・リスニング

Part 1

No. 1	2	No. 5	4	No. 9	3
No. 2	3	No. 6	1	No.10	3
No. 3	2	No. 7	4		
No. 4	3	No. 8	3		

Part 2

No.11	4	No.15	1	No.19	2
No.12	1	No.16	3	No.20	2
No.13	2	No.17	2		
No.14	3	No.18	3		

Part 3

No.21	2	No.23	3	No.25	4
No.22	3	No.24	4		

Part 4

No.26	1	No.27	3

一次試験・筆記	**1**	問題編 p.114～116

(1) ― 解答 ③

訳 携帯電話は現代社会において常に身近にある存在になった。ほとんどの人は，携帯電話のない暮らしを想像できないかもしれない。

語句 1「留め金」　　　　　　　　　　2「（就労などの）期間」
3「定着したもの」　　　　　　　4「破裂」

解説 動詞 fix「～を固定する」から連想されるように，本来 fixture は流し台や便器など「建物内に固定された備品」を意味するが，問題文のように，ある状況や時代などに「定着したもの［人］，いつもそこにある存在」の意味でも用いられる。

(2) ― 解答 ②

訳 コリンには車の代金を一括で支払うだけのお金がなかったので，2 年間月々800ドルの分割払いで完済した。

語句 1「性質，気質」　　　　　　　　2「分割払いの 1 回分」
3「（法律の）制定」　　　　　　4「思案，熟考」

解説 名詞 installment は動詞 install とは意味上のつながりがないので，単独で覚えておく必要がある。「（連続小説・連続番組などの）1 回分」という意味もある。

(3) ― 解答 ④

訳 メラニーが上司に賃上げを求めたとき，自信なさげな口調から，彼女がいかに緊張しているか明らかだった。

語句 1「けばけばしい」　　　　　　　2「陽気な」
3「尊大な」　　　　　　　　　　4「自信のない」

解説 nervous だったということは，自分の要求が受け入れられるかどうか不安で，diffident「自信のない，おずおずした」話し方だったと考えられる。

(4) ― 解答 ④

訳 その教派は，信者が一緒に住みすべてを共有することのできる農村地域に生活共同体を設立した。私的所有は一切認められなかった。

語句 1「挽歌」　　　2「前兆」　　　3「貯蔵所」　　　4「生活共同体」

解説 第 1 文の where 以下と第 2 文がそのまま commune「生活共同体，コミューン」の定義になっている。動詞 commune「親しく語らう」とは発音が違うので確認しておこう。

(5) ― 解答 ②　　　　　　　　　　　　　　　　　　正答率 ★75%以上

訳 その有名な記者は，別のジャーナリストの仕事を剽窃したことで首になった。彼の記事は，その別のジャーナリストの記事とほとんどまったく

同じだった。

語句 **1**「～を和らげる」 **2**「～を剽窃する」
3「～に予防接種をする」 **4**「(困難などが)～につきまとう」

解説 他人の文章やアイデアなどを盗んで自分のものとして発表することを plagiarize「～を剽窃する，盗用する」と言う。名詞 plagiarism「剽窃，盗用」も覚えておきたい。

(6) ― 解答 **3**

訳 地元の鉄鋼工場が閉鎖されてしまったので，かつてにぎわった町の市街地には営業していない商店が立ち並んでいる。ほとんどの店主は店を放棄した。

語句 **1**「修辞学の」 **2**「不安定な」 **3**「廃れた」 **4**「大望を抱く」

解説 工場が閉鎖して寂れた商店街の様子。defunct は，接頭辞 de-「反対，逆の」と function「機能」から，「機能していない」といった意味だと推測できる。

(7) ― 解答 **2**

訳 国王をたたえて催された式典にその大使が出席しなかったことは，接受国から侮辱と見なされ，既に悪くなっていた関係をさらに悪化させた。

語句 **1**「解明」 **2**「侮辱」 **3**「袋小路」 **4**「最後通告」

解説 国と国の関係を悪化させたのだから，大使の行為は affront「侮辱」と見なされたことになる。affront には「～を侮辱する」という動詞の意味もある。

(8) ― 解答 **1**

訳 米国国境警備隊は，その脱獄囚がカナダへの国境を越えようとするところを何とか逮捕した。彼は直ちに刑務所に戻された。

語句 **1**「～を逮捕する」 **2**「～を略奪する」
3「～の地位を高める」 **4**「～を順応させる」

解説 apprehend は catch，arrest「～を逮捕する」の堅い語。なお，名詞 apprehension には「逮捕」の意味もあるが，むしろ「不安，心配」の意味で覚えておきたい。

(9) ― 解答 **1**

訳 アンソニーは新しい仕事の初日を楽しんだ。雰囲気は和やかだったし，彼を温かく迎え入れるよう同僚たちは精一杯のことをした。

語句 **1**「和やかな，快適な」 **2**「錯乱した」
3「ほんのわずかの」 **4**「本当とは思えない」

解説 genial は人や振る舞いが「親切な，愛想のいい」という意味だが，接頭辞 con-「共に」が付くと，「人を幸せな気分にさせる，一緒にいて楽しい」というニュアンスが加わり，人だけでなく場所・環境・仕事などについても用いられる。

21年度第1回 筆記

215

(10) – 解答 **1**

訳　A：さっき知ったんだけど，学校のオーケストラで第二バイオリンに降格されたよ。もっと練習しなきゃとはわかっていたんだけど。

B：うーん，がんばればきっと前のポジションを取り戻せるよ。

語句　**1**「格下げされる」　　　　　**2**「危うくされる」
3「反復される」　　　　　　**4**「きちんとしまわれる」

解説　relegate *A* to *B* は「A を B（低い地位など）に降格する，格下げする」という意味。previous position は第一バイオリンだったことになる。

(11) – 解答 **2**

訳　その政治家がソーシャルメディアで殺人脅迫を受けた後，そうした行為は非難に値し罰せられるべきだと多くの報道機関が述べた。

語句　**1**「数え切れない」　　　　　**2**「非難されるべき」
3「ぎこちない」　　　　　　　**4**「徳のある」

解説　reprehensible は，動詞 reprehend「～を叱責する，非難する」の形容詞形。道徳的・倫理的に問題のあることについて多く用いられる。

(12) – 解答 **3**　　　　　　　　　　　　　正答率 ★**75%以上**

訳　自動で動くよう作られている車両の数が増加するにつれ，ドライバーは，車が自分で運転する間，自由にくつろいだり仕事を片付けたりできるようになる。

語句　**1**「無気力に」　**2**「わびしげに」　**3**「自律的に」　**4**「意味論的に」

解説　autonomously は国・組織・人などについて「自律的に，自立して」という意味で用いられることが多いが，機械にも使われる。「自動運転車」は autonomous vehicle [car] と言う。

(13) – 解答 **2**

訳　公演の最後の夜，そのオペラ歌手は観客の喝采に酔いしれた。生涯最高のパフォーマンスをしたと彼女にはわかっていた。

語句　**1**「大声で叫んだ」　　　　　**2**「（称賛などに）浸った」
3「まごついた」　　　　　　　**4**「踏みつけた」

解説　bask は bask in the sun「日光浴をする」といった使い方が基本だが，問題文のようにも用いられる。太陽の心地よいぬくもりを全身に受けるように，称賛を浴びて喜びを味わっているという意味合いである。

(14) – 解答 **1**　　　　　　　　　　　　　正答率 ★**75%以上**

訳　種を植える前には，有効期限を確認することが大切だ。種が古過ぎれば，その多くが発芽しない可能性が高い。

語句　**1**「芽を出す」　　　　　　　**2**「～を未然に防ぐ」
3「（剣などで）突く」　　　　　**4**「（法律など）を廃止する」

解説　種が古ければ，芽が出ないかもしれない。sprout は，「大量に出現する，急速に成長する」という意味も重要。その意味ではしばしば up を伴う。

216

(15) – 解答 **1**

訳 A：とても美しい夜ね！　あそこにあるあの星座の名前は何？
B：あれはオリオン座。中央に並んでいる3つ星でわかるよ。

語句 **1**「星座」　　　**2**「大量出国」　　　**3**「教義」　　　**4**「救済」

解説 語幹 stella は「星」の意味で，stellar「星の」という形容詞もある。constellation は，「（有名人などの）一団，（関連あるものの）集まり」という意味も覚えておきたい。

(16) – 解答 **4**

訳 公式報告書によると，いくつかの外国政府が民主主義を転覆させるためにインターネットを利用していた。報告書は，有権者に影響を与えようとさまざまな人気のあるウェブサイトに掲載されたフェイクニュース記事を示した。

語句 **1**「唾液を（過度に）分泌する」　　**2**「（重い物）を持ち上げる」
3「～をなだめる」　　　　　　　　　**4**「（政府など）を打倒する」

解説 subvert は，革命やクーデターのように暴力・武力を用いるのではなく，秘密活動を通じて，あるいは問題文のように情報を操作するなどして，間接的に既成の体制を転覆させることを言う。

(17) – 解答 **4**

訳 ロデリックは去年自動車事故に遭ったが，相手の運転手の過失だったので，幸い損害に対する責任は一切なかった。

語句 **1**「影響されない」　　　　　　　**2**「暗示する」
3「触知できない」　　　　　　　　**4**「責任がある」

解説 liable for ～ は「～に対して（法的に）責任がある」という意味。名詞は liability「（法的）責任」だが，それぞれ多義語なのでほかの意味も確認しておこう。

(18) – 解答 **2**

訳 新しい国立博物館の開会式の来賓は，フォーマルな服装を着用しなければならなかった。ジーンズとTシャツ姿の少数の人たちは，入り口で入館を拒否された。

語句 **1**「美人コンテスト」　　　　　　**2**「服装」
3「話し方」　　　　　　　　　　　**4**「摩滅」

解説 attire は clothes，clothing「服装」の堅い語で，改まった服装に用いることが多い。動詞を使った be attired in ～「～に身を包んでいる」も覚えておきたい。

(19) – 解答 **3**

訳 その子供には年少のころから，他人が考えていることを言い当てる不思議な能力があった。そのようなものはそれまで見たことがないと教師たちは言った。

21年度第1回　筆記

217

（語句）**1**「衝動的な」　**2**「牧歌的な」　**3**「奇怪な」　**4**「非常に不快な」

（解説）uncanny は，理屈では説明できない信じ難いことについて用いる形容詞。ややニュアンスは違うが，unearthly，preternatural などの類義語も確認しておこう。

(20)－解答 **①**

（訳）その俳優は最近，最新映画で演じた役で万人の称賛と数々の賞を受け，今やキャリアの絶頂にある。

（語句）**1**「頂点」　　**2**「想像の産物」　**3**「逆戻り」　　　**4**「渦」

（解説）pinnacle は「（教会の）小尖塔，（山の）尖峰」から転じて，比喩的に「（成功・人生などの）頂点，絶頂」の意味でも用いられる。

(21)－解答 **④**

（訳）上司は枝葉末節にこだわり過ぎだ，とレザは思っている。いつも上司がささいで取るに足りない細部について話し合いたがるので，彼はフラストレーションを感じている。

（語句）**1**「見苦しい」　　　　　　　　**2**「憤った」
　　　　3「政治に無関心な」　　　　　**4**「枝葉末節を気にかける」

（解説）pedantic は日本語の「ペダンティックな，学問や知識をひけらかす」と違い，「枝葉末節にこだわる」が最も一般的な意味。

(22)－解答 **①**

（訳）会議は正午までには終わるはずだったが，午後1時半になってもまだ続いていた。そのころには，ほとんどの人はとてもおなかがすいていた。

（語句）**1**「終わる」　　　　　　　　　**2**「大金をしぶしぶ払う」
　　　　3「（靴など）を履き慣らす」　**4**「あふれ出る」

（解説）文脈から，空所には「終わる」という意味の句動詞が入るとわかる。wind up は，特に会議・演説・協議などが「終わる」場合に用いられる。

(23)－解答 **③**

（訳）新総理大臣の経済政策は，インフレを抑え込むことに重点を置いている。可及的速やかに物価を制御すると彼は約束した。

（語句）**1**「～を打診する」　　　　　　**2**「～を縫い合わせる」
　　　　3「～を厳しく抑制する」　　　**4**「～をしまい込む」

（解説）名詞 rein「（馬を御する）手綱」から，句動詞 rein in は「（人・事）を厳しく抑える」という意味になる。名詞を用いた keep a tight rein on ～ も同じ意味。

(24)－解答 **③**

（訳）刑事は殺人の実行犯が誰かわかるまで，数カ月を費やして事件を巡る状況を掘り下げた。

（語句）**1**「（文章・言葉で）～を攻撃する」　**2**「～の向きを変える」
　　　　3「～を探る」　　　　　　　　　　**4**「～に備える」

解説 dig は「掘る」が基本の意味。dig into ～ は比喩的に，情報をつかんだり秘密を暴いたりするために「～を探る，探求する」という意味で用いられる。

(25) – 解答 **2**　　　　　　　　　　　　　　　　　　　　　　正答率 ★75%以上

訳　Ａ：カーロス，今年の夏，休みを取る日にちは決めた？　そろそろ私たちの休暇の予定を立てられたらと思うんだけど。

Ｂ：まだなんだよね。明日上司と話して，それから決めるよ。

語句　**1**「尻込みする」

2「～を決定する」

3「（部屋など）から家具などを取り去る」

4「尻込みする」

解説　settle on ～ は，選択肢の中から「～を［に］決める，選ぶ」こと。settle on a date「日にちを決定する」のように選択のテーマを提示する使い方と，settle on April 1st「4月1日に決定する」のように具体的な選択肢を示す使い方がある。

一次試験・筆記 **2** 問題編 p.117 ～ 119

全文訳 **ジェダイ教**

　SF映画『スター・ウォーズ』シリーズに基づくジェダイ教は，世界中に相当数の信奉者を持つポップカルチャー哲学である。その実践者が手本にしようとするのは，この映画に登場する一団の魂の戦士，すべての創造物の基礎を成し自分たちに超自然的能力を与えてくれるエネルギーである「フォース」という現象を自在に操る者たちだ。信奉者たちはジェダイ教を正当な宗教と見なしているが，ジェダイ教はフィクションに根差す精神的実践としてしばしば嘲笑の的となる。しかし，信者たちはそれに応えて，ほかの宗教の多くの信者がそれらの宗教の起源すべてを文字どおりに受け取っているわけではない，と指摘する。主要な宗教は道徳的教訓や精神的教訓を伝えるために一般的に物語を用いるが，こうした物語には，例えば言葉を話す動物といった空想的な要素がしばしば含まれており，実際の歴史上の出来事を述べたものではないことを強く示唆している。だがこのことがそうした宗教にとって必ずしも不名誉とはならないのと同じように，フィクションに出自を持つことがジェダイ教の正当性を左右すべきではない，とジェダイ教の実践者たちは感じている。

　しかし，映画に基づく哲学を信奉することは，皮肉な状況を引き起こすこともある。ジェダイ教の場合，信奉者たちは，衣装や模造武器といった装備類に相当な金額を熱心に投資することでよく知られている。映画の多くの要素は関連商品の購入を促すよう意図的に作られていると論じることもできるが，そうした振る舞いは，映画で詳述されている物質的財産の過剰な所有の禁止に反するように見える。ほとんどの信奉者はこの矛

盾をあっさり無視している。リサイクルなどの対策を取って所有物を減らそうと試みる人も確かにいるのだが。

　公的な認知を得ることは，ジェダイ教に困難をもたらしている。英国では，免税資格の申請が，ジェダイ教はまとまりも信仰の統一的体系も持たないという根拠で却下された。だが公的に（宗教としての）指定を獲得することがかなわずとも，ジェダイ教は，西洋において宗教それ自体の受け取られ方が変化していることの証左である。西洋文化は，例えば仏教のように，多くの西洋人には容易にそれとわかる神という概念を持たないかもしれない，あるいはキリスト教に見られるタイプの崇拝を持たない東洋の宗教の影響を受けてきているので，宗教的慣行を特徴付けて正当とするのに用いられるような明確な境界線を引くのは困難になっている。評論家はしばしば，ジェダイ教は，権威主義的で高度に体系化された組織の衰退と，信者の個人的充足感に焦点を当てる集団の台頭の双方を例証するものだと説明する。

> 語句　emulate「～を見習う」，underlie「～の基礎を成す」，anchored in ～「～にしっかり根を下ろした」，ridicule「あざけり，嘲笑」，discredit「～の信用を傷つける」，paraphernalia「装備，道具」，purposely「故意に」，expound「～を詳細に説明する」，inconsistency「矛盾，不一致」，tax-exempt「免税の」，designation「指定，選定」，legitimize「～を正当とする」，exemplify「～を例証する」，authoritarian「権威主義の」，fulfillment「充足感」

(26) ― 解答 ④

解説　空所文の however から，以下ではジェダイ教への嘲笑に対する反論が書かれていると考えられる。空所の次の文では，信奉者がジェダイ教の正当性を主張する根拠として，主要な宗教の教えに空想的な要素が含まれている事実が挙げられている。つまり，**4**のように，宗教の起源は文字どおりに受け取られるべきものではなく，フィクションが含まれる点において多くの宗教とジェダイ教は同列だ，とジェダイ教の信者は指摘していることになる。

(27) ― 解答 ②

解説　第2段落で述べられているのは，映画は過度の物質的所有を戒める内容なのに，ジェダイ教信者が映画の関連グッズを大量に購入している矛盾した現状である。**2**がこれを ironic situations「皮肉な状況」とまとめている。

(28) ― 解答 ③

解説　西洋における何の証拠なのかを考える。続く文では，東洋の宗教の影響を受けた西洋文化において宗教の正当性が揺らいでいることが述べられ，最後の文では，権威主義から個人主義への移行が取り上げられている。つまり，**3**のように，西洋では宗教観それ自体が変化していることになる。

220

全文訳 **ウェブスター第3版**

　米国で最も著名な辞書制作会社メリアム・ウェブスター社が1961年に『ウェブスター新国際辞典第3版』を出版したとき，この辞書が現代にとって画期的な参照ツールとして迎えられることを同社は期待した。言語学の当時新しいトレンドに影響された『ウェブスター第3版』は，英語が日常生活において普通の人々によって実際にどのように書かれ話されているかに焦点を当てる，革新的な「記述主義的」アプローチを採用した。しかし批判的な人たちは，この辞書の著者たちは無責任な振る舞いをしたと非難した。辞書は「規範的」でなければならないと彼らは主張した。規範的とは，辞書の役割は正しい用法と発音に関して権威を持って判断することだ，ということである。規範主義の放棄により英語は転落の一途をたどり言語学的無秩序状態に陥りつつある，と苦情を言う人すらいた。彼らが特に激怒したのは，ain'tのような俗語が是認されるとされたことで，『ウェブスター第3版』は，ain'tは「多くの教養ある話し手によって……口語で用いら」れていると主張した。

　しかし，『ウェブスター第3版』は辞書に対するアメリカ人の姿勢に起因していたとも言える。辞書は1700年代の終盤から，高等教育を受けたエリートからと同じように，下層階級の人々からも十分に受け入れられていた。社会の周縁に追いやられ抑圧されたマイノリティーは，自分たちに禁じられた読み書きの力を獲得する道として辞書を用い，この国への移民は，辞書を言語的同化と文化的同化を補助する不可欠な学習ツールと見なしていた。『ウェブスター第3版』はこの平等主義的考え方を体現するもので，例えば，シェークスピアと聖書からだけでなくハリウッドの俳優などの非伝統的な出典からの文も活用し，利用しやすさと包摂性を一層強化した。

　表面的には，『ウェブスター第3版』がエリートと学者の間に引き起こした騒ぎは，ain'tのような語に「不正確」「語法に反する」といった見下した用語でラベルを付けるべきなのか，それとも「非標準」といったもっと当たり障りのない用語でラベルを付けるべきなのかに関する争いだった。だがもっと深いレベルでは，1960年代に起きたフェミニズム運動の拡大と若者による権威の拒否が例証するように，善悪に関する絶対的理念が徐々に消失し順応への圧力が衰えつつあった根源的な文化的転換を反映していた。したがって，そうした運動の文脈で考えれば，『ウェブスター第3版』は言語学の分野における先駆的な仕事であるだけでなく，社会的変化を反映したものでもある。

> **語句** groundbreaking「草分け的な」, descriptivist「記述主義的な」, prescriptive「規範的な」, authoritative「権威のある」, pronouncement「宣告，判断」, abandonment「放棄」, prescriptivism「規範主義」, slippery slope「先行き不安な状態」, irate「激怒した」, endorsement「承認，是認」, cultivated「教養のある」, marginalize「〜を主流から外す」, oppress「〜を抑圧する」, epitomize「〜の典型である」, egalitarian「平等主義の」, nontraditional「非伝統的な」, inclusivity「包摂性，誰にでも開かれていること」, disparaging「軽蔑する」, nonstandard「非標準的な」

21年度第1回　筆記

221

(29) – 解答 **①** ....

解説 空所には，『ウェブスター第3版』を批判する内容が入る。空所前後の記述によると，辞書は本来規範的でなければならないのに『ウェブスター第3版』は記述主義的アプローチを採用し，英語を無秩序状態に陥れている，というのが批判者の主張。それを irresponsible「無責任な」という語でまとめた **①** が正解である。

(30) – 解答 **④** ....

解説 空所後を読むと，当時米国ではエリートだけでなく下層階級の人々も平等に辞書を利用するようになっており，『ウェブスター第3版』の大衆的路線はその状況に対応するものだったことがわかる。それに合致する選択肢は **④** のみ。

(31) – 解答 **②** .... 正答率 ★**75%以上**

解説 空所文の such movements は，前の文の the growing feminist movement and the rejection of authority by young people を指す。その文によると，『ウェブスター第3版』を巡る騒動はそうした運動が例証する根源的な社会的転換を反映していたのだから，この辞書は「社会的変化の反映」だとすると文脈に合う。

一次試験・筆記 **3** 問題編 p.120〜128

全文訳 **顕示的消費**

　需要に関する経済法則によると，物品の価格とその需要には負の相関関係がある。したがって，企業が製品を大幅に値上げすれば，もっと手ごろな価格で同等の製品を供給する競合他社に切り替える動機を消費者に与えるはずである。しかし1899年に，経済学者ソースティン・ヴェブレンは「顕示的消費」という用語を作り，社会の特定の層はある一定の製品の市場価値には無関心で，自らの富と卓越を誇示する機会を与えてくれる物なら何にでも惜しみなくお金を使うものだと論じた。これらの商品——希少な高級ワインや手作りの腕時計といった物品——は，以後「ヴェブレン財」として知られるようになった。普通の消費財と違い，ヴェブレン財の値上げは，かなりの値上げであっても，富裕な消費者への販売量には悪影響を与えないし，かえって訴求力を増すこともあるかもしれない。ヴェブレンはウィリアム・ランドルフ・ハーストやアンドリュー・カーネギーといったアメリカの大富豪を観察して理論の基礎としたのだが，彼らの豪勢なコンサートホールと大邸宅と博物館は，いかなる実用的目的で建てられたにせよ，それと同じくらい所有者の富を反映させるために建てられたように見えた。そうした誇示は「常日ごろから自分と同類だと見なしている人たちより勝るよう促す」生得の欲望の表出だ，とヴェブレンは考えた。

　しかし，顕示的消費は社会のほかの層でも観察されており，その層では，豪勢さの明

らかな誇示は，購入者の実際の地位が持つ富を超えた富を暗に示している。そうした人たちにとって，ぜいたく品の購入は，自分がより高い社会階級の一員に見えるかもしれないように用いるツールと考えられている。経済学者の指摘によると，貧困から連想される恥辱を避けるため，人々は価格の変化などお構いなしに，明らかに富の指標となる物に散財する傾向がある。好例は，新興経済国がぜいたく品市場を動かす上で果たす役割である。ロシアや中国やサウジアラビアなどの成長市場の消費者は，米国や日本などの先進国より平均収入がかなり低いにもかかわらず，最近数十年で，ぜいたく品の売り上げを伸ばす必須の原動力になった，と経済学者は述べる。実際，経済学者が言うには，さほど裕福ではない消費者が富裕な人たちを手本にしようと，収入に見合わない支出をしてステータスシンボルを購入するのは普通のことである。

　しかし，ヴェブレンの理論が描くイメージは不完全である。最近の研究によると，資産をひけらかす富裕な人々は経済的成熟の1つの段階を意味するもので，この明らかに節度を欠いた出費は，富の格差が縮小するにつれて徐々に消える傾向がある。個人や階級や国がより高いレベルの富を享受し出すと，多くのパターンの「非顕示的消費」が現れ始め，専用のサービスを利用できる権利がますます珍重され貴重になる。ぜいたく品はステータスシンボルとしてなお重要性らしきものをいくぶん保持するが，これらのサービスが支出に占める割合は次第に増えるようになり，自分磨きと排他性を優先するようになる。そういう事情なので，ライフコーチを雇ったり，高級ヘルスクリニックの会員になったり，完全招待制のイベントに参加したりといった経験の方が，単にデザイナーウォッチを所有することより，個人が所属する経済的階級をよく実証するものになるのである。

（語句）coin「（新語）を作り出す」，unconcerned「無関心な」，lavishly「気前よく」，handcrafted「手作りの」，opulent「豪勢な」，affluence「富，裕福」，innate「生得の」，outdo「～に勝る」，opulence「豪勢さ」，stigma「汚名，恥辱」，splurge on ～「～に湯水のようにお金を使う」，case in point「適例」，emerging「新興の」，affluent「裕福な」，emulate「～を見習う」，flaunt「～をひけらかす」，sought-after「需要が多い」，semblance「見かけ，～らしさ」，prioritize「～を優先する」，exclusivity「排他性」

(32) − 解答　❶　　　　　　　　　　　　　　　　　　　正答率 ★75%以上

問題文の訳　「ヴェブレン財」についてわかることの1つは何か。

選択肢の訳　**1** ヴェブレン財が一部の消費者に持つ人気は，商品それ自体の価格より，それらが意味する富の度合いによって定められる。

2 ヴェブレン財は頻繁に需要の変化を被るので，それらを生産する製造業者はしばしばかなりのリスクを冒して生産する。

3 それらの商品は価格が下がる時期を頻繁に経るので，格安品を探す消費者がしばしば引き寄せられる。

4 ヴェブレン財は品質が優れているので，普通の消費財よりも需要の法

則に従う可能性が高い。

解説 第1段落第3文に，anything that provided opportunities to display their wealth and prominence というヴェブレン財の定義が書かれている。そして第5文から，富裕層は価格に関係なくヴェブレン財を買い続けることがわかる。これらの特徴に合致するのは**1**。**4**の「需要の法則に従う可能性が高い」が当てはまるのは普通の消費財の方である。

(33) – 解答 ③

問題文の訳 この文章の記述によると，経済学者は以下の記述のどれと意見が一致する可能性が最も高いだろうか。

選択肢の訳
1 ぜいたく品を購入する傾向は，より高い社会階級についい最近上がった人たちの間で最も強い。
2 発展途上国の富裕な人々の方が，同じようなレベルの富を持つ先進国の人々より，ぜいたく品を手に入れやすい。
3 ぜいたく品を買う余裕がないにもかかわらず，低所得層の出身であるように見えるのを避けるためにぜいたく品を買う人たちがいる。
4 ぜいたく品は最初富裕層に非常に人気があっても，貧しい人々が購入し始めるとぜいたく品としての地位を失う。

解説 第2段落に，裕福ではない人たちの購買行動についての経済学者の考えが書かれている。第3文 Economists point out ... が**3**の内容とほぼ同じ。本文の avoid the stigma associated with poverty を選択肢では avoid appearing as though they are from a low-income background と言い換えている。

(34) – 解答 ②

問題文の訳 この文章の筆者は，ソースティン・ヴェブレンの理論は以下のことを説明していないと示唆している。

選択肢の訳
1 社会のすべての層の人々がさらに高いレベルの富を蓄積するのを妨げる，最近の景気下降の循環。
2 地位を象徴するものとしてのぜいたく品の使用の衰退につながる，経済成長の結果としての金銭的繁栄の増大。
3 社会で富と地位を誇示する手段としてのぜいたく品を拒否する，すべての資産集団にわたりある割合で存在する人々。
4 より低い経済的階級の構成員が手に入れられる非顕示的ぜいたく品の販売促進がより普通の出来事になること。

解説 第3段落ではヴェブレンの理論が incomplete である理由が説明されている。社会がより豊かになると，富裕層でなくても買えるぜいたく品より，exclusive や exclusivity という語が示すように，利用者が限定された排他的なサービスが経済的階級を証明するものになる。これに合致するのは**2**である。

全文訳　化石燃料補助金

　2017年に各国政府が化石燃料企業に対し5.2兆ドルの補助金を交付したことを，国際通貨基金（IMF）の報告書が明らかにした。化石燃料関連の汚染が毎年数百万人の死の原因となっている証拠に照らして考えると，化石燃料の利用を支援することは倫理的に問題があるように思えるし，二酸化炭素排出量を減らすという各国政府の誓約に完全に反するようにも思える。しかし，補助金の総計が税前の補助金と税後の補助金両方を含む点において，この総計は誤解を招くものだ。前者はほとんどの人が「補助金」という語を聞いて思い浮かべるもの——生産コストを下げ，その結果消費者価格を引き下げることを目的に石油会社に支給される現金や，税の軽減措置といったものである。しかし，報告書に書かれた補助金の大半はさまざまな税後のタイプだ。これらは，私たちの化石燃料への依存の結果，納税者にとってさらなる重荷となるもので，石油流出事故の後始末の費用から交通渋滞と交通事故の増加に至るあらゆるものである。多数の批判的な人がIMFによる補助金の定義に異議を申し立て，そうしたコストをこの計算に含めるべきかどうかに関しては明らかに主観が大きく関与していると指摘する。税後の補助金を除外すれば金額は4,240億ドルとなり，最初の合計のほんの一部に減少する。

　税後の補助金を含めることは人を惑わすものだったかもしれないが，その社会的コストをより注意深く見ると不安になる。社会の多数の人は，化石燃料に基づくエネルギー消費がもたらす経済的恩恵と生活様式の恩恵から実際にメリットを得ているのだが，米国で毎年記録される約20万の大気汚染関連死者は，一部の人が払わざるを得ない不幸な代償を反映している。さらに，調査が示すところによると，化石燃料使用が結果的に個人の生活にどの程度プラスあるいはマイナスの影響をもたらすかには，人種的不均衡と社会経済的不均衡がある。例えば，研究によると，白人アメリカ人は自分たちが被るより17％多くの大気汚染の原因を作り出すが，一方黒人アメリカ人とヒスパニック系アメリカ人は，自分たちが原因となるより優に50％を超える大気汚染にさらされている。

　しかし，税後の補助金は間接的な性質であるが故に，税前の補助金より対処するのがずっと難しい。そして税前の補助金は世界中で減ってはいるのだが，撤廃はもろ刃の剣かもしれない。税前の補助金が消費者への直接の金銭的負担を減らすのは確かだから，撤廃すれば低所得世帯への圧迫が大きくなるだろうし，化石燃料よりさらに大量の汚染物質を放出するもっと安価な燃料を用いるよう，非常に貧しい人たちを追い込む場合もあるだろう。同時に，この補助金が奨励する活動の結果として，不釣り合いに多い苦悩と苦難を経験するのはまさにこれらの世帯なのである。各国政府にとってのより効果的な戦略は，より幅広い社会的コストに重点を置くことだ，と専門家は言う。例えば，化石燃料を採掘して生産する企業に，放出する排出物に対して課税し，そのお金を，それらの企業の活動から最も多くの影響を受ける人たちに再分配する新規構想があってもよい。そうすれば，低所得世帯への影響を軽減すると同時に，化石燃料産業にある程度の説明責任を課すことになるだろう。また，もっと重要なことかもしれないが，結果的に化石燃料の価格が上昇し，よりクリーンなエネルギー源の研究と開発に報奨金を出すことによって，化石燃料がもたらす被害の程度を軽減することになるだろう。

語句 pretax「税引き前の」，posttax「税引き後の」，handout「補助金」，tax break「税の軽減措置」，oil spill「石油流出（事故）」，subjectivity「主観（性）」，societal「社会の」，socioeconomic「社会経済的な」，disparity「不均衡」，double-edged sword「もろ刃の剣」，pollutant「汚染物質」，disproportionate「不釣り合いな」，redistribute「～を再分配する」，accountability「説明責任」，mitigate「～を軽減する，和らげる」，incentivize「～に報奨金を出す」

(35) – 解答 ④

問題文の訳 この文章の筆者によると，国際通貨基金が報告した補助金の総計は誤解を招くものである。なぜなら，

選択肢の訳 **1** この組織が，税後の補助金はそうあるべきだと自らが考える推計に直接基づいて税前の補助金の額を計算しているからである。

2 この補助金の総計が，有害な温室効果ガスの排出量を削減するという各国政府の約束の将来的コストを考慮に入れていないからである。

3 税前の補助金は，生産コストを下げたり，より安価な燃料コストを一般大衆に渡したりする上でしばしば有用ではないことを，この組織が無視しているからである。

4 この補助金の総計は，何をもって補助金とするのかという通念に合致しない，納税者が払うさまざまなコストの大きな部分を含んでいるからである。

解説 第1段落では補助金を pretax と posttax に分けているが，語の意味にとらわれて考え過ぎることがないようにしたい。pretax は第4文に書かれているように，一般にイメージされる補助金のこと。posttax は第6文で the consequence of our dependence on fossil fuels と説明され具体例が2つ挙げられていることから，化石燃料を使用することで納税者が間接的に負担しなければならない環境的・社会的コストだと考えられる。したがって **4** が正解。

(36) – 解答 ③ 　　　　　　　　　　　　　　正答率 ★75%以上

問題文の訳 第2段落で，この文章の筆者は化石燃料について何を明らかにしているか。

選択肢の訳 **1** 化石燃料使用の現在の流れが続けば，より多くの化石燃料を消費する人たちが最も深刻な健康への影響を受けることになる。

2 化石燃料を燃やすことから帰結する大衆へのマイナスの影響の最悪のものは，大気汚染とは無関係であることがわかっている。

3 マイノリティーが化石燃料補助金から受ける恩恵と，彼らが化石燃料使用から被るマイナスの影響の間には，不均衡が存在する。

4 一部のマイノリティーが化石燃料を消費する特定のやり方は，化石燃料が最終的にもたらす汚染の量にほとんど影響しない。

解説 第2段落では，化石燃料について2つのことが述べられている。1つは，

化石燃料は恩恵ももたらすが，大気汚染により多くの人が亡くなっていること。もう1つは，人種や社会経済的背景によって，化石燃料が与える影響に不均衡があること。後者が **3** の内容と一致する。本文で例として挙げている Black and Hispanic Americans を選択肢では minorities とまとめ，disparities を imbalance と言い換えている。

(37) – 解答 **2**

問題文の訳 以下のどれが，専門家が推薦する戦略の一部である可能性が高いか。

選択肢の訳
1 化石燃料企業に払う税後の補助金を撤廃し，空気の質の改善に取り組む産業にそのお金を向け直すこと。
2 低所得世帯が確実に金銭的な利益を得られるようにすると同時に，化石燃料企業が，自分たちが引き起こす汚染の責任を直接負うようにさせる政策を導入すること。
3 クリーンエネルギー産業の企業に税前の補助金を交付し，低所得世帯がクリーンエネルギーをより手に入れやすくすることに対してそれらの企業に褒賞を与えること。
4 税前の補助金のいかなる削減も，税後の補助金の減額が実行されるのと同じ割合で確実に実行されるようにすること。

解説 第3段落半ばの Experts say ... 以下に，専門家の意見が書かれている。具体的な提案は，化石燃料企業の排出物に課税して汚染に対する責任を負わせ，そのお金を低所得世帯に分配すること。本文の impose ... industry を hold ... responsible と言い換え，低所得世帯へのお金の分配を benefit financially と表した **2** が正解である。

全文訳 **植物の知性**

中枢神経系——それもとりわけ脳——が知性の必要条件であることを科学者は当然視し，思考することができるのは人間と動物だけだと昔から主張してきた。この見解に基づき，知性の研究は，IQ テストなど，筆記問題に答えたり物理パズルを解いたり行動によって記憶術を実証したりといったことをする能力の客観的測定に枠組みが限定されてきた。

しかし，植物神経生物学として知られる新興分野の支持者は，中枢神経系の欠如は必ずしも植物が何らかの形態の知性を持つ妨げにはならないと論じて，この科学的総意に異を唱えてきた。植物にある通常の生物学的・化学的・遺伝的メカニズムでは，植物が示す非常に高度な幅広い行動の数々を十分に説明できない，と彼らは主張する。したがって，植物は単に置かれた環境における受動的要素なのではなく，実際は，適切な反応を組織的に導き出すために，多様な環境要因からの刺激を感知し評価することができるのだ，と唱道者たちは主張する。しかし，そうした主張は科学界から懐疑で，それどころかあからさまな敵意で迎えられてきた。

西オーストラリア大学のモニカ・ガグリアーノの研究は，触れられたり邪魔されたり

すると防御するように葉をくるりと丸めることで知られる植物オジギソウを用いて，植物神経生物学の物議をかもす主張の一部が正しいことを証明しようと試みた。ガグリアーノの実験の内容は，毎週何度か，50以上のオジギソウを制御された無害な落下する動きにさらすことだった。時がたつと，植物の一部が防御する反応をしなくなったことに彼女は気付いた。これは，危険が差し迫ったものではないと植物が学習したことを示していた。落とされることに植物が反応しなかったことの原因が疲労かそれに類することにあるかもしれない可能性を排除するため，ガグリアーノは植物の一部を突然揺さぶる動きにさらした。落とされることへの順応は緩やかだったのに，揺さぶる動きは直ちに植物を通常の防御行動へと戻した。再び落下する動きにさらすと，植物は以前学習したことを「思い出した」。これは，植物が経験に基づいて，落とされることへの反応を意図的に変えていることを示唆していた。

　こうした研究は，植物は脳を持たないかもしれないが，環境的刺激に対する反応における植物の行動は脳のような情報処理システムの証拠だ，という主張の高まりを裏付けるものである。この説を支持する科学者たちは，生物学的レベルでは，動物の神経系に見られる化学信号伝達システムは植物にも確認されているとも述べている。

　植物の知性という考えに裏付けを与える研究が増えているにもかかわらず，この分野の一層の調査を提唱するガグリアーノなどの人たちは，そうした研究の妥当性を疑う人たちから批判を浴びている。ガグリアーノの実験に直接反応する一部の人たちは，植物を落下させることは自然界の普通の出来事ではなく，したがって，実験で用いた植物が行ったとガグリアーノが言う種類の学習の確かな誘因と考えることはできない，と論じる。そうではなく，ガグリアーノの植物の行動は進化的適応の帰結，つまり多くの世代にわたって自然がプログラムした自動的反応なのだ，と彼らは説明する。それに応えてガグリアーノは，自分が実験で用いた刺激は人工的なものだったのだから，置かれた自然環境では生じないことに植物が進化的適応を経ることができたなどということは理にかなわない，と指摘する。植物の反応が生得のものだったはずがないという彼女の主張は，彼女が用いた植物の中に，ほかより速く学習したものがあったことからもさらに裏付けられる。

　イタリアのフィレンツェにある国際植物ニューロバイオロジー研究所の所長ステファノ・マンクーゾは，この論争に別の方法で取り組んでいる。彼の研究は植物の根の異常な電気的活動量と酸素消費量を明らかにしたが，これはもしかすると「根脳」の存在を暗に示しているのかもしれない。植物神経生物学の強固な主張者であるマンクーゾは，植物の知性は群れ行動に観察される分散型知性に似ていると考えている。例えば鳥の群れでは，鳥は，飛ぶときは互いに適度な距離を保つといった，集団の集合的利益にかなうルールに従う。このタイプの集合的行動は，植物の個々の根がその生物全体のためになるよう協調して振る舞うやり方と似ていなくもないのではないか，と彼は言う。

　植物神経生物学を巡る論戦は，知性に関するより広範な論争を再び活発化させている。マンクーゾによると，私たちが知性をほかの生物に適用したがらないのは，心理的根拠によるバイアスのせいかもしれない。彼の意見では，例えば私たちは，自分たちが作る

機械の人工知能という考えを受け入れることができるが，それは，機械が私たちに奉仕するものであり，私たちの手に成る創造物だからである。それに引き換え，私たちが植物の知性に対して抱く敵意は，植物のない世界は人間にとって破滅的なものになるだろうが，一方その逆は植物にとっておそらく問題にならないだろう，という暗たんたる認識の現れなのかもしれない，と彼は考えている。マンクーゾの視点を考慮すると，植物の知性は細胞間で交換される電気信号の結果でしかないと単純化することは，不当に尊大だと考えられるかもしれない。

語句 prerequisite「必要条件」，proponent「支持者」，emerging「新興の」，neurobiology「神経生物学」，preclude *A* from *do*ing「A が〜するのを阻む」，skepticism「懐疑心」，validate「〜の正しさを立証する」，mimosa「オジギソウ」，discount「〜を軽視する，勘定に入れない」，mounting「増えている」，ascribe *A* to *B*「A を B に帰する」，innate「生得の」，analogous to 〜「〜に似た」，reignite「〜に再び火をつける」，somber「暗い，暗たんとした」，simplification「単純化」，dismissive「尊大な，軽蔑的な」

(38) – 解答 ④

問題文の訳 なぜ植物神経生物学は科学界で物議をかもしているのか。

選択肢の訳
1 植物神経生物学は，人間の被験者の知性レベルを確定するために科学者が用いるのとまさに同じ手法をほかの生物にも応用すべきだと主張している。
2 植物神経生物学は，植物の行動に観察される生物学的・化学的・遺伝的プロセスは人間と動物のプロセスとは作用の仕方が異なると提唱している。
3 植物神経生物学は，人間の中枢神経系の基礎となっていると以前は思われていたメカニズムが，科学者がずっと考えてきたようには機能しないと暗に示している。
4 植物神経生物学は，知性の背後にある根本的メカニズムに関して，大多数の科学者が抱いている考えに反対する主張を行っている。

解説 知性を持つのは人間と動物だけというのが従来からの説（第 1 段落）だが，植物神経生物学は植物にも何らかの知性があると唱えて科学界から疑問視されている（第 2 段落）という大まかな流れが理解できれば，4 が正解だとわかる。植物神経生物学は，生物学的・化学的・遺伝的メカニズムだけでは植物の行動を説明できないと言っているだけであり，2 のように植物は人間と動物とは異なると主張しているわけではない。

(39) – 解答 ③

問題文の訳 モニカ・ガグリアーノがオジギソウで行った実験が示唆するのは，

選択肢の訳
1 この植物は脅威を突き付けられたときに遅れた防御行動を示したのだから，危険に素早く反応することはできない，ということである。

2 記憶したことに基づいて行動できるこの植物の能力は，いかなる時においてもこの植物が感じている疲労の程度に大きく左右される，ということである。

3 この植物は，さまざまなタイプの感覚入力に対して異なる反応を示すのみならず，それらを区別する能力を証明している，ということである。

4 揺さぶられることに対するこの植物の反応の仕方は一貫していなかったのだから，学習速度は種の間で同じではない，ということである。

解説 ガグリアーノの実験は第3段落で詳述されている。オジギソウを上から落とす実験を繰り返すと，次第に葉を丸める防御行動を取らないものが現れた。次に揺さぶるという別の動きには直ちに防御行動を示したが，再び落とすと，学習したことを思い出し，防御行動を取らなかった。落とす・揺さぶるという動きを sensory input と表した **3** が正解。ガグリアーノはオジギソウの反応に fatigue が関与しないことを証明しようとしたのだから，**2** は誤りである。

(40) ‒解答 ①

問題文の訳 この文章によると，ガグリアーノは以下の記述のどれと意見が一致する可能性が最も高いだろうか。

選択肢の訳 **1** 自然界では経験しない刺激を用いて植物をテストすることは，植物の反応が実際に学習に基づいていることを証明する助けとなる。

2 植物が何世代もかけて適応するやり方は，ほとんどの研究者が考えているよりも，人間が学習するやり方に実は似ている。

3 植物は神経系を有しているという科学者間の総意は，植物の行動を動物の行動と比較することを十分に正当化する。

4 植物の情報処理システムは人間のものよりずっとゆっくりと働くが，だからと言って必ずしも劣っているわけではない。

解説 第5段落に，ガグリアーノへの批判とガグリアーノの反論が書かれている。批判者は，自然界では生じない手法を用いて得た植物の反応は学習ではなく進化的適応だと言うが，それに対しガグリアーノは，人工的な刺激に進化的に適応することはあり得ないし，植物の学習速度に違いがあったことからも，生得の反応とは言えないと主張する。**1** がガグリアーノの反論と一致する。

(41) ‒解答 ③

問題文の訳 ステファノ・マンクーゾは植物の知性に関して暗に何と言っているか。

選択肢の訳 **1** もし研究者が人間以外の動物を植物と比較することにすれば，植物神経生物学分野ははるかに急速に進歩するだろう。

2 人間と植物がさまざまな行動を練り上げるやり方は多少類似しているとはいえ，そのことが同じように知性に関連すると推定するのは無責任である。

3 植物における知性という考えに対する人間の態度は，私たちが植物と自分たちとの関係をどのように理解し合理化するかに関連するかもしれない。

4 植物の根と鳥の脳の電気的活動量が似ていることは，それらの作用の仕方も似ているかもしれないことを示唆する。

解説 最終段落のマンクーゾの主張によると，人間以外の生物に知性を認めたがらない考え方は心理的バイアスに基づく。それは，人間は植物なしでは生存できないが植物は人間なしでも構わないという認識が，人間が創造物の頂点に立つという考えと相いれないことから来る敵意である。それに合致するのは **3**。選択肢の rationalize は理屈を用いてそうした不都合な真実を隠そうとすることで，この文章では植物の知性を電気信号で説明しようとする尊大な態度を指す。

一次試験・筆記 **4** 問題編 p.128

解答例　Of the numerous foreign-policy tools used by governments to navigate globally contentious situations, economic sanctions are extremely effective for upholding laws and treaties, settling disagreements in an indirect manner, and even forging international support.

In cases where a country's actions violate international law, economic sanctions can yield effective results. Dictatorships, for example, typically rely on imported resources for their militaries and illegal activities. When these nations refuse calls to engage in diplomatic discussions, economic sanctions can be used to restrict the flow of specific resources and curb the proliferation of the offending activities.

Economic sanctions are also a nonconfrontational approach to resolving international disputes. Some foreign-policy tools, such as military intervention or diplomatic sanctions, can exacerbate tensions by elevating the risk of armed warfare or shutting down crucial avenues of negotiation. Economic sanctions, however, avoid the use of force while still effecting a positive outcome.

Furthermore, economic sanctions can be instrumental in garnering multilateral support. The decision to levy economic sanctions is commonly regarded as a way for a country to reinforce its commitment to issues such as human rights. Such stances are often universally praised and can encourage other nations to follow suit.

Strengthening solidarity on the international stage is no doubt a welcome benefit of economic sanctions, but in times when there is a need to enforce international law or foster peaceful resolutions, the true usefulness of such sanctions in foreign policy becomes particularly apparent.

トピックの訳 「経済制裁は役に立つ外交政策ツールか」

解説 全体の構成は，自分の立場を明示する導入の段落，3つの理由について論じる3つの段落，自分の立場を再確認する結論の段落の5段落という基本に則ったものである。経済制裁は extremely effective だとして，トピックに対する全面的な Yes. の立場を表明している。3つの理由としては，「法律と条約を守ること」「不和を間接的に解決すること」「国際的支持を築くこと」を挙げている。それぞれやや抽象的な言い回しだが，続く段落で具体的に論じられている。

最初の理由については，独裁国家を例に挙げ，国際法を破るそうした国は輸入した資源を用いて軍事活動や違法活動をしているのだから，経済制裁を科すことでそうした資源の流入を止められるとしている。最初の段落で述べている laws and treaties を，ここでは international law とまとめている。2つ目の理由については，軍事的干渉や外交制裁はむしろ緊張を悪化させる恐れがあり，経済制裁のように正面からの対決を避けるやり方の方が国際紛争の解決策として有効だとしている。nonconfrontational「対決姿勢ではない」という語が，「間接的に解決する」ことに相当する。そして3つ目の理由については，例えば人権問題への取り組みは普遍的に称賛される姿勢なので，そのような問題を理由とした経済制裁は国際的な支持を得やすいと述べている。

結論の段落では，3つ目の理由を Strengthening solidarity on the international stage と言い換え，それが経済制裁の有効性それ自体を論じたものというより経済制裁によるメリットの考察である点を考慮して，ほかの2つの理由とは区別し，その2つの理由を言い換えた enforce international law と foster peaceful resolutions が経済制裁の有用性を真に示すものだと締めくくっている。

反対の立場なら，食糧や医薬品など必需品の禁輸は相手国の国民を苦しめることになり人道主義的に問題がある，国連が経済制裁を決議したとしても抜け駆けをする国が出てくれば実効性が担保されない，経済制裁は対象国からの敵意や憎悪をあおる可能性があるのだから話し合いによる問題解決に勝るものはない，などの理由が考えられるだろう。

| 一次試験・
リスニング | **Part 1** | 問題編 p.129 ～ 130 | ▶MP3 ▶アプリ
▶CD 3 **1** ～ **11** |

No.1 － 解答 **②**　　　　　　　　　　　　　　　　　正答率 ★**75%以上**

スクリプト　★： So, Mrs. Rowlands, has the medicine I prescribed for your back pain last month made a difference?

☆： Honestly, Doctor, I've been reluctant to even try it.

★： Why?

☆： I read online that it can cause sleeplessness and irritability. I have so much trouble with insomnia that I'd rather put up with back pain than risk aggravating the problem.

★： Well, I've prescribed that medication to many patients, and none of them has ever experienced problems.

☆： I'd still feel better if you could give me something else.

Question: Why did Mrs. Rowlands not take the medicine?

全文訳　★： さて，ローランズさん，先月処方した腰痛の薬で少しはよくなりましたか？

☆： 本当のことを言うと，先生，使ってみたいという気持ちすら起きないんです。

★： どうしてですか？

☆： ネットで読んだんですが，不眠といらいらの原因になることがあるそうです。私は不眠症でとても苦労しているので，問題を悪化させるリスクを冒すくらいなら，腰痛は我慢しようと思うんです。

★： うーん，あの薬はたくさんの患者さんに処方してきましたが，問題があった人は1人もいませんよ。

☆： それでも，別の薬を出していただいた方がありがたいです。

質問：なぜローランズさんはその薬を服用しなかったのか。

選択肢の訳　**1** 腰痛が前よりひどくなくなった。

2 副作用が心配だった。

3 その薬は安全ではないかもしれないと医師がそれとなく言った。

4 その薬は腰痛に効かないと耳にした。

解説　女性の2つ目の発言の sleeplessness と irritability は薬の side effects「副作用」。続けて言っている insomnia が「不眠症」の意味だとわかれば，女性が副作用である sleeplessness を心配していると判断できる。

No.2 － 解答 **③**　　　　　　　　　　　　　　　　　　　　　　　　

スクリプト　☆： Hi, Al. I haven't seen you for . . . well, since you left the company. Have you found another job yet?

★： Yes, I work for Plexar now. I miss you guys, but I'm much

21年度第1回　リスニング

233

happier there.

☆ : Good for you. What makes Plexar so much better, besides the products?

★ : That's just it. All my clients know we sell high-quality products, so they trust me. I get far fewer complaints than I did with MediaSavvy, and my sales volume's through the roof.

☆ : I'll bet. Let me know if they have any openings in marketing, would you?

★ : Sure, Linda. I will.

Question: What can be inferred about the man's previous job?

全文訳 ☆ : こんにちは，アル。久しぶり……えーと，あなたが会社を辞めて以来ね。もう別の仕事は見つかった？

★ : うん，今はプレクサーで働いている。君たちに会えなくて寂しいけど，プレクサーにいる方がずっと幸せだよ。

☆ : よかったわね。プレクサーの方がずっといいというのはどうしてなの，製品のほかに。

★ : それが決め手なんだよ。うちが高品質の製品を売っていると僕の顧客はみんな知っているので，僕を信頼してくれる。苦情はメディアサビーのころよりはるかに少なくなったし，僕の売上額はうなぎ上りさ。

☆ : そうでしょうね。マーケティングで求人があったら教えてもらえるかな。

★ : いいよ，リンダ。そうするよ。

質問：男性の前の仕事について何を推測できるか。

選択肢の訳　**1**　彼はスタッフとうまくいっていなかった。
　　　　　　2　社員の入れ替わりが激しかった。
　　　　　　3　彼は多くの苦情に対応しなければならなかった。
　　　　　　4　製品の品質がもっとよかった。

解説 男性の発言の I miss you guys から，人間関係は良好だったと考えられるので，**1** は誤り。**2** についての話はない。新しい職場では I get far fewer complaints ... と言っているので，**3** が正解。品質がいいのは Plexar の方なので，**4** は誤りである。

No.3 – 解答 ❷ ••••••••••••••••••••••••••••••••••••••

スクリプト ☆ : Mike, have you read this newsletter from Kate's school?

★ : Not yet. Is there anything interesting?

☆ : Well, it appears there's a proposal to open a snack shop on the school grounds. I don't like the sound of that.

★ : Sounds convenient. But I know what you're getting at. It's related to the meeting last semester about healthier school meals, right?

☆ : Exactly. What's the point of encouraging healthy eating habits if there's a shop selling junk food at school?

★： Well, we don't know yet what control the school will have over it.

☆： True, but I'm not convinced it'll be much.

Question: What is the woman concerned about?

全文訳 ☆： マイク，ケイトの学校からのこの学校便りは読んだ？

★： まだだけど，何か興味深いことが載っている？

☆： えー，学校の構内に軽食の店を開く提案があるみたい。なんだか気に入らないわ。

★： 便利そうじゃないか。だけど言いたいことはわかるよ。もっと健康にいい給食についての先学期の会議に関係があるんだよね？

☆： そのとおりよ。ジャンクフードを売る店が学校にあったら，健康的な食習慣を奨励する意味がどこにあるっていうの。

★： うーん，学校がその店をどれだけ管理できるかは，まだわからない。

☆： そうだけど，大して管理できるとは決して思わないわ。

質問：女性は何を心配しているか。

選択肢の訳　**1**　給食の質の低下。

2　軽食の店を開くという提案。

3　地域に手近な飲食店がないこと。

4　給食の費用の上昇。

解説　女性の 2 つ目の発言にある proposal to open a snack shop と同じ **2** が正解。続く会話から，女性は給食の改善を求めているのに，snack shop ができるとその努力が無意味になると思っていることがわかる。snack shop のせいで給食の質が下がるとは言っていないので，**1** は誤り。

No.4 – 解答 ③

スクリプト ☆： I'm surprised to see you eating lunch in the cafeteria, Tatsuo.

★： Yeah, I usually prefer to get away from the office, but I'm preparing for the company's stock exchange listing.

☆： Oh right, that's pretty exciting. It's going to mean big things for the company. It's scheduled for next year, right?

★： That was the plan, but listing requirements have become stricter of late. With the global slowdown, it's more difficult to list. I've gotten even busier.

☆： Well, I hope it doesn't take too much out of you.

Question: What does the man say?

全文訳 ☆： あなたがカフェテリアで昼ご飯を食べているなんて，驚いたわ，タツオ。

★： うん，普通は会社の外に行く方が好きなんだけど，会社の証券取引所上場の準備をしているんだよ。

☆： ああ，そうだったわね。結構わくわくする。会社にとってとても大事なことになるもの。来年の予定よね？

★： 計画ではそうだったんだけど，最近は上場の要件が厳しくなっているんだ。世界的に景気が減速しているから，上場は前より難しい。僕は一層忙しくなったよ。

☆： まあ，負担になり過ぎないといいけどね。

質問：男性は何と言っているか。

選択肢の訳　**1**　会社を辞めるつもりでいる。

　　　　　　　2　その年の多くは出張で不在である。

　　　　　　　3　現在抱えているプロジェクトが複雑になった。

　　　　　　　4　上司が締め切りを延ばさない。

解説　男性が外出せずに社員食堂でランチを食べているのは，listing「上場」の準備のため。男性は 2 つ目の発言で，上場の要件が stricter になったので忙しくなったと言っている。stricter を complicated と言い換えた **3** が正解。

No.**5** – 解答 ④ ⋯⋯⋯⋯⋯⋯⋯⋯⋯⋯⋯⋯⋯⋯⋯⋯⋯⋯⋯⋯⋯⋯⋯⋯⋯⋯⋯

スクリプト　★： I see the "For Sale" sign on the Wilsons' house is still there.

　　　　　　☆： That's strange. I thought that place would sell in a flash. It's in a lovely spot.

　　　　　　★： Well, it's a buyer's market at the moment.

　　　　　　☆： Now you mention it, they said something about that on the news last night.

　　　　　　★： If the Wilsons are in a hurry, they'll have to rethink their asking price.

　　　　　　☆： That's a shame, though. It looks like pretty good value to me.

Question: Why does the man think the house is still for sale?

全文訳　★： ウィルソンさんの家の「売り出し中」の看板はまだそのままだね。

　　　　☆： おかしいわ。あの家はあっという間に売れると思ったのに。すごくいい場所にあるから。

　　　　★： まあ，今は買い手市場だし。

　　　　☆： そう言えば，昨日の夜のニュースでそんなような話をしていたわ。

　　　　★： ウィルソンさんたちが急いでいるなら，希望価格を考え直さなければならなくなるね。

　　　　☆： でも，それは気の毒だわ。私にはかなりお値打ちに思えるけど。

質問：その家がまだ売り出し中なのはなぜだと男性は思っているか。

選択肢の訳　**1**　宣伝が十分にされていない。

　　　　　　2　家の立地のせいで買い手に敬遠されるのかもしれない。

　　　　　　3　その地域ではもっといい家が手に入る。

4 家の売却希望価格が高過ぎるのかもしれない。

解説 男性が2つ目の発言で言っている buyer's market は，需要より供給が多いため価格が下がっている状態のこと。つまり，男性の次の発言の rethink their asking price は「今の希望価格は高過ぎるので考え直して値下げする」ことを意味する。したがって**4**が正解。

No.6 - 解答 ①

スクリプト
★: Lesley, how nice to see you. I didn't know you shopped here.

☆: I just started recently. I'm trying to be more careful about what I eat. The prices are a little steep, though.

★: True, but you have to be prepared to fork out a bit extra for organic food.

☆: I guess so.

★: And you get the satisfaction of knowing you're making a contribution to the environment.

☆: It's a tough choice, though. If I don't notice any improvements in my health, I may switch back to my regular place.

Question: What do we learn about the woman?

全文訳
★: レズリー，奇遇だね。君がここで買い物をしているとは知らなかったよ。

☆: 最近来るようになったばかり。食べる物に前より気を使うようにしているの。価格はちょっと高いけどね。

★: そうだけど，オーガニック食品にはちょっと余分に払う覚悟がなきゃね。

☆: そうみたいね。

★: それに，環境に貢献していると知る満足感を得られるし。

☆: 難しい選択だけどね。健康にまったく改善が見られなければ，いつもの店に戻るかもしれない。

質問：女性について何がわかるか。

選択肢の訳
1 オーガニック食品を買うのをやめるかもしれない。
2 買い物の予算を減らした。
3 環境を助けることに熱心である。
4 もっと安いオーガニック食品店を見つけた。

解説 オーガニック食品に熱心な男性に対し女性は現実的で，効果がなければ I may switch back to my regular place と最後に言っている。いつも買い物をしている店に戻るということは，**1**のようにオーガニック食品をやめると示唆していることになる。**3**が当てはまるのは男性である。fork out「（大金）を払う」。

No.7 - 解答 ④

スクリプト
☆: You're looking kind of stressed, honey. Everything OK?

★: Yeah. I'm just trying to figure out how to adjust our budget to accommodate the new car expenses.

☆： I thought we'd worked out manageable payments.

★： For the car itself, we did, but insurance costs quite a bit more for a sports car. And it really goes through gas.

☆： It's fun to drive, but if it doesn't make economic sense, we can do without it.

★： It hasn't come to that just yet. I'm sure we can figure out a way to cut corners elsewhere.

Question: What will the couple probably do?

全文訳 ☆： 何だかストレスがたまっているみたいね，あなた。大丈夫？

★： うん。予算をどうやりくりして新車の出費を工面するか，解決策を考えているんだ。

☆： 無理なく支払えるよう計算したと思ったけど。

★： 車それ自体の計算はしたけど，スポーツカーは保険が少しばかり高くつくんだよ。それにガソリンをすごく食うし。

☆： 車を運転するのは楽しいけど，経済的に割に合わないなら，なしで済ませてもいいわよ。

★： まだそこまでの話ではないね。ほかのところで費用を削れる方法がきっと見つかるよ。

質問：この夫婦はおそらくどうするか。

選択肢の訳 **1** 保険会社に連絡する。

2 車の支払いについて再交渉する。

3 もっと燃費のいい車両を購入する。

4 ほかのことに支出するお金を減らす。

解説 夫は新車の保険やガソリン代をどう捻出するか頭を悩ませている。妻は we can do without it と言って車を手放すことを提案しているが，夫は最後に cut corners elsewhere の方法を考え出すと言っている。これは車以外の出費を減らすという意味なので，**4** が正解となる。

No.**8** – 解答 ③ ・・・・・・・・・・・・・・・・・・・・・・・ 正答率 ★**75%以上**

スクリプト ☆： Hi, Sam. How's the job search going?

★： I got an offer that I'm considering from a firm in the city. Great salary, but a lot of business trips, and a two-hour-a-day commute, which I'm not sure I can handle.

☆： What does your wife think?

★： She understands my reluctance. But she'd like to put a dent in our debt and start a college fund for the kids.

☆： The commute sounds tough, but she does have a point.

★： She sure does. The question is whether it's worth the extra stress and time away.

Question: What is the man's main concern?

全文訳　☆： こんにちは，サム。職探しの調子はどう？

★： 市内の会社からオファーをもらって検討中。給料はすごくいいんだけど，出張が多いし，通勤に1日2時間かかるんで，うまくこなせるかどうか自信がないんだ。

☆： 奥さんはどう思っているの？

★： 僕が乗り気じゃないのをわかってくれている。だけど彼女は，借金を減らして，子供たちの大学進学資金を準備し始めたいと思っている。

☆： 通勤は大変そうだけど，奥さんの言うこともももっともね。

★： そうなんだよ。問題は，ストレスと家から離れる時間が増えるだけの価値があるかどうかだね。

質問：男性の主な懸念は何か。

選択肢の訳　**1** その仕事の給料が思ったほど高くない。

2 妻がお金を重視し過ぎる。

3 その仕事は生活様式の変化を彼に強いるだろう。

4 家族がさらに借金を抱えるかもしれない。

解説　新しい仕事のオファーを受けるべきか男性は悩んでいるが，その理由は，出張が多く通勤時間が長いこと。それを change his lifestyle とまとめた **3** が正解。男性の妻がお金を重視しているのは確かだが，女性の she does have a point という指摘に男性は She sure does. と答えているので，**2** のように too much とまでは考えていない。put a dent in ～「～を減らす」。

No.**9** - 解答 ③

スクリプト　★： OK, ma'am. You're all set with new tires, but when I was changing them I found a problem with the brakes.

☆： Really? I haven't noticed anything unusual.

★： Well, your front brakes are fine, but the problem is with your rear ones. The pads are worn and need to be replaced.

☆： I hadn't planned on that expense. Will they last a couple more months?

★： Possibly, but you risk causing damage to the brake drums and may end up having to replace them as well.

☆： Well, I certainly don't want to pay even more. If I leave it here today, would you be able to replace the pads?

★： Unfortunately, I'll have to order the parts.

☆： How soon can you get it done, then?

★： Let's see. The earliest would be next Monday morning. Will that work for you?

☆： Yes, that's fine. How much can I expect all this to cost?

★： About $300, including labor.

☆： Wow, that's a lot.

★： We do offer a payment plan, so you can break up the cost into four monthly payments.

☆： That would really help me out. Thanks.

Question: What does the woman decide to do?

全文訳 ★： さあ，お客さま。新しいタイヤの取り付けはこれで完了ですが，交換しているときブレーキに問題を見つけました。

☆： 本当？　特に異常には気付かなかったけど。

★： えー，前ブレーキは大丈夫なんですが，問題があるのは後ろブレーキですね。パッドがすり減っていて，交換が必要です。

☆： その出費は予定外だわ。あと2，3カ月もたないかしら。

★： もつかもしれませんが，ブレーキドラムの損傷の原因になるリスクがありますし，結局ブレーキドラムも交換する羽目になるかもしれませんよ。

☆： うーん，それ以上払うことになるのは絶対に嫌だわ。今日こちらに置いていったら，パッドを交換していただけますか。

★： 残念ですが，部品を注文しなければなりません。

☆： それじゃ，いつごろまでにやってもらえますか。

★： えっと，一番早くて来週月曜日の午前中ですね。それで問題ありませんか。

☆： ええ，それで結構です。全部まとめていくらかかると思えばいいでしょう。

★： 工賃を入れて300ドルくらいです。

☆： まあ，大金ね。

★： 支払いのプランをご用意していますから，費用は4回の月賦に分けていただくこともできます。

☆： そうしてもらえると本当に助かるわ。ありがとう。

質問： 女性はどうすることに決めているか。

選択肢の訳 1　車のブレーキドラムを交換する。

2　もっと安い修理工場に行く。

3　できるだけ早く車を修理してもらう。

4　修理代金を前払いする。

解説 タイヤ交換の際にブレーキに異常が見つかったことから会話が進んでいく。女性の3つ目の発言の I certainly don't want to pay even more は，パッド交換ならまだしも，ブレーキドラム交換にはお金を使いたくないという意味なので，**1** は誤り。続けて日程の話になり，早くて月曜

日の午前中と言う男性に対し女性は that's fine と答えているので，**3** が正解となる。最後に分割払いで話がまとまっているので，**4** は誤りである。

No.10 解答 ③

スクリプト
☆： So, Dan, what do you think of the candidates we've interviewed so far?

★： I think Philip Johnson could be a good addition to our team.

☆： Mary?

○： Hmm . . . I'm not sure. Philip's still young, which is a plus, I guess, since he can grow with the job . . .

★： He also graduated from a good university, and he has some sales experience in our industry. Hopefully, that means he'd require less training.

☆： I guess so, but Philip seems too quiet and shy. I have to say, none of the interviewees seemed really outstanding. There's no one who's really "wowed" me.

○： I agree. We haven't seen a candidate with a proven track record of boosting sales. We're looking for someone who's proactive, someone who can expand our customer base.

☆： I know it's a lot of work, but personally I'd rather continue this process in the hopes of finding a candidate who meets all our criteria.

★： I still think someone like Philip is worth considering.

☆： Look, why don't we keep him as a backup for now? Meanwhile, Dan, can you let our recruiting agencies know the position is still open?

★： OK, if you're sure. I'll also let them know that the rest didn't make the grade.

Question: What do the two women think?

全文訳
☆： では，ダン，これまで面接してきた候補者たちのことをどう思う？

★： フィリップ・ジョンソンは僕たちのチームのいい戦力になるかもしれないと思う。

☆： メアリーは？

○： うーん……よくわからない。フィリップはまだ若いから，その点はプラス材料じゃないかな，仕事とともに成長できるんだから……

★： それに彼はいい大学を卒業しているし，僕たちの業界で少し営業の経験がある。ということは，きっと研修が少なくて済むんじゃないかな。

☆： そうかもしれないけど，フィリップはあまりに物静かで内気な感じね。

21年度第1回 リスニング

241

はっきり言って，面接を受けた人の中で特にずば抜けた人はいないと思えた。私を本当に「あっと言わせた」人はいないわね。

○： 同感だわ。売り上げを伸ばしたという確かな実績を持った候補者には出会えていない。私たちが探しているのは，先を読んで行動する人，私たちの顧客基盤を広げることができる人よ。

☆： とても大変なのはわかっているけど，個人的には，私たちの基準をすべて満たす候補者が見つかることを期待して，できればこの作業を続けたいわ。

★： それでも，フィリップのような人は検討に値すると思うけど。

☆： ねえ，取りあえず彼を補欠としてキープしたらどうかしら。それと同時に，ダン，人材紹介会社にポストはまだ空いていると伝えてもらえる？

★： わかった，君が本当にそれでいいなら。残りの人たちは基準に達しなかったとも伝えておくよ。

質問：2 人の女性はどう思っているか。

選択肢の訳　**1**　紹介会社は理想的な候補者を数人見つけた。

2　ダンは期待値を下げるべきだ。

3　フィリップ・ジョンソンの営業記録はずば抜けていない。

4　ダンが最終的な採用の判断を下すべきだ。

解説　社員の採用に関する男女 3 人の会話。男性はフィリップ・ジョンソンを推す理由の 1 つに営業経験を挙げているが，それに対して女性の 1 人は none of the interviewees seemed really outstanding と述べ，もう 1 人の女性も，確かな営業実績のある候補者はいなかったと言っている。つまり 2 人とも，フィリップの営業実績が outstanding「ずば抜けた」ものではないと考えていることがわかるので，**3** が正解。期待値が高いのはダンではなく女性たちなので，**2** は誤り。make the grade「要求された水準に達する」。

242

A

(スクリプト) **Electricity and the Brain**

As we age, our bodies become less nimble. The same thing can also happen to our brains. While occasional bouts of forgetfulness may not be serious, mental decline can be a sign of more-severe conditions like dementia or Alzheimer's disease. However, neuroscientist Robert Reinhart believes electrical stimulation can help. In a controlled study, Reinhart applied electrical currents to parts of the brain involved in short-term memory, also known as working memory. He found that by using electricity to synchronize brain waves in certain areas, working memory could be significantly improved, and learning ability could also be enhanced.

Such results seem promising. Furthermore, using electrical stimulation therapy may not be confined to improving working memory or helping us to become better learners. It is hoped it can also be used to help treat brain disorders including autism, schizophrenia, and Parkinson's disease. Poor synchronization of brain waves in different areas of the brain is believed to be a factor in such conditions. However, while electrical stimulation to synchronize brain waves proved effective in Reinhart's study, its viability as a long-term treatment has yet to be determined.

Questions

No.11 What is one thing Robert Reinhart's research illustrates?

No.12 What does the speaker suggest about electrical stimulation therapy?

全文訳　**電気と脳**

年を取ると，私たちの体の敏しょう性は低下する。同じことが私たちの脳にも起こり得る。時折短期的に忘れっぽくなっても深刻ではないかもしれないが，知能の衰えは，認知症やアルツハイマー病といったより重度の疾患の兆候のこともある。しかし，神経科学者ロバート・ラインハートは，電気刺激が助けになり得ると考えている。対照研究で，ラインハートは，短期記憶に関与する脳の部位に電流を流した。短期記憶は作業記憶としても知られる。電気を用いてある領域の脳波を同期させると，作業記憶を著しく改善することができ，学習能力も強化され得ることを彼は発見した。

こうした結果は期待できるように思える。さらに，電気刺激療法を用いることは，作業記憶を改善したり，私たちがよりよい学習者になる助けになったりすることにとどまらないかもしれない。電気刺激療法は，自閉症と統合失調症とパーキンソン病を含む脳の病気の治療を助けることにも使えると期待されている。そうした疾患では，脳の異なる領域で脳波がうまく同期しないことが1つの要因だと考えられている。しかし，脳波

を同期させる電気刺激はラインハートの研究では有効だとわかったものの，長期的治療として実現できるかどうかはまだ確定していない。

（語句）nimble「敏しょうな」，bout「（病気などの）短い期間」，dementia「認知症」，neuroscientist「神経科学者」，synchronize「～を同期させる」，autism「自閉症」，schizophrenia「統合失調症」，viability「実現可能なこと」

No.11 解答 ④ 〔正答率 ★75%以上〕

（質問の訳）ロバート・ラインハートの研究が例示する1つのことは何か。

（選択肢の訳）
1 私たちの脳は，体が年を取るのと同じようには年を取らない。
2 電気刺激は精神に重大な問題を引き起こすかもしれない。
3 学習は脳のほかの機能と関係がない。
4 脳波を同期させると記憶機能が改善する。

（解説）第1段落後半でラインハートの研究が手短に述べられている。by using electricity to synchronize brain waves ... working memory could be significantly improved を 4 が簡潔にまとめている。中ほどの electrical stimulation can help の help は精神疾患を助けるという意味なので，2 は誤り。

No.12 解答 ①

（質問の訳）電気刺激療法について話者は何を示唆しているか。

（選択肢の訳）
1 記憶の改善と学習を超えた潜在的利用法がある。
2 これまで知られていなかった疾患を特定するのに役立ってきた。
3 長期的効果を証明した。
4 脳の病気の治療には適さないとわかった。

（解説）第2段落冒頭の may not be confined to ... を has potential uses beyond ... と言い換えた 1 が正解。3 の長期的効果については，最後の文で has yet to be determined と言っているので，まだ証明されていないことになる。

B

（スクリプト）**Madagascar's Biodiversity**

Madagascar has one of the highest levels of biodiversity on Earth, with up to 90 percent of its plants and animals found nowhere else. The island split from other landmasses about 80 million years ago, which allowed the flora and fauna there to evolve in isolation. Scientists also believe that significant variations in its landscape contribute to biodiversity. The mountain range running down the middle of the island separates a rain forest on one side from desert-like plains on the other. This combination allowed the development of unique habitats that have encouraged a variety of plant and animal adaptations.

Unfortunately, Madagascar's biodiversity is threatened by human activities that are causing climate change. The island's isolation as well as its terrain, rainfall, and other variables make it difficult for researchers to predict how different species will respond to alterations in their environment. One method being used by researchers is to study how species on the island reacted to past environmental changes. This could help identify which plants and animals are vulnerable today. A concern with this model, however, is that it involves examining environmental fluctuations which occurred over tens of thousands of years. The human causes of climate change, in contrast, have been occurring for a far shorter period of time.

Questions
No.13 What is one reason given for Madagascar's biodiversity?
No.14 How are researchers trying to identify Madagascar's vulnerable wildlife?

全文訳　**マダガスカルの生物多様性**

　マダガスカルの生物多様性は地球でも最高レベルの1つで，その動植物の最大90%はほかのどこにも見られない。この島はおよそ8千万年前にほかの大陸塊から分離し，そのため島の動植物相は孤立して進化することができた。科学者は，島の風景が変化に富んでいることが生物多様性に寄与しているとも考えている。島の中央を走る山脈が，片方の熱帯雨林をもう一方の砂漠のような平原から切り離している。この組み合わせが，多様な動植物の適応を促してきた特異な生息環境の発達を可能にしたのである。

　残念なことに，気候変動の原因となっている人間の活動によって，マダガスカルの生物多様性は脅かされている。島の孤立だけでなく地形や降雨量などの変動要因が，置かれた環境の変化にさまざまな種がどう対応するか，研究者が予測することを困難にしている。研究者が用いている1つの手法は，島の生物種が過去の環境変化にどう反応したかを調査することである。これは，今日どの動植物が変化に弱いかを特定する上で役立つかもしれない。しかし，このモデルに関する1つの懸念は，数万年にわたって生じた環境変動の検証が必要なことである。それに比べて，気候変動の人為的原因が生じているのははるかに短い期間である。

　〔語句〕landmass「大陸塊」，flora and fauna「動植物相」，terrain「地形」

No.13 解答

質問の訳　マダガスカルの生物多様性の1つの理由として挙げられているのは何か。
選択肢の訳　1　かつてうっそうとした熱帯雨林に覆われていた。
　　　　　2　いくつかのまったく異なる生態学的環境がある。
　　　　　3　ほかの大陸塊から多くの種を引き付けた。
　　　　　4　現代文明から孤立したままである。
解説　第1段落で，マダガスカルの生物多様性の理由が2つ挙げられている。1つは，大昔から大陸から切り離されていること。もう1つは，中ほど

で significant variations in its landscape contribute to biodiversity と言っているように，熱帯雨林と砂漠に似た平原といった多様な環境があること。**2** が 2 つ目の理由に合致する。

No.14 解答 3 .... 正答率 ★75%以上

質問の訳 研究者はマダガスカルの変化に弱い野生生物をどのように特定しようとしているか。

選択肢の訳
1 ほかの島の野生生物と比較することによって。
2 地元の人たちをガイドとして募集することによって。
3 過去の気候の変化を検証することによって。
4 ほかの国で用いられている手法を模倣することによって。

解説 第 2 段落の冒頭で climate change というキーワードが提示されている。中ほどに出てくる environmental changes と後半に出てくる environmental fluctuations は，climate change を言い換えたものと考えられる。研究者はこれらと生物種との関係を調べているのだから，**3** のように気候変動を調べていることになる。

C

スクリプト **Operation Gunnerside**

During World War II, Germany initiated a secret nuclear program with the goal of building an atomic bomb. German scientists, however, faced an obstacle: their production strategy involved an extremely rare substance known as heavy water, which contains a different form of hydrogen to that of regular water. This difference allows heavy water to slow the movement of neutrons, which is essential for the correct chain reaction required for an atomic explosion to take place. Heavy water was therefore key to the German program's success. Only one facility produced heavy water at the time: a hydroelectric power plant in Norway called Vemork.

After Germany occupied Norway, the US and Britain decided to attack Vemork to halt Germany's nuclear progress. However, as the heavy-water reactor was in the basement of the building, air strikes would have failed. Therefore, in a mission known as Operation Gunnerside, a small unit of British-trained Norwegian soldiers was sent to destroy the reactor with explosives. The soldiers obtained detailed information about the building's layout, enabling them to sneak in, set the explosives, and escape. Operation Gunnerside was one of the most important steps toward stopping Germany's wartime nuclear program.

Questions

No.15 What is one thing we learn about heavy water?
No.16 Why was Operation Gunnerside necessary?

全文訳　**ガンナーサイド作戦**

　第2次世界大戦中，ドイツは原子爆弾の製造を目標に，秘密の核プログラムに着手した。しかし，ドイツの科学者たちはある障害に直面した。彼らの生産戦略には，通常の水とは違う形態の水素を含む，重水として知られる極めて珍しい物質が必須だった。重水はこの違いにより中性子の動きを遅くすることができるのだが，この中性子の動きは核爆発が起きるのに必要な正しい連鎖反応に欠かせない。したがって，重水はドイツのプログラムが成功するための鍵だった。当時重水を生産する施設は1つしかなかった。ノルウェーのベモルクという水力発電所である。

　ドイツがノルウェーを占領した後，米国と英国はドイツの核開発の進展を止めるためにベモルクを攻撃する決断を下した。しかし，重水炉は建物の地下にあったので，空爆をしたとしても失敗しただろう。それ故，ガンナーサイド作戦として知られるミッションで，英国で訓練を受けたノルウェー兵の小部隊が爆薬で炉を破壊すべく送り込まれた。兵士たちは建物の設計図の詳細な情報を手に入れ，そのおかげで彼らは忍び込んで爆薬を仕掛け，脱出することができた。ガンナーサイド作戦は，ドイツの戦時核プログラムを止めるための最も重要なステップの1つだった。

　語句　neutron「中性子」，hydroelectric power plant「水力発電所」

No.15 解答 ①

質問の訳　重水についてわかる1つのことは何か。

選択肢の訳　1　ドイツの核プログラムは重水に頼っていた。
　　　　　2　重水は原子が分裂するのを防ぐ。
　　　　　3　ドイツの科学者たちは重水が危険だと思った。
　　　　　4　どんな中性子も重水を通り抜けられない。

解説　重水については第1段落で説明されている。極めて珍しい物質であること，通常の水とは水素の形態が違うこと，中性子の動きを遅くすること，ドイツの核開発の鍵だったがノルウェーの水力発電所でしか生産されていなかったことである。**1** が，ドイツの核開発に欠かせなかったことを depended on it と表している。

No.16 解答 ③

質問の訳　なぜガンナーサイド作戦が必要だったか。

選択肢の訳　1　ドイツは米国から核技術を盗んでいた。
　　　　　2　英国は核プログラムを開発していなかった。
　　　　　3　ベモルクに空襲しても成功しなかっただろう。
　　　　　4　米国はベモルクに重水を生産してもらう必要があった。

解説　ガンナーサイド作戦は，ベモルク発電所を攻撃してドイツの核開発を止めることが目的だった。第2段落の前半で，重水炉が地下にあったので air strikes would have failed と言っており，**3** が failed を not ... succeeded と言い換えている。空爆で重水炉を破壊するのは無理なの

247

で，小部隊による潜入作戦が行われた，というのが話の展開である。

スクリプト **The World's First Computer?**

In 1901, divers near the Greek island of Antikythera discovered an ancient Roman shipwreck full of artifacts, including a shoebox-sized bronze mechanism in a wooden case. The mechanism was largely ignored until the mid-twentieth century, when science historian Derek de Solla Price began to study it. In the early 1970s, he had x-ray and gamma-ray images of the mechanism taken. After analyzing the results, Price theorized the device was an "ancient analog computer," constructed around 87 BC. The technology available to him at the time was limited, and the images he took were difficult to interpret conclusively. However, Price believed the mechanism's inscriptions and gear system were designed to track the movements of planets and stars.

In the following decades, a mechanical engineer analyzed the inner workings of the mechanism using more-advanced imaging technology. According to the engineer, dials on the front and back would have conveyed information about the movements of the sun, the moon, and individual stars. Although no other such ancient device has ever been found, many historians believe the mechanism's complexity means it must have had a predecessor. This theory is supported by first-century-BC writings of the Roman statesman Cicero, which describe similar types of astronomical-calculator devices.

Questions
No.17 What is true of Derek de Solla Price's observations of the mechanism?
No.18 What do Cicero's writings suggest about the mechanism?

全文訳　**世界初のコンピューター？**

　1901年に，ギリシャのアンティキテラ島の近くにいたダイバーたちが，工芸品でいっぱいの古代ローマの沈没船を発見したが，工芸品の中には木箱に入った靴箱大の青銅の機械装置があった。この機械装置は，科学史家デレク・デ・ソーラ・プライスがその調査を始めた20世紀半ばまでおおむね無視されていた。1970年代初頭に，彼は機械装置のエックス線画像とガンマ線画像を撮ってもらった。結果を分析した後，プライスは，この装置は「古代のアナログコンピューター」で，紀元前87年前後に組み立てられたという説を立てた。当時彼が利用できた科学技術は限られており，彼が撮った画像からは決定的な解釈が困難だった。しかしプライスは，機械装置に刻まれた文字と歯車装置は惑星と星の動きを追うためのものだと考えていた。

　続く数十年の間に，ある機械工学者が，より進んだ画像処理技術を用いて機械装置内部の仕組みを分析した。その工学者によると，表と裏の目盛りは，太陽と月と個々の星の動きに関する情報を伝えたのだと思われる。そうした古代の装置はほかに見つかったことがないが，この機械装置の複雑さからすると，先行するものがあったに違いないと

多くの歴史家は考えている。この説は，同様のタイプの天文計算機装置を記述している，ローマの政治家キケロの紀元前 1 世紀の著作に裏付けられる。

> 語句　shipwreck「難破船，沈没船」，artifact「工芸品」，theorize「～という学説を立てる」，conclusively「決定的に」，inscription「碑文，銘」，imaging「画像処理」

No.**17** 解答 **2**

質問の訳　デレク・デ・ソーラ・プライスのこの機械装置の観察について正しいのは何か。

選択肢の訳
1　エックス線を使えば観察はもっと決定的なものになっただろう。
2　彼が用いた画像処理技術が観察の正確さを制限した。
3　機械装置が青銅製でなく木製であることが観察で明らかになった。
4　彼の分析はローマの科学者たちの分析と違っていた。

解説　プライスの観察はエックス線画像とガンマ線画像によるものだが，この技術は limited だったので画像は difficult to interpret conclusively だったと第 1 段落の後半で言っている。これを全体的に言い換えた **2** が正解。imaging technology はエックス線とガンマ線のこと。

No.**18** 解答 **3**

質問の訳　キケロの著作はこの機械装置について何を示唆しているか。

選択肢の訳
1　機械装置はこれまで見つかっている同様の古代の装置より古い。
2　機械装置が明らかにした情報には不正確なものもあった。
3　機械装置はその種のもののうち最初のものではなかったかもしれない。
4　機械装置の当初の用いられ方は効率的ではなかった。

解説　キケロの名前は最後に出てくるが，その文は This theory is supported by ... で始まる。This theory がその前の the mechanism's complexity means it must have had a predecessor を指すと理解できれば，この機械装置が最初に作られたものではないという内容の **3** を選ぶことができる。

E

スクリプト　**The Chicago Fire**

The Chicago Fire of 1871 is one of the most infamous disasters in US history, killing nearly 300 people and leaving one in three residents homeless. The fire's exact cause is still unknown, but it is believed to have started in a barn in the southwest of the city. Firefighters responded immediately, but they accidentally went to the wrong location. As a result, the fire rapidly spread out of control, intensified by a severe regional drought and the proximity of wooden structures in the city. Thousands of buildings, including the entire downtown business district, were destroyed. Among them was the facility that controlled the city's water supply. This left Chicago helpless, and the blaze burned unchecked for two days.

Despite the widespread devastation, reconstruction began immediately. Officials introduced stricter fire and building codes, and great progress was made in public health thanks to new infrastructure that reduced water pollution. The reconstruction effort attracted prominent architects, resulting not only in careful replanning of the city center but also the erection of the world's first skyscraper. The rebuilding also attracted many new residents. The pre-fire population had been approximately 300,000, but by 1890, the city's population had increased to over 1 million.

Questions

No.19 What is one thing we learn about the Chicago Fire of 1871?

No.20 What is one thing that happened following the fire?

全文訳 **シカゴ大火**

　1871年のシカゴ大火は米国の歴史で最も悪名高い大惨事の1つで，300人近い人が亡くなり，3人に1人の住民が住む家をなくした。火災の正確な原因は今でも不明だが，市の南西部の納屋が火元だと考えられている。消防士は直ちに反応したが，誤って違う場所に行ってしまった。その結果，深刻な地域的干ばつと市内の木造建造物が近接していたことで勢いを増した火災は，急速に広がって手が付けられなくなった。中心部のビジネス地区全体を含む数千もの建物が全焼した。その中には，市の水道を制御する施設もあった。これでシカゴはお手上げ状態になり，炎は歯止めなく2日間燃えた。

　広範囲に荒廃したにもかかわらず，直ちに復興が始まった。役人はより厳格な火災基準と建築基準を導入し，水質汚染を減らした新たなインフラのおかげで公衆衛生は大きく進歩した。復興の取り組みは有力な建築家を引き付け，その結果都心部が入念に再設計されただけでなく，世界初の超高層ビルが建設されることとなった。建物の再建は多くの新住民を引き付けもした。火災以前の人口は約30万だったが，1890年には市の人口は100万以上に増えていた。

　語句 proximity「近いこと，近接」，unchecked「抑制されない」，devastation「破壊，荒廃」，replanning「再計画，再設計」，erection「建設」，rebuilding「再建」

No.19 解答 ②

質問の訳 1871年のシカゴ大火についてわかる1つのことは何か。

選択肢の訳 1　市内に住むホームレスの人たちが火元だった。

2　環境状態が火災の急速な拡大の手助けをした。

3　ビジネス地区の建物には影響がなかった。

4　消防士たちは火災を抑え込んだと思った。

解説 第1段落中ほどで火災が拡大した理由について intensified by a severe

250

regional drought and the proximity of wooden structures in the city と言っているが，この2つの理由を Environmental conditions とまとめた **2** が正解。**1** は放送文に出てくる homeless という語を使った引っかけ，ビジネス地区は全部焼けたのだから **3** は誤り，火災は under control ではなく out of control だったのだから **4** も誤りである。

No.20 解答 ② 正答率 ★75%以上

質問の訳 火災に続いて起きた1つのことは何か。
選択肢の訳
1 新しい建築物の高さが制限された。
2 復興の結果人口が増加した。
3 有名な建築家たちが功労に対して法外な請求をした。
4 役人たちは復興を加速するため火災基準を無視した。

解説 第2段落は火災後の復興について述べている。最後に人口の変化に触れて，新住民の流入により火災前の30万から1890年には100万以上に増えたと言っているので **2** が正解。stricter ... building codes が導入されたとは言っているが，skyscraper が建設されたことから，**1** のように高さを制限する基準ではなかったことがわかる。

一次試験・リスニング **Part 3** 問題編 p.133～135 ▶MP3 ▶アプリ ▶CD 3 18～23

F

スクリプト

You have 10 seconds to read the situation and Question No. 21.

Despite our commitment to the highest manufacturing standards, we are now looking at undertaking a product recall, which is needed to prevent any possible injuries. I've drawn up a plan to assign roles and spell out exactly what steps are required to carry out such a recall. The priority for senior members of the legal team is to explore any possible lawsuits we could be facing. For junior legal staff, I want you to look into any legal procedures we need to follow for this kind of recall, then write up your findings so all of us can quickly and easily understand and review them. You will also all need to thoroughly review the guidelines for making changes to our current contracts, including supplier contracts, but that can come later. As we make progress on these steps, the manufacturing department will need to conduct a thorough review of production standards.

Now mark your answer on your answer sheet.

全文訳

　わが社は最高の製造基準を守ると約束していますが，製品のリコールをすることについて今検討しています。これは，どんなけがの可能性も防ぐために必要なことです。役割の分担と，そうしたリコールを実行するにはいったいどのような段階が必要かを明確に説明した計画書を作成しました。法務チームの上級メンバーの優先課題は，わが社が受けるかもしれない可能性のあるどんな訴訟についても調査することです。下級法務スタッフの皆さんにしてほしいのは，この種のリコールで従う必要のあるどんな法的手続きについても調べ，それから調査結果を書類にまとめて，私たち全員が手早く簡単に理解し見直しができるようにすることです。また皆さん全員が，供給業者の契約を含むわが社の現在の契約に変更を加えるためのガイドラインを徹底的に見直す必要がありますが，それは後で構いません。これらのステップが進展すれば，製造部は生産基準の徹底的な見直しを行うことが必要になります。

No.21 解答 ②

状況の訳　あなたは最近，自動車部品製造会社で未経験者向けの仕事を始めたところである。法務部で働いている。スタッフ会議で社長が次のことを言う。

質問の訳　あなたはまず何をする必要があるか。

選択肢の訳　**1** 製品の製造基準を見直す。
　2 リコールの法的要件の要約をつくる。
　3 既存の契約を修正する手続きを確認する。
　4 会社が受けるかもしれない訴訟を調査する。

語句　spell out「～を明確に説明する」

解説　状況でポイントになるのは entry-level job と legal department だと思われる。リコール対策の進め方について話す社長は，まず senior members に訴訟の調査をするよう言うが，これは entry-level ではないので **4** は外れる。続けて junior legal staff にしてほしいこととして，リコールに必要な法的手続きを調べて書類にまとめるよう言っている。あなたは junior だと考えられるので，**2** が正解となる。**1** は製造部がすること，**3** は that can come later なので，まずするべきことではない。

G

スクリプト

You have 10 seconds to read the situation and Question No. 22.

It's a good thing you asked about your passport. A lot of travelers assume they can go abroad on any valid passport, but that's not always true. Canada is more lenient than other countries about allowing foreigners in with only a few months remaining on their passport, but I'd still advise you to renew it to be on the safe side. The Japanese consulate downtown is helpful in these situations. You don't have much time, so you should go tomorrow and have your passport renewed right away. Take all necessary documents, a photo, and anything else listed on their website. It usually takes five days, but it might be quicker, considering the circumstances. I wouldn't advise purchasing a ticket until you've done that, as you might not be able to reschedule, and you won't get a refund if you cancel.

Now mark your answer on your answer sheet.

全文訳

パスポートのことをお尋ねいただいてよかったです。有効なパスポートならどんなものでも外国に行けると思い込んでいる旅行者が多いですが,必ずしもそうではありません。パスポートの期限が数カ月しか残っていない外国人を入国させることについては,カナダはほかの国より寛大ですが,それでも安全策を取ってパスポートを更新するようお勧めします。中心街にある日本領事館がこうした状況では役立ちます。あまり時間がありませんから,明日行ってすぐにパスポートを更新してもらうのがいいでしょう。必要な書類全部と写真,あと領事館のサイトに載っているものがほかにあれば持って行ってください。普通5日かかりますが,状況を考えればもっと早いかもしれません。それが片付くまでは,チケットは購入しないようお勧めします。予定を変更できないかもしれませんし,キャンセルしても払い戻しを受けられませんから。

No.22 解答 ③

状況の訳　あなたは米国に住んでいて,家族の急な用件で1週間後に飛行機でカナダに行く必要がある。日本のパスポートは2カ月後に失効する。旅行代理店の人が次の話をする。

質問の訳　あなたは何をすべきか。

選択肢の訳
1　カナダの空港で係員に相談する。
2　一時パスポートをネットで申請する。
3　新しいパスポートをもらいに中心街に行く。
4　カナダに着いた後で日本領事館を訪ねる。

語句　lenient「寛大な」,consulate「領事館」

解説　旅行代理店の人のアドバイスは明快で,有効期限が数カ月あるパスポートでも入国できないことがあるので,念のためすぐにパスポートを更新するのがいい,というもの。更新できる場所については The Japanese consulate downtown と言っており,それを単に downtown と表した**3**が正解である。

スクリプト

You have 10 seconds to read the situation and Question No. 23.

Welcome to Brookton Primary School. On the morning your daughter starts school, you'll receive some permission forms for school outings. You'll be asked to sign and return those within a day or two. We require all students to be fully vaccinated before the first day of the term, and any family doctor can provide the immunizations if they haven't been completed. If they have been completed, written proof of immunization should be submitted. School starts next month, so time is of the essence for those. I understand you're also requesting after-school care. For this, we'll need a letter from your employer stating your work hours and commuting time. We can provide temporary care until 6 p.m. for two weeks to give you time to get that letter. Finally, here is a list of our uniform requirements. We have a grace period of one week before the uniform is required.

Now mark your answer on your answer sheet.

全文訳

ブルックトン小学校にようこそ。娘さんの学校初日の午前中に，学校の遠足の承諾書を何枚かお受け取りいただきます。署名して 1 日か 2 日以内に戻していただくようお願いします。学期初日の前にワクチン接種が完了していることを生徒全員に義務付けており，済んでいなければ，どこのかかりつけ医でも接種を受けられます。接種済みの場合は，書面のワクチン接種済み証明書を提出していただくことになります。学校は来月始まりますから，済んでいない生徒には時間がとにかく重要です。確か放課後の保育もご要望でしたね。これについては，勤務時間と通勤時間を明記したあなたの雇用主からの手紙が必要になります。その手紙をもらう時間を差し上げるため，2 週間，午後 6 時まで一時的保育を提供できます。最後ですが，こちらが当校で必要な制服のリストです。制服が必須になるまで 1 週間の猶予期間があります。

No.23 解答 ③

状況の訳 あなたと家族は最近外国に引っ越した。あなたは娘を小学校に入学させるところである。娘は日本でワクチン接種を済ませた。学校の事務職員が次の話をする。

質問の訳 学校初日の前にあなたは何をすべきか。

選択肢の訳 1 署名した承諾書を提出する。
2 医師に娘の健康診断をしてもらう。
3 ワクチン接種済み証明書を提出する。
4 あなたの雇用主から手紙をもらう。

語句 outing「遠足」，of the essence「極めて重要な」，grace period「猶予期間」

解説 選択肢にはする必要があることとないことが混在しているので，学校が始まる前にしなければならないことに集中して聞く。1 の承諾書は学校初日の後に提出することになる。ワクチンは接種済みなので 2 の必要はない。3 は来月学校が始まるまでに提出しなければならないので，これ

が正解である。**4**は学校が始まってから2週間の余裕があるので，必ず初日の前にする必要はない。

（スクリプト）

You have 10 seconds to read the situation and Question No. 24.

Unfortunately, you don't currently qualify for Gold membership renewal next year. It is still possible to meet the criteria, however. As a rule, you need to spend a minimum of $4,000 a year on travel through E-Zonia, or book at least two weeks' accommodation at qualifying hotels. You've spent about $2,000 in total so far but trying to reach the minimum would take you beyond the budget you mentioned. Still, I see you've stayed for 10 days at our partner hotels. You've already mentioned you plan to travel during the Christmas holidays, so we can book you something for then if you'd like. Just four more nights would do the trick, and that can be done within your budget. For future reference, you might also want to consider obtaining an E-Zonia credit card, as you'll save an additional 5 percent on all flight bookings made through our website.

Now mark your answer on your answer sheet.

（全文訳）

残念ですが，現在は来年のゴールド会員更新の資格をお持ちではありません。ですが，基準を満たすことはまだ可能です。原則として，Eゾニアを介した旅行に1年で最低4千ドル使っていただくか，資格を満たすホテルで少なくとも2週間の宿泊を予約していただく必要があります。今のところ総額で2千ドルほどお使いですが，最低額に届くようにしようとすると，先ほどおっしゃった予算を超えることになります。それでも，当社のパートナーホテルに10日間宿泊されています。クリスマス休暇中に旅行するご予定だと既に伺いましたので，よろしければその時のためにこちらで何か予約をお取りすることもできます。あとたった4泊で目的達成ですし，それならご予算内で収まります。今後のご参考までに，Eゾニアのクレジットカードを作ることを検討された方がいいかもしれません。当社のサイト経由で予約するすべての航空便がさらに5％お得になりますから。

No.24 解答 ④

（状況の訳）Eゾニア・トラベルのゴールド会員資格が間もなく切れるので，あなたは更新したいと思っている。あなたの年間総予算は3千ドルである。代理店の係員が次のアドバイスをする。

（質問の訳）あなたは何をすべきか。

（選択肢の訳）
1 支出をEゾニアの最低額まで引き上げる。
2 Eゾニアのクレジットカードを申し込む。

3 年末までにEゾニアを介して航空便を予約する。
4 Eゾニアのパートナーホテルで4泊予約する。

(語句) do the trick「目的を達する」

(解説) 係員が最初に提示している更新の条件は，1年で最低4千ドル使うことか，指定のホテルで少なくとも2週間の宿泊を予約すること。前者は係員も言っているように予算オーバーなので，必然的に後者を選ぶことになる。Just four more nights would do the trick が，あと4泊予約すれば更新条件をクリアするという意味だと理解できれば，迷わず**4**を選ぶことができる。

(スクリプト)

You have 10 seconds to read the situation and Question No. 25.

Government regulations have become stricter, and staff at any branch can explain the new procedures. If you're unable to visit a bank branch here in the US personally, you'll need to do everything online. Access your account online and click on the "Make a Payment" option. Then, click on "Wire Transfer." To complete the wire transfer form, you'll need a single-use security access code. To get that, you'll need to complete a two-stage authentication process, so the first thing you have to do is complete the two security questions you set up when you originally opened your account. Once you've done that, you need to enter your account password. After those steps are done, you can request the code to be sent to your preregistered e-mail address. You can then complete the transfer online, but you'll have to reenter your password for any subsequent transfers.

Now mark your answer on your answer sheet.

(全文訳)

政府の規制が以前より厳しくなり，どの支店のスタッフも新しい手続きの説明ができます。こちらのアメリカの銀行支店にご自分で行くことができないのなら，全部ネットでする必要があります。ネットでアカウントにアクセスし，「支払いをする」というオプションをクリックしてください。次に「電信送金」をクリックします。電信送金の書式に記入するには，使い捨てのセキュリティーアクセスコードが必要になります。それを手に入れるには2段階の認証プロセスを完了する必要があるので，まずしなければならないのは，最初に口座を作ったときに設定した2つのセキュリティー質問に対し答えを記入することです。それが終わると，口座のパスワードを入力する必要があります。これらのステップが終わった後で，あらかじめ登録したメールアドレスにコードを送ってもらうよう要請できます。そうするとネット送金を完了することができますが，ほかに続けて送金する場合はパスワードを再入力しなければなりません。

No.25 解答 ④

状況の訳 あなたは海外に住むアメリカ市民である。アメリカの銀行口座から娘の口座に送金したい。銀行に電話すると,係員が次の話をする。

質問の訳 アクセスコードを入手するには,あなたはまず何をすべきか。

選択肢の訳
1 アカウントのパスワードを変更する。
2 メールアドレスを再確認する。
3 自ら銀行の支店を訪ねる。
4 2つのセキュリティー質問に答える。

語句 single-use「1度だけ使用する,使い捨ての」, authentication「認証」

解説 to obtain an access code のようなポイントとなる要素が状況ではなく質問に含まれている場合もあるので,先読みでは注意したい。中ほどの you'll need a single-use security access code. To get that が聞き取れたら,次にアクセスコードの入手方法に関する情報が話されるはずなので,聞き逃さないこと。2段階の認証プロセスがあり,1つ目は complete the two security questions なので **4** が正解となる。

問題編 p.135

スクリプト

This is an interview with Gary Stevens, a jewelry seller in New York.
I (Interviewer): We have Gary Stevens with us today. Welcome, Gary.
G (Gary Stevens): Thank you for having me.
I: Could you tell us a little bit about what you do?
G: Well, I run my own business buying and selling jewelry in New York. I sell to private customers as well as other jewelers in the trade. I can help customers order what they like through a catalog, or I can have something custom-made for them.
I: I see. What are some of the issues that customers often face?
G: When buying something, customers are often tempted by the biggest stones, but this isn't always indicative of the quality of the jewelry as a whole. Likewise, customers are not aware of how valuable a piece of jewelry might be before they attempt to sell it to us. Something that they think is cheap costume jewelry might have diamonds in it, whereas an impressive-looking piece might not be worth much. Sometimes, customers return to my store asking to buy back a sentimental piece that they've already sold me. This is possible when I still have the item in question, but in a situation where a gold ring is scrapped, for example, you cannot simply

put it back together. Especially in the case of family heirlooms, it's often better to just keep it in the family. As a word of advice to customers, I'll say, "Before you sell us your jewelry, it's important that you think about this decision carefully."

I: Is there a benefit to working in a place like New York City?

G: New York has a large jewelry district, and while this does mean competition for customers, it also allows jewelers to help one another. Someone who, for example, is skilled at resetting stones can do repairs for someone else without that expertise. There are many different companies that work in a wide variety of styles using different metals, and sometimes if we know someone who can meet a customer's needs, we can refer the customer to that person.

I: Could you tell us about some recent trends in the industry?

G: Due to the sharp increase in the price of gold and silver, people are increasingly selling their jewelry just for the value of the metal. While this can be an attractive option at first, to me it seems like a shortsighted decision. Fine jewelry is a work of art just like an expensive painting or a sculpture, but the work of talented jewelers is disappearing forever because people are more interested in making a quick profit. Before someone decides to scrap something, I always ask them to consider it carefully.

I: Lastly, do you have any words of wisdom for new jewelers or people interested in becoming one?

G: First of all, it's important to have a lot of background knowledge. By studying gemology or something similar, one can identify the cut and quality of stones used, and can tell genuine items from, for example, cut glass made to look like a stone. Precision and attention to detail are also necessary when making jewelry. If you happen to ruin a diamond or expensive stone while cutting and sculpting it, it can be difficult to fix your mistake.

I: Gary, thank you very much for your time.

G: It was my pleasure.

Questions

No.26 What is an issue Gary says many people face when selling their jewelry?

No.27 What does Gary say about selling jewelry for the price of the metal?

`全文訳`

これはニューヨークの宝飾商であるギャリー・スティーブンズとのインタビューです。

聞き手 (以下「聞」): 今日はギャリー・スティーブンズをお招きしています。ようこそ,

ギャリー。

ギャリー・スティーブンズ（以下「ギ」）：呼んでいただきありがとうございます。

聞：お仕事について少し教えていただけますか。

ギ：えー，宝飾品の売買をする自分の店をニューヨークで経営しています。個人のお客さんにも，業界のほかの宝飾店にも販売しています。お客さんが気に入ったものをカタログで注文するお手伝いもできますし，オーダーメイドでお客さんに何かお作りすることもできます。

聞：なるほど。客が直面する問題にはどういったものがありますか。

ギ：何か買うとき，お客さんは一番大きな宝石に引き付けられることが多いですが，これは必ずしも宝飾品全体としての品質を示すものではありません。同様に，1点の宝飾品を私たちに売ろうとする前は，お客さんはそれがどれだけ価値があるかもしれないのかを知りません。安物のコスチュームジュエリーだと思ったものにダイヤモンドが使われているかもしれませんし，一方，見た目は見事なものが，それほど価値がないかもしれません。時々お客さんが私の店に戻ってきて，既に私に売ってしまった思い入れのあるものを買い戻したいと言うことがあります。問題の品物を私がまだ持っていれば可能ですが，例えば金の指輪がスクラップにされてしまった状況では，元の形に戻すことはできっこありません。特に家族の家宝の場合は，とにかく家族で取っておく方がいいことが多いです。お客さんへの忠告の言葉として，「当店に宝飾品を売る前に，その決断についてよく考えることが重要です」と言っておきたいです。

聞：ニューヨーク市のような場所で働くことにメリットはありますか。

ギ：ニューヨークには大きな宝飾店街があり，これは確かにお客さんの獲得競争を意味しますが，宝飾店が助け合うことも可能になります。例えば，宝石をはめ直す技術に優れている人は，その専門技術がない別の人の代わりに修理をすることができます。さまざまな金属を用いてバラエティーに富んだスタイルで仕事をするさまざまな会社がたくさんあり，時には，お客さんのニーズを満たすことのできる知り合いがいれば，そのお客さんをその人に回すことができます。

聞：業界の最近の動向について少し教えていただけますか。

ギ：金と銀の価格が急速に上がっているので，金属の価値だけで宝飾品を売る人が増えています。これは最初は魅力的な選択のこともありますが，私には近視眼的な決断のように思えます。ファインジュエリーは高価な絵画や彫刻のような芸術作品ですが，才能のある宝石職人の作品は永遠に姿を消しつつあります。それは，手っ取り早くもうけることへの関心が強くなっているからです。何かをスクラップにすると決める前に，よく考えてほしいと私はいつも言います。

聞：最後に，新米宝石職人や，宝石職人になることに興味がある人に，何か先人のお言葉を頂けますか。

ギ：まず何よりも，背景知識をたくさん持っていることが大切です。宝石学や同様のことを学べば，使われている宝石のカットと品質を特定できますし，本物と，例えば宝石に似せて作られたカットガラスを区別できます。正確さと細部への注意も，宝飾品

を作る際には必要です。ダイヤモンドや高価な宝石をカットして彫刻している間に偶然駄目にしてしまうと，間違いを修正するのは難しいことがあります。
聞：ギャリー，お時間を頂きありがとうございました。
ギ：どういたしまして。

> 語句　indicative of ～「～を示す」，costume jewelry「コスチュームジュエリー（ファッション性を優先して人工の宝石などを用いた宝飾品）」，heirloom「先祖代々伝えられた家財」，shortsighted「近視眼的な」，fine jewelry「ファインジュエリー（天然の宝石や貴金属を用いた高級宝飾品）」，gemology「宝石学」

No.26 解答

> 質問の訳　宝飾品を売るときに多くの人が直面する問題は何だとギャリーは言っているか。

> 選択肢の訳
> 1　彼らは自分の宝飾品の価値を十分には理解していない。
> 2　彼らは思い入れのある無価値な品物に過度に愛着を持っている。
> 3　彼らは金と銀の市場価格に依存し過ぎである。
> 4　彼らはその宝飾店の評判を調べるのをしばしば怠る。

> 解説　客が直面する問題について聞かれたギャリーは，3つ目の発言で，客が目を奪われる大きな宝石が宝飾品の品質を表すとは限らないと言い，続けて，宝飾品を売ろうとしている客について，customers are not aware of how valuable a piece of jewelry might be と述べている。1がこれと同じ内容である。2の sentimental pieces への愛着についても発言しているが，worthless だとは言っていない。

No.27 解答

> 質問の訳　宝飾品を金属の値段で売ることについてギャリーは何と言っているか。

> 選択肢の訳
> 1　一部の宝飾品製造者が職を去る結果になっている。
> 2　金の高価格にもかかわらず，彼の利益を減らした。
> 3　貴重な芸術作品を破壊することに似ている。
> 4　昔よりも行われる頻度が減っている。

> 解説　質問の selling jewelry for the price of the metal に対応するのは，ギャリーの5つ目の発言中の selling their jewelry just for the value of the metal である。metal，つまり金と銀の高騰に目がくらんで宝飾品を手放すことを shortsighted だと批判するギャリーは，Fine jewelry is a work of art just like an expensive painting or a sculpture と宝飾品を芸術作品にたとえ，スクラップにされることを憂えている。それに合致するのは 3 である。

二次試験・面接　トピックカード　A 日程　問題編 p.136

ここでは，A日程の5つのトピックをモデルスピーチとしました。
A日程

1. Should democratic nations try to force democracy on other nations?

I strongly disagree that democratic nations should try to force their system of government on other countries. First of all, the whole concept of democracy is based on freedom. Democracy requires willing participation and must be the decision of the country's own citizens in order to be successful. Therefore, democratic nations should give aid and provide education to encourage the natural evolution of democracy instead of using force. Another reason is based on history. There are many examples of unsuccessful attempts to use military action to bring about democratic changes. For example, in recent decades in Afghanistan, the attempt to introduce democratic changes by entering the country and occupying it cost many thousands of lives and the endeavor was largely unsuccessful. Finally, efforts to impose democracy can harm a country's reputation. Many places around the world resent the actions that America has taken by invading, imposing economic sanctions, and manipulating politics around the world. Trying to impose democracy while ignoring any oppositions from the international community only does more harm than good. When you consider the basic democratic principle of freedom, the examples of history, and the harm to countries' reputations, it seems clear that attempting to force democracy on other countries is a mistake.

> 解説　「民主主義国家は他国に民主主義を強要すべきか」
>
> 強く反対する立場からのスピーチなので，冒頭で明瞭にその立場を述べている。①民主主義の根幹は自由意思なので強要するべきではない，②歴史的にも民主主義を強要して失敗した例には大きな犠牲が伴った，③民主主義を強要した側の評判が落ちるリスクがある，という3つの理由に対して具体例を加えて議論を展開している。②と③はアメリカを例に取っており，②をさらに展開したものが③となっている。このように先に話したものを利用して論点を深めるアプローチを用いるのもよい。

2. Information in the Internet age — too much or not enough?

In my opinion, there is no such thing as "too much information" as long as you can make a distinction between what is real and what is fake. Firstly, the spread of information in the Internet age has brought incredible technological changes. For example, medical science is helping people to live longer, healthier lives. Also, new technologies like smartphones and AI are driving economic growth and making people's lives more convenient. Secondly, greater access to information is bringing peace to the world. The spread of information through things like social media, news programming, and even movies and music is creating a new world culture that is helping to overcome old problems like racism and national rivalries. The better people understand each other, the less likely they are to come into conflict. Lastly, greater access to information is helping people to make better decisions if they have enough literacy. In the past, checking facts was difficult, but now, when politicians make claims or when people get medical advice, it's possible to check whether the information is true on the Internet. This is leading to a better-informed, better-educated general public. Based on the reasons I've given, I think it's obvious that increasing the availability of information on the Internet makes the world a much better place.

解説 「インターネット時代の情報——情報過多か情報不足か」

正面から答えるのではなく，条件付きながらも「情報過多ということはあり得ない」と聞き手の興味を引く切り出し方になっている。そこから，情報が多いことの利点を①インターネットによる情報の拡散は多くの技術的発展に寄与してきた，②人々が正しい情報を得やすいほど世界平和が実現しやすくなる，③正しい情報が伝わることで人々はよりよい判断ができる，という3つにまとめている。技術革新，世界平和，個人の生活の向上，と重複しない観点から，正しい情報が広く十分に与えられることの重要性を強調している。

3. Could genetic engineering be the solution to human health problems?

Although many people fear the idea of genetic engineering, I think it could be a solution to human health problems because it could cure diseases, increase human lifespans, and help people to overcome disabilities. Recently, a technology called CRISPR has been invented, which allows scientists to alter people's genes. Using CRISPR, it will someday be possible to prevent inherited illnesses, such as Huntington's disease. CRISPR also has the potential to lead to treatments for cancer and other deadly illnesses that kill millions of people. I've read that scientists also believe it may be possible to prevent cells from aging through genetic engineering. There are some plants and animals that live for hundreds or even thousands of years, and by combining their DNA with ours, it may be possible for humans to live much longer than they do now. Finally, genetic engineering offers hope to people with disabilities, such as people who are paralyzed or visually impaired. If cells, tissue, and bones can be regrown through genetic engineering, people who thought they would never walk or see again may someday regain these abilities. In conclusion, I believe that scientists should make every effort to pursue genetic engineering in order to improve human health.

解説　「遺伝子工学は人類の健康問題の解決策となるか」

　　　冒頭で「自分とは異なる立場」,「自分の意見」そして「3つの理由」のすべてを網羅する計画性の高いスピーチ。準備時間内にきれいに構成を決められればぜひトライしてみたいスタイルだ。ここでは遺伝子工学が多くの健康問題を解決できるはずだ,という立場から,以下の3点を強調している。① CRISPR(ゲノム編集技術の1つ)が深刻な病を治療できる可能性,②遺伝子操作によって実現される長寿,③身体の障害の克服,である。科学関連のトピックは知識がないと話せないので,常に情報をアップデートしておこう。

4. Is there too much emphasis on technology in professional sports today?

　While some people may say there is too much emphasis on technology in professional sports today, I think that the changes have mainly been beneficial. One important reason is that technology has greatly improved the performance of professional athletes. These days, athletes and coaches are able to analyze athletes' technique using slow-motion cameras and sophisticated computer systems. By seeing their mistakes and improving their efficiency, many athletes have been able to break world records. This also makes watching sports more exciting for spectators. Next, thanks to advances in sports medicine, injuries now heal faster, and even serious injuries that previously forced athletes to retire can now be healed. Health management using medical data has extended the lifespan of athletes as well. Finally, instant replays have made sporting events fairer. In the past, biased referees often affected the outcome of games. Now, though, officials and fans can see exactly what happened, so there are fewer bad calls because referees know their decisions will be reviewed. Furthermore, if bad calls are made, instant replays make it easier to correct them. As I've discussed, technology is improving athletic performance, making sports safer, and improving referees' decisions. For these reasons, I think there should be more, not less, emphasis on technology in sports.

解説　「今日のプロスポーツにおいてテクノロジーは重視され過ぎているか」

　　　冒頭部分では While some people may say ～, I think ～「一部の人

263

は〜という意見かもしれないが，私は〜と思う」という発話の定型パタ
ーンを使っている。定型パターンをいくつか持つと労せずに聞き手に正
確な意図を伝えられるので，ぜひ覚えておきたい。ここでは反対の立場
から，プロスポーツにおけるテクノロジーの重要性を強調している。理
由として，①データ分析によるパフォーマンスの向上，②スポーツ医学
の発展，③試合における審判の公平性の向上，の3点にテクノロジーが
寄与したとしている。

5. Agree or disagree: A single world government would benefit the planet

I'm opposed to the idea of a single world government. Please allow me to
explain why I believe it would be bad for the human race as a whole. First, a
world government would threaten human advancement. Currently, all
countries are in serious economic competition with each other. But without
borders, there would likely be fewer large companies that control their
industries and put effort into developing science or technology. This could
greatly slow down the progress of humankind. Another problem is that a
world government would likely be dominated by just a few powerful countries.
Politicians would tend to favor their own regions, giving them economic
benefits and working for their own interests rather than the good of all the
people in the world. Finally, it would be dangerous if there was that much
power in a single organization. Today, if one government is taken over by a
dictator, other countries and military alliances are able to act together to
weaken, contain, or overthrow the government that is causing problems. This
would be impossible, however, if one government controlled the entire world.
For these reasons, I think that the current system in which each country has its
own government is more beneficial to humankind.

解説 「賛成か反対か：単一世界政府は地球のためになる」

反対の立場から3つの考え得る理由，①競争がなくなることで人類の進
歩が停滞する可能性があること，②単一世界政府の下では一部の強国だ
けが恩恵を受ける可能性があること，③1つの組織に強大な力を与える
のは相互監視が効かなくなるので危険であること，を示している。この
ような「もし〜だったら」タイプのトピックの場合，1級レベルの話者
であれば，仮定の話と現実の話をきちんと分けて話せることが重要だ。
もしあなたが自信をもって仮定法を使えなければ，今日から練習を始め
よう。

2020-3

一次試験
筆記解答・解説　　p.266〜284

一次試験
リスニング解答・解説　p.285〜312

二次試験
面接解答・解説　　p.313〜316

解 答 一 覧

一次試験・筆記

1

(1)	3	(10)	3	(19)	1
(2)	2	(11)	1	(20)	3
(3)	4	(12)	2	(21)	2
(4)	1	(13)	1	(22)	1
(5)	1	(14)	1	(23)	2
(6)	4	(15)	1	(24)	3
(7)	4	(16)	4	(25)	1
(8)	1	(17)	4		
(9)	3	(18)	4		

2

(26)	3	(29)	2
(27)	3	(30)	3
(28)	4	(31)	2

3

(32)	4	(35)	3	(38)	2
(33)	2	(36)	4	(39)	1
(34)	3	(37)	2	(40)	4
				(41)	2

4　解答例は本文参照

一次試験・リスニング

Part 1

No. 1	2	No. 5	1	No. 9	3
No. 2	4	No. 6	1	No.10	2
No. 3	3	No. 7	4		
No. 4	4	No. 8	2		

Part 2

No.11	3	No.15	2	No.19	4
No.12	1	No.16	3	No.20	2
No.13	2	No.17	3		
No.14	4	No.18	4		

Part 3

No.21	1	No.23	2	No.25	1
No.22	4	No.24	3		

Part 4

No.26	3	No.27	2

| 一次試験・筆記 | **1** | 問題編 p.138 〜 140 |

(1) ― 解答 ③

訳 RC コンピューターズの新社長は，前社長が下したいくつかの決定を覆した。それらの決定は誤りで，会社の売り上げを損なっていると彼は考えていた。

語句 1「〜を永続させた」　　　　　2「〜に序文を付けた」
3「〜を覆した」　　　　　　　4「〜を十分に満足させた」

解説 前任者の決定が誤りで不利益を与えると新任者が考えるなら，その決定を「覆す」のが普通だと考えられる。override の類義語に overrule，overturn があるが，overturn は「（判決）を覆す」という意味で用いられることが多い。

(2) ― 解答 ②

訳 ブレンダンは子供のころから，バスケットボールチームのグリーンビル・ウルブズの熱烈なサポーターだ。毎シーズン，彼はできるだけ多く彼らの試合を見に行く。

語句 1「捕まえにくい」　　　　　2「熱烈な」
3「飾り立てた」　　　　　　4「無感動な」

解説 第 2 文から，ブレンダンがウルブズの大ファンだとわかる。ardent の類義語は avid，fervent，passionate など。

(3) ― 解答 ④

訳 その教会が子供向けに週末の宗教教育プログラムを提供し始めてから，毎月新しい家族が加わり，会衆の数が着実に増えた。

語句 1「仕切り」　　2「編集」　　3「抑制」　　4「会衆」

解説 congregation は，礼拝のため教会に集まる信徒たち，つまり「会衆」を表す集合名詞。動詞 congregate は一般的に「集まる」という意味で用いられるが，名詞になると宗教的な意味を帯びる。

(4) ― 解答 ①

訳 通貨の価値が今年突然下落したため，輸入品の価格が急上昇した。

語句 1「価値の低下」 2「翻訳，演奏」 3「境界，区別」 4「摘出，抽出」

解説 輸入品の値上がりは，例えば円安のように自国の通貨価値が「下落」した場合に起こる。depreciation の反意語は appreciation「価値の上昇」。

(5) ― 解答 ①

訳 新税が非常に不評だったので，財務大臣は，世間の批判が弱まるまで待ってから何かそれ以上の税金を導入することにした。

語句 1「弱まった」　　　　　　　2「染み込んだ」
3「腐食した」　　　　　　　4「〜をそそのかした」

266

解説 新税が不評な間に別の税金を導入するとさらに大きな反発を招く恐れがあるので，大臣は批判が「弱まる」のを待つことにしたのだと考えられる。abate は，強風や激しい感情などが「衰える，弱まる」という意味。

(6) ― 解答 ④

訳 Ａ：あなた，私はこの新しい家がいいと思うけど，今住んでいる家が売れなかったらどうなるかしら。

Ｂ：今の家が売れた場合に購入する契約をするよ。だから，今の家が売れなかったら，新しい家は買わなくてもいいんだ。

語句 1「全員出席の」 2「恐ろしい」 3「子の」 4「依存する」

解説 contingent on [upon] ～ は「～に依存する，左右される」という意味。今の家が売れたら新しい家を買うが，売れなかったら買わない，という契約を結ぶことになる。

(7) ― 解答 ④

訳 ルーシーはその自動車事故で軽い脳振とうを起こし，地元の病院で手当てを受けた。今後 2，3 週間は頭が痛むでしょう，と医師は言った。

語句 1「慰撫」 2「大都市圏」 3「妙な仕掛け」 4「脳振とう」

解説 日本語では日常的に使われる病名や医学用語，例えば脳に関する語であれば stroke「脳卒中」，infarction「梗塞」，dementia「認知症」，blood clot「血栓」などは英語でも覚えておきたい。

(8) ― 解答 ①

訳 塔のてっぺんまで上るのは，観光客たちが予想していたより骨が折れるとわかった。上り切ったころには，彼らのほとんどは疲れ果てていた。

語句 1「骨の折れる」 2「動揺した」 3「残虐な」 4「老いぼれた」

解説 てっぺんに着いたらほとんどの人は疲れ果てていたのだから，塔を上るのは身体的に相当きつかったのだ。arduous は「骨の折れる，難儀な」という意味。

(9) ― 解答 ③

訳 その市に引っ越したとき，ティムには古くて荒れ果てたアパートを借りるお金しかなかった。訪ねて来た母親は，彼が暮らす汚らしい状況にショックを受けた。

語句 1「巨大な」 2「補助の」 3「汚い」 4「不注意による」

解説 第 1 文から，ティムの住環境はかなりひどいとわかる。squalid は「汚い，むさくるしい」という意味。名詞 squalor「不潔，むさくるしさ」も覚えておきたい。

(10) ― 解答 ③

訳 その戦時指導者の新しい伝記に多くの人が憤慨した。彼らは著者を，証明されていないうわさを伝えて偉人をおとしめたと非難した。

語句 1「逸脱している」 2「～を懇願している」

3「～を中傷している」　　　　　**4**「(卵) を抱いている」

解説 多くの人は「証明されていないうわさを伝えて」いると非難しているのだから，その伝記は戦時指導者（＝偉人）をネガティブに描いていると考えられる。

(11) – 解答 **1**

訳 敵国が突然国境の部隊を増員したことを大統領は懸念していた。自国が強大な隣国に侵略され併合されるかもしれない，と彼は危惧した。

語句 **1**「併合された」　　　　　　　　**2**「産出された」
3「ためらった」　　　　　　　　**4**「提供された」

解説 「アネックス」は「別館」の意味で日本語になっているが，動詞 annex は「～を（武力で）併合する」という意味。その名詞「併合」は annexation。

(12) – 解答 **2**

訳 人は教育機関を卒業生の成功で判断する傾向があるが，学校がどれだけ優れているかを決める基準はそれだけではない。

語句 **1**「寓話」　　　　**2**「基準」　　　　**3**「主唱者」　　　　**4**「宣伝文」

解説 yardstick は「1 ヤードの物差し」が原義で，そこから比喩的に「（評価・判断などの）基準，尺度」という意味で用いられるようになった語。

(13) – 解答 **1**

訳 若手政治家のころ，ラメシュは将来のリーダーだと広くもてはやされた。しかし，重い病にかかった後，彼は政治家としてのキャリアを諦めざるを得なかった。

語句 **1**「褒めそやされた」　　　　　　**2**「砕かれた」
3「発酵された」　　　　　　　　**4**「皮をむかれた」

解説 praise，laud，commend は実績に基づいて「～を称賛する」という意味だが，tout は，実績の有無にかかわらず世間にアピールするために「～を褒めそやす」というニュアンスで用いられる。

(14) – 解答 **1**

訳 ヨーロッパの多くのチーズは鼻につんとくる香りを持つことでよく知られているが，そうしたチーズを食べるのが好きな人たちはその匂いをまったく気にしない。

語句 **1**「鼻につんとくる」　　　　　　**2**「攻撃的な」
3「物寂しい」　　　　　　　　　**4**「暗い，濁った」

解説 文の後半を裏返せば，好きではない人には匂いが気になるということになる。pungent は，快・不快を問わず味や匂いが舌や鼻を強く刺激するさまを表す。

(15) – 解答 **1**

訳 A：ジーナ，疲れ切った顔ね。どうしたの？
B：1日ずっと，姉の3人の子供の世話をしていたの。たった2，3時

間ですっかり疲れ果てたわ。

（語句）　**1**「くたくたに疲れた」　　　　**2**「曲がって」
　　　　3「耐え難い」　　　　　　　　**4**「公然の」

（解説）　frazzled は，身体的にも精神的にも疲れ切ったというニュアンスの語。名詞 frazzle を用いた be worn to a frazzle「くたくたに疲れる」という表現もある。

(16) － 解答　**4**

（訳）　犯人が銀行のセキュリティーについて熟知していたことから，犯人には銀行組織内部に<u>共犯者</u>がいたはずだと警察は考えた。

（語句）　**1**「有権者」　　**2**「専制君主」　　**3**「社交的な人」　　**4**「共犯者」

（解説）　セキュリティーに関する情報を漏らす「共犯者」が銀行内部にいた，と考えると文脈に合う。accomplice の類義語は confederate。また，complicit「共謀した」，complicity「共犯，共謀」といった関連語もまとめて覚えておきたい。

(17) － 解答　**4**

（訳）　Ａ：総理大臣についての最新の世論調査は見た？
　　　　Ｂ：うん，ぼろぼろだね。前回の公開討論会の後，彼の支持率は<u>たったの</u> 10％に下がったよ。

（語句）　**1**「率直な」　　**2**「毒性の強い」　　**3**「怒りっぽい」　　**4**「ごくわずかの」

（解説）　paltry は主に数量について「ごくわずかの，たったの」という意味。類義語は meager，measly など。反対に数量の大きさを強調する形容詞には staggering，whopping などがある。

(18) － 解答　**4**

（訳）　ビジネスパートナーが顧客に過剰請求をしていると知ったローランドは，辞職してその会社とのあらゆる関係を<u>断った</u>。彼はそうした行為にかかわりたくなかった。

（語句）　**1**「～の前兆となった」　　　　　　**2**「～を徐々に教え込んだ」
　　　　3「～を本国に送還した」　　　　　**4**「～を断った」

（解説）　sever は，「（物）を切断する，切り離す」ことにも，「（関係・連絡など）を断つ」ことにも用いられる。名詞は severance。

(19) － 解答　**1**

（訳）　その殺人は<u>計画的な</u>ものだったと警察は結論付けた。殺人犯が犯罪を一から十まで詳細に計画していたことは証拠から明らかだった。

（語句）　**1**「前もって計画された」　　　　**2**「つらい思いをした」
　　　　3「糸を通された」　　　　　　　**4**「少しずつ集められた」

（解説）　pre（前もって）＋ meditated（熟考された）と分解すると，語の意味を類推できる。premeditated は，犯罪や攻撃など他者に害を及ぼす行為について用いられる。

(20) – 解答 **3**

訳 ガルシア氏は，部下の1人が寝坊して仕事に遅刻したその日に図々しく昇給を願い出たことにあきれ返った。

語句 1「偽物」 2「憤怒」 3「図々しさ」 4「敬虔」

解説 遅刻したその日に昇給を求める振る舞いは「図々しさ」以外の何物でもない。gall は have the gall to *do*「図々しくも～する，厚かましくも～する」というフレーズで用いられることが多い。

(21) – 解答 **2**

訳 新製品を独創的な方法で売り出す当初の試みはほんの少ししか成功しなかったので，その会社は販売戦略を考え直すことにした。

語句 1「心から」 2「わずかに」 3「猛烈に」 4「熱心に」

解説 販売戦略を考え直すということは，当初の試みはうまくいかなかったことになる。marginally は (very) slightly と同義で，「わずかに，ほんの少し」という意味。

(22) – 解答 **1**

訳 一部の生徒が最終試験で不正をしたことを知った学校管理者たちは，関与した全員にすぐさま罰を与えた。

語句 1「（罰）を与える」 2「～を引きはがす」
3「～に配線工事をする」 4「～に没頭する」

解説 dish out には「～を（気前よく）配る，与える」という意味があり，目的語は money や advice のように人が喜ぶものもあれば，punishment や criticism のように人に嫌がられるものもある。

(23) – 解答 **2**

訳 フランクリンは，妹が宝くじで5千万ドル当てたという知らせに驚嘆した。知っている人が突然そんな金持ちになるなどと思ったこともなかった。

語句 1「吹き飛ばされた」 2「驚嘆した」
3「たたき壊された」 4「煮こぼれさせた」

解説 句動詞 blow away には，「～を撃ち殺す；～に大勝する」などのほかに，「～を驚嘆させる，感動させる」という意味がある。

(24) – 解答 **3**

訳 若いトラは生後18カ月になるころには自力で生きていくことができるのだが，2歳半くらいまでは母親と一緒にいるのが普通だ。

語句 1「～のへりに沿って進む」 2「～より遅れる」
3「～をやりくりする」 4「～とけんかをする」

解説 fend for *oneself* は「自分で自分の面倒を見る，独力でやっていく」という意味。動詞 fend には fend off「（攻撃・批判など）から身を守る，～をかわす」という句動詞もあり，こちらも覚えておきたい。

(25) −解答 **1** ....

訳 その報道カメラマンはホテルの従業員から，映画スターがそのホテルで休暇を過ごしているという裏情報を聞いたので，写真を撮ろうと急いでホテルに行った。

語句 **1**「内報を受けた」　　　　　　**2**「倹約された」
3「よく検査された」　　　　　**4**「詰まった」

解説 tip off は多くの場合「(警察) に内報する，密告する」という意味だが，問題文のように「(人) に秘密の情報を教える」という意味でも用いられる。

一次試験・筆記 **2** 問題編 p.141 ~ 143

全文訳 **ミッチェル地図**

　1750 年，イングランドに住むアメリカの医師ジョン・ミッチェルは，英国の高官ハリファックス伯爵から，北アメリカの地図を作製する任務を与えられた。当時，英国とフランスの関係は緊張しており，フランスが軍事的防御施設を建設していた北アメリカ植民地領土の支配権を巡る論争が続いていた。これらの植民地の経営責任者だったハリファックスは，こうした侵犯に抵抗する活動への政府の支持を結集しようと決意していた。彼がミッチェルに作るよう委託した地図は，この目的を達した。ミッチェルは北アメリカに対する英国の権利の主張の支持者で，この偏向は，地図の初期の版に彼が引いた境界と，英国の領土権の主張に関する多数の注釈に顕著に表れていた。その心情は，引き続き出版された地図ではさらに明白で，フランス領と認められる土地はもっと減っていた。これは世論と政界の意見を動かす力となり，植民地の利害を巡って両国が激しく競い合うこととなった一連の出来事を促進した。

　続いて起きた紛争でフランスが敗れた結果，英国は大量の領土を獲得したものの，戦争に注ぎ込んだ莫大な金額のせいで英国の国家債務は急増した。この損失を埋め合わせようと英国は 1765 年に印紙法を成立させたが，これはアメリカ植民地に最初の直接税を課すものだった。報復として植民地全域で抗議が噴出し，最終的にアメリカ独立戦争を招いた。1 つ軍事紛争が終わった後にこれほど早く別の紛争が起きたのだから，フランスに対する英国の勝利は明らかに高い代償を伴っていた。

　英国とそのアメリカ植民地の間で 8 年にわたって戦われた独立戦争は，1783 年に終結した。これはアメリカ人にとって明るい前途を予感させる結末であり，アメリカ人は英国の支配から自由になっただけでなく，領土の新境界線を画定するために英国とアメリカの交渉者がミッチェルの地図を用いたおかげで，土地をたんまり手に入れたのである。地図作製の裏にあった当初の意図と，戦争の余波が残る中で地図が最終的に果たした役割との対照を考えると，ミッチェル自身は——もし存命で調印を見届けていれば——まず間違いなく，自分の地図がそのように利用されたことを認めなかっただろう。

271

ミッチェルの地図は，フランスとの争いを鼓舞する助けとなる上で重要な役割を果たすことによって，究極的には，アメリカの英国からの独立への道を開いたのである。

語句 high-ranking「高位の」，ongoing「進行中の」，fortification「防備用施設」，annotation「注釈」，sway「（意見など）に影響を与える」，ensuing「続いて起こる」，exact「（税金など）を課す」，erupt「（暴力などが）発生する」，retaliation「報復」，culminate in 〜「〜で頂点に達する」，auspicious「縁起のよい，幸先のよい」，grasp「掌握，支配」，aftermath「結果，余波」，disapprove of 〜「〜を非とする」

(26) – 解答 **3** ....

解説 空所の前の文の intrusions は，フランスがアメリカ植民地に軍事拠点を築いていたこと。政府の支持を得てこれに対抗することがハリファックスの意図だったのだから，ミッチェルの地図が世論と政界の意見を動かしてフランスとの競争が激化した，という空所後の内容から考えると，地図はハリファックスの思惑どおりの成果を上げた，つまり「目的を達した」ことになる。

(27) – 解答 **3** ....

解説 空所文の前半は，フランスとの戦いが終わったら独立戦争が起きるという，紛争が相次いだ状況を指す。第2段落によると，対フランス戦で抱えた債務を埋め合わせるために英国が導入した印紙税への反発が引き金となって独立戦争が起きたのだから，フランスに対する勝利は，アメリカを失うという「高い代償を伴っていた」と考えると筋が通る。

(28) – 解答 **4** ....

解説 第1段落によると，ミッチェルは英国のアメリカ植民地政策の支持者で，地図では英国の領土が広くなるように境界を引いた。そして第3段落では，アメリカの領土を画定する際にその境界線が用いられ，アメリカは a generous amount of land を手に入れたと書かれている。自分の地図が英国に不利になるよう利用されたのだから，ミッチェルが生きていれば反対していただろうと考えられる。

全文訳 **演技と脳**

　俳優の役目は，考え方が自分とは大きく違うこともあるさまざまな異なる登場人物になり切ることである。しかし，これは時に俳優に害を及ぼすこともあるのではないかと言われてきた。俳優の演技の成功に決定的に重要なのは「不信の停止」として知られる現象で，何かと言うと，批判的思考を捨て，俳優は実際には演じられている登場人物ではないとわかっていても無視するよう，観客を納得させることである。だが，不信の停止が可能になるのは，演じる登場人物に俳優が没入できるからであり，多くの俳優は，登場人物の感情に浸り切ろうとしゃにむに努力することは心理的に悪影響を及ぼすと主張する。これが特に当てはまると言われるのは，家庭内暴力や性的暴行を題材とする物

272

語で俳優が人物を演じる場合である。

　この懸念は真剣に受け止められるべきだと今では思われる。カナダの大学の研究チームが，俳優がいろいろな条件下で一連の質問に回答する様子を観察した。条件の１つは，自分自身として，そしてまたシェークスピア劇の役の準備をした後で「登場人物として」回答することだった。被験者が劇の登場人物に「なって」いたときは，自己関連情報の処理に関連する脳の領域の活動が大きく減少したことを研究者たちは発見した。これが示唆するのは，俳優は登場人物に変容するとき，自らのアイデンティティーを危うくするリスクを実際に冒しているということである。

　カナダの研究者たちは，質問には外国のアクセントを使って回答し，しかしそのアクセントで自然に話すだろう人に「なる」ことなく回答するよう俳優たちに指示することによって，自己に関する自分たちの考えをさらに深く検証した。この実験中に観察された脳の活動は，単に普通でない話し方をするだけで自己の弱体化が助長され得ることを示唆した。これは，一般人が参加した別の研究によって裏付けられる。その研究では，被験者は自分の性格と友人の性格について質問された。その後，自分の性格について再度質問されると，被験者は，自分の性格についての認識を友人の性格についての認識に近づくよう無意識のうちに変化させていたことを示唆するようなやり方で回答し，一般人の脳ですらアイデンティティーを処理する際はある程度の不安定さを経ることを物語っていた。この研究結果は，単に俳優には限られない人々の自己感覚のもろさを強調しているように思われる。

　　　語句　inhabit「～に宿る，存する」，mind-set「考え方，意見」，disbelief
　　　「不信」，cast aside「～を捨てる」，take a toll「悪影響を及ぼす」，
　　　compromise「～を危うくする」，subconsciously「無意識に」，
　　　fragility「もろさ」

(29) – 解答　**2**

　解説　空所前の however から，俳優の役目は登場人物になり切ることだという前の文に対する異論，あるいはその否定的側面に関する記述が続くと予想される。段落後半にあるように，観客を納得させるために役になり切ろうとすることは「心理的に悪影響を及ぼす」と多くの俳優は言うのだから，「俳優に害を及ぼすこともある」ことになる。

(30) – 解答　**3**　　　　　　　　　　　　　　　　正答率 ★75%以上

　解説　空所が段落冒頭の文にあるので，この段落をまとめるような内容が入ると考えられる。素の自分としての回答と役になり切ったときの回答を比較した研究で，後者では「自らのアイデンティティーを危うくするリスク」があることがわかった。これは，第１段落では仮説として扱われていた「俳優に害を及ぼす」という懸念が研究で裏付けられたことを意味する。したがって，「この懸念は真剣に受け止められるべき」が文脈に合う。

(31)−解答 ②

解説 第3段落では，俳優に外国のアクセントで回答させた研究と，一般人に自分と友人の性格について答えさせた後で自分の性格だけについて答えさせた研究について書かれている。いずれも，外国のアクセントまたは友人の性格に引きずられる回答だったのだから，「単に俳優には限られない」という研究結果が得られたことになる。

一次試験・筆記 **3** 問題編 p.144 ～ 152

全文訳 **ビジネスと持続可能性**

　2015年に国際連合は持続可能な開発目標（SDGs）を全会一致で採択したが，これは，貧困への取り組みと環境保護によって，より繁栄した持続可能な地球の未来を実現する力となることを各国政府と事業者と一般市民に等しく求める構想である。多くの事業者がSDGsを熱心に受け入れているように思える一方で，これらの企業が言うことと実際にすることの間には気がかりな断絶があるように見える。世界的な投資運用会社PIMCOが行ったある調査によると，多数の会社が企業報告でSDGsに言及していることは，SDGsの存在と重要性に関する意識の広がりを示している。しかし，目標に向けた数値化可能な進展を示す数字を挙げた会社は10分の1に満たず，この調査報告書の執筆者たちは，「ほとんどの企業は，事業価値を付加できる活動と目標を特定するための専門的知識をいまだに持っていない」と結論付けた。

　この落差が，SDGsが比較的新しくなじみのないことの結果かもしれないのは確かだが，もっとシニカルな見方をしている人たちもいる。数多くの企業が，企業が実際よりも環境に関心を寄せていると一般大衆を欺いて思わせる試みを指す用語である「グリーンウォッシング」をしていると非難されているのである。17のSDGsのうち相当数は，クリーンエネルギーや生態系の保護・回復といった課題を直接扱うもので，批判者たちの指摘によると，既に進行中のプロジェクトだけでなく既存の実践を取り上げ，それらをSDGs目標に似た形に仕立て上げることはいとも簡単であり，SDGsは曖昧な言葉遣いのせいでこうした行いには非常に弱い。加えて，一部の企業は，SDGsコンプライアンスの名の下に二枚舌を使っているという非難も受けている。環境保護団体に多額の寄付をして世間のイメージをよくしようとしながら従業員には生活賃金を払わない，というのがその一例である。SDGsの意図は普遍的に有益な革新と変容への触媒になることだったのだから，こうした行いは明らかに誤りである。

　グリーンウォッシングを疑われる企業に対する非難はSDGs報告をしばしば好意的でない見方で描くが，この慣行を巡る論争には希望を持てる側面があるかもしれない。いかなる程度のSDGs報告であっても，持続可能性の実践について，企業をそれまで以上の精査にさらす。近年では，最も腰の重い企業ですら持続可能性の取り組みを拡大するよう世論が駆り立てるのが極めて一般的になっているが，それにもかかわらず，こ

のことがグリーンウォッシングをしているという非難の殺到を招くのは避けられない。しかし，グラスゴー・カレドニアン大学ロンドン校の講師エリカ・チャールズは，多国籍企業の実践におけるほんのわずかな，広報活動に触発された変化でも，重大な「影響と波及効果を同業他社に与え，事業への取り組み方法を見直すようにさせる」こともあるのではないかと言う。こういった理由から，批判者は不十分な報告だと理解したものに対する非難を多少自制することが肝要だ，と主張する人もいるだろう。メディアからの過度に厳しい反発に思いとどまって，企業がまったく何もしなくなるかもしれないからである。環境の持続可能性を装って行われる企業の取り組みが失敗したり不誠実なものだったりしても，結局のところまったく無駄な努力ではないのかもしれないと思える。

> 語句 unanimously「全員一致で」，disconnect「断絶」，reference「～に言及する」，quantifiable「数量化できる」，disparity「相違，不均衡」，in the pipeline「進行中で」，wording「言葉遣い，言い回し」，double-dealing「二枚舌，言行不一致」，beef up「～を増強する」，living wage「生活賃金（最低限の生活を維持するために必要な賃金）」，catalyst「触媒，触発するもの」，transformation「変化，変容」，miss the mark「的を外す，失敗する」，unflattering「好意的でない」，silver lining「明るい希望」，uncompromising「妥協しない，頑固な」，avalanche「殺到」，miniscule「微小な」，ripple effect「波状効果」，backlash「（社会的な）反発」，insincere「誠意のない」，wasted「無駄な」

(32) – 解答 4 　　　　　　　　　　　　　　　　　正答率 ★75%以上

問題文の訳 PIMCO が行った調査によると，

選択肢の訳
1 企業が設定した SDGs 目標に向けた進展の 2015 年以来の減速は，目標が利益に悪影響を与えると企業が恐れていることを示している。
2 国際連合の動機に対する不信感が，多くの企業が SDGs の重要性をなかなか認めようとしていない主な理由である。
3 企業は発表する報告書の数字を改ざんすることで，SDGs に違反していることを隠そうとしているように見える。
4 多くの企業は SDGs に賛同しているが，事業に有益な方法でどのようにそれらを実行するかを決められないでいる。

解説 第 1 段落からわかるのは，多くの企業が SDGs の理念を受け入れながら，どのように企業活動に組み込めばいいのか戸惑っている現状である。それに合致するのは 4。本文の many businesses ... embrace the SDGs を many corporations approve of the SDGs と，add business value を beneficial to their business と言い換えている。

(33) – 解答 2

問題文の訳 企業が「グリーンウォッシング」をしていると非難される 1 つの理由は何か。

選択肢の訳　1　SDGsのいくつかの不明瞭な言葉遣いが大きな混乱を招いているので，企業の方針に関する誤解がほぼ確実に生じる。
2　一部の企業は，自分たちが既にしていたことをSDGsに沿って行動する取り組みの一部に見せかけようと試みている。
3　SDGsの多くに設定されている非現実的な目標が，個々の目標すべてを満たしているふりをするよう一部の企業に強いている。
4　SDGsの多くは環境とは無関係なのだから，それらに重点を置き，環境関連の目標はないがしろにした方が楽だということを企業は知っている。

解説　第2段落では，企業への批判が2つ取り上げられている。1つは，SDGs以前からしていることをSDGsへの取り組みに見せかけ，「やっている感」を演出すること。もう1つは，多額の寄付と低賃金のように表の顔と裏の顔を使い分けていること。**2**が前者と一致する。**1**の「SDGsのいくつかの不明瞭な言葉遣い」は本文にあるが，企業が都合のいいように利用しているだけで，企業についての誤解を招く原因になっているわけではない。

(34) – 解答

問題文の訳　エリカ・チャールズの論評は，この文章の文脈ではどう解釈するのが最適か。

選択肢の訳　1　大企業は，同業他社に影響を与えて環境規制に抵抗させることによって，SDGs報告を骨抜きにしようとしている。
2　批判者は1つの産業の最大手企業に重点を置くのではなく，グリーンウォッシングの責任を問われる全事業者に目を向けることが重要である。
3　重要とは思えない小さな変化を大企業が実行するときは，過度に批判的になるのは賢明ではないかもしれない。
4　大企業のSDGs報告の大半は非常にいい加減に行われているので，全面的に新しいシステムを開発する必要がある。

解説　第3段落第1文の the practice は greenwashing を指す。これに silver lining「希望を持てる側面」があるということは，この段落では greenwashing のポジティブな面を扱うと予想される。わずかな変化が一石を投じて業界全体を変えることもあり得る，というチャールズのコメントと，何もしないよりはグリーンウォッシングの方がましなのだから厳し過ぎる非難で企業を委縮させるべきではない，という続く内容から，**3**が正解。

全文訳　**家賃統制**

米国全域の主要な大都市での住居費急騰に直面し，多数の自治体は，低所得住民が安

定した住宅利用機会を確保できることを目的とする家賃統制法を課している。一般にこれらの法律は市が運営する委員会によって定められ，住居費が毎年ごくわずかな率以上に上昇しないことを保証する。表面上は，家賃統制は弱い市民を経済的苦境から保護するものと見なすことができるものの，これらの制限は経済学者からほぼ一様に糾弾されている。彼らの主張によると，家賃統制には家主の収入を制限する効果があるのだから，法律は新規の不動産物件を建てるインセンティブを減少させる。利用できる賃貸物件が乏しくなるのは避けられず，需要と供給の原理に従って，家賃統制を免除された住宅の家賃は急激に押し上げられる。加えて，家賃統制された物件に居住する幸運に恵まれた借家人は，自分の経済状況がよくなってもその物件にとどまり続ける傾向があり，より所得の低い人たちが利用できる住宅供給に与える悪影響を大きく拡大させる。そうであるなら，家賃統制法が改善しようとするまさにその問題を法自体が悪化させるのは明白だ，と経済学者は主張する。

　一方，家賃統制支持派は，建設されて間もない住宅は一般に家賃統制法を免除されていると指摘する。実際，これまでの研究が示すところでは，市場に以前から存在する不動産物件に家賃統制規制が課せられている都市では，ほとんどの規制は新規の住宅建設に悪影響を与えない。しかし経済学者の主張では，その代わり家主は家賃統制によって，賃貸不動産を販売用物件に変えたり，さらには長期居住者に売ったりといった手段を講じることを余儀なくされ，賃貸住宅の供給不足をさらに助長する。

　経済学者と家賃統制支持派両者が一致している点が1つある。家賃を制限すれば，金銭的に恵まれない人々が自宅から強制退去させられるリスクが下がることである。さらに，サンフランシスコ住民の住所と移住の履歴を調べた研究者の調査では，家賃統制された物件に住んでいた低所得層，特にマイノリティーは，家賃統制された物件から退去した後も市内に居住し続ける可能性がより高かった。これは低所得層の一部には明るい調査結果だが，賃貸物件の供給不足に由来する安価な選択肢の欠如のために住宅を見つけることのできないほかの人々の問題にこの対策は対処していない，と経済学者は言う。

　しかし，経済学者がしばしば見逃すのは，住宅の安定性の問題である。米国の税法は，税の減免という形で，持ち家の所有者にかなりの給付金を与えている。つまり，家を購入するのに十分な資金を持たない人は，これらの給付金を利用できないのである。したがって家賃統制がなければ，低所得の借家人は金銭的苦境のために立ち退かされるリスクが特に高くなる。強制的な引っ越しが心身の健康に与える有害な影響は多くの文書で裏付けられており，男性より女性への影響の方が深刻だと証明されている。妊娠中にストレスを受ける女性の子供が長期的な心理的影響を被ることを考えれば，これは特に気がかりであり，また，住居がほとんど安定しない子供の方が，高校を卒業する確率も低い。家賃統制を公然と非難する際に経済学者が挙げる量的な論拠に幾分の妥当性があるのは確かだが，家賃統制のより広くより有益な意味合いを市の職員たちは見逃してはならない。

　　　語句　skyrocket「急騰する」，municipality「自治体」，drive up「（価格など）を急速に上昇させる」，amplify「～を増強する，拡大する」，

aggravate「～を悪化させる」，preexisting「以前から存在する」，for-sale「販売用の」，shortfall「不足」，displace「～を強制退去させる」，vacate「～を立ち退く」，subset「部分集合」，tax break「税の軽減措置」，evict「～を立ち退かせる」，decry「～を公然と非難する」

(35) − 解答 ③

問題文の訳 家賃統制について経済学者が共通して批判していることの1つは，

選択肢の訳
1 近年の建設ブームに起因する家賃の急上昇を家賃統制が補えていないことである。
2 賃貸アパートを規制する市の委員会が，家賃統制されている物件から人々を強制的に出て行かせるよう，家主から容易に影響され得ることである。
3 ほかの人たちほど経済的に恵まれていないかもしれない住民が利用できる住居の選択肢を，家賃統制が実際には制限していることである。
4 家賃統制は市内で利用できるアパートの供給を増やす助けとなるが，アパートの需要を減らす一因にもなることである。

解説 問題文の common criticism made by economists は，第1段落第3文の universally condemned by economists に対応している。同段落の続く記述によると，家賃収入が低いと新しい物件が建たない→家賃統制されていない物件の家賃が上がる→家賃統制されている物件を借りている人たちが出て行かない→さらに所得の低い人たちが借りる物件が不足する，という結果を招く。これに合致するのは **3** である。

(36) − 解答 ④

問題文の訳 家賃統制支持派は以下の記述のどれに最も賛同する可能性が高いか。

選択肢の訳
1 家賃統制は一時的な住宅不足の結果かもしれないが，不足は長期的には建設の増加によって相殺される。
2 築年数がたった多くの建物は家賃統制の適用を受けないのだから，賃貸住宅不足は実際には新規建設事業の欠如の結果である。
3 家賃統制法に対応して家主が取る対策は，実際には住宅を利用できる可能性が増える結果になる傾向がある。
4 家賃統制法は通例既に利用可能な賃貸不動産にしか影響しないので，家賃統制は経済学者が主張するほど住宅市場に影響しない。

解説 第2段落前半に家賃統制支持派の主張が書かれている。新規に建設される住宅には家賃統制が適用されないのだからさして悪影響は受けない，というのが彼らの考えで，家賃統制が新規住宅建設へのインセンティブをそぐという経済学者たちの主張と対立する。したがって **4** が正解である。

(37) − 解答 ②

問題文の訳 この文章の筆者は最終段落で家賃統制について暗に何と言っているか。

278

選択肢の訳 1 家賃統制法に関する経済学者の警告は現時点ではほとんど意味を成さないが，この問題は将来の世代によって再考される必要がある。

2 家賃統制法にいかなる欠点があろうと，経済学的分析だけでは測れない重要な役割を社会で果たしている。

3 家賃統制法が住宅市場に与える悪影響は，家賃統制法がもたらし得る社会的恩恵より大きい。

4 家賃統制法がより豊かな人々に与える恩恵は，最終的には社会全体が利用できるようになる。

解説 最終段落では，housing stability の問題を取り上げている。住まいが安定しなければ心身の健康が侵され，子供の将来にも悪影響を与える。家賃統制にはこうしたマイナス面を防ぐ役割もあるというのが筆者の考えで，経済学者の主張に一理あることは認めながらも，家賃統制を肯定的に捉えている。経済学者による批判を drawbacks とまとめ，本文の the quantitative arguments economists make を economic analysis と短く言い換えた **2** が正解。

全文訳 ## ナセルと汎アラブ主義

1952 年，陸軍将校のグループが，英国の支援を受けるエジプトの君主制から権力を奪い，国王ファルーク 1 世を国外に追放した。反乱軍は自由将校団として知られるエジプト軍隊内部の民族主義運動の一部で，このグループは，指導者であるガマル・アブデル・ナセルという若いエジプト人将校の反植民地イデオロギーを中心に結成されていた。クーデター時の公式のトップは陸軍上級将校である戦争の英雄ムハンマド・ナギーブで，ナセルは彼を名目だけの長に据えた。ナセル自身はその役回りに必要な威信を当時は欠いていたので，彼は新政権に正統性を与えるため，ナギーブが一般大衆から集めるとてつもない声望を利用していたのである。しかし，身の程をわきまえずナセルに反旗を翻そうとしたナギーブは権力の座から排除され，黒子から表舞台に立ったナセルが 1954 年に国の指導者の地位に就いた。

政権を担っていた長い年月の間に，ナセルはエジプトを作り変えた。彼は，無償の教育と医療，住宅供給の改善，労働改革を含む遠大な近代化プログラムを策定した。君主制の間の土地所有の封建制度によって富の不平等な配分が生まれていたが，ナセルは，農民に有利なように条件を改善し，個人が所有できる土地の量を制限する改革でこれに対処した。ナセルは庶民の出であり，人民の味方を自任していた。彼のイデオロギーは「ナセル主義」として知られるようになったが，社会主義と富の再配分に根差すものであり，また彼以前の支配者と違い，ナセルは汚職と無縁だった。

しかし，だからと言って彼の統治が温情的だったわけではない。異論は容赦なく弾圧され，ナセルは民主主義へのあからさまな軽蔑を表明した。彼は，中東全域におけるアラブ統一，すなわち汎アラブ主義というビジョンを達成するには，自身の平等主義的社会プログラムと苛烈な施行戦術はどちらも欠かせないと考えていた。統一されたアラブ

世界でエジプトが盟主としての役割を担うことになるとすれば，まずエジプトは，ナセルの政策に害を及ぼす可能性のある敵は誰であっても確実に政治の舞台から遠ざけながら，国内的に経済を強化し社会福祉を改善しなければならなかった。

反植民地主義がナセルの外交政策の基本であり，彼はアフリカ全土の解放運動を支援した。自身のカリスマと演説の才に助けられたナセルは，エジプト社会を変容させたのみならず，ほかのアラブ諸国の熱望の対象となり得るモデルも示した。ナセルが国際的に注目を浴びるようになったのは，1956 年，戦略的かつ経済的に重要なスエズ運河を国有化したときのことである。スエズ運河はエジプト領土内に位置するにもかかわらず，英国とフランスが共同で所有し運用していたのだが，エジプト兵たちが運河の支配権を奪った。イスラエルとフランスと英国の三軍がエジプトに侵攻し，スエズ地域のエジプト軍を直ちに打ち負かして「スエズ危機」として知られるようになったものを突然引き起こした。しかし，エジプトは外交分野でもっと大きな成功を収めた。ソビエト連邦は，その地域での将来的な影響力拡大をもくろんで当時エジプトの歓心を買おうとしており，西側帝国主義の事例と見なすものを激しく非難した。ソ連政府は，侵攻者が撤退しなければ西側ヨーロッパへの核攻撃も辞さない構えすら見せた。恐れおののいた米国はソ連政府との対立を回避するため舞台裏で介入し，結果的にヨーロッパとイスラエルの侵攻者は屈辱的な撤退をした。ナセルは西側に公然と逆らってスエズ危機を切り抜けたのみならず，見込みの低い賭けに勝利したのだが，しかしその幾分かは米ソ政府の思いがけない仲裁によるものだった。それにもかかわらず，ナセルの行動の結果，中東全域で大衆から賛美の声が湧き上がり，中東内で彼の指導者としての役割が強化された。

ナセルが権力の絶頂にあったとき，アラブ統一は真に実現可能に思われた。植民地支配を脱した中東諸国は連帯して共に立ち上がり，独立した地政学的ブロックとしての自己同一性を獲得した。だが，1958 年に成立した，エジプトとシリアの連合国であるアラブ連合共和国は，ナセルが課した中央集権化政策にシリアが不満だったせいで短命に終わった。アラブ諸国の統一が可能だという考えは，エジプトが周辺アラブ国家を率いてイスラエルとの破滅的な戦争を行った 1967 年に打ち砕かれた。この戦争の結果，相当な領土が失われただけでなく，また，アラブ人の魂は消えることのない深い傷を負ったのである。

ナセルの人気は 1970 年に亡くなる前の年月で衰えたが，たとえ今日の不和と争いが汎アラブ主義の見通しを暗くしているとしても，中東の至る所で彼は相変わらず多くの人から偶像視されている。ナセル後のエジプトでは貧富の隔たりが変動し続け，社会的平等というナセルの目標が成就する可能性は低そうである。しかし，ナセルの統治への郷愁にもかかわらず，エジプト人は彼のカリスマに目がくらみ欠点が見えなかったのだ，と主張する評論家もいる。欠点とは例えば，彼の富の再配分政策が，今日まで続く労働人口の国家への過度の経済的依存を助長したことである。そうした非難は確かにもっともだが，結局のところ，常にナセルの人気は業績というより主として彼のイデオロギーの産物だったのだから，この郷愁はおそらくこの先も長く存続することだろう。

（語句）anticolonialist「反植民地の」，coup「クーデター」，figurehead「名

目だけの長」, legitimize「～を合法と認める」, overstep「～を（踏み）越える」, defy「～に（公然と）反抗する」, remake「～を作り直す」, far-reaching「遠大な」, feudal「封建制度の」, benign「慈悲深い，優しい」, dissent「不賛成，異議」, egalitarian「平等主義の」, bolster「～を強化する」, precipitate「～を突然引き起こす」, court「（好意など）を得ようと努める」, avert「～を回避する」, humiliating「屈辱的な」, long odds「あまり見込みのないこと」, fortuitous「偶然の，思いがけない」, intercession「仲裁，とりなし」, adulation「賛美」, consolidation「強化」, geopolitical「地政学的な」, centralization「中央集権化」, abiding「持続する」, psyche「魂，精神」, icon「偶像」, disunity「不和」, fluctuate「変動する」, fruition「達成，実現」, failing「欠点」, overreliance「過度の依存」

(38) – 解答 ②

問題文の訳 自由将校団について何が推測されるか。

選択肢の訳
1 ムハンマド・ナギーブがグループの指揮権構造を変えようと試みた後，ガマル・アブデル・ナセルはグループを解散する必要があるだろうと考えた。
2 ナギーブの名声のためグループの行動は広範な支持を受けたが，彼が地位を失ったことは，彼が必要不可欠な人物ではなかったことを示していた。
3 グループが権力を握った後どの程度の民主主義を認めるかについて，ナセルとナギーブの間に対立があった。
4 その主義主張はナギーブの考えに基づいていたが，ナセルは，クーデターが暴力的でなく確実に平和的に行われるようにするには自分が統御しなければならないと感じた。

解説 第1段落が自由将校団によるクーデターを簡潔にまとめている。ナセルはナギーブの名声を利用してクーデターを実行したが，結局ナギーブを排除して自ら権力の座に就いた。つまり，**2**のように，ナギーブはお飾りにすぎなかったことになる。**1**と**3**に関する記述はない。自由将校団はナセルの反植民地イデオロギーの下に結集したのだから，**4**は前半を読んだだけで誤りだとわかる。

(39) – 解答 ①

問題文の訳 この文章の筆者によると，ナセルの苛烈な政治的政策の主たる理由は何だったか。

選択肢の訳
1 エジプトが主導してアラブ世界を統一するという彼の究極の目標は，国内政策が障害なく導入されることを必要とした。
2 普通の人々の富の増加と教育向上は，社会主義を支持する政敵の台頭を招くかもしれない，と彼は恐れていた。

20年度第3回　筆記

3 自身が庶民の出であり富を持たないことで，エジプト人大衆もほかの政治家たちも彼を弱い指導者と見なすようになるだろう，と彼は恐れていた。

4 君主制への彼の反対はほとんどの人に共有されておらず，ほとんどの人は，前の政権下の方が生活の質はよかったと考えていた。

【解説】第3段落前半に，問題文と同じ harsh という語がある。この段落によると，ナセルは，アラブ統一を主導するには国内基盤の安定が必須と考え，苛烈な政治を行った。異論を弾圧し敵を政治の舞台から遠ざけるという本文の内容を without obstacles とまとめた **1** が正解である。

(40) – 解答 ④

【問題文の訳】以下の記述の中で「スエズ危機」の帰結を最もよく表しているのはどれか。

【選択肢の訳】
1 最初は勝利に思えたものが，エジプトと非常に重要な西側同盟国との関係に修復不能なダメージを与えたことがわかった。

2 危機が終わりに近づくとナセルはわずかに優勢になったが，エジプトの軍事的敗北は長期的成功が不可能なことを証明した。

3 当初ナセルはソ連政府の側についているように見えたが，危機の終わりに際しての彼の政策変更は，彼が実際は米国と同盟を結んだことを証明した。

4 ナセルは西側列強に対して大きな政治的勝利を勝ち取ることができたが，とはいえその一部は彼の力が及ばない要因によるものだった。

【解説】第4段落中ほど以降がスエズ危機の記述に充てられている。軍事的には敗北したエジプトだったが，ソ連と米国の外交的介入によって最終的には勝利を得た。段落後半で the fortuitous intercession「思いがけない仲裁」と書かれているように，核攻撃をちらつかせて影響力拡大を狙うソ連と，ソ連との対決を恐れる米国という，ナセルの思惑を超えた国際政治事情を **4** が factors beyond his control と表している。

(41) – 解答 ②

【問題文の訳】この文章の筆者は，多くの現代エジプト人がナセルと彼の統治についてどう感じているかをどのように説明しているか。

【選択肢の訳】
1 エジプトの労働者階級は，ナセルを個人としては尊敬しているものの，イスラエルとの戦争がもたらしたダメージについては彼を許していない。

2 ナセルの政策に起因する変化による影響よりも，ナセルがエジプトのために示した哲学とビジョンによる影響を多く受けている。

3 ナセルが導入した全エジプト人のための社会福祉と教育における変化は，彼に続く指導者たちの欠点にもかかわらず，長期的利益をもたらしている。

4 ナセルの個性とカリスマが彼の統治中にエジプト人をどれだけ鼓舞したかを理解できない人々によって形作られている。

解説 ナセル時代への郷愁が今も根強く残ることについて，最終段落に説明がある。ナセル人気は彼の accomplishments ではなく ideology によるものだ，という最終文がポイント。**2** が accomplishments を the changes that arose from his policies と言い換え，ideology を the philosophy and vision と言い換えている。ideology とは，エジプトの指導下によるアラブ統一という理想のことである。

一次試験・筆記 **4** 問題編 p.152

解答例 Beneath globalization's seemingly positive effects of international trade and integrated markets lie worrying issues. Centralized authoritative bodies, suppression of local economies, and the exploitation of foreign labor are just some of the problems accompanying a more globalized world.

As economies grow more interconnected, further regulation of trade and business becomes necessary. More powerful nations, however, are often quick to seize upon this by establishing central trade commissions and all-encompassing laws, leading to smaller countries having less autonomy to make their own decisions regarding how money, labor, and products flow through their economies.

In addition to drawing power away from developing countries, globalization also stifles their local economies. The rising desirability of certain products grants corporations that create them greater financial leverage to purchase land and materials in poorer countries. By doing so, corporations appropriate valuable local resources for foreign markets that could be better used for local consumption.

Even more concerning is the treatment of foreign labor. Manufacturing is often outsourced to poorer countries to slash costs, which, some argue, provides jobs for low-income communities. In reality, this fosters an unhealthy reliance on large companies, which are then free to exploit local labor — including children — with low wages and poor conditions.

From the perspective of developing countries, it is clear the problems arising from one-sided regulatory pressure, monopolization of smaller economies, and the abuse of poor, vulnerable workers are aspects of globalization that, if ignored, will only continue to worsen.

トピックの訳 「賛成か反対か：グローバリゼーションは今日の世界においてプラスに働く力である」

解説 　グローバリゼーションは，経済・政治・文化・情報・テクノロジーなど多方面から論じることができるトピックである。この解答例は論点を経済に絞り，disagree の立場からグローバリゼーションを批判している。第 1 段落でポイントとして挙げているのは「中央集権化した権威機関」「地域経済の抑圧」「海外労働力の搾取」の 3 つ。第 2 段落以降でそれぞれのポイントを 1 つずつ詳述し，最終段落で 3 つのポイントを再確認して結論とする，基本的な 5 段落構成のエッセーである。

　最初のポイントについては，貿易とビジネスの規制は大国の主導下で作られる委員会や法により決定されるので，小国が自律的に意思決定することができなくなるとしている。2 つ目のポイントについては，地域経済を潤すべき特産品や資源が企業に吸い上げられて海外に流出し，地域経済を圧迫すると論じている。そして最後のポイントについては，海外の安価な労働力を求める大企業によって，子供を含む労働者が搾取されていると指摘している。いずれも，グローバリゼーションは先進国と発展途上国の格差を埋めるものではなく，むしろ拡大させるものだという視点で貫かれており，非常に説得力のある内容になっている。

　トピックに agree の立場を取るなら，第 1 段落冒頭に書かれているように，国際貿易と統合市場のメリットについて述べることができる。例えば，貿易の自由化は世界的な経済成長を促す，市場が統合され関税が撤廃されれば消費者はより安価で質の高い製品やサービスを利用することができる，発展途上国は先進国の技術を取り入れることで自国の発展につなげることができる，など，一般的にグローバリゼーションの恩恵と考えられるポイントは数多い。

　この解答例の表現面で注目したいのは，第 1 段落と最終段落でのポイントの大胆な言い換えに加え，第 3 段落冒頭で In addition to drawing power away from developing countries，第 4 段落冒頭で Even more concerning is と，長いつなぎ言葉を用いていることである。例えば Secondly，In addition，Furthermore などの簡単な副詞（句）で済ますのではなく，このように前の段落の内容を受ける形で次の段落につなぐことで，全体の流れが非常にスムーズになっている。

284

一次試験・リスニング Part 1

問題編 p.153〜154

No.1 - 解答 ②

スクリプト ★: That was the last interviewee. Looks like we have some decent candidates for the manager position.
☆: I'm not convinced we should stop looking yet.
★: But the position has been open for over a month. I've been covering as best I can, but it's a struggle.
☆: I know, but the job requires a very specific skill set.
★: Several applicants seem to meet most of our requirements. Perhaps you should adjust your expectations a little. I mean, we could wait forever for the perfect person.
☆: I'm not so sure. I don't want to jump the gun.
Question: What does the man imply?

全文訳 ★: 面接を受けるのはあの人が最後だったね。マネージャーのポジションにふさわしい候補者が何人かいるようだ。
☆: 探すのをやめた方がいいとはまだ確信できないわ。
★: だけどこのポジションは1カ月以上空席のままだよ。僕ができる限りカバーしているけど、四苦八苦している。
☆: そうだけど、この仕事にはとても特別なスキルセットが必要よ。
★: 何人かの応募者は僕たちの条件のほとんどを満たしているように思える。君の期待は少し修正が必要なんじゃないかな。つまり、完璧な人を待っていても切りがないかもしれない。
☆: それはどうかしら。私は早まったことはしたくない。
質問: 男性は暗に何と言っているか。

選択肢の訳 1 女性は自分のスキルセットを向上させることを考えるべきだ。
2 女性が設定している基準は高過ぎる。
3 彼はそのポジションの候補者として考慮に値する。
4 適任者が見つかるまで彼がカバーすることができる。

解説 今回の応募者に適任者が数名いると考える男性は、意見を異にする女性に対して、3つ目の発言で Perhaps you should adjust your expectations a little. と言っている。つまり、女性の期待(=基準)は高過ぎると思っていることになる。jump the gun「早まったことをする」。

No.2 - 解答 ④

スクリプト ☆: Frank, will you be available on Friday for a feedback session about last month's sales figures?
★: Friday? I've got two meetings in the morning, and I promised a

client I'd visit their office that afternoon.

☆： Frank, you know I've been telling you to delegate more.

★： Believe it or not, I took your advice to heart. But my whole staff is working overtime now, so I can't ask them to do more.

☆： Then you have to ask your boss to bring additional sales staff on board.

★： I wish it were that easy. As you know, the president wants to cut costs.

☆： Yeah, but without a properly functioning sales team, the company's future would be pretty hopeless. I think you have a strong case, so don't give up so easily.

Question: What does the woman suggest that the man do?

全文訳 ☆： フランク，金曜日に，先月の売上高に関するフィードバックセッションに出る時間はある？

★： 金曜日？　午前中に会議が2つあって，その日の午後はクライアントのオフィスを訪問する約束がある。

☆： フランク，ほかの人にもっと仕事を振るよう，ずっと言い続けているじゃない。

★： まさかと思うかもしれないけど，ご忠告は心に染みたよ。でも，今は部下全員が残業をしているから，もっとやってくれとは頼めないんだ。

☆： じゃあ，追加の営業スタッフを入れてくれるよう，上司に頼まないと。

★： そう簡単だといいんだけど。知ってのとおり，社長はコストを削減したがっているから。

☆： そうね，だけど，きちんと機能する営業チームがなければ，会社の将来に希望があまり持てなくなる。あなたには十分な論拠があると思うから，そんなに簡単に諦めちゃ駄目よ。

質問：女性は男性が何をすることを提案しているか。

選択肢の訳 1　営業スタッフに相談する。

2　フィードバック会議の日時を変更する。

3　部下の給料を削減する。

4　追加のスタッフを頼む。

解説 部下も忙しいので自分で仕事をたくさん抱え込んでいる男性に，女性が改善策を述べている。女性は3つ目の発言で ask your boss to bring additional sales staff on board と提案し，男性が否定的な答えをすると，最後の発言で，営業チームの重要性を力説している。つまり，スタッフの増員を頼むべきだという提案は一貫していることになる。

No.**3** – 解答 **3** ●

スクリプト ★： Hi, Lisa. How are you enjoying your violin classes?

286

☆： They're good but very demanding.

★： Yeah, I studied with Mrs. Jackson for years.

☆： I've been playing since I was a kid, but she has me working on the basics.

★： It's just to perfect your technique.

☆： I know, but she's such a slave driver!

★： You do know that she's the most sought-after teacher in New York, and a virtuoso herself.

☆： That's true.

★： It'll be tough, but if you stick with Mrs. Jackson, you won't regret it.

Question: What do we learn about Mrs. Jackson?

全文訳
★： やあ，リサ。バイオリンの授業は楽しい？

☆： いい授業だけど，とてもきついわね。

★： そうだよね，僕は何年もジャクソン先生の下で学んだから。

☆： 私は子供のころからずっと弾いているのに，先生は基礎をやらせるのよ。

★： それは君の技術を完璧にするためだよ。

☆： わかるけど，先生はすごいスパルタ教師だわ！

★： 先生がニューヨークで最も引っ張りだこの教師で，彼女自身が名演奏家だと，君も知っているだろう。

☆： そのとおりね。

★： 大変だけど，ジャクソン先生についていけば後悔することはないよ。

質問：ジャクソン先生について何がわかるか。

選択肢の訳
1 ニューヨークの交響楽団で演奏している。
2 バイオリンを教え始めたばかりだ。
3 生徒に多くを要求する。
4 初心者を担当する方が好きだ。

解説 女性は最初の発言で授業は very demanding だと言い，3つ目の発言で先生は slave driver「厳しい教師，人使いの荒い人」だと述べている。したがって **3** が正解。ジャクソン先生の活動拠点はニューヨークだが，交響楽団に所属しているとは言っていない。virtuoso「名演奏家」。

No.**4** – 解答 ④

スクリプト
☆： Hey, Patrick, you better watch out for the boss today.

★： Why? What's up?

☆： She needed to make a bunch of copies this morning, but the copy machine was still broken.

★： Oh no. I was supposed to call and get the maintenance company to come. It totally slipped my mind.

20年度第3回 リスニング

287

☆： Don't worry too much. She tends to blow things out of proportion, but she usually forgives and forgets pretty quickly.

★： Well, I'll get on it now and stay under her radar for the rest of the day.

Question: Why is the man worried?

全文訳
☆： ねえパトリック，今日は上司に気を付けた方がいいわよ。

★： どうして？　何があったの？

☆： 今朝彼女はコピーを大量に取る必要があったんだけど，コピー機が壊れたままだったの。

★： しまった。僕がメンテナンス会社に電話して，来てもらうことになっていたんだ。すっかり忘れていたよ。

☆： 心配し過ぎることはないわ。彼女は何でも大げさに騒ぎがちだけど，たいてい結構早く許してくれるし，忘れるから。

★： うーん，コピー機の件はすぐに何とかして，後は今日1日彼女の目を逃れることにするよ。

質問：男性はなぜ心配しているのか。

選択肢の訳
1 彼は上司と会う約束を守らなかった。
2 彼は上司の代わりにコピーを取るのを忘れた。
3 彼はうっかりコピー機を壊した。
4 彼はコピー機を修理してもらわなかった。

解説
女性は2つ目の発言で，今朝上司が使おうとしたらコピー機が壊れたままだったと話し，男性はそれに対して I was supposed to call and get the maintenance company to come. と言っている。コピー機の修理依頼は男性の担当だったことがわかるので，**4** が正解。get on ～「～に取りかかる」，stay under *A's* radar「Aの目を逃れる」。

No.**5** – 解答 ①

スクリプト
★： So, Janet, did the boss like our ideas for the new TV ad campaign?

☆： Actually, he said our budget is going to be halved.

★： That's insane. That won't be nearly enough.

☆： Tell me about it. He wants to put more ads on the radio. Thinks it's a more cost-efficient way to reach our target market.

★： Not according to our marketing polls.

☆： He also suggested we try another direct-mail campaign and see how that pans out.

★： Well, I guess we'll just have to do what he wants.

Question: What does the boss want these people to do?

全文訳
★： それで，ジャネット，新しいテレビ広告キャンペーンの僕たちのアイデアを上司は気に入ってくれた？

☆： 実はね，私たちの予算は半分になると言われたわ。

★： むちゃくちゃだ。それじゃ到底足りないよ。

☆： 本当よね。彼はラジオでもっと広告を流したいの。うちのターゲット市場に届くには，その方がコスト効率がいいと思っているのよ。

★： 僕たちのマーケティング調査によるとそうじゃない。

☆： ダイレクトメールキャンペーンをまたやってみて，どんな結果になるか様子を見てはどうかとも言われたわ。

★： うーん，彼が望むようにするしかなさそうだね。

質問：上司はこの人たちにどうしてほしいのか。

選択肢の訳　**1**　広告戦略を変更する。

　　　　　　2　テレビ広告の結果を待つ。

　　　　　　3　もっとマーケティング調査を行う。

　　　　　　4　ダイレクトメールキャンペーンを中止する。

解説　女性が上司の意向を男性に伝えている。上司の希望は put more ads on the radio と try another direct-mail campaign なので，2 人が最初に提案したテレビ広告という戦略は却下されたことになる。したがって正解は **1**。pan out「（結局〜に）終わる」。

No.6 – 解答 ①

スクリプト ☆： Tom, long time no see. How's everything with your new job at the ad company?

★： In one word, stressful. The majority of ads I create are for engineers, so I have to get all the technical details right, and that's not easy.

☆： And I guess you have a lot of tight deadlines.

★： Yes, but that's nothing new. The problem is I have to do a lot more research now, too.

☆： You always did great work at RCB Graphics, so I'm sure you'll get used to it soon.

★： Thanks. I hope you're right.

Question: What is the man's concern?

全文訳 ☆： トム，久しぶり。広告会社での新しい仕事はうまくいっているの？

★： 一言で言うと，ストレスがたまるね。僕が作る広告の大半はエンジニア向けだから，技術的な詳細を全部正確に理解しなければならなくて，それが楽じゃないんだ。

☆： それに厳しい締め切りをたくさん抱えているんでしょうね。

★： うん，でもそれは今に始まったことじゃない。問題は，今では前よりずっと多くの調査をしなければならないことなんだ。

☆： あなたは RCB グラフィックス社ではいつも立派な仕事をしていたんだ

から，きっとすぐに慣れるわよ。

★：ありがとう。そうだといいんだけど。

質問：男性の懸念は何か。

選択肢の訳　**1**　彼はまだ十分な能力があると感じていない。
2　RCB 社での彼の顧客は不満を抱いている。
3　彼は厳しい締め切りを抱えることに慣れていない。
4　彼は RCB 社の製品は売れないだろうと思っている。

解説　男性は，新しい仕事はストレスがたまると述べ，技術的詳細の正確な理解の必要性と調査量の増加をその理由に挙げている。そして，すぐに慣れると励ます女性に対しても I hope you're right. と控えめに答えていることから，自分が今の仕事に competent「十分な能力がある」とは思っていないことがわかる。厳しい締め切りは nothing new だと言っているので **3** は誤り。

No.7 – 解答 ④

スクリプト　★：I think I've been tricked!

☆：Tricked? By whom?

★：A salesman came to my door. He was so persuasive I didn't know how to say no.

☆：Oh no, you didn't buy something, did you?

★：Well, he said it was a revolutionary new filing system. But when the package arrived this morning, it was just a plastic box. For $100!

☆：Have you tried to contact him?

★：I rang the number he gave straightaway, but it turns out there's no such number.

☆：I think you're going to have to chalk this one up to experience.

Question: What does the woman think?

全文訳　★：だまされたみたいだ！

☆：だまされた？　誰に？

★：セールスマンが訪ねてきたんだ。すごく説得力があったから，断りようがなくて。

☆：あらまあ，何か買わなかったでしょうね。

★：うーん，革命的な新型ファイリングシステムだと言っていた。だけど今朝荷物が届いたら，ただのプラスチックの箱だった。100 ドルしたんだよ！

☆：連絡してみた？

★：教えてもらった番号にすぐ電話したんだけど，結局そんな番号はないんだよ。

290

☆： この件をいい経験としなければならないでしょうね。

質問：女性はどう思っているか。

選択肢の訳　**1**　男性はその番号に電話し続けるべきだ。
　　　　　　2　男性はこの経験を使ってセールスマンになるべきだ。
　　　　　　3　男性はファイリングシステムを利用するべきだ。
　　　　　　4　男性はお金を取り戻す望みを捨てるべきだ。

解説　女性の1つ目と2つ目の発言は男性に話を促すための発話で，女性の考えは最後の発言にある。chalk ～ up to experience は「（失敗など）を貴重な経験として覚えておく，教訓とする」という意味なので，今回の件については諦めた方がいいと思っていることになる。したがって**4**が正解。

No.**8** – 解答 **2**

スクリプト　★： So, what do you think of the office space, Ms. Kato?

☆： The location is outstanding, but it's quite a bit more spacious than what we were originally looking for.

★： I understand that, but given the way your firm has been expanding over the past two years, it might make sense to allow yourself some flexibility.

☆： Good point. On a square-meter basis the price is certainly reasonable. And I'd hate to have to think about relocating again, at least not for several years.

Question: What will the woman probably do?

全文訳　★： それで，このオフィス物件はどう思われますか，カトーさま。

☆： 立地は素晴らしいけれど，私たちが最初探していたより少し広々としていますね。

★： それはわかりますが，そちらの会社がこの2年でどれだけ成長してきたかを考えると，多少は柔軟性を持たせておくのが賢明かもしれませんよ。

☆： 確かにそうね。平米当たりだと賃料は確かにお手ごろです。それに，少なくとも数年は，また移転しなければならないなんて考えるのも嫌だし。

質問：女性はおそらくどうするか。

選択肢の訳　**1**　もっと便利な場所を探す。
　　　　　　2　このオフィス物件を借りることに決める。
　　　　　　3　よそでもっと狭いところを探す。
　　　　　　4　数年以内にまた引っ越す。

解説　不動産屋と客の会話。女性の a bit more spacious という発言を受けて，男性は allow yourself some flexibility と提案しているが，これは，会社のさらなる成長を見越してこの広いオフィスを借りておくということ。女性の最後の発言から，提案に対して前向きな気持ちになっている

ことがわかる。

No.9 – 解答 ③

スクリプト

★: This is a great apartment. I think it would suit your parents well.

☆: Yeah, the location is great, and it's in the vicinity of the train station. It might need a few modifications for them, though.

★: Well, let's think about what they'll need. Your dad's still fairly strong, so the outside steps shouldn't be a problem for him.

☆: Yeah, but I think a ramp would be better, especially if Mom needs a wheelchair, which is looking increasingly likely.

★: I'm sure a ramp could be added. Maybe even a wheelchair lift, if it comes to that.

☆: There's also no handrail to support them if they were to slip. Mom's going to want to bring her friends over, and they're all in their 70s or 80s.

★: Safety's definitely a concern. And since we're on the subject, there's no outdoor light by the walkway leading to the steps.

☆: I'm thinking we could probably take care of what we've discussed, which would keep costs down.

★: Maybe, but let's ask the agent if the building's owner could do them first, or even if they're possible. If not, we can look at some other places before we decide.

Question: What is one thing these people say about the apartment?

全文訳

★: 素晴らしいマンションだね。ご両親にぴったりだろうと思う。

☆: ええ，立地が素晴らしいし，駅にも近い。両親のために少しリフォームする必要があるかもしれないけど。

★: じゃあ，ご両親が必要になるものを考えてみよう。お父さんはまだまあまあ達者だから，外の階段は問題にならないはずだ。

☆: ええ，だけどスロープの方がいいだろうと思う。特にママが車椅子が必要になったらね。そうなりそうな感じがどんどん強くなっているし。

★: スロープはきっと足せるよ。ことによると車椅子用の昇降機も。必要になればだけど。

☆: 足を滑らせでもしたときに体を支える手すりもないわ。ママは友達を連れて来たがるだろうし，みんな70代か80代だもの。

★: 安全性は確かに懸念材料だ。その話になったついでだけど，階段につながる通路に外灯がないね。

☆: 今話し合ったことはたぶん自分たちで何とかできるんじゃないかしら。そうすれば費用を安く抑えられるだろうし。

★: そうかもしれないけど，ビルのオーナーがそうしたことを最初にやって

くれるかどうか，あるいはそもそもそうしたことが可能かどうか，業者に聞いてみよう。無理なら，決める前にほかの物件を当たってみてもいいんだし。

質問：この人たちがこのマンションについて言っていることの1つは何か。

選択肢の訳　**1**　公共交通機関に十分近くない。
　2　自分で修理するとお金がかかり過ぎるだろう。
　3　高齢の訪問客には危険かもしれない。
　4　外にスロープを作るスペースがない。

解説　女性の高齢の両親にマンションを探している夫婦の会話。女性の最初の発言の it's in the vicinity of the train station から，**1** は誤り。また女性は最後の発言で，それまで話していたリフォームを自分ですれば which would keep costs down と言っているので，**2** も誤り。男性の3つ目の発言の I'm sure a ramp could be added. から，**4** も誤り。女性が3つ目の発言で，母親が招くであろう高齢の友人たちにからめて，手すりがないので危ないといったことを述べているが，それが **3** と合致する。

No.10 解答　②

スクリプト　☆：Thanks for coming to this meeting. I wanted to catch up on progress with the English program at our affiliated elementary school. Did you get everything sorted out?

★：Quite the opposite. We observed classes and talked with teachers, and it's the same old story. The two part-timers are doing great in the circumstances, though.

○：Yes, but one of them told me she may give notice if things continue as they are.

☆：You're kidding. Give me some specifics.

★：Well, curriculum development is so far behind schedule that teachers often have no materials for classes.

☆：But that's Helen's job, not theirs. That's the whole reason we sent her out from the university.

★：Exactly. And that seems to be the heart of the problem. Helen seems to be leaving work early and isn't getting the curriculum done.

○：I also hear that some of the teachers are afraid to confront her, too, since they think she's their boss.

☆：But she's not. Margaret is.

★：That's not how they see it.

○：So, what can we do? Are you considering pulling Helen out of the elementary school?

★ : We're not there yet. I suggest we sit down with her and have a frank discussion. We need to set clear goals and then monitor things more carefully.

☆ : OK, and we also need to make clear that Margaret's in overall charge of the English program and make sure that she's being more proactive.

Question: What is one of the problems at the elementary school?

全文訳　☆ : 今日は集まってくれてありがとう。うちの付属小学校の英語プログラムの進捗状況を教えてもらいたかったの。万事うまく処理できた？

★ : 正反対です。授業を視察して教師たちと話したんですが，よくある話ですよ。この状況で，2人の非常勤教師はとてもよくやっていますけどね。

○ : ええ，だけどそのうち1人に，このままこんなふうに続くのなら辞表を出すかもしれないと言われました。

☆ : そんなばかな。詳しいことを教えて。

★ : えー，カリキュラム開発が予定よりずっと遅れていて，教師に授業の教材がないこともしばしばなんです。

☆ : だけどそれはヘレンの仕事で，教師たちの仕事じゃないわ。そのためだけに大学から彼女を派遣したのよ。

★ : そのとおりです。そしてそれが問題の核心のようです。ヘレンは仕事を早退して，カリキュラムを終わらせていないようなんです。

○ : 教師たちは彼女を上司だと思っているので，直談判するのを怖がっている人もいると聞いています。

☆ : だけど彼女は上司じゃない。上司はマーガレットよ。

★ : 彼らはそういう見方はしていないんです。

○ : じゃあ，どうすればいいでしょう。小学校からヘレンを外すことを検討しますか？

★ : それはまだ早いでしょう。彼女と膝を交えて率直に話し合うことを提案します。明確な目標を定めて，もっと慎重にいろいろ見極める必要があります。

☆ : わかった，それに，マーガレットが英語プログラムの全体責任者であることをはっきりさせて，彼女がもっと能動的に動くようきっちりさせる必要もあるわね。

質問：小学校の問題の1つは何か。

選択肢の訳　1　カリキュラムのレベルが生徒に合っていない。

2　ヘレンが責任を果たしていない。

3　マーガレットが強過ぎて過度に威張り散らしている。

4　教師たちが教材を作り過ぎている。

294

解説 小学校で起きている問題の内容は，男性の2つ目の発言以降で述べられている。カリキュラム開発が遅れていて教材が足りない→それはヘレンの仕事だ→ヘレンがサボってカリキュラムを終わらせていない，と続く会話の流れから，**2**が正解。本当はマーガレットがbossなのに教師たちはヘレンをbossと見なしているのだから，**3**は誤り。

A

(スクリプト) **Political Beliefs**

Many people assume that people's political beliefs are the result of choices made based on logical thinking and the observation of reality. Recent research, however, has questioned this assumption. A study by researcher Chris Fraley, for example, has suggested that children raised by strict, authoritarian parents often have conservative views as adults. On the other hand, children who grow up in households where they are given more freedom and allowed to express their opinions tend to identify themselves as liberal when they reach adulthood.

Other researchers have found evidence that the reasons for one's political beliefs are at least partially biological. For instance, a study by two political scientists demonstrated that conservatives tend to react faster and more intensely than liberals to negative stimuli such as shocking photos. This "negativity bias," the scientists say, appears to be hard-wired into the brain. Moreover, DNA comparisons in another study also indicated that liberals and conservatives have differences in certain genes that affect how the brain reacts to threats or how open it is to new ideas. It is therefore possible that nature, as well as nurture, shapes our political beliefs.

Questions

No.11 What did Chris Fraley's research suggest?
No.12 What do the two political scientists believe about "negativity bias"?

全文訳 **政治的信念**

人々の政治的信念は論理的思考と現実の観察に基づいて行われる選択の結果だ，と多くの人は想定する。しかし，最近の研究が，この想定に異議を唱えている。例えば，研究者クリス・フレイリーによる研究は，厳格で権威主義的な親に育てられた子供は大人になるとしばしば保守的な考えを持つことを示唆している。一方，より多くの自由を与えられ，意見を述べることを許される家庭で育つ子供は，成人に達すると自らをリベラルだと認識する傾向がある。

人の政治的信念の理由が少なくとも部分的には生物学的なものである証拠を発見した研究者もいる。例えば，保守的な人の方がリベラルな人より，ショッキングな写真などのネガティブな刺激に対してより速くより激しく反応する傾向があることを，2人の政治学者による研究が証明した。この「ネガティビティバイアス」は脳のシステムに組み込まれているように思える，とこの学者たちは言う。さらに，別の研究におけるDNAの比較も，脅威に対する脳の反応の仕方や脳が新しい考えにどのくらい開かれているかに影響するある特定の遺伝子が，保守的な人とリベラルな人では違うことを示した。したがって，育ちだけでなく生まれも，私たちの政治的信念を形成することがあり得るのである。

> 語句 authoritarian「権威主義の」，hard-wired「（脳などに）深く刻み込まれた」，nurture「養育，育ち」

No.11 解答 ③

質問の訳 クリス・フレイリーの研究は何を示唆したか。

選択肢の訳
1 厳格な親の子供の方が反抗する可能性が高い。
2 家族の価値観は政治的信念とほとんど関係がない。
3 どのように育てられるかが人の政治的考えに影響する。
4 人は親とは違う視点を取ろうとする。

解説 第1段落で述べられているフレイリーの研究によると，厳格で権威主義的な親の子供はしばしばconservativeに育ち，自由に意見を述べられる家庭の子供はliberalに育つ傾向がある，という違いがある。つまり，3のように，育つ環境がpolitical viewsに影響を与えることになる。

No.12 解答 ①

質問の訳 2人の政治学者は「ネガティビティバイアス」についてどう考えているか。

選択肢の訳
1 生物学的要因が原因に思える。
2 人にネガティブな刺激を無視させる。
3 成人の間の脳でだけ発達する。
4 保守的な人よりリベラルな人の方に多く影響する。

解説 第2段落によると，政治学者が言っているのは，negativity biasはbe hard-wired into the brainに思えるということ。これは「脳に生得的に備わっている」という意味で，政治的信念の理由の一部はbiologicalなものだという段落冒頭の記述に対応している。したがって1が正解。

B

スクリプト **Households and Marriage**

According to the US Census Bureau, people living in married households in the US are now outnumbered by those living in other types of household arrangements. Various factors are responsible for this change, including the tendency of younger adults to live together before getting married. The senior-citizen demographic is another factor behind the change, because when one spouse dies, a "single-person household" is created. For a number of reasons, including greater wealth, elderly people who lose a spouse are tending to live on their own rather than move in with their families as they may have in the past. What is more, elderly people are less likely to remarry than younger adults are.

Another notable fact is that college graduates tend to postpone marriage until they have greater financial stability. Reduced job opportunities and lower salaries also seem to be making it harder for some people with less education to get married and start a family. Both factors may be contributing to the lower number of married households. Interestingly, however, when college graduates eventually do get married, they are now less likely to divorce, resulting in lower divorce rates overall.

Questions

No.13 What is one cause of the declining number of married households?

No.14 What has been observed among college graduates?

【全文訳】 **世帯と結婚**

米国国勢調査局によると，米国では既婚世帯に住む人より，ほかのタイプの世帯構成に住む人の方が今では数が多い。この変化を引き起こしている要因はさまざまだが，若年層の人たちが結婚前に一緒に住む傾向はその１つである。一方の配偶者が死ぬと「単身世帯」ができるから，高齢者の世代人口もこの変化の背後にある別の要因である。資産の増大などいくつかの理由で，配偶者を亡くした高齢者は，昔なら家族と同居を始めたかもしれないが，むしろ１人暮らしをする傾向にある。さらに，高齢者は若年層より再婚する可能性が低い。

もう１つの注目すべき要因は，経済的により安定するまで大卒者が結婚を遅らせる傾向があることである。雇用機会の減少と給料の減少も，学歴の低い一部の人が結婚し家族を持つことをより困難にしているように思える。両方の要因が，既婚世帯数の減少の一因なのかもしれない。しかし，興味深いことに，大卒者が最終的にいざ結婚してみると，離婚する可能性は低く，その結果離婚率が全体的に低下している。

（語句） outnumber「～より数で勝る」，demographic「世代人口」

No.**13** 解答 ❷

質問の訳 既婚世帯数が減少している原因の１つは何か。

選択肢の訳 1 若い大人の比率の低下。

2 配偶者が死んだ後１人で暮らす高齢者。

3 再婚する離婚者の減少。

4 離婚率の上昇につながる資産の増大。

解説 第1段落で，既婚世帯数減少の理由を2つの年齢層に関して述べている。1つは，若年層が結婚前に一緒に住むこと。もう1つは，elderly people who lose a spouse are tending to live on their own であること。後者を言い換えた **2** が正解である。

No.14 解答 ④

質問の訳 大卒者の間に何が観察されているか。

選択肢の訳 1 家族を養おうと苦労している。
2 学歴の高い配偶者を見つけようとする傾向がある。
3 しばしば結婚してすぐに子供を持つ。
4 今ではもっと年齢を重ねてから結婚する。

解説 第2段落では college graduates について，経済的に安定するまで結婚を遅らせること，実際に結婚したら離婚する可能性が低いことの2点が述べられている。結婚を遅らせることを **4** が get married later in life と言い換えている。

C

スクリプト **Positive Psychology**

Psychology has traditionally focused on classifying and treating mental illness. In recent years, however, a movement known as positive psychology has been attempting to revolutionize the profession. Rather than focusing on the treatment of mental illness, positive psychology seeks to actively prevent it by helping people build feelings of fulfillment and self-worth. One of its central principles is that one's circumstances in life play a much smaller role in determining happiness than most people imagine. Accordingly, people who win the lottery, or even suddenly suffer a serious physical injury, will frequently return to their previous level of contentment within a matter of months. Positive psychology therefore seeks to help individuals find peace of mind through altering their attitudes and ways of looking at the world.

Positive psychology, however, is not without its critics. According to noted psychologist Paul Wong, since there are limitations on time and financial resources, changing the focus of psychology to individuals who are currently free of mental dysfunction could have serious consequences. Logically, if more resources are devoted to that group, people with existing mental issues are more likely to be neglected.

Questions

No.15 What is one of the main ideas behind positive psychology?

No.16 What is one criticism Paul Wong makes of positive psychology?

全文訳 **ポジティブ心理学**

心理学は伝統的に，精神病を分類し治療することに重点を置いてきた。しかし近年，

ポジティブ心理学として知られる運動が，この専門職に革命を起こそうと試みている。ポジティブ心理学は精神病の治療に重点を置くのではなく，人が充足感と自己価値感を築くのを助けることによって，積極的に精神病を予防しようと努める。その中心原則の1つは，幸福を決定する上で人生の境遇が果たす役割はほとんどの人が思うよりずっと小さい，ということである。したがって，宝くじを当てた人は，あるいは突然体に重傷を負った人ですら，しばしばほんの数カ月のうちに以前の満足度に戻ることになる。それ故，ポジティブ心理学は，個人の考え方と世界の見方を変えることを通して個人が心の平静を見つける手助けをしようと努める。

しかし，ポジティブ心理学を批判する人がいないわけではない。著名な心理学者ポール・ワンによると，時間と金銭的資源には限りがあるのだから，心理学の重点を現時点で精神的機能障害を持たない個人に変えると，重大な結果を招くかもしれない。論理的には，その集団により多くの資源を割けば，現に精神的問題を抱える人たちがないがしろにされる可能性が増すことになる。

語句 self-worth「自尊心」，contentment「満足」，dysfunction「機能障害」

No.15 解答 ②

質問の訳 ポジティブ心理学を支える主な理念の1つは何か。

選択肢の訳
1 精神病は直ちに治療されなければならない。
2 外的要因は人を幸福にするものではない。
3 人はもっと個人主義でなくなるべきだ。
4 精神病は人が思うよりもありふれている。

解説 質問の one of the main ideas は，第1段落中ほどの One of its central principles に対応している。その文の one's circumstances in life を External factors と，determining happiness を what make people happy と言い換えた **2** が正解。

No.16 解答 ③

質問の訳 ポール・ワンのポジティブ心理学に対する1つの批判は何か。

選択肢の訳
1 伝統的療法より高額である。
2 効果が出るまで長時間かかる。
3 精神病患者の治療に影響を与えるかもしれない。
4 精神病の予防に何の効果もない。

解説 第1段落によると，ポジティブ心理学は精神病を prevent「予防する」ことを重視する。それに対する批判者として第2段落で登場するポール・ワンは，限られた時間と金銭的資源を予防に回すことに疑義を呈している。**3** が，最後の文の people with existing mental issues are more likely to be neglected を全体的に言い換えている。

20年度第3回 リスニング

D

Radium Poisoning

　Radium is now known to be an extremely hazardous substance, but when first discovered, it was actually used as a health tonic. Radium glows in the dark, so it was also used to paint the faces of clocks and dials used by the US military during World War I. The company that made them employed women as they were considered better suited to the delicate work of painting because of their slender fingers. The women would paint with radium all day, frequently inserting the brushes between their lips to ensure they had very fine points.

　Eventually, however, the women began dying of radium poisoning. Their employer denied responsibility, claiming that radium was harmless. However, the research that the employer relied on was conducted by the radium industry, whose scientists had a clear interest in claiming that radium was safe. In the years that followed, lawsuits were brought against the company. Eventually, the courts ruled against the company. It was one of the first cases in the US in which an employer was held accountable for its employees' health issues.

Questions

No.17 What is one way the women were exposed to radium?
No.18 What does the speaker say about the women's employer?

全文訳　**ラジウム中毒**

　ラジウムは極度に危険な物質だと今ではわかっているが，発見された当初は，強壮剤として実際に用いられた。ラジウムは暗闇で発光するので，第1次世界大戦中に米軍が用いた時計の文字盤と目盛りに塗装するためにも用いられた。それらを製造した会社は女性を雇用したが，それは，女性の方が指がほっそりしているので塗装という繊細な作業に向いていると考えられたからだった。女性たちは一日中ラジウムで塗装し，ブラシの先端がきちんととがっているよう，ブラシを唇の間に挟むこともしばしばだった。

　しかし，最終的に女性たちはラジウム中毒で死に始めた。雇用主は，ラジウムは無害だと主張して責任を否定した。しかし，雇用主が依拠した研究はラジウム産業が行ったもので，産業の科学者たちには，ラジウムが安全だと主張することに明白な利害関係があった。続く年月の間に，その会社に対する訴訟が相次いだ。最終的に，法廷は会社を有罪とする判決を下した。これは，雇用主は従業員の健康問題に対して責任があるとされた，米国で最初の裁判の1つだった。

　　　語句　poisoning「中毒」，health tonic「強壮剤」

No.17 解答 ③

　　質問の訳　女性たちは1つにはどのようにしてラジウムに被ばくしたか。
　　選択肢の訳　**1** ラジウムを含む強壮剤を与えられた。

2 指にラジウムを塗る必要があった。
3 ラジウムで覆われたブラシを口の中に入れた。
4 ラジウムを用いて自分が使うブラシをきれいにした。

解説 第1段落の最後で述べられている the brushes は，ラジウムを塗るために使ったブラシだと考えられる。それを唇に挟んだということは，3のように，口の中に入れたことになる。強壮剤はラジウムが用いられた一例，指は女性がラジウム塗装の仕事に雇われた理由として挙げられているだけである。

No.18 解答 ④

質問の訳 女性たちの雇用主について話者は何と言っているか。
選択肢の訳
1 塗料の中のラジウムは危険ではないと証明した。
2 女性たちの被ばく量が低いことを示した。
3 訴訟を避けることに成功した。
4 偏った研究結果を用いた。

解説 第2段落の However, the research ... の文がポイント。雇用主はラジウム産業が行った研究に依拠したと述べた後の whose scientists had a clear interest in claiming that radium was safe から，研究に携わった科学者が研究結果をゆがめた可能性があることを話者は示唆している。それを biased を用いて表した 4 が正解である。

E

スクリプト **Technology in Our Bodies**

A technology company in the state of Wisconsin was recently the first in the United States to implant microchips into the hands of some of its workers. Now those employees can unlock doors, operate office equipment, log into computers, and buy items from vending machines at the company with a simple wave of the hand. Supporters of this technology view such implanted devices as cutting-edge, efficient, and inevitable. Some people insist that enhancing human bodies with technology will be necessary for them to be able to compete against machines, robots, and artificial intelligence in the workplaces of the future.

Among critics, the biggest issues are security and privacy. Such technology could eventually contain tracking devices that would allow managers to monitor their workers' movements even outside the workplace. Another concern is that outside parties could access private data. Although the manufacturer maintains the implanted devices are secure, they cannot rule out hacking entirely. Health concerns are another issue. Any device implanted into the body carries the potential for infection or migration away from the implant site. Furthermore, although such devices have been approved by the US Food and Drug Administration, the long-term health effects of implanted devices are unknown.

Questions

No.19 What do supporters say about implanted microchips?

No.20 Why are some people against placing microchips into people's bodies?

【全文訳】 **体内のテクノロジー**

　ウィスコンシン州のテクノロジー企業が，最近，米国で初めて一部の労働者の手にマイクロチップを埋め込んだ。今ではそれらの従業員は，単に手を振るだけでドアのロックを解除し，オフィス機器を操作し，コンピューターにログインし，会社の自動販売機で品物を買うことができる。このテクノロジーを支持する人たちは，そうした埋め込まれた装置は最先端で効率的で不可避だと考える。人体をテクノロジーで向上させることは，将来の職場で人体が機械，ロボット，人工知能と渡り合うために必要となるだろうと主張する人たちもいる。

　批判的な人たちの間で最大の争点は，安全とプライバシーである。そうしたテクノロジーは，最終的に，管理者が労働者の動きを職場外でも監視することを可能にする追跡装置を含むようになるかもしれない。もう１つの懸念は，外部の第三者が個人データにアクセスするかもしれないことである。埋め込まれた装置は安全だと製造者が主張しても，製造者はハッキングの可能性を完全に排除することはできない。健康に関する懸念も，もう１つの争点である。体に埋め込まれたどんな装置も，感染の可能性や埋め込んだ場所から移動する可能性を秘めている。さらに，そうした装置が米国食品医薬品局の認可を得ているとはいえ，埋め込まれた装置が健康に与える長期的影響は未知である。

　【語句】 cutting-edge「最先端の」

No.19 解答 **4**

【質問の訳】 支持する人たちは埋め込まれたマイクロチップについて何と言っているか。

【選択肢の訳】 **1** ロボットの利用を進歩させる。
2 会社のセキュリティーを大きく向上させる。
3 人間が生き残るために必須である。
4 将来の職場では避けられない。

【解説】 第１段落半ばの Supporters of this technology ... 以下の２文が支持者の主張。まず，cutting-edge, efficient, and inevitable とこのテクノロジーの特徴を挙げ，続いて，将来の職場でロボットなどと渡り合うために必要だと具体的に述べている。inevitable を unavoidable と言い換えた **4** が正解である。

No.20 解答 **2**

【質問の訳】 なぜ一部の人は人の体にマイクロチップを入れることに反対なのか。

【選択肢の訳】 **1** このテクノロジーは簡単に盗まれるかもしれない。

302

2 そうした装置の安全性はまだ定かでない。
3 マイクロチップは不正確なデータを作成するかもしれない。
4 埋め込まれた物は健康問題を引き起こすことが知られている。

[解説] 批判者の意見は第2段落でいくつか挙げられている。労働者が職場の外でも監視される可能性，ハッキングにより個人データが盗まれる危険性，装置が人体に及ぼし得る健康被害。最後の文で言っている the long-term health effects of implanted devices are unknown を **2** が短くまとめている。

一次試験・リスニング Part 3　問題編 p.157〜158

F

[スクリプト]

You have 10 seconds to read the situation and Question No. 21.

The watch you've chosen is high quality, and with the right care it could last for generations. As a mechanical watch, it doesn't have a battery; a similar quartz diving watch would need a new battery every few years. Since it's automatic, it will remain accurate if you wear it a couple of times a week, as the movement of your arm will wind it. To make sure the parts stay in working order, I recommend having it serviced by a professional. Once every five years is standard, but once every three years is recommended if you go scuba diving four or more times a year. Also, after using this watch while diving, remember to clean it with a soft toothbrush and fresh water. Avoid using any detergents or other cleaners, as they may destroy the waterproofing.

Now mark your answer on your answer sheet.

[全文訳]

お選びいただいた腕時計は高品質で，正しく手入れすれば何世代ももちます。機械式時計なので，電池はありません。似たようなクオーツ式のダイバーズウォッチなら，数年おきに新しい電池が必要になります。自動巻きですから，週に2，3回着ければ腕の動きで巻いてくれるので，常に時間が正確です。間違いなく部品が正常に作動しているようにするには，専門家に点検修理してもらうことをお勧めします。5年おきに1回が標準ですが，年4回以上スキューバダイビングに行かれるのでしたら，3年おきに1回がお勧めです。また，ダイビング中にこの時計を使った後は，柔らかい歯ブラシと真水で必ず洗ってください。合成洗剤などの洗浄剤は防水を駄目にするかもしれないので，一切使わないようにしてください。

No.21 解答 ①

状況の訳 あなたはダイバーズウォッチを買うところで，店員がメンテナンスについて説明している。あなたはたいてい年に5回スキューバダイビングに行く。

質問の訳 あなたは何をすべきか。

選択肢の訳
1　腕時計を3年おきに点検修理してもらう。
2　推薦された洗浄剤とブラシを買う。
3　交換部品を少し手元に用意しておく。
4　電池を5年おきに交換する。

語句　detergent「合成洗剤」

解説　it doesn't have a battery と言っているので**4**は誤り。parts に関しては専門家に点検修理してもらうよう言っているので**3**も誤り。点検修理は5年に1回が標準だが年4回以上スキューバダイビングに行くなら3年に1回がいいと言っているので，年に5回という状況の条件から，**1**が正解。洗浄剤は使わず歯ブラシと真水で洗うよう言っているので，**2**は誤りである。

スクリプト

You have 10 seconds to read the situation and Question No. 22.

I know you've called the airline without satisfaction, so hold off on that route. International law requires airlines to provide compensation for the value of your bags and contents up to $3,400, so they have to do something eventually. You've already submitted an itemized list of the contents and value of your baggage with your claim form. It's a shame you don't have any receipts for the items because that would strengthen your case. It's likely you'll get offered travel vouchers for the airline as compensation instead of cash. You said you want to avoid a lengthy legal battle, so waiting to see if their voucher offer is acceptable makes sense. Otherwise, taking the airline to court is an option. I can file the claim for you, but my fees are likely to exceed the amount of damages you will be awarded.

Now mark your answer on your answer sheet.

全文訳

航空会社に電話しても満足のいく結果は得られなかったわけですから，そっち方面は取りあえずやめておきましょう。国際法は航空会社に対して，あなたのかばんと中身の価値に対して最大3,400ドルの補償をするよう定めていますから，航空会社は最終的に何かしなければなりません。あなたは既に，荷物の中身と価値を箇条書きしたリストを請求書と一緒に提出しています。品目の領収書があれば立場が強くなりますから，1枚もお持ちでないのは残念です。現金の代わりに，補償としてその航空会社で使える旅

行クーポンの申し出がある可能性が高いです。長く続く法廷闘争は避けたいというお話でしたから，あちらのクーポンの申し出が受け入れられるものかどうか様子見をするのが妥当です。そうでなければ，裁判で航空会社を訴えるのも選択肢です。私が代わりに請求を申し立ててもいいですが，私の報酬は，受け取られる補償金の額を上回る可能性が高いです。

No.22 解答 ④

状況の訳 航空会社が数週間前にあなたの荷物を紛失し，あなたは何らかの補償をしてほしいと思っている。あなたは定期的に飛行機に乗る。弁護士が次のアドバイスをする。

質問の訳 あなたは何をすべきか。

選択肢の訳
1 現金で解決するよう航空会社に電話をする。
2 弁護士に法廷で代理人を務めてもらう。
3 領収書付きの請求書を提出する。
4 旅行クーポンの申し出を待つ。

語句 hold off on ~「~を先に延ばす」，itemize「~を箇条書きにする」

解説 電話は既に試みてうまくいかなかったので hold off on that route と弁護士が冒頭で言っていることから，1 は誤り。claim form は提出済みで，なおかつ you don't have any receipts なので 3 も誤り。waiting to see if their voucher offer is acceptable makes sense と弁護士はアドバイスし，定期的に飛行機に乗るのならクーポンは有用なので，4 が正解。弁護士料金が補償金を上回るだろうと最後に言っているので，2 は現実的な選択肢ではない。

H

スクリプト

You have 10 seconds to read the situation and Question No. 23.

Hi, this is Keith from the head office. It's 5:30 p.m. now. Our new client, Bill Fleischman, just called me to discuss the contract we sent him last week. He wants to ask you some questions before he'll agree to sign it. He said he'd be in his office for another two hours. If you can call him before he leaves, that would be great. If not, he'd like you to call him in the morning as he has to head to Brazil on business in the afternoon. If you're not free to talk in the morning, maybe you should e-mail him a response to his questions. He wants to know if he'll be allowed to sell competing products from other manufacturers and if we can revise the contract to specify that.

Now mark your answer on your answer sheet.

全文訳

やあ，本社のキースです。今，午後 5 時半です。うちの新規の顧客のビル・フライシ

ュマンさんからさっき電話があって，先週こちらから送った契約書について話し合いたいということでした。契約書へのサインに同意する前に，あなたにいくつか質問したいそうです。あと2時間オフィスにいるという話でした。彼が退社する前に電話できれば一番いいです。無理なら，彼は午後出張でブラジルに向かわなければならないので，午前中に電話してほしいとのことです。午前中に話す余裕がなければ，質問への回答をメールするのがいいかもしれません。彼が知りたいのは，ほかの製造会社の競合商品を売っても構わないか，それを明記するよううちが契約書を修正できるか，ということです。

No.23 解答 ②

状況の訳 あなたは出張中である。3時間以上前に同僚があなたに残したボイスメールを聞く。あなたは明日の午前中，正午まで会議に出る。

質問の訳 あなたは何をすべきか。

選択肢の訳
1 顧客に修正した契約書を送る。
2 顧客の質問にメールで回答する。
3 顧客から電話が来るのを待つ。
4 ブラジルから戻った後で顧客に連絡する。

語句 specify「～を明確に記す」

解説 顧客が今日オフィスにいるのはあと2時間と話者は言っており，3時間以上過ぎているので顧客は既に退社している。明日の午前中は正午まで会議なので電話できない。話者のもう1つの提案は maybe you should e-mail him a response to his questions で，それに従うことになる。したがって **2** が正解。

スクリプト

You have 10 seconds to read the situation and Question No. 24.

The American money-market account you're in has been earning 4 percent interest, but that'll fall to 2 percent at the end of the month. You've got several options for your holdings. Our top earner is an American real-estate investment trust that delivered 5 percent growth last year. Real estate is cyclical, though, so it's not the safest choice. Another possibility is transferring your money to our Australian money-market account. This guarantees 4 percent interest for six months. Foreign exchange rates do fluctuate, but the Australian dollar is also predicted to remain stable after that guarantee period, too. Or you could shift your money to a Japanese bond-investment fund. That's a low-risk option, but it also means it won't deliver more than 2 percent interest. Anyway, I think those are your best options at present.

Now mark your answer on your answer sheet.

全文訳

　お持ちのアメリカのマネーマーケット口座はずっと4％の利回りを出していますが，今月末に2％に下がります。運用資金に対する選択肢はいくつかあります。当社の稼ぎ頭は，昨年5％の成長を達成したアメリカの不動産投資トラストです。ですが不動産には周期がありますから，最も安全な選択肢ではありません。別の可能性は，当社のオーストラリアのマネーマーケット口座にお金を移すことです。これは，半年間4％の利回りを保証します。外国為替レートは必ず変動しますが，オーストラリアドルはその保証期間の後もずっと安定しているとも予測されています。あるいは，日本の債券投資ファンドにお金を移してもいいかもしれません。そちらは低リスクの選択肢ですが，つまり，2％を超える利回りは達成しないということでもあります。ともかく，今のところ以上が最善の選択肢だと思います。

No.24 解答 ③

状況の訳 あなたはファイナンシャルアドバイザーと投資について話し合っている。運用資金に対し最低3％の利回りは稼ぎたいが，リスクを最小限にもしたい。

質問の訳 あなたはお金をどうすべきか。

選択肢の訳
1 アメリカのマネーマーケット口座に置いておく。
2 アメリカの不動産投資トラストに投資する。
3 オーストラリアのマネーマーケット口座に移す。
4 日本の債券投資ファンドに移す。

語句 cyclical「周期的な」，fluctuate「変動する」

解説 耳慣れない金融用語に惑わされず，at least 3 percent interest と minimize your risk という2つの条件に関する内容に集中して聴く。アメリカのマネーマーケット口座は利回りが2％に下がる。アメリカの不動産投資トラストは5％だが，最も安全な選択肢ではない。オーストラリアのマネーマーケット口座は半年間4％が保証され，その後も安定が見込まれる。日本の債券投資ファンドは低リスクだが2％。条件に合うのは3のオーストラリアのマネーマーケット口座である。

スクリプト

You have 10 seconds to read the situation and Question No. 25.

The main drawing is held on Saturday, so check the results online or in the newspaper. The process for collecting your winnings varies. If you win under $600, just take your winning ticket to any lottery retailer and collect the cash. If you win $600 or more, download a claim form and take your winning ticket and a valid photo ID to a lottery district office. And don't throw your tickets away if you don't win on Saturday, as our state has a second-chance lottery.

To enter, create an account on the state lottery website. Some states require you to mail in your tickets, but here you just submit lottery ticket numbers through your account. Your chances on the second drawing actually increase, since a lot of people don't know about it or don't bother to enter.

Now mark your answer on your answer sheet.

全文訳

主な抽選は土曜日に行われるので，結果はオンラインか新聞で確認してください。当選金を受け取る手順はさまざまです。当選金額が600ドル未満なら，どこでもいいので宝くじ売り場に当たり券を持って行き，現金を受け取るだけです。当選金額が600ドル以上なら，請求用紙をダウンロードし，当たり券と有効な写真付き身分証明書を持って宝くじの地区事務所に行ってください。それから，土曜日に当たらなくても券を捨てないでください。私たちの州では外れくじの再抽選がありますから。登録するには，州の宝くじサイトでアカウントを作ってください。券を郵送するよう求める州もありますが，こちらでは，アカウント経由で宝くじ券の番号を送信するだけで済みます。多くの人はこのことを知らないか，わざわざ登録したりしませんから，再抽選で当たる確率は実際上がります。

No.25 解答 ①

状況の訳　あなたは初めて宝くじ券を買っている。当たる確率を上げたい。販売員が次のアドバイスをする。

質問の訳　最初の抽選で当たらなかったらあなたはどうすべきか。

選択肢の訳
1 オンラインアカウントを開設し券の番号を送信する。
2 宝くじのサイトから請求用紙をダウンロードする。
3 州の宝くじ事務所に券を送る。
4 どこでもいいので宝くじ売り場に外れ券を持って行く。

語句　winnings「賞金，当選金」

解説　質問の if you do not win on the first drawing に該当するのは，中ほどの if you don't win on Saturday である。最初の抽選で外れても second-chance lottery があり，参加する人が多くないので Your chances on the second drawing actually increase だと言っている。登録に必要なのは create an account on the state lottery website と submit lottery ticket numbers だから，1 が正解となる。

一次試験・リスニング Part 4　問題編 p.159

スクリプト

This is an interview with Emily Lee, who works in investor relations.

I (Interviewer): Thanks for tuning in, everyone. Today, we're talking with Emily Lee. Welcome.

EL (Emily Lee): Nice to be here.

I: So, what is investor relations?

EL: Well, many Japanese companies have international investors, and my company makes reports and communicates all the financial and nonfinancial information to these investors so they can decide how they would like to continue investing in the future.

I: And what sort of challenges do you face in your job?

EL: There are many, many challenges in this job, but one of the main ones is scheduling. So, in Japan, the fiscal year ends in March, which means everything piles up in the summer. When that happens, I sometimes have five or six reports going simultaneously, and that can be a lot of pressure, because you don't want there to be any mistakes. I have seen colleagues stay overnight, through weekends, not sleep, in order to meet deadlines from clients. Because of this, there can be quite high turnover in the IR field. So, many people only last between two to three years before they think they'll move on to a different job, in a different industry altogether, or stay in the IR industry, but not be client-facing. Morale can be a little bit low when you lose some of your favorite, or most competent, coworkers over time, but I feel that it makes the people who stay gel together all the better. And when you have people who are experienced and know what they're doing, it makes the workflow much easier as well.

I: So, what are the annual reports aimed at?

EL: Their main purpose is to explain the financial situation of a company, because these investors are abroad. They're not on the ground to see what the actual circumstances are, so the report explains to them how a company has done over the past year, and what they're planning to do in the future. That includes midterm management plans, and what their nonfinancial goals are. So, things relating to charity work, or anything that could relate to corporate social responsibility.

I: Could you tell us briefly what corporate social responsibility is?

EL: Corporate social responsibility is how a company addresses their social responsibility to the planet and to the communities it operates in. So, for example, the social side can be organizing charity events, or art events, in the community for people to participate in for free. Another example is the environmental side, where a company will try to lower its emissions volumes in order to hit certain goals put out by the United Nations.

I: And do you think that most companies take CSR seriously?

EL: I think most companies do, if only because they must. Certain things have come into law, due to the environmental impact of how companies operate on the planet. There is also something called the SDGs, which is the sustainable development goals put out by the United Nations in 2015. For example, how to promote clean water, how to promote less inequality in the world — and companies will use these goals as guidelines for how they can operate.

I: Well, Emily, thanks so much for coming in today. That was very interesting.

EL: Thanks for having me.

Questions

No.26 What is one thing Emily implies about working in the investor relations industry?

No.27 What does Emily think about corporate social responsibility?

全文訳

これはインベスター・リレーションズの仕事をしているエミリー・リーとのインタビューです。

聞き手（以下「聞」）：皆さん，お聴きいただきありがとうございます。今日は，エミリー・リーとトークします。ようこそ。

エミリー・リー(以下「エ」)：よろしくお願いします。

聞：さて，インベスター・リレーションズとは何ですか。

エ：えー，多くの日本企業には国際投資家がいて，私の会社は，それらの投資家が将来的に投資し続けたいと思うかどうかを決められるよう，報告書を作り，あらゆる財務情報と非財務情報を彼らに伝えています。

聞：それで，お仕事ではどういった難題に直面しますか。

エ：この仕事には実にたくさんの難題がありますが，主なものの１つはスケジュール管理です。つまり，日本では会計年度が終わるのは３月で，ということは，何やかやと夏にどんどんたまるわけです。そうなると，時に５つか６つの報告書を同時に動かすことになり，間違いは１つもないようにしたいですから，すごくプレッシャーになることがあります。顧客の締め切りに間に合わせるため，同僚が週末ずっと眠らずに泊まりがけで居残りしているのを目にしてきました。このため，IR分野では離職率がかなり高いことがあります。つまり，まったく違う業界の違う仕事に転職しよう，あるいはIR業界に残っても顧客と対面はしないと思うようになるまで，多くの人は２年から３年しか続かないんです。時がたつうちに一番好きな同僚やとても有能な同僚の何人かを失うと士気が少し下がることもありますが，そうしたことは，残った人たちの結束をかえって強くすると感じます。そして，経験を積んで万事のみ込んでいる人たちがいると，業務の流れがずっと容易にもなります。

聞：では，年間報告書は何を目標にしているのですか。

エ：主な目的は企業の財務状況を説明することですね，これらの投資家は外国にいますから。彼らは実際の状況がどうなのかを現場で見ることはできませんから，企業が過去1年間どんな具合だったか，今後何をする計画なのかを，報告書が投資家に説明するんです。それには，中期経営計画と，企業の非財務目標が何なのかが含まれます。つまり，慈善事業に関する事柄や，企業の社会的責任に関連するかもしれないものは何でもです。

聞：企業の社会的責任とは何なのか，簡潔に教えてもらえますか。

エ：企業の社会的責任とは，事業を行う場である地球と地域社会に対する社会的責任に，企業がどのように取り組んでいるかということです。つまり，例えば社会的側面としては，人々が無料で参加できるようなチャリティーイベントやアートイベントを地域社会で組織することがあり得るでしょう。別の例は環境的側面で，その場合企業は，国際連合が発表する一定の目標を達成するために排出物の量を減らそうとします。

聞：それで，ほとんどの企業は CSR を真剣に受け止めていると思いますか。

エ：そうせざるを得ないからだとしても，ほとんどの企業はそうしていると思います。企業の地球での事業運営が環境に与える影響のため，一定の事柄は法制化されています。SDGs というものもあり，これは，2015年に国際連合が発表した持続可能な開発目標です。例えば，きれいな水をどのように広めるか，世界の不平等の縮小をどのように進めるかといったことですが——企業はこれらの目標を，どのように事業を行えるかの指針として用いることになります。

聞：さて，エミリー，今日はお越しいただきどうもありがとうございました。とても興味深いお話でした。

エ：お招きいただきありがとうございました。

（語句）turnover「離職率，転職率」，gel together「結束する」，workflow「仕事の流れ」，on the ground「現場で」，midterm「中間の」

No.26 解答

質問の訳　インベスター・リレーションズ業界で働くことについて，エミリーが暗に言っていることの1つは何か。

選択肢の訳
1　会計年度が3月に終わるので，人々は夏に自由な時間がある。
2　卓越したチームワークは，ほかの業界よりも転職する人が少ないことを意味する。
3　仕事のプレッシャーに対応できる人たちは，たいてい信頼できる同僚になる。
4　新人は顧客と仕事をする前に3年の経験が必要だ。

解説　エミリーは3つ目の発言で，インベスター・リレーションズ（IR）業界の難題の1つとして，スケジュール管理の難しさを挙げている。そして，そのプレッシャーのせいで離職率が高いが，やめずに残った人たちの結束が強くなり，経験を積んだ人が残れば業務がはかどるといったこ

とを言っている。やめずに残ることを「プレッシャーに対応できる」，結束が強くなることを「信頼できる」と表した **3** が正解。

No.27 解答 **2**

質問の訳 企業の社会的責任についてエミリーはどう思っているか。

選択肢の訳 1 企業の環境保護を支援するため，国際連合はもっと多くのことをしなければならない。

2 企業の大多数は，企業の社会的責任が事業にとって重要だと今では感じている。

3 投資家は，地域社会で仕事をしようとする企業の取り組みに資金を出すべきだ。

4 多くの企業は，チャリティーイベントとアートプロジェクトに集中するため，企業の社会的責任を無視している。

解説 エミリーは5つ目と6つ目の発言で企業の社会的責任について話している。聞き手が言っている CSR が唐突な印象を与えるが，話の流れから，corporate social responsibility の頭文字だと見当がつく。ほとんどの企業は CSR を真剣に受け止めているか，という聞き手の質問に I think most companies do と答えていること，また，企業は SDGs（持続可能な開発目標）を指針とするだろう，という発言から，エミリーは **2** のように思っているとわかる。

312

ここでは，A日程の5つのトピックをモデルスピーチとしました。

A日程

1. Would the global economy benefit from a single world currency?

　A single currency would definitely benefit the global economy. It would boost global trade, make investing easier, and encourage tourism. First, let's consider global trade. Today, when businesses import or export goods, there are usually additional costs because their money may need to be converted to a foreign currency. If we adopted a global currency, this additional cost would vanish, making trade between foreign countries more accessible. Investors would also benefit. Whenever people invest abroad, they have to worry not only about whether the investment itself will rise in value, but about the price of the foreign currency. If everyone used the same currency, this risk would be eliminated, making investing simpler and more profitable. Finally, it could be good for the tourism industry. It would save people the trouble of exchanging currencies, so they'd be more likely to go abroad. Furthermore, it would be easier to understand prices, encouraging people to spend more. Since tourism is an important part of the world economy, this could have a significant economic impact. In conclusion, we are currently living in an era of globalization, so the potential advantages related to global trade, investment, and travel make it clear that we should have a single world currency.

> 解説　「単一の国際通貨によって世界経済は恩恵を受けるか」
> 　賛成の立場を取る根拠は3つ，①貿易におけるコストの削減，②投資の際のリスクの軽減，③海外旅行での利便性，である。重複しない理由を出すことで広い視野から単一国際通貨が世界経済にもたらす利点を説明できている。さらに，自分が仮定していることは仮定法，事実は現在形，と明確に分けて話し，聞き手に誤解を与えない発話となっている。最後のまとめも既出の表現の繰り返しではなく，言い換え表現を使って同じ主張を述べることで発話レベルの高さをアピールできている。

2. Can labor unions effectively support workers in the modern business world?

　In my opinion, labor unions are gradually losing their ability to support workers in the modern business world. Union membership is decreasing, corporations are becoming more powerful, and labor laws are weakening. In the years after World War II, the majority of Japanese workers were union members, but now only certain occupations, like teachers and government workers, tend to have strong unions. While unions are helping to maintain wages and benefits in some workplaces, the majority of workers have no organization to protect them. Another problem is that companies are becoming much more powerful these days. In today's world, companies can easily use outsourced or temporary workers instead of regular full-time employees. Workers know that if they strike or try to form unions, they can easily be replaced, and this puts them in a weak position when negotiating with companies. Finally, labor laws are becoming weaker around the world and this reduces the power of labor unions. Such laws usually make it difficult for unions to encourage workers to become members. Without a high number of members, unions cannot help workers effectively. Although there are a few jobs where unions are still important, in general, they have lost most of their power to protect workers.

解説 「現代のビジネス環境において労働組合は効果的に労働者をサポートできているか」

否定の立場から3つの理由として①労働組合の組合員が減少している，②労働者より企業が強い立場になっている，③労働法の力が弱まっている，と述べている。理由のそれぞれに事実に基づいた具体例を挙げていることで，主張の信頼性を高く維持することができている。労働組合の問題は考えたことがないという人もいるだろう。本番のスピーチで，挙げた理由のすべてに具体例を思い付けなかったとしても焦らずに，出せる具体例を丁寧に，わかりやすく説明するようにするとよいだろう。

3. Agree or disagree: The traditional family unit has lost its central role in modern society

I think traditional families are still extremely common in modern society. I'd like to talk about mainstream values, finances, and government policies to explain my opinion. First of all, although I am personally supportive of the rise of non-traditional family units, I accept the fact that the majority of people around the world value the idea of having a nuclear family. TV programs and movies still largely reinforce society's ideal of two-parent households. Traditional families also have an advantage when it comes to their personal finances. Many housing or car loan institutions still generally give the best rates to married couples, with or without children. Also, it is well known that many companies give better healthcare, pension, and paid leave benefits to employees who are married and have children. Lastly, government policies are mainly based on the idea that people will live in traditional families. Married couples receive various tax benefits, and welfare and educational services are also based on the assumption that people will be living in traditional family units. Based on things like values, finances, and government policies, it seems clear that traditional family units still have a central role in modern Japanese society.

解説「賛成か反対か：伝統的な家族単位は現代社会においてその重要な役割を失った」

反対の立場から 3 つの理由として①伝統的な家族単位の価値観は社会に根付いている，②融資や年金など経済面で有利である，③国の政策は家族単位を標準に作られるので税制や教育などにおいても恩恵を受けやすい，を挙げ，根拠としている。このスピーチのように，設問にある traditional family unit とは何か（ここでは核家族），という定義を先に示しておくと論理を展開しやすい。賛成の立場を取る場合，シングルペアレントや同性婚などが世間で認知を得つつあることを中心に意見を展開するとよいだろう。

4. Do the advantages of jury trials outweigh the disadvantages?

I believe jury trials have many benefits. They create less bias, make the legal system more open, and offer hope of making trials fairer. First, without jury trials, cases would be decided by highly educated elites who may have biases against the underprivileged. However, since juries are made up of people from all walks of life, they give accused criminals an opportunity to be judged by their peers. Another important reason for having jury trials is that ordinary people get to participate in the justice system. Most people know little about what happens in courts except for what they see on TV shows. However, when ordinary people experience being in juries themselves, they learn more about the justice system and there is increased public awareness of what is happening in court. Last but not least, they may help to lower Japan's extremely high conviction rate. Critics often say that people have very little chance of being found not guilty in Japanese criminal trials. However, having larger groups of diverse people could lower the odds that an innocent person will be found guilty. Although jury trials may not be perfect, I believe their advantages far outweigh the disadvantages.

解説「陪審裁判制度の利点は欠点を上回るか」

陪審裁判制度を積極的に肯定するスピーチ。3 つの根拠として，①裁判官などエリートだけによる判断ではなくさまざまな経験を経た人に判断

315

してもらえる，②一般の人が裁判にかかわることによって司法への理解を深められる，③さまざまな人々がかかわることによって有罪判決の率を下げられるのではないか，を挙げている。裁判に関するトピックは知識がないと対応が難しいのももちろんだが，法律関連の正確な英語表現を最低限知っている必要がある。海外の司法ドラマや映画なども参考にして，日ごろから発話練習しておこう。

5. Will the human race one day be the cause of its own downfall?

I think that it is unlikely for humanity to one day cause its own downfall. Technology, environmentalism, and space exploration are factors that will help us to survive. Although some people worry that there are problems which may bring down human civilization, technology is often the solution. For example, as the world faces overpopulation, food insecurity will likely become a major issue. Scientists are working on methods to create sustainable food sources in non-traditional ways, such as growing plants in closed spaces using artificial sunlight. Next, humans will find a way to overcome the climate change crisis. Many citizens, especially from the younger generation, are pressuring their governments to take the issue very seriously, and things like investment in renewable fuels and pollution regulations will be able to save the climate in time. Finally, exploring space will ensure the survival of humans. There are currently many efforts to explore whether humans may be able to live on Mars someday. Once humans have colonized Mars, we have two planets to live on, so even if there were a global catastrophe on one planet, the people on the other would survive. I know some people are afraid humans will destroy themselves, but when you consider technology, the environmental movement, and space exploration, extinction seems unlikely.

解説 「人類はいつか自分たち自身を破滅に追い込むだろうか」

否定の立場の意見を，主にテクノロジーを理由に絞って展開している例。このようにテクノロジーという枠の中でさらに細分化した3点をサポートとして使うことでスピーチの具体性を上げることができる。ここでは，①食料危機に対応するためのさまざまな技術的解決，②気候変動に関しての若い世代からの圧力と再生可能燃料への投資，③宇宙開発を通しての火星移住などの可能性，というテクノロジーによる解決方法を紹介し，人類はさまざまな危機に直面してはいるが絶滅はしないだろうと結論付けている。

MEMO

旺文社の英検®書

★ **一発合格したいなら「全問＋パス単」！**
旺文社が自信を持っておすすめする王道の組み合わせです。

★ 【過去問集】過去問で出題傾向をしっかりつかむ！
英検® 過去6回全問題集 1〜5級
音声アプリ対応 / 音声ダウンロード / 別売CDあり

★ 【単熟語集】過去問を徹底分析した「でる順」！
英検® でる順パス単 1〜5級
音声アプリ対応 / 音声ダウンロード

【模試】本番形式の予想問題で総仕上げ！
7日間完成 英検® 予想問題ドリル 1〜5級
CD付 / 音声アプリ対応

【参考書】申し込みから面接まで英検のすべてがわかる！
英検® 総合対策教本 1〜5級
CD付

【問題集】大問ごとに一次試験を集中攻略！
DAILY英検® 集中ゼミ 1〜5級
CD付

【二次対策】動画で面接をリアルに体験！
英検® 二次試験・面接完全予想問題 1〜3級
DVD+CD付 / 音声アプリ対応

このほかにも多数のラインナップを揃えております。

旺文社の英検® 合格ナビゲーター https://eiken.obunsha.co.jp/
英検合格を目指す方のためのウェブサイト。
試験情報や級別学習法、おすすめの英検書を紹介しています。

※英検®は、公益財団法人 日本英語検定協会の登録商標です。

株式会社 旺文社　〒162-8680　東京都新宿区横寺町55
https://www.obunsha.co.jp/